VIRGINIA/WEST VIRGINIA GENEALOGICAL DATA FROM REVOLUTIONARY WAR PENSION AND BOUNTY LAND WARRANT RECORDS

Volume 3 -- Iams through Myres

Compiled By
Patrick G. Wardell
Lt. Col., U.S. Army Retired

HERITAGE BOOKS
2008

HERITAGE BOOKS
AN IMPRINT OF HERITAGE BOOKS, INC.

Books, CDs, and more—Worldwide

For our listing of thousands of titles see our website
at

www.HeritageBooks.com

Published 2008 by
HERITAGE BOOKS, INC.
Publishing Division
100 Railroad Avenue #104
Westminster, Maryland 21157

Copyright © 1992 Patrick G. Wardell

All rights reserved. No part of this book may be reproduced or transmitted in any form or by any means, electronic or mechanical, including photocopying, recording or by any information storage and retrieval system without written permission from the author, except for the inclusion of brief quotations in a review.

International Standard Book Number: 978-1-55613-657-3

FOREWORD

This book is the third of several volumes of genealogical data pertaining to Virginia people and to their families that has been extracted from some 2,670 reels of microfilm at the US National Archives. Family history researchers can view the complete records at the the National Archives or may obtain copies of the microfilms by mail or may purchase reels for home viewing. For the convenience of users of this volume, pertinent microfilm reel and file numbers for each serviceman's record are indicated.

Most of the bounty land warrant records for Revolutionary War servicemen were destroyed by fires in Washington, DC, in 1800 and 1814. However, the pension records are fairly complete and they are replete with excellent source data. Records include affidavits of the applicants and their witnesses, local court actions, Congressional actions, extracts from family bibles, discharge papers, service certificates, marriage certificates, as well as letters from descendants requesting data on Revolutionary War ancestors. Those letters often contained additional genealogical data which is also provided herein.

This book includes not only data on the men who entered the Army or the Sea Service from Virginia but also those who entered from other states or countries but were born, married, or lived at one time in Virginia or had members of their families reside in Virginia before or after the Revolutionary War.

Not all of the Revolutionary War veterans or their widows or family members applied for pensions or bounty land warrants. Those who did apply were not always successful for various reasons, such as insufficient proof of service or marriage, or failure to submit the required documents or forms to the National Pension Office, or to the Government Land Office. In some cases, the veteran or his spouse died before the pension or warrant could be approved. The mails at the time being slow and government bureaucracy being even slower, considerable time passed between application and approval. Many frustrated applicants solicited the help of their Congressmen to speed up the process. Proof of marriage was often difficult to obtain because of the loss of public records, particularly in Virginia where fire destroyed courthouses in a number of counties. Affidavits from witnesses to service or marriage were often difficult or impossible to obtain when the applicants were of advanced age or had moved out of state.

There were, of course, fraudulent claims. Some were discovered when the claims were made, while others were found out later. Some people who had been awarded pensions were dropped from the rolls as a result.

Laws for receiving pensions and bounty land were not consistent, since Congress made a number of changes after the first awards were allowed. Consequently, some claimants who were initially rejected were able to submit a successful claim later. However, some who waited too long missed out because of a rules change.

The reader's attention is invited to the many variations in the spelling of names, which was prevalent in those early days. When looking for a particular surname, the reader should also look for similar sounding names; e.g. ALLEN vs. ALLAN, STEWART vs STUART, BRIAN vs BRYAN, NEAL vs NEILL, or CAREY vs CARY.

Variations in ages of the claimants from one court appearance or affadavit to another were prevalent. Not having public records of births in those times, as well as the failing memory of elderly and aged claimants and witnesses, were the main causes of discrepancies.

Some of the microfilmed documents were very difficult to read, especially when the handwriting of the preparers of court documents or family bible entries was poor, or the ink was badly faded or blotched. The compiler of this book often was obliged to make an educated guess as to the names and dates recorded.

An index which lists all people who are not the subject of an entry is provided. Women are listed by both maiden and married names, when known.

This work is a companion piece to the book, WAR OF 1812: VIRGINIA BOUNTY LAND & PENSION APPLICANTS, by the same compiler, published by HERITAGE BOOKS, INC, in 1987.

General Abbreviations

adm	administrator	LWT	last will and testament
ae	age	m	mother
aec	age about	MB	marriage bond
afb	applied for bounty land warrant	ML	marriage license
AFF	affidavit	mbnn	mentioned but not named
afp	applied for pension	md	married
AKA	also known as	mns	mentions
b	born	mvd	moved
bc	born about	NKG	no kinship given
BLAR	bounty land application rejected	o	of (used with /)
BLW	bounty land warrant	PAR	pension application rejected
bro	brother	PN	pension, pensioned
c	about	POW	prisoner of war
ch	child, children	QLF	query letter in pension or bounty land warrant record
co	county		
d	daughter		
dd	died	R	microfilm reel number for record
decd	deceased		
desc	descendant	recd	received
esf	entered service from	res	resident, residence
f	father	RW	Revolutionary War
gdc	grandchild(ren)	s	son
gdd	granddaughter	sis	sister
gdf	grandfather	sol	soldier
gdm	grandmother	sub	substitute
gds	grandson	surv	surviving
gtd	granted	svc	military service
h	husband	w	wife
JP	justice of the peace	wid	widow
KIA	killed in action		
liv	living		

===

Volume 4 will start with NABORS, Nathan/Nathaniel, Reel #1800

IAMS, John Frederick, esf 1780 Prince Georges Co, MD, where b; res after RW Pittsylvania Co, VA; mvd to Wilkes Co (area later Oglethorpe Co), GA, thence Grainger Co, TN, where PN 1833 ae 67-68; dd there 1/24/39; md 1789 Mary JOHNSON in Wilkes Co, GA; wid PN ae 80 Grainger Co, TN 1844 where res 1848 ae 81; surname also spelled IIAMS. F-W434 R1389
ICE, Adam; esf c1776 Monongalia Co, VA, where b 6/1/1760; afp there 1837, & PAR. F-R5470 R1389
  Andrew, b 1758 Hampshire Co, VA; esf 177 Monongalia Co, VA, where res; mvd 1832 to Henry Co, IN, where PN later same year; dd 3/13/37 & PN due paid to estate adm Jesse ICE (no kinship given); QLF states sol buried near Muncie, IN. F-S32336 R1389
IDEN, John, b 12/5/1752 Bucks Co, PA; esf 1777 Loudoun Co, VA; PN there 1832; res 1838 with s mbnn Knox Co, OH, address P O Frederickstown, where sol had recently mvd from VA; AFF there then by James IDEN (kinship not given) on behalf of sol; QLF 1940 from desc V Gilmore IDEN, New York, NY; QLF states sol dd 6/6/47, when P O address Andrews, Morrow Co, OH. F-S2302 R1389
ILES, Samuel, b 8/17/1745 near Bristol, England; to Baltimore, MD, ae 18; esf 1777 res Queen Anne Co, MD; res Alexandria, VA, for 3 years after RW, thence 1806 Kent Co, DE, thence 1806 Madison Co, KY for 6 years, thence Pendleton Co, KY, thence 1824 Fayette Co, IN, where afp 1832 res Harrison Township; state/o MD reported sol esf 1778 in 4th MD Regiment & deserted 1780; sol PAR, desertion. F-R5474 R1389
  William, esf 1779 Halifax Co, NC, where b 3/5/1763; went to Nansemond Co, VA, where esf; returned home to Halifax Co, NC, after svc; afp 1843 St Landry Parish, LA & PAR; s William AFF 1844 Caddo Parish, LA that sol very old & infirm. F-R5475 R-1389
IMHOOF, Frederick, esf 1781, when day laborer with no family; BLW492 gtd 1810 when res Berkeley Co, VA; PN aec 72 Frederick Co, VA, 1820; surname also spelled IMHOFF. F-S380-68 R1390
INGHAM, Thomas, see INGRAM, Thomas. F-S4419 R1391
INGLE, Henry, esf 1780 Buckingham Co, VA, where b 6/1761; afp 1835 Russell Co, VA, & PAR, insufficient proof of svc. F-R5481 R1391
  John, see ENGLE, John. F-S38861 R1391
  Michael, esf 1775 in VA regiment; PN 1818 Washington Co, TN, ae not given. F-S38860 R1391
INGLISH, John, esf VA; gtd BLW181 Adams Co, OH, 1804; surname also spelled ENGLISH. F-BLW181 R1391
INGRAHAM, William,, b 1758 Granville Co, NC, where orphaned at early ae; esf 1776 Montgomery Co, VA, where res; mvd to Hawkins Co, TN, for 15 years, thence Wayne Co, KY, for c7 years, thence Clay Co, KY, for c1 year, thence Madison Co, KY, for 1 year, thence Orange Co, IN, for c3 years, thence Marion Co, IL, for 7 years, thence Bledsoe Co, TN where PN 1834. F-S21314 R1392

INGRAM, Andrew, b 1752 Granville Co, NC; esf 1779 Montgomery
    Co, VA where res; mvd after RW to Holston, Hawkins Co, TN,
    thence 1819 to Floyd Co, IN, where PN 1834 res Township of
    Greenville; dd 7/25/48. F-S32338 R1392
  Edwin, b 4/17/1751 Southampton Co, VA; esf 1779 Anson Co, NC
    where res; res after RW Salisbury, NC, mvd to Richmond Co,
    NC, where PN 1832; legislature of NC in 1786 gave vote of
    thanks to sol for his svc & offered him gift of 500 pounds
    which he declined; bro Samuel res 1832 Richland District,
    SC; sol dd 5/11/43; QLF 1937 from great gdd (on f's side)
    Mrs J T JENKINS, Star, NC, who great gdd (on m's side) of
    RW sol Hugh MONTGOMERY; QLF 1937 from great gdd Mrs Mickie
    SEWARD, Star, NC to President ROOSEVELT claiming money due
    sol Edward T INGRAM, she being d of Saunders M INGRAM, who
    served in Mexican War & Civil War, further her maiden name
    Mickie LORENS & she md Richard H SEWARD now decd, further
    she now wid ae 52 with d aec 18 & d ae 10. (PN Office res-
    ponse to Mrs SEWARD stated no money due her for svc of sol
    since money was voted by state of NC & not by US Congress)
    F-S9741 R1392
  Jeremiah, esf 1776 in VA regiment; PN 1832 Adair Co, KY, ae
    73; QLF 1930 from desc John C INGRAM, New York, NY, he al-
    so desc/o sol s John who esf 1780 in PA regiment; QLF 1923
    from Willis M JOHNSTON, Louisville, KY whose d desc/o sol;
    QLF 1913 from great great gdd Mrs J H GILKESON of Lebanon,
    KY. F-S15184 R1392
  Samuel, b 8/1/1765 Southampton Co, VA; esf Anson Co, NC when
    res there with f John; mvd 1833 to Montgomery Co, AL where
    afp 1835 when eldest s William res with him; PAR. F-R5485
    R1392
  Sarah, former wid of Lemuel THOROWGOOD. (F-R5486)
  Thomas, esf c1777 Southampton Co, VA, where b 6/6/1762; mvd
    c3 years after RW to Northampton Co, NC for c5 years, then
    to Chatham Co, NC for c2 years, thence back to Northampton
    Co, NC for c12 years, thence Halifax Co, NC for c15 years,
    thence Wilson Co, TN, where PN 1833 when res there for c2
    years; res 1835 Lebanon, TN. F-S4419 R1392
INLO, Thomas, esf 1777 VA; afp ae 80 Walton Co, GA, 1836; PAR.
    F-R5488 R1392
INSCOE, William, b 3/10/1756 Essex Co, VA; esf 1777 VA sub for
    f James; esf 1778 VA sub for bro James; PN 1834 Mecklen-
    burg Co, VA; last PN payment dated 3/4/41. F-S11363 R1393
IRBY, David, b 1758 Halifax Co, VA; esf 1776 Pittsylvania Co,
    VA; PN there 1832. F-S5602 R1393
  Douglas/Douglass, esf 1775 VA; PN 1820 Botetourt Co, VA, ae
    69 when w ae 53 & ch Elizabeth ae 25, Sally ae 22, & Polly
    ae 21 res with him; occupation carpenter; md Hannah CAND-
    LER, Campbell Co, VA, who dd c1833; they had 7 ch; sol dd
    5/15/43 Roanoke Co, VA leaving ch: Mary (w/o Pliny H BERRY
    of Washington Co, TN), Tabitha (w/o John T COWAN) & Eliza-
    beth; d Mary BERRY AFF 1856 ae 53 res Jonesboro, Washing-
    ton Co, TN, that only surv ch/o sol then were self, Eliza-

IRBY (continued)
beth (never md, res Lee Co, VA), & Tabitha COWAN (wid, res Russell Co, VA). F-S38069 R1393

John, B 8/5/1761 Richmond Co, VA, in Northern Neck near Chesapeake Bay; res ae 13-14 Dinwiddie Co, VA, when mvd with f to Charlotte Co, VA; esf there 1777; went 1780 to visit uncle Joseph IRBY (res on Saluda River in SC), found that uncle had been killed by Tories; sol then esf there; mvd 1789 from Halifax Co, VA to York District, SC, thence 1807 Lincoln Co, NC where PN 1833; dd 5/9/43; md 3/12/1788 Anne who PN ae 78 Lincoln Co, NC, 1845; ch births: Joshua Mason 11/9/1790, Thomas Kendrick 4/30/93, Nansey 5/7/96, Betsey 12/9/1800, William 1/26/1804, & Joseph 5/10/06; s Joseph K res 1845 Cleveland Co, NC; sol cousin Richard HANKS AFF ae 73 Lincoln Co, NC, 1834. F-W5003 R1393

William, esf 1776 Culpeper Co, VA, where b & raised; later esf Halifax Co, VA, where parents res; when returned from svc, he found parents had mvd to SC; sol joined them & esf there; dd 9/30/1828 Laurens Courthouse, SC; sons & heirs-at-law, Dr William ae 62 & Colonel James H ae 60, afp 1853 there as f's LWT executors & PAR, neither sol or w had ever afp; AFF 1851 Greenville District, SC by John MATTOX ae 88 (b & raised Culpeper Co, VA) that he & sol esf together Culpeper Courthouse, VA. F-R5492 R1393

IRON, Robert, svc in Indian Wars, VA, 1790-95; no RW svc; esf Greenbrier Co, VA, to fight indians; gave s Silas power of attorney to afb when sol res Lewisburg, Highland Co, OH, 1854 ae 84; BLW27032 gtd sol; no claim for PN; QLF 1934 from desc John O BOYD, New York, NY states sol surname was actually IRION, further querier's gdm mbnn ae 88 in 1934. F-BLW27032 R1393

IRVIN, Andrew, esf 1780 Bedford Co, VA, where res; dd 1830 ae 82 Clinton Co, OH; md 1774 Elizabeth MITCHELL, Bedford Co, VA; wid PN ae 92 Fayette Co, OH, 1841 res Jefferson Township, her afp being made by s Stephen; ch births: Robert 8/6/1775, Jane 1/3/77, Mary 9/1778, Stephen 10/3/80, Lucinda 6/1782, Caleb 1/1785 or 2/1785, Joshua 9/1787, John 5/1790, Elizabeth 5/1792, & William 3/1796; s Stephen M md 3/16/1809 Jane WHITSETT who b 12/10/1790; s William M md (1) 3/22/1818 Frances ROGERS (b 5/6/1799, dd 8/5/1821), & md (2) 4/29/1824 Letticia MILLS, who b 9/17/1801; other births: Robert W IRVIN 2/15/1819, Will IRVINE (7/16/1821 & dd 2/11/1825), Caleb IRVIN 2/11/1825, James Andrew IRVIN 11/13/1829, Aylett Rains IRVIN 9/9/1831, Elizabeth Margaret IRVIN 2/12/1834, Amanda Melvina IRVIN 3/5/1810, Chrissa Narcissa IRVIN 3/14/1812, Tabitha Russell IRVIN 12/2/1814, Joseph Andrew IRVIN 2/24/1817, Isaiah W IRVIN 6/20/1819, Stephen IRVIN 12/21/1821, Elizabeth Jane IRVIN 9/27/1824, Mary Margaret IRVIN 6/30/1827, John Clifford IRVIN 3/10/1830, William Griffith IRVIN 7/25/1832, Elizabeth JANUARY 12/11/1800, & Virginia Ann BARRERE 1/4/1822: marriages: Hanson LAWRENCE & Amanda M IRVIN 10/2/1828, Stephen M

IRVIN (continued)
 IRVIN & Elizabeth BARRERE 4/16/1835, Isaiah W IRVIN & Virginia Ann BARRERE 7/29/1841; QLF 1922 from desc Viola Irvine (Mrs Harry C) WEBSTER, Marceline, MO, states sol s of Alexander & w (Miss GAULT) of Scotland who came to America 1725-31 & settled Bedford Co, VA, further sol's d Jane md querier's great gdf William MITCHELL of Bourbon Co, KY who b there 1767 & later member of KY state legislature, & dd there 1851, further querier's parents M G KENDRICK & Sarah E WILSON were 1st cousins, their m's being sis's who were d's of William & Jane Irvin MITCHELL, further querier's f (b 2/22/1832, dd 1/15/1920) a Civil War sol from MO, further querier's kinswoman Lucinda BOYD of Cynthiana, KY was gdd of sol. F-W9045 R1394
 Hannah, former wid of Thomas WHITLOW. (F-W7861)
 William, esf 1775 Bedford Co, VA; PN 1818 Steuben Co, NY res Wayne; res there 1820 ae 63 when had w ae 60. F-S44975 R1394
IRVINE, James, est Halifax Co, VA, where b 9/4/1755; mvd 1796-1797 to Jessamine Co, KY for 2 years, thence Green Co (later Adair Co), KY; PN 1832 Adair Co, KY. F-S4422 R1394
 James, esf 1776 Lunenburg Co, VA, where raised; mvd 1797 to Jessamine Co, KY, where PN 1818 ae 68; res there 1820 ae 64 when had w aec 62; res there 1835 ae 77; QLF states sol dd 1851 ae 97; QLF states sol b 1754 Mecklenburg Co, VA, & dd 1851 ae 97 Jessamine Co, KY. F-S36611 R1394
 John, esf 1782 Augusta Co, VA; PN aec 64 Rockbridge Co, VA, 1832 when blind & had no w or children. F-S39763 R1394
 Matthew, surgeon in Colonel Henry LEE's VA regiment; BLW 342 issued 4/11/1807 res Charleston, SC. F-BLW342 R1394
 William, b 9/26/1763 Halifax Co, VA, where esf 1779 sub for bro Samuel; res there to 1795, thence Fayette Co (area later Jessamine Co), KY, thence 1815 Orange Co, KY, where PN 1833; QLF states sol s Samuel bc 1783-4. F-S16422 R1394
IRWIN, John, see IRVINE, John. F-S39763 R1394
ISAACS, Samuel, b 1759 Frederick Co, VA; mvd to Ninety-Six District, SC, where esf 1776; mvd to Wilkes Co, NC where esf in regiment commanded by f Colonel ISAACS who taken POW by British, carried to England, & later released; sol mvd to Pendleton Co, SC where esf 1787 against indians; mvd later 1787 to Franklin Co, GA where home destroyed 1788 by indians but w & ch escaped; mvd 1807 to Lincoln Co, TN, where PN 1833; md c1777; surname also spelled ISAAKS; QLF states sol f also named Samuel, who dd in SC; QLF 1910 from desc Mrs F L MONTGOMERY, Muskogee, OK; QLF states sol dd c1845 Bedford Co, TN. F-S5600 R1395
ISBELL, Benjamin, b 3/18/1763 Goochland Co, VA, where esf 1778 or 1779 sub for bro Lewis; res after RW Buckingham Co, VA, & Hanover Co, VA, for 7 years, thence Goochland Co, VA; PN there 1832. F-S9358 R1395
 Christopher, b 1754 Goochland Co, VA, where esf 1775 sub for James ISBELL; later esf there sub for William ISBELL (kin-

ISBELL (continued)
ship not stated for either); mvd after RW to Hanover Co, VA for c4 years, thence Loudoun Co, VA, for 1 year, thence Amherst Co, VA, where PN 1833. F-S9357 R1395
Daniel, esf as fife major in VA Line; gtd VA BLW 6/29/1784; dd 5/4/1797; md 5/18/1783 Franka d/o John LAND, Wilkes Co, NC; wid md (2) 3/20/1801 Bennet TILLY/TILLEY, Jessamine Co KY, who also RW sol (dd 3/15/43); wid PN ae 76 Macon Co, MO, 1844; wid bro Thomas LAND AFF ae 61 Jessamine Co, KY, 1844. F-W9856 R1395
Henry, esf Goochland Co, VA, where b 10/3/1760; res Caroline Co, VA, after RW, thence Fluvanna Co, VA, thence Goochland Co, VA, where PN 1832. F-S9359 R1395
Henry, esf 1776 Charlotte Co, VA; PN 1818 Bullitt Co, KY; res ae 61 Jessamine Co, KY, 1820. F-S35461 R1395
James, b 4/3/1760 Orange Co, VA; esf 1780 VA/NC; mvd from Madison Co, VA, 1817 to Warren Co, KY, where PN 1833; dd there 4/1/40; md 8/5/1819 Mary/Polly SIMPSON there; wid PN there 1854 ae 74; gtd BLW26782 there 1855; res there 1869 aec 75; dd 6/29/71; surname also spelled ISABEL. F-W7862 R1395
Pendleton, esf 1775 in VA regiment; PN 1818 Greenville District, SC; dd 3/1829; md 3/1828 Margaret LAWHON, Pendleton District, SC; wid PN ae 80 Pickens District, SC, 1853; gtd BLW34930 there 1855 ae 81; gave power of attorney 1856 to Samuel ISBELL of Fair Play, Anderson District, SC, who was present at her marriage to sol (kinship not stated). F-W5308 R1395
Thomas, esf 1775 Albemarle Co, VA; dd 10/27/1819; md Discretion HOWARD 2/21/1782, when both res Wilkes Co, NC; wid PN ae 78 Caldwell Co, NC, 1843; dd 6/24/48; ch births: Prudence 9/5/1783, Benjamin 10/19/85, John 2/11/88, & Thomas (date not given); QLF 1926 from Miss Emma HAMPTON, Cleveland, TN, states sol b Albemarle Co, VA & had bro's James, Francis, William, & Livingston who all esf in same company with sol, further she desc from sol on her f's side & desc from sol bro Livingston on her m's side. F-W7862 R1395
ISNER, Thomas, raised in Randolph Co, VA where esf as spy; afp ae 76 there 1834; PAR, svc was after RW. F-R5502 R1395
ISOM, Elijah, esf 1775 Henry Co, VA; esf 1778-79 Amherst Co, VA; afp 1832 McMinn Co, TN; afp ae 89 there 1846; PAR both times. F-R5503 R1395
ISRAEL, John, b 1765 Albemarle Co, VA; esf 1781 Wilkes Co, NC, where res; mvd 1811 to Butler Co, OH, thence 1821 to Johnson Co, IN where PN 1832 res Franklin Township; QLF states sol dd Johnson Co, IN. F-S17510 R1395
John, b 12/24/1754; esf 1776 VA; taken POW & released 1779 in NY; PN ae 68 New York, NY 1818; res 1826 Westchester Co NY when had w Nancy. F-S44973 R1395
IVES, Thomas, esf 1777 Portsmouth, VA; PN ae 57 Knox Co, TN, 1818; res there 1820 when had w aec 57, s ae 12-13, d aec 16, & younger d ae not given. F-S38863 R1396

IVIE, Anselem/Anselm, esf 1228 Brunswick Co, VA; PN there 1818 ae 60; res there 1820 ae 64-5, occupation farmer, when had large family including w & ch: Anselm ae 26, Sally aec 23, Benjamin aec 19, Lucinda aec 17, & Washington aec 13. F-S38070 R1396

IVY, David, esf 1781 Brunswick Co, VA, where b 6/11/1752; mvd 1816 to Halifax Co, NC, thence 1823 Williams Co, TN, where PN 1832. F-S4417 R1396

William, VA sea svc; esf before 1777 aboard ship SCORPION as lieutenant; later was 1st lieutenant aboard ship LIBERTY; an S H PARKER of Richmond, VA, inquired 1853 about any PN due sailor; no action taken on query per PN Office. F-R46 R1386

JACK, James, b 6/22/1748 Cumberland Co, VA; mvd aec 6 months with m to Mecklenburg Co, NC, where sol gdf dd; sol esf there early in RW; mvd after RW to Loudoun Co, VA, thence 1803-1808 Harrison Co, VA, thence 1817 Monongalia Co, VA; PN 1830 Tyler Co, VA; res there 1842; dd 2/24/45 leaving s's & d's mbnn; bro John res near Charlotte, NC; QLF says sol md Margaret HOUSTON. F-S8750 R1397

James, esf 1777 Berkeley Co, VA; PN ae 75 Greene Co, TN 1832 F-S2644 R1397

JACKMAN, Joseph, esf 1777 Fauquier Co, VA, where b 1755; mvd 1797 to Lincoln Co, KY, thence 1800 Washington Co, KY, thence 1829 Callaway Co, MO, where afp 1835; PAR, svc less than 6 months; dd 10/6/46 Audrain Co, MO, leaving wid Phebe who res there 1853. F-R5508 R1397

JACKO, William, see JACO, William. F-S36612 R1397

JACKSON, Andrew, b 5/30/1754; esf 1777 Monongalia Co, VA where res during RW; afp 1833 Franklin Co, IN & PAR, svc against indians on frontier not truly RW svc; dd 11/47 IN, leaving ch mbnn; QLF states sol s/o Thomas & Elizabeth who had mvd from MD to Morgantown, Monongalia Co, VA, further sol md 3 times, ch by 1st w being: (1) Thomas b 1773 VA who dd near Gilmore, IN, (2) Rachel b 1775 VA who md Mr NICHOLS & res near Danville, IN, (3) James b 1776 VA who dd 1848 near Orangeburg, Preble Co, OH, (4) Catharine, (5) Elizabeth b 1782 VA who md Mr JONES & dd 1857 near Shelbyville, IN, further sol 1st w dd 3/5/1798, his ch by 2nd w being: (1) Cynthia 1802-1883, (2) Andrew 1805-1851, (3) William 1806-1851, (4) McKinney 1808-1830, (5) Sarah 1811-1879, (6) Malinda 1816-1817. F-R5510 R1397

Churchwell, b 2/15/1758 Orange Co, VA; esf 1780 Burke Co, NC where res during RW; mvd to Jefferson Co, TN, for 2 years, thence Anderson Co, TN, for c30 years, thence Marion Co, TN where PN 1833. F-S4432 R1398

Drury, b 6/21/1754; esf 1776 Culpeper Co, VA; PN 1818 Madison Co, VA, when res Shenandoah Co, VA; res 1820 Culpeper Co, VA, when had w aec 60 & widowed d, who had 2 small ch. F-S38075 R1398

Francis, b 8/1757 Amelia Co, VA, where esf before Battle of Guilford; PN 1832 Woodford Co, KY; QLF 1927 from desc Do-

JACKSON (continued)
nald L STONE of Indianapolis, IN; QLF states sol md Sally TYLER in 1778. F-S13524 R1398

George, b 6/10/1759; esf Amelia Courthouse, VA; PN 1818 Garrard Co, KY; res there 1820 when had w aec 50, s's ae 20 & aec 18 (both res TN), md d ae 19, d aec 15, d aec 13, & d aec 6; dd 2/19/31. F-S36613 R1398

George, heirs afp 1832 for svc/o sol as captain of VA volunteers, & PAR; claim sent 1856 to US House of Representatives & was never returned; QLF states sol res Clarksburg, Harrison Co, VA, s of John of Jackson's Fort (later Buckhannon, WV), who also RW sol. F-R15396 R1398

Henry, esf 1780 Chesterfield Co, VA, where b 1761; PN 1832 Powhatan Co, VA. F-S5609 R1398

Isaac, BLW12259 & 14060 issued 2/10/1794. F-BLW12259 R1399

Isaac, esf Botetourt Co, VA; PN aec 80 Mason Co, VA, 1822 when had aged w. F-S38072 R1399

Isaac, esf in VA regiment; PN ae 77 Edgecomb Co, NC 1832; dd there 4/25/42; md there 7/4/1798, 1800, 1801 or 1802 Winifred BRAKE/PROCTOR; wid PN there 1850 ae 82; only ch b 20 Oct in 2nd year of marriage & dd aec 8; QLF states sol (b 1754 & md Elizabeth CLAIBORNE) was s of Isaac, who b 1718. F-W944 R1399

James, b 1757 Orange Co, VA; esf 1778 Burke Co, NC, where res; mvd c1801 to Pike Co, KY where PN 1833; QLF 1909 from desc Mrs S W FOSTER, Atlanta, GA, who also desc/o RW sol's Walter & Benjamin JACKSON of NC, & of RW sol's Thomas COBB of GA & Robert MOTLEY of NC. F-S38077 R1399

James, BLW12262 issued 5/5/179-. F-BLW12262 R1399

James, esf 1776 VA; PN ae 57 Madison Co, VA, 1818; res there 1823 ae 63 when family w ae 57 & ch: Betsy ae 33, Polly ae 21, Patsy ae 19, Tabitha ae 15, Joseph ae 19, & Humphrey ae 14; occupation then millwright. F-S38071 R1399

John, esf 1778 Louisa Co, VA, where res; dd 9/4/1829; md Katharine/Catharine WHITE, Hanover Co, VA 10/27/1787; wid PN ae 72 Louisa Co, VA, 1842 when ch included Elisha; gtd BLW 36219 there 1855; QLF 1929 from desc Mrs W O DABNEY; QLF 1910 from gdd Mrs J C QUARLES, Jeffersonville, IN, states sol w dd just before Civil War ae 90; QLF 1904 from desc Fredericka Fleming HOFFMAN of Philadelphia, PA, states sol wid dd 4/26/1859; QLF 1903 from Allan Douglas CARLILE of Pittsburgh, PA, desc/o a RW sol George JACKSON, b Lewis Co VA, eldest s of John who emigrated from England to Calvert Co, MD 1748, mvd to Moorefield, Hardy Co, VA, thence Jackson's Fort (later Buckhannon, WV) with f George. F-W3425 R1399

John E, esf 1775 ae 17 Amelia Co, VA, with 2 older bro's; dd 7/8/1810; added middle initial E after RW so as to distinguished from other RW sol John JACKSON; md 3/30/1793 Jane BAILEY (MB 3/27/93) Lunenburg Co, VA; wid PN aec 75 Nottoway Co, VA, 1846 when s Thomas AFF res there then AFF sol survived by wid & 6 ch (4 s's & 2 d's); wid gtd BLW36721

JACKSON (continued)
   there in 1855; records contains copy/o LWT of Edward JACK-
   SON of Nottoway Co, VA, dated 10/19/1789 listing w Abigail
   & ch: Daniel, Milliman HAMOCK, Edward, Lucy, William Parrish, Mary HOWARD, John, Silvaner FRANK, Phebe WHITESIDES,
   Benedick, Moses, Ephraim, Woody, Ambrose, & Reubin. F-
   W3823 R1399
John, esf 1779 Bedford Co, VA; mvd to Madison Co, KY, thence
   1807 Knox Co (area later Laurel Co), KY, where dd 2/10/33;
   md 1/24/1787 Mary HANCOCK (MB1/15/1786 signed by sol & another John JACKSON), Madison Co, KY; wid afp ae 77 Laurel
   Co, KY 1846 & PAR, less than 6 months svc; eldest s Jarvis
   (b 1/18/1788) AFF then there sol & w had 8 ch, 6 of which
   liv then, & that f preparing afp when dd; births in family
   bible (all surname JACKSON): John 6/10/1762, Polly 10/29/
   1762, Jarvis 1/18/1788, George 8/12/1790, Caty 4/17/1793,
   Handcock 5/12/1796, Lee 5/10/1800, John 10/2/1803, Humphrey 9/14/1806 & Stephen 7/25/1809; AFF 1846 Garrard Co, KY
   by John BUFORD (b 2/12/1765 Bedford Co, VA) that he served
   in RW with sol; s Jarvis exec/o m's LWT 1848 Laurel Co, KY
   F-R5519 R1399
John C, esf 1778 Amelia Co, VA, where b 1744; PN 1833 Franklin Co, KY; QLF states a VA RW sol John JACKSON md Elizabeth CUMMINS; QLF 1923 from desc Louis P BARNETT, Columbia
   MO. F-S2648 R1399
Jonathan, esf 1775 Westmoreland Co, VA, where b 1755; mvd c
   1790 to Mecklenburg Co, VA, where PN 1832; mvd to Grainger
   Co, TN, 1836 to be with ch mbnn; dd 6/24/42; QLF 1938 from
   desc Mrs J Louis CRUM, Columbia, MO, states she desc/o sol
   d Sarah & h John STANFIELD. F-S1836 R1399
Jonathan, esf 1776 King George Co, VA; PN ae 74 Washington
   Co, TN, 1818; res there 1820 when had w & 9 ch, all ch having mvd away from home, except d ae 39 (with 3 ch) & d ae
   27 (1 ch) both widows; occupation shoemaker; dd 3/1/35; md
   8/9/1779 Mary by announcement of banns in church, King and
   Queen Co, VA; wid PN ae 86 Washington Co, TN, 1843; s William (b 3/31/1789) AFF 1844 he 5th ch/o parents; birth data in file (all surname JACKSON): Loyd 1/13/1810, Nancy
   6/27/1813, Alexander 2/6/1815, John T 7/22/1816, Rebeccha
   11/6/1817, Johnathan 6/4/1819, Elizabeth 2/11/1821 & James
   T 2/22/1823; sol 1st ch b on day sol returned from RW svc.
   F-W15 R1399
Joseph, esf 1777 Bedford Co, VA, where b; POW of British and
   indians with Daniel BOONE 1778-83; settled 1800 Madison Co
   KY, thence c1802 Bourbon Co, KY, near town of Paris, where
   PN 1832 ae 75; dd there 5/10/44; md 8/20/1801 Charlotte
   PAYNE, Madison Co, KY; wid PN ae 68 Adams Co, IL, 1853 res
   Gilmer; gtd BLW 1855 res Knox Co, MO; QLF states sol b on
   12/15/1756 & buried Bourbon Co, KY. F-W7884 R1400
Josiah, esf 1780 Amelia Co, VA, where b; mvd 1786 to KY; PN
   ae 85 Clark Co, KY, 1832 when had s Francis F; dd 8/5/36
   there; md 11/19/1809 Sarah RAY alias Sarah STROPES, Madi-

JACKSON (continued)
son Co, KY when she liv with her m & stepf; wid Sarah/Sally PN & also gtd BLW73543 Clark Co, KY, 1852; AFF then by sol gds Josiah A JACKSON ae 48 there; wid & sol had 2 ch/o which 1 dd aec 8 & other went off to MS when about grown & never heard of afterward. F-W9332 R1400
Mark, b 11/12/1742 Brunswick Co, VA; esf 1779 Ninety-Six District, SC where res; PN 1832 Maury Co, TN. F-S1675 R1400
Mathew, esf 1781 Halifax Co, VA; afp Spartanburg District, 1853 ae 88; PAR, insufficient proof of svc. F-R5520 R1400
Moses, esf c1780 Shenandoah Co, VA, where res; mvd 1802 to Gallatin Co, KY; dd 5/1821; md 1778 Christiana, Shenandoah Co, VA; wid PN ae 76 Gallatin Co, KY, 1836 when s Hugh (b 5/3/1780) AFF for m; wid gtd PN increase there 1851 ae 94. F-W9073 R1400
Obadiah, esf 1778 Amelia Co, VA; mvd from Davidson Co, TN to Simpson Co, KY, where PN 1832 ae 73. F-S4434 R1400
Philip, esf 1775 Amelia Co, VA, where b 5/11/1753; mvd 1826 to Pike Co, GA, where PN 1833; dd there c1838; md 1797-98 Ann VINSON, Hancock Co, GA; wid PN ae 65-70 Pike Co, GA, 1850; gtd BLW30774 there 1855 ae 75; res 1856 Spalding Co, GA when ch: William (b 2/1799, decd), Charles (b 12/1800, decd), Nancy (b 3/1803, res Hancock Co, GA, md ae 17), John M (b 10/1804, res TX), & Woody (b 12/1806, res near m). F-W11931 R1400
Reuben, BLW12276 issued 12/13/1791. F-BLW12276 R1401
Reuben, esf 1776 in VA regiment; PN 1820 Henrico Co, VA, ae 72; res there 1820 with w ae 69 & s ae 23. F-S38074 R1401
Samuel, b 1756 Prince William Co, VA, where esf 1775 at Dumfries; mvd 1798 to Mason Co, KY, thence 1820 Floyd Co, IN, where PN 1834; mvd 1841 to Morgan Co, IL where dd 3/12/44; md Spring 1782 Vashti, Culpeper Co, VA, who dd Morgan Co, Co, IL, 1848 ae 83; ch liv 1855: Lucy STANSBERRY, Nancy DANIELS, Polly WELDON, Charles, Zephaniah, John, & Kessiah (ae 53, res Morgan Co, IL with h Reuben WRIGHT, ae 64); ch afp then for PN due m, & PAR. F-R5329 R1401
Thomas, b 5/1757 VA; esf early in RW when res on Santee River, Sumter District, SC; mvd to KY, then to TN, then to Wilkinson Co, MS, then to East Feliciana Parish, LA, where PN 1832, & res 1833; w dd long before sol who dd 11/20/44; surv ch: Chesley (eldest, res there 1853), Charlotte DEES, Temperance WILKENSON, Elsafin, Eliza ANDREWS, & Elizabeth FERGUSON; s Elsafin/Elsapah/Ellzey esf res near Clinton, LA, for War of 1812, dd 8/17/1874 when res Summit, Pike Co MS, divorced 1st w Mary 11/18/1857 East Feliciana Parish, LA, & she dd 5/1/68 at res of her s J H JACKSON there; Elsafin md (2) 5/12/60 Miss Martha E CAUSEY, Liberty Township, Amite Co, MS who PN ae 35 for h War of 1812 svc 1879 res near Summit, MS & dd 3/5/1915, her ch by Elsafin being Thomas (b 12/6/61), Eula AYCOCK (b 6/21/64), Bertha QUIN (11/26/67), & Elsie QUIN (b 10/17/74); Elsie QUIN afp 1937 McComb, MS, due m, & PAR, under current law PN not allowed

JACKSON (continued)
 for ch or gdc/o War of 1812 sol's; QLF states sol md Frances when res near Clinton, LA. F-S31166 R1401
William, esf 1777 Dorset Co, MD where b 1759; PN 1834 Davidson Co, NC, when res Grayson Co, VA; dd 6/22/49; md Jemima BURNETT, 8/8/1814; wid PN ae 66 Carroll Co, VA, 1853. F-W7883 R1401
William, esf 1776 near Juniata, PA; later esf Baltimore, MD; esf 1780 Petersburg, VA; mvd c1784 to Buckingham Co, VA; gtd BLW1791; PN ae 64 Blount Co, TN, 1818; res there 1820 when had w Peggy ae 56 & s Lorenzo aec 15; a neighborhood committee sent letter to PN Office claiming sol was member of British army, who deserted when CORNWALLIS was in Carolinas, came to Albemarle Co, VA, thence Augusta Co, VA, & Shenandoah Co, VA, taught school in VA until mvd to Greene Co, TN; sol dropped from PN rolls; PN restored 1823 when sol went to court & proved he wrongfully defamed by neighbors; res 1837 Lauderdale Co, AL. F-S38079 R1401
William, esf 1776-7 Amelia Co, VA where b 1758; PN 1832 Wilson Co, TN. F-S1676 R1401
William, b 3/10/1764 Prince Edward Co, VA; mvd when small ch to Amelia Co, VA; esf there 1779; mvd after RW to NC for 2 years, thence TN, where PN Davidson Co, TN, 1832 when res there over 35 years; cousin William JACKSON Sr AFF there then ae 74 he esf with sol Amelia Co, VA. F-S4431 R1401
William, free man of color, esf 1780-81 Amherst Co, VA; mvd after RW to Bedford Co, VA where PN 1825 aec 65 when had w aec 74-5 & niece aec 35 (had 4 small ch); dd 4/10/30; md Summer 1783-4 Nicy/Nicey HILL, a free woman of color; wid PN ae 77 Bedford Co, VA, 1839. F-W7877 R1401
JACO, William, esf 1777 VA; PN ae 82 Pike Co, OH, 1818; res ae 84 Bracken Co, KY, 1821, when res with s-in-law. F-S36612 R1402
JACOB, John Jeremiah, esf 1776 in MD regiment; gtd BLW1405; PN ae 61 Hampshire Co, VA, when w very feeble; res 1820 Allegany Co, MD, with w's s; dd 3/23/39; md (2) 7/4/1821 Susan J McDAVITT, Allegany Co, MD; wid PN ae 58 Hampshire Co, VA 1853 res Romney when had s-in-law John W VANDIVER; gtd BLW 15431 there 1855; last PN payment made to her there 1866; sol surname also spelled JACOBS. F-W11930 R1402
JACOBS, Benjamin, esf 1778 NC; PN aec 60 Middlesex Co, VA, occupation farmer, 1818; res there 1820 ae 65 when w Frances ae 63. F-S38073 R1402
 David, esf 1777 PA where b; PN aec 55 Tyler Co, VA, 1818; ch res at home 1820: Jacob 6 5/17/1811, John b 11/22/13, & Prudence b 5/29/20; sol dd 5/18/35 there; wid Elizabeth (b 10/1788) res there 1836; QLF states sol middle name Hickman. F-S38865 R1402
 John, b 3/26/1763; esf 1780 Fredericksburg, VA; PN Scott Co, KY, 1833; dd 11/1/47; md 2/12/1784 Ann PRICE, Stafford Co, VA; wid PN there 1848 ae 80, when s John AFF there ae 51; sol bro Robert AFF there then; wid gtd BLW41581 Owen Co,

JACOBS (continued)
KY, 1855 ae 87; ch births: Zachariah 11/24/84, William 9/19/87, John 6/7/89, Matthew 9/30/91, Mary 2/21/94 (dd 7/23/06), Elijah 5/21/95, Allen 11/29/97, Benjamin 3/16/99 Elizabeth 12/27/1801, Melinda 5/19/04, Nancy 10/24/06 (dd 3/13/30), & Mary 12/25/08; other births: Eliza Ann 12/17/1821, Sefrona JACOBS 2/20/1826. F-W9071 R1402

John, esf 1777 in VA regiment; dd 2/11/1831; md 10/30/1783 Sarah WRIGHT by announcement of banns in Elk Run Church in Fauquier Co, VA; ch births: Deborah 6/12/1784, Jacob 2/6/1786, Toliver 4/4/88, Ephraim 3/15/90, Margret 10/18/93, Pernelleper 5/30/94, John W 11/18/96, Polly H 3/18/1800, Sally H 12/7/02, Aquilla 10/18/05, Elijah 5/6/08 & Alexander 5/4/11; wid PN ae 80 Gallatin Co, KY 1843; dd 12/27/48 leaving ch: Deborah EMBY, Jacob, Toliver, Ephraim, Margaret STANFORD, Priller EMBRY, Polly H WRIGHT, Sally H LEMION, Aquilla, Elijah, & Alexander who all gtd PN due m 1851 Franklin Co, KY, after s Aquilla afp Gallatin Co, KY, for her surv ch. F-W9069 R1402

Samuel, esf 1776 Culpeper Co, VA; PN ae 72 Washington Co, IN, 1832; dd 1/26/40 Johnson Co, IN; md 10/24/1833 Lydia GROVES, Washington Co, IN; wid PN 1858 Lawrence Co, IN, ae 53; gtd BLW82006 there 1856; QLF 1909 from desc Harold BLAKE; QLF 1931 from desc Ruth CRALLE, Inglewood, CA, says sol md (1) 1782 Elizabeth MARTIN (1762-?) & they had 9 ch including Bennett, James, Milburn, Martin, & Elizabeth, further sol & 2nd w had ch: George Arnold, Mason & Amanda, further wid md (2) Abraham LEMON; QLF 19-- from Estelle C (Mrs Charles H) WATSON, Evanston, IL who desc/o Peter MARTIN (f/o sol 1st w) b Prussia 2/8/1741, came to Orange Co, VA, where esf, md 9/1761 Sarah REDDING, & res later Woodford Co, KY. F-W11921 R1403

William, esf 1776 Frederick Co, MD, where b 6/19/1755; after RW mvd to Frederick Co, VA, then to Hardy Co, VA, then to Hampshire Co, VA, thence Morgan Co, OH, where PN 1832 res Olive Township; w Sarah dd c1834; sol dd 6/3/36; d Elizabeth md 1810 Pall COFMAN/COFFMAN, Hampshire Co, VA, & she afp & afb 1851 Perry Co, OH ae 66 when she referred to her bro William of VA & her sis Catharine SPRAGE of Guernsey Co, OH; AFF 1851 by John COFFMAN, Perry Co, OH that at one time sol & w res with him. F-S2289 R1403

William, esf 1776 Winchester, VA; PN 1818 Floyd Co, KY, ae 63 when had w & ch mbnn; bro Roley AFF there then; sol res there 1820. F-S36614 R1403

William, b 3/23/1766 Fauquier Co, VA where res when esf 1777 Fredericksburg, VA, as waggoner; afp 1833 Fauquier Co, VA, 1833, & PAR, svc as teamster not considered military svc; elder bro John RW sol. F-R5536 R1403

JAGGERS, Nathan, esf 1775 Craven Co (area later Chester District), SC; esf 1781 in VA regiment; mvd after RW to Lancaster District, SC for 4 years, thence Bedford Co, TN for 2 years, thence near Huntsville, AL, for 1 year, thence

JAGGERS (continued)
   White Co, IL, where PN 1832; dd 8/19/39 leaving 2 ch mbnn;
   QLF states sol buried White Co, IL.   F-S32339 R1403
JAMERSON, Robert, esf 1777 Augusta Co, VA, where b 1762; PN
   1833 Ralls Co, MO; last PN payment in file dated 1841. F-
   S16885 1/2 R1403
JAMES, Ann, former widow of Matthew LEWIS. (F-W7909)
   David, b 1764 Pembrokeshire, Wales; esf 1781 Loudoun Co, VA,
   where res; res after RW SC, KY & TN; PN 1833 Henry Co, TN;
   QLF 1913 from desc Clara C BRADFORD, Webb City, MO. F-
   S1674 R1404
   Isaac, esf 1781 Northumberland Co, VA where b 3/16/1758; mvd
   c1785 to Hampshire Co, VA, where PN 1833, when s mbnn had
   gone West 5-6 before; sis Nancy BRANDON AFF ae 67 Preston
   Co, VA 1833; QLF states sol res 1840 Hampshire Co, VA. F-
   S18053 R1404
   John, esf 1776 Sumter District, SC, where b near Statesburgh
   5/14/1761; PN 1833 that district, res Clarendon, where he
   always lived, except for 10 months in VA in 1782-1783; QLF
   1925 from desc Mrs Rachel M DYAR, Adairsville, GA, states
   sol f John Sr, b 1715-20, mvd from VA to SC & also RW sol;
   QLF 1910 from desc Mrs Wells THOMPSON of Bay City, TX. F-
   S18051 R1404
   Joseph, esf 1775 in VA regiment; PN ae 66 Scott Co, KY 1818;
   QLF states sol b 1750 Culpeper Co, VA, dd KY, md Polly, &
   their ch included John, who md Miss NALL/NALLEY. F-S35462
   R1405
   Joshua, b 1754 Northumberland Co, VA; esf 1778 Warren Co, NC
   where res; mvd after RW to Halifax Co, VA, where PN 1832.
   F-S20895 R1405
   Michael, VA sea svc, esf aboard ship LIBERTY; dd leaving in-
   fant d who dd shortly after him; sol also left sis Bridget
   & sis Susan SAVAGE + halfbro Thomas JAMES, halfbro Robert
   JAMES, halfsis Peggy BEEL, halfsis Elizabeth SAVAGE & half
   bro John EWING; sis Bridget dd before 1833 leaving heirs:
   John C MAPP the Younger, William H MAPP, Alfred H H MAPP &
   Robins W W MAPP; sis Susan SAVAGE dd before 1833, leaving
   ch: Michael, Susanna w of Hezekiah P WESTCOAT, George (dd
   before 1833 leaving ch: John & George) & Ann R RODGERS (dd
   before 1833 leaving ch: Robert, James, Edward, & Jane);
   halfbro Thomas JAMES dd before 1833 leaving ch: Elizabeth
   w of James POULSON, Cassandra w of John C MAPP, Rosey w of
   Jeptha JOHNSON, Robert, Ann JACOB, Peggy SAVAGE & gdc Margaret (only ch of his decd s William) w of John T JAMES;
   halfbro Robert JAMES dd before 1833 leaving ch: Thomas &
   Ainsley DENNIS + gdc: William (only ch of decd d Susan CA-
   GUS), Robert C, Abel & Susan w/o James DOWTY (all ch/o decd d Sally JAMES), Evelyn JAMES, & great gdd Maria SCOTT
   (d/o Maria SCOTT who d/o decd d Sally JAMES) + gdc: Elizabeth & Wallace (ch/o decd d Rosey & her h Arthur ADDISON);
   halfsis Peggy BEEL dd before 1833 leaving ch: William AD-
   DISON, Elizabeth HUNTING & Robert ADDISON (dd leaving a ch

JAMES (continued)
  mbnn); halfbro John EWING dd before 1833 leaving s Victor; halfsis Elizabeth SAVAGE living 1833; 1/2 pay PN gtd heirs F-R47 R1405
William, b 9/30/1758 Southampton Co, VA; esf 1780 Caswell Co NC where res; PN 1832 Adair Co, KY; dd there 7/24/42; md 1/1781-2 Mary, NC, who b 6/25/1762; wid PN 1843 Adair Co, KY; never had any ch. F-W2943 R1405
William, esf 1777 Gloucester Co, VA; PN there 1832 ae 74; dd there 4/13/41; md 4/15/1815 Frances CLETHERLAN (MB same date with Frances MITCHAEL per Co Clerk), York Co, VA, parish of Yorkhampton; wid PN 1853 Gloucester Co, VA, ae 72; gtd BLW26965 there 1855. F-W1875 R1405
William, b 4/14/1759 Culpeper Co, VA; esf 1781 Montgomery Co VA; mvd to Jessamine Co, KY for 10 years, thence Scott Co, KY, for c2 years, thence Edgar Co, IL, where afp 1832 when res there 3 years; wid mbnn 1842. F-R5550 R1405
JAMESON, David, b 8/19/1752 Orange Co, VA; esf 1775 Culpeper Co, VA; PN there 1832 when res there almost 60 years; member VA Assembly; Co JP; dd 10/20/39; sis mbnn res KY 1832; QLF 1920 from desc Mrs M C ANDERSON, Arkadelphia, AR. F-S3607 R1406
David, b 3/10/1757; esf 1776 Greenbrier Co, VA; PN Bourbon Co, KY, 1832; QLF states sol dd Paris, KY, & LWT probated 9/2/1833. F-S31167 R1406
George, see JEMERSON, George. F-R5551 R1406
John, esf 1777 VA; BLW1164 issued 9/10/1789; surname also spelled JAMIESON; no other data in file; QLF states a John JAMISON of VA md Frances RANSOME of Richmond, VA. F-R15404 R1406
John, b 10/22/1763 near Staunton, Augusta Co, VA, where esf 1779 sub for f George; PN 1832 Barren Co, KY; QLF states sol dd there 1832; QLF 1914 from great gds Samuel F POTTINGER, Washington, DC; QLF 1906 from desc Forrest POTTINGER, Washington, DC. F-S4427 R1406
John, b Ireland; came with f to America 1773, settled 1st in York Co, PA, mvd to Holston, Washington Co, VA, where res during RW; esf there 1775; afp there 1833 ae 81; PAR, insufficient proof of svc; dd there 8/9/37; md 1780 Nancy HAYTOR; wid dd there 4/9/38 or 4/11/39; surv ch who afp in 1853 there, & PAR: Mrs Margaret HAYTER & Mrs Martha/Patsy McHAFFY/McHAFFEY; ch decd in 1853: Susanna, Mary, Jane, Sally, William, John, & Edward A; several gdc mbnn; QLF states sol md Nancy HARDY; QLF 1924 from great gds J E JAMISON, Roanoke, VA. F-R5552 R1406
William, b 1759 Prince William Co, VA where esf 1780 sub for bro John; mvd 1817 to KY, where PN 1832 Bath Co. F-13527 R1406
JAMIESON, Samuel, esf 1781 Albemarle Co, VA; dd 4/11/1805; md 2/1769 Margaret CRAIG, per her statement (wit AFF wid md 1772-3); wid b 6/1753; PN 1842 Albemarle Co, VA; births of ch: Hannah 4/25/1774, Jane 1/3/76 (dd 12/24/1803), Eliza-

13

JAMIESON (continued)
12/6/77, Mary 4/18/80, Catherine 11/17/82, William 10/9/84
John 1/23/87, Thomas Wharry 1/17/89 (dd 1/28/04), Samuel
3/17/91, Alexander 11/20/93, & Robert 7/2/96; other JAMIE-
SON births: Alexander 1/16/1732, Thomas 11/7/1737, Mary
12/26/1742, John 2/21/1747, Samuel 7/13/1753, & Mary 10/6/
1760; Thomas CRAIG dd 4/16/1798; Hannah (d of sol & w) md
Tilman J MAUPIN, & she AFF 1842 Albemarle Co, VA, their ch
births: Samantha 9/14/1830, Cynthia Jane 11/11/32, Mary
Lidna 5/30/33, & William Bernard 8/18/37; Sintha Dabney
MAUPIN dd 3/9/1821 ae 18; Wellington MAUPIN dd 9/10/1829
ae 5 months. F-W5112 R1406
JAMISON, Robert, see JAMERSON, Robert. F-S16883 1/2 R1406
JANES, Benjamin, esf 1779 Henrico Co, VA, where b 9/1760; PN
1832 Smith Co, TN. F-S1959 R1406
JANIS, Jean Baptiste, esf 1779 with Col George Rogers CLARK of
VA to fight indians; esf 1781 VA for RW; PN 1830 St Louis,
St Genevieve Co, MO, ae 74 by special act of US Congress;
dd 10/1830; a Frenchman. F-S15901 R1406
JARED, Joseph, esf 1779 Loudoun Co, VA, where b 1/2/1760; mvd
after RW to Bedford Co, VA, then 1810 to Jackson Co, TN,
where PN 1833; QLF 1939 from great great gdd Mrs Betty Jared STEINER, Mackinaw, IL, states sol was b an only ch, &
was orphaned ae 18, & lived with m's people, his f Israel
coming to Loudoun Co, VA, from Scotland 1745; QLF states
sol dd 3/4/1835, buried in JARED Cemetery, Buffalo Valley,
TN; QLF 1925 from desc Mrs Millie HOFFNAGLE, Roseville, IL
states sol middle name Jackson & he res for time in Botetourt Co, VA. F-S1539 R1407
JARMAN, William, esf in VA regiment; gtd NC BLW4210 12/12/1796
PN 1828 Anson Co, NC; dd there 5/16/45; md there 10/1785
Mary HAMER who b 5/1764; wid PN there 1846; res there 1848
sol surname also spelled GERMAN. F-W4003 R1407
JARREL, Solomon, esf 1776-7 Orange Co, VA; PN ae 70 Monroe Co,
VA, 1818. F-S38076 R1407
JARRELL, John, see GARRELL, John. F-W7874 R1407
  William, esf 1779 Orange Co, VA, where res; PN there 1832 ae
79; dd 4/4/34 Madison Co, VA; md 12/24/1789 Elizabeth d of
Merryman MARSHALL, Orange Co, VA; wid afp ae 77 Greene Co,
VA, 1844, & PAR, insufficient proof of marriage & svc; ch
included 1st (a d) mbnn. F-R5557 R1407
JARVIS, Field, b 4/25/1756 Westmoreland Co, VA; mvd 1773 to
Bedford Co, VA, where esf 1777; mvd 1781 to Botetourt Co,
(area later Monroe Co), VA; PN latter Co 1833; signature
on AFF there 1835 witnessed by Field A JARVIS & Sally JAR-
VIS (no kinship stated); QLF states LWT of a John JARVIS,
dated 10/30/1744, Westmoreland Co, VA, listed sons John &
Field + d's Elenor, Catherine, & Jane. F-S5606 R1408
JEAN, Philip, b 10/27/1762 Brunswick Co, VA; mvd aec 10 with f
to Warren Co, NC where esf 1780; mvd c1787 to Guilford Co,
NC, where PN 1832; dd 11/18/47; md 6/22/1786 Sally PEEPLES
(MB 6/20/86 signed by Drury PEEPLES), Guilford Co, NC; wid

JEAN (continued)
  b 1/4/1766; PN 1848 Guilford Co, NC when her bro Wyatt AFF
  there ae 68; ch births (record faded & blotched): Smith
  5/7/1787, Wyatt 3/22/89 (dd 1807), Nancy 11/1/92, Betsy
  3/10/1802, Wyatt 8/27/08, & Sally 10/11/11. F-W3824 R1408
  William, b 1759 Brunswick Co, VA; esf 1776 Bute Co (area later Warren Co), NC; mvd to Halifax Co, NC where again esf,
  thence Guilford Co, NC, thence Stokes Co, NC, thence c1820
  Surry Co, NC, where PN 1832, when Methodist preacher for c
  40 years; mvd 1834 to Cool Springs, Lafayette Co, MO where
  gtd transfer of PN payments 1836; wid Elizabeth res there
  1844 & recd sol PN residual there 1845. F-S7071 R1408
JEANNERAL, Claude Francois (AKA Henry BRADFORD, because local
  citizens had trouble pronouncing his real name); svc 1779-
  1783 in French army in RW; gtd BLW20476 for svc in 20th US
  Infantry in War of 1812; PN ae 72 Frederick Co, VA, 1820
  for that svc, res Newtown Stephensburg; occupation weaver;
  family then w Elizabeth ae 52, s Vance ae 12, & d Betsy ae
  8; dd 3/17/32 there; md there c1805 Elizabeth, who had ch
  by prior marriage (James BRADFORD b 1/5/1783 & Henry BRAD-
  FORD b 10/5/84); wid afp 1838 ae 75 as Elizabeth BRADFORD,
  alias Elizabeth JEANNERAL, there stating she had md 1st h
  7/1782; PAR, h svc in RW not in American army; dd there c
  6/9/42; Goren L WHITE, adm of her estate, afp there 1853
  for her ch by sol (Vance b 5/5/1808, Betsey b 8/23/12) who
  res there then; ch PAR, f not in American army in RW, thus
  not entitled per PN Act of 1832. F-R1125 R1408
JEFFERIES, William, BLW12266 issued 4/8/1794. F-BLW12266 R1408
  William, esf Fauquier Co, VA; PN ae 73 Garrard Co, KY, 1832;
  res 1845 Morgan Co, MO. F-S16886 R1408
JEFFERS, Gawin, see JEFFRIES, Gowin. F-S32341 R1408
  John, see JEFFREYS, John. F-W26158 R1408
JEFFRESS, Thomas, esf Nottoway Co, VA, where b 6/10/1761; dd
  5/9/1822 Lunenburg Co, VA; md 9/2/1794 Mary C/Polly HAMLET
  (MB 8/9/74), Charlotte Co, VA; wid afp ae 78 Lunenburg Co,
  VA, 1852, & PAR; eldest ch mbnn b 9/4/1797; wid aunt of T
  H AVERETT, member of Congress from VA. F-R5565 R1409
JEFFREYS, John, esf Halifax Co, VA, where b 1733; blind when
  mvd with s Thomas to Orange Co, NC; dd there 12/4/1834 as
  John Sr, leaving no wid; s & only heir Thomas gtd PN due f
  there. F-S8754 R1409
JEFFREYS, John, esf 1780 Brunswick Co, VA, where bc 1765; mvd
  1808 to Orange Co, NC, where PN 1832; dd 4/15/45 Alamance
  Co, NC; md (per wid claim & witness Andrew JEFFRIES) 1822
  (MB 12/8/24 between John JEFFERS & Dilly BALLARD signed by
  Andrew & Eaton JEFFERS), Orange Co, NC; wid PN ae 80 Ale-
  mance Co, NC, 1853; gtd BLW26840 there 1855; sol bro Drury
  AFF Orange Co, NC, 1837; surname also spelled JEFFRIES.
  F-W26158 R1409
  William, esf 1777 Richmond Co, VA, where b 1758; mvd 1780 to
  Pittsylvania Co, VA where esf 1781; res there 10 years af-
  ter RW, thence Halifax Co, VA, for 15 years, thence Pitt-

JEFFREYS (continued)
   sylvania Co, VA, where PN 1832; surname also spelled JEFF-
   RES. F-S18470 R1409
JEFFRIES, Alexander, b 1762 King & Queen Co, VA; esf 1781 Fau-
   quier Co, VA, where PN 1832; QLF 1922 from great gdd Mrs W
   R MORRISON, Kokomo, IN, states sol dd after 1841; QLF says
   sol left wid. F-S8755 R1409
   Gowin, esf King & Quieen Co, VA, as fifer where b 1756; mvd
   1827 to Vigo Co, IN; afp 1829 Orange Co, IN, res Northeast
   Township, signature witnessed by Gowin JEFFRIES Jr, & PAR;
   PN 1833 Vigo Co, IN; res there 1834. F-S32341 R1409
   Isaac, BLW1157 issued 1/29/1799 to Richard JEFFRIES & other
   heirs; BLW2703 issued 1/29/1799 to Richard & Ann JEFFRIES,
   only surv heirs. F-BLW1157 R1409
   John, b 2/7/1760; esf 1777 Essex Co, VA; PN 1832 Tippecanoe
   Co, IN, res Fairfield Township. F-S16888 R1409
   Reuben, b 1/25/1762 Stafford Co, VA; esf 1781 Culpeper Co,
   (area later Rappahannock Co), VA, where res; PN 1833 latter Co when res there 40 years; dd there 6/26/37; md 1/22/
   1787 Anne, d of Edward HORE of Brunswick Parish, Stafford
   Co, VA; wid dd 5/20/41 Rappahannock Co, VA leaving ch William, Reuben, Nancy, & Celia, w/o Rodham JONES; ch gtd PN
   due m 1841; QLF 1931 from Mrs M J COTHRAN, Knoxville, TN,
   great gdd of Moses JEFFRIES of Rappahannock Co, VA, states
   she probably desc of sol. F-W20178 R1409
   William, esf VA; mvd c1812 to KY where PN 1829 Jefferson Co,
   when res Henry Co; dd there 5/30/50; md 1/4/1790 Nancy
   CONNELL, Spartanburg District, SC; wid PN ae 83 Henry Co,
   KY, 1853; ch births: Susanah 4/4/1791, Martha Livana 9/6/
   96, George C 9/5/98, Elizabeth 9/10/1800, James Gillett
   12/17/02, Josiah 1/25/06, Washington 12/17/08, Henry 1/5/
   10, Jane 4/10/12, Mariah P 1/14/14, & John 6/11/16; family
   bible listed sol w as Elizabeth; d Susan KING AFF Henry Co
   KY 1854 she 1st ch/o sol & w Nancy, that sol only married
   once, that sol & w illiterate, that Mr PERRY who wrote entries in bible for sol erred in listing Elizabeth as w of
   sol instead of Nancy, further Susan's bro's & sis's res IN
   & MO except sol youngest ch Mariah who res with m; AFF by
   wid cousin Jesse CONNELL, Henry Co, KY, 1854; wid gtd BLW
   275 there 1855 ae 89; sol surname also spelled JEFFRIS.
   F-W9076 S1409
JEFFRYS, Thomas, see JEFFRESS, Thomas. F-R5565 R1409
JEMERSON, George, captain in rangers VA & KY; never afp; dd
   5/1/1834 Ashtabula Co, OH; md 4/9/1797 Elener GREEN, Nia-
   gara, NY; wid afp & afb 1850 Wyoming Co, NY; PAR & BLAR.
   F-R5551 R1409
JEMISON, John, esf 1775 Greenbrier Co, VA; PN ae 67 Bourbon Co
   KY, 1819; res there 1820 with w & gds; had 3 other ch then
   who res with their md sis. F-S36623 R1409
JENIFER, Daniel, hospital surgeon in MD Line; BLW1082 gtd to
   heirs 2/24/1824; heir then was s Walter H, per Fairfax Co,
   VA, court. F-BLW1082 R1409

JENINGS, William, see JENNINGS, William. F-W27144 R1409
JENKINS, Anthony, esf 1776 Culpeper Co, VA where b; mvd 1818 to Lincoln Co, KY, thence Knox Co, KY, thence 1825 Mercer Co, KY; PN there 1832; dd 4/22/37, w having dd 10/1836; s Anthony gave power of attorney 1853 to agent to claim any PN due f. F-S16426 R1410
Caleb, esf ae 16 Gloucester Co, VA; PN there 1832 ae 72. F-S8757 R1410
Charles, BLW12273 issued 7/14/1792. F-BLW12273 R1410
Charles, esf 1779 VA; PN ae 75 Burke Co, NC, 1821 when had w aec 70 & no ch of their own res with them, but 4 orphaned ch res with them then; occupation farmer. F-S41693 R1410
Edward, esf c1776 Frederick Co, VA; VA BLW4881 issued 1/21/1799; dd there c1820; md c1776 Mary who dd there c1843; 7 ch including Stephen (eldest), Edward Jr & Adam (youngest, with whom wid liv as late as 1841); only surv ch Adam afp 1855, & PAR, no PN to ch per current PN law; Adam had w & 4 sons then; sol s Stephen md & res near Frederick Co, VA & dd c1852; sol s Edward Jr served in War of 1812, mvd to OH or IL, & not heard of for some years in 1855; QLF 1937 from great gdd Mrs Jessie W RHONEMUS; (file includes following record of an Edward JENKINS of Frederick Co, VA, who esf 1813 Newtown, VA for War of 1812; gtd BLW ae 68 Guernsey Co, OH, 1850: mvd to Peoria, IL; gtd BLW there 1855; dd there 2/2/56; md 1811 Sarah, d of John CUMMINS, near Winchester, VA, who dd 10/27/37 OH; BLW44592 gtd sol's only surv minor ch Martha DENNIS, who b 8/2/36 OH & res 1856 Guernsey Co, OH; sol s George res 1856 Peoria, IL; sol d Lucinda TATTERSHALL res 1856 Peoria, IL, & AFF there then; a George TATTERSHALL res there then, kinship to Lucinda not stated). F-R5573 R1410
Ezekiel, esf 1779 Loudoun Co, Va; PN 1832 Clarke Co, IN, ae 69. F-S16163 R1410
Job, b 1/6/1752; esf 1776 Frederick Co, VA; mvd 1789 to near Harrodsburg, KY, thence Bedford Co, TN, thence Davidson Co TN, where PN 1818; res Jackson Co, TN, 1819; res 1820 St Clair Co, IL, occupation farmer when had w ae 69 & d ae 25 res with him; dd intestate 1/6/32 Morgan Co, IL, & s John N appointed adm of his estate; md 1784 (per wid AFF, 1778 per several witnesses) Elizabeth NEAL, Fairfax Co, VA; wid b 1/10/1752; ch: James Harness (dd aec 14), Job, Jonathan (dd 1806 ae 16), John Neale, Elizabeth, Mary, James (dd c 1832) & Martha (dd c1829); PN 1842 Pike Co, IL when s John N AFF he b VA 1/24/1789; d Mary (b 12/24/93) & her h John ROACH (b 9/1794) both AFF 1851 there they md 2/6/1822, & their ch births: Joshua Harnes 12/22/1823, Isaac Clarke & twin Jacob Buckley 6/24/25, Nancy Jane 9/21/27, William Jinkens 11/2/30, & James Nowlen 1/3/34 (dd 11/26/44), further sol wid dd there 1/8/45, further Mary ROACH then only surv ch of sol & w. F-W26806 R1410
John, esf 1777 VA; gtd BLW2174; PN 1823 Hardy Co, VA aec 65; sol res 1839 Shelby Co, IL with d & s-in-law with whom sol

JENKINS (continued)
  had lived for 15 years; QLF states sol dd there. F-S36632 R1410
John, esf 1778 VA; one of heirs, nephew Rufus THOMAS, gave power/o attorney 1828 Bedford Co, VA to agent to afb; BLAR F-none R1410
John, esf 1780 VA, afb ae 70 Fayette Co, OH 1831 & BLAR; afb 1832 there 1832, & BLAR again. F-none R1410
John, esf Spotsylvania Co, VA where b 1760; mvd 1812 to Harrison Co, KY, where PN 1832; QLF states sol left wid Sarah F-S16425 R1410
John, esf 1780 Henry Co, VA; PN ae 73 Pike Co, VA, 1832; dd there 7/20/47; md 2/28/1797 Mary RUTHERFORD, Greene Co, GA who PN ae 77 Pike Co, GA, 1854; gtd BLW2846 there 1855 ae 76 P O address Barnesville; ch births: Sally B 12/2/1797, Polly W 6/16/1801, Lewisa 8/10/03, Jesse 11/1/04, Frances A 11/17/10, John R 3/4/13, & Mahalah 10/1/15; s John R res 1855 Pike Co, GA; sol sis Mary STAR res there 1854 ae 85; sol bro James A liv 1832. F-W7894 R1410
Reuben, esf 1777 Westmoreland Co, VA where b 1759; mvd after RW to Frederick Co, VA, thence Randolph Co, VA, then to Preston Co, VA, where afp 1833; PAR. F-R5574 R1411
Richard, AKA Jawdeck JENKINS, b Shenandoah Co, VA; mvd when ch to Culpeper Co, VA, where esf 1781; PN ae 82-3 Page Co, VA 1833; dd 9/10/34; md 9/2/1793 Jemimah HOLDWAY, Culpeper Co, VA; wid PN ae 77 Page Co, VA, 1840; gtd BLW87087 there 1859 ae 94. F-W7893 R1411
William, b 1762 Chesterfield Co, VA; esf 1779 Henrico Co, VA where res; res after RW Wilkes Co, NC, thence Iredell Co, NC, thence Ashe Co, NC, thence Surry Co, NC, where PN 1833 F-S7070 R1411
William, esf 1777 Orange Co, VA; PN aec 53 Harrison Co, KY, 1819; dd 7/17/30; md 12/1783 Kisiah/Keseah QUIN, Spotsylvania Co, VA; wid PN ae 72 Fayette Co, KY, 1838; dd 12/15/52; ch in 1821: Cynthia MOORE ae 16, twins Elijah & Elisha ae 15, Susan STINNETT, Sarah/Sally, Nancy ADAMS, Fanny EVE, Peggy DAVIS, Polly MOORE, & Elizabeth GEORGE; ch surv m: Elisha (adm/o m's estate, res Fayette Co, KY), Sarah, Nancy ADAMS, & Susan STINNETT, all liv 1854 except Nancy; wid other ch dd before her, leaving ch; Marwood JENKINS (kinship not given) AFF ae 58 Fayette Co, KY 1858 where he res that sol & w md at home of Marwood's f. F-W2944 R1411
William, esf 1776 VA; dd 8/26/1844 Wilkes Co, NC; wid also dd there, leaving ch: Jesse, Hiram, Tabby, Nancey, George Washington, Adolphus, Adison, Jackson, David, Solomon, & Susan; all decd 1883 except Jesse & Hiram, who afb there & BLAR, afb as minor ch when not minors; sol & w never afp. F-BLW335774 (rejected application number) R1411
JENNINGS, Edmund, b 1751 Bedford Co, VA; esf 1774 Fincastle Co VA where res; mvd to Gordon's Station, KY Territory, & esf there 1781; mvd after RW to Western TN, thence AR, thence Owen Co, KY, where PN 1832 when res there with s mbnn; res

JENNINGS (continued)
  1834 near Nashville, Davidson Co, TN, where mvd to be near children; dd 12/6/40 leaving wid mbnn; QLF states sol dd Davidson Co, TN & f may have been Jonathan. F-S4439 R1412
James, b 2/4/1757 Buckingham Co, VA; esf 1777 Prince Edward Co, VA, where res; mvd 1779 to Surry Co, NC where esf; mvd 1808 to Buncombe Co, NC, where PN 1832; dd there or Yancy Co, NC 12/4/37; md 3/1781 or 1788 Hannah MARTIN, Surry Co, NC, who b 12/25/1762; wid PN 1841 Buncombe Co, NC; gtd BLW27580 there 1855; had no minor ch in 1856; QLF states sol md (2) Hannah MARTIN; QLF 1905 from great gds Frank CARTER, Asheville, NC; QLF states a RW sol James JENNINGS. who esf Amelia Co or Prince Edward Co, VA, md Philadelphia BRUCE. F-W7897 R1413
John, bc 5/15/1752-3 Gloucestershire, England; esf 1780 Berkeley Co, VA; res after RW Bedford Co, VA; mvd 1810 to Fayette Co, PA, where PN 1836; mvd 1841 to Preston Co, VA to res with s mbnn; QLF states sol on 1840 Census of Preston Co, VA ae 92, res with Jonathan JENKINS; QLF states a John JENNINGS came from London, England, to Tazewell Co, VA, & probably served in RW, he s of William & had s Miles & Samuel Odd. F-S13529 R1413
John, VA sea svc, esf as sailing master on schooner PATRIOT, later commander of ship FLY; dd VA 1803 leaving 5 ch, 2 of which dd under ae; LWT 1801 appointed Mary JENNINGS (kinship not stated) executrix; s Thomas gtd 1/2 pay PN Hampton, VA, 1837 for self, sis Ann A MAURICE/MORRIS/NORRIS, & sis Jane w/o Thomas H WILLIAMS of Portsmouth, VA; s Thomas decd 1845 when Thomas H WILLIAMS res Portsmouth, VA; QLF states sol from Elizabeth City Co, VA, md Lydia BATTS, mvd after RW to NC but later returned to VA. F-R48 R1413
Royal, b 1762 Henrico Co, VA; mvd with f to Prince Edward Co VA, thence Charlotte Co, VA, where esf 1889; res after RW NC, thence Grainger Co, TN, where PN 1833 when res there c 38 years; dd 2/1/39; children mbnn; QLF states sol given name also spelled Rial. F-S1541 R1413
William, b 2/26/1761; esf 1777 Prince Edward Co, VA, where res; mvd c1786 to TN, where PN 1832 Lincoln Co; res 1836 Shelby Co, AL; dd 7/14/40; md 1/18/1787 Polly KIDD, who b 11/4/1771; wid PN 1844 Shelby Co, Al; ch births: Martin 4/4/1787, Nancy 9/4/89, Elizabeth 1/1/92, Allen 12/28/94, Nancy Allen 3/14/96, William K 7/19/98, Salley 2/10/1801, Webb 5/11/02, William Calvin 6/20/03 or 6/20/05, Robert 4/18/08, Lucreecy 5/12/10, Sophy 5/27/12 (dd 6/6/12), & James W 12/31/13; other bible data: James JENNINGS & Mary BEVELL md 8/4/1836, John B SMOOT (b 3/4/1795, dd 7/12/40) md 12/30/1820 Salley W JENNINGS, (dd 1/12/42); wid res Parish of Claiborne, LA, 1851 with s James W & family; surname also spelled JENINGS; QLF states sol buried Harpersville, AL; QLF 1896 from desc D W SHOFNER, Erin, TN; QLF states a William JENNINGS, b 1726 Hanover Co, VA, dd 1793 Nottoway Co, VA. F-W27144 R1413

JENNINGS, William, esf VA; dd 10/10/1791 Hampton, VA; Thomas
CLARKE of Elizabeth Co, VA, adm/o sol estate; gds James R
JENNINGS res 1845 Washington, DC; gds William W R JENNINGS
res Norfolk, VA 1849, who bro of Mrs Thomas CLARKE, India-
na, Amanda, James, & Mrs ROBINSON; PN gtd to James R JEN-
NINGS for all heirs 1846; QLF states sol esf Fauquier Co,
VA; QLF states a Robert JENNINGS gtd BLW 1834 for RW svc/o
f William JENNINGS Jr who s/o William who dd 1775 Nottoway
Co, VA, further Robert md Agnes DICKERSON, & they res 1793
Wilkes Co, GA, in which year sol dd. F-R15422 R1413
William, VA sea svc, esf 1777 aboard ship PATRIOT; PN ae 80
Elizabeth City Co, VA, 1838; dd 8/21/38; QLF 19-- from his
great great gdd Mrs T H BAKER, Louisville, KY, also great
great great gdd of RW sol James LYNCH; QLF 1925 from desc
Mrs Hazel Moren KOHLMORGAN, Norristown, PA, states sol esf
from res in Fauquier Co, VA; QLF 1914 from Mrs Ollie Bal-
linger McKEEVER. F-S5615 R1413
JERNIGAN, George, b 1753 Nansemond Co, VA; esf 1778 Dobbs Co,
NC, where res; PN 1832 Wayne Co (area formerly Dobbs Co),
NC. F-S8756 R1414
JESSE, William, b 11/14/1758 Essex Co, VA; esf 1780 Powhatan
Co, VA; PN 1832 Prince Edward Co, VA; dd there 12/24/41;
md 1/6/1784 Elizabeth NIX (MB 1/4/1785 per Co Clerk), Powhatan Co, VA; sol & w mvd from that Co to Amelia Co, VA,
thence Prince Edward Co, VA; wid PN ae 75 that Co 1843,
when d Dianna AFF family bible showed parents married 1/6/
1784; ch births: Anderson 11/26/1786, Judith 11/1/88, Sarah 3/8/90, Ann 4/1/92, Mary 12/14/93, Elizabeth 4/1/96, &
Dianna/Dianner 4/20/99 (md Mr FORD); a Disey FORD witness
for sol wid 1843, & D A FOARD witness for sol wid 1848 (no
kinship given). F-W8325 R1414
JESSEE, Thomas, b 1/1754 Amelia Co, VA; esf 1781 Cumberland Co
VA, where had mvd ae 8 with f; mvd several years after RW
to Prince Edward Co, VA for c2 years, thence Goochland Co,
VA, for c2 years, thence Henrico Co, VA, VA, thence 1815
Adair Co, KY where afp 1836 res near Columbia; PAR, insuf-
ficient proof of svc. F-R5581 R1414
JETER, Dudley, b 9/20/1754 VA; esf 1775-76 Wake Co, NC, where
res; afp DeKalb Co, GA, & PAR. F-R5584 R1414
Fielding, esf 1779 Richmond, VA; PN 1818 Fayette Co, KY, ae
56; res there 1820 when had w, 2 d's, & s aec 18; dd 9/27/
43 leaving no wid; s John afp 1853 Fayette Co, KY; no indicated action on John's afp. F-S36629 R1414
James, b 1759 Amelia Co, VA; esf Chester District, SC, where
res; PN 1832 Union District, SC; wid mbnn liv 1839. F-
S21840 R1414
Littleton, esf 1775 near Fredericksburg, VA; PN aec 64 Fayette Co, KY, 1818; res there 1821 when had 5 ch, 3 s's of
which eldest aec 18, & 2 d's, liv at home who dependent on
him for support; dd 5/20/42 or 5/26/42 Lexington, KY; md
9/7/1786 per Co clerk, (2/19/1789 per sol wid) Jane ALSOP,
Caroline Co, VA; wid PN ae 71 Fayette Co, KY 1843 res Lex-

JETER (continued)
ington; s Hugh res there 1853; Fielding, sol younger bro, b 1/1763, res there 1843; QLF 1936 from desc Mrs John Kenneth PATTERSON, Santa Barbara, CA who desc from sol s Hugh who dd Bloomington, IL. F-W9077 R1414

JETT, William, esf Fauquier Co, VA where b 1764; PN there 1834 & dd 4/23/51. F-S16885 R1414

William Storke, esf 1779 King George Co, VA, where b 9/27/1763 near Leeds (area later Westmoreland Co); PN 1832 res there; dd c1844 leaving s Charles C of that Co who res Oak Grove; QLF 1926 from desc Miss Eva JETT of Reedsville, VA; QLF 1920 from desc Miss May PINCKARD of Forsyth, GA; QLF 1895 from sol gds John L MARYE, Alexandria, VA, states his m Jane Christian MARYE, d of sol, liv then; QLF 1917 from Custie Jett (Mrs C F) HAGANS, Bristol, VA, desc of a VA RW sol Stephen JETT whose LWT recorded 1832 Washington Co, VA F-S5614 R1414

JEWELL, Elisha, b 1762-63 Montgomery Co, MD; esf 1780 Loudoun Co, VA, where res; PN 1832 Fairfax Co, VA; dd 5/13/34; md 1789 Mildred HODGKINS (MB 11/20/89) Loudoun Co, VA; wid b 8/26/1763; PN 1838 Fairfax Co, VA. F-W7890 R1415

Jonathan, esf 1780 Loudoun Co, VA; afp ae 74 Barren Co, KY, 1834, & PAR. F-R5586 R1415

Joseph, b 10/13/1752 Hunterdon Co, NJ; mvd 1772 to NY where esf 1776 res Orange Co; mvd 1784 to Augusta Co, VA for several years, thence Botetourt Co, VA, thence 1808 Cumberland Co, KY, where PN 1832 totally blind when d Catherine LEWIS AFF there, her signature witnessed by Richard & Thomas LEWIS (kinship not stated); sol dd 8/1/40. F-S15480 R1415

William, esf 1779 Augusta co, VA; 1st w dd c1817; md (2) in 3/1818 or 4/1818 Mary ARMS, Scott Co, VA, then mvd to Hawkins Co, TN, where PN 1832 ae 89; dd there 11/24/44; wid afp there 1855 ae 74, when res c15 miles from Rogersville; Absalum BUREM, adm of wid estate, AFF there 1856 she dd on 3/17/56 before PN gtd, leaving d Tabitha, w of Matthew MANESS, & ch/o decd s Joseph (Robert, Joseph, & Nancy) whose wid Susan still liv; heirs gtd wid PN 1856 & gtd BLW82174 in 1858; surname also spelled JEWEL. F-W11946 R1415

JINKINS, Absalom, esf 1776 Hanover Co, VA, where b 1759, where PN 1832, when sis Mary Ann JINKINS ae 70 & nephew Burrell JINKINS both AFF Richmond, VA. F-S5616 R1417

Anthony, see JENKINS, Anthony. F-S16426 R1417

JINNINGS, James, see JENNINGS, James. F-W7897 R1417

JOB, Enoch, esf 1776 Shenandoah Co, VA, where res; PN aec 70 Cole Co, MO, 1828 when 2nd ae 52 & no ch res with him; dd there 4/189/43; md (3) Sarah, Cooper Co, MO; wid PN ae 72 Moniteau Co, MO, 1853; surname also spelled JOBE. F-W1193 R1417

JOHN, Elhanan, esf VA; dd of disease 6/26/1847 Monterey, Mexico, while a private in VA Volunteers; md (2) Catharine who PN ae 34 Philadelphia, PA, 1848, when sol surv ch: Anna

JOHN (continued)
    Jane ae 13, Edwin ae 12, Martha ae 10, Milton ae 8, Annetta ae 5, & Mary ae 4. F-W3260 R1417
JOHNS, George, esf 1777 Alexandria, VA; PN ae 69 there 1818, city then part of DC; res there 1820 when only family with him was w ae 78; dd 2/14/22. F-S36025 R1417
    James, esf 1777 Buckingham Co, VA where res; dd 10/1817 near Lexington, Fayette Co, KY; md 12/25/1765 Mary GANNAWAY, Cumberland Co, VA; wid afp ae 87 Russell Co, KY, 1837, & PAR; dd there 3/2/45 leaving s William (res Allen or Barren Co, KY, who dd before 1852) & d Susannah ACRES who afp ae 70 Russell Co, KY, 1852 & PAR; sol eldest ch Betsy aec 70 & h James WARRINER aec 64 both AFF 1837 Pulaski Co, KY, they md 3/1793; James WARRINER AFF ae 79 Russell Co, KY, 1852. F-R593 R1417
    Thomas, esf 1776 Amherst Court House, VA; PN ae 77 Harrison Co, KY, 1819; AFF 1824 to JP, Clermont Co, OH, that he had recently mvd there from KY; QLF states a Thomas JOHNS md Nancy LAYNE before 1810 probably in Amherst Co, Bedford or Fluvanna Co, VA, & they mvd to Floyd Co, KY, thence c1830 to Lawrence Co, KY, where he dd after 1834 & she dd later; F-S41707 R1417
    Zachariah, b c1765 c30 miles from Winchester, VA; esf 1781 VA; mvd ae c25 to Rutherford Co, NC where afp 1853, & PAR; sol was illiterate; eldest bro Moses KIA in RW. F-R5594 R1417
JOHNSON, Abraham, esf 1778 Hampshire Co, VA, where b 10/1754; mvd after RW to Belleville, Wood Co, VA, thence 1810 Sullivan Co, IN, where PN 1833 res Haddon Township; f was sol at Braddock's Defeat in French & Indian War; QLF states sol dd IN; QLF states sol w Elizabeth & they had s Peter. F-S16427 R1418
    Alexander, esf 1778 Fauquier Co, VA; mvd at end of RW to NC for c3 years, thence KY for c9 years, thence Ross Co, OH, where dd 7/14/1819 ae 64; md c1786 Jane MILLER, Fauquier Co, VA who afp ae 81 Ross Co, OH 1838, & PAR, insufficient proof/o marriage; dd there 10/31/43 at home/o s Simon leaving ch: Simon, Susannah & John; had 7 ch: eldest Sarah bc 1787, Catharine bc 1789, Susannah bc 1792, John bc 1785, Simon b 3/23/1798, Thornton, & Delphina; s John mvd West c 1832, & presumed decd in 1852; s Simon & d Susannah wid of Barney MINNEY afp Ross Co, OH, both res Levin Township, & PAR, same reason as m. F-R5631 R1418
    Andrew, b Fall 1758 Germantown, PA; esf 1776 Bucks Co, PA, res Warwick Township; mvd ae 21 to NJ where esf 1797-2 New Brunswick against indians; mvd to Preston Co, VA, where md Elizabeth, whose f John was murdered by indians & she captured & held for 11 years; sol dd 3/21/46 survived by ch: Rebecca CASTLE, Mary Ann SENATE, Sarah, Isaac, & Jesse. F-S15905 R1418
    Andrew, b 3/1761 Rockingham Co, VA; f's house on south bank of Potomac River burned, & family mvd to Guildford Co, NC,

JOHNSON (continued)
  where sol esf 1782; mvd to KY, thence Franklin Co, IL; afp there 1834 & PAR, insufficient proof/o svc. F-R5599 R1418
Arthur, b 8/7/1757; esf 1775 Brunswick Co, VA; PN 1818 Gibson Co, IN; res 1822 & 1824 Posey Co, IN; in 1838 had mvd to White Co, IL, to be near children & grandchildren; dd 10/16/39; md 1/2/1779 Lucy HARMON, when both res Brunswick Co, VA; wid b 1/1/1759; PN 1840 White Co, IL, res with s; res 1843 Posey Co, IN; ch births: John 9/27/1779, Sampson 1/19/81, Nancy 12/30/83, Ritter 1/17/85, Elizabeth 7/2/87, Nathaniel 5/13/89, George 2/7/91, Benjamin 8/27/92, Winny 6/24/94, Arthur L 6/31/97, William M 12/11/98, & Lucy 5/1/1800; s John md 3/6/1800; d Ritter md 10/15/1801 John WILLIAMS, s George md 10/19/1816 Anna WILLIAMS; s Benjamin md 1/4/1821 Polly OLMON; a Zadock JOHNSON bc 4/1802 & member of family of sol 1820; QLF 1917 from great great gdd Mrs D E MITCHELL of St Paul, MN, states sol dd Edgar Co, IL; QLF 1927 from Louis R HAMILL, Matanzas, Cuba, states sol dd at Endfield, White Co, IL, further querier desc of another VA RW sol Andrew JOHNSON, b 1747 Augusta Co, VA, dd 3/1824 Grandview, Edgar Co, IL, md Elizabeth HARRISON who b 1742, dd 1830. F-W10152 R1418
Bailey, esf in VA regiment; md 1/1783-4 Hannah MUFFETT, Fauquier Co, VA; mvd to PA where sol dd 9/1805; wid PN ae 73 Ross Co, OH, 1838 res Twin Township; ch births (not including ch who dd in infancy): Metilday 12/19/1781 (note from PN Office states she illegitimate ch), Adin 11/7/83, John 12/10/86, Daniel 4/20/89, William 7/18/91, Melinday 7/11/93, James 11/22/95, Elijah 11/6/98, Jesse 6/6/99, Henery 5/6/1801, & Bailey 8/6/02 (surname for all in bible JOHNSTON); ch of d Metilday GATES: Bailey b 8/1/1800 & Hannah b 9/25/1801; sol surname also spelled JOHNSTON; QLF 1924 from great great gds A F UZZELL of Jamaica, NY; QLF 1935 from great great gds Lee S McCOY of Cedar Rapids, IA; QLF 1907 from desc Daisy S (Mrs George S) WILSON, Indianapolis IN; QLF 1913 from gds Stephen JOHNSON of Prairie City, IA F-W4006 R1418
Benjamin, esf Charles Co, MD, res near Annapolis as a bound boy, when ran away to join army; PN ae 76 Fayette Co, VA, 1834; dd there 7/15/34; md 8/7/1829 Elizabeth McGRAW, Kanawha Co, VA; wid md (2) 4/26/36 James PRICE, Fayette Co, VA, who dd 1859 IN; wid PN ae 63 Fayette Co, WV, 1866 when had recently mvd from there to Kanawha Co, WV; gave oath/o allegiance then to US; res 1878 Hawks Nest, Fayette Co, WV with her children. F-W27761 R1419
Benjamin, b 8/2/1758; esf c1777 Cumberland Co, VA, where was raised; md 1782 there Phebe who b 2/24/1765; sol dd 1826, leaving wid Phebe who dd 2/1/47 leaving ch: Dudley, Polley M TAYLOR, Cyntha BAKER, William W, & Cicero; ch births: Nancy 6/28/1783, Elizabeth 2/14/85, Rebecha 2/10/87, Dudley 11/6/89, Polly M 5/1/93, Cyntha L 10/2/94, Lucy M 1/25/97, William W 8/31/99, Cicero M 1/1/1803, & Albert B

JOHNSON (continued)
1/27/05; other births: Nancy BRYAN 2/8/1805, Nancy M, d of William & Lucy JOHNSON, 7/9/1825, Martha E JOHNSON 6/14/1828, Lucy Mannen, d of Cicero & Marthy J JOHNSON, 6/11/1831; Mary Jane JOHNSON 2/12/1834, Pheby Ann JOHNSON 12/2/1835; Nancy Jamima JOHNSON 7/29/1838, Juliet Lavina JOHNSON 1/28/1841, & Martha J, d/o Cicero JOHNSON, 2/19/1803; deaths: Lucy M JOHNSON 4/7/1840 & Mary Jane JOHNSON 4/8/1840; s Cicero afp 1853 Franklin Co, TN 1853; s Dudley afp 1854 there; both PAR. F-R5651 R1419

Benjamin, esf Lynchburg, Campbell Co, VA; dd 2/29/1834 Red Horse Shoals, Kanawa Co (area later Putnam Co), VA; md Rebecca OLDAKERS, Campbell Co, VA, 12/15/1794; afb Mason Co, VA, 1858 aec 88 & gtd BLW291229; also afp then & PAR, insufficient proof of marriage; res then 18 miles from Court House; births in bible: Susan GIVINGS, d of Lucy, b 7/11/1823, Cornell JOHNSON 1/1/1829; deaths: Isaac OLDAKERS 11/25/1840, Margaret BELVILL 12/21/1840. F-R5652 R1419

Benjamin, esf 1779 Bedford Co, VA where res; afp ae 77 Kanawha Co, VA, 1833; PAR, less than 6 months svc; QLF states s Lemuel b 1782, md 1806 Lucy COX & gave f power of attorney when esf 1814 in War of 1812. F-R5674 R1419

Cave, esf 1778 Orange Co, VA; mvd 1779 to Bryant's Station, KY Territory, where esf in company of brother Captain Robert; res there until end of RW; PN 1833 Scott Co, KY, ae 72 res in adjacent unnamed Co, when Richard M JOHNSON, s/o sol bro Robert, of Scott Co, KY, interceded for sol to get PN; sol res 1847 Boone Co, KY; QLF states sol b Orange Co, VA & res at one time Dearborn Co, IN; QLF states sol dd in Boone Co, KY. F-S8767 R1419

Charles, b 4/24/1758; esf 1776 Albemarle Co, VA, where res; PN 1832 Goochland Co, VA; QLF 1917 from desc Nora Johnson (Mrs F C) SMITH of Chicago, IL; QLF 1936 from Mrs Edwin J SNEAD, Fork Union, VA, states she desc/o VA RW sol Charles JOHNSON b 9/27/1753 (s/o Christopher b 11/22/1731 & Eliza-MOORMAN b 4/20/1738), esf 1776, & md Mary/Molley b 1758. F-S5643 R1419

Clabourn, esf 1777-8 Goochland Co, VA, where b 6/7/1760; res in VA in Chesterfield, Hanover, Louisa, & Nelson Counties before mvd c1826 to Howard Co, MO, where PN 1833; last PN payment in record 3/4/1839 in MO; QLF 1903 from desc P T TALBERT, Washington, DC. F-S16892 R1419

David, b 1757 Ireland & came to America before RW; esf York Co, PA; res after RW Philadelphia, PA where college teacher, thence Washington Co, TN, for 2 years, thence Cannonsburg, PA, for 8 years teaching at Jefferson College, then to Charleston (later called Wellsburg), VA, for 3 years, thence Beaver, PA, where PN 1832 when res there 28 years; dd there 3/6/37; md 5/8/1785 Catharine, Philadelphia, PA; wid PN aec 74 Beaver Co, PA, 1838 when s Thompson M made AFF there; wid res there 1848 ae 84: QLF states sol md Anna Catharine who dd c9/1853. F-W5009 R1420

JOHNSON, David, b 9/17/1763 Morris Co, NJ; esf 1780 in VA regiment when res near Ten Mile Creek, Washington Co, PA; PN 1833 Parke Co, IN, res Union Township; res 4/1845 Knox Co, OH, with s Levi; res 9/1845 Brooke Co, VA with s Amos, sol then totally blind; last PN payment in record 3/1850 in WV S-5641 R1420
David, b 10/10/1759-60 Frederick Co, VA; mvd aec 11 to Montgomery Co, VA; mvd 1773 to head of Clinch River where esf 1775; PN 1832 Jackson Co, IN. F-S32349 R1420
Dilmus/Dalmath/Dillamus, b 4/5/1761; esf 1777 Fluvanna Co, VA; mvd 1781 to Albemarle Co, VA, thence Fluvanna Co, VA, thence Amherst Co, VA for 7-8 years, thence c1808 Logan Co KY for c1 year, thence Christian Co, KY, where PN 1832; dd 8/29/1838-9; md 1786-7 Nancy, Fluvanna Co, VA; wid afp aec 81 Christian Co, KY, 1844 but dd there 12/23/45 before gtd PN; s David AFF there 1844 aec 47; wid surv ch 1852: Elizabeth PATTON, William ae 61, Martha LOCKHART, David, & Hannah LACEY who afp then; only ch res there then William, Martha, & Hannah; ch gtd PN due m. F-W2662 R1420
Edmond, b 1763 Caroline Co, VA; esf 1779 Lunenburg Co, VA, where res; mvd to GA, thence 1788 Natchez, MS, then to St Landry Parish, LA, where PN 1833 as Edmond Sr. F-S30509 R1420
Ellis, b Brunswick Co, VA; esf 1775 Mecklenburg Co, VA where res; res there after RW, thence Spartanburg District, SC, where PN 1833 ae 73; dd there 9/12/40; md 3/1 or 3/28/1816 there Mary BRIBE at home/o Joseph McMILLEN (ae 79 in 1854) & w Sally (ae 74 in 1854) who both res there 1854 (no kinship given); wid PN ae 78 there 1853; gtd BLW26767 there 1855; QLF 1937 from decse Mrs R L WILKINSON, Savannah, GA, who also desc of RW sol's Samuel PRYOR (res ae 83 Lincoln Co, NC), Peter HILLIARD (res ae 86 Edgefield Co, NC), William DAY (res ae 83 Pickens District, SC) & John RIDGEWAY of SC F-W7941 R1421
Enos, esf 1777 Montgomery Co, VA; PN ae 77 Hawkins Co, TN, & dd there 6/4/36; md (1) Sarah & their ch births: Susannah 12/27/1781, Mary 1/24/83, Ann 9/1/1784, Rebecker 3/1/86, Rachel 10/10/87, Rhoda 6/27/89, Kinsey 12/-/92, William 10/11/03, Ellet 11/17/95, James 6/8/1800, Johney 1802, & John 1806; md (2) 7/20/1806 Levina HUTTON, Jefferson Co, TN, & their ch: Betty 7/11/1807, Lucy 11/22/08, Pleasant Miller 11/21/10, Levina 10/4/12, Hester 10/14/14, Wila B 10/14/16, Jane Ceney 12/4/18, Dicey 12/28/20, Anner 3/4/23 & Noble Washington 7/13/25; wid PN ae 67 Hawkins Co, TN 1854; gtd BLW26160 there 1857; PN restored there 1866 ae 84. F-W11959 R1421
George, esf 1778-9 Fauquier Co, VA, where b 11/25/1747; mvd c1781 to Wilkes Co, NC, where esf soon after arrival; PN there 1832; QLF states sol dd c1828, had bro Bailey who RW sol. F-S7096 R1421
George, esf 1778 Shepherdstown, Berkeley Co, VA; mvd 1780 to Bedford, PA, thence 1789 Borough of Berlin, Brothers Vall-

JOHNSON (continued)
 ey Township, Somerset Co, PA where PN 1833 ae 79; QLF says sol md Catharine LAHR/STUART; QLF states sol buried Berlin, Somerset Co, PA, had w Catharine, & they had ch William & Sarah; QLF says sol had bro Stewart; QLF states sol dd Berlin, PA, 1837. F-S23731 R1421

Gideon, b 11/7/1754 Amelia Co, VA, s of Gideon Sr & Ursula ALLEN; esf 1775-6 Guilford Co, NC; res after RW that part of Guilford Co which became Rockingham Co; mvd 1819 to Davidson Co, TN, thence 1826 Williamson Co, TN where PN 1832 & res there 1840; bro Abner AFF then ae 74 Maury Co, TN he served in RW with sol; QLF sol md Nancy ALLEN, & their ch included Mary who md Mr PILLOW & Nancy who md James COTTON F-S4456 R1421

Gideon, see JOHNSTON, Gideon. F-S38089 R1421

Giles, esf 1779 Charles City Co, VA; PN there 1818 ae 62; wid's agent sent letter to PN Office 1843 from Richmond, VA; no action indicated on letter. F-S3090 R1421

Hardy, only record in file is AFF 1835 of acquaintance that sol emigrated from VA c1805 to Cumberland Co, NC & claimed he RW sol. F-R5616 R1421

Henson, esf 1780 Frederick Co, VA, where b; mvd after RW to to KY, thence IN, where PN 1832 Harrison Co when res Posey Township 13 years; gtd BLW26778 there 1855; dd 1/9/58; QLF 1908 from great gdd Lizzie PERIMMER, Corydon, IN. F-S16171 R1421

Howell, b 1/18/1762 Chesterfield Co, VA; mvd at early ae to Mecklenburg Co, VA; esf 1781 VA; PN 1832 Spartanburg District, SC; dd there 1/13/46; md 10/23/1796 Holly CROWDER in NC; wid PN ae 73 Spartanburg Co, SC, 1853; gtd BLW26766 ae 76 there 1855; PN restored there 1867 when lived near Walnut Grove & Poolesville since 1861; gtd PN increase there 1868; ch included eldest William L, b 1/6/1796, who res York District, SC, 1853. F-W4468 R1421

Isaac, esf 1779 in VA regiment; later transferred to PA regiment; PN 1818 Bullitt Co, KY; res there 1820 ae 72 when had w ae 65-66, s (b 10/21/1799), & md d liv with him; occupation farmer; dd 10/21/33; QLF 1928 from Mrs A D PADEN, Indianapolis, IN, whose gdm was gdd of sol, further sol w was Christina. F-S36642 R1422

Isaac, b Charles City Co, VA; f mvd family to Northampton Co NC for 1 year, thence Brunswick Co, VA where sol esf 1779; res there 13-14 years after RW, thence Montgomery Co, NC, for 30 years, thence 1826 Carroll Co, TN where PN 1833 aec 70; QLF 1922 from great great gdd Mrs S A MOSE, Williamsburg, KY. F-S21326 R1422

Jacob, name on list of invalid pensioners paid annual allowance of $50 by PN Office VA Agency; decd in 1835; rest of record lost in Washington, DC, fire 1914. F-none R1422

Jacob, name on list of VA pensioners who paid disability for wounds suffered at Waxsaws Battle; no other data in file. F-none R1422

JOHNSON, James, esf 1779 Point of Fork, VA; PN ae 58 Shelby Co KY 1818; res there 1823 ae 59 when had w ae 59 & ch: Sarah ae 35, Mary ae 22, Nancy ae 19 & Abel ae 15 + orphaned gdd Lucy JOHNSON ae 4; in 1843 had mvd to Ripley Co, IN, to be near children; gtd BLW1963; QLF 1917 from great gdd Mrs G L LOUDERMILK, La Grange, MO, states sol b Scotland, walked with crutches for rest/o life as result of RW wound, had 5 s's & 3 d's, dd 1835-45 Versailles, IN, ae almost 100; QLF states a VA RW sol James JOHNSON of Shelby Co, KY, had s Lanty, s David, & d Margaret (md James BEARD of Shelby Co, KY). F-S36664 R1423

James, BLW12257 issued 4/16/1794. F-BLW12257 R1423

James, esf 1775 Isle of Wight Co, VA, where b 4/27/1747; PN there 1833; QLF 1912 from Charles W HART, Cornet, VA, says his w great gdd of sol, further sol dd 8/1845 ae 99; same querier wrote 1924 from Norfolk, VA, stating his own w dd before 1924. F-S15904 R1423

James, b 1759 Louisa Co, VA, reared Bedford Co, VA; esf 1776 Amherst Co, VA, while visiting bro; res after RW Campbell Co (area formerly Bedford Co), VA; mvd to SC for 2 years, thence Sullivan Co, TN, for 6 years, thence Wayne Co, KY, for 33 years, thence Washington Co, MO, where PN 1833; sol bro John res there then; QLF 1910 from Mary Johnson STRONG of Indianapolis, IN, who desc of sol bro John who dd Washington Co, OH, 1834-5 at home of s Josiah. F-S16891 R1423

James, esf 1778 Lunenburg Co, VA; mvd c1799 to KY, where PN ae 63 Shelby Co 1820 when res there 9 years; res then with w & s ae 17; dd 8/11/39; QLF 1917 from great great great gdd Mrs H L PENDLETON, Prairie Du Chien, WI, who desc of sol eldest s William Sanford (b 1791, dd ae 83 Brodtville, Grant Co, WI), states sol s John De Jarnet b 1799 & dd ae 83 KY, further sol b Fauquier Co, VA, s of Mary (SANFORD) JOHNSON, further sol mvd from VA to Bourbon Co, KY; QLF states sol b 1757 Fauquier Co, VA, & dd 1839 Shelby Co, KY F-S35471 R1423

James, esf 1776 Wheeling, Ohio Co, VA; PN ae 64 Montgomery Co, KY, 1818; res there 1821 ae 68. F-S36636 R1423

James, esf 1776-7 Amelia Co, VA; PN there 1832 ae 88; dd 6/7/43; md c1786 Esther, Augusta Co, VA; wid PN there 1843 ae 75; living 1846; sol surname also spelled JOHNSTON. F-W7934 R1423

James, esf 1781 VA; afp aec 76 Mecklenburg Co, VA 1841; PAR. F-R5628 R1423

John, esf 1779 in Armand's Corps of VA Continental Line; s & heir William gtd BLW1362 Bedford Co, VA. F-BLW1362 R1424

John, esf 1776 King William Co, VA; PN 1818 Hanover Co, VA, ae not given; res there 1820 when had w ae 30-40, 4's, & 1 dd (eldest ae 13, youngest ae 5); QLF 1930 from great gdd Nora Johnson SMITH, East St Louis, IL, states sol bc 1758, dd c1835, md Jemima LEWIS who survived him. F-S38082 R1424

John, b 1763 MD; esf 1782 near Fredericksburg, VA, as teamster for French army; esf later Stafford Co, VA where res;

JOHNSON (continued)
    res there after RW for c27 years, when mvd to Clark Co, KY
    where afp 1832, & PAR, svc only with French army. F-R5634
    R1424
John, esf 1779 Hanover Co, VA, where b 5/14/1762; mvd c10
    years after RW to KY for c8 years, then to Marion Co, IN,
    with children; PN there 1835; gtd BLW26351 Fulton Co, IN,
    1855 res Rochester; s-in-law mbnn 1857 ae 62; bro Richard
    res 1835 ae 75 Sumner Co, TN where minister; QLF 1908 from
    Albert W BITTERS, Rochester, IN, whose w Emma E (nee SHEL-
    TON) great gdd of sol, further sol only RW sol buried Ful-
    ton Co, IN & buried Shelton Cemetery near Rochester, tomb-
    stone inscription says sol dd 8/7/1860 ae 96, 2 months, &
    24 days, further sol middle initial M, further sol dd at
    res of s-in-law Thomas SHELTON who was gdf of querier's w;
    QLF 1923 from Mrs Fanny Gibbs PUTNAM, Mt Carmel, IL gdd on
    f's side of War of 1812 sol Jacob JOHNSON who b 9/29/1785
    VA s/o John & Sarah whose other ch Rebecca, Elizabeth, Ma-
    ry, Hannah, John, & David, all b VA, further John & Sarah
    mvd 1798 to KY, thence 1802 Gibson Co, IN. F-S32345 R1425
John, esf 1778 in VA regiment; PN aec 63 Garrard Co, KY 1818
    when had 12 s's & 5 d's, of whom 9 ch then res with him;
    res there 1821 ae 66 when had w, 5 s's & 3 d's (eldest aec
    15, youngest aec 5) res with him; surname also spelled
    JOHNSTON. F-S35480 R1425
John, b 8/1748; esf 1775 in VA regiment; PN 1818 Scott Co,
    KY; res there 1820 when had no family; dd 3/27/1825; QLF
    states sol md Anne HONEYCUT, & dd KY; surname also spelled
    JOHNSTON. F-S36026 R1425
John, esf Orange Co, VA, early in RW; gtd VA BLW 6/20/1783;
    dd 2/24/1820 Orange Co, VA; md 3/9/1789 Elizabeth DODD,
    Spotsylvania Co, VA; wid PN ae 85 Garrard Co, KY, 1853.
    F-W9086 R1425
Joseph, esf Cumberland Co;, VA; s of James, who res 3 miles
    north of Cartersville, VA; gtd VA BLW for svc; mvd 1786 to
    Lynchburg, VA, where dd 1802; md 5/19/1786 Elizabeth, d of
    Benjamin ANDERSON, Goochland Co, VA; wid md (2) 1803 Nath-
    an WILLIAMSON, who dd 10/6/1836; wid apf ae 73 Amherst Co,
    VA, 1843, & PAR, insufficient proof/o marriage to sol; AFF
    then there by Reverend Lewis SHADOWN ae 90 who md in 1784,
    & came to Amherst Co, VA; several ch mbnn. F-R11631 R1426
Joseph, b 10/20/1755 Frederick Co, VA; mvd ae 14 with f to
    New River, VA, thence ae 18 with f to Clinch River, VA, &
    esf there 1774; esf 1775 Montgomery Co, VA, where res; md
    5/18/1776 & mvd with f-in-law's family to New River, VA, &
    esf there; esf 1777 Montgomery Co, VA; mvd 1781 to Powells
    Valley (area later in Lee Co), VA where esf; mvd c1786 to
    Knox Co, KY, for 14 years, thence Hawkins Co, OH, for 2
    years, thence Jackson Co, IN, for c5 years, thence Monroe
    Co, IN, where PN 1833; sis Elizabeth MONDAY then res KY;
    mvd 1841 to Fleming Co, KY, where bro Ebenezer res; Ebene-
    zer AFF there then ae 81 he also RW sol; sol stated at one

JOHNSON (continued)
time be b 1760 NJ & esf PA; surname also spelled JOHNSTON. F-S31782 R1426
Joseph Payne, b 7/4/1747; esf 1776 in VA regiment; PN 1818 Wilkes Co, GA; res there 1824 with w older than he. F-S38095 R1426
Josiah, esf VA; illiterate; dd 12/18/1839; md 7/24/1789 Susan MASTIN, Charlotte Co, VA; wid afp ae 75 Pittsylvania Co, VA 1840; PAR, insufficient proof of svc; Abraham JOHNSON, ae 57, one/o legal heirs, gave power/o attorney Pittsylvania Co, VA to agent 1853 to afp & PAR. F-R5665 R1426
Micah, esf 1775 New Kent Co, VA where b 8/14/1756; mvd after RW to Franklin Co, VA, thence 1822 Patrick Co, VA, thence 1828 Howard Co, MO, where afp 1834, & PAR; dd there 1844 & wid dd aec 95; heirs afp 1856 & PAR. F-R5648 R1427
Moses, esf 1777 Winchester, VA; PN 1818 Ohio Co, KY; res ae 71 there 1820 when had w aec 66-7 & no ch liv with him; PN address transferred 1834 to Lawrence Co, IL where children liv; res 1836 White Co, IL; surname also spelled JOHNSTON. F-S36024 R1427
Nahum, esf 1775 Amelia Co, VA, where b 11/1750; PN Charlotte Co, VA, 1833. F-S7079 R1427
Obadiah, esf 1780 Cumberland Co, VA; PN ae 67 Goochland Co, VA 1832; dd there 6/7/40; LWT 8/26/35, with codicils dated 9/17/36 & 9/17/38, probated there 7/20/40, lists w Polly, s Monroe, s Anderson, d Louisiana PERKINS, d Mary JENKINS, d Kitty TANDY, & d Susan JOHNSON, + gdc Reuben, Augustine, & Elizabeth Ann (ch of Reuben GEORGE & decd w mbnn) + gdd Martha (d of Susan JOHNSON); md 10/1/1786 Mary MERRYMAN, Cumberland Co, VA; wid afp ae 77 there 1843, & PAR, insufficient proof of marriage; co court clerk AFF records lost in fire before 1800; AFF 1843 by Elizabeth/Betsey HIPPEN, halfsis of sol wid, aec 65, she witnessed marriage in Cumberland Co, VA; wid dd 7/24/44 Goochland Co, VA, leaving ch: Monroe, Anderson, Susan JOHNSON, Catherine HERNDON, Louisiana PERKINS, & Mary JENKINS, all liv 1854; s Monroe, adm of m's estate, afp 1852 there, & PAR. F-R5646 R1427
Philip, esf 1777 Hales Hollow, Essex Co, VA; PN ae 60 Montgomery Co, KY, 1818 occupation farmer; res there 1820 when had 5 ch liv with him, including Berry ae 19, Langston ae 15 & Clement ae 10, a cripple; mvd c1824 to Ripley Co, IN; dd 7/11/35; surname also spelled JOHNSTON; QLF states sol b 1742; QLF states a Philip JOHNSON, dd 1788, md Elizabeth BRAY, & was member/o RW Committee of Safety, James City Co VA. F-S36657 R1427
Richard, esf 1778 in Lee's Legion, VA; PN 1829 Abingdon, VA, ae not given, where had gone to obtain evidence of RW svc, he then res of Madison Co, AL, & formerly res Halifax Co, VA; dd 8/30/42; md 9/15/1784 Frances PHELPS, Halifax Co, VA, who b 4/29/1759; wid PN 1844 Madison Co, AL; QLF 1929 from great gdd Mrs Floyd GILLIAM, Huntsville, AL; QLF 1908 from desc Mrs Martha Byrne PENNEY, Memphis, TN, states sol

JOHNSON (continued)
   b Halifax Co, VA; QLF states sol esf Halifax Co, VA, & dd near Brannsboro, AL; QLF states sol res 1840 Madison Co, AL ae 82, per 1840 Census; QLF states sol wid Frances dd 11/1845, & sol dd Maysville, AL, & they both buried there. F-W11956 R1428
Richard, BLW12275 issued 4/13/1791. F-BLW12275 R1428
Richard, esf 1777 Hanover Co, VA; PN 1832 Sumner Co, TN, ae 72. F-S2664 R1428
Richard, b 4/1762 Hanover Co, VA; esf 1781 Albemarle Co, VA; PN there 1832. F-S8766 R1428
Richard, esf 1775 Southampton Co, VA sub for bro Jordan; mvd 1800 to Johnston Co, NC, thence 1833 Greene Co, AL, where PN 1833 ae 72; last PN payment in record 1840. F-S16896 R1428
Robert, b 4/7/1759 Albemarle Co, VA; esf 1780 Bedford Co, VA where res; mvd 1787 to Knox Co, TN where PN 1832. F-S1838 R1428
Roland, b Amelia Co, VA; esf 1781 Lunenburg Co, VA, where res; mvd 1783 to Spartanburg District, SC where PN 1832 ae 74. F-S21846 R1428
Samuel, esf 1776 Wilkes Co, NC, s of Jeffrey who res on Yadkin River c9 miles below Wilkesboro, NC, during RW; f dd there after RW; sol PN 1809, disability from wounds recd at Battle of Kings Mountain; dd 9/15/34 at res on Roaring River, Wilkes Co, NC, ae 75; md 6/25/1782 Mary d/o Ambrose HAMONS/HAMMONS (MB 6/24/1782 signed by John JOHNSON), that Co; wid PN there 1839 aec 79; ch births: Robert 10/25/1783 (md Miss BORAN, sis of below named William BORAN), Nancy 10/3/85 (md Mr GAMBILL), Cloe 9/3/88, Samuel B 5/18/90, Ambrose 5/15/92-3, Mary/Polly 6/9/96 (md William BORAN), Rachel (md Mr FORRISTER), Lewis c1800 (md ? before 1834), & John S 1803 (referred to 1854 as Colonel John S); ch who survived m: Ambrose, Lewis, John S, Mrs Clay GAMBILL, Nancy GAMBILL & Rachel FORRISTER (all of Wilkes Co, NC) & Mary BORAN of Grayson Co, VA; sol nephew George was s/o William JOHNSON, who was RW officer; Nancy GAMBILL AFF 1853 Ashe Co, NC; QLF 1925 from great gds L W JOHNSON of Rock Hill, NC, states sol b 1757 near Richmond, VA, & mvd to Wilkes Co, NC, querier desc of 2nd s/o sol. F-W5012 R1428
Samuel, b 12/1744 Bucks Co, PA; esf 1779 Amelia Co, VA where res; mvd to Granville Co, NC where esf; PN 1832 Daviess Co KY, when bro John res SC; QLF 1932 from desc Nora Johnson (Mrs F C) SMITH, East St Louis, IL states sol dd KY c1833; QLF 1937 from Jack C McCUNE of Rock Island, IL, states he gds of Richard M JOHNSON, decd IL Civil War sol who gds of either RW sol John JOHNSON or RW sol Samuel JOHNSON (who PN Daviess Co, KY, & md Lydia PHELPS; QLF 1932 from desc Mrs W B NORMENT, Henderson, KY. F-S16430 R1428
Samuel, esf 1776 Essex Co, VA; PN there 1818; dd 2/11/20; md 2/5/1780 Patsey who b 1/13/1764; wid PN 1837 Essex Co, VA; dd 6/30/50 or 6/27/50; ch: Philip, Lawson (ae 27 in 1823 &

JOHNSON (continued)
  only surv ch 1837), & 2 d's mbnn; gdc: Robert & Isabella
  JOHNSON; great gdd: Catharine CARTER. F-W7939 R1428
Silas, BLW12277 issued 6/22/1793. F-BLW12277 R1429
Silas, esf 1780 in Lee's Legion, VA Line; PN ae 57 Muskingum
  Co, OH, 1818, occupation farmer, when res with him w Sarah
  ae 49 & ch: Silas ae 17, Tunis ae 14, Henry ae 11, & Peter
  ae 6; also had 2 s's mbnn liv nearby. F-S41705 R1429
Solomon, esf Accomac Co, VA where b 1759; afp 1844 Sevier Co
  TN, when res there c30 years & PAR, name listed then by PN
  Office on roll/o decd RW sol's; afp again there stating he
  b 1765 Accomac Co, VA, & esf there 1782; PAR, did not per-
  form actual military svc in period stated. F-R5664 R1429
Teresha/Terisha, esf 1781 Mecklenburg Co, VA where b; afp ae
  70 Henderson Co, TN, 1832; PAR. F-R5667 R1429
Thomas, esf 1776 Philadelphia, PA; PN ae 66 Jefferson Co, VA
  1818; res there 1820 ae 69 when res with him w aec 60 & a
  sickly d (& her 3 ch, eldest aec 9). F-S38882 R1429
Thomas, esf Louisa Co, VA where b 3/28/1751; PN 1834 Augusta
  Co, VA; QLF 19-- from desc W H SIMMONS, Springfield, TN, a
  desc/o sol d Eliza md Dr Martin, s/o John WALTON of Louisa
  Co, VA, further John & Martin WALTON both RW sol's (Martin
  (PN record F-S3473). F-S18064 R1429
Thomas, esf 1775 Charlottesville, VA; PN ae 61 Albemarle Co,
  VA, 1818; res there 1820 occupation blacksmith when family
  w Nancy ae 48 & s William D ae 6. F-S38100 R1429
William, esf 1775 Charlotte Co, VA; PN ae 76 Goochland Co,
  1832; dd 6/3 or 6/9/33; md 12/25/1784 Elizabeth WOODSON,
  Goochland Co, VA, who b 6/4/1758; wid PN there 1839; QLF
  1930 from great gdd Mrs Nora Johnson SMITH, East St Louis,
  IL (compiler's note: for several years, this lady wrote
  numerous queries to PN Office, claiming to be great gdd of
  various VA RW sol's of surname JOHNSON/JOHNSTON, apparently using this strategy to obtain data for a comprehensive
  history of those surnames in the RW). F-W7932 R1430
William, b 7/28/1754 Amelia Co, VA; mvd when small ch with f
  to Johnston Co (area later Washington Co,), NC; mvd aec 17
  with f to Rowan Co (area later Surry Co), NC where sol esf
  1776; PN 1832 Wilkes Co, NC, where mvd after RW. F-S7095
  R1431
William, b 4/6/1751 Fauquer Co, VA; esf 1776 Wilkes Co, NC,
  where res; bro mbnn wounded at Battle of Kings Mountain, &
  sol helped him get home; PN 1832 Wilkes Co, NC; QLF states
  sol md Mary PARKER after RW. F-S8764 R1431
William, b 1/5/1761 Chesterfield Co, VA; esf 1889 Brunswick
  Co, VA, where res as sub for f; mvd to Montgomery Co, NC,
  where esf 1781; PN 1832 Anson Co, NC, res Sneedsborough;
  QLF states sol listed as head of family on 1840 Anson Co,
  NC, census. F-S2661 R1431
William, b 8/2/1757; esf 1776 Amelia Co, VA when res Bedford
  Co, VA; esf latter Co 1779; PN 1832 Wayne Co, KY. F-S1226
  R1431

JOHNSON, William, esf 1779 Fairfax Co, VA; PN ae 74 Pendleton Co, KY, 1832. F-S13583 R1431
William, b 1761 Bucks Co, PA; esf 1778 Loudoun Co, VA, where res; mvd 1789 to KY, where PN 1834 Woodford Co; dd there 2/17/41 leaving no wid or ch, never having been md; Robert JOHNSON adm of estate (no kinship given). F-S30510 R1431
William, b 3/1756; esf 1777 Westmoreland Co, VA; mvd to KY c 1803 where PN 1833 Grant Co. F-S46050 R1431
William, esf 1779 Caroline Co, VA; PN aec 56 Hawkins Co, TN, 1818; dd 11/16/32 or 11/17/33 Grainger Co, TN; md 9/30 or 10/1/1790-1 Nancy BRIANT, Northampton Co, NC; wid PN 1844 aec 71 Campbell Co, TN; res 1856 Union Co, TN; dd 4/14/62 or 5/20/62; ch: eldest Patsy aec 55 in 1855, 2nd Betsy (2 years younger), 1st s Reuben (2 years younger than Betsy), 4th Julia (md Daniel WIDOWS & res 1820 NC), William, James (res 1869 Union Co, TN aec 67), youngest Ann (1820 aec 17, md soon after 1820 William DAUGHTRY, Hawkins Co, TN who in 1845 aec 64); s James only surv ch 1875, P O address Cross Roads, Union Co, TN; gds mbnn 1856; sol wid gave oath of allegiance 1869 Union Co, TN, when PN restored after Civil War. F-W24 R1431
William, esf 1779 Fairfax Co, VA, where esf 1779; esf 1780 Alexandria, VA; mvd 1783 from res Fairfax Co, VA, to KY, where res Harrison Co & other Co mbnn, thence 1829 Marion Co, MO, where PN 1832 res Fabius Township as William, Sr; dd there 6/19/38; md 3/2/1793, per wid AFF or 3/23/93 per Co clerk certificate, Margaretta, d/o Peter TITTLE, at her f's res, Bourbon Co (area later Harrison Co) KY; wid PN ae 73 Lewis Co, MO, 1843 when res with s John C (only 1 of ch mentioned); res there 1848 & dd before 1855 leaving children mbnn. F-W10151 R1431
William, b 10/1759; esf 1780 Albemarle Co, VA sub for f; esf 1781 again sub for f; mvd to Madison Co, KY, thence 1832 Estill Co, KY, where PN 1832; md twice; 2nd w never afp; d Nancy/Alsey md Micager PITTMAN who adm/o estate of sol & wid's estate 1855 when he afp, & PAR; QLF 1911 from great gdd Mrs Nora SMITH, East St Louis, IL; QLF 1939 from relative Miss Louise M JOHNSTON, Chicago, IL. F-R5650 R1431
William, esf 1777 Fauquier Co, VA when res Prince William Co VA; mvd 1781 to Greenbrier Co (area later Monroe Co), VA; afp ae 76 latter Co 1836; afp there 1837; PAR both times. F-R5672 R1431
William, esf King William Co, VA, & svd part time as wagonmaster; dd 1826-7 leaving wid mbnn who dd 1837; neither he nor wid afp, since had enough assets to live on; AFF 1837 by s Colin JOHNSON, Albemarle Co, VA, that his bro Robert D of TX then guardian for infant sisters Mary Ann & Elizabeth, other sol ch being Benjamin S, Colin, Judith J HOPKINS, Ann W w of William ELLIS, William F, Seymour & Owen D; s Owen D afp 1853 by letter from Galveston, TX, for all of sol heirs, & PAR, sol dd before 3/1831; sol dd Goochland Co, VA. F-R5673 R1431

JOHNSON, William E, VA sea svc, esf 1778 as surgeon's mate; he had no ch, but left estate to niece, who md Mr TOMPKINS, & had several ch, one of which md Mr TABB of Gloucester Co, VA, & their s John L TABB, whose only child md Nathaniel MITCHELL; MITCHELL afp 1853 New Lisbon, OH where res & gtd 1/2 pay PN arrears due sailor. F-R49 R1431
  Zopher, b in the Forks of Delaware, PA; res near Winchester, VA, when esf 1781 as sub for bro Joseph; mvd to Greene Co, TN, where PN 1832 ae 70 when res 40 years; res 1836 Greene Co, PA. F-S1840 R1431
JOHNSTON, Archibald, b 1/17/1750-1 Frederick Co, VA; esf 1777 Loudoun Co, VA, where res; res after RW Fairfax Co, VA, & mvd 1816 to Shelby Co, KY, where PN 1834; lost PN certificate in fire 1839 there & gtd replacement; QLF states sol md Jemima O'BANNON, & res with s Parrinenus when PN. F-S38091 R1432
  George, esf 1776 Martinsburg, Berkeley Co, VA; PN ae 88 Jefferson Co, VA, 1820 when no family res with him. F-S38088 R1432
  Gideon, esf 1775 in VA regiment; PN 1818 Fauquier Co, VA, ae 69; res there 1820 when mentioned s William & d Elizabeth w/o William THOMPSON; dd 12/6/25; gds William H JENNINGS res there 1850; QLF 1924 from desc Chester H FARTHING of East St Louis, IL. F-S38089 R1432
  Isaac, see JOHNSON, Isaac. F-S36642 R1432
  James, esf 1778 Culpeper Co, VA, where b 1764; mvd 1792 to KY, where PN 1832 Henry Co; gtd BLW34964 there 1855; QLF 1902 from Belle (Mrs W F) WILLIAMS of Kirkwood, MO, great gdd of VA RW sol James JOHNSON whose wid Sarah gtd PN & dd 1830-32; QLF states sol had s's James & John; QLF from desc Nora Johnson SMITH, East St Louis, IL. F-S1225 R1432
  James, esf 1776 Culpeper Co, VA; PN ae 77 Giles Co, VA, 1832 F-S5640 R1432
  James, b 1/17/1761; esf 1780 VA; PN 1819 Buncombe Co, NC; dd 7/2/52 at Shaw's Creek, Henderson Co, NC; md 7/22/1791 Ann COLE, Greenville District, SC, who b 1/5/1772; wid PN 1852 Henderson Co, NC; gtd BLW17592 there 1855; dd 1/24/57; ch births: Hugh 7/29/1794, Sarah 2/19/96, Uranah 12/27/97, James 1/22/99, Malinda 5/29/1800, Ann 11/25/02, Joseph 2/2/05, Noble 4/26/07, & Mary 8/11/10; d Ann OSBORN living 1852; d Malinda REES liv 1855; s Noble & w Charlotte res 1853 Henderson Co, NC; surname also spelled JOHNSON. F-W7935 R1432
  James, esf in VA regiment; PN 1828 Henry Co, VA; dd 4/30/41 or 1842 there; md there 4/23/1789 Joice/Joyce WELLS; wid PN there 1845 ae 77 res Turkey Cock; gtd BLW121 there 1855 QLF states sol b Charlotte Co, VA, res Turkey Cock Creek, at Leatherwood Store, Henry Co, VA, 1810-1840; surname also spelled JOHNSON; QLF states sol esf 1777 in 14th VA Regiment; QLF 1905 from J C EDWARDS, O'Fallon, MO, whose d S S a desc of sol. F-W7945 R1432
  John, b 8/30/1752; esf 1781 Cumberland Co, VA, where res; PN

JOHNSTON (continued)
    1832 Smith Co, TN; P O address 1836 Dixon Springs, Sumner Co, TN, when nephew H H JOHNSTON res there; sol dd 2/15/37 F-S1958 R1433
John, b 1732 Ireland; esf Berkeley Co, VA where res; PN 1833 (area then Morgan Co, VA); surname also spelled JOHNSON. F-S8763 R1433
John, esf 1777 Culpeper Co, VA, where b 1757; PN as John Sr 1832 Henry Co, KY; surname also spelled JOHNSON; QLF 1931 from desc Nora Johnson (Mrs Frank) SMITH, of East St Louis MO; QLF 1908 from J L VINZANT, Indianapolis, IN; QLF says sol dd 8/2/32 Henry Co, VA leaving ch Jack, Sandford, Polly (w/o Thomas FRANK) decd, & Matilda (w/o John BERRY) decd, further ch of Polly FRANK were Thomas T, Mary, Will S, Elvisa, & John, further ch/o Matilda BERRY were Thomas T & Mary, further sol survivors gtd BLW7659 issued 3/25/1834, further sol gtd BLW issued 5/20/23. F-S31168 R1433
Joseph, esf 1780 in VA regiment; PN 1819 ae not given, Henry Co, VA; dd 3/17/20. F-S36654 R1433
Lewis, esf Essex Co, VA; dd c3/1819; wid dd c4/1822, leaving ch: Lucy J BURRUSS, Mary (dd leaving d Elizabeth GOODWIN liv 1854) & Matilda (dd 1854 leaving ch Lewis & Lucy MILLER); d Lucy afp & afb 1854 Louisa Co, VA, & PAR, sol & wid dd before passage of law to allow PN to ch; BLAR, sol name not listed on return of "War's men." F-R5642 R1433
Martin, b 2/1/1758 VA, s of William & Sarah; esf 1776 Culpeper Co, VA; PN 1818 Clark Co, KY where dd 7/3/20; md Nancy WRIGHT, Culpeper Co, VA, 3/1/1779; wid b 3/27/1762; wid PN 1839 Clark Co, KY; ch: (1) William b 9/11/1780, md 12/22/1800 Elizabeth LAURENCE, who b 11/2/1781, sol wid res with him 1840 Clark Co, KY, (2) Frances/Fanny b 6/3/1783, md 2/4/1802 John JOHNSON, who b 12/25/1774 & dd before 1840, (3) George W b 7/31/93, md 9/6/1820 Murtila MURPHEY, & res 1840 TN; ch of s William births: Matilda 10/2/1801, Martin 6/2/03 (md 3/8/1822 Lucy SANDERS), Henry 3/9/05, Nancy 5/29/06, Betsey 2/28/08, William 3/11/10, Frances 2/8/12, George H 11/197/13, Cinthy 10/4/15 & John Roberts 2/17/18; other data: Laurence JOHNSTON b 10/7/1821, Cornelius SPRY b 1/6/1801, & Asa S WRIGHT md 9/9/1819 Martilda JOHNSTON; sol bro George AFF ae 84 Henry Co, KY, 1840; wid bro William WRIGHT decd in 1840; surname also spelled JOHNSON; QLF states sol wid dd 9/9/1843 Clark Co, KY; QLF 1938 from W Wayne SMITH, Moscow, ID, whose w Margaret Eunice WINN a desc of sol. F-W436 R1433
Peter, esf in Lee's Legion, VA; member of Society of Cincinnati; PN 1828 Abingdon, VA; dd 12/18/31; md (2) 12/13/1828 Ann, d of John BERNARD (formerly of Buckingham Co, VA) & w Hennington (d of Judge Poage/Powel CARRINGTON), Richmond, VA; BLW gtd wid, Abingdon, VA; wid mvd soon after h dd to Richmond, VA, where PN 1853; AFF then by Peter Jr, s/o sol by 1st w, ae 60 that sis mbnn, res Washington, DC, had family bible; sol was judge when md Ann, & marriage license

JOHNSTON (continued)
  was dated same as marriage; J W WILLS, wid's nephew & only "true heir", afp 1869 Richmond, VA, for her PN arrears, he then clerk in office/o the Register/o Bankruptcy, 3rd Congressional District/o VA; he AFF sol wid dd 6/29/65, & her LWT of 8/7/60 gave PN arrears to her niece Miss Henningham BLAIR; WILLS stated sol wid mentally incompetent when made LWT & he her only loyal heir, sol wid had dd before restoration of PN's after Civil War, and he gave oath of allegiance for her; Walter D BLAIR of Prince William Co, VA, was executor of sol wid LWT, she dying aec 91; copy of LWT in sol PN record & lists her niece Louisa E, w of executor Walter D BLAIR, & other niece Henningham BLAIR; LWT had a codicil dated 2/22/62; LWT probated 11/21/65 Richmond, VA; sol surname also spelled JOHNSON. F-W27629 R1434
  Richard, esf 1776 Caroline Co, VA; PN ae 74 Fredericksburg, VA; dd 10/29/34; bro Larkin also RW sol; s Fayette AFF in 1832 f gtd VA BLW 1808-9. F-S5639 R1434
  Richard, esf 1777 in VA regiment; PN ae 56 Monongalia Co, VA 1818; res 1820 Preston Co, VA, when had no family res with F-S38873 R1434
  Robert, esf 1780 Lancaster Co, PA; PN ae 68 Frederick Co, VA 1818; res 1820 Berkeley Co, VA; dd 12/10/32; QLF 19-- from great great gdd Eunice R PORTER, Washington, DC, says sol b NJ & dd VA (area now Barbour Co, WV). F-S38872 R1434
  Samuel, b 10/1758 King George Co, VA; mvd to Fredericksburg, VA, ae 21 where esf 1780; res Westmoreland Co, VA, after RW, thence Washington Co, VA where PN 1832 when occupation saddler & when res there 26 years. F-S18066 R1434
  Stephen, BLW12279 issued 5/11/1793. F-BLW12279 R1434
  Thomas, esf 1776 Pittsylvania Co, VA, res on Sandy River c3 miles above Halifax; PN ae 73-74 St Clair Co, AL, 1832 res Coosa Valley; dd there 12/29/32; md 4/1785 Rachel MULLEN, Washington Co, VA; wid PN ae 75 McMinn Co, TN, 1845, & res there 1849; surname also spelled JOHNSON. F-W254 R1434
  William, b 3/1759 near Shenandoah River; mvd ae 4-5 to SC, where esf 1775 Fairfield District, res on south bank, Little Waters Creek; PN ae 76 that District 1835. F-S18062 R1434
  William, b Amelia Co, VA; esf 1777 Valley Forge, PA, in VA regiment; mvd after RW from Amelia Co, VA to Prince Edward Co, VA, thence Henrico Co, VA, thence NC, thence SC, then to Guilford Co, NC, thence Salisbury, NC, thence Columbia Co, GA, thence Washington Co, GA, thence Hancock Co, GA, thence Baldwin Co, Ga, thence Bibb Co, GA where PN 1835 ae 81; last PN payment in record 1837; QLF states sol had 24 ch including Morgan P who res Three Notch, Bullock Co, AL, further sol bro James KIA in RW; QLF states sol b 1753 & dd 1839 Bibb Co, GA. F-S31780 R1434
  William, BLW1166 issued 7/5/1799. F-BLW1166 R1434
JOHNSTONE, Peter, esf 1776 in VA regiment; PN 1829 Harrison Co VA; res 1832 Monongalia Co, VA; dd 9/6/40 when PO address

JOHNSTONE (continued)
   Pruntytown, Harrison Co, VA; QLF states sol once high sheriff of Harrison Co, VA, & was made bankrupt by his depu-
   ties. F-none R1435
JOINER, Jonathan, b Southampton Co, VA; esf GA where res; res
   after RW Halifax Co, NC, for 20 years, thence Jackson Co,
   KY, thence Hardiman Co, KY, where PN 1833 ae 80; dd there
   7/25/35; md 1789 Elizabeth, Halifax Co, NC; wid PN ae 82
   Hardiman Co, KY, 1846; ch births (surname spelled JOYNER):
   Sally 6/25/1791, Poley 9/11/92, Thomas 1/18/96, Jonathan
   8/4/99 (dd 0/15/1804), & Henry 3/13/1802; surname spelled
   also JOYNER. F-W300 R1435
   Moses, see JOYNER, Moses. F-R5683 R1435
   Nathan, b 1/15/1761 on Meherrin River, VA; mvd to Edgecomb
   Co (area later Nash Co), NC, aec 4 where esf 1778-9; w De-
   lilah dd 3/20/1795 Nash Co, NC, where sol afp 1833, & PAR;
   dd there 8/17/1825; LWT probated there 11/1825; ch births:
   Mary 2/24/1775, Matthew 9/4/76 & Jonas 6/23/84; ch Matthew
   & Jonas gave power of attorney 1852 to agent to afp, which
   PAR, & PN office deemed claim fraudulent. F-R5684 R1435
JOLLEY, Boling, b Dinwiddie Co, VA, where esf 1781 when res
   there with f; mvd after RW with f to Chatham Co, NC, where
   md w mbnn; afp ae 76 Morgan Co, IL, 1842; PAR, less than 6
   months svc; QLF 1917 from U S Congressman from IL for sol
   great gdd Mrs Julia R MAYFIELD, Trinidad Co, IL who stated
   sol's given name was BOURLAND; QLF states sol dd Morgan Co
   IL; QLF 1925 from great gdd Mary Clark WORKMAN of Springfield, IL. F-R5686 R1435
JONES, Abraham, esf 1779 in VA regiment; PN 1828 Buckingham Co
   VA; res there 1832 ae 71 when gtd BLW1893. F-S46452 R1436
   Albridgton, esf VA; res 1807 Southampton Co, VA, when sold
   his BLW359 to Thomas D HARRIS of Henrico Co, VA. F-BLW359
   R1436
   Alexander, esf 1779 in VA regiment; PN 1818 Prince Georges
   Co, MD; res there 1820 ae 60, occupation farmer, when had
   w Mary aec 40 & ch: John aec 21, William aec 19, Lucy aec
   14, Nancy aec 10, Mary aec 8, Henry aec 5 & Charles aec 3.
   F-S34939 R1436
   Ambrose, b 8/10/1756; esf 1777 Augusta Co, VA; PN 1821 Floyd
   Co, KY; dd 6/12/33; md 12/30/1784 Martha CRAGE/CRAIG,
   Greenbrier Co, VA; wid b 8/10/1766; PN 1840 Morgan Co, KY;
   ch births: William 10/23/1785, Priscilla 2/18/87, Nancy
   3/17/80, Jienny 5/3/92, John 11/24/93, Richard 6/8/95,
   Barbary 4/19/97, Sinthy 6/13/99, James 10/24/1801, & Ambrose 12/31/03; s John res 1840 Morgan Co, KY; d Polly liv
   1845; QLF 19-- from desc Miss Lillian SHERLAND, South Bend
   IN; QLF 1909 from desc Miss Jeanette EMERSON, Plymouth, IN
   who also desc of RW sol Isaac SWAIM & w Hannah. F-W9083
   R1436
   Benjamin, esf 1776 King William Co, VA where b 3/28/1754; PN
   1832 Stokes Co, NC; QLF states sol res there with Elizabeth JONES (no kinship given) 1840, family records having

JONES (continued)
  been destroyed; QLF 1921 from desc Miss Rose E RICHARDSON, Moberly, MO; QLF 1934 from desc Bertram M JONES, Montebello, CA states sol dd 1833, further sol d Aquilla md Lettie d of William HOOPER (Declaration of Independence signer), Stokes Co, NC. F-S7076 R1436
Benjamin, see JANES, Benjamin. F-S1959 R1436
Benjamin, esf 1775-6 Orange Co, VA, where res; dd 12/27/1820 NC; md 5/12/1773-4 Elizabeth FOSTER, Orange Co, VA who afp aec 88 Coffee Co, TN, 1840; PAR, insufficient proof of six months svc in military capacity; sol hauled cannon balls & lead for troops; 4 ch mbnn, 1 liv at time sol esf; sol bro Morton AFF aec 92 Coffee Co, TN, 1840 that he c2.5 years younger than sol & they raised in Orange Co, VA; QLF 1934 from W C KENNAMER, Yonkers, NY, states he either great gds or great gdnephew of sol, further sol w Elizabeth was sis of Frankey FOSTER who md sol bro Morton, further sol had s Hugh & s Gabriel. F-R5699 R1436
Berryman, b 1757 Amherst Co, VA; mvd when ch with f to Augusta Co, VA, where esf sub for bro Valentine; mvd after RW to Greenbrier Co, VA, where PN 1832. F-S5632 R1436
Cadwallader, b 9/11/1745 Lunenburg Co, VA; esf Charlotte Co, VA where res; res there several years after RW, thence Rutherford Co, NC, for 3-4 years, thence Wilson Co, TN where PN 1832; res there 1833; dd there 7/23/34; QLF 1917 from desc Mrs Elizabeth AURNER, State Center, IA; QLF 1917 from great great great gds W R JONES, Yellville, AR, states sol s/o William who also RW sol. F-S1543 R1437
Charles, esf 1775 Bedford Co, VA; PN aec 76 Adair Co, KY, 1828 when had w aec 66 & 2 unmd d's (aec 21 & aec 23); referred 1829 to d Dorcas TAYLOR & another d mbnn who md on 12/14/1821, d Catharine who became of ae in 1826, & d Betsy Ann who became of ae in 1827; sol dd 1840; surv ch 1852 were: William T (res Cumberland Co, KY), Levi, Chesley, Lucy WINFREY, Frances TAYLOR, Sally NEAT, Betsey Ann WHITE & Catharine STAPLES; QLF 1897 from DAR agent of Kansas City, MO for sol desc G R JONES; QLF 1925 from U S Congressman from NY for constituent Mrs G R REED, who desc of sol. F-S36647 R1437
Charles, BLW1169 issued 2/24/1797. F-BLW1169 R1437
Charles, VA sea svc; esf VA, & served until 1781; dd 1810; adm/o his estate, William WOODWARD of Norfolk, VA, gtd 1/2 pay PN due sol. F-R50 R1437
Churchill, esf 1777 in VA regiment; afb 1806 res Chatham (no state given); BLW304 issued 1/3/1807; QLF states sol lived 1748-1828, res Chatham, Stafford Co, VA, md 3 times & left no ch, further only bro William (1750-1845) of "Ellwood", Spotsylvania Co, VA, md ae 78 Lucy GORDON ae 16 who had d Betsy Churchill who md Major J Horace LACY of Chatham; QLF 1931 from desc Mary F HASSELL, Raleigh, NC. F-BLW304 R1437
David, b 1/26/1755; esf 1777 Louisa Co, VA where res; PN Robertson Co, TN, 1832. F-S1677 R1437

JONES, David, b 1/1761 Pittsylvania Co, VA; esf 1777 Henry Co, VA, where res; mvd after RW to KY, thence MO where PN 1833 Cooper Co; QLF 1926 from desc Maud BOYD, Nampa, ID, states sol md Jane RUBAL & mvd to AL, thence MO; QLF states sol b 1/20/1761 Richmond, VA, md in KY to Mary, d of Dr RUBLE, & they mvd to MO in 1811 where both dd. F-S17517 R1437
David, b 1759 King George Co, VA; esf 1776 Kanawha Co, VA; res after svc Nelson Co, KY, thence Jefferson Co, IN where PN 1833; dd there 5/6/35; md 24/1789 or 2/4/1780 Rebecca RUTHERFORD, Nelson Co, KY; wid PN ae 73 Jefferson Co, IN, 1838 res Shelby Township. F-W10150 R1437
Edward, BLW12278 issued 5/11/1792. F-BLW12278 R1438
Edward, b NC; esf Washington Co, VA where res; PN ae 75 Sumner Co, TN, 1832 when res TN over 40 years. F-S5622 R1438
Edward, b 4/7/1759 Richmond, VA; esf 1777 in VA regiment; PN 1832 Stokes Co, NC. F-S45872 R1438
Edward, esf VA; dd 1807 Caroline Co, VA; md 6/7/1792 Frances who PN aec 84 Caroline Co, VA 1843; children mbnn. F-W7908 R1438
Elijah, esf 1778 Nansemond Co, VA; PN there 1832; res there 1833 ae 72. F-S8762 R1438
Elisha, esf 1777 Hanover Co, VA, where res; PN 1832 ae over 70 Pittsylvania Co, VA. F-S5633 R1438
Freeman, b 1763 Brunswick Co, VA; f killed in skirmish with British when sol ae 12-14; mvd with m & family to Rutherford Co, NC, where esf 1779; res there c12-14 years after RW, thence Knoxville, TN for c4 years, thence near Bowling Green, Warren Co, KY, for c7 years, thence near Bletcher's Lick, Smith Co, TN for c4 years, thence Madison Co, AL for c10 years, thence St Clair Co, LA, for 7-10 years, thence Pickens Co, AL, where PN 1833; dd there 8/26/35; md Christian/Christina PARES, Rutherford Co, NC, 11/7/1785; wid PN 1847 Hancock Co, MS; re 1849 aec 82 Newton Co, MS, her P O address Decatur, AL; s Freeman res 1848 Gainesville, Hancock Co, MS; QLF 1914 from Hobart HUSON of San Diego, TX, states his w desc of sol who came from Ireland, esf in RW, md Christina PARRISH in KY, & lived in KY, AL, & MS; QLF states sol b Ireland. F-W7900 R1438
George, esf 1781 Fauquier Co, VA, where b 11/17/1762; mvd from Culpeper Co, VA, to OH, where PN 1832 Madison Co, res Pike Township; QLF states sol dd c1840. F-S4455 R1439
George, esf 1776 VA; PN ae 80 Williamson Co, TN, 1826 where had been school teacher; w then ae 79; their 2 d's & 1 s mbnn had families, & had not res with them for c40 years; an Erasmus JONES (kinship not given) AFF there in behalf/o sol; QLF 1933 from Maben JONES, Columbia, SC, gds/o War of 1812 William D JONES who s/o RW sol Michael JONES of Buckingham Co, VA, further f of Michael believed to be Publius JONES Sr who res on Falling River, Campbell Co, VA, further s's of Publius were Michael (of Buckingham Co, VA), Publius Jr, George, Daniel, Erasmus, & Douglas (all of Campbell Co, VA). F-S38888 R1439

JONES, George, esf 1778 King George Co, VA; dd 10/10/1812; md 2/25/1784 Sarah WILLIAMS, Shenandoah Co, VA; wid PN ae 78 Stafford Co, VA, 1838. F-W7923 R1439
George, b 10/4/1753 Prince William Co, VA; esf 1776 Fauquier Co, VA, where res; mvd c1808 to KY where PN 1833 Henry Co; dd 2/9/35; md 9/22/1780 Mary RHODES, Loudoun Co, VA, who b 4/11/1760; wid afp 1838 Henry Co, KY but claim not forwarded to PN Office by agent before she dd 4/1842; ch births: James 1/21/1781, Tholemiah 2/24/1785, William 1/7/89, Lettice 11/13/91, Solomon 9/8/93, Samuel 11/29/95, John 7/3/98, & Daniel 2/15/1801; Thomas A BERRYMAN, adm of wid estate, afp 1843 Henry Co, KY, for following ch who survived her: Solomon, Tholemiah, Lettice, William, John, Daniel J, & Samuel (last 3 then res IN, others then res KY); ch gtd PN due m; Francis, s of sol youngest s Daniel & w Celia, b 12/30/1830. F-W9082 R1439
Gray, b Sussex Co, VA, where esf 1780 sub for f; mvd 1816-17 to Bedford Co, VA, where PN 1833 ae 73; dd there 6/13/40; md 9/3/1790 Elizabeth WINFIELD, Sussex Co, VA; wid PN 1852 Bedford Co, VA, ae 82; res there 1855 ae 83 when gtd BLW 33731; ch births: Winfield 11/13/1791, Priscilla 9/1/96, Salley 2/19/98, Meriah 4/6/1801, Francis 2/19/05, Martha 3/1/07, & Robert Edward 4/14/13; s Winfield postmaster at Stoney Creek Warehouse, Sussex Co, VA, 1833; QLF says sol b 1764, s of Edward & Elizabeth; QLF 1911 from desc Mrs Charles L WOODS, Rolla, MO. F-W3690 R1439
Harrison, bc 1758; esf Cumberland Co, VA; PN 1785 for disability Richmond, VA, having lost leg at Battle of Guilford Court House; mvd to Cumberland Co, VA, thence Morgan Co, GA, thence Marshall Co, MS where PN 1840 when s Weldon AFF there; dd 1/12/41 leaving wid mbnn; s Harrison Jr AFF 1839 Baldwin Co, GA, other sol ch liv then were John P & Weldon (a doctor); QLF 1916 from Mrs A BURTON, Whitesboro, TX who desc/o sol sis mbnn; QLF states sol dd at home of gdd, Mrs Jacob THOMPSON, whose h was member of US Congress & Secretary of Interior for President BUCHANAN. F-S25603 R1439
Henry, b 1762 Dinwiddie Co, VA; esf 1780 Brunswick Co, VA, where res; mvd after RW to NC, thence GA, thence AL, where afp 1839 Barbour Co; PAR, svc less than 6 months; QLF 1905 from desc Morgan D JONES of Montgomery, AL; QLF 1915 from desc J Herbert JONES, Meridian, MS, states sol md (1) Sally LIGHTFOOT, (2) Polly HOGAN in GA, & (3) Eleanor/Nelly PAYNE in AL, mvd shortly after War of 1812 to Conecuh Co, AL, mvd c1825 from Covington Co, AL, to Barbour Co, AL, & res near Louisville where dd 5/5/51. F-R5704 R1439
Henry, b 12/7/1751 King George Co, VA; esf 1775 Fauquier Co, VA, where res; PN 1834 Hardy Co, VA; dd 2/6/38; md Rachel 9/17/1776, who b 4/19/1758; wid PN 1840 Hardy Co, VA; d Cassandra b 2/22/1779; d Leusendy b 8/20/1783; Edmond N JONES (kinship not given) b 5/13/1790. F-W4249 R1439
Henry, esf 1776 VA against Cherokee indians; dd Floyd Co, VA 10/9/1831; md 5/26/1817 Casander JAMES, Franklin Co, VA;

JONES (continued)
   wid afp aec 76 Floyd Co, VA 1853, & PAR; afb there 1855 ae 76 & gtd BLW33558; res there 1860. F-R5692 R1439
Isaac, b 3/30/1761 NJ; mvd with parents to Frederick Co, VA, where esf 1777; mvd 1778 to Guilford Co, NC, & esf there 1779; mvd to Jefferson Co, GA, thence Wilkinson Co, GA, & thence Telfair Co, GA, where PN 1832 when res there for 10 years. F-S31777 R1439
James, esf 1777 Fredericksburg, VA; PN ae 57 Stafford Co, VA 1818; res there 1820, when had w Molly aec 57 & d Letitia ae 22; gtd BLW1876. F-S45890 R1440
James, b 1753 Charlotte Co, VA; mvd 1777 to Ninety-Six District, SC, where esf 1779; afp 1834 Butler Co, KY, & PAR, less than 6 months svc; afp 1843, & PAR. F-R5706 R1440
James, b 6/17/1752; esf 1780 Powhatan Co, VA; PN Robertson Co, TN, 1832. F-S2656 R1440
James, esf 1775 King William Co, VA, where b 7/1/1749; PN there 1832; last PN payment in record 1840. F-S5624 R1440
James, b Dublin, Ireland; became citizen of VA before RW, & esf in VA regiment; PN 1818 Logan Co, KY res Russellville; res 1820 Warren Co, KY, occupation farmer. F-S35472 R1440
James, esf 1776 Fauquier Co, VA, where b 4/20/1758; PN there 1832 res Culpeper Co, VA; last PN payment in record 1841. F-S45873 R1440
James, b 1762 Charles Co, MD; esf 1780 Fairfax Co, VA; PN 1833 Tyler Co, VA, res on Long Run branch/o Arnolds Creek; dd 11/19/50 Ritchie Co, VA; md 5/18/1791 Sarah RAVENSCROFT in Allegheny Co, MD; wid b 3/18/1776; PN 1854 Ritchie Co, VA, when res with s Jessie I (ae 42); other ch: John who b 1792, Anne, & Samuel; wid gtd BLW1591 there 1855; QLF 1907 from gds Dr W S JONES, Central Station, WV whose d Mrs Sarah L PATTON, d Mrs Nannie WEEKLEY, d Mrs Laura B STEWART, & d Mrs G V ECHOLS (res Mannington, WV) then seeking data to join DAR, further sol ch were: John, Samuel R, James R, William, Thomas S, Jesse I, Anne, Priscilla, Easter, Ruth, & Sarah. F-W5008 R1440
James, b 11/16/1760 Prince William Co, VA; esf 1777 Fauquier Co, VA, where res; s of Peter & Elizabeth; PN 1832 Monroe Co, VA; dd 3/16/49; md 10/27/1781 Mary, d of William & Susannah LEACH, Fauquier Co, VA; wid b 10/10/1763; PN 1849 Monroe Co, VA; ch births: James 12/6/1782, Samuel 3/21/84, & Betsy (dd 1/3/1832); other data: John & Jean/Joan JAMES md 12/10/1822, Archibald & Susannah CAMPBELL md 10/29/1817 F-W7917 R1440
James, esf 1778 Amherst Co, VA, where res; esf 1782 Montgomery Co, VA; PN ae 72 Wayne Co, KY, 1832 res Otter Creek; dd there 1/10/44; md there 12/19/1834 Sarah/Sally BROWN; wid PN ae 70 Putnam Co, MO, 1854 where had mvd with s Elijah & s Jesse; gtd BLW57645 there 1855 ae 70; res there 1865, when lost PN certificate replaced; res 1866 Clinton Co, KY, ae 81; s Alexander res there 1854. F-W26165 R1440
James, b 4/1759; esf Orange Co, VA where res; afp there 1832

JONES (continued)
& PAR, less than 6 months svc; dd there 1/28/41; md 9/15/ 1785 Catharine/Caty ROBINSON/ROBBERTSON/ROBERSON; wid afp ae 84 Orange Co, CA 1854, & PAR; gtd BL33534 there 1855 ae 87; ch births: Thomas 7/4/1786, Betsey 7/23/88, James 1/10/91, Fielding 1/30/92, John 10/16/94, Lucy 2/14/97, Israel 12/4/98, Caty 1/18/1801, Priscilla/Zillah 1/25/03, Richard 2/16/05, Alse 1/9/07 (dd 6/26/08), Churchwell 4/13/09, Milly 6/17/12, & David 10/7/16; surv ch: James, Elizabeth FORKNER/FAULKNER, Fielding, John, Lucy MASON, Israel, Catharine MASON, Priscilla JOHNSTON, Richard, Churchwell, & Milley MASON; Richard & Priscilla JOHNSTON AFF 1854 Orange Co, VA; QLF states sol w d of Ensign John ROBINSON of Orange Co, VA, & she dd 1857 ae 90 Orange Co, VA. F-R5693 R1440

Jesse, esf 1777-8 Caroline Co, VA; PN there 1818 aec 80; res there 1820 with w; no other family there. F-S38086 R1440

Joel, BLW's 12256 & 12667 issued 7/14/1792. F-BLW12256 R1440

John, b Brunswick Co, VA; esf Rutherford Co, NC, where res; mvd after RW to Knox Co, TN, for number of years, then to Bledsoe Co, TN, for several years, then to Marion Co, TN, where PN 1832 ae 73-4 when res there 15 years; dd 11/23/39 or 11/23/41; md 3/1789-90 Mary who PN ae 77 Marion Co, TN; ch births (record torn & faded): James 9/17/1790, Milbury/ Milberry 1/2 or 6/2/179-, -man 5/21/1794, Joseph 5/27/96, Philip 5/16/9-, William 2/10/1800, -tey 11/24/18--, & Sophronia 18--. F-W373 R1441

John, b 4/3/1746 Morris Co, NJ; esf 1776 Henry Co, VA, where res; afp 1832 Grayson Co, VA; PAR, less than 6 months svc. F-R5714 R1441

John, b 1761 on Leatherwood Creek, Henry Co, VA; esf 1779 Surry Co, NC, where res during RW; mvd to Lincoln Co, NC, thence Spartanburg District, SC where esf for War of 1812, thence Burke Co, NC, thence Washington Co, TN, where afp 1852, & PAR, insufficient proof of 6 months svc; BLW35719 gtd there 1855. F-R5719 R1441

John, BLW12255 issued 7/7/1792. F-BLW12255 R1441

John, BLW12261 issued 7/30/179- (torn). F-BLW12261 R1441

John, esf 1777-8 Albemarle Co, VA where b 5/8/1750; mvd 1790 to Franklin Co, VA, thence 1796 Smith Co, TN, thence 1832 Maury Co, TN where PN 1832; w mbnn; QLF 1929 from desc Mrs A B WHITLEY, Nashville, TN, states sol w Barshaba b 12/28/ 1758, sol dd c1841 Giles Co, TN, res 1840 with eldest ch Hezekiah/Hizar who b 7/5/1776, further querier also desc/o RW sol Capt James OSBORNE of NC (res there 1790) s of Capt Alexander OSBORNE of NC; QLF 1929 from desc Mrs J H TRAVIS of Greenville, IN, states sol res 1840 Giles Co, VA, with s Hezekiah. F-S1678 R1441

John, b Spotsylvania Co, VA; esf 1778 Orange Co, VA; PN 1832 ae 66 Madison Co, VA, where mvd c1793; last PN payment in record 1840. F-S5629 R1441

John, b 1758 Culpeper Co, VA; esf 1779 Halifax Co, VA, where

JONES (continued)
res; PN there 1832; dd 3/17/37; QLF 1925 from great great gdd Mrs J A GARRARD of La Grange, TX, states sol md a Miss BARTON, sis of Pattie BARTON. F-S5631 R1441
John, b 2/1/1760 Albemarle Co, VA; esf 1779 Amherst Co, VA, where res; mvd 1787 from VA to KY, where PN 1830 Calloway Co. F-S31171 R1441
John, b 9/5/1763 Brunswick Co, VA; esf 1778 Mecklenburg Co, VA where res; esf 1779 Brunswick Co, VA where res; PN 1834 Garrard Co, KY; dd 2/6/38 leaving ch mbnn. F-S31174 R1441
John, esf 1776 King George Co, VA; PN ae 83 Caroline Co, VA, 1818; QLF list following marriages/o possible VA RW sol's: Butler BAKER & Susanna, Charles HEIGDEN & Mary MITCHELL, Samuel DISHMAN & Susanna BAKER, Samuel DISHMAN & Polly, William JONES & Elizabeth BUCKNER, John JONES & Anne MADISON. F-S38085 R1441
John, esf Dinwiddie Co, VA; afp there 1832 aec 76 when memory very poor; PAR, less than 6 months svc. F-R5715 R1441
John, b 2/3/1758; esf Mecklenburg Co, VA; afp there 1832, & PAR, insufficient proof of svc. F-R5716 R1441
John, esf 1776 VA; PN ae 65 Albemarle Co, VA 1818; dd there 7/15/49; md there 12/4/1821 Susan MARTIN; wid PN 1853 ae 70 there. F-W299 R1441
John, b 1762 St Marys Co, MD; esf 1780 Botetourt Co, VA, res there; PN 1834 Claiborne Co, TN; dd 2/14/42; md 9/15/1792 Mary, d of James FITZPATRICK, Bath Co, VA, where she b & raised; wid PN ae 69 Claiborne Co, TN, 1843; ch births: Nancy 12/31/1794, Elizabeth 11/11/96, John 12/20/98 (res 1843 Claiborne Co, TN), Moses 10/29/1800, & Thomas Fitzpatrick 10/29/02; other births: Joseph SAMPSON 9/3/1753, Matilda Clementina JONES 9/27/1840, & Nancy JONES 10/2/1842; marriages: Hezekiah JONES & Anna CESTERSON 6/9/1829, Eleanor JONES & Abraham GOBBLE 1/1/1824, Jane JONES & Covington COLLINSWORTH 2/17/1839. F-W372 R1441
John, b 6/8/1769; esf 1781 VA; dd 5/17/1840 Nelson Co, KY; md 8/6/1789 Jane SANDS (MB 7/31/89 showed consent of her f James), Nelson Co, KY; wid PN ae 83 there 1852; 10 ch, including following births: William 8/20/1790, Margaret 4/3/92, Elizabeth 12/23/94, James 5/17/99, Robert C 12/14/1801 & Samuel H 8/13 or 8/15/04; wid gtd BLW 38852 aec 84 there 1855 when following ch living: Elizabeth, Mary, William, & James. F-W9084 R1441
John, esf VA early in RW; PN ae 77 Lincoln Co, TN, 1829 when family w & ch: Clarissa ae 19, John ae 18, Reuben ae 16, Hetty ae 14, Nancy ae 10, Newton ae 9, Thomas ae 8, & Edmond ae 6; dd there 12/23/31; md (2) 1/31/1809 Leah CARTER in Bedford Co, VA; wid PN ae 73 Fayetteville, Lincoln Co, TN, 1860; d Clarissa JEFFRIES, then a wid, AFF there 1861 ae 51; QLF 1930 from desc Miss Pearl FLETCHER of Rockdale, TX, who requested PN Office also send data on sol to Mrs George P PREWETT, Taylor, TX. F-W10149 R1441
John, b 2/2/1755 Culpeper Co, VA; esf 1774 Greenbrier Co, VA

JONES (continued)
(area later Kanawha Co) for Dunsmore War; esf 1776 for RW Greenbrier Co, VA; PN 1835 Kanawha Co, VA, where dd; md 11/17/1775 Frances MORRIS, Culpeper Co, VA; wid PN ae 78 Kanawha Co, VA, 1838; Jane HANSFORD AFF then there sol wid was sis/o her f; a John HANSFORD Jr (no kinship given) was JP there then; QLF 1919 from desc Frances C BURGESS, Glen Lyn, VA, states sol w sis of Leonard MORRIS of Kanawha Co, VA; QLF 1938 from great great great gdd Mrs Joseph BAKER, New Paris, OH, states sol came from Wales to Culpeper Co, VA, md Frances d/o Levi MORRIS of VA, further 5 s's of sol & w res Wayne Co, IN: William, Edmund, Thomas, John, & Levi M. F-W7920 R1441

John, b 2/20/1762 Rowan Co, NC; esf VA (area later Woodford Co, KY) for Indian Campaigns in KY 1783-84; res after svc Madison Co, KY, thence Bath Co, KY where afp 1847 when res 54 years there; PAR, svc done after RW. F-R5718 R1441

Joseph, b 7/6/1758-9 NJ; mvd ae 2-3 with f to Loudoun Co, VA for 6 years, thence Culpeper Co, VA, thence 1779 Burke Co, NC, where esf 1780; returned to Culpeper Co, VA, where esf 1781; PN 1832 Giles Co, TN. F-S2652 R1442

Joseph, esf 1776 Hampshire Co, VA; PN 1824 Greene Co, TN, ae 69 when had w, 2 s's, & d mbnn; dd there 4/22/26; md 1786 Joanna in Greene Co, IN (area later Greene Co, TN) who never afp, & dd there 8/15/42; births of 6 eldest ch: Polly 3/7/1787, Caleb 2/8/89, Susanna 10/29/91, Sally 5/11/93, John 5/17/94 & Anna 4/5/96; ch who survived m: Caleb, Sally w/o David BRUMLEY, Betsy wid/o William BRUMLEY, Thomas, Samuel, & Joseph, all res 1852 Greene Co, TN, when wid ch Polly, Susanna, John, & Anne all decd; d Polly dd c1833, leaving h Jacob FARNS, who AFF 1852 ae 66 Greene Co, TN; s Thomas, adm of m's estate, afp then there ae 52 for self & surviving siblings, & PN gtd. F-W943 R1442

Joseph, esf 1775 Caroline Co, VA, where b 5/8/1751 s of Thomas & Sarah; mvd 1776 to New Kent Co, VA where esf 1776-7; mvd back to Caroline Co, VA, where esf 1777; PN 1832 Owen Co, KY; dd 12/5/37; md 11/12/1779 Sarah CHANDLER, Caroline Co, VA, who b 2/5/1761 d/o Robert & Lucy; wid PN 1838 Owen Co, KY; ch births: Thomas Woolfolk 5/13/1782, s ? 9/11/84, all other bible data illegible; QLF states sol had d Anne who md Nicholas AMOS, other ch/o sol probably Abraham, Joseph, & Thomas. F-W9079 R1442

Joshua, b 8/1760 Bucks Co, PA; esf 1776 Philadelphia Co, PA, where res; mvd c1792 to Harrison Co, VA where PN 1832; QLF 1905 from desc Miss Eleanor FREEMAN of Denver, CO, states sol res Harrison Co, VA, 1840. F-S5628 R1442

Joshua, b 4/25/1761; esf Northumberland Co, VA, where res; mvd after RW to Bourbon Co, KY, thence Pendleton Co, KY, thence Grant Co, KY where PN 1833; dd 1/6/44 when minister of Methodist Church; md 4/1791 Mary, Frederick Co, VA, who b 2/1767; wid afp 1844 Grant Co, KY, & PAR, insufficient proof of marriage; ch births: Elizabeth 2/5/1792, Sarah

JONES (continued)
   7/11/95, William W 7/23/97, Mary 12/13/99, & Mariah 2/10/
   1807; other birth data: Jane JONES 10/22/1786, & Rebecca
   JONES 8/16/1788; only surv ch William W res 1855 Grant Co,
   KY. F-R5726 R1442
Josiah, b 1752 Cumberland Co, VA; esf 1775 VA; mvd to Burke
   Co, NC, thence Rutherford Co, NC, where esf 1780, thence
   Greenville District, SC, thence Anderson District, SC; afp
   there 1833 & PAR, insufficient proof/o svc. F-R5722 R1442
Lewellen/Lewellin, esf 1779 Charlotte Co, VA; PN ae 58 Camp-
   bell Co, VA, 1818; dd there 10/30/21; md 2/26/1789 Catha-
   rine VERNON, Charlotte Co, VA; wid PN ae 75 Campbell Co,
   VA; ch mentioned in 1820: Nancy ae 23, Richard ae 22, Jo-
   seph ae 19, Elizabeth ae 16, Catharine ae 12 & Polly ae 8;
   wid res 1843 Campbell Co, VA, ae 75 when gtd PN increase.
   F-W7906 R1442
Lewis, VA sea svc, 2 years svc; dd 2/1800; LWT of 8/29/1799
   probated 2/17/1800 Loudoun Co, VA, listed w Milly, & ch:
   Loftis (eldest s), Lewis, Judith, Molly, Lucy, & Sally; md
   10/4/1789 Milly CHILTON (MB of 10/3/89 signed by Merryman
   CHILTON), Lancaster Co, VA; wid PN ae 70 there 1838; dd on
   1/30/45 or 1/31/45 there at res of nephew Ralph H CHILTON,
   leaving no ch; QLF 1893 from great gds W HENDLEY, Washington, DC, states his m, maiden name SMITH, a gdd of sailor;
   QLF 19-- from desc Helen BONAR, Streator, IL, states sail-
   or gtd VA BLW1200 on 6/26/1783. F-W7904 R1442
Lucretia, former wid of Elijah SMITH. (F-W10504)
Matthew, b 8/29/1760 Isle of Wight Co, VA; esf 1777-8 Franklin Co, NC; mvd after RW back to Isle of Wight Co, VA, for
   3 years, thence NC for 3 years, thence Putnam Co, GA where
   afp 1832; PAR, less than 6 months svc. F-R5729 R1442
Matthew, esf 1778 Southampton Co, VA, where b 3/18/1758 Not-
   toway Parish; mvd after 1801 to Montgomery Co, KY, thence
   Clark Co, KY, thence Bath Co, KY, thence Owen Co, KY where
   PN 1833 res Wayne Township; eldest s mbnn 1833; dd 1/18/37
   QLF 1926 from N E AUSTIN, Woodburn, OR whose w desc/o sol,
   states sol md Mary CRUMPLER/CRUMBLE, & they had s Thomas b
   1785 Southampton Co, VA; QLF states sol dd 1836 Hendrick
   Co, IN. F-S32348 R1442
Morton, esf 1780 Orange Co, VA, where b 8/10/1747; mvd 1794
   to Wilkes Co, NC, thence 1818 Bedford Co, TN, for 7 years,
   thence Frankliln Co, TN, where PN 1832; dd 11/8/41 Coffee
   Co, TN; md 11/13/17-- Frankey, who PN ae 90 Coffee Co, TN,
   1842 when her sis Elizabeth JONES AFF there aec 90; wid
   decd in 1844; had 7 ch including eldest Gabriel (b 11/29/
   1766) & 2nd ch Hugh (b 10/8/1768, res 1842 Coffee Co, TN);
   COMPILER'S NOTE: sol w probably sis of the Elizabeth (FOS-
   TER) JONES who afp 1840 Coffee Co, TN, aec 88 for RW svc/o
   her h Benjamin JONES, who was bro of Morton JONES (see PN
   record of Benjamin JONES, F-R5699 R1436). F-W7903 R1443
Moses, b 9/1762 Isle of Wight Co, VA; esf 1782 Gates Co, NC;
   PN 1832 Franklin Co, IL; QLF 1906 from SAR agent of Kansas

JONES (continued)
   City, MO, for sol desc J Logan JONES. F-S32347 R1443
Moses, esf Caroline Co, VA; dd 1826; md 12/23/1779-80 Sarah/
   Sally ROBERSON, Caroline Co, VA; wid PN 1837 Spotsylvania
   Co, VA, ae 78. F-W5113 R1443
Nicholas, b 11/14/1762 Caroline Co, VA where esf 1780 as sub
   for f; mvd 1784 to Spotsylvania Co, VA, thence 1811 to KY
   wher PN 1832 Clark Co, when res there nearly 14 years; res
   1835 Bartholomew Co, IN, then known as Nicholas Sr, where
   mvd to be with children & grandchildren. F-S16169 R1443
Nicholas, b 7/3/1760; esf 1780 Amherst Co, VA; dd Rockbridge
   Co, VA, 4/7/1834; md 7/3/1783 Amarella, d of John CAMDEN,
   Amherst Co, VA; wid b 3/25/1765; PN 1838 Rockbridge Co, VA
   when sis Hyse CAMDEN AFF there ae 76; ch births: Nancy
   6/29/1784, Sally T 4/3/86, Elizabeth W 3/25/88 (md Mr Mc-
   CLURE & dd 3/17/1830), Levina C 5/1/90, Susan 9/26/92,
   Winston J 3/28/95, Rhoda L 8/14/97 (dd 5/7/1827), William
   P 1/9/1800, Wesley C 12/3/02 (dd 7/9/1813) & John Nicholas
   1/11/04; ch living 1838: Nancy (w of James McDANIEL, res
   Kanawha Co, VA), Levina (w of John BRUSTAN, res KY), Wins-
   ton (res OH), Susan L (w of Halbert McALLISON), William, &
   John Nicholas (last 3 res Rockbridge Co, VA); wid res 1845
   Rockbridge Co, VA, when sol younger bro Lane AFF there ae
   75; AFF then there by Nancy CAMDEN, who b 1/2/1777 Amherst
   Co, VA; AFF then there by Washington CAMDEN aec 63 (kin-
   ship not given for Nancy & Washington). F-W7907 R1443
Peter, esf 1776 Dinwiddie Co, VA; PN 1823 Warren Co, NC, ae
   70, occupation planter, when only family d Sintha; only ch
   Cynthia P HAWES afp there 1837 ae 45 her f dd 2/10/33 lea-
   ving no wid, & she was their only ch. F-S8772 R1443
Philip, esf 1780-1 Amelia Co, VA; PN 1832 Logan Co, KY, ae
   70; res 1838 Johnson Co, AR, where children liv. F-S32342
   R1443
Richard, esf 1775 York Co, PA; PN 1818 Harrison Co, VA; res
   there 1820 ae 80 when liv with him w ae 75, an orphaned ch
   Sally ae 10, & a ch Mary BECK ae 15 (no kinship given for
   either ch); dd 9/1/22. F-S38081 R1444
Richard, esf NC in VA regiment; discharged Henrico Co, VA;
   PN ae 80 Chesterfield Co, VA 1818; res there 1820 when his
   only family a md d mbnn; res there 1821 (a cripple) with
   stepd Martha WATKINS aec 40 & her ch William P aec 6, Mary
   aec 4, Thomas aec 3 & infant aec 5 months. F-S38097 R1444
Richard, esf Charlotte Co, VA, 1781; PN ae 63 Rutherford Co,
   TN, 1824 when had w Sally ae 45 & ch: Learnah b 7/3/1809,
   Applin b 1/14/11, Elizabeth ae 12, Jane Nunnelly b 7/26/14
   & Levi b 4/29/1816; dd there 6/2/35; md 10/20/1808 Sarah/
   Sally JACKSON, Charlotte Co, VA; wid PN ae 78 Rutherford
   Co, NC, 1853. F-W2123 R1444
Richard, BLW12260 issued 4/12/179-. F-BLW12260 R1444
Richard, BLW12280 issued 10/17/1791. F-BLW12280 R1444
Richard, per AFF 1847 by bro John ae 83 Madison Co, VA, sol
   esf VA as minuteman; PN Office stated sol did not serve as

JONES (continued)
bro claimed; PN Office letter 1848 stated no law in force then granting PN to children/o RW sol's. F-none R1444
Richard, b 5/9/1745 on Rappahannock River, Essex Co, VA; esf Brunswick Co, VA where res; PN 1832 Barren Co, KY; s Sampson AFF there 1833 ae 60. F-S2654 R1444
Richard, b/5/5/1763 Amelia Co, VA; esf 1780 Charlotte Co, VA where res; esf 1781 Amelia Co, VA, while visiting kin; res after RW GA, thence 1820 Lincoln Co, TN, thence 1821 Giles Co, TN, where PN 1832; QLF states sol res there 1835. F-S4441 R1444
Richard, b 1/6/1748 Wales, & came to America ae 8; esf 1780 Rockbridge Co, VA, where res; PN 1832 Weakley Co, TN. F-S4444 R1444
Samuel, esf Petersburg, VA; dd 6/6/1816; md 2/11/1790 Patsey EANS (MB2/6/90), Amelia Co, VA; wid PN ae 74 Chesterfield Co, VA, 1843, she formerly res Amelia Co, VA; d Frances A WORSHAM AFF 1843 ae 43 Chesterfield Co, VA; wid res there 1848 ae 80+; file contains part of PN record of another VA RW sol Samuel JONES, who esf 1776 in 8th VA regiment & who had recently mvd 1831 from Brown Co, OH, to Clinton Co, OH & had requested new PN certificate 1829 at Clermont Co, OH (COMPILER'S NOTE: this Samuel apparently the Samuel/o file F-S41709 below); QLF 1917 from great great gdd Mrs William Roscoe MUSE, Roanoke, VA, states sol md Patsey EANES, also he esf 1776. F-W3826 R1444
Samuel, b 9/23/1756; esf 1776 in 6th VA Regiment; PN 1818 Christian Co, KY, when stated he had left his RW discharge in Dinwiddie Co, VA. F-S13554 R1444
Samuel, b 7/1762; esf Winchester, VA; PN 1818 Brown Co, OH; occupation farmer; res there 1821 when family w Elizabeth ae 45 & ch: Catherine ae 17, Lewis ae 18, Elizabeth ae 13, Matilda ae 11, Westly ae 9, Stephen ae 7. F-S41709 R1444
Samuel Z, b 1/30/1759 Gloucester Co, NY; esf in PA regiment; PN 1833 Lewis Co, VA; dd there 4/16/46; PN Office dropped his name from rolls 1834 when determined his proof of svc of 6 months or more not sufficient; QLF states sol buried near Jane Lew, WV. F-S18474 R1444
Solomon, esf 1776 VA; later esf NC & GA; PN aec 66, occupation planter, McIntosh Co, GA, 1827 when had w Nancy aec 55, s John res SC, & d Sarah res MS. F-S38083 R1445
Stephen, b Dinwiddie Co, VA; esf 1781 Bedford Co, VA, where res; PN there 1833 ae 70; dd 1/3/34; md 12/28/1782 Mary GIBBS, Bedford Co, VA; wid PN ae 74 there 1839; QLF states sol's d Mary/Polly md Nicholas SMITH; QLF 1926 from great great great gdd Miss Jane MACON of Brunswick, GA. F-W7916 R1445
Strother, esf 1776 VA; William Strother JONES, gds & one of heirs, afb 1849 Frederick Co, VA; other heirs then: David W BURTON & w Frances L, James F JONES, Francis B JONES, Burnly JONES, & infant heirs of decd Marshall JONES (Maria & Marshall JONES); BLW2442 gtd to above heirs; sol d Nancy

JONES (continued)
  Ann contested 1849 award of BLW to other heirs; afb 1855, & no indication of action on claim shown. F-BLW2442 R1445
Taverner, esf 1777 Culpeper Co, VA, where b 1755; PN there 1832 (area then Madison Co, VA); dd c3/4/41 leaving wid, who gtd his PN arrears 1842. F-S5627 R1445
Thomas, esf 1779 Prince William Co, VA; PN 1828 Shelby Co, KY, ae 68; gtd BLW1648 there 1830; dd 10/3/33; md 12/1787 Elizabeth, Prince William Co, VA; wid PN ae 70 Shelby Co, 1838 when her sis Peggy DAVIS AFF there ae 68; ch births: James 4/3/1789, Richard 10/11/90, John Wheeler 11/6/93, Abraham 5/27/97, Maria 5/30/99, William 6/17/1804, illegible name 8/11/06, & Henry 7/21/10; wid gtd BLW228 1855 ae 96 Shelby Co, KY. F-W3020 R1446
Thomas, esf 1776 Frederick Co, MD where b 1/1/1752; esf Randolph Co, NC & later transferred to VA regiment; res after RW Randolph Co, NC, where PN 1833. F-S8760 R1446
Thomas, esf NC; dd 6/12/1832 Bartholomew Co, IN; md 8/1/1785 Mary CLARKSON (MB 7/30/1793 with Polly CLARKSON with consent of her m wid Elizabeth CLARKSON, per Co clerk), Charlotte Co, VA; sol & w res there 3 years, thence KY; wid afp & afb ae 79 Bartholomew Co, IN, 1845; PAR & BLAR, not enough proof/o identity with sol/o the same name on NC records; dd 7/30/51; her youngest bro Drury present at marriage, & other bro's were William, Joseph, & Thomas (last 2 res c1840 Mercer Co, KY); wid surv ch 1851: Margaret w/o Archibald THOMSON, Leanah w of George BAKER, Godfrey, Thomas S, Joseph & Smith D; s Thomas adm/o m's estate; s Godfrey afp ae 48 Johnson Co, IN, 1852 for all PN's & BLW's due m's heirs; PAR & BLAR. F-R5735 R1446
Thomas, esf 1789 Amelia Co, VA where b 5/4/1763; mvd 1781 to Stokes Co, NC, where PN 1832. F-S7077 R1446
Thomas, BLW12258 issued 4/13/1791. F-BLW12258 R1446
Thomas, b 3/1751 SC; during RW res Charlotte Co, VA, & Halifax Co, VA; esf 1780 Charlotte Co, VA; res after RW Campbell Co, VA, thence 1819 OH where PN Jackson Co when res c 5 years in Madison Township; mvd to Williams Co, OH, where dd 2/28/38; Charles CASE (no kinship given) afp for PN arrears 1847 Bryan, Williams Co, OH which gtd. F-S4453 R1446
Thomas, esf 1776-7 Caroline Co, VA, where b 9/10/1755; soon after RW mvd to Spotsylvania Co, VA, where PN 1833; dd on 12/16/44. F-S5630 R1446
Thomas, esf 1775 Amherst Co, VA; PN ae 73 Mercer Co, 1818; res 1832 Putnam Co, IN, where mvd with Andrew BUNTIN (no kinship given) with whom he had res for 15 years; last PN payment in record 1837. F-S36656 R1446
Thomas, b 3/6/1757; esf 1776 Frederick Co, VA where res; mvd 1784 to Bourbon Co, KY, where PN 1832; QLF states sol dd there 1833; QLF says sol b 1754 Augusta Co, VA, dd Bourbon KY 7/1/33; QLF 1921 from desc Mrs May Hughes MILLER, High Hill, MO; QLF 1925 from great great gds S D MITCHELL, Lexington, KY; QLF states sol md kin/o James GARRARD, who was

JONES (continued)
  member of VA legislature & was later 2nd governor of KY.
  F-S46053 R1446
Thomas, b 1762 Loudoun Co, VA; mvd to Fauquier Co, VA where esf near end of RW; mvd to Henry Co, VA, & esf there; res there after RW for many years, thence Wythe Co, VA for 3-4 years, thence Sullivan Co, TN where PN 1832; dd 7/26/42 md 12/24/1786 Susan/Susannah RAMSEY (MB 12/23/86) Bedford Co, VA; wid PN ae 73 Sullivan Co, TN, 1843; gtd BLW26429 there 1855; ch births: Susannna 1789, Mary 9/21/92, Squire 4/10/94, Rebecky 11/9/95, Elizabeth 2/1-/98, William 2/10/1800, Daniel 8/5/02, Betsey 1/1/05, John 11/17/06, & Eliza 5/30/09. F-W43 R1446
Thomas, esf 1776 Amherst Co (area later Nelson Co), VA; BLW 5418 issued 7/30/1817; PN latter Co 1832 ae 77; dd there 7/8/33 at Jonesboro; md 10/17/1780 Catharine CLARKSON who b 6/1/1760; wid PN there 1838; res there 1844; ch births: Hezekiah 3/3/1782, Clarkson 12/9/83 (dd 11/13/85), Shelton 1/21/85, Joshua 1/28/87, & John C 7/1-/91. F-W7905 R1446
Tim, man of color who esf 1776-7 Point of Forks, VA, as sub for master Rolling JONES, who had enlisted during drunken frolic, then sent slave to sub for him; lost leg at Yorktown; gtd freedom after RW for svc; PN ae 86 York Co, VA, 1833. F-S18063 R1447
William, esf 1779 Petersburg, VA; PN ae 65 Pittsylvania Co, VA;, 1827 occupation carpenter & bricklayer, when w (b in same year as he) only family; dd 12/15/32 ae 72; md Mary, Amelia Co, VA, 10/1782; wid afp 1839 ae 77 Wilson Co, TN & dd same year; wid PAR, per current law no PN allowed to wid of sol's who liv 1832; ch mbnn afp & PAR since m not gtd PN; QLF 1919 from desc Mrs G P GLENN, Norman, OK; QLF 1914 from desc Miss A Jane MACON, Brunswick, GA. F-R5727 R1447
William, esf 1780 Annapolis, MD; PN 1818 Fairfax Co, VA, ae 56; res there 1820 occupation farmer with w ae over 37 & youngest ch (d aec 18), all older ch having mvd away; sol had added middle initial L to distinguish self from other William JONES; PN address transferred 1828 to Washington, DC; dd 3/26/39; md 12/27/1819 Mary who md (2) James TILLETT who dd; wid PN ae 70 Loudoun Co, VA, 1853; gtd there 1855 BLW13899. F-W6292 R1447
William, b 5/7/1758 Brunswick Co, VA; esf 1776 Franklin Co, NC, where PN 1832; res there 1834. F-S8765 R1448
William, b 7/20/1755; mvd when sm ch with parents to Guilford Co, NC, (area later Carroll Co, TN); esf 1781 Guilford Co, NC; mvd 1803 to Sumner Co, TN, thence Carroll Co TN where afp 1836 & PAR, less than 6 months svc. F-R5757 R1448
William, esf Amherst Co, VA; md c1778 Ann, d of James & Ann FREEMAN, & mvd to Sumter District, SC; dd 2/12/1809; wid md (2) 12/1/1811 John PARKER (dd 11/1831); wid dd 6/3/47

48

JONES (continued)
Sumter District, SC, leaving 9 ch by sol including: eldest Elizabeth who dd before f, James, Elizabeth J, Leonard, & Wiley; family bible (torn, faded) births (all with surname JONES): James 10/17/1782, Elizabeth 12/5/84, Mary 12/1/86 (md 11/1805), Peggy 5/11/ 89, Nancey 12/14/91, Eli 1/15/94 William 4/11/17-- (above sol, md 2/12/--), Leonard 6/18/98 Wiley 10/7/17--, Betsey Ann 9/3/1805, Sarah 12/23/07, Susanah 1/26/10, & Margaret 6/30/12; d Elizabeth J afp 1854 there for self & her bro's Leonard & Wiley who res Marengo Co, AL, & PAR, insufficient proof/o svc; AFF by Susannah B JONES (m of Edgar b 7/1831), Sumterville, Sumter District, SC; AFF then there by Martha DEAS (m/o James bc 1831); Eli FREEMAN, bro/o sol wid, acted as agent 1786 for his m Ann. F-R7934 R1448

William, BLW12264 issued 4/13/1791. F-BLW12264 R1448
William, BLW12274 issued 11/2/1792. F-BLW12274 R1448
William, b 3/3/1759 Frederick Co, VA, where esf 1776 Battletown; PN 1832 Hickman Co, KY. F-S13549 R1448
William, b 1761-2 MD; esf 1780 Montgomery Co, VA, sub for f with whom res; res after RW Amherst Co, VA, then 1810 to Clermont Co, OH, where PN 1851 res Union Township; gtd BLW 78030 there 1856 ae 91; res there 1858. F-S16172 R1448
William, esf 1778 Albemarle Co, VA where b; PN 1833 Boone Co MO, ae 77; dd 1839. F-S16890 R1448
William, esf 1776 in VA regiment; PN ae 70 Casey Co, KY 1825 when had neither w nor ch res with him; dd 1/27/1833. F-35492 R1448
William, b 12/13/1759 Fauquier Co, VA where esf 1778 Warrenton; res there & Culpeper Co, VA, until 1828 when mvd to Perry Co, OH, where PN 1832 res Hopewell Township; dd Somerset, that Co, 7/24/34; md 6/24/1784 Mary FISHBACK, Fauquier Co, VA, who b 1/15/1760; wid PN 1841 Perry Co, OH, res Pike Township; res 1860 Somerset Co, OH, when gtd BLW 26780; liv 1859 ae 98 (blind); s mbnn res 1834 Alexandria, VA; 2 d's (1 single, & other with large family) liv 1855; s-in-law George CHAPPELEAR res 1843 Perry Co, OH; sol elder bro James AFF 1841, Rappahannock Co, VA, also RW pensioner, he present at sol's wedding with his younger & elder sis mbnn; QLF 1932 from desc Mrs T Temple HILL, Washington, DC, who also desc of RW sol's Peter DUDLEY of King & Queen Co, VA, Ambrose JEFFRIES of King & Queen Co, VA, & William WALLIS of Culpeper Co, VA; this querier later letter states she not desc of above William JONES, but great gdd/o VA RW William JONES who md Ann/Nancy (d of John EUSTACE & w Alice PEACHY), further her William md 12/14/1780 Warrenton, VA, & dd c1815; QLF 1922 from US Congressman of IN for constituent Mrs PERRY who great gdd/o sol. F-W4463 R1448
William, esf aec 18-19 Henrico Co, VA where bc 1760; dd 1/1/ 1835 Yancy Co, NC, when too ill to complete afp; md c7/4/ 1788 Dorothy HAMPTON, Wythe Co, VA, where she b & raised;

JONES (continued)
  wid dd there 7/28/54 never having afp, leaving ch: Laban, Viney w/o Elijah SHEPHERD, Malindy w of James RUNIONS (all res Macon Co, NC), Susannah w of Gabriel MADCAP (res Madison Co, NC), Thursee w/o John ROBERSON (res KY), Dorothy w of John SHEPHERD (res Yancy Co, NC), Preston (res KY), Alford (res Yancy Co, NC), & William B (res Washington Co, TN); birth record/o ch illegible except for Alford b 4/13/1809, & Dorothy/Dolly b 3/25/1806; s Alford afp 1855 Yancy Co, NC, for self & surv siblings (Thursee then decd); PAR, insufficient proof of svc & marriage of sol & w. F-F-R5698 R1448
  William, esf 1776-7 VA; dd 11/12/1828 Halifax Co, VA, where md 10/9/1776 Martha; wid mvd to Carroll Co, TN & afp ae 87 there 1843; PAR, insufficient proof of svc; dd there 8/18/43; had 11 ch; ch who survived m: Mary wid of John CHISM, Elizabeth, Jane, Temperance w of Lemuel BROWN, Sarah w of Royal WYATT, & William (ae 42 in 1844); QLF states sol md Patsy BROWN who survived him. F-R5724 R1448
  William, esf 1776 VA; PN ae 70 Jasper Co, GA, 1829 when had ch: Jane ae 18, Lucy ae 16, Nancy ae 14, Milly ae 12 & Joseph ae 8; dd there 2/15/41 or 2/20/41; md 1/5/1808 Emilia /Milly PATERSON, Greene Co, GA; wid PN 1854; gtd BLW9197 ae 79 Jasper Co, GA, 1855. F-W11950 R1448
  Williamson, bc 1759 Essex Co, VA; esf 1776 Caroline Co, VA, where res, sub for bro John & later esf sub for bro James; mvd after RW to Fayette Co, KY for c4 years, thence Franklin Co, KY, thence Harrison Co, IN, thence Morgan Co, IN, where PN 1832 when res there c 8 years. F-S17516 R1448
JOPLING, Thomas, esf 1776 VA; PN ae 73 Nelson Co, VA, 1828; dd 3/20/37 or 3/29/37; md 11/25/1790 Mary/Molly, d of James STEPHENS, while res Amherst Co, VA; wid PN ae 69 Nelson Co VA 1840. F-W7927 R1449
JORDAN, Freeman, b 4/14/1760 Nottoway Co (area formerly part/o Amelia Co), VA; esf 1777 Amelia Co, VA; PN 1832 Nottoway Co, VA, when res Brunswick Co, VA; last PN payment in file 1839. F-S5618 R1449
  George, esf 1776 Culpeper Co, VA; PN ae 78 Anderson Co, KY, 1832; QLF 1894 from gds Thomas R JORDAN, Tacoma, WA, says sol P O address Lawrenceburg, KY; QLF states sol b Culpeper Co, VA, 1/26/1754, dd 3/1/1842, md in VA Martha, who b 4/11/1766 Culpeper Co, VA. F-S31176 R1449
  Henry, esf VA; PN ae 58 Williamson Co, TN, 1818; res there 1820 when had w aec 55, & 6 ch including Henry, Rachel, & Sarah; QLF states sol settled Chester Co, SC, before 1790. F-S38887 R1449
  John, esf 1778 Philadelphia Co, PA, where res; member of Society of Cincinnati; BLW1165 issued 2/14/1791; PN 1829, ae not given, Botetourt Co, VA, where res; dd 5/4/35; md Catharine BEALE 4/21/1789 Shenandoah Co, VA who b 9/25/1764; wid PN 1838 Botetourt Co, VA; dd 2/22/36; QLF 1930 from desc Mrs R H EDWARDS of Camden, NJ; QLF 1924 from desc Mrs

JORDAN (continued)
   Estaline Paxton WALKER, Blacksburg, VA, whose m gdd/o sol.
   F-W34261 R1449
John, esf Greenville Co, VA, where b 5/8/1756 s of Burrel &
   Amy; dd 8/17/1828 Washington Co, GA; md 2/19/1786 Winni-
   fred/Wineford d/o George JORDAN, Northampton Co, NC; wid b
   9/9/1763; ch births: Britain/Brittain 6/18/1787, Green H
   4/26/89, Priscilla 8/17/91, Patience 9/22/93 (md Mr SAF-
   FORD), Burwell 9/30/179-, John 4/16/1800 & Mary 7/2/02 (md
   John H NEWTON & dd 1/22/1893 or 2/22/1893, leaving ch Olivia M who md Lamar COBB, Helen C who md H H CARLTON, & Edwin D); wid dd 7/6/1847 leaving ch: Green, Burwell, John,
   Patience SAFFORD, & Mary NEWTON; sol sis Mary b 2/6/1755;
   sol bro Burrel b 9/15/1757; wid sis or halfsis of Hezekiah
   JORDAN; d Mary NEWTON gtd PN by special act of Congress in
   1889 when she res Athens, GA, with s-in-law US Congressman
   Henry H CARLTON; Mary dd at home/o s-in-law Lamar COBB Jr,
   who was executor/o her h John's LWT; QLF states sol buried
   near Davisboro, GA, where he res. F-W29726 R1449
John, esf 1776 VA; BLW1127 & BLW 2550 issued 5/7/1793; gtd
   disability PN 1811, for wound at Battle of Edge Hill, when
   res Albemarle Co, VA; PN there 1827 ae 68 when had no family. F-S38098 R1449
Peter, esf 1776 Frederick Co, VA; mvd 1798 to Mercer Co, KY,
   on Salt River where PN 1818 ae 69; res there 1820, occupation farmer, when had w & 4 ch (s aec 18 & 3 d's) living
   with him; other ch had already left home; dd there 8/2/24;
   md c12/10/1786 Susannah SHULL, Frederick Co, VA; wid PN
   aec 76 Mercer Co, KY, 1838; JP Peter JORDAN, her nephew,
   took her afp statement at her home, she too feeble to come
   to Court; eldest ch May DISSOWELL/DISPONETT AFF there then
   ae 51; s John M, b 1789, AFF there then ae 49; wid sis Mrs
   Magdalena HATFIELD AFF then ae 68 Franklin Co, IN; last PN
   payment to wid in file 1840. F-W9091 R1450
Richard, b Surry Co, VA; esf Pitt Co, NC, where PN 1932 aec
   73; res part of time since RW in Anson Co, NC; dd leaving
   wid Anna who afp 1835; no action taken by PN Office, since
   needed certificate from War Department. F-S7087 R1450
Sharshall, b 3/15/1747-8 s of Thomas & Mary; esf 1776 Culpeper Co, VA; mvd from VA 1794-5 to Clark Co, KY, where dd
   9/28/1813; md 11/19/1771 Efferilla, Culpeper Co, VA; wid
   b 4/27/1755; PN ae 88 Clark Co, KY, 1843; ch births: Lucy
   9/19/1772, Thomas 9/25/74, Richard 11/10/76, Jonas 12/19/
   78, Jane 9/11/81, Elizabeth 6/27/86, Milley 10/26/88, Catey 4/14/94, & Sharshall 4/16/97; d Milley md 9/15/1816 to
   Morgan JOHN; AFF 1843 by s Sharshall, Mercer Co, KY ae 46.
   F-W9090 R1450
Thomas, esf in VA regiment; gtd PN 1786 for disability from
   wounds at Battle of Trenton; dd 7/24/1817; md 10/17/1791 a
   wid Anna BARBEE (MB 10/26/91) Fauquier Co, VA; wid afp ae
   87 Page Co, VA, 1838 when s Gabriel AFF; dd 11/5/38 there
   before apf acted on, leaving d Mary McDONALD & s Gabriel;

JORDAN (continued)
  s Gabriel res Luray, Page Co, VA 1855; QLF 1918 from great
    gds Sidon HARRIS, Austin, TX. F-R5759 R1450
  William, b 1/9/1762 Surry Co, VA; esf 1779 Edgecomb Co, NC,
    where res; mvd to Edgefield District, SC, thence Elbert Co
    GA, thence Newton Co, GA, thence Randolph Co, AL where afp
    1844; PAR, less than 6 months svc; heirs Christopher JOR-
    DAN, Burel JORDAN, Samuel NUNIS, & Elizabeth KEY afp there
    1856, & PAR; d Elizabeth KEY afp 1860 Carroll Co, GA, sta-
    ting her f dd c1852, & she PAR. F-R5770 R1450
  William, b 1/20/1760 on Schuylkill River, near Philadelphia,
    PA; mvd aec 13 to Augusta Co, VA, where esf 1779; mvd 1783
    to Albemarle Co, VA, where PN 1832. F-S8274 R1450
  William, esf Caroline Co, VA, sub for bro Armistead, where b
    5/16/1754; PN 1834 Nelson Co, VA; last PN payment in file
    1838. F-S10929 R1450
JORDEN, George, see JORDAN, George. F-S31176 R1450
JORDON, William, esf 1777 Culpeper Co, VA, where b 2/15/1756;
    PN there 1832. F-S5620 R1450
JOSEPH, William, esf St Mary's Co, MD; afp & afb ae 90-95 Lee
    Co, VA, 1853; PAR & BLAR, insufficient proof of svc. F-
    R5775 R1451
JOUETT, Matthew, captain in VA line; BLW1126 & BLW2510 issued
    7/15/1789 to John LOUETT, legal heir; records lost in Wa-
    shington, DC, fire 1800; QLF states Army Adjutant General
    Office gave sol death date as 11/15/1777. F-BLW1126 R1451
JOY, Richard, esf 1779 Loudoun Co, VA; wounded 5 times in two
    battles (Guilford & Eutaw Springs); PN ae 67 Henrico Co,
    VA, 1820 minus leg, when no family liv with him, except d
    aec 38 + boy aec 19, boy aec 12 & girl aec 7; res Richmond
    VA, 1822. F-S25182 R1452
JOYCE, George, esf 1779 Charlotte Co, VA, where b 10/25/1759;
    mvd with bro to Guilford Co, NC, where f had plantation;
    esf there 1780; mvd from there 1806 to KY where PN Bullitt
    Co 1835; dd 9/15/35; surv ch 1838: Thomas, Richard, Alicia
    w of William C MOORE, George, Alexander, Mary w of William
    VAUGHAN, & Delila w of John RAWLINGS; d Sarah md Johnson
    TODD, & dd several years before f, leaving ch: Elizabeth,
    Simpson, Andrew, Eliza & Jane (last 2 under ae 21); s John
    afp arrears 1838 Bullitt Co, KY, for sol heirs, which gtd.
    F-S30511 R1452
JOYNER, Joshua, esf Southampton Co, VA, where b 1758; PN there
    1832; dd there 9/24/41, leaving wid Sarah & s Thomas; md
    11/15/1812 Sarah, who PN ae 78 Southampton Co, VA, 1853;
    gtd BLW 26092 there 1855; gtd PN increase there 1856. F-
    W7924 R1452
  Moses, esf 1776 Southampton Co, VA; PN ae 74 Franklin Co, NC
    1832; dd 7/16/36; md 10/10/1783 Honor BRADSHAW/BRATCHER,
    Southampton Co, VA; wid dd c3/31/40; s William (b there)
    afp aec 61 Franklin Co, NC 1850 stating m never recd PN, &
    he had liv bro & sis older than he; PAR. F-R5683 R1452
JOYNES, Levin, BLW1163 issued 11/24/1792. F-BLW1163 R1452

JUNIOR, Anthony, esf 1776 Halifax Co, VA where res; afp aec 79 Jasper Co, GA, 1838, & PAR. F-R5789 R1455
JUSTICE, George, esf 1776 in VA regiment; PN ae 70 Accomac Co, VA, 1818; res there 1720 when s mbnn. F-S38889 R1455
Richard, esf Accomac Co, VA where b 1749; dd 5/17/1850 there leaving no wid but ch: Teackle, Samuel, & Margaret; never afp; s Teackle afp for sol ch & gtd PN. F-S8775 R1455
Simeon, b 6/4/1765 Pittsylvania Co, VA; mvd with f to Rutherford Co, NC, for short time, thence Ninety Six District, SC, where esf 1777 Ft Rutledge with f John & bro John; res SC to 1795 thence TN for 4 years, thence Buncombe Co, NC, for c8 years, thence 1807 Sandy River, Floyd Co, KY, where PN 1820, occupaton farmer, when family w Susanah ae 65-70; dd 1/16/46; md (2) Delphia JOHNSON (marriage license 10/4/34), Perry Co, KY; wid PN ae 67 Letcher Co, KY, 1854; gtd BLW36722 Perry Co, KY. F-W7946 R1455
Thomas, b 1/11/1765 Halifax Co, VA; esf 1781 Rutherford Co, NC; PN 1832 Bedford Co, TN. F-S1842 R1455
JUSTUS, Moses, b 1755 MD; esf 1774 Mecklenburg Co, NC; mvd to New River, VA, where esf 1781; mvd to East TN, thence West TN, thence IN, thence Schuyler Co, IL, thence McDonough Co IL where res when PN 1832 Schuyler Co, IL. F-S32351 R1455
KAIN, Thomas, BLW12298 issued 5/22/1792. F-BLW12298 R1456
KAMPER, Tilman, see CAMPER, Tilman. F-W8573 R1456
KANADAY, John, see CANNADAY, John. F-R1654 R1456
KAPPLINGER, Christley, b 3/10/1750 PA; brought aec 2 by f & m to Rockingham Co, VA, where esf 1780; PN there 1832. F-S8776 R1456
KARNEY, Gilbart/Gilbert, esf 1779 Pittsburgh, PA, in 15th VA Regiment; PN 1818 Monmouth Co, NJ; res there 1820 aec 67 Middletown when family w Ruth aec 50. F-S33347 R1456
KARR, James, see KERR, James. F-R5888 R1456
KARREN, Barney, b 1753 Co Monaghan; came with f & 4 bro's to America; sol esf 1776 Winchester Co, VA, where res; mvd to Hampshire Co, VA, where esf 1781; PN 1832 Randolph Co, VA; bro's John & Edward esf in PA regiment & both KIA; bro Peter esf in VA regiment. F-S15906 R1456
KAUFFMAN, George, see COFFMAN, George. F-R2102 R1456
KAUFMAN, John, b 12/25/1757 PA; mvd c1765 to Fredericktown, MD, with parents; esf 1777 Hagerstown, MD, where res; mvd to Alexandria, VA, where esf 1781; afp 1845 Augusta Co, VA when res there 42 years; PAR. F-R5798 R1456
KAUTZMAN, John Valentine, VA sea svc, esf VA on ship TEMPEST; taken POW 1781 for c2 years; gtd VA BLW30541 5/7/1784; petitioned VA 1787 Henrico Co, VA, for pay during captivity; w dd at their Elizabeth City Co, VA, res long before sol; sol dd 1788, leaving gdc John & Judith WILLIAMS, his only descendants, they being ch of d Ann who md Samuel WILLIAMS of King & Queen Co, VA where Ann & Samuel dd; sol LWT left PN claim to Mistress Mary BOND (spinster of Richmond, VA), & left money to Sarah, d/o William & Elizabeth BARKER; gdc John res Henrico Co, VA, & Judith res King & Queen Co, VA,

KAUTZMAN (continued)
  gtd PN due f 1839. F-R59 R1457
KAVANAUGH, Rutha, former wid of Travis BOOTON. (F-W9382)
KAY, James, b 9/1759; esf 1776 King George Co, VA, where res; PN 1825 for disability from wound at Battle of Brandywine; res 1833 Boone Co, KY; formerly res Fayette Co, KY; dd on 7/12/33; QLF 1928 from great gds Frederick R KAY, St Louis MO states sol f James, further sol res after RW Waynesburg in Greene Co, PA; QLF from C W KAY (no kinship given), New Orleans, LA, states sol b 9/15/1759, & dd Georgetown, KY. F-S31179 R1457
KAY, Robert, BLW1211 issued 7/18/1791. F-BLW1211 R1457
KEA, Charles, esf in 4th VA Regiment; res 1808 Surry Co, VA, when John KEA (no kinship given) AFF there; PN 1818 Chester District, SC; res there 1820 ae 71, occupation farmer, when family liv with him d aec 25 & gds aec 12. F-S39039 R1457
  Henry, b Surry Co, VA; mvd at early ae to Edgecomb Co, NC, where esf; PN there 1832 ae 79. F-S8783 R1457
KEARNEY, Edward, esf 1777 Kent Co, DE, where b 5/10/1753 & res during RW; PN 1833 Ohio Co, VA; after PN office reexamination/o claim found insufficient proof/o svc, his name was dropped from PN rolls 1836; sol dd 5/2/42 Ohio Co, VA, at home of only surv ch Ann, w of Benjamin BIGGS; w dd before sol; d Ann afp there 1860 & PAR; QLF 1926 from sol gds D E BIGGS, Parkersburg, VA, who ae 7 when sol dd near West Liberty, VA (now WV). F-S15495 R1457
KEARNS, Michael, BLW12291 issued 5/12/1792. F-BLW12291 R1457
KEATH, William, b Franklin Co, VA; esf 1780 Mongtomery Co, VA, ae 18-19 when res with parents there; mvd to Wayne Co, KY, where PN 1832 ae 71; dd there 10/19/38; md there 1/30/1828 Mary/Polly DAVENPORT; wid md (2) Thomas McINLIN who dd in Montgomery Co, IN, 1852; wid PN ae 55 Putnam Co, IN, 1855, & gtd BLW36646 there then. F-W26150 R1457
KEATON, Zacharia James, esf 1777-8 near Charlottesville, VA, when res Albemarle Co, VA; mvd to Henry Co, VA, where area became Patrick Co, VA, thence Wilson Co, TN where apf 1840 when res there 26 years; PAR. F-R5803 R1457
KEBLINGER, Adam, see KEEBLINGER, Adam. F-W1618 R1457
KEEBLE, William, esf Fauquier Co, VA; PN ae 63 Blount Co, TN, 1818; dd there 12/30/34; md 12/17/1799 Mary KEEBLE, Fauquier Co, VA; wid PN ae 65 Blount Co, TN, 1849; gtd BLW 14518 there 1855; dd before 1858; ch referred to in 1829, res there: Rebecca ae 19, Richard ae 18, Walter ae 13, Charlotte ae 5 & June ae 4; QLF 1922 from desc P M KEEBLE, Maryville, TN, states sol buried at old KEEBLE home farm in east end of Blount Co, TN. F-W1880 R1457
KEEBLINGER, Adam, esf 1779 Shenandoah Co, VA where b 8/15/1762 s/o Daniel; PN 1832 Albemarle Co, VA; dd there 7/15/44; md c1785 Elizabeth, d of Philip PRENTZ/PRINCE, (MB 10/22/1785 signed by Jacob KIBLINGER & with consent of both f's) Shenandoah Co, VA; wid PN 1858 Albemarle Co, VA ae not given;

KEEBLINGER (continued)
   surname also spelled KIBLINGER, KELTLINGER, & KEBLINGER;
   QLF 1931 from desc Mrs W S CRUM of West Lafayette, IN, who
   also desc/o SC RW sol James PARNELL/PORNELL; QLF 1925 from
   desc E C KLEPINGER, Chicago, IL, says sol res Fredericksville Parish, Albemarle Co, VA. F-W1618 R1457
KEELE, Richard, esf 1776 Henry Co, VA; md there, then mvd to
   frontiers of NC on Nolachucky River, where esf for Battle
   of King's Mountain; PN aec 74 Rutherford Co, NC, when res
   with one/o s's mbnn, 1832 having just mvd from Bedford Co,
   TN, where had res c17 years. F-S1977 R1457
KEELING, Edmund, esf 1780 Charlotte Co, VA; afp 1834 Abbeville
   District, SC, ae 71; PAR, less than 6 months svc. F-R5812
   R1459
KEEMLE, John, esf in VA regiment as surgeon's mate; PN ae 65+
   Eastern District of PA 1818 where res "the Northern Liberty"; res 1820 aec 68 Penn Township, Eastern District/o PA,
   when had 4 d's: eldest Rebecca aec 30, Eliza aec 25, Maria aec 15, & Caroline aec 12; sol then "too feeble to be
   doctor but now making soap", & res with eldest s mbnn; res
   1823 ae 70 Philadelphia Co, PA with d's: Rebecca, Eliza, &
   Maria "who keep a little school." F-S5652 R1459
KEEN, Abram, esf 1777 Halifax Co, VA, where res when RW began;
   mvd to Amelia Co, VA, 1777 where esf 1781; mvd to Mecklenburg Co, VA, 1785 where PN 1839 ae 77 as General (not RW
   rank) KEEN; res there 1847. F-S11710 R1459
John, BLW12294 issued 7/7/1792. F-BLW12294 R1459
John, esf 1780 VA; PN ae 63 Campbell Co, KY 1823 when w mbnn
   ae 60. F-S37127 R1459
KEEP, James, BLW12297 issued 7/3/1795. F-BLW12297 R1460
James, esf 1777 Frederick Co, VA, where res near Winchester;
   PN ae 61 Alleghany Co, PA, 1818 res Ross Township; res ae
   63 there 1820, when "sickly wife" only family at home; QLF
   1894 from gds J W BOXELL, St Paul, MN. F-S39804 R1460
KEETON, David, esf 1777 Albemarle Co, VA where b 1756; res af-
   ter RW Henry Co, VA, thence Patrick Co, VA, then c1810 to
   Gallia Co, OH where PN 1832 res Huntington. F-S2685 R1460
Isaac, b 1763 Albemarle Co, VA; esf 1718 Botetourt Co, VA,
   where res, in NC regiment; PN 1834 Morgan Co, KY; dd there
   2/6/44; md 8/5/1793 Margaret WADE, Clark Co, KY; wid PN ae
   80 Morgan Co, KY, 1845. F-W9097 R1460
John, esf 1780 Spotsylvania Co, VA, where b 3/24/1763 near
   Fredericksburg; PN 1832 Franklin Co, KY, when sis Nancy &
   her h Reuben HULETT res there; res Frankfort that Co 1834;
   res 1855 Owen Co, KY, when gtd BLW26475; surname also was
   spelled KEATON. F-S13614 R1460
KEGER, John, esf 1782 Winchester, VA, when res Frederick Co;
   PN ae 56 there 1818; res there 1820 ae 57 occupation laborer. F-S38118 R1460
KEISINGER, Andrew, b 12/25/1756 Lancaster Co, PA; mvd aec 10
   to Greenbrier Co, VA where esf 1774, 1776, & 1779 to fight
   indians; mvd after RW to Montgomery Co, VA, then 1815 to

55

KEISINGER (continued)
Knox Co, TN, thence Grainger Co, TN, thence Monroe Co, IN, thence Owen Co, IN where afp 1834; PAR, less than 6 months svc. F-R5818 R1460

KEITH, Alexander, esf 1775 in VA regiment; PN ae 75 Orange Co, IN, 1818 when dd res there over 25 years; res there 1820 when family w Phebe ae 55 & ch: Polly ae 23, Nancy ae 19, Jane ae 17, & Susannah ae 13; dd 5/14/28; QLF 1933 from Miss Ruth SWINEBROOD of Memphis, TN, desc of another VA RW sol Alexander KEITH, who esf 1771 in 6th VA Regiment, md Miss YANCY/YANCEY of SC, & dd 1824 Rodney Landing, Jefferson Co MS. F-S36672 R1461

Daniel, esf in 12th VA regiment; PN ae 69 Rockbridge Co, VA, 1819; res there 1820 occupation laborer when had no family whatsoever. F-S38115 R1461

John, esf 1779 SC; taken POW by British; esf in VA regiment 1780 when released; PN ae 68 Putnam Co, GA 1820 occupation shoemaker when had w Nancy aec 55 & ch Membrance ae 9; dd 2/10/42 Twiggs Co, GA; md there (2) 8/1/1832 to Mrs Nancy WEST (marriage license 7/31/32); wid PN ae 51 Bibb Co, GA, 1834 when res in adjacent Twigg Co, GA; md there (3) William SMITH who dd 3/30/52; AFF there 1853 by James KENT he md d of sol's w in 1841; wid gtd BLW178992 there 1855; sol surname also spelled KEETH. F-W11478 R1461

Thomas, esf 1775 Fauquier Co, VA where res; dd Fall of 1805 while visiting GA, w & other ch remaining in VA, with 1 s accompanying him; md 5/25/1775 Judith BLACKWELL (MB 5/23/75) Fauquier Co, VA; wid PN there 1836 ae 77; dd 4/17/57; ch included eldest s Marshall & s Isham; gds John T JAMES mentioned 1842, who res 1845 Warrenton, VA; nephew James MARSHALL, bro of Chief Justice MARSHALL, AFF 1837 res at "Fairfield"; file mentions Captain John CHILTON of 3rd VA Regiment, who KIA Battle of Brandywine, h/o of sis of Thomas KEITH's w Judith, who dd before RW, & their son Major Joseph CHILTON res 1838 Fauquier Co, VA, further Mark A CHILTON, nephew of Captain John CHILTON, AFF Captain CHILTON md d of Captain John BLACKWELL; in 1845 Jane TAYLOR, wid of George Keith TAYLOR, res Fauquier Co, VA, AFF she niece/o Captain Thomas KEITH & a sis of Chief Justice MARSHALL; QLF states sol s John Marshall (AKA Marshall KEITH) md Elizabeth JONES; QLF 19-- from sol great great gdd Mrs S P JOHNSTON of Aurelian Springs, NC; QLF 1906 from gds James KEITH, who president of VA Supreme Court of Appeals, states sol dd GA when visiting a s there. F-W5119 R1461

William, see KEATH, William. F-W26150 R1461

KELCH, Leonard, b 1763 Salem Co, NJ; esf 1781 Hampshire Co, VA & later esf 1782 Big Pigeon River, NC against Cherokee indians; afp 1834 Tyler Co, VA, & PAR. F-R5823 R1462

KELKNER, Henry, esf 1777 Berks Co, PA; PN ae 62-63 Montgomery Co, VA 1820, occupation laborer, when only family liv with him aged w; surname also spelled KIRKNER. F-S38114 R1462

KELLAM, Housten/Houston, b 1756 Accomac Co, VA, where esf res

KELLAM (continued)
St George's Parish; PN there 1832; dd 1/13/47 or 1/15/47; md there 6/5/1822 Elizabeth RODGERS; wid PN there 1853 ae 84; QLF 1927 from possible desc Mrs E E ADAMS, Richmond, VA. F-W4354 R1462

Spencer, esf 1781 Accomac Co, VA; PN there 1829 ae 69, occupation sailor, when family w Margaret aec 70; dd 2/9/37; md 11/28/1827 Margaret, wid of John RODGERS; wid PN there 1853 ae 65; gtd BLW95517 there 1855. F-W1178 R1462

KELLAR, John, esf 1776 Lancaster Co, PA, where b 1/11/1758 s/o a physician who dd c1808; mvd 1790 to VA, thence 1809 to OH where PN 1833 Clark Co; QLF 1913 from desc Mary KELLAR, North Olmsted, OH. F-S4465 R1462

KELLER, Abraham, esf VA, a captain in Illinois Regiment of VA troops; killed by indians 4/1786; AFF 1846 Jefferson Co, VA, by nephew Abraham, who s of sol bro Isaac, ae 64 who b that Co that sol survived by wid Mary who had a d soon after sol dd & that ch dd as infant, further sol wid md (2) William LYNN by whom she had number of ch & res many years at Shippingport, then mvd to OH; sol eldest brother Jacob res Bourbon Co, KY, & had an only s (dd there before 1846, leaving family); adm of sol estate gtd VA 1/2 pay PN; QLF 1909 from possible desc John W KELLER of New York, NY. F-R15580 R1462

George, b 4/19/1758 near Stoverstown, Shenandoah Co, VA; esf 1779 Augusta Co, VA, where res; mvd c1786 to Monongalia Co VA, where PN 1832; res 1851 Taylor Co, VA; QLF 1935 from great great gds Harry L KELLER, Plant City, FL, states sol listed as RW pensioner 1840 Monongalia Co, VA, census, res then with John KELLER. F-S5649 R1462

George, b 10/14/1760; esf 1780 Augusta Co, VA where res; afp there 1841, & PAR, less than 6 months svc; dd 3/1/41; md there 5/7/1786 Sophia MOWRY/MOURY; wid afp there 1854 ae 88, & PAR; decd 1860 when had ch liv there including Samuel. F-R5827 R1462

George, esf 1781 Shenandoah Co, VA; afp there 1836 ae 73, & PAR; dd there between 10/19/36 & 11/7/36, leaving w Christena; LWT 6/6/1836 probated there 11/7/36, listed w Christena & Reuben, s/o Abraham PENCE (no kinship stated). F-R5828 R1462

KELLEY, Elias, b 8/3/1762 New Castle, DE; esf 1778-9 PA when res VA; after boundary line drawn between VA & PA, he res PA; mvd to VA, thence 1791 to KY, thence 1805 to Clark Co, IN, where PN 1832. F-S16175 R1463

Griffin, b 1770 Spotsylvania Co, VA; mvd 1786 to KY where he esf before 1790 Fayette Co against indians; PN for wound disability 1846 Clark Co, KY; dd there 3/17/55; md 12/26/1793 Sarah/Sally SUTTON, Bourbon Co, KY; wid afp Clark Co, KY, 1855 for h svc in Indian Wars 1790-95; PAR, no proof of sol's death as result of that svc; res ae 85 Scott Co, KY, 1858; sol had bro Joseph, who md Nancy; surname also spelled KELLY. F-R15571 R1463

KELLEY, James b 1758; esf 1778 Bedford Co, VA, where res; mvd to KY c1817; PN there 1832 Daviess Co; QLF 1928 from great great gdd Mrs N J BELL, Waterloo, NE, states sol came from Kilkenny, Ireland, md Rose KISER & their ch: John, Janice, Joseph, Mordecai, Samuel, Absalom, Charles, Susan, Elizabeth, Mary, Nancy, & Judy; surname also spelled KELLY. F-S16433 R1463

James, esf c1778 VA, drum major; dd 6/24/1811; md 6/24/1786 Elizabeth CRUTCHFIELD; wid afp ae 74 Caroline Co, VA, 1840 & PAR, insufficient data for PN Office to determine which one of 5 different VA sol's named James KELLEY was her h; wid res Hanover Co, VA, 1847 when AFF by Sarah LEWIS (d of William SUTTON) ae 70 at res of her h Robert LEWIS, King William Co, VA, that sol & w res 14 years on land of her f in latter co, VA; children mbnn; surname also spelled KELLY. F-R5841 R1463

John, esf 1777 in 11th VA Regiment; wounded Battle of Brandywine; PN ae 62 Muskingum Co, OH, 1818; res there 1820 with w Elizabeth ae 62 & ch: Abigail (a wid) ae 33, Sarah ae 23 & s John ae 8; s Joseph also res in that Co; surname also spelled KELLY; QLF says sol dd 6/11/1853 ae 98 Union Township, Muskingum Co, OH & buried in Rich Hill Cemetery; QLF 1907 from J M DALZELL, Washington, DC, whose w gdd of sol, says sol res near New Concord, OH & dd Zanesville, OH F-S41717 R1463

John, esf 1777 Pittsylvania Co, VA; res there 24 years, then to Stokes Co, NC for c34 years, thence Logan Co, (area later Simpson Co), where PN ae 70, latter Co, 1832 when res there c24 years; dd 4/3/1838; md 2/1779 Ann TEMPLETON, Pittyslvania Co, VA, who 4 years older than he; they both illiterate; wid PN ae 83 Simpson Co, KY, 1839; 2 ch mbnn; s Joseph res there 1840 ae 50; wid res there 1844 ae 86; her bro John TEMPLETON res 1840 Pittsylvania Co, VA; sol surname also spelled KELLY. F-W9095 R1463

William, esf 1778 VA; PN ae 67 Elbert Co, GA 1827 when had w Philadelphia aec 60, s William ae 13, & d Rutha ae 10; dd 6/29/47 Elbert Co, GA; md (2) 2/1833 Lucinda HARRIS, Anderson District, SC; wid md (2) 11/7/48 Jesse WHITMOND/WHITMAN, Elbert Co, GA, who dd 10/8/55, Marietta, GA; wid PN there 1856 ae 40; gtd BLW43528 Cobb Co, GA, 1856 while res Marietta, GA; in 1868 "had no sons large enough to engage in the War of the Rebellion" when PN restored Cobb Co GA, after Civil War; sol surname also spelled KELLY; QLF 1937 from great great gdd (on f's side) Maud McLure KELLY, Birmingham, AL. F-W25993 R1463

William, esf 1780 Culpeper Co, VA, where b; PN ae not given Mercer Co, KY 1832; dd there 9/22/54; md Sally ATKINSON there 7/1831 (8/12/30 per Co clerk to Sally ADKISSON); wid PN & gtd BLW3466 there 1855 ae 78; surname also spelled KELLY. F-W13595 R1463

William, b 1/10/1760 VA; esf aec 16 on Eastern Shore of VA; res VA several years after RW, thence Dorchester Co & So-

KELLEY (continued)
    merset Co's, MD, for c11 years, thence IN, where afp 1845 Spencer Co; PAR, insufficient proof of svc; dd there 3/18/46 leaving wid mbnn; surv ch 1847: William J ae 57 of Warrick Co, IN, Jacob, & Elizabeth RUBLE, both res Spencer Co IN. F-R5833 R1463
KELLY, Beal, b 12/11/1750 MD; mvd to Prince William Co, VA, thence 1778 Boonesborough, KY Territory where esf; PN 1832 Warren Co, KY; res 1834 Rockcastle Co, KY. F-S15490 R1466
Benjamin, b 1761 King & Queen Co, VA; esf 1775 SC; esf 1779 Granville Co, NC, where res; res after RW Mecklenburg Co, VA, thence Warren Co, NC, thence Buncombe Co, NC where apf 1850, & PAR; res there 1853. F-R5838 R1466
Edmond, b 12/1754; esf SC; later esf in VA regiment; PN 1827 by NC; afp then Newberry District, SC, & PAR; dd intestate there 10/6/42 leaving no wid or survivors; afp 1851 there by adm of estate James D MANSFIELD ae 24, & PAR. F-R5840 R1466
George, esf 1783 VA; res Buckingham Co, VA after RW; dd 1820 there; md there 1792 Nancy, who md (2) Thomas DEWITT, who dd 1837; wid afp ae 73 Cocke Co, TN, 1844, & PAR. F-R2922 R1466
Henry, BLW13292 & 13574 issued 9/2/1789; svd in Lee's Legion F-BLW13292 R1466
James, b 10/22/1759 Pittsylvania Co, VA; mvd just before RW to Greenbrier Co, VA, where f shortly thereafter killed by indians; sol then mvd with m & family back to Pittsylvania Co, VA; sol esf 1777 Kershaw Co, Camden District, SC, mvd there shortly after RW where 7 ch b in period of 14 years, thence Green Co, TN, for 3-4 years, thence Williamson Co, TN, for 2-3 years, thence Maury Co, TN, thence c1823 Hickman Co, TN, thence 1834 to Maury Co, TN, where afp 1833 ae 74; claim returned for further proof of svc; PN there 1835 aec 75; last PN payment in file 1840 in TN. F-S1544 R1466
James, b 8/1756 Ireland; to VA 1773; esf 1777 Greenbrier Co, VA; res after RW VA, KY, TN, then c1820 to Cooper Co, MO, where PN 1833; last PN payment in file Cole Co, MO, agency 1842; QLF states sol res Moniteau Township near Booneville MO, further sol b Kilkenny, Ireland, & md Rosa KEISER; QLF states sol dd Cole Co, MO, 1840. F-S16903 R1466
James, esf 1778 near Morgantown, Monongalia Co, VA, where res; mvd c1808 from KY to Clark Co, OH where PN 1832 ae 79 res Greene Township; dd there 4/30/37; md 9/1783 Catharine STEWART, Monongalia Co, VA, who b Tyrone, Ireland; wid PN ae 80 Clark Co, OH, 1847 res Greene Township; ch births: Rachel 8/4/1784, Joseph 12/23/85, John 3/3/89, Samuel 3/3/91, Thomas 8/1/92, Nathan 5/12/94, Mary 3/24/96, James 11/5/98, Catharine 6/7/99, Stewart 6/13/1801, Francis 5/12/03, & Leah 1/7/06; s James res 1847 Clark Co, OH; wid res there 1851 with s Samuel; d Rachel KIRKPATRICK mvd c 1808 to Clark Co, OH with h & several ch mbnn; QLF states sol b 1752 VA; QLF 1925 from desc Mrs M W SITTON, Live Oak

KELLY (continued)
CA; QLF states sol b 1752 Scotland; sol AKA James KELLEY; file contains data on a War of 1812 sol James KELLEY/KELLY who esf 1812 Chillecothe, Ross Co, OH, md 9/1849 Barbara LEACH, Ross Co, OH & he PN 1871 ae 77 Fountain Co, IN when res with s Alexander Leach at Harveysburg. F-W7969 R1466
John, esf 1776 in 12th VA regiment; PN 1819 Barren Co, KY; res there 1820 ae 63 occupation farmer with w, b 11/1760, & an orphan boy William McGINNIS (no kinship given) aec 14 F-S36674 R1466
Richard, esf 1780 Frederick Co, VA, where b 3/26/1763; PN 1832 Carter Co, TN; QLF 1930 from desc John Alexander KEL-LY, Haverford, PA, states sol dd 1853; QLF says a Richard KELLY md 1773 Maria GIBBS, & they came to VA where he esf. F-S1680 R1467
Thady/Thaddy, esf VA as captain of artillery; dd soon after 1/1788; adm of estate Richard RANDOLPH afp 1847 & gtd 1/2 pay PN. F-R15579 R1467
Thomas, esf aec 16 PN in VA regiment; PN aec 60 Jefferson Co KY, 1821 occupation laborer when had w & 7ch liv with him; QLF states a Thomas KELLY came to America with CORNWALLIS, deserted British army, joined American troops in VA, & mvd c1802 to near Lexington, KY. F-S36031 R1467
William, b 11/2/1755 Chester Co, PA; esf 1777 Winchester, VA where res; mvd after RW to PA for c13 years, thence KY for c26 years, thence IN, where PN 1832 Switzerland Co, when res with s William; sol bro Thomas AFF there then ae 68; dd 1/21/33-4; md 9/14/1786 Sarah PRESSOR, Fayette Co, PA, at house of Henry PRESSOR; wid AFF she lost marriage certificate when res c1795 Clark Co, KY; wid PN ae 74 Switzerland Co, IN 1838; res there 1840 ae 75; ch births: Nancy 4/13/1787, Catharine 12/30/89, Mary 2/17/92, Elizabeth 9/20/95, twins Thomas & Rachel 7/31/97, Lydia 12/11/1800 & William 3/20/03; AFF by wid sis Rebecca STEPHENS, Boone Co KY, 1841; AFF then by eldest ch Nancy SPARKS & by d Lydia Ann, Switzerland Co, IN; surname also spelled KELLEY. F-W10165 R1467
William, esf 1776-7 Accomac Co, VA; BLW1947 issued 6/8/1833 there to only ch: Daniel, Richard & Nancy w/o Ralph SMITH; surname also spelled KELLEY. F-BLW1947 R1467
KELSO, Alexander, b 3/30/1758 Augusta Co, VA; esf 1775 Washaw Settlement, SC, where res; mvd 1776 to Botetourt Co, VA, thence later 1776 Bedford Co, VA, thence Sullivan Co, NC where esf 1780; discharged from svc 1780 when res Washington Co, NC; esf there 1781 & 1782 against indians; res after RW Jefferson Co, TN, thence Knox Co, TN, thence 1828 Morgan Co, IN, where PN 1832; dd there c9/2/35; md 5/1781 Margaret BALCH, Washington Co, NC who b Fall 1755; wid res Mecklenburg Co, NC during early part of RW from where fled with others to Little Limestone, NC, where res till md; PN 1838 Morgan Co, IN, res Jackson Township; res 1843 Monroe Co, IN res Perry Townsip; ch included eldest s Charles (ae

KELSO (continued)
58 when res Jackson Township, IN, 1843), & James W (ae 47 when res Monroe Co, IN, 1843, veteran of War of 1812); wid had sis mbnn & bro's James, William, Amos, John, & Stephen B BALCH; her bro William ensign/o NC troops in RW; her bro John in RW Battle of Ramson's Mill; her bro's James, Amos, & William, all in RW Battle of Gates Defeat; her bro John res 1837 Jefferson Co, TN, & bro Stephen B pastor of Presbyterian Church at Georgetown, DC, after RW (he had s Thomas B res MD Eastern Shore & d mbnn who md General MACOMB; sol bro mbnn sub for him for one tour in RW; surname also spelled KELSOE & KELSOO; QLF 1908 from great gds Clarence E KELSO, Manistique, MI, states sol dd Morgantown, IN; QLF 1908 from desc Wilber M KELSO, Chicago, IL; QLF 1938 says sol buried in old cemetery, west of Morgantown, IN, near John Williams Farm. F-W9493 R1468

James, b 1761 Augusta Co (area later Rockbridge Co), VA; esf 1781 latter Co; PN 1832 Bath Co, VA; QLF says sol was res Rockbridge Co, VA, in 1835. F-S18068 R1468

KELTLINGER, Adam, see KEEBLINGER, Adam. F-W1618 R1468
KEMP, Adria, former wid of William ENGLISH. (F-W7970)
James, esf VA as quartermaster officer for military hospitals erected in VA 1776-1781; dd 12/15/1795 Richmond, VA; s Thomas, a physician, esf at beginning of RW & served to late 1781 as surgeon's mate, & later was representative to VA legislature for Princess Anne Co; sol's sis mbnn md Robert NISBET of Richmond, VA, & she dd 2/1/1846; her s William, who res 1832 St Louis, MO, md heiress/o Colonel John SPOTSWOOD; her s Archibald dd 4/16 or 4/17/1849; her d Agnes M (AKA Nancy) md Mr BIGELOW & had s Robert M; 1/2 pay PN gtd to sol's heirs; QLF states sol middle name Beckett. F-R15581 R1469

Reuben, esf 1780 Harrod's Station, KY Territory, where res; PN ae 78 Crawford Co, IN, 1832. F-S16901 R1469

Thomas, s/o above James KEMP, esf 1775 as surgeon's mate; dd 1789 or 1792 Princess Anne Co, VA, leaving wid mbnn & ch: Frances, James, & Sarah; wid decd in 1832 when sol's heirs were James KEMP of Princess Anne Co, VA & Sarah wid/o William WILKINS of Norfolk, VA; heirs gtd BLW by VA; William R WILKINS of Petersburg, VA, appointed adm/o sol estate by Princess Anne Co Court, & he afp for all heirs, & PAR, insufficient proof of svc; sol gds Thomas T KEMPE res 1848 Norfolk, VA; QLF states sol md to Esther MAXEY. F-R15582 R1469

William, BLW12293 issued 12/13/1791. F-BLW12293 R1469
KEMPER, Charles, b 6/27/1756 near Warrenton, Fauquier Co, VA, where esf 1777 while res on f's farm; PN 1833 that Co res near Warrenton; dd 12/1/41; md that Co 11/29/1786 Susanna MAWZEY; wid PN there 1843 ae 77; s mbnn 1843; QLF 1931 from Mrs W F SIMMONS, Del Norte, CO, whose gdm was d/o Alexander KEMPER, whose f was William KEMPER, only s of sol, further sol was s of John KEMPER II (b 5/1722 Germantown,

KEMPER (continued)
  VA), further William Kemper md Sarah HILS; QLF 1913 from desc Gladys KEMPER, Granville, IL, states sol b Germantown VA & had s William; QLF states sol bro JOHN b 1740 who res Fauquier Co, VA, further sol had bro Peter also an RW sol; QLF states Peter KEMPER dd c1829 Cincinnati, OH. F-W20292 R1469
KEMPLEN, William, esf 1777 Philadelphia, PA; mvd to Franklin Co, VA, c1786 where PN 1818 ae not stated; res there 1821 with w, s aec 12, s aec 10, s aec 7 & d aec 5; dd 12/9/36; md 12/1789 Elizabeth, d of Gasper GARLICK (MB 11/24/1788), Montgomery Co, VA; ch births: Ann 5/20/1791, John 7/13/93, Mary 9/14/95, William 4/24/97, George 7/16/99, Elizabeth 8/20/1801, Thomas 7/22/05, Nicholas 2/26/08, & Henry 10/4/10; wid PN ae 68 Franklin Co, VA, 1841 when s Nicholas AFF there; wid gtd BLW38511 there 1855. F-W7971 R1469
KENDALL, Aaron, esf 1781 Stafford Co, VA, where b; esf later 1781 sub for bro Moses; mvd 1805 to OH, then 1827 back to Stafford Co, VA, where PN 1833 ae 69; last PN payment in record 1842; QLF states sol dd there. F-S15909 R1470
  Benjamin, esf Prince William Co, VA, for svc with Illinois Regiment of General George Rogers CLARK; dd 2/16/1817; md 9/1/1786 Elizabeth, d of Alexander JAMESON of Overwharton Parish, Stafford Co, VA; per that Co Clerk marriage dated 8/29/1776; wid afp ae 72 Hardin Co, KY, 1839 & PAR, insufficient proof/o svc; s Enoch AFF there then he b 6/26/1787 F-R5857 R1470
  Custis, BLW1209 issued 6/26/1789, captain in VA Line. F-BLW 1209 R1470
  Francis, esf Prince William Co, VA, where res since ae 6; PN ae 78 Culpeper Co, VA, 1832; dd 2/13/35; LWT probated Rappahannock Co, VA, 3/9/35; md 1/3/1823 Malinda CRISMOND who md (2) 9/3/35 James HITT, who dd 10/20/53; wid PN 1854 ae 61 Rappahannock Co, VA; gtd BLW2360 there 1855; her PN restored 1867 there after Civil War. F-W25775 R1470
  George, b King George Co, VA; esf Falmouth, VA; afp 1834 ae 93 Prince William Co, VA, & PAR; dd 5/2/47 leaving ch: Robert, Catharine STEWARD & Mary M (md 1820 Ransom F HICKERSON, Stafford Co, VA); d Mary M afp & afb 1854 Stafford Co VA, when only surv ch/o sol; PAR & BLAR. F-R5859 R1470
  Jeremiah, b 1758 Stafford Co, VA, where esf 1775 res with f; f dd c12/1777; sol allowed to come home then from Valley Forge; PN 1833 Fayette Co, PA, res German Township; QLF says sol md Rhoda McINTYRE in VA; QLF says sol dd Fayette Co, PA, 1843; QLF 1916 from Mrs Paula Kendall ROGERS, Tennile, GA, gdd of a VA RW sol Jeremiah KENDALL who mvd 1795 to Washington Co, GA, dd there, & wid remained there, further he had bro Harry who also VA RW sol. F-S23743 R1470
  Peter, esf 1777 Stafford Co, VA; PN aec 57 Fleming Co, KY, 1818; dd there 3/1825; md there 10/9/1817 Nancy KING, who dd there 5/17/55 ae 67; sol s Warder b 12/1802; surv ch of sol (all ch by w Nancy) afp 1857 Fleming Co, KY; they were

KENDALL (continued)
  Harrison O (ae 35 res there), Peyton & Henry (aec 39); PAR F-R5860 R1470
KENDRICK, Abel, b 3/14/1759 Hanover Co, VA; esf 1779 Union District, SC; mvd c1807 or 1814 to Franklin Co, GA, thence Jackson Co (area later Hall Co), GA; afp 1834 latter Co, & PAR, less than 6 months svc; dd there 8/23/36, leaving wid Judy/Juda & 7 ch; wid dd 9/28/36 Forsythe Co, GA, at home of Henry H & Elizabeth BEALL (kinship not given) with whom she had res since h dd; s Robert res ae 62 Marietta, Cobb Co, GA 1852; QLF states sol gtd land for RW svc in 1827 GA Land Lottery, further 1790 Census lists sol res Ninety-Six District, Union Co, GA, further sol res Floyds District of Hall Co, GA, 1827. F-R5861 R1471
  Benjamin, esf 1776 Culpeper Co, VA, where res; PN 1786 for disability from wound at Battle of Brandywine; PN 1818, ae not given, Bourbon Co, KY; res there 1822 P O Address Paris; dd 6/12/30; md 6/13/1778 Frankey, Fauquier Co, VA; wid afp ae 78 Bourbon Co, KY, 1838, & dd 11/9/38 before PN gtd; surv ch who gtd PN 1838: Elizabeth PUTNAM, Nancy CUMMINS, Joseph, Fanny SMITH, Frankey, Dosha CORBIN, William, & Joanna CORBIN; sol bro William (res 1818 Bourbon Co, KY) & bro Benoni res Culpeper Co, VA, during RW; AFF 1838 by Benjamin & Nancy CORBIN of Boone Co, KY, for sol wid (no kinship given); AFF 1838 by Robert B CUMMINS (kinship not stated), Jacksonville, Bourbon Co, KY; QLF 1905 from great great gdd Mrs Jennie Kendrick SEELEY, address not given; QLF states sol b MD, & w named Nancy; QLF 1917 from great gdd Ola C (Mrs Thomas) GIBBON, New Brighton, NY, says sol d Temperance md Mr McWHINNEY, they querier's grandparents, further sol had d Sarah, d Elizabeth & s William; QLF 1938 from Roberta Armstrong (Mrs Joseph Kirby) MAHONEY, El Dorado, AR, gave this VA KENDRICK data: Abraham KENDRICK dd Warren Co, VA, his LWT listing ch Catharine, Abraham, Benjamin, Jacob, & Christopher, further s Benjamin md 10/18/1785 Annie FUNK, & dd Warren Co, VA, & their ch: (1) Mary md Baylor JACOBS & mvd to MO, (2) John, mvd to KY, (3) Jacob, (4) Christopher md 1818 Mary WAY, & they had s James Way res 1938 Front Royal, VA, (5) Samuel md Clarenda SPENGLER, settled "Matin Hill", Strasburg, VA & d there (their d Eleanor Frances md David English ARMSTRONG, & they res El Dorado, AR, & their d was querier Roberta A above), (6) Elizabeth md Abraham BRINKER & dd Denver, CO & (7) Catherine md John STEPHENSON & dd Front Royal, VA, further David English (b El Dorado, AR) s/o James W ARMSTRONG (b GA) who s/o B ARMSTRONG & Caroline DAVIS, further Caroline DAVIS sis of David English DAVIS & Thomas DAVIS (md MS); QLF 1895 from great gds John L KENDRICK, Riverside, OH, states sol one of 7 bro's in Battle of Brandywine & he buried at Jacksonville, KY. F-W9098 R1471
  Benoni, esf 1779 Culpeper Co, VA; PN aec 60 Bourbon Co, KY, 1818; res there 1820 aec 62, occupation farmer, with s-in-

KENDRICK (continued)
 law mbnn, when sol w decd c15 years; sol given name shown incorrectly as Benson on list of RW pensioners res Bourbon Co, KY, 1835. F-S36030 R1471
Daniel, esf 1777 Culpeper Co, VA, serving in same company as bro's Benoni, Benjamin & William; never afp since "did not need a a pension"; mvd from Culpeper Co, VA, 1812 to Scott Co, KY, thence 1819 Campbell Co, KY, where dd 11/1/42 leaving wid & ch: John, Jacob, Daniel Beard, Jane WIGGENTON & Catherine JEWETT (all res there); md 5/11/1779 Winnifred/ Winifred (MB 5/3/79, with consent/o her f Samuel DAY) Culpeper Co, VA; wid PN ae 91 Campbell Co, KY, 1852. F-9491 R1471
Jacob, esf in VA Line & wounded Battle of Guilford; afp aec 87 Cocke Co, TN, 1830 & PAR, name not on any rolls/o sol's of VA Line. F-R5863 R1471
William, b 10/19/1747 (old style) Hanover Co, VA; esf 1779 Mecklenburg Co, VA, where res; PN 1832 Shelby Co, KY, when family mbnn; surname also spelled KENDRICKS; QLF states sol md Miss HUMPHREY & they had d Susanna b 7/4/1784, further sol at one time res Washington Co, KY, & dd KY; QLF 1927 from desc E G CHAPMAN of Minneapolis, MN. F-S31182 R1471
William, esf 1779 Culpeper Co, VA where res; PN 1818 Bourbon Co, KY; res there 1820 ae 71; res 1833 Schuyler Co, IL having recently mvd there from KY; dd 12/29/35; md 6/3/1783 Fanny MITCHEL, Culpeper Co, VA; wid PN ae 75 Brown Co, IL, res near Mt Sterling; ch included Sally, James, John, Mitchell, & Francis; QLF states sol b 12/29/1757 Culpeper Co, VA, md 1782 Fanny MITCHEL, dd Mt Sterling, IL, 6/1836, & wid dd there 1854, sol s/o Jacob whose family name originally McKENDRICK when ancestors came to America, F-W26743 R1471
KENEDA, William, esf 1780 Culpeper Co, VA, where b 1755; mvd 1786 to Lincoln Co, NC, thence 1818 Williamson Co, TN; PN there 1833; QLF states sol buried TN as William KENNEDY. F-S4468 R1471
KENNADAY, Joseph, b 10/1763; esf 1780 Rockbridge Co, VA, where res; PN 1833 Boone Co, KY. F-S31181 R1471
KENNADY, John, see CANNADAY, John. F-R1654 R1471
KENNAHORN, William, esf 1776 Accomac Co, VA, where res; PN ae 70 there 1818; res there 1829 ae 82 occupation cooper with w Delaney ae 50; dd there 11/30/40; md there 1/14/1824 as widower to Delaney BUTLER; wid PN there 1853 ae 78, & gtd BLW8175 there 1855 ae 82; dd 5/6/62; adm/o her estate William MOORE ae 56 gave power/o attorney 1866 to agent there to secure restoration/o wid's name to PN rolls for PN lost during Civil War. F-W26642 R1471
KENNEDAY, Sherwood, b 10/14/1760 Halifax Co, VA; esf Guilford Co, NC 1778 where res; esf 1779 Randolph Co, NC where res; PN 1832 Davidson Co, NC; dd 4/6/42; surname also spelled KENNEDY. F-S8779 R1471

KENNEDY, Charles, b NJ; mvd 1779 to Jefferson Co, KY Territory where esf 1780; PN ae 69 Trigg Co, KY 1832 when res there c26 years. F-S13617 R1472
David, b 9/21/1767 NC; esf 1780 Kennedy's Station, KY Territory; PN 1833 Garrard Co, KY, when sis mbnn res TN; dd there 9/21/50; md 7/29/1794 Jane COX, Madison Co, KY; wid PN there 1855 ae 71 when children mbnn. F-W7973 R1472
James, esf 1781 in VA regiment; dd 3/10/1828; s Granville as adm/o f's estate, gtd 1/2 pay PN Henrico Co, VA, 1849 when res Stanardsville, VA; QLF 1924 from John C KENNEDY, Harwood, MO, who desc/o RW sol John KENNEDY (VA or NC), settled near Roxboro, Person Co, NC, after RW & dd after 1820; QLF 1914 from Mrs C H WINE, Culpeper Co, VA, who desc/o VA RW sol James KENNEDY, who came from Scotland/Ireland & esf VA, md 1790 Barbara SMITH, Louisa Co, VA. F-R15594 R1472
Jesse, esf 1775-6 VA; dd 1799/1800 Amherst Co, VA; md there 10/1780 Susannah (MB 10/16/80 with consent/o f Joseph DILLARD); wid md there (2) 4/1805 Thomas ALFRED (MB 4/5/1805) who dd 1832; wid afp there 1847 ae 83 for RW svc/o both h; PAR, insufficient proof/o svc for both; 2nd h Thomas in VA sea svc; surname/o 1st h also spelled KENADY. F-R93 R1472
John, esf in VA regiment near Portsmouth, VA soon after Battle of Great Bridge; PN 1818 Davidson Co, TN; res there ae 68 in 1820 when liv with w ae 40 & ch Pierce ae 13, Robert ae 11, James ae 8, Jesse ae 6, & Shadrick ae 2. F-S38890 R1472
John, BLW2091; surname also spelled CANADY. F-BLW2091 R1472
Joseph, mvd from Burke Co, NC 1776 to KY Territory where esf 1777, thence later 1777 Charlotte Co, NC where esf sub for uncle Mr KENNEDY same year; returned to KY 1779 where esf; appointed ensign 1780 at Kennedy's Station there in company of bro Captain John; captured by indians 1780 & held for 1 year; esf 1782 Lincoln Co, KY Territory, against indians; PN ae 62 Madison Co, KY, 1832; QLF states sol dd there 1844, LWT probated there, b 1760, md (1) Martha/Patsy PERRIN, md (2) Elizabeth MORRISON who b 1779 & dd 1844. F-S13600 R1472
Joseph, see KENNADAY, Joseph. F-S31181 R1472
William, esf 1776 in VA regiment; PN ae 60 Brunswick Co, VA, 1818; res there 1820 ae 70; dd 11/30/24 Augusta Co, VA; s George S res there 1858; QLF states sol b VA, md Miss McCLURE, & they res near Staunton, VA. F-S38117 R1472
KENNER, Rodham, VA sea svc, esf 1777 Fredericksburg, VA, as steward & gunner aboard ship PAGE, later on ship DRAGON, & later on ship JEFFERSON all commanded by his uncle Captain James MARKHAM; later esf Fauquier Co, VA, for army svc; PN 1832 Logan Co, KY; dd there 8/24/42 leaving wid Elizabeth, who still liv there 1851. F-S1228 R1473
KENNERLEY, Samuel, b 2/1754 or 3/54 Culpeper Co, VA; esf 1777 Augusta Co, VA; PN 1834 Botetourt Co, VA; dd St Louis, MO, 2/3/40; ch included Samuel Lockhart who dd Fall 1843; sol bro/o William; surname also spelled KENNERLY; QLF says sol

KENNERLEY (continued)
   dd at res of s Captain George Hancock, Jefferson Barracks, MO, 2/3/1840. F-S16900 R1473
Thomas, b 10/24/1750 Culpeper Co, VA; esf 1780 Augusta Co, where res; mvd after RW to Walker Co, GA (area later Oglethorpe Co); res latter Co 19 years, thence Overton Co, TN, thence Cumberland Co, KY, thence Franklin Co, TN, where PN 1832. F-S1843 R1473
William, b 2/4/1752 Culpeper Co, VA; esf 1774 Augusta Co, VA where res; PN there 1833; last PN payment in file 1839; QLF states sol dd 1840 Greenway Court, VA. F-S8781 R1473
KENNON, Richard, esf VA Line & was captain; ch 1842: Dr George T of Henrico Co, VA, Erasmus decd of Mecklenburg Co, VA, Commodore Beverly of Washington, DC, William H of Powhatan Co, VA, Dr Richard decd of Norfolk, VA, & Sarah S decd who w/o decd Commodore Arthur SINCLAIR; ch of sol s Erasmus in 1842: William, Richard, Roberta, Sally w of William D LIGON, Lucy w/o Edward A WILLIAMS, Nancy w of Oliver KENNON, Elizabeth w/o Dr Silas H HARRIS, & George decd (who left 2 ch, d Alice being only one liv, res Mecklenburg Co, VA); w/o sol s Richard & their only ch Emily E res 1842 Norfolk VA; ch/o sol d Sarah S SINCLAIR in 1842: Arthur, Elizabeth w/o William C WHITTLE, George T, William Henry, & Gilberta M LaFayette (the d's res Mecklenburg Co, VA & s's all commodores in US Navy); sol s Dr George T afb 1842 Henrico Co VA, for self & all heirs; BLW2298 for 300 acres issued on 11/42/1842; QLF states sol s/o William & w Elizabeth LEWIS & that sol also md an Elizabeth LEWIS, further RW sol Robert MARTIN of King & Queen Co, VA, & Prince Edward Co, VA md Mary VENABLE & they had s Dr George MARTIN who md Mary, d/o Richard KENNON. F-BLW2298 R1473
William, see CANNON, William. F-W5897 R1473
KENNEY, Richard, see KINNEY, Richard. F-W10175 R1473
KENSOR, Michael, see KINSER, Michael. F-W8001 R1473
KENT, Absolam, b 10/16/1752 Fairfax Co, VA; esf 1779 Fayette Co, VA; mvd 1805 to Harrison Co, OH, where PN 1834 res Archer Township; dd 8/12/39 leaving wid mbnn; sol sis mbnn 1834. F-S8784 R1474
Alexander, esf 1777 in 10th VA Regiment; PN ae 67 Halifax Co VA, 1820 occupation farmer, when family w, d (a wid), & s, all mbnn; res there 1823; d 4/8/40 & wid dd 4/28/43; only surv ch Alexander Jr gave power of attorney to agent 1853 Gilmer Co, VA, to afp arrears. F-S38113 R1474
Daniel, ensign VA Line; dd intestate c1811 leaving ch John, Judith, & Jane who all dd intestate Lancaster Co, VA ; sol heirs 1833: d Judith CURRELL + Frances A B & Jane W R both ch/o d Jane W EDMONDS, + Daniel s/o s John; in 1845 heirs (all surname CURRELL) William, John Y, Ann B, Sarah L, & Maria K, all of Lancaster Co, VA, gave power/o attorney to afp; in 1853 George WADDY, deputy sheriff of Lancaster Co, VA, & adm/o sol estate, afp for sol heirs which were above name CURRELL children, + Jane Edmonds Haseltine KENT; 1/2

KENT (continued)
PN gtd heirs 1853. F-R15583 R1474
John, b 10/1/1748; esf 1778 in 2nd VA Regiment; afp 1828 Columbia Co, GA, when had large family to support; PAR, name not on VA rolls or on BLW rolls; dd 2/14/1846 Columbia Co, GA; md 2/29/1792 Susan who afp ae 95 Columbia Co, GA, 1855 & PAR; ch mbnn. F-R5875 R1474
Peter, esf 1777-8 Fairfax Co, VA where b 3/5/1760; mvd c1791 to Wilkes Co, GA, thence 1825 Greene Co, TN where PN 1833; dd 12/23/43; md 5/7/1779 Sarah Ann COOPER, Fairfax Co, VA, who b 2/13/1761; wid PN 1844 Greene Co, TN, when d Harriet JOHNSON AFF there ae 40 that she 8th ch; ch births: Elizabeth 2/11/1780, Ann Perry 10/27/83, John 7/4/91, & Sarah Reynolds 4/1/1802. F-W85 R1474
Robert, b 1/20/1762 Albemarle Co, VA; esf 1777 Fluvanna Co, VA where res; PN there 1833; dd 5/9/45; md 9/23/1782 Sarah COCKE (MB 9/19/82 signed by Pleasant COCKE), Fluvanna Co, VA; wid PN there 1850 ae 87; ch mbnn. F-W27875 R1475
Thomas, b 1746 Prince William Co, VA where esf 1780 when already md; mvd after RW to Loudoun Co, VA, thence Columbiana Co, OH, where PN 1833. F-S4466 R1475
KENTON, Simon, b 4/3/1755 VA; esf 1774 for Lord Dunsmore's War in KY Territory; esf there for RW with Gen. George Rogers Clark; PN 1830 by special act of congress as general when res OH; dd 4/29/36; large family mbnn; QLF states sol 2nd w buried in Co, where city of Rensselaer now stands; QLF 1929 from desc Mattie M (Mrs W A) RINEHART of Palmyra, MO. F-S41719 R1475
KEPHART, Henry, see KIPHART, Henry. F-S31190 R1475
KEPPS, Jacob, b 11/11/1760; esf 1778 Rockingham Co, VA, where res; mvd 1786 to Shenandoah Co, VA, where PN 1832 res near Newmarket; dd there 4/20/49; md there 1/24/1786 Elizabeth ZIRKLE; wid PN there 1851 ae 85; gtd BLW 35835 there 1855; surname also spelled KIPPS & KIPS. F-W7993 R1475
KERBY, Christopher, b f9/10/1760 Halifax Co, VA; esf 1779 Surry Co, NC where res; mvd after RW to Greene Co, TN, thence Washington Co, AR, where PN 1835. F-S32356 R1475
Jesse, b 10/23/1757; esf 1780 Henry Co, VA where res; mvd to SC, thence KY, where PN 1832 Warren Co; dd 12/17/52; newspaper obituary in file states sol had 13 ch, 135 gdc, 303 great gdc, & 7 great great gdc, for a total of 458 descendants when he dd; md 3/18/1778 Sophia who b 9/23/1760; wid PN 1853 Warren Co, KY; ch births (2 dd young, not listed): ? (probably Jesse R below) 1/27/1779, Nancy 20/23/81, Lucy 11/27/83, William 2/15/85, Sirus 12/2/87, Elizabeth 1/27/90, ? 3/6/1792 (b SC), Isaiah 8/5/94, John 2/27/97, Poley 2/26/99, & Tully 11/11/1802; s Jesse R AFF 1853 Warren Co, KY, he res there nearly 56 years; QLF states sol md Sophia CHOICE & was probably bro of VA RW sol Edmund KIRBY who md Sarah, d/o General William D SHEPHERD (settled before 1770 in Surry Co, NC, area later Stokes Co, NC); QLF states sol res Bowling Green, KY; QLF 1894 from desc Mrs W A ATCHISON

KERBY (continued)
  of Nashville, TN; QLF 1914 from A L ANDERSON, Lincoln, IL, whose w desc/o sis/o sol, further sol had bro Leonard T, & their f also RW sol. F-W9489 R1475
  Leonard T, b 10/4/1760 Pittyslvania Co, VA; esf 1778 Henry Co, VA, as sub for f David; mvd from Pittsylvania Co, VA, to SC, thence KY, thence TN, thence back to KY, where PN 1832 Warren Co, when Jesse KIRBY AFF there he had served 2 tours in RW with sol (no kinship given); QLF states sol dd Warren Co, KY. F-S31183 R1475
  William, 11/19/1759; esf 1779 Hanover Co, VA; PN 1818 Albemarle Co, VA; ch 1821 included Nancy ae 12, Martin ae 10 & Minor ae 5; dd 8/17/48; md Elizabeth McDANIEL soon after end of RW; wid PN ae 85 Albemarle Co, VA, 1851 when d mbnn w of William T SMITH res there; wid gtd BLW 17717 when res Nelson Co, VA, 1855. F-W7998 R1475
KERCHEVAL, John, b 9/12/1762 Spotsylvania Co, VA; esf Frederick Co, VA, 1776 when res there; PN 1834 Fleming Co, KY; dd there 10/1/39; md 12/1784, 1/1785, or 1/23/1785 Jane, Frederick Co, VA; wid PN ae 80 Mason Co, KY, 1843, res at Mays Lick; s John B res 1834 Detroit; s Thomas B mentioned; QLF 1924 from desc Mrs John M PREWITT of Mt Sterling, KY; QLF states sol f also RW sol & they res Winchester, VA F-W3023 R1476
  John, esf Essex Co, VA where res; dd 10/21/1823; md 7/8/1790 Elizabeth LACKLAND, Fayette Co, KY; wid PN 1843 ae over 74 Scott Co, KY, when s George AFF Woodford Co, KY; wid gtd BLW38507 there 1855 aec 90; ch births: John 2/3/1792, Joseph & twin George 11/25/93, William 5/2/97, Charles 1/10/1800, Elizabeth 7/18/04, & May 5/19/05; QLF 1898 from SAR agent for sol great gds G G PARRY, St Joseph, MO. F-W9490 R1476
  William, b 8/15/1748 Orange Co, VA; mvd ae 13 to Augusta Co (area later Frederick Co), VA, where esf c1778; afp 1836 Logan Co, KY, & PAR, insufficient proof of svc; QLF 1927 from US Congressman for sol desc Mrs P H LOGGINS of Corsicana, TX. F-R5882 R1476
KERNES, William, b 5/1757; esf 1776-7 Fauquier Co, VA; PN 1819 Bath Co, KY; dd 8/20/42, or 8/22/42; md 2/25/1829 Sarah, Bath Co, KY; wid PN there 1854 ae 46; gtd BLW38512 there 1855; PN increased there 1870 aec 63 res Owingsville; sol surname also spelled KERNS. F-W7965 R1476
KERNEY, John, esf 1776 Berkeley Co, VA; dd before 1847 leaving heirs Thomas KERNEY, Mrs BLUE w of Colonel J BLUE, Mrs Solomon BLUE, Mrs MINOR, & Mrs Susan St AUBIN (kinship not given for heirs); John BOYLE referred to sol as his f-in-law in 1847; James FAULKNER, adm/o sol estate, afp for sol heirs, & gtd 1/2 pay PN due sol; QLF states sol dd 1805, soon after moving with w Susannah from Berkeley Co, VA, to KY. F-15613 R1476
KERR, David, b 2/4/1756 Augusta Co, VA; esf 1775 res Abbeville District, SC; res for time after fall of Charleston in Ro-

KERR (continued)
    wan Co, NC, where esf; PN 1833 Abbeville District, SC when
    res on farm where mvd to 1762; dd 12/16/35; md 2/24/1792
    Sarah who dd 10/15/40 never having afp; sol referred 1833
    to sis Mrs ROBERTSON, who then res Pendleton District, SC;
    surv ch who afp 1857: Martha VANLANDINGHAM (res Hickman Co
    TN ae 64), Rachel E SIMS (res Talledega Co, AL, ae 57) & s
    John Y (res Randolph Co, AL, who b 2/4/1803); AFF then by
    John L SIMS, Randolph Co, AL, (kinship to sol d Rachel not
    given); ch PAR. F-R5890 R1476
  David, b 2/18/1757; esf 1776 res Albemarle Co, VA; PN 1832
    Scott Co, KY; QLF states sol dd there; QLF 1917 from great
    gdd Miss Marie Louise SMITH of Lexington, KY, who gdd (on
    her m's side) of VA RW sol Colonel Stephen TRIGG; QLF 1900
    from great gds W N HOOD, Kenwood, MS. F-S31186 R1476
  David, esf 1780 Bedford Co, VA; PN ae 69 Wilkes Co, GA when
    res Oglethorpe Co, GA. F-S38111 R1476
  James, esf ae 14 Bedford Co, VA, against indians; f shortly
    bound him out to hatter's trade; sol later esf as minute-
    man in 7th VA Regiment; BLW1146 issued 10/28/1809 to sol
    under name of James KARR; dd 9/30/1818; md 12/1783 Ruth
    GADDY (MB 12/13/83 signed by Bartholomew GADDY, with con-
    sent of bride's f George), Bedford Co, VA; wid afp 1843 ae
    78 Wayne Co, IL; PAR, insufficient proof of svc; ch Benja-
    min & John AFF there then that their sis Anna b 6/11/1784.
    F-R5888 R1476
KERRY, Barney, see KARREN, Barney. F-S15906 R1476
KERSEY, John, b 4/1757 Hanover Co, VA; esf 1774/8 Charlotte Co
    VA where mvd as ch with f; mvd after RW to near Calloway's
    Iron Works, Franklin Co, VA, for c14 years, thence Warren
    Co, TN, where PN 1833. F-S1679 R1477
  John, b 11/2/1756 at lower end of Louisa Co, VA, where esf 2
    times for f Thomas; PN there 1832; legal heir James W KER-
    SEY's letter to PN Office 1887 claimed sol never received
    any PN money, never gtd BLW, & dd soon after PN approved;
    heir's res then Locust Creek, that Co; no action on heir's
    claim indicated in file; last PN payment to sol in file is
    dated 1833. F-S5507 R1477
  John, b 3/11/1764 Pittsylvania Co, VA; went to KY 1779 where
    esf 1780 in Colonel Daniel BOONE's regiment when res Lex-
    ington Station; PN 1832 Nicholas Co, KY; res 1837 Boone Co
    IN, where had recently mvd from KY to be near children; a
    Benjamin KERSEY (kinship not given) AFF then there he had
    arranged for transfer of sol PN address. F-S16435 R1477
  William, see CASEY, William. F-W29906.5 R1477
KESLER, Jacob, b 7/1757 Berks Co, PA; esf 1775-6 York Co, PA,
    where res; later esf NC; res after RW Rockingham Co, VA,
    thence Greenbrier Co, VA, thence Preble Co, OH, where PN
    1832 when res Harrison Township c19 years; QLF states sol
    dd aec 84 near Lafayette Co, IN. F-S2688 R1477
KESLING, Teter, see KISLING, Ditrich. No F# R1477
KESNER, Jacob, see KISNER, Jacob. F-S45886 R1477

KESTER, Joseph, b PA; mvd ae 9 with family to VA where settled near Brocks Gap, Rockingham Co, VA; esf there 1780 sub for Conrad KESTER (no kinship given); mvd to Harrison Co, VA, where PN 1832 ae 79; res 1837 Delaware Co, OH, where had mvd to be near children; dd 7/2/39, leaving wid & children mbnn. F-S2690 R1477
KESTERSON, John, esf 1781 Fauquier Co, VA, where b; PN 1832 ae 73 Greene Co, TN as John Sr; last PN payment in file 1839. F-S4467 R1477
KESTLER, Frederick, esf 1776 Northumberland Co, PA, where res; esf 1777 Lancaster Co, PA; esf 1781 Augusta Co, VA, where res; mvd after RW to Wilkes Co, GA for 20 years, thence KY for c3 years, thence Jefferson Co, IN, thence 1831 Clark Co, IN, where PN 1832; dd there 3/9/36; wid Catharine dd there 1/20/37; heirs authorizing agent 1853 there to afp (kinship not given): Samuel KESTLER, Emanuel KESTLER, Susanna GILTNER, & Tirsah GILTNER, their signature witnessed by Anderson GILTNER. F-S16177 R1477
KETTERMAN, Daniel, b 1762 Berks Co, PA; esf 1781 Hampshire Co, VA, where res; PN 1833 Hardy Co, VA; last PN payment in file 1844. F-S15908 R1477
KEY, George, esf 1777 Buckingham Co, VA; esf 1779 Bedford Co, VA; res there c33 years when mvd 1831 to Calloway Co, MO; PN there 1833 ae 80; dd 1/15/36; md 1785 Sucky (MB 8/22/85 with consent of her f John CRAGHEAD), Bedford Co, VA; wid Susannah (nickname Sucky) PN ae 74 Calloway Co, MO, 1840; her bro Robert CRAGHEAD AFF there then. F-W10162 R1478
Henry, b 2/1763; esf 1780 in VA Regiment; served under General JACKSON in War of 1812; PN 1824 Albemarle Co, VA; dd 2/22/36; QLF states sol bro/o Tandy, Thomas, Martin, John, Jesse, James, Harry, William, & Walter, their f res Albemarle Co, VA, until they grown. F-S38116 R1478
John, esf in VA regiment; PN ae 65 Lunenburg Co, VA 1825; dd there 1/14/37 or 2/20/37; md 1808 or 1809-12 Fathy LESTER there; wid PN & gtd BLW67535 there 1856 ae 70; 15 ch mbnn. F-W10163 R1478
Price, esf Spotsylvania Co, VA, early in RW; mvd 1792 to KY, where PN ae 60+ Clark Co, 1818; res there 1820 ae 66 when res with w aec 60 & s aec 17; dd 7/4/29 Barren Co, KY; md 3/17/1786 Sarah McQUEEN, Fauquier Co, VA, who b 1760-1767; wid PN 1839 Barren Co, KY; nephews Alexander KEY & Peyton KEY AFF then Mason Co, KY; wid gtd BLW31285 Montgomery Co, KY 1855; dd 9/7/55; children mbnn; Anderson JOHNS AFF 1855 Mongtomery Co, KY, where res, he md d of sol over 40 years ago, & their d Sally Ann PETTIT (sol gdd) then res there. F-W3021 R1478
Tandy, b 10/29/1754 Fluvanna Co, VA; esf 1777 Buckingham Co, VA, where res; mvd 1779 to Fluvanna Co, VA, where esf; mvd to Albemarle Co, VA, thence 1814 back to Fluvanna Co, VA, where purchased plantation; PN there 1834; QLF 1936 from great great gdd Miss Lucia KEY of Cuthbert, GA; QLF 1936 from desc Mrs J E EVANS, Auburndale, FL, states sol middle

KEY (continued)
   name Clark; QLF 1930 from desc Frances L DANCE of Atlanta, GA; QLF states sol had s Joseph bc 1765, who had s Tandy b 1786; QLF states sol f Martin who also had other s's John, Walter, Henry, Thomas, William Bibb, Jesse, Joshua, Martin & James; QLF states a John Walter KEY b 5/11/1751 Bedford Co, VA; QLF states sol f John md Miss TANDY & sol md Agnes WITT. F-S18069 R1478
   William, VA sea svc, esf 1779 in VA regiment, Dinwiddie Co, VA, where res; esf 1780 as marine aboard ship NANCY; res Dinwiddie Co, VA several years after RW, thence Warren Co, NC, for 7-8 years, thence Sumner Co, TN where PN 1832 when Methodist preacher; dd 1/19/34; md 1793-4 Elizabeth GAINS, Halifax Co, VA; wid res 4/1844 Sumner Co, TN, & dd 7/28/44 leaving ch: Thomas, Peterson, Nancy DAVIS, James, Alfred C, Harriet ROBERSON, & William; s James res Sumner Co, TN, 1844, 1845, & 1855; 2nd d mbnn md Mr. DUNCAN & dd IL, leaving 7 ch, 5 of whom were of age in 1846; s James AFF 1846 Gallatin, TN, his m md ae 22; Sarah STONE AFF 1854 Sumner Co, TN, she sis/o sol wid & of Nancy GAINS & of John GAINS who all had mvd from Halifax Co, NC, to Sumner Co, TN; sol bro Bingham res aec 70 there 1832 & AFF he md c1783 Susan, & their s Macklin/McLin bc 1786, & was res Sumner Co, TN, 1846; Bingham was RW sol who afp & PAR, less than 6 months svc, & his record is in bro William's file, & has no file number; sol sis Mildred res Sumner Co, TN, 1832; sol s James afp 1852 for self & all sol heirs 1852 & 1854 Sumner Co, TN, & PAR, proof/o date of parents' marriage; QLF 1924 from great great gdd Mrs T J DARLING Jr of Tallulah Falls, GA. F-R5895 R1478
   William B, esf 1776 Fluvanna Co, VA, where b 10/2/1759; esf 1781 Albemarle Co, VA, where res; mvd c2 years after RW to Elbert Co, GA where PN 1833; QLF 1938 from great great gdd Mrs Sally Bell HAWKINS of Marshall, TX, states sol middle name Bibb; QLF 1934 from desc Litsey Lloyd SESSIONS of Okmulgee, OK; QLF states sol dd Elbert Co, GA; QLF states sol md Mourning CLARK, & dd 1836 Elbert Co, GA. F-S31787 R1478
KEYER, John, see KEGER, John. F-S38118 R1478
KEYS, James, b 1756 Augusta Co, VA; mvd 1773 to Washington Co, VA, where esf 1774 against indians & 1775 in RW; PN there 1833. F-S15907 R1478
   Matthew, esf 1780 Chesterfield Co, VA, where b 2/5/1761; mvd 1795 to Franklin Co, VA, thence 1811 Knox Co, TN, where PN 1832; QLF states sol dd there ae 74. F-S1681 R1478
   William, b 4/10/1756 Prince William Co, VA, where f William res during RW; esf there early in RW sub for f; mvd 1819 to Harrison Co, VA, where PN 1832; dd 1/30/33 leaving wid Elizabeth. F-S18070 R1478
KEYSACKER, George, esf 1781 Berkeley Co, VA where res; afp aec 74 Crawford Co, IN, 1834; PAR, less than 6 months svc; dd IN 1851 leaving 3 heirs mbnn; bro Aron of Berkeley Co, VA,

KEYSACKER (continued)
   decd in 1834; sis Mary md Barney MILLER; they res Brecken-
   ridge Co, KY, 1834. F-R5899 R1479
KEYSER, Andrew Sr, b 12/16/1758; esf 1780 Shenandoah Co, VA;
   PN 1832 Pge Co, VA;   QLF states sol f Charles KISER/KEYSER
   fought with General BRADDOCK's troops; QLF 1908 from desc
   Dr I LeSAGE, Huntington, WV, (on m's side) states sol b on
   Mill Creek, Shenandoah Co, VA; QLF 1822 from desc Miss Jo-
   sephine LeSAGE, Huntington, WV. F-S5651 R1479
   Jacob, esf 1779 Frederick Co, MD; PN ae 62 Harrison Co, VA,
      1818; dd there 2/6/34; md 10/1785 Pamelia JOHNSTON (MB da-
      ted 10/11/85), Loudoun Co, VA, who b 4/6/1764 & was from
      Shelburne Parish, that Co; wid PN 1839 Harrison Co, VA; dd
      11/5/44; 8 ch including Hester (md Mr ROSIER), George (res
      Harrison Co, VA), Pamelia, Elizabeth, Jonas, & Joseph (bc
      1806); surname also spelled KAYSER. F-W7952 R1479
   William, esf Gloucester Co,VA; mvd c1802 from Hanover Co, VA
      to Bath Co, VA where PN 1832 ae 77; dd c2/3/37; md 12/1783
      Kesiah/Keziah; wid PN ae 76 there 1841; ch births: Polley
      1/29/83, John 10/10/84, William 11/20/85, Elizabeth 10/13/
      87, Christopher 5/30/89, Cat 1/26/92, Fleming 1/26/94, Da-
      vid 7/10/96, James 5/1/99 & Sally 9/13/1806; s Fleming AFF
      1841 Bath Co, VA; s-in-law Robert BRINCKLEY AFF then there
      he md sol d Elizabeth 12/3/1805; births of ch of neighbor
      Richard SNEED: Salley 2/22/1782, Keturah 6/9/85, Elizabeth
      12/25/87, Jean 5/6/89, William 10/22/92, & Richard 5/23/95
      F-W3427 R1479
KIBLER, John, esf 1776 Hagerstown, MD;   PN ae 58 Berkeley Co,
   VA 1818; family there 1820 w Mary aec 46 & ch: John ae 24,
   Jacob ae 22, Margaret ae 19, Elizabeth ae 17, George ae 12
   Nancy ae 9, & Mary Ann ae 4; dd there 6/22/27; md (1) 1781
   Mary MUMFORD (marriage license 4/28/1781) Berkeley Co, VA;
   md there (2) 1796 Mary RIFFE (MB 1/1796); wid PN 1852 ae
   84 Wayne Co, OH; gtd BLW30753 there 1855 aec 90; s John
   AFF ae 67 Hancock Co, OH 1853 he s/o sol by 1st w; d Nancy
   w/o Michael BAUM AFF there 1855 she d/o sol by 2nd w & was
   b 3/6/1810, further sol had 9 ch. F-W5014 R1479
KIDD, Benjamin, esf 1777 Buckingham Co, VA, where b 1752; afp
   1838 Surry Co, NC, & PAR; s & legal heir Jesse gave power
   of attorney 1852 Mt Airy, NC, to afp. F-R5906 R1480
   George, esf 1777 Amelia Co, VA where b; afp there 1836 ae 73
   & PAR, less than 6 months svc; dd there 11/24/44; s & heir
   Asa afp there 1846. F-R5907 R1480
   James, b 4/22/1766 Granville Co, NC; f mvd shortly after sol
   b to Albemarle Co, VA; esf there 1781; PN 1832 Nelson Co,
   VA; dd leaving wid Lucy. F-S18481 R1480
   James H, esf 1779 Mecklenburg Co, VA, where b 1764; PN 1832
   DeKalb Co, GA, when bro William res Oglethorpe Co, GA. F-
   S16436 R1480
   Robert, esf 1778 VA in Colonel George Rogers Clark's regi-
   ment; PN ae 75 Monroe Co, IL, 1835. F-S32367 R1480
   William, b 12/16/1763 Mecklenburg Co, VA, where esf 1778 sub

KIDD (continued)
  for f James; mvd 1799 to Oglethorpe Co, GA, where PN 1832; bro/o RW sol James; QLF states sol f also RW sol; QLF says sol living Oglethorpe Co, GA 1840 as William Sr. F-S31796 R1480
KIDWELL, Mathew, esf 1777 Charles Co, MD where b 6/8/1752; mvd aec 30 to Frederick Co, VA, for 2 years, thence Pendleton Co, VA, for 15 years, thence White Co, TN, for 2 months, thence KY, where PN 1832 Monroe Co; QLF 1927 from desc Mrs Erna Kidwell CHADWICK, Montgomery City, MO who also desc/o Hezekiah KIDWELL of Fairfax Co, VA. F-S30523 R1480
KIESINGER, Andrew, see KEISINGER, Andrew. F-R5818 R1480
KILBERN, Henry, b 6/10/1763; esf 1781 Mongtomery Co, VA; esf 1786 Lincoln Co, KY, against indians; mvd after that svc to Greenbrier Co, VA, thence KY, where afp 1842 Rockcastle Co, when res Pulaski Co; PAR; surname also spelled KILBURN F-R5912 R1481
KILBY, John, MD sea svc; b 9/15/1758 near Vienna, Dorchester Co, MD; esf 1776 aboard ship STURDY BEGGAR; captured & taken to England, thence France, where released; esf there aboard ship BON HOMME RICHARD, which commanded by Captain John Paul JONES; later esf aboard ship ALLIANCE; PN 1818 Hanover Co, VA; res there 1823 when had w ae 43, who had been wid of William Augustus TALLEY; QLF 1926 from great gdd Mrs Alva Turrentine HOLMAN of Norfolk, VA. F-S38119 R1481
KILGORE, Charles, esf in VA regiment; PN 1809 for svc disability; PN 1820 ae not given Greene Co, TN. F-S699 R1481
  Charles, b 1763-64 Orange Co, VA; mvd shortly before RW to Washington Co, VA, where PN 1778; mvd 1787 to Greene Co, TN, thence Pendleton Co, SC, thence back to Washington Co, VA, thence Wayne Co, KY, thence Lawrence Co, IN, thence Daviess Co, IN where PN 1833 res Wallis Township; dd there 11/20/44; md Avarilla in VA; wid PN ae 90 Daviess Co, IN, 1856 & gtd BLW44506 then; s Hiram ae 64 in 1854; a Reuben KILGORE, b 1795, mentioned (no kinship given); QLF states sol s of RW sol Charles, who md Winnie CLAYTON; QLF 1930 from desc Mrs S N TAYLOR, states when sol fought at Battle of Kings Mountain, he res of Nicklesville, Scott Co (area then Russell Co), VA. F-W7994 R1481
KILLEY, William, see KELLEY, William. F-R5833 R1482
KILLION, Jacob, esf Orange Co, NC where b 3/16/1755; mvd after RW to Greenbriar Co, VA, then to Madison Co, KY, then to Fleming Co, KY, thence Scott Co, IN where PN 1832 as Jacob Sr; w dd 2/18/1828; res 1838 Sangamon Co, IL where had mvd to live with his 2 ch mbnn. F-S32362 R1482
  John, esf Stokes Co, NC & recd BLW from NC; f Michael KIA in RW; dd 1816 Surry Co, NC; md Becky WILBORN, Stokes Co, NC; wid afp ae 90 Scott Co, VA, 1858; afp ae 102 VA 1860; PAR both times. F-R5918 R1482
KIMBLE, Jacob, esf 1776 Morris Co, NJ, where b 1758; mvd to Frederick Co, VA, where esf 1781; PN 1832 Greene Co, PA,

KIMBLE (continued)
   1832 res Aleppa Township; dd there 6/22/38; md there 1/19/ 1816 Mary EDDY at home/o her f; wid gtd BLW94033 Pleasants Co, VA, 1859; AFF then by Michael EDDY, Monroe Co, OH, he md sis/o wid on same day & same place that wid md sol; wid PN ae 67 Monroe Co, OH, 1860 when res with relatives, her occupation "washwoman for some years past"; AFF then there by wid sis Catharine ECHEBERRY; wid decd in 1880, per AFF Catharine TRIMBLE (no kinship given). F-W10178 R1484
Robert, esf 1776 in 5th VA Regiment; esf 1779 PA; PN 1822 ae 65 Spartanburg District, SC, when family w Fanney ae 46-50 & ch: Archibald aec 19, Nancy ae 17, & Martha ae 15. F-38896 R1484
KIMBRELL, Thomas, b Dinwiddie Co, VA; esf 1778 Brunswick Co, VA; mvd to SC where esf against Tories & indians; afp ae 78 there Spartanburg District 1838, & PAR; surname spelled also KIMBRILL. F-R5927 R1484
KIMMEY, Isaac, esf 1777 Norfolk, VA; dd 1/13/1817 Brookville, Franklin Co, IN; md 5/21/1780 Margaret, Florida, Orange Co NY, who b 3/15/1757; wid afp 1844 Berrien Co, MI, & PAR. F-R5977 R1485
KINCAID, James, b 3/10/1763 Albemarle Co, VA; esf with elder bro Joseph 1776 when they res with f in Castlewood Settlement on Clinch River c25 miles north of Abingdon, VA; sol & bro Joseph mvd 1779 with f to KY Territory where James & Joseph esf; Joseph KIA 8/19/1782 in Battle of Blue Licks; sol esf 1787 Mercer Co, KY, against indians & again 1791; mvd to Boone Co, MO, after res 50 years in KY, thence Lafayette Co, MO, where PN 1833; dd 7/8/41; QLF 1924 from desc Samuel S PARKES ae 95, Richmond, KY. F-S16907 R1485
John, b 3/10/1760 Amherst Co, VA; esf 1781 Greenbrier Co, VA where res; PN 1834 Fayette Co, VA having previously res in Kanawha Co, VA. F-S19367 R1485
John, b 1/11/1755 Augusta Co, VA; esf 1778 Botetourt Co, VA; PN 1833 Alleghany Co, VA; dd 8/11/35; md 7/25/1787 Alice DEAN, Botetourt Co, VA, per wid AFF; that Co clerk certified record showed sol md Alcy ELLIOTT that day; wid PN ae 72 Alleghany Co, VA, 1842; gtd BLW38513 there 1855 ae 89. F-W3428 R1485
Joseph, esf 1779 in militia "in defense of western frontiers of VA"; dd Woodford Co, KY; s Thomas U appointed adm/o f's estate by court there 1835; s Thomas afp there 1850, res Versailles, & PAR, svc in militia only. F-R15697 R1485
Robert, b 2/28/1764 Prince Edward Co, VA, s/o John; esf 1781 Lincoln Co, NC, where res; PN 1833 Burke Co, NC; dd there 6/26/36; md 6/1802 Elizabeth GUTHREY, Lincoln Co, NC; wid PN ae 71 Burke Co, NC 1853; large family of ch including s John who ae 67 in 1854; wid gtd BLW13206 there 1855; QLF 1927 from desc Lily Doyle DUNLAP, Ansonville, NC. F-W26186 R1485
Robert, b 7/14/1761 Albemarle Co, VA; esf 1776 Washington Co VA; PN 1834 Bath Co, KY; dd 10/20/44; md 1808-1809 Rebecca

KINCAID (continued)
   EVANS, Clark Co, KY; wid PN & gtd BLW84019 aec 70 Bath Co,
   KY, 1859 res Owingsville; 11 ch mbnn.   F-W10177 R1485
KINCHELOE, Thomas, b 10/8/1761 Fairfax Co, VA; mvd aec 1 with
   f to Fauquier Co, VA, where esf 1777; mvd to Davis Settlement on waters of Chaplin, Nelson Co, KY, thence Breckenridge Co, KY, where was Co court justice c1800; PN there
   1832 res Hardinsburg; dd 11/20/45; md (1) 8/24/1780 Hannah
   ROBINSON who b 8/24/1762 & dd 11/10/1791; md (2) 12/2/1794
   Nancy EDWARDS who b 4/18/1779; ch births by 1st w: William
   7/12/1781 (md 10/13/1799), Joseph 6/2/83 (md 3/5/1805),
   Peggy 8/4/85 (dd 1/20/1818, md 2/5/1809 Richard PURKINS, &
   he dd 8/23/1809), Molly 8/24/1787 (dd 8/24/91), & Caty
   8/24/89 (dd 8/24/92);   ch births by 2nd w: John 5/8/1796
   (dd 8/18/1817), Phillip 2/4/98 (md 10/9/1823 Caroline
   STITH), Hannah Robinson 2/17/1800 (dd 12/24/1814), Lewis
   11/7/01 (md 4/28/1828 May FONTAINE), Thomas Jefferson
   10/28/03 (dd 9/29/182-), Jesse White 12/22/05 (md 5/26/
   1829 Claracey RENO), Allen 3/17/08, & Purkins 3/28/10; ot-
   her data: Juley dd 1/22/1818, William RENO dd 8/23/1826,
   R Perkins KINCHELOE md 12/27/1832 Mary PATE; wid PN 1849
   Hardinsburg, KY; QLF states sol wid dd 6/29/1869; QLF 1939
   from desc Lewin D McPHERSON, Bremen, GA.   F-W1620 R1485
KINDER, Peter, esf 1780 Wythe Co, VA; dd 9/22/1807; md 1774
   Margaret, who afp ae 88 there 6/1845 & dd 10/23/45; George
   WINDER (kinship not given), adm/o sol wid estate, afp 1845
   & PAR.   F-R5931 R1485
KINDLE, William, esf 1776 Culpeper Co, VA; PN ae 72 Greene Co,
   TN, 1832; res 1838 aec 84 Perry Co, TN, where had mvd to
   live with only s George.   F-S2705 R1485
KINDRED, Thomas, b Northumberland, England; mvd with f 1774 to
   Albemarle Co, VA, where esf 1777; mvd to Goochland Co, VA,
   where esf; bro's William, Bartholomew & Edward served with
   him in siege of Yorktown; sol returned to Albemarle Co, VA
   after RW, thence 1808 to Roane Co, TN, thence Morgan Co,
   TN, where PN 1832 ae 72; QLF 1858 from George L BESTOR of
   Peoria, IL, concerning PN due sol's one surv s Edward; no
   action indicated by PN Office on query.   F-S4476 R1485
  William, b 1744 Cumberland Co, England; came to America 6-7
   years before RW began; esf Goochland Co, VA, early in RW;
   later esf Albemarle Co, VA; PN 1832 Madison Co, KY. F-
   S13636 R1485
KINDRICK, John, b 12/25/1752; esf Pittsylvania Co, VA; mvd c8
   years after RW to Columbus, GA, for 15-16 years, thence
   Limestone Co, AL, for 3 years, thence Monroe Co, MS, where
   afp 1836 ae 83 res Athens Town; PAR; s & heir Silas F gave
   power of attorney 1854 Monroe Co, MS, to agent to afp; PAR
   F-R5933 R1485
KING, Andrew, b 1753 VA; esf 1779 Henry Co, VA, where res; after RW res NC, thence Claiborne Co, TN where PN 1833, when
   only w res with him; dd there 11/14/34; md 1778 Sally, Rockingham Co, NC; wid PN ae 82 Grainger Co, TN, 1842; still

KING (continued)
   res there 1844; large family of ch mbnn. F-W374 R1486
Arthur, b 2/25/1752 Fairfax Co, VA; esf 1777 Wake Co, NC res
   there; mvd 1811 to Darlington District, SC, thence Bedford
   Co, TN 1823, thence Lincoln Co, TN, where afp 1835, & PAR.
   F-R5934 R1486
Charles, esf 1775 Cambridge, MA; applied for duty with General WASHINGTON personal guard, & accepted 1776 in VA Line;
   PN ae 63 Brooke Co, VA, 1819 as Charles Sr; mvd to Washington Co, OH, where res 1820 with w Elizabeth ae 44, her
   d Elizabeth ae 14, her s Caleb ae 10, & her d Catharine ae
   8; mvd soon after to Muskingum Co, OH. F-S2700 R1486
Charles, b 4/5/1750 Hanover Co, VA; res there with f until
   of ae; mvd then to Botetourt Co, VA where esf 1774; PN Alleghany Co, VA, 1833; dd 3/18/36; md 8/1787 Rebecca BESS
   (MB 8/21/87), Botetourt Co, VA; wid PN ae 87 Alleghany Co,
   VA 1839 when s John res Covington, that Co; QLF states sol
   had s James V (md c1830, settled Frederick Co, VA, & later
   mvd to Fayettte Co, OH) & s Samuel V. F-W20334 R1486
Cornelius, b 11/21/1753 New Castle Co, DE; esf 1774 Tygart's
   Valley, Randolph Co, VA, where res; mvd 1779 to Western VA
   (area later KY), where esf 1779 against Shawnee indians;
   mvd after RW to Nelson Co, KY, thence Orange Co, IN, then
   to Morgan Co, IN, where PN 1832; surv ch mbnn 1840; QLF
   1928 from great great gds H A DAVEE of Seviersville, TN,
   states sol dd Morgan Co, IN. F-S17527 R1486
Elisha, BLW324 issued 2/14/1807. F-BLW324 R1487
George, esf 1779 Berkeley Co, VA, where b 5/12/1751; mvd to
   KY for 16 years, thence 1815 Decatur Co, IN where PN 1832;
   dd 2/7/38; md 10/15/1775 Mary SAUNDERS, Berkeley Co, VA;
   wid afp ae 88 Decatur Co, IN, 1839 & PAR, no proof of date
   of marriage; dd 1/17/42 ae 90; ch births: James 1776 (md
   1796 Miss BRUCE, & they had s John R), William 1778-9, Edward 1781 (md c1805 in Garrard Co, KY), John B, George W
   3/13/98 (md in Pulaski Co, KY), Jeremiah, Phebe DUNLAP,
   Elizabeth KENNEDAY, Easter SLOME, Rebecca, & Sarah RECTOR;
   ch Phebe, Rebecca, James, & William all decd in 1851 when
   s George W afp 1861 Decatur Co, IN, for all heirs, & PAR;
   s John R then res St Louis, MO; s George W res 1854 Decatur Co, IN; QLF 1908 from desc Mrs Daisy D JONES of Hunniwell, KS; QLF 1910 from desc Miss Addie M POTTER, Waucoma,
   IA; QLF 1920 from great gdd Allie Denney BROWN, Hillsdale,
   OR, states sol buried at Kokomo, IN. F-R5960 R1487
George, b 1750 on Chesapeake Bay, Northumberland Co, VA; esf
   1781 Amelia Co, VA, where res; esf later 1781 Lunenburg Co
   VA, where res; mvd 1798-9 to Henry Co, VA, for c20 years,
   thence Cumberland Co, KY, where PN 1833. F-S31189 R1487
George, esf 1780 Fauquier Co, VA; mvd 1818 to Richland Co,
   OH, where PN 1828 ae 67; dd 12/5/38; md 1797 Mary d/o Priscilla BOWLING; wid PN ae 73 Ashland Co, KY, 1840 when res
   Vermillion Township; only ch John b 1798 Fauquier Co, VA;
   sol m Jane ae 89 & sol w m Priscilla ae 76 res 1828 Rich-

KING (continued)
land Co, OH, with sol & w. F-W2736 R1487
Gerrard, b 7/1759 Charles Co, MD; esf 1777 Prince William Co VA, where res; PN 1836 Hamilton Co, OH, when res there c40 years; dd 6/7/40 Waynesville, OH, & buried Friends Burying Ground there; md 1791 Keziah THRUSTON (MB 1/29/71 between her & Garrett KING, signed by James THRUSTON), Martinsburg in Berkeley Co, VA; witness to marriage Henry HAUK AFF ae 80 Warren Co, OH, he & his w md 2/26/1793 at Martinsburg, VA, & he knew sol & w in states of MD & VA; wid PN 1852 Warren Co, OH, when s John AFF there. F-W7984 R1487
Henry, esf 1779 Brunswick Co, VA where b 1/1760; mvd 1802 to Rockingham Co, NC where PN 1846; dd there 10/1852 when had 2 d's res there mbnn; they still liv 1859; s Thomas H res 1859 Granville, Jackson Co, TN when referred to f as Henry B KING. F-S8792 R1487
Jacob, esf Hanover Co, VA, where b; PN there 1832 ae 70; dd there 11/5/38; md there 1/5/1829 Elizabeth TYREE (MB 1/3/29 signed by David Jones TYREE); wid PN ae 62 Richmond, VA 1853; gtd BLW26041 there 1855; dd 9/5/65 Essex Co, VA leaving ch Jacob J/I & Mrs Nathaniel CROW; Littleton G FOGG, adm/o wid estate, ae 35 applied 1868 for restoration/o her PN after Civil War 1868 for her 2 ch. F-W7988 R1488
James, b 10/6/1760 Sussex Co, DE, where esf 1776 sub for bro John who was also RW sol (dd c1790); mvd after RW to Norfolk Co, VA, for 28 months, thence back to Sussex Co, DE, for 4 years, thence Pitt Co, NC, for 2 years, thence Edgecombe Co, NC, for 20 years, thence 1811 Roberson Co, NC, thence 1846 Cumberland Co, NC, where afp 1848; PAR, insufficient proof of svc; afp again 1852 & PAR. F-R5952 R1488
James, b 6/1757 near Staunton, VA; esf 1779 Sullivan Co, TN, (area then NC); mvd to Hawkins Co, TN, thence Grainger Co, TN, thence KY, thence Davidson Co, TN, thence Wilson Co, TN, thence Franklin Co, TN, thence Madison Co, AL, thence Henderson Co, TN, where PN 1833. F-S4477 R1488
James, esf in 2nd VA Regiment; PN 1819 Edgefield District, SC; res there 1824 ae 63 occupation farmer when had w + d Amelia aec 16 & s Joshua aec 3 + stepch: Jackson aec 10, Jesse aec 7 & Reuben aec 5; res 1841 Lincoln Co, GA with d mbnn whose h dd 1839. F-S31794 R1488
Jesse, esf 1776 VA; PN ae 77 Surry Co, VA, 1832; dd 1/27/46. F-S5559 R1488
John, esf 1778 MD; PN ae nearly 70 Montgomery Co, VA, 1829, occupation farmer, when had 2 single d's, md d & her h & 1 ch res with him; s aec 21 mbnn who res with f 1818, whom f gave farm when s got md. F-S5553 R1488.
John, b 11/25/1761 Loudoun Co, VA; esf 1780 Bedford Co, PA, res there; res after RW Mason Co, KY, then to Bracken Co, KY where PN 1832; QLF states sol dd there. F-S30521 R1488
John, b 1754; esf 1777-8 Augusta Co, VA where res with f; PN 1832 Jackson Co, GA; dd there 6/22/40; md 5/17/1792 Eleanor, d of David KERR of Coddle Creek Settlement, Rowan Co,

KING (continued)
   NC; wid PN ae 73 Jackson Co, GA, 1843; gtd BLW26694 there 1855; ch births: Jenny McDowell 2/13/1793, John 2/5/95, David Kerr 12/20/1801, Abigail 3/7/04, James 3/19/06, Dovey 3/24/08 & Eleoner Elijah 11/18/11; sol sis Jane McCUTCHEON AFF 1832 Hall Co, GA. F-W7986 R1488

John, b 1/12/1758; esf 1777 in VA regiment; PN 1819 Spartanburg District, SC; dd 3/25/42; md 3/2/1790 Sarah LEMASTERS (b 9/17/1774 Amherst Co, VA) Spartanburg District, SC; wid PN 1843 there; ch births: Edmund 12/1/1790 (md 1/30/1830 Nancy EMBERSON), William 3/19/92 (md 1825 Rhoda SMITH), Mary 3/8/94, Ann 11/7/96, Lucy 11/15/98 (md 12/15/1816 James W COOPER), Elizabeth 9/6/1800 (md 1/30/1823 John EASLY), Martha 10/20/01 (md 12/15/1830 John GOSSETT), Philip W 10/22/03 (md 8/1/1829 Dolly BROWNING), Sarah 1/22/06 (md 11/11/1828 Hiram WHITE), s 12/6/08 (dd ae 3 weeks), Margaret 11/2/09 (md 10/11/1827 David REID), John 3/28/12, & Minerva 5/25/15 (dd 2/5/1817); wid res 1849 Spartanburg District, SC, when PN increased; QLF 1920 from great gdd Mrs Frances M FOLGER, Hollywood, CA. F-W9100 R1488

John, esf VA; PN 1806 PA for disability from wound at Battle of Guilford; res 1830 Bracken Co, KY; dd there 4/8/37 when occupation minister; md 4/27/1786 Catherine/Caty (wid of Philemon HAWKINS), Fayette Co, KY; wid d/o Lewis CRAIG who mvd to KY Fall 1781 & res Fayettte Co, KY, for many years; wid afp ae 79 Bracken Co, KY 1838; PAR, insufficient proof of 6 months svc; ch births: Philip 2/13/1787 (War of 1812 sol, res 1839 Augusta, Bracken Co, KY), John 9/15/90, Elizabeth 3/5/93, Mary 6/5/96, William 1/26/98, Anne 8/2/1800 & Lucinda 1/15/02; wid bro Major Lewis CRAIG (b Orange Co, VA, & mvd to KY with f) res 1838 aec 60 Mason Co, KY. F-R5936 R1488

Julian, esf 1777 in 3rd VA Regiment; PN ae 62 Orange Co, VA; res there 1820, when had w Margaret aec 70 & gds John KING (b 2/1808) res with him. F-S38120 R1489

Miles, b 11/2/1747 Elizabeth City Co, VA, where esf 1776 at Hampton; one of first men to be elected to VA state legislature after RW; dd 6/9/1814 or 8/1814; md 4/27/1782 Martha KIRBY, Elizabeth City Co, VA; wid b 11/1765; PN 1838 Norfolk, VA where dd 1/29/1849; QLF 1898 from desc Calvert K MELLEN of Buffalo, NY; QLF states sol dd 6/30/1814. F-W20342 R1489

Nancy, former widow of Jesse TUCKER. (F-W7987)

Nathaniel, esf 1778 Westmoreland Co, VA where b c1755; PN ae 80 there 1832; dd 4/2/39. F-S10248 R1489

Parks, b 1750 Brunswick Co, VA; esf 1779 Warren Co, NC; mvd to GA, thence Fayette Co, AL, where afp 1834; PAR, less than 6 months svc. F-R5963 R1489

Philip, b 5/22/1760 Louisa Co, VA; mvd 1774 to Westham, VA, where esf; later esf 1780 Goochland Co, VA; taken POW, escaped, returned to f's house in Louisa Co, & rejoined his regiment; res after RW Richmond, VA, for c2 years, thence

KING (continued)
    Cumberland Co, VA, thence Louisa Co, VA, for 6 years, then to Sullivan Co, TN for c8 years, thence Hawkins Co, TN for c8 years, thence Warren Co, TN, where PN 1833; dd 8/14/36; md Nancy in VA who dd 10/22/40; ch who afp 1841: William, Nancy LESTER, Drury, Catharine BURUM, Wilson C N, Thomas Jefferson, & Lucy BONNER; ch PAR, insufficient proof/o parents' marriage. F-R5961 R1489

    Sabrit, esf 1778 Albemarle Co, VA; PN ae 58 there 1819; dd 4/1838; md 10/15/1835 Jerusha/Jarucia HERRING, Albemarle Co, VA; wid PN ae 65 Greene Co, VA, 1853; sol given name also spelled Seybert & Sibert. F-W9253 R1490

    Stephen, esf 1780 Henry Co, VA; PN 1832 Franklin Co, VA, ae 81; QLF states sol md Lurana MAUPIN, & she survived him. F-S5551 R1490

    Thomas, b Hanover Co, VA; esf Orange Co, NC; PN aec 87 there 1833; dd there 12/26/34; LWT 1/8/1832, probated there 1834 listed w Elizabeth, youngest s Thomas, d Dicey, & d Marsha Ann; md 2/1819 Elizabeth BROWN, Orange Co, NC; wid PN 1854 there ae 68; gtd BLW13017 there 1855; QLF 1923 from great great great gdd Mrs Minnie King HAY, Raleigh, NC, who also great great great gdd of NC RW sol William P RIGGAN. F-W26185 R1490

    Vincent, b 1756 near Rappahannock River, VA; esf 1778 Wake Co, NC, when res near Raleigh, where mvd when quite young; PN 1833 that Co; dd there 8/9/36; md there 10/10/1784 Margaret, d of John RILEY (MB 10/1/84 with Peggy RAYLA); wid PN there 1839 aec 76; ch mbnn; wid AFF her correct surname RILEY. F-W4007 R1490

    William, b 7/4/1754; esf 1777 Prince William Co, VA; PN 1820 Fauquier Co, VA; QLF 1931 from great great gdd Mrs Cora King REYNOLDS of Montgomery, AL, great gdd of sol s George Compton KING (b 4/4/1798 Fauquier Co, VA). F-S39121 R1490

    William, esf 1777 Fauquier Co, VA, where b 3/1760 or 3/1763; PN 1833 Bracken Co, KY; last PN payment in file 1841; QLF 1925 from desc Mrs Raymond G GUNALL of Washington, DC. F-S30524 R1490

    William, esf Bedford Co, VA, before GATES Defeat; PN ae 77-8 Montgomery Co, VA, 1833; res 1837 Washington Co, IN, where had recently mvd to get out of slavery state & to res with some of ch in IN. F-S32364 R1490

    William, esf 1778 Henrico Co, VA; PN ae 80 Campbell Co, VA; dd 12/27/35; md c1788 Mary WOODSON, Cumberland Co, VA, & they mvd soon after to Campbell Co, VA; wid PN ae 74 there 1839; AFF then by wid sis Martha RIDDLE, ae 63, Buckingham Co, VA; AFF same Co then by Drury WOODSON (kinship not given) ae 67. F-W7982 R1490

KINGSTON, John, esf 1780 Henry Co, VA; dd 3/21/1831 Morgan Co, TN; md 1792 Eleanor CAFFREY at home/o her f John (MB 1/21/92), Campbell Co, VA; ch births: William 1/13/1793, John H 2/8/95, Polly 1/12/97, Betsy 6/12/99, Nicholas 9/26/1801, Bernard 1/13/04, twins George & Edmund 4/26/07, & Nancy

KINGSTON (continued)
6/12/09; wid b 3/10/1766; PN 1838 Morgan Co, TN; her cousin Sally RECTOR (b 1/17/1772) AFF there then she present at sol wedding on 2/15/1792; wid res 1843 Clinton Co, KY; res Jamestown, TN, 1848; sol surname also spelled KINGTON. F-W1513 R1492

KINKADE, Robert, VA sea svc, esf c1776 in 1st VA Regiment; esf 1780 aboard ship HYDER ALI; afp 1819 but never PN because had too many assets then; dd 1/3/32 Hardin Co, KY, aec 90; md 12/2/1784 Mary/Molly, Washington Co, PA; wid afp ae 71 Hardin Co, KY 1839 & PAR; AFF then there by John VEECH, ae 59, h of d Mary Ann; wid dd aec 76 there 1/17/44; births/o ch: Mary (10/28/1786 (md John VEECH), Isabella 1/17/89 (md Mr BUNCH), James 12/9/1800, Sarah 1801 (md Mr FLETCHER), Patsey 1806, Arthur 1814, & George W (date not given); PN gtd 1854 to surv ch James (res Harden Co, KY), George W, Isabella BUNCH, Sarah FLETCHER, & Arthur, all res IL; QLF states sol b Ireland. F-W9102 R1492

KINKAID, John, b 1748 Lancaster Co, PA; esf 1778 in PA regiment when res Yogohania Co, VA; PN ae 85 Allegheny Co, PA, 1833; md ? Carlisle, PA; dd Allegheny Co, PA 10/16/33 leaving no wid, but d Elizabeth DUNCAN & d Hannah TORRENCE; d Elizabeth AFF there 1850 ae 70 her f a cooper & a blacksmith; AFF then there by William DUNCAN that he res in sol household when sol dd; sol surname also spelled KINCAID. F-S22345 R1492

KINKEAD, Joseph, see KINCAID, Joseph. F-R15697 R1492

Thomas, b 3/1764; esf 1780 Augusta Co, VA, where res, as sub for f mbnn; PN 1832 Pendleton Co, VA; last PN payment in file 1841; QLF states sol res 1840 Highland Co, VA. F-S5997 R1492

KINLEY, Benjamin, esf 1777 in VA regiment & KIA; LWT 4/21/1777 Augusta Co, VA, probated 3/24/1781 Rockingham Co, VA, gave all estate to nephew Benjamin BERRY (res Monmouth, NJ) except for 5 shillings to nephew Henry BERRY; LWT executives were Archibald & John HOPKINS; Benjamin BERRY dd intestate 1832 Rockingham Co, VA, aec 75 leaving ch: McKinley, John, George, David, Ellen SWATZ, & Rhoda FULS; McKinley BERRY dd intestate, leaving w Catherine & ch: Margaret ANN FRAYER, Phebe Jane FREED, Elizabeth DOUGHERTY, Catharine SINDEN & Archibald; surv heirs/o Benjamin BERRY afb & gtd BLW 2457. F-BLW2457 R1492

KINNARD, David, esf 1777 in 1st VA Regiment; PN ae 74-5 Culpeper Co, VA res Brumfield Parish; surname also spelled KINNAIRD. F-S5557 R1492

KINNEY, Richard, esf in 12th VA Regiment; mvd to Mercer Co, KY thence Oldham Co, KY, thence Scott Co, KY, thence Jefferson Co, IN, where afp ae 69; res 1820 Scott Co, IN, occupation farmer, when family w Susanna ae 58 & ch: George ae 23, Clayman ae 21, & James Reed ae 14; PN gtd 1821 after schedule of property examined; dd 4/25/38; md 1782 Susan SHADD near Moorefield, Hardy Co, VA per wid AFF; Henry Co,

KINNEY (continued)
    VA, court clerk certified MB 10/22/1787 between a Richard
    KINNEY & Susannah BEARD; ch births: Mary 1783, Sarah 1784,
    Saul/Solomon, Rachel 1790, John, George, Claborn, Katha-
    rine, James b 2/4/1808, & Rosa; wid bc 7/1763; PN ae 79
    Scott Co, IN, 1843 when ch George, Saul, Claborn, & Rosa
    decd; AFF then by s James & w Sarah; s James gave power of
    attorney to agent 1847 Scott Co, IN, to afb for following
    heirs of sol: self, sol d Katharine MORGAN, sol d Rachel
    DEAN, sol d Sally WILKINSON, sol gdc William, Harrison,
    Lucinder, Emily, & Susan (all ch of decd s Saul), sol gdc
    John Madison, Betsy, William, & Claborne (all ch of decd s
    Claborn) & sol gdd Mary d/o decd s Richard; BLW2415 issued
    to those heirs 10/12/1847; QLF 1892 from gds William KIN-
    NEY, Columbia, CA, s of sol Solomon, states sol s George
    dd without issue, further sol gds William gave power/o at-
    torney to agent to afb; no action indicated by PN Office
    on his afb. F-W10175 R1493
KINNISON, Jacob, b 5/16/1757; esf 1777 Greenbrier Co, VA; PN
    1834 Pocahontas Co, VA; last PN payment in file 1838. F-
    S16905 R1493
KINSAUL, John, b 1759 Princess Anne Co, VA; esf Pitt Co, NC;
    PN there 1832; surname also spelled KENSAUL; QLF 1929 from
    great gds S A MOORE, Boling, TX. F-S8790 R1494
KINSER, Michael, esf 1780 Wythe Co, VA; PN 1788 there for dis-
    ability from wounds at Battle of Camden; dd 11/1823; md 9/
    4/1783 or 1784 Elizabeth, Montgomery Co, VA, or Wythe Co,
    VA; wid b 6/19/1765; PN 1844 Wythe Co, VA; QLF states two
    bro's Michael & Philip KINZER/KINSER/KINCER PA RW sol's &
    mvd later to Montgomery Co, VA where dd; QLF states sol bc
    1740, LWT probated 12/10/1822 Wythe Co, VA. F-W8001 R1494
KIPHART, Henry, b 1761 PA; esf 1782 Shenandoah Co, VA, where
    res; mvd after RW to MD, thence 1818 Henry Co, KY, where
    PN 1833; sis mbnn then; QLF states sol dd KY 1841 & had s
    Jake. F-S31190 R1495
KIPPERS, John, b 3/4/1762; esf 1776 Amherst Co, VA; res after
    RW Greenbrier Co, VA; mvd c1832 to MO where PN 1835 Monroe
    Co; QLF 1920 from great gdd Mrs M S MEISNER, Atlanta, MO;
    QLF 1922 from great great great gdd Maud N (Mrs M A) ROM-
    JUE, Macon, MO, states sol dd & buried MO. F-S15914 R1495
KIPPS, Jacob, see KEPPS, Jacob. F-W7993 R1495
  Michael, esf 1777 Rockingham Co, VA, where res; afp 1834 ae
    74 Montgomery Co, VA & PAR; dd 6/1835; md 4/26/1782 Catha-
    rine MILLENBARGER, Rockingham Co, VA; wid afp aec 80 Mont-
    gomery Co, VA, 1840 & PAR; AFF then by sol bro Jacob, She-
    nandoah Co, VA, he served in RW with him; sol s John liv
    1841 ae 55. F-R5984 R1495
KIPS, Jacob, see KEPPS, Jacob. F-W7993 R1495
KIRBY, John, esf 1779 Spotsylvania Co, VA; PN 1819 Scott Co,
    KY, ae 60; res there 1820 with w mbnn & ch: Betsey ae 22,
    Polly ae 20, Suckey ae 16, & John ae 13; dd 3/1836 leaving
    wid Nancy BENNETT (his 2nd w) who md (2) John GRISHAM; sol

KIRBY (continued)
- s Michael res ae 57 Scott Co, KY, 1857; s William gtd BLW 61287 there 1857 as only ch/o sol less than ae 21 in 1855, he b 5/22/1835; sol wid dd before 3/1855. F-S335502 R1495
- William, see KERBY, William. F-W7998 R1495

KIRK, James, esf 1780 Stafford Co, VA, where res; PN ae 75 Marion Co, KY, 1834; gtd BLW26411 there 1855; dd there 1/21/57; md there 7/30/1840 Mahala CHAMBERLAIN; wid PN 1857 ae 39 there; QLF 1932 from desc Margaret McGiffin McILVAINE, Peoria, IL, states sol b 3/23/1759, & dd near Lebanon, KY; QLF states sol b VA, & md (1) Ann HORTON; QLF states sol d 2nd w/o William McELROY. F-W10171 R1495
- Jemima, former widow of Daniel McCARTY. F-R5988 R1495
- John, b 10/10/1754; esf 1776 Fauquier Co, VA, where res; PN 1832 Giles Co, VA. F-S5558 R1495
- John, esf 1775 in VA Line when res PA; later esf in PA unit; PN ae 66 Allegany Co, PA 1821; dd 1825; last PN payment in file 1829 (compiler note: apparently payment of sol PN arrears to wid); QLF 1858 & 1859 from d Jane LEWIS of Cassville, TN states her m survived sol & never gtd PN; no PN Office response to Jane in file. F-S39819 R1495
- Robert, esf 1780 VA; BLW1214 issued 1/21/1790; PN ae 72 Livingston Co, KY, 1827 when res with s Harvey, who then had own family to support; QLF 1887 from Dr R N ROSS, Lonoke, AR, states sol his gdf-in-law, further sol res 1821 with sons John, George, James, & Harvey, sol having afp in 1820 but had too many assets then to qualify for PN. F-S35511 R1495
- Thomas, esf 1779 Fauquier Co, VA where res; dd Lauderdale Co AL, 5/18/1831 when making arrangements to afp; md 12/1787 Nancy WEBB wid/o Simeon WEBB, (MB12/15/87 signed by Joseph KIRK), Montgomery Co, VA; wid PN ae 78 Lauderdale Co, AL, 1840, she having been res there since 1820, res previously Shelby Co, KY; gave power of attorney 1840 to Allen KIRK (no kinship given) Lauderdale Co, AL, to afp increase; res 1844 ae 85 Tippah Co, MS; gave power of attorney to Sarah DAVIS (no kinship given) of Salem, MS, 1845 to collect PN. F-W7992 R1495

KIRKHAM, Michael, b 8/29/1746; esf 1776 VA; esf 1779 Clarke's Station, near Danville, KY Territory; PN 1833 Woodford Co, KY. F-S31187 R1495

KIRKLAND, John, b Prince George Co, VA; reared Dinnwiddie Co, VA, where esf 1776; mvd after CORNWALLIS Surrender to KY (area later Mercer Co), where esf against indians 1782; PN ae 78 Mercer Co, KY, 1832; dd Fall 1837; s John gave power of attorney 1853 there to agent to collect PN due f; QLF states sol b Scotland & dd Mercer Co, KY. F-S13634 R1496

KIRKPATRICK, Abraham, BLW1210 issued 11/5/1789; captain in VA Line; QLF states sol served in 8th & 4th VA Regiments. F-BLW1210 R1496
- James, BLW12300 issued 12/13/1791. F-BLW12300 R1496
- Robert, esf 1775 Camden District, SC, where b 1/19/1754; mvd

KIRKPATRICK (continued)
after RW to Powell's Valley, VA where captured by indians; after release mvd to Madison Co, KY, thence Green Co, KY, thence Jackson Co, TN, where PN 1832; dd 2/24/35; one of heirs then John KIRKPATRICK (kinship not given). F-S1845 R1496

KISENCEDERS, Martin, esf 1782 Winchester, VA; PN ae not given Crawford Co, PA, 1818; dd 12/5/19; ch who afb there 1847: Sarah PORTER, Margaret HICKMAN, Joseph, & Benjamin; ch gtd BLW2416, issued 4/15/1847 to James PORTER (kinship not given). F-S39823 R1497

KISLING, Ditrich, esf Rockingham Co, VA, where res; PN 1832 ae 75 Warren Co, OH, res Clear Creek Township; QLF 1933 from desc James L SAYLER, Chicago, IL whose m Elizabeth KESLING was great gdd of sol. F-S16178 R1497

Jacob, esf 1781 Rockingham Co, VA, where b 1760; PN that Co 1832; QLF 1926 from desc Mrs J S MACY of Indianapolis, IN; QLF 1923 from great gds Charles E KEMPER of Staunton, VA, states Mrs Mary V YANCEY of Harrisonburg, VA, great gdd of sol; QLF 1916 from desc Mrs A Kemper SPENCE of Wytheville, VA who also desc/o RW sol May BURTON of Orange Co, VA; QLF states sol dd c1835; QLF 1920 from Frank B CRAWFORD, Winchester, VA, whose w great gdd/o VA RW sol George HOUSTON/ HUSTON of Rockingham Co, VA. F-S5554 R1497

KISNER, Jacob, b 5/6/1763 PA; esf 1779 Greenbrier Co (area later Monroe Co), VA; mvd after RW to KY, thence Gibson Co, TN, where PN 1833. F-S45886 R1497

KITCHEN, Benjamin, b 1763 Southampton Co, VA; esf 1776 Nash Co NC, where res; res after RW Washington Co, GA; mvd 1798 to Natchez, MS, thence 1816 Rapides Parish, LA, thence Catahoula Parish, LA, where PN 1833; dd there 1849; md there (2) c1822 Lavica WILSON & had 4 or 5 ch by her; s Benjamin (by 1st w) served in 1813 in Creek War & dd of disease during siege of New Orleans in War of 1812; s William H (by 1st w) liv 1832; wid md (2) Daniel NICHOLSON; her s Benjamin by sol afb 1855 ae 15 as only minor ch/o sol & gtd BLW 47613 (under Act of 1855 minor ch/o RW sol's authorized to receive BLW's); sol elder brother Benjamin res Nash Co, NC then; QLF 1933 from desc Robert Hunter PERSON, Alexandria, LA, whose m Martha Louise (d of Robert P HUNTER & Martha L RANSDELL) was desc of sol, & also of RW sol William PRINCE (Princeton University & town/o Princeton named for latter) F-S31797 R1497

Daniel, esf 1778 Leesburg, VA; PN ae 72 Fairfax Co, VA, 1830 when had ch Daniel ae 24 & Polly ae 21; ch Elisha & William res Fairfax Co, VA, 1824; dd 1/25/38; md 2/1/1786 Molly BARKER of Cameron Parish (MB 1/27/86 with Mary BARKER), Loudoun Co, VA; wid PN ae 76 Fairfax Co, VA 1840. F-W8005 R1497

James, b 10/25/1765; esf 1779-80 Stafford Co, VA; PN Warren Co, IN, 1832; mvd c1839 to Fulton Co, IL, where res 1841 with d Mrs William HALL. F-S31192 R1497

KITCHEN, James, esf 1776 Greenbrier Co, VA; res Russell Co, VA 1801; dd 3/23/32 Lawrence Co (area later Carter Co) KY; md 1/10/1780 Jane, who b 10/1763; wid afp 1844 Carter Co, KY; PAR, insufficient proof of marriage, & of svc of 6 months; dd there 11/20/49 leaving ch: Andrew, William, Mary w of William WATSON, Elizabeth w of Jesse KISEE, & John; s John afp 1852 there ae 67 for self & above siblings, & PAR; s Andrew AFF there 1854. F-R5997 R1497
 John, b 4/25/1757; esf 1781 Henry Co, VA, where res; PN 1832 Anderson Co, TN, when res there 33 years; dd 8/29/45; md 1/1796 or 2/1796 Mary WHITTEN who PN ae 90 Anderson Co, TN 1860. F-W2737 R1497
 Thomas, esf VA Buckingham Co, VA, before Battle of Guilford, where b 4/27/1764; md in Campbell Co, VA, & res there for c4 years; mvd after RW to SC for c16 years, thence GA for 14 years, thence Posey Co, IN, for c2 years, thence Gibson Co, IN, where afp 1847 when res there for 27 years, & PAR; surname also spelled KITCHENS; bro-in-law of John GARREL. F-R5998 R1497
KITE, John, esf 1780 Rockingham Co, VA, where b; PN ae 71 Hawkins Co, TN, 1835; bro George AFF then there aec 67. F-S21334 R1497
KITTLE, Jacob, b 7/26/1757 Sussex Co, NJ; esf 1776 Northampton Co, VA, where res; mvd 1779 to Tygarts Valley, Augusta Co (area later Randolph Co), VA; captain/o company of rangers & spies there 1792 against indians; PN 1832 Randolph Co, VA; last PN payment in file 1837; QLF states sol res there 1840. F-S13630 R1497
KLINE, John Nicholas, usually called Nicholas, b 1761 Berks Co PA; esf 1776 Allentown, Northampton Co, PA, where res; mvd 1783 to Philadelphia, PA, thence DE, thence 1798 Loudoun Co, VA, where PN 1832. F-S8796 R1498
 Philip, esf 1780 Frederick Co, VA, where res; dd 6/23/1842 intestate Hampshire Co, VA; md there 3/31/1791 Elizabeth SWITCHER/SWITZIR; wid liv 1854; ch then: Joseph, Mary, Daniel, Elizabeth, Rebecca, Abraham, Barbara, Philip, John, Michael, & Eva; sol bro Anthony then res Frederick Co, VA, ae 79; adm of sol & wid estates, Philip KLINE, afp 1862, & PAR, insufficient proof/o RW svc; s Michael res then Clayton, Montgomery Co, OH: QLF states sol b 1/1/1760, surname also spelled KLEIN, CLYNE, & CLINE). F-R6004 R1498
KLUNCK, Henry, esf 1777 Marsh Creek, VA, in 11th VA Regiment; PN 1818 Chambersburg, Franklin Co, PA; res there 1826 ae 66 when had w Elizabeth ae 58 & s mbnn; dd 6/26/33; surname also spelled CLUNG; QLF 1912 from desc Mrs Eva J H DOOLEY, Marion, IN. F-S39824 R1498
KNAPP, John, esf 1777 Hampshire Co, VA; PN ae 57 Pickaway Co, OH, 1819; res there 1820 when had w ae 64 & s ae 24 mbnn; res 1833 Lyme Township, Huron Co, OH; QLF states sol wid Prude/Prudence. F-S41735 R1500
KNICK, William, esf 1778 Frederick Co, MD; md 12/25/1784 Flora at her f's home, Winchester, VA; res there for 12-14 years

KNICK (continued)
   after marriage, then mvd to Rockbridge Co, VA where sol dd 2/11/89; wid PN there 1843 ae 87, when half sis Mrs Mary CUNNINGHAM AFF there ae 74; wid dd there 4/28/45, leaving ch: Catharine w of John CUNNINGHAM of Fayette Co, OH, William of Miami Co, OH, Betsy w/o John ARMSTRONG of same Co, Polly w/o Thomas MORRIS of Lewis Co, VA, John & Adam, both of Rockbridge Co, VA; wid LWT of 4/4/1845, probated Rockbridge Co, VA, 6/2/45, appointed s Adam as executor of LWT & left to him all her PN & any BLW due her; surv ch gtd PN there 1845; AFF there then by Richard MORRIS, b 10/1782, that he merchant there 41 years, that sol eldest ch Katy CUNNINGHAM aec 60 & sol youngest ch Adam aec 37; AFF then there by Charles ARMENTROUT, b 1/15/1773, he res there c50 years; AFF there then by Henry McCORKLE, b 2/14/1791, res there Collierstown, that Co, that he raised that Co; sol surname also spelled NICK. F-W9104 R1501
KNIGHT, Austin, esf 1781 Amherst Co, VA; dd there 9/1817; md there 3/23/1789 Elizabeth HAM, (MB 2/24/89 between Orson KNIGHT & Betsey HAM); wid PN ae 70 there 1843; dd there on 12/25/43, having just recd PN certificate; wid left s William & d Ann MAYS; s William, as adm/o m's estate, afp due her 1844 & stated sol given name always pronounced Austin. F-W8010 R1502
Christopher, drafted VA for short time & his f served as his substitute; afp 1835 VA, & PAR; very little data in file. F-R6023 R1502
Henry, esf 1781 Sussex Co, VA, where b 2/15/1760; mvd c1803 to Rockingham Co, NC, for c3 years, thence Guilford Co, NC for c20 years, thence back to Rockingham Co, NC, where PN 1833. F-S7124 R1502
James, esf 1776 Frederick Co, VA; PN ae not given, Jessamine Co, KY, 1830; dd 11/3/31; md 10/21/1783 Elizabeth, who b 1/1766; wid PN 1839 Jessamine Co, KY; ch births: James 1/10/1785, William 2/7/87, Marques D F 2/18/89, Polly 1/29/92, Jane Watts 3/10/94, George 10/18/96, Abigail 4/17/99, James William 4/25/1801, Nancy Daugherty 8/28/03, Amanda F 8/29/05 & Grant 1/17/09; other birth: Elijah NEAL 5/2/1839; QLF 1911 from gds M A BURTON, Nicholsville, KY, states sol wid liv 1850. F-W2946 R1502
John, esf 1776 in VA regiment as surgeon's mate; PN 1828 ae 75 Shelby Co, KY; dd there 3/12/38; md 10/14/1784 Mary/Polly d of Richard & Elizabeth STEPHENSON, Fayette Co, PA; wid PN 1838 Shelby Co, KY, & dd there 7/31/39; ch births: George Beall 3/14/1787, John Alexander 5/8/89, Richard Stephenson 12/8/91, Joseph Winlock 4/20/94, Betsy Sommers 2/26/96 (dd 2/5/1809), Sarah/Sally Lane 4/23/99 (md John HALL), Effie/Effey Winlock 1/4/1801 (md John M ALLEN), Mary Brock 10/1802, Helen Steele 1/4/05 & Jane/Jean Isabella 7/27/07 (md 11/13/1828 John LANE); gdd Sarah LANE b 9/16/1829; births of sol wid's sisters: Sally 9/26/1766, Effey 3/22/70, & Betsey 1/14/73; wid sis Effey md 1787 Joseph

KNIGHT (continued)
  WINLOCK, Fayette Co, PA, & Joseph AFF ae 70 Shelby Co, KY, 1828 he was RW sol in 7th VA Regiment; QLF states sol was stepson-in-law of VA RW sol Robert BEALE. F-W12051 R1502
  Moses, b 8/27/1763 Brunswick Co, VA; esf 1779 SC near border of NC; afp 1833 Richmond Co, NC, & PAR, insufficient proof of svc; w Frances dd 5/6/1828, & sol dd 10/1/36; surv ch who afp 1853: Anna wid of Daniel McINTOSH, John A, Elizabeth w/o Caleb CURTIS, & Frances w of Culliver J BRITT Jr; ch PAR; QLF 1908 from great gdd Mrs Anna R HENDERSON, Williamstown, WV. F-R6028 R1503
  Peter, esf 1777 Stafford Co, VA, where b 4/3/1760; mvd to Harrison Co, VA, where PN 1832; last PN payment in file 1838. F-S5660 R1503
  William, esf 1776 Middlebrook, VA; PN ae 58 Spotsylvania Co, VA, 1818; res there 1820 when had 2 d's & 1 s; dd 12/6/40 there; md there 3/27/1819 Mary OAKES; wid PN ae 83 there 1853; gtd BLW43510 there 1856. F-W8009 R1503
KNIGHTEN, Thomas, b 3/22/1753 Caroline Co, VA; esf 1780 Craven Co (area later Sumter Co), SC where res, in Colonel Knighton's regiment (no kinship stated); esf 1781 Culpeper Co, VA where res; PN 1832 St Clair Co, IL; surname spelled also KNIGHTON; QLF states sol buried IL. F-S32368 R1504
  William, esf 1778 in 16th VA Regiment; PN aec 62 Orange Co, VA, 1818; res there 1820 occupation miller, with w Susannah aec 50 & d Lydia aec 17; surname also spelled KNIGHTER F-S38123 R1504
KNIPE, Henry, b 1751 Germantown Township, Philadelphia Co, PA, where esf 1775; PN 1831 Frederick Co, VA, occupation shoemaker, when w decd & only family d aec 55, they having res there for 42 years; had afp 1822 & PAR. F-S38123 R1504
KNOWLES, John, b 1749 Beliminah, Co Antrim, Ireland, Parish of Chochel; esf 1775 Cumberland Co, PA; res after RW Augusta Co, VA, thence Amherst Co, VA, thence Pendleton Co, VA, thence 1807 White Co, TN, where afp 1833, & PAR; dd 3/21/38 leaving no wid; s William afp aec 52 White Co, TN, 1851 for sol surv ch: self, Sally aec 68, John aec 66, & Elinder aec 58; ch PAR. F-R6038 R1504
  William, esf 1776 VA Line; md 1778 Mary DONAHO in MD, & they mvd to Augusta Co, VA, where res on plantation/o Judge Archibald STUART on South River; sol dd 9/1811 there; wid PN ae 84 that Co 1839; ch births: twins unnamed bc 1780 & dd in early infancy, 3rd ch unnamed 1782, 3 other ch unnamed, Jane 5/2/1783, Elender 10/27/84, Salley 8/2/86, Robert 9/16/88, William 1/11/89, Samuel 1/11/91, Archibald 8/17/93, Cathran 10/17/95, John 3/8/99, & Susan 5/3/1800; other birth: William (s of James SOMERFIELD & Cathrane MATHENY) 6/23/1827; marriages: Robert KNOWLES & Susannah BROOKS on 2/13/1811, James MATHENY & Catharine KNOWLES on 4/6/1820. F-W4257 R1504
KNOX, James, esf 1775 in 8th VA Regiment; res 1822 Shelby Co, KY, when had w Ann; niece Margaret (wid of Samuel TAGGART)

KNOX (continued)
    then had s James Knox TAGGART; sol then referred to James Knox & Joseph Winlock (s's of Dr Benjamin LOGAN), also to James Knox s of William MONTGOMERY; sol dd Shelby Co, KY, before 9/5/31; BLW1832 issued 4/6/1832 to LWT executors Henry CRITTENDEN, Nudegate OWSLEY, & Mark HARDIN; QLF says sol d Jane md 3/15/1820 Josiah BUCHANAN, Washington, Co, VA, further Robert BUCHANAN b 1741 (s of Samuel), dd 1832, was VA RW sol, & was f of above Josiah BUCHANAN; QLF 1908 from desc Mrs Oscar BARTHOLD, Weatherford, TX, who was also desc of William ROGERS of Orange Co, VA, who served in French & Indian War in 1758; QLF states sol dd 12/4/1822 Shelby Co, KY, md (2) Ann MONTGOMERY, wid/o General Benjamin LOGAN, & she dd ae 76 Shelby Co, KY, 10/18/1825. F-BLW1832 R1506

KOON, Philip, esf 1776 Harrison Co, VA; indians killed sis & 2 bro's there; mvd to Monroe Co, OH, thence Belmont Co, OH, thence Washington Co, OH, where afp 1834 ae 77; PAR, less than 6 months svc. F-R6053 R1507

KOONTZ, Phillip, b MD; mvd ae 19 to VA, where res 2 years on South Branch, thence Augusta Co (area later Rockingham Co) VA; esf 1781 Augusta Co, VA; PN there 1832 aec 80; last PN payment in file 1840; QLF states sol b 1745. F-S5661 R1507

KREMER, Conrad, esf 1777 PA; PN ae 77 Frederick Co, VA, 1825 res Winchester; res there 1819 with w Catharine; res there 1825 with w ae 63, s Peter, s George & gdc ae 6 mbnn; QLF states sol buried Winchester, VA; QLF 1906 from great gds Chester M LAWRENCE of Arvada, CO; QLF 1912 from desc Miss N L MAYNARD, Winchester, VA, states sol w possibly Catharine, d of RW sol Peter HELPHENSTINE; QLF states sol w Catharine HELPHENSTINE; QLF 1918 from great great gdd Alice GILBERT of Niles, OH; QLF states sol had d Mary. F-S19372 R1508

KROESEN, Isaac, esf 1780 Shepherdstown, Berkeley Co, VA; PN ae 78 there 1832. F-S5663 R1508

KRYSTAR, John, b 4/1752; esf 1777 Fauquier Co, VA; wounded in battle, then transferred to be interpreter for General LAFAYETTE; PN 1836 Williamson Co, TN, occupation tanner, his w then aec 73; in 1826 had 5 s & 1 d, all of whom res PA. F-S38902 R1509

KYCENCEDER, Martin, see KISENCEDERS, Martin. F-S38923 R1509

KYLE, Anna, former widow of Mathias MAUK. (F-R6064)

KYMES, Coonrod, b 1763 near Fredricktown, Frederick Co, MD; f mvd when sol ch to Loudoun Co, VA, where sol esf 1782; mvd after RW to Rockbridge Co, VA, thence Green Co, TN, thence Murray Co, TN, thence c1815 to Lincoln Co, TN, where afp 1832; PAR, svc less than 6 months. F-R5928 R1509

LACKEY, Adam, b Baltimore Co, MD, son of Alexander; esf 1777 Pittsylvania Co, VA; mvd after RW to NC, thence TN, thence IL, where PN ae 73 Lawrence Co 1832; dd 2/13/36 there; md 10/1810 Catharine, on Tennessee River near Muscle Shoals, TN; wid PN ae 75 Lawrence Co, IL, 1854. F-W8030 R1510

LACKEY, Henry, esf PA; res near Berkeley Co, VA, for 3 years; dd 1/31/1812; md 3/14/1781 Mary JENKINS, Berkeley Co, VA, per wid AFF; MB 2/25/1785 there per Co Clerk; wid afp ae 102 Grayson Co, TX, 1852; PAR, insufficient proof of svc. F-R6073 R1510

Thomas, esf 1781 Winchester, VA, when res Berkeley Co, VA; PN ae 70 Washington Co, TN, 1/1829; dd 7/4/29; md 23 June c1780 Elizabeth; wid PN 1837 ae 78 Washington Co, TN; ch: John, Joseph, Nancy, Peggy, Elizabeth, & Jane; QLF states sol wid res 1840 Washington Co, TN, & had descendents res Blount Co, TN, in 1916. F-W8023 R1510

LACKLAND, John, b 6/9/1756; esf Rockbridge Co, VA; PN Scott Co KY, 1832. F-S13692 R1510

LACKY, Andrew, b 10/25/1762 Lancaster Co, PA; mvd with f to Augusta Co, VA & esf there 1777 at Staunton; mvd to Monongalia Co, VA, thence Fayette Co, KY, for c4 years, thence Madison Co, KY, thence Estill Co, KY, where PN 1837; surname also spelled LACKEY. F-S30533 R1510

LACY, Elijah, b 10/14/1764 Hanover Co, VA; mvd 1770 to Goochland Co, VA where esf 1778 with bro Matthew & cousin Ellit LACY when m liv & f decd; mvd 1805 to Fayette Co, KY, then to Woodford Co, KY, thence 1825 Owen Co, KY where PN 1832; dd 4/25/46 Morgan Co, IN, at home/o s Jesse; md 10/26/1787 Frankey HOLLAND, Louisa Co, VA who b 4/8/1766; wid PN 1847 Owen Co, IN, where res 1849 Ray Township; ch births: Polley 10/5/1788, Jesse 7/10/90, Stephen 6/1/92, Peter 6/14/94, Eliza 5/8/96, & Patsey 12/29/97; d mbnn md Stephen F HANCOCK of Owen Co, IN. F-W10189 R1511

Mathew, esf 1779 Goochland Co, VA; bro/o Charles who esf Hanover Co, VA; dd 3/7/1823; md 4/8/1772 Susanna who PN 1838 ae 88 Goochland Co, VA; had several small ch when sol serving in RW; John RICHARDS AFF 1838 Goochland Co, VA, he md sis of sol wid; QLF states sol dd Richmond, VA & md Susanna RUTHERFORD in Goochland Co, VA. F-W8077 R1511

LADD, William, esf 1781 New Kent Co, VA, where b 2/8/1760; PN there 1833; dd there 5/9/34; md there 12/17/1778 Mary, who PN there 1843 ae 84; had 8 ch including eldest John who ae 63 in 1845. F-W8079 R1511

LADY, Philip, b 6/7/1758 Lancaster Co, PA; mvd to Loudoun Co, VA, where esf 1780; PN 1834 Estill Co, KY. F-S30529 R1511

LAFFOON, James, esf 1779 Lunenburg Co, VA, where b; PN aec 69 Fayette Co, KY, 1832 when res there c27 years; younger bro Simon res there 1832; QLF 1940 from desc Mary Louise MORGAN of Dallas, TX, states sol dd 1851; QLF 1914 from great gds Dr C A LAFFOON of Champaign, IL; QLF 1909 from Joseph McCOY, St Louis, MO, states w desc of sol. F-S13694 R1512

Nathaniel, b Brunswick Co, VA; mvd when very young with parents to Lunenburg C, VA where esf 1780; mvd c1806 to Wake Co, NC, thence c1810 to Warren Co, NC where PN 1832 ae 86; res 1835, nearly blind, Wake Co, NC, with one of d's mbnn. F-S8813 R1512

LAFO, Mary, former wid/o Jacob WHITE; her surname also spelled

LAFO (continued)
  LAFOY & LAFONG. (F-W8076)
  LAFON, Richard, esf VA Line; dd 8/1824 Jessamine Co, KY; md 11/13/1794 Anna MAXEY (MB 11/11/94 with Anne MAXEY, signed by Ephraim MAXEY) Powhatan Co, VA; wid PN aec 74 Jessamine Co, KY, 1848; gtd BLW75063 there 1857 ae 83; ch mbnn; certificate of MB from Powhatan Co clerk contains data: Henry GARDNER md 12/20/1794 Sarah FARLEY there. F-W1785 R1512
LAIDLEY, Thomas, PA sea svc, b 1/1/1756 Argyleshire, Scotland; esf 1776 in PA army when res Philadelphia, PA; esf 1777 on ship RESOLUTION as gunner & shortly thereafter promoted to ship's captain; PN 1833 Cabell Co, VA, res with s mbnn; dd 3/17/38 leaving wid mbnn; QLF states sol md 6/18/1778 Sara OSBORNE in PA; QLF states sol buried at Huntington, Cabell Co, WV. F-S15596 R1512
LAIN, Charles, esf 1780 Amherst Co, VA, where res; PN 1832 ae 73 Roane Co, TN; dd 11/6/43 Bradley Co, TN; md 1/6,7 or 8/1801 Sarah/Sally LEISTER (MB 1/6/1801 with Sally LEISTER), Cocke Co, TN; wid PN ae 76 Bradley Co, TN, 1853; gtd BLW 26750 there 1855, when AFF there by Samuel & Lavina BURTEN (no kinship stated); PN restored there 1865 ae 92 when res with d Mrs BURTEN. F-W26193 R1512
  Gisborn (AKA LAINE, Gisborne), esf 1778 Princess Anne Co, VA where res; mvd from Norfolk Co, VA to Halifax Co, NC, then c1815 to Wilson Co, TN where PN 1832 ae 79. F-S4496 R1512
  Joseph, see LANE, Joseph. F-W1783 R1512
  Joseph, esf 1779 Bedford Co, VA, where b 11/17/1759; mvd after RW to Halifax Co, VA, for 16-17 years, thence Pittsylvania Co, VA, where PN 1832; dd 4/12/37; md 12/20/1775 Sarah HALL, Halifax Co, VA; wid PN ae 86 Pittsylvania C, VA, 1841; ch births (family bible pages badly faded & blotched & partially illegible): Isham 12/1778, Pleasant 11/8/1782, Robert Hall 5/3/84, Elias 1/11/88, Patesie Ellinton Hall 10/23/90, Joel, Nancy, John 3/13/95, Sare 3/13/98 & Will L 5/27/1800; other birth: Henrie, s of Drury LAIN, 8/8/1784; wid bro Isham HALL AFF 1842 Campbell Co, VA. F-W5123 R1512
LAINE, Henry, esf 1776 Hunterdon Co, NJ where res; dd 6/3/1831 ae 87 Wheeling, Ohio Co, VA; md 1779 Mary, Hunterdon Co, NJ; wid b 4/16/1760; afp 1840 Marshall Co, VA, & PAR. F-R6128 R1512
LAINHART, Isaac, b 4/5/1755 NJ; mvd when very young with f to NC, thence Cumberland Co, VA, thence Bedford Co, VA, where esf 1777; mvd several years after RW to KY, where PN 1832 Madison Co, when res there 30 years; surname also spelled LAINHEART. F-S30532 R1512
LAKE, Asa, esf 1779 VT; mvd to OH where res Jackson & Hancock Co's; dd 8/1843; md 9/1788 Chloe ABBOTT, Hampshire Co, VA; wid afp ae 82 Hancock Co, OH, 1851; PAR, wid did not sufficiently establish her h as same Asa who listed on VT RW rolls, & also h served less than 6 months; ch births: Rachel 1/18/1789, Lorenzo 1/2/90, Sarah 5/8/92, John 11/29/93, Joseph 4/20/95, Silas 7/26/97, Milton 10/22/98,

LAKE (continued)
  Esther 3/5/1800, Ira 12/30/01, Asa 7/12/05, Lidia 7/28/09, & Martha 3/30/13; QLF states sol b CT, & mvd with parents to VT before end of RW. F-R6087 R1513
Elizabeth Q, former wid of John PRYOR. (F-W12064)
LAMASTER, Joseph, see LEMASTER, Joseph. F-W797 R1514
LAMB, Thomas, b 1/1/1751 Spotsylvania Co, VA; esf 1776 Orange Co, VA, where res; mvd after RW to Madison Co, KY where PN 1832; last PN payment in file 1836. F-S30531 R1514
LAMBAUGH, Joseph, esf 1781 Loudoun Co, VA, where res near Noland Ferry; PN ae 69 Lawrence Co, OH, 1832. F-S8816 R1515
LAMBERT, Charles, b 5/3/1754 Albemarle Co, VA; esf Bedford Co, VA; res after RW Richmond, VA, thence Henrico Co, VA, then to Hanover Co, VA, thence Bedford Co, VA where PN 1832 res Russell Parish; bro George AFF there then held family bible; dd 11/7/39; md 1785 Nancy (MB 3/17/1785 between sol & Nancy SNEAD alias JONES) Hanover Co, VA; wid PN ae 77 Henrico Co, VA, 1843; res 1849 Richmond, VA. F-W8021 R1515
George, b 10/28/1748 (old style) Albemarle Co, VA; esf 1775 Bedford Co, VA; PN there 1832 res Russell Parish; dd 1/30/1837. F-S8810 R1515
James, b 3/25/1758 near Hagerstown, MD; res Rockingham Co, VA all during RW; esf 1774 in Tygert's Valley on Monongahela River against indians; esf ae 19 Augusta Co, VA, for RW; mvd to KY, thence OH, thence IN, where afp 1841 Dearborn Co when res there 27 years; PAR, insufficient proof/o svc; afp again 1844 Ripley Co, IN when res Dearborn Co, IN & PAR; dd 1847; md Jane, wno gave power/o attorney 1854 at Dearborn Co, IN, to agent to afp; children mbnn 1850. F-R6099 R1515
Lambert, John, b 2/1760 Albemarle Co, VA; esf 1781 Bedford Co, VA, where res; PN 1832 Mercer Co, KY. F-S15445 R1515
Lambert, John, esf 1776 Prince William Co, VA; PN 1832 ae 79 Columbia Co, GA; dd there 11/25/33; md there 3/1809 Rachel MOORE; wid PN ae 72 there 1853; gtd BLW17586 there 1855 ae 65; children mbnn res there 1857. F-W9111 R1515
Mathias/Matthias, b 3/15/1755 near Frederickstown, MD; esf Augusta Co, VA, where res; mvd several years after RW to Clark Co, KY for c18 years, thence Madison Co, KY where PN 1834 when res there 33 years; bro Abraham AFF there then he also RW sol; dd 4/4/39; md 1/27/1796 Elizabeth WILLIAMS in Madison Co, KY; wid PN aec 83 there 1850 when had 3 ch by sol liv; s John AFF there then ae 51. F-W1784 R1515
Meredith, esf Hanover Co, VA; afp ae 84 Green Co, KY, 1845 when res Hart Co, KY, near Co line; PAR. F-R6100 R1515
LAMKIN, John, esf 1776 in VA regiment; PN ae 79 Culpeper Co, VA, 1818; dd 7/20/30 or 7/27/30; md 2/10/1785 wid Mary LEE (nee STORY), Fauquier Co, VA; wid PN ae 76 Culpeper Co, VA 1838 when P O address Wheatley, that Co; had 8 ch, including William (dd young), Joanna (res ae 50 with m 1839), John b 8/1791 (res 1839 Culpeper Co, VA), & Thomas LAMKIN; surname also spelled LAMPKIN. F-W8018 R1515

LAMKIN, Sampson, esf in VA Line; afp ae not given Richmond Co, GA, 1828; PAR, insufficient proof of svc. F-R20395 R1515
LAMME, Nathan, esf 1776 in 10th VA Regiment; PN 1831 Greene Co OH; BLW1831 issued there 5/26/32 ae 76, P O address Bellbrook; earlier granted 4,000 acres by VA; QLF states sol dd 1835 ae 89 near Bellbrook, OH. F-S46454 R1516
 Samuel, esf Augusta Co, VA, where res; dd 1/1/1826; md 7/27/1826 Agnes STEEL, Fayette Co, KY; wid afp ae 81 Harrison Co, KY, 1851 & PAR, insufficient proof/o svc; large family of ch mbnn; QLF states sol b near Staunton, Augusta Co, VA md Agnes STEELE & mvd to Cynthiana Co, KY where he dd; QLF 1913 from desc Louise H J (Mrs A C) DANIELS of Pueblo, CO, states sol md Agnes STEELE; QLF states sol wid Agnes "Nancy" STEELE dd 1860-1861; QLF 1926 from great gdd (on m's side) Lamme Frizell (Mrs Raymond) RATLIFF, Cincinnati, OH, states sol mvd from Augusta Co, VA to Harrison Co, IN 1787 further sol wid d/o David STEELE who was RW sol in 13th VA Regiment & mvd to Fayette Co, KY, from VA, further sol bro Nathan LAMME also RW sol. F-R6103 R1516
LAMON, Robert, b 1755 Co Tyrone, Ireland; esf 1776 Westmoreland Co, PA; mvd 1777 with f & family to Cumberand Co, PA, where esf 1777 with bro William; mvd 1780 to Charlotte Court House, Mecklenburg Co, NC, where esf 1781; res after RW McCord's Ferry, NC, for 2 years, thence PA, thence Berkeley Co, VA, for 9 years where md w mbnn, thence Scott Co KY, thence 1824 Boone Co, KY, where PN 1833; 4 older bro's also RW sol's, they all decd in 1833; surname also spelled LEMON; QLF 1934 from desc Mrs W T ROBERDS, West Point, MI; QLF 1929 from desc Malenna M (Mrs G W) ROGERS, Great Falls MT, states sol md Isabel JENNINGS; QLF 1928 from desc Mrs S C FORD, Great Falls, MT, also desc of RW sol Daniel MAUPIN who esf Albemarle Co, VA; QLF states sol w Mary McGOWAN (dd 1837); QLF 1916 from great gdd Laura M WALKER, Kansas City, MO, states sol dd Boone Co, MO. F-S16916 R1516
LANCASTER, Thomas, esf 1775 Orange Co, VA where res; dd 7/25/1828 Pendleton Co, KY; md there Michey OWENS; certificate of consent for marriage dated 11/23/1813; wid afb there 1855 aec 62 & BLAR, insufficient proof of svc & marriage. F-BLW Rej 180089-1855 R1517
 William, b 11/17/1745 Hanover Co, VA but christened in King William Co, VA; esf 1779 Orange Co, VA, where res; mvd c 15 years after RW to KY for c28 years, thence IN where PN 1832; dd there 11/4/43; md (2) 9/11/1813 Sarah BLADES in Bracken Co, KY, wid/o MD RW sol John Levy BLADES (of Worcester Co, MD, who dd there 1/1784 or 2/1784, had d Sarah S & s Zadock, b 5/1777, who mvd to KY with widowed m); sol wid PN 1845 ae 90 Switzerland Co, IN, res Craig Township, for svc of 1st h John Levy BLADES (see F-W9500); s Mallory LANCASTER, by 1st w, md Catharine, & res Switzerland Co, IN, 1844. F-S16912 R1517
LAND, John, esf 1776 Orange Co, VA; PN aec 63 Madison Co, KY, 1819; family res with him 1821 w Nightingale & ch: Moses,

LAND (continued)
Elizabeth ae 16, Nightingale ae 14, & gds William Henry ae 11; dd there 9/22/46; md 1787 Nightingale, Pendleton Co, VA; wid mvd shortly after h dd to Decatur Co, IN, & there dd 11/17/49; s John J afp 1850 Garrard Co, KY for sol surv ch: self, Joseph ae 56, Rosanah ae 54, & Moses ae 48; ch PAR. F-R6112 R1517

Lewis, esf 1776 Orange Co, VA; PN ae 70 Greenville District, SC, 1832; dd there 7/28/54; md there 8/27/1842 Obedience WEST; wid PN there 1855 ae 64; res there 1857 when gtd BLW 31784. F-W26200 R1517

Moses, esf 1780 Orange Co, VA; PN 1820 St Clair Co, IL, ae 59; res there later 1820 ae 61 with w ae 63 mbnn; QLF 1920 from gds Henry C FIKE, Warrensburg, MO; QLF states sol res St Clair Co, IL, 1840 ae 76 per 1840 Census; QLF 1917 from desc Mrs Ada R LUNESCH of O'Fallon, St Clair Co, IL; QLF 1907 from great gds J B MIDDLECOFF, Duluth, MN, states sol b VA 1764, dd 1848 near Mascoutah, IL & had s Philip; QLF 1924 from great gdd Ida J Land HOUSTON of Belleville, IL. F-S36037 R1517

LANDALE, Charles, see LANGSDON, Charles. F-W441 R1517

LANDER, Charles, b 12/28/1754; esf 1775 Loudoun Co, VA, where res; PN 1832 Bourbon Co, KY; QLF states sol dd there; QLF states sol dd KY 1833; QLF 1925 from desc Miss Lelah FORMAN, Mays Lick, KY, states sol b 12/29/1754, dd 8/14/33, & md Catherine FORMAN; QLF states sol dd 8/10/33 Bourbon Co, KY. F-S31198 R1517

Nathaniel, b 8/30/1760; esf 1781 Hampshire Co where res; mvd to Clark Co, KY, thence c1815 to Breckenridge Co, KY where PN 1832; AFF there then by Jacob LANDER (no kinship given) he res Hampshire Co, VA, when sol esf. F-S30536 R1517

LANDERDALE, William, see LAUDERDALE, William. F-S4505 R1517

LANDERS, John, b 9/15/1757 Granville Co, NC where esf early in RW; esf Prince Edward Co, VA, while on visit to uncle; mvd after RW to Columbia Co, GA, for 9 years, thence Caswell Co, NC, for c29 years, thence DeKalb Co, GA, where PN 1832 when res there c40 years; minister of the gospel then; dd 10/30/40 leaving wid Mourning; QLF states sol dd DeKalb Co GA. F-S16444 R1518

Thomas, esf 1778 Albemarle Co, VA, where res; PN ae 75 Alleghany Co, VA 1834; dd 8/1839; md 3/1791 Nancy BIGGS, Botetourt Co, VA; wid PN 1846 Alleghany Co, VA; gtd BLW31288 1855 ae 94 Monroe Co, VA; ch included eldest s who bc 1793 F-W3831 R1518

LANDMAN, Newman, esf 1776 Richmond Co, VA; PN 1818 Culpeper Co VA ae 63; res there 1821 ae 63 when w mbnn, who bedridden for 12 years; requested PN transfer Muskingum Co, OH, 1836 when res Perry Co, OH where had recently mvd from VA to be near his children; AFF then by William LANDMAN (no kinship given); surname also spelled LANDMON. F-S4737 R1518

LANDRES, Kimbrow/Kimbro, esf 1776-7 Albemarle Co, VA; PN ae 65 Switzerland Co, IN, 1818; dd 5/26/31; md Keziah HUMBLE (MB

LANDRES (continued)
7/21/1798) Louisa Co, VA; wid PN ae 80 Switzerland Co, IN, 1843; s-in-law Aaron STURGEON liv 1829.   F-W1623 R1518
Thomas, see LANDERS, Thomas.   F-W3831 R1518
LANDRUM, James, esf 1780 Amherst Co, VA, in company of f Captain Young LANDRUM; PN ae 70 Greene Co, TN 1832 when known as Reverend; dd 1/15/40; md 12/22/1788 Mary Clark ALFORD (MB 12/13/1787 signed by William ALFORD), Amherst Co, VA; wid PN ae 77 Jefferson Co, TN, 1843; d (eldest ch) mbnn bc 1789; QLF 1932 from desc Vera Fay McCUTCHEN, Clayton, MO, who also desc/o RW sol Nicholas DAVIS of Prince Edward Co, VA, who md Mary HAYES, & they had s Nicholas, further Captain Young LANDRUM dd Greene Co, TN; QLF states sol bro of Young LANDRUM Jr who md Joanna Goode SEVIER, Greene Co, TN & she dd 1841; QLF 1913 from N F HOWARD, Greeneville, TN, great gds of RW sol George LANDRUM of Amherst Co, VA, who chaplain during RW, mvd 1800-1815 to TN & left wid who PN. F-W800 R1518
Thomas, esf 1778 Orange Co, VA, where b 10/6/1759; PN Oglethorpe Co, GA, 1832; dd 4/13/33; QLF states sol also War/o 1812 veteran, & md Nancy BELL, further VA RW sol Zachariah BUTLER given land grant in Wilkes Co, GA, md Mary EDWARDS, & their s Patrick (md Elizabeth HUBBARD) drew land in Elbert Co, GA in GA land lottery 1838, further VA sol Joseph BELL md Elizabeth MOSELY & settled in GA, further RW sol Tandy KEY came from VA to GA where dd 1839 Jackson Co, was War of 1812 sol also.   F-S31811 R1518
Thomas, esf 1777 VA; PN ae 60 Scott Co, KY, 1818; decd in 1833; ch mbnn gtd PN due f 1845; surname also spelled LANDREM; QLF 1908 from desc Sue HAYNER, Macon, MO, states sol dd c1827 Scott Co, KY.   F-S35512 R1518
Thomas, VA sea svc, esf as surgeon's mate; dd 1/1811; LWT of 1/10/1811; Mary MARTIN AFF 1834 Elizabeth City Co, VA, she an heir/o sol; Elizabeth W COLLINS, adm/o sol estate 1845, gtd PN due sailor for heirs.   F-R61 R1518
LANDS, Ephraim, b 1732 Orange Co, VA; esf 1776 Amelia Co, VA; mvd after RW to Henry Co, VA, thence Stokes Co, NC, where PN 1832; dd there 10/4/36; md 9/1792 Polly BOLIN, Rockingham Co, NC, who b 2/1761; wid PN 1840 Stokes Co, NC; res there 1848 when gtd PN increase; ch births: Unity 5/1793 & Zachariah 8/31/95; both ch mvd to western country where dd before m; niece Sally (Bolin) SHELTON AFF ae 63 Stokes Co, NC 1840 she witness when sol md Polly.   F-W4066 R1518
Lewis, see LAND, Lewis.   F-W26200 R1518
LANE, Aquilla, b 5/18/1753; esf 1779 Orange Co, VA, where res; taken POW & released; esf 1781 NC; dd 11/24/1819; md 2/1/1780 Agnes FITZGERALD, Washington Co, NC (area later TN); wid afp 1845 Jefferson Co, TN, & PAR, insufficient proof/o svc; ch births: Esther 11/7/1780, Garret 6/18/82, Ranson 10/17/84, Jane 3/6/87, Tidence 4/18/89, Theney 9/21/91, John King 1/7/94, Clear 4/4/96, Anna 4/4/98, Pleasant W 4/20/1800 (md 8/21/1823 Mary H CALTHARP, their d Mary Catha-

LANE (continued)
  rine), Adelina 9/17/02, & Thomas Jefferson 10/9/04 (md on 7/25/1822 Vany PANGLE, & d Mary H b 12/25/1823); s Thomas J AFF 1/1852 his m "died some four years since"; QLF 1920 from great gds J M PHILLIPS of Wichita, KS, states sol bro Isaac also RW sol, they both sons/o Tidence LANE; QLF 1905 from desc Mrs George J SCHLICHER of Cuero, TX; QLF states sol f Tidence was Baptist minister, res 1760 Pittsylvania Co, VA, mvd soon after to Randolph Co, NC, thence 1779 Washington Co, TN, further sol bro John gtd BLW 11/10/1784 by NC for RW svc, & bro Samuel gtd BLW 1809 & 1810 by NC for RW svc; QLF 1910 from desc E St Clair THOMPSON. F-R6116 R1519
Drury, esf 1780 Bedford Co, VA, where b 2/14/1756; res 1781 Campbell Co, VA; mvd c1819 to Bedford Co, TN where PN 1832 ae 77; dd 7/28/37; md 8/15/1778 Carolina Matilda HALL by publication of banns in Hat Creek Church, Bedford Co, VA; wid PN ae 82 Rutherford Co, TN 1838; res there 1842 ae 85; ch births: eldest Henry 3/10/1780, Isham H 2/28/82, Sarah 1/4/85, Mary 11/11/88, Drury 2/14/91, Rutherford 6/12/94, Horatio G 3/18/97, Henry 10/16/1801 & William 2/27/04; AFF 1838 by s Isham H, Bedford Co, TN; AFF 1839 Rutherford Co, TN, by William BLAKELEY, ae 74 he aec 15 when sol & w md, & he served in RW with sol after wedding; sol younger bro of Joseph. F-W8015 R1519
Henry, b 11/26/1745 on Southanna River; esf 1780 Spotsylvania Co, VA, where res; afp 1832 Amherst Co, VA, & PAR, svc less than 6 months. F-R6122 R1519
Isaac, b 2/14/1760; esf 1776 Pittsylvania Co, VA, where res; mvd with f to Washington Co, TN, then to Grainger Co, TN, then to Claiborne Co, TN, then to McMinn Co, TN, where PN 1832; dd there 11/9/51; md 5/1782 Sarah RUSSELL, Washington Co, NC; (ceremony performed by Reverend Tidence LANE); wid gtd BLW34621 McMinn Co, TN, 1855 ae 95; afp then there & PAR, insufficient proof of marriage; ch included Tidence C who res there 1844; QLF states sol w d of Colonel Thomas RUSSELL who RW sol; QLF 1928 from desc Ray H WALLS, Greencastle, IN, states sol s/o Tidence; QLF 1917 from desc Mrs W R LANDRUM, Trenton, TN; QLF 1915 from great gdd Miss Sarah E DUTY, Farmington, IA, who also gdd of TN War of 1812 sol Joab HILL. F-R6137 R1520
Isham, b 1757 Louisa Co, VA; f & family res Albemarle Co, VA during RW; sol esf there 1778; PN 1832 Madison Co, KY when res there c23 years; QLF 1937 from desc Miss Virginia ENGLE, Berea, KY, who also desc/o RW sol Richard LAMB of Albemarle Co, VA & of RW sol James CHICK who PN Knox Co, KY; QLF 1898 from gds Isham G LAIN, Bloomington, IL; QLF says sol md Lucinda/Cinda LAMB; QLF states sol res Madison Co, KY, 1840 ae 82. F-S13705 R1520
James, esf 1777 Uniontown, PA, in VA company which later became part of 9th VA Regiment; PN ae 69 Lewis Co, KY, 1818 occupation school teacher; res there 1820 when w aec 70, &

LANE (continued)
their 6 ch all md; res 1827 Rush Co, IN, where had mvd to
be near 2 sons res there; Joseph LANE (kinship not given)
AFF there then; QLF states sol dd IN, & was buried there.
F-S35517 R1520

James, b 12/22/1746 Great Britain; came aec 14 to Rockbridge
Co, VA, where esf 1776 Lexington; PN 1832 Grainger Co, TN;
dd c2/4/35; md there c8/17/1830 Temperance JENNINGS who PN
there 1853 aec 65; gtd BLW26818 there 1855 aec 67; res Anderson Co, TN, 1866 when PN restored after Civil War; P O
address Wallace Crossroads, that Co 1869 when PN increased
& dd 8/14/72; John LESTER adm of her estate 1875; QLF 1880
from sol gds Henry S LANE, Marshall, TX. F-W8026 R1520

James, b 10/14/1753; esf Hanover Co, VA; dd 12/10/1798; md
1/2/1789 Rachel ANTHONY, who b 3/8/1763 & dd 8/12/1838; ch
births: Joseph A 9/15/1789 (dd 12/13/1808), Mark A 2/12/91
James 8/22/92 (dd 12/20/1808), Micajah A 12/24/93, William
T 10/12/95 & Sarah A 10/29/97; s Micajah A afp 1855 Wilkes
Co, GA for self & only other surv sibling Mark A (res Cobb
Co, GA), & they PAR, insufficient proof of svc & marriage;
Margaret A CALLAWAY dd 8/21/1845 ae 29. F-R6133 R1520

John, esf 1778 NH; seriously wounded, taken POW, & released;
discharged Hampton, VA; res Richmond, VA, after RW; mvd to
Manchester, Chesterfield Co, VA, where PN 1819 ae 93; res
1821 Henrico Co, VA; dd 7/14/23; d mbnn; gdd Mrs William
CLARK res 1851 Richmond, VA; QLF states sol gtd PN by VA
1807, & his w Ann Maria also gtd PN 1807 by VA for extraordinary service at Battle of Germantown where she wounded
seriously, further sol & w had s John (dd unmd) & s Thomas
(md Sally KELLY, Henrico Co, VA, & they had 2 ch, of which
Louisa w/o William CLARK & she liv 1851, & other ch decd);
QLF states sol w fought as a man, & was first & only woman
PN by VA for RW svc; QLF 1932 from Hazel Lane (Mrs D A)
LEHMAN, Harrisburg, IL, desc/o John LANE (b 1729) & w Mary
(b 1733) of VA. F-S38129 R1520

John, esf 1776 Spotsylvania Co, VA; PN 1818 Knox Co, TN, aec
64; res 1820 Wilkes Co, NC, ae 66 when only family w aec
60; sol liv 1839. F-S41740 R1520

John, b 10/5/1755; esf VA Line; dd 1/13/1824; md 2/21/1781
Margaret, sis/o Thomas BURNS, Prince Georges Co, MD; wid b
11/22/1761; ch births: Truman 7/18/1782, Ann Truman 11/2/
83, Mary Smith 8/4/86, Jemima Waddey 3/4/89, Elizabeth
7/4/91, Maryanne 1/21/92, Sarah 9/17/96, & Hiram 3/18/99;
wid PN ae 84 Montgomery Co, KY, 1843; res 1844 Marion Co,
KY. F-W27146 R1520

Joseph, esf 1780 Amherst Co, VA; mvd c1796 to TN, where PN
Roane Co 1832; dd 3/13/46; md during latter part of RW to
Rebecca BOWMAN, Amherst Co, VA; wid PN aec 94 Bradley Co,
TN, 1846; res there 1849 ae 100; Amherst Co clerk sent AFF
that only marriage record of a Joseph LANE in his Co was a
MB 9/30/1795 between Joseph LAIN & Patsey WRIGHT with consent of her f Kelliss WRIGHT & they were md same day, also

LANE (continued)
- a William LAYNE md there 1794 Rebecca BERRY; sol eldest ch Anderson bc 1782 & dd 1815; 3rd ch Sarah b 6/5/1785, md Mr HYTEN/HYTON; s John res Cleveland, TN, 1846 ae 56; d Polly PRIGMORE AFF McMinn Co, TN, 1849 she b 9/18/1785, md 1807 Thomas PRIGMORE (b 19/6/1787), & their ch births: Mahala 10/27/1808, Kezia 12/16/09, Levinia 3/20/11, Sally 4/25/12 Malinda 1/15/14, Ruth Kelley (date not given), & Lucinda Greene (date not given); Bersheba BOWMAN AFF 1846 sol wid was sis/o her h; Winiford RENTFROE (d of Philip STEPHENS) AFF 1849 ae 66 her m was sis/o sol; sol d Sarah HYDEN res 1846 Brady Co, TN; sol surnamed also spelled LAIN. F-W1783 R1520
- Larkin, esf 1781 Spotsylvania Co, VA, where b 2/22/1762; mvd to Louisa Co, VA, thence KY, thence IN where PN 1833 Parke Co 1833; QLF 1913 from Quincy SWAIN, Rockville, IN, whose d desc of sol. F-S15442 R1521
- Richard, b 1/20/1760 Hanover Co, VA; mvd with f Daniel to Orange Co, VA, where esf 1781; mvd to Spotsylvania Co, VA, where afp 1845 & PAR; dd there; his exec s Fountain H afp 1850 & PAR; heirs who afp 1877: Miss Rebecca LANE, Waller LANE, Fountain H LANE, Margaret A LANE, Martha G HILMAN, & John L HILMAN (gds of William HILMAN); heirs PAR. F-R6136 R1521
- Thomas, esf 1776 Surry Co, VA, where b 1751; afp 1834 there, & PAR, insufficient proof of svc. F-R6138 R1521
- Turner, esf ae 16 Hanover Co, VA, where b 1/9/1762; mvd 1783 to GA, thence 1786 Washington Co, VA, thence 1895 Bourbon Co, KY, thence 1807 White Co, TN, where PN 1832 as Turner, Sr when ch mbnn; part of svc sol sub for elder bro James; dd 8/13/40; QLF states sol dd White Co, TN. F-S1916 R1521
- William, b 3/10/1754; esf 1775 in VA regiment; PN 1824 Charlotte Co, VA; res there 1824; ch then: Sally (b 1/10/1779) Betsy (b 1/24/81), & Esther (b 1786). F-S38124 R1521

LANEY, John, b 9/9/1758 Lancaster Co, PA; mvd to Frederick Co, VA, where esf 1779; mvd 1805 to Washington Co, PA, for 4 years, thence OH where PN 1833 Mason Co; younger bro William AFF then Harrison Co, KY. F-S18486 R1522
- William, b 8/12/1760 Lancaster Co, PA; esf 1780 Frederick Co VA where res; mvc c1790 to KY, where PN 1832 Harrison Co; elder bro John res 1832 Brown Co, OH. F-S13684 R1522

LANG, John H, b 6/24/1751 Germany; esf in French army; sailed Brest, France 7/1/1782 for America; afp 1832 Goochland Co, VA; PAR, RW svc in foreign army. F-R6172 R1522

LANGDON, Judith, former widow of Thomas HAYS. (F-W20375)

LANGFIT, Philip, esf 1776 in 3rd VA Regiment; PN ae 60 Prince Co, VA, 1818; res there 1820 with w ae 58 mbnn, d Dolly ae 27 & d Lucy ae 19; QLF states sol bro/o William. F-S38126 R1522

LANGFITTE, Francis, esf 1776 in 11th VA Regiment; PN 1826 Wood Co, VA, ae 65, when w Embly ae 64 & d Nancy GLASSCOCK aec 30; QLF states sol md sis of John HANCOCK, further sol bro

LANGFITTE (continued)
　Thomas KIA RW, bro Philip RW sol & bro William (b 1735, dd 1831, md Margaret CAMPBELL, Indian War & RW sol). F-S38131 R1522
LANGHAM, Elias, esf 1777 Yorktown, VA; BLW1789 issued 8/10/1789; also gtd BLW by VA; member/o the Society of the Cincinnati; PN ae 59 Madison Co, OH, 1818; res there 1821 ae 71 occupation surveyor, when had 6 ch mbnn; QLF 1935 from desc Margaret R SANDELS, Tallahassee, FL, who also desc of Colonel Wharton RECTOR, army paymaster stationed c1825 in AR, who gtd BLW Crawford Co, AR, & dd 1842; QLF states sol dd 4/3/1830 at res/o Honorable Samuel BASKERVILLE, Madison Co, OH. F-S41747 R1522
　James, esf 1779 VA; PN ae 60 Jasper Co, GA, when occupation farmer, & had w aec 30 & ch: James Washington ae 12, John Madison ae 8, Mary Ann ae 6, Marshal Jackson ae 4, Samuel Hammond ae 2, & Jane ae 8 months; dd 10/28/29 there; md there 7/24/1808 Elizabeth MARTIN; wid md (2) Elijah GOLDSBY, who dd 6/1842; wid PN there 1856 ae 62; gtd BLW84041 Conecuh Co, AL, 1856, when her ch by sol liv: James W, Samuel H, John M, Thomas T, Mary Ann, Jane & Martha Ann; wid res there 1867 ae 79 when gave oath of allegiance to US, & PN restored after Civil War. F-W11070 R1522
　Joshua, esf 1776-7 Bedford Co, VA; dd Fall 1836 Amherst Co, VA, while res Co Poorhouse; s Isham afp ae 68 Bedford Co, VA, 1844; s Joshua gave power of attorney to agent 1854 in Bedford Co, VA, 1854; both PAR. F-R6146 R1522
LANGLEY, William, esf c1779 Petersburg, VA; dd 7/24/1815 Camden, SC, where had been res several years & had been postmaster; md 9/18/1783 Lucy (b 8/27/1763), d of James HOWZE, SC; wid afp 1841 Fairfield District, SC, & PAR, insufficient proof of svc; several s's & 1 d res there then, including s Samuel, who was physician; QLF 1931 from Mary Langgley (Mrs Fred W) STRIEBY, Washington, DC, states her f's gdf William B LANGLEY & William B's f William LANGLEY Sr both RW sol's. F-R6147 R1522
LANGLY, James, b 3/23/1762 Hampton, VA; mvd to Orange Co, NC, where esf 1780; res after RW Santee Hills, SC, thence Augusta Co, GA, thence Eatonton, GA, thence Troup Co, GA, where PN 1833 ae 70. F-S31813 R1523
　John, b 12/15/1760 on James River, VA; mvd when infant with f to Ninety-Six District, SC where esf while res on Little River; f dd & m md again; mvd to near Kinston, Dobbs Co, NC, for c13 years (md there), thence Iredell Co, NC, for 1 year, thence Randolph Co, NC, for 3 years, then to Camden, Kershaw District, SC, for 6 years, thence c1805 Wilson Co, TN, thence 1821 Hickman Co, TN, thence 1833 Maury Co, TN, where PN 1833. F-S4502 R1523
LANGSDEN, Charles, BLW12314 issued 3/22/1790. F-BLW12314 R1523
　William, BLW12315 issued 4/22/1794. F-BLW12315 R1523
LANGSDON, Charles, esf 1779-80 Hillsburg, NC, in VA regiment; mvd after RW to Mercer Co, KY, thence Bullitt Co, KY where

LANGSDON (continued)
   PN 1819; res there 1820 aec 58-59 occupation farmer with w aec 58, d aec 23, & s ae 16; dd 10/11/31 leaving ch: John (res 1837 Bullitt Co, KY), Elizabeth w of Royal LANGSDEN, Mary, William (res 1837 Jefferson Co, KY) & Charles (res OH or MI 1837) all ae 21+ at f's death; md 12/18/1781 Edith at house/o her f Richard BURKS, Burks Old Store, (MB 12/15/81 between Charles LANDALE & Edith BURKS) Prince Edward Co, VA wid b 4/11/1759; apf 1837 Jefferson Co, KY; PAR, md after termination of h svc; PN ae 77 there 1843 when wid had furnished Co clerk's certification of MB which showed marriage in 1781, not in 1788 as she had previously wrongly stated; wid sis of Amelia RAIN & Elizabeth BURKS; surname spelled LANGSDALE & LANDALE. F-W441 R1523

LANHAM, Greenberry, esf 1780-1 VA; dd 11/30/1810; md 5/25/1785 Catharine; wid afp ae 81 Casey Co, KY, 1844 when sis Mary COFFEY AFF there; wid decd in 1853, when heirs A J LANHAM, Pleasant LANHAM, & Mathers LANHAM gave power of attorney to agent to afp; wid & heirs PAR. F-R6151 R1523

John, esf in 1st MD Regiment & discharged 1779 for total disability; PN 9/4/1789 for that disability & paid by VA agency; dd Fall 1801 Charles Co, MD; md Susanna there c1 year after RW; wid appointed adm of h's estate 1802; PN due sol paid to William BARRY 1806, then adm of sol estate; wid PN 1826 Annapolis, MD; dd c5/15/1838 leaving s John & d Betty (w/o Robert BIER?, res Baltimore, MD); ch afp then & PAR, since not eligible for PN under current PN laws; PN Office noted F-number should have been F-R6152. F-S30534 R1523

Thomas, b 1757 Prince Georges Co, MD; esf 1776 near Bladensburg, MD, in MD regiment, while res with parents whose farm lay in both Prince Georges Co, MD, & Montgomery Co, MD; mvd after RW to Wheeling, WV, thence Madison Co, KY, where PN 1836, when res there c50 years; bro Stephen AFF there then he b 1760 Prince Georges Co, MD. F-S30534 R1523

LANIER, Lewis, bc 1756; esf 1778 Sussex Co, VA; mvd to NC where again esf; mvd c1790-2 to GA where res Greene Co, St Marys, Jefferson, Bullock & Screven Co's; member of state legislature/o NC & GA; dd 2/12/1839 leaving wid Esther & ch: Noel, James, Isaac L, Amy KELLY, Elizabeth McCALL, Sarah STRICKLAND, Mary McCALL, & Thomas B (eldest s by 1st w); md (1) Nancy, d of General Thomas BUTLER, Essex Co, VA, during RW, & she dd; md (2) 1803-05 Esther THORN; s Thomas B f of 10 ch in 1847; s Thomas B afp ae 54 Screven Co, GA, 1846; PAR, for insufficient proof of svc; QLF states sol md (2) Hester THORNE whose maiden name was BUTTS; QLF 190- by great great gdd Mrs W M JOHNSTON, Eufaula, AL, states sol desc/o Thomas LANIER who settled on grant of land which now includes city of Richmond, VA. F-R6153 R1523

LANKFORD, William, b 10/11/1763; esf 1779 King & Queen Co, VA, where res; PN 1833 Chesterfield Co, VA; QLF 1934 from desc Mrs Clara GARRISON, Houston, TX; QLF 1898 from gds (on m's side) W L MOODY, Galveston, TX, whose f Jameson MOODY (War

LANKFORD (continued)
   of 1812 sol) was s/o VA RW sol Lewis MOODY of Essex Co, VA
   F-S8823 R1523
LANNUM, Joseph, esf 1777 Amherst Co, VA; PN ae 77 Campbell Co,
   TN, 1833; dd 11/11/37; agent wrote PN Office for balance
   due to sol wid 1837; no wid shown in file & no indication
   of any action on agent's letter. F-S1846 R1523
LANTER, Jacob, esf 1778 Orange Co, VA, where b 8/11/1762; mvd
   1810 to Montgomery Co, KY, thence 1820 Harrison Co, KY; PN
   there 1833; dd 7/1/37 Campbell Co, KY; md 1784-5 Mary WEBB
   Orange Co, VA; wid PN ae 70-71 Harrison Co, KY, 1838 when
   AFF there by Hannah LANTER ae 73-74 that she witnessed sol
   marriage to Mary; wid had 10 ch; dd 4/1/49 Decatur Co, IN,
   survived by ch: Larkin, Archibald, William, John, James, &
   Delilah FEAR; had bro-in-law Henry CLAYTON; William H FEAR
   adm/o wid estate there 1849; AFF there 1850 by John H FEAR
   F-W10191 R1524
   Peter, esf Orange Co, VA; mvd to Bourbon Co, KY, thence Gar-
   rard Co, KY, where dd 8/14/1811; md Fall 1785 Hannah, d of
   John WEBB, Orange Co, VA; wid PN 1839 Bourbon Co, KY, ae
   73 when d Joanna HUFFMAN AFF she b 6/10/1787; wid res 1843
   ae 70 Fayette Co, KY; res 1849 Grant Co, KY, aec 80; gtd
   BLW40005 there 1855 ae 90. F-W9114 R1524
   Thomas, esf 1775 Orange Co, VA, where b 6/8/1758 & raised c
   12 miles from Co Court House; mvd 1805 to Montgomery Co,
   KY, thence Madison Co, KY, where PN 1833 ae 75; AFF then
   there by Milley WEBB ae 77 she b & raised Orange Co, VA, &
   she knew sol since childhood. F-S31199 R1524
LAP, John, b 1757 Anspiker, Germany; esf 1779 Stamford, CT;
   mvd after RW to Baltimore, MD, thence Bedford Co, PA, then
   to Monongalia Co, VA, thence 1818 Preston Co, VA where afp
   1834 when family only aged & infirm w; PAR, he Hessian deserter, & unable to prove 6 months svc with American army;
   surname also spelled SAP. F-R9200 R1524
LAPRADE, John, esf 1780 Chesterfield Co, VA where b 2/23/1765;
   PN there 1832. F-S5666 R1524
LAPSLEY, Samuel, esf VA; dd 1786 Fort Pitt (now Pittsburgh,
   PA) on way home to VA while on trip to KY; md 10/1785 Margaret IRVIN (MB 10/3/1785 bet sol & Peggy IRVINE), Lincoln
   Co, KY; wid md (2) 6/18/1798 Reverend John LYLE, Mercer Co
   KY, who dd 7/1825; Sally Woods b 7/29/1786, d/o sol & Mar-
   garet, gtd BLW1301 10/29/1792 as his heir-at-law, & she md
   Mr WITHERSPOON; wid ch births by 2nd h Reverend LYLE: John
   R 8/8/1800, Abraham T 9/9/01, & Joel Andrew 5/24/03; wid
   afp Fayette Co, KY but dd there 10/21/42 before claim sent
   to PN Office; s John R LYLE afp for her ch 1844 there, &
   gtd; John LYLE (ruling elder of Timber Ridge Church, Rockbridge Co, VA, b 7/10/1746 there when area in Augusta Co,
   VA, & his w Nora REID b 2/1743, their ch births: Andrew
   3/1768, John (2nd h/o Margaret IRVIN above) 10/20/69, Joel
   12/19/74, William 9/19/79, Martha 10/1781, Jane 5/28/82
   (md Mr FINDLAY); wid s Abraham T LYLE md 7/1820 Frances H

LAPSLEY (continued)
  HUNDLEY, their ch births: John Andrew 10/5/1823 & Joel Irvin 3/10/1826; wid s John R LYLE md 1/1/1833 Sarah M IRVIN F-W9149 R1524
LARENCE, Isaac, esf 1779 Camden District, SC where b 1762; esf 1780 NC; esf 1780 MD; mvd after RW to Westmoreland Co, PA, thence Forks/o the Potomac, Hampshire Co, VA, thence Mason Co, KY, thence Hendricks Co, IN, where PN 1833, res Washington Township; res 1842 Clark Co, IL; res 1846 Boone Co, IN; surname also spelled LAWRENCE. F-S32373 R1525
LAREW, Abraham, esf 1776 VA; PN ae 73 Hamilton Co, OH, 1828 when only family w Martha ae 63. F-S41742 R1525
LARGE, Joseph, b 1761 Pittsylvania Co, VA; esf 1781 Lincoln Co NC, where res; mvd to Sullivan Co, TN, thence Jefferson Co TN, where PN 1833; s John AFF ae 54 there 1844 his f dd on 10/9/42 leaving w Mary & ch: William, Thomas, Jacob, Adam, Elizabeth, Pheba COOK, Lucy CARMAN, Debora & Sarah HARPER; wid dd 11/7/1843, leaving ch John, William, Thomas, Jacob, Adam, Elizabeth, Phebe COOK, Lucy CARMAN, Deborah & Sarah; s John afp there then for self & siblings for PN due m; ch PAR. F-R6163 R1525
LARGENT, James, esf 1776 Hampshire Co, VA, where res; PN ae 77 Champaign Co, IL, 1832. F-S3857 R1525
 Nelson, esf 1781 Hampshire Co, VA where b 9/27/1762 about 18 miles from Romney; mvd to Fleming Co, KY, for c15 years, thence Champaign Co, OH for 10-12 years, thence 1830 Montgomery Co, IN where afp 1834; PAR, less than 6 months svc; surname also spelled SARGENT. F-R6166 R1525
LARKIN, James, esf Augusta Co, VA; PN ae 65 Monroe Co, VA 1818 F-S38130 R1526
LARKINS, Presley, esf 1777 ae 12-13 VA as fifer, when res near Stover Town; esf ae 28 TN against indians; esf 1810-1811 ae 47-48 New Port, KY, against British & indians; afp ae 72 Floyd Co, IN, 1835; PAR, insufficient proof of RW svc & no PN authorized for svc on frontiers against indians; res 1851 Johnson Co, KY. F-R6168 R1526
LARRANCE, John, esf 1778 in VA regiment; POW 1780, escaped after taken to England & returned to America after RW; PN ae 68 Gwinnett Co, GA, 1828, res Lawrenceville; gtd BLW1493 there 1829; dd there 1/29/41; md 9/3/1788 Beheathaland SMITH, Pittsylvania Co, VA; wid PN ae 72 Gwinnett Co, GA, 1843; gtd BLW13414 there 1855; file contains list of following marriages from Pittsylvania Co, VA, clerk for 12-month period beginning 1787: Jeremiah WALKER & Mary MALLICOAT, John LINSEY & Ann WITCHER, John KESSEE & Betsey PASSONS, John LARRANCE & Behesland SMITH; surname spelled also LAWRENCE; QLF 1939 from great great gdd Kathleen Lawrence GRIFFIN, Atlanta, GA, further sol s George b 1780 NC mvd to Jasper Co, GA, md Sarah MOSELEY (b 1797 NC, dd 9/28/1869), mvd to Paulding Co, GA where dd 1850, had s George who esf 1862 Civil War in 60th GA regiment, md 3/25/1847 Eliza (d/o Oliver BRINTLE & Sarah BROWN/o Paulding Co, GA)

LARRANCE (continued)
& their ch liv 1895: George M, Mrs Sarah C SHELTON, & Mrs
Ida GRAHAM. F-W5310 R1527
  Rodham, esf 1781 Fauquier Co, VA where b 6/20/1762; mvd 1811
to Barren Co, KY, where PN 1832. F-S31195 R1527
LARROWE, Peter, see LERUE, Peter. F-R6171 R1527
LARUE, Peter, see LERUE, Peter. F-R6171 R1527
LARY, John, b 3/9/1751; esf Prince William Co, VA, where res;
PN 1832 Shenandoah Co, VA; last PN payment in file 1837.
F-S8812 R1527
LASHLEY, Edmun/Edmund, b 1/30/1763 Cabin Point, Surry Co, VA;
esf 1779 Wake Co, NC; PN 1833 Pike Co, GA; res Pulaski Co,
GA, when house burned down & family bible lost; dd 5/6/41;
md 3/13/1783 Delilah OLIVE, d/o John, Wake Co, NC; wid was
eldest ch in her family & was sis/o John & Berry OLIVE who
dd Columbia Co, GA; wid PN 1846 ae 94 Pike Co, GA; d Sarah
AFF ae 56 there 1851 she 7th ch/o sol & wid; wid liv 1852;
other ch included Elijah. F-W8014 R1528
  Howell, see LESLEY, Howel. F-S8825 R1528
LASLEY, John, b 11/11/1760; esf 1778 Montgomery Co, VA; after
RW res Tazewell Co, VA, thence KY where PN 1833 res East
Fork of Little Sandy River; surname also spelled LESLEY;
QLF 1931 from Miss Frances F LASLEY, Mullins, SC, who was
great great gdd of a John LASLEY, b 5/5/1744 Scotland, md
there 12/28/1772 Frances BICKLY (b there 2/19/1755), came
to America soon after & settled near Co Courthouse, Louisa
Co, VA, he member of Illinois Regiment of VA troops 1781;
QLF 1937 from desc Mrs Henry E DAVIS, Williamsburg, VA also desc of RW sol Auldin WILLIAMSON. F-S30687 R1528
LATHAM, John, b Stafford Co, VA, where esf 1781 sub for John
LATHAM (no kinship given); PN aec 68 Harrison Co, VA, 1832
res on headwaters of Booth's Creek; dropped from PN rolls
1835 when PN Office determined his svc less than 6 months;
QLF states sol w Susan; QLF 1931 from great great gdd Mrs
Gertrude E ROBINSON, Delaware, OH; QLF 1928 from desc Mrs
Emma McDONALD of Fairmont, NE; QLF states sol md Miss SINCLAIR; QLF 1904 from W O OWEN who desc of a VA RW sol John
LATHAM, who settled Culpeper Co, VA, after RW, md Frances
Dinsmore FOSTER, & their s Philip md Dorothy GRAY & latter
couple great grandparents of querier. F-S8811 R1528
  Samuel, b 1759 Northumberland Co, VA; mvd aec 7 to Guilford
Co, NC, where res during RW; esf there 1775; mvd after RW
to SC, where res on Saluda River for 2-3 years (md there),
thence East TN for 2-4 years, thence IL for c6 years, then
to West TN where res in several Co's before settling Hickman Co, where afp; PAR, less than 6 months svc; res there
1834 when afp again & PAR. F-R6175 R1528
LATIMER, James, see LATTEMER, James. F-R6176 R1529
  William, esf 1779 Brunswick Co, VA; PN 1832 Pendleton Co, ae
70; dd 3/24/38; md 11/12/1815 Elizabeth HOLLIDAY, Scott Co
KY; wid PN ae 65 Harrison Co, KY 1853; QLF 1917 from desc
Mrs A D BUSHNELL, Chicago, IL. F-W26192 R1529

LATTEMER, James, b 8/19/1756 Scotland; emigrated 1775 to York Co, PA, where 1776; esf 1777 in VA troops as wagoner; afp 1832 Washington Co, PA res Canton Township; PAR, less than 6 months svc; dd 6/8/1848; md 1785 Sarah (dd 10/20/1807); d Margaret LATTIMER afp ae 57 Perry Co, OH, 1852; her PAR. F-R6176 R1529
LAUCK, Peter, see LAUK, Peter. F-R6183 R1530
LAUDERDALE, William, b 1741-2 MD; mvd when infant with parents to Botetourt Co, VA, where esf 1777; mvd 1792 to Sumner Co TN where PN 1833; QLF states sol bro of James & John, also RW sol's. F-S4505 R1530
LAUGHLIN, Thomas, b 1763 Hanover Township, PA; esf 1778-9 Washington Co, VA; later esf Sullivan Co, NC (area later TN) PN 1833 Whitley Co, KY; dd there 3/29/44; md Spring/Summer 1785 Elizabeth DUNCAN, Washington Co, VA, who b 7/14/1762; PN 1845 Whitley Co, KY; children mbnn; wid cousin Burton LITTON AFF ae 63 there 1844, earlier res Washington Co, VA F-W9112 R1530
   Thomas, esf 1776 in VA regiment;   PN ae 67 St Landry Parish, LA, 1826 occupation loom maker, when had d ae 14 & d ae 4. F-S36682 R1530
LAUK, Peter, b 12/31/1753; esf 1775 Winchester, Frederick Co, VA; PN there 1832; dd 10/2/39; md 10/27/1779 Emily HEISKELL; wid afp there 1840 ae 79, & PAR; children mbnn; QLF 1912 from desc Mrs William MacDONALD of Keyser, WV, states family record shows sol md Amelia HEISKELL; QLF states sol bro Simon also RW sol. F-R6183 R1530
LAURENCE, Joseph, see LAWRENCE, Joseph. F-S31810 R1530
   Thomas, esf 1777 Pauldings Precinct (later Washington Co), NY; mvd c1703 to Montgomery Co, VA, where PN 1833 aec 69; dd 6/12/35; md there 3/29/1824 Catharine KESLER (MB same day, signed by James SIMPKINS); wid md (2) 1/12/37 Robert SIMPKINS, who dd 6/21/48; wid PN aec 56 Montgomery Co, VA, 1853; gtd BLW29688 there 1855; PN restored there after Civil War 1866; gtd PN increase there 1868 ae 72; surname also spelled LAWRENCE. F-W2632 R1530
   Thomas, see LAWRENCE, Thomas. F-S31205 R1530
LAUTER, Jacob, see LANTER, Jacob. F-W10191 R1530
LAVENDER, Charles, b Amherst Co, VA, where afp early in RW; md there 1785 Lucinda BALLEW (MB 12/21/85 between Charles LAVENDER Jr & Lucy BALLEW); mvd shortly after marriage to NC & sol killed by lightning 5/5/1802 when res Edgefield District, SC; wid then mvd to McDowell Co, NC, for c2 years, thence Spartanburg District, SC, thence 1822 Jackson Co, GA, where afp 1845 ae 79; dd there 6/14/46 at home of s Charles before claim approved; s Charles, as adm/o m's estate afp for surv ch: self, Simeon (res Lamar Co, AL) Willis (res Choctaw Co, MS); s Charles ae 51 in 1853; sol bro of William & Winston, also RW sol's; wid f mbnn res 1789 Edgefield District, SC; wid bro Joseph BALLEW b Amherst Co VA, AFF ae 86 McDowell Co, NC, 1854, his bro John esf with sol & KIA early in RW; William C LAVENDER & John E LAVEN-

LAVENDER (continued)
DER (nephew of Simeon LAVENDER), res 1855 Jackson Co, GA.
F-W8025 R1530
William, esf 1778 VA; PN ae 70 Amherst Co, VA 1830; dd 1/17/35; md 4/4/1781 Sarah d/o John STRATTON of Amherst Co, VA; wid b 2/1768; PN there 1838; dd 3/16/40; d & gdc mentioned 1830; sol & w had "many" ch. F-W8080 R1530
LAW, Henry, b 1/4/1759 Henrico Co, VA; esf 1781 Henry Co, VA, where res; mvd 1816 from Franklin Co (formerly part/o Henry Co), VA, to Green Co, KY, for c2 years, thence Russell Co, KY, where PN 1833; last PN payment in file 1842. F-S31196 R1531
Jesse, b 1/9/1758 Henrico Co, VA; esf 1777 Pittsylvania Co, VA, where res; PN 1832 Oldham Co, KY; dd 11/14/39 Trimble Co, KY; md 12/1/1780 Mary/Polly WILLIS, Pittsylvania Co, VA; afp ae 43 Jefferson Co, IN, when res with s-in-law Francis BARN(E)S, & PAR, proof of marriage; dd there 4/23/44-5; ch: Joel, Willis, John, Elizabeth, Sally, Avyrilla, Daniel & Anderson; eldest s Joel dd c1835 aec 54 Edgefield District, SC; ch who survived m: Elizabeth w of Dick LEMASTER, Sally w of John BARNES, Avyrilla (bc 1789, md 3/29/1806 Francis BARNES), Daniel, & Anderson; Susannah, wid of s Joel, AFF ae 51 Jefferson Co, IN 1850; s Anderson afp for self & siblings 1852 Trimble Co, KY & PAR, proof/o parents' marriage. F-R6188 R1531
John, esf 1781 Henry Co, VA, where res; PN ae 85 Franklin Co VA 1832. F-S8809 R1531
LAWLER, Nicholas, b 9/10/1743 Northumberland Co, VA; esf 1777 Fauquier Co, VA, where res; mvd 1817 to KY for 3 years, thence Jefferson Co, IN, where PN 1833. F-S32372 R1531
LAWLESS, Augustine/Austin, esf 1779 VA; res 1823 Cumberland Co VA, occupation farmer, ae 73 when w Sally ae 73 & widowed d with 3 ch res with him; PN ae 75 Adair Co, KY 1824 when w aec 75 & no ch res with them; dd 10/15/32; md 11/4/1781 Cumberland Co, VA; 1st ch dd when infant; wid PN 1837 ae Russell Co, KY 1837 when her 2nd ch Jesse AFF there ae 55; other ch births: Polly 10/1784 (md Mr STATIN), Susanna 12/1785 (md Mr HAMBLETON), Edward 12/1786, Reuben 1/1788, Benjamin 1/1789, William 5/1790, John 6/1792, & James 8/1794; wid res there 1844 ae 90. F-W2950 R1531
John, b 3/11/1751; esf 1776 Fauquier Co, VA, where res; mvd to Bourbon Co, KY, thence Pendleton Co, KY, where PN 1818 occupation farmer; res 1820 Grant Co, KY; dd there 8/12/47 at home of Urial TONGATE; md 2/7/1780 Mary/Polley STODARD, Stafford Co, VA, who b 1/1755; wid PN 1848 Grant Co, KY; res 1849 there with s-in-law Mr TONGATE; had 9 ch; 2nd ch Henry res there 1848 ae 63; Urial TONGATE & Mason TONGATE AFF for wid there then; wid res there 1848 ae 93 when oldest woman in Co; res there 1849; QLF 1936 from great great gdd Mrs Maggie G Longstreet STOFER, Burns, KS, states sol md Mary CARUTHERS & their d md Uriah TONGATE, whose d md Martin H BRAND, whose d md William L LONGSTREET, who was f

LAWLESS (continued)
of querier, who md Bursy STOFER, s of Civil War sol Jacob; QLF 1927 from desc Margaret E THOMPSON of Saginaw, WI says sol had s John Jr b 6/1/1795 in VA. F-W9109 R1531
LAWRANCE, James, b 3/25/1764 King William Co, VA; esf 1779 Lunenburg Co, VA; mvd after RW to SC, where PN 1833 Spartanburg District; last PN payment in file 1849; surname also spelled LAWRENCE. F-S21858 R1531
LAWRENCE, Absolam, esf 1781 VA; PN 1818 Henrico Co, VA; res there 1821 ae 58 occupation farmer when had no family. F-S40910 R1531
Jacob, b Frederick Co, VA; esf 1781 Fayette Co, PA, when res there; PN there 1832 ae 71; mvd c1846 to Adams Co, OH, to be near children; dd there before 1857; surname spelled also LAURANCE. F-S4521 R1531
John, see LARRANCE, John. F-W5310 R1532
Joseph, b 1755 Albemarle Co, VA, s/o Richard; esf there soon after marriage; mvd to Surry Co, NC, where esf 1777; stepm Isabella LAWRENCE had record of his ae there; PN 1832 Monroe Co, IN, when res Green Co, IN; last PN payment in file 1839. F-S31810 R1532
Thomas, esf 1777 Louisa Co, VA, where res; mvd several years after RW to Mason Co, KY, thence Logan Co, KY, where PN ae 77 res Butler 1832. F-S31205 R1532
William, b 4/1/67; esf 1778-9 Fredericktown, Frederick Co, MD; PN 1819 Pendleton Co, VA; res there 1820 with w Elizabeth ae 48 when had ch Jonas b 6/1800, Margaret b 11/1802, Feliska ae 12, Patsey ae 9, Rebecca ae 7, Sally ae 5 & Jacob b 6/27/1818; BLW1968 issued there 9/25/33; res 1843 in Franklin Co, VA; QLF states sol md 1791 Elizabeth FRIEND & he buried near Franklin, VA (now WV). F-S38128 R1532
LAWREY, Giles, b 1733 Westminster, England; esf 1776 Culpeper Co, VA, where res; PN there 1833. F-S5670 R1533
LAWS, David, b 1744 Halifax Co, VA; esf 1776 Wilkes Co, NC, where res; PN there 1832; dd there 12/2/41; md 2/1778 Martha MITCHELL at home of her f on Moravian Creek, that Co, wid PN that Co 1843 ae 82; res there 1845; children mbnn. F-W5125 R1533
John, esf 1776 Fauquier Co, VA where PN 1818; res there 1820 ae 63 when family w Margaret ae 40, d Sally ae 4, & s John H ae 18 months; res 1829 OH where mvd to be with his children; dd 2/27/40; QLF 1927 from desc Glenna B (Mrs Horace H) BAKER, El Paso, IL, who also desc of VA RW sol William GUSTINE (b 1552, dd 1790, w dd 1824). F-S41754 R1533
LAWSON, Benjamin, esf 1777 Portsmouth, VA; PN 1819 Charlotte Co, VA, ae not given. F-S38127 R1533
Benjamin, esf 1777 in VA regiment where was lieutenant; BLW 1225 issued 3/1/1827 to s & heir Fabius, Richmond, VA; QLF states a VA sol General Benjamin LAWSON, esf Botetourt Co, VA, was res 1774 near Abingdon, Washington Co, VA where he was a young lawyer. F-BLW1225 R1533
Claiborne Whitehead, bro/o Benjamin above, esf c1776; KIA at

LAWSON (continued)
   Battle of Buford's Defeat 6/22/1780, a captain of VA Line; BLW1460 issued to nephew Fabius & other heirs 1828 Henrico Co, VA. F-BLW1460 R1533
Drewry, b Pittsylvania Co, VA; esf 1780 Henry Co, VA, where res; afp ae 79 Hawkins Co, TN, 1835; PAR, svc less than 6 months. F-R6201 R1533
Jacob, b 1781 Bedford Co, VA; esf 1779 Henry Co, VA, where res; PN 1832 Hawkins Co, TN; dd there 9/5/33; md 8/1784 at Captain AMIS's there to Polly; wid PN ae 74 there 1839; dd 7/10/44 home of s Lazarus; d Betsy b 8/1784, liv 1839; ch who survived m: Lazarus (1845 ae 51), Matilda (md Anderson CAMPBELL of that Co), Lewis (res McMinn Co, TN), Russell, Reynolds, Elizabeth (md William FINNELL) & Anna (md Thomas HAYNES of Bradley Co, TN, who decd in 1845), they all liv 1845. F-W86 R1533
James, b 3/1760; esf 1777-8 Hampshire Co, VA, where res; mvd c1823 from Adams Co, OH, to Greenup Co, KY, where PN 1832; bro mbnn liv then; QLF states sol dd Greenup Co, KY; QLF 1907 from gdd Mrs Mary J ARNOLD of Lakeport, Lake Co, CA, states sol b 3/11/1760, dd 11/11/1844 near Greenupsburg, KY & was also War of 1812 sol from Adams Co, OH. F-S30530 R1533
John, esf 1778 in VA Line; PN 1828 Washington Co, KY, res on Glenn's Creek, ae not given; BLW1697 issued 12/31/1831; QLF states a VA RW sol John LAWSON dd ae 83 Nelson Co, KY, md Ellen PIERCE. F-S46502 R1533
John, b Bedford Co, VA; esf Cumberland Co, NC, sub for David LAWSON (kinship not given); PN ae 78 Morgan Co, TN, 1832; dd 6/4/38; md on 4th Sunday of January 1775 Anna LAWSON, Stokes Co, NC; ch John, Betsy, & Joshua b before Battle of Guilford, 11 more ch afterward; ch included eldest Betsy, John, Joshua, Lydia, Patsey, Runels, William, Staples, & Meliela (9th ch, ae 44 in 1840); wid afp ae 81 Morgan Co, TN, 1838 & PAR, insufficient proof/o marriage; sol halfbro Randolph (c2 years younger than sol) AFF 1840 Fentress Co, TN, who also RW sol; sol s William AFF 1842 ae 54 Morgan Co, TN, he having md Delilah BOLIN, Hawkins Co, TN, & they had s Harmon; wid afp 1844 ae 80+ Morgan Co, TN, & again PAR. F-R6199 R1533
John, b 9/7/1760; esf 1777 King & Queen Co, VA, where res; md 11/17/1779 Frances, Ware Parish, Gloucester Co, VA when res adjoining Pitts Parish, they being Quakers; mvd 1798 from Gloucester Co, VA, to Halifax Co, VA; sol PN Smith Co TN 1832; dd 4/2/37; wid b 10/5/1763; PN 1838 Smith Co, TN; res there 1848, when gtd PN increase; William NEELEY AFF 1841 there he md sol only ch Elizabeth (b 4/8/1782), Halifax Co, VA; wid gdd of Daniel HUNTER (b 10/10/1678, dd 11/4/1743) & w Mary; James WASHER b 2/14/1785. F-W376 R1533
Mormon, b 1751 Bedford Co, VA; esf 1778 Henry Co, VA, where res; mvd from Lee Co, VA, to Stokes Co, NC, thence Hawkins Co, TN, where PN 1834 when res there 30 years; dd 9/16/42

LAWSON (continued)
   Hancock Co, TN; md (2) Elva COLLINS, Lee Co, VA; wid PN ae 85 there 1855; gtd BLW39226 there 1857 ae 82; ch included Peter, Mormon, & Phoebe. F-W9501 R1533
   Nathan/Nathanal, b 3/15/1755 King William Co, VA; esf Charlotte Co, VA, where res; mvd 1802 to Washington Co, KY; PN there 1832; bro Joshua AFF there then. F-S31197 R1533
   Reuben, esf 1776 Pittsylvania Co, VA, where b 1760; esf 1780 Montgomery Co, VA; mvd c2 years after RW to Hawkins Co, TN thence c1825 Roane Co, TN, thence 1833 Monroe Co, TN where PN 1833. F-S1547 R1533
   Thomas, b 1754 Albemarle Co, VA; esf 1775 Mecklenburg Co, NC where res; PN 1832 Iredell Co, NC; dd 5/19/45. F-S44492 R1533
   William, esf 1779 Franklin Co, NC, where res; esf 1781 Montgomery Co, VA at uncle's home; PN ae 68 Scott Co, VA 1832; dd 1/30/52; QLF states sol known as William Sr; QLF states sol William Sr listed on 1840 Census ae 86 as RW PNer. F-S10969 R1533
   William, b 1758 Halifax Co, VA, where esf 1781 sub for John LAWSON (no kinship given); mvd after RW to Adair Co, KY, for 12 years, thence Gibson Co, IN, for 15 years, thence Wabash Co, IL where PN 1833 res Mt Carmel. F-S32374 R1533
LAWTON, Robert, see LORTON, Robert. F-R6454 R1534
LAWYER, John Adam, esf 1776 Lancaster Co, PA; md 10/5/1776 or 11/5/1776 Margaretta CONRAD, at Lutheran Church, Tulser Howan? Township in Berks Co, PA; 1st ch b 1777; mvd to VA 1780; dd 1799; wid afp ae 83 Frederick Co, VA 1837, & PAR, insufficient proof of svc; ch Eve Maria NEWCOM & Elizabeth BOLES/BOWLES gave POA to agent 1854 to afp Frederick Co, VA; their signatures witnessed by James BOWLES & James Edward BOWLES (no kinship given); surname also spelled LAYER & LAWIER. F-R6211 R1534
LAY, William, thought he b VA; esf 1779 Salisbury, Wilkes Co, NC; res after RW there, thence Pendleton Co, SC, thence c 1810 Warren Co, TN, thence Wayne Co, TN where afp 1840 aec 80; afp aec 83 there 1842; both PAR. F-R6213 R1534
LAYLAND, William, esf in 8th VA Regiment; BLW381 issued 12/26/1807. F-BLW381 R1534
   Jacob, esf Cuilpeper Co, VA; PN ae 73 Cocke Co, TN 1832. F-S4504 R1534
LAYNE, Anthony, esf 1778 Goodchland Co, VA where b 10/20/1759; PN there 1832. F-8822 R1535
   Robert, esf 1779 Goodland Co, VA, where b 7/11/1758; mvd to Albemarle Co, VA where esf 1780; res there c20 years after RW, thence Kanawha Co, VA, for c5 years, thence Clark Co, OH, where PN 1832 when s Lewis mentioned; QLF states a Robert Lane esf VA, later PN, & dd Springfield, OH. F-S4489 R1535
   Samuel, b 1/14/1759 Goochland Co, VA; esf 1777 Fluvanna Co, VA, where res; res after RW Bedford Co, VA, thence Patrick Co, VA, thence Floyd Co, KY, thence c1829 Lawrence Co, OH,

LAYNE (continued)
  where PN 1832. F-S4493 R1535
LAYTON, John, esf 1776 Middlesex Co, VA; decd in 1833 when s
  John afp there, & PAR. F-R15775 R1535
  Robert, esf 1775 Fauquier Co, VA; PN ae 86 Spotsylvania Co,
    VA; gtd VA BLW then; dd 3/6/38 leaving no wid but ch: Ri-
    chard (res 1842 Danielsville, VA), John, Elizabeth GORDON
    (res ae 75 Spotsylvania Co, VA, 1854); ch Robert & Ann EL-
    LIS dd before f; latter survived by ch Elizabeth C & Mary
    V ELLIS. F-S46638 R1535
LAZEAR, Hyatt, esf 1776 Frederick Co, VA, where b 1744; mvd to
  Washington Co, PA, where esf 1779; mvd to Pittsburg, PA,
  thence Lewis Co, TN, where afp & PAR; Co court considered
  him "an infamous character" who made frequent afp's, when
  he actually only served against indians & not in any regu-
  lary constituted military units. F-R6219 R1535
LEACH, Andrew, esf in VA regiment; dd 1814 VA; md 7/18/1786-87
  -88 Mary, d of Mrs Elizabeth PILCHER/PITCHER, Stafford Co,
  VA; BLW6914 issued 6/18/1831 to sol ch Elizabeth CRAIG,
  Nancy, & Sarah STANLEY, & to ch of decd s John LEITCH (Mary Belinda, Angelina, & Emelene Virginia); wid afp ae 71
  Washington, DC but dd 1 week later on 7/24/1838; PN gtd to
  surv ch Elizabeth CRAIG & Sarah STANLEY; QLF states sol
  esf Stafford Co, VA. F-W24521 R1536
  Burdett, b 8/13/1763 Fauquier Co, VA; esf 1780 Little York,
    PA, sub for bro George; also bro/o Valentine who had fami-
    ly bible; PN 1832 Franklin Co, GA, where dd 5/7/35; md Ju-
    dith, d of Joseph & Rachel COOK, Wilkes Co, GA, 2/4/1798;
    wid b 8/12/1779; PN 1853 Franklin Co, GA; ch births: Bet-
    sy 11/27/1799, Polley 8/12/02, Susan 1807, Milly 1810, Ra-
    chel 1812, George 1814, & William 1816; wid gtd BLW38519
    Wood Co, TX, 1855; surname also spelled LEECH & LEITCH.
    F-W3567 R1536
  George, esf 1777 Fauquier Co, VA; wounded in battle, & bro
    Thomas served as sub for 3 months to finish enlistment; PN
    ae 75 Wood Co, VA, 1832 when res there c25 years; mvd 1837
    to Jackson Co, OH where dd 2/20/38; md 12/29/1785 Ann BIG-
    BEE, Fauquier Co, VA; wid PN ae 73 Jackson Co, OH 1848 res
    Lick Township; res 1848 Washington Township, that Co; res
    there 1855 when gtd BLW3764; dd there 7/22/56 at home of s
    Thomas W; ch births: Fanney 12/28/1786, Susanah Bigbee
    11/16/88, Willis 12/16/90, Luis 5/1/93, Thomas Whiting
    2/17/97, Amelia 7/14/99, Mary 2/4/1804, & George 2/14/0-;
    most of ch res OH 1837; a Thomas W LEACH was JP of Jackson
    Co, OH 1870; QLF states sol md Nancy BIGBY; QLF states Le-
    wis LEACH, War of 1812 sol, md Sarah McKENZIE; QLF 1924
    from desc Mrs M B GIBBONS, Parkersburg, WV. F-W27584 R1536
  John, esf 1777 in VA regiment; mvd soon after RW to Orange
    Co, NC; afb 1800 there & BLW78 issued 11/14/03; dd c1803;
    md 1785 Elizabeth at home/o her f Melichy HATMAKER, Orange
    Co, NC; wid PN there 1842 ae 81. F-W5313 R1636
  Thomas, b 4/1764 Prince William Co, VA, s of James; esf 1781

LEACH (continued)
  Fauquier Co, VA; mvd 1810 to Wood Co, VA, where PN 1832; bro George res there then; last PN payment in file 1837; QLF states sol res 1840 at home of John COOPER, Wood Co, VA; QLF 1907 from J L BUCKLEY, Parkersburg, WV, states his w (maiden name LEACH) great gdd of sol. F-S8837 R1536
LEAGUE, Edmond (AKA LEGUE, Edmund) esf 1777 b 12/9/1759 Amelia Co, VA, where esf 1777; PN 1832 Smith Co, TN where res for 27 years; dd 9/17/38; md 4/10/1792 Mary at home of f John BEADLE (MB 4/1/1793 per Co clerk) Amelia Co, VA; wid PN ae 74 Smith Co, TN, 1839; had 6 ch including Ryleigh who b 1/17/1799, res 1843 Carthage, TN, md 2/26/1829 Jane (b 5/13/1811), & they had Mary b 11/13/1830 & Cinthia Jane b 1/26/33; QLF 1930 from desc Bess L MADISON of Shepherd, TN. F-W378 R1537
  James, esf 1776-7 in 15th VA Regiment; PN 1818 Prince Edward Co, VA, ae 75; res there 1820 occupation farmer when had d Martha ae 40 (her ch: Caty Ann ae 7, Judy ae 5, & s Branch aec 1); QLF states sol mid name Adams. F-S38134 R1537
LEAK, James, b 2/1765 Culpeper Co, VA; esf 1780 Caswell Co, NC where res; after RW res NC, SC & GA; PN ae 68 Pike Co, GA; QLF states a James LEAKE b 4/19/1764 (ancestors came from England c1685), md Mary (d/o Robert SHARP, & she dd 11/19/1808), & his bro Mathew KIA in RW. F-S31822 R1537
  John M, esf c1777 Amherst Co, VA, where b 1758; PN 1833 Rutherford Co, TN; dd 8/24/40 when s Mask liv. F-1550 R1537
  Walter, 11/31/1781 Buckingham Co, VA; esf 1779 Anson Co, NC, where res; taken POW by British, escaped & returned to regiment; PN 1832 Richmond Co, NC; QLF 1934 from desc Mrs J M SLOAN of Gastonia, NC, who also desc of RW sol William PICKETT of NC; QLF states RW sol William LEAKE, b 1734, dd 1797, md Judith MOSELEY, & dd Anderson Co, NC, further sol Walter LEAK md Hanna, Carolina Co, VA, she d/o RW sol William PICKETT, who md Mary TERRY of VA or NC, & dd 1795 Anderson Co, NC, & further VA RW sol James TERRY md Mollie RAIFORD. F-S7136 R1537
LEAKE, William, b 10/1/1759; esf 1777 Albemarle Co, VA, where res, as sub for f mbnn; PN there 1833; dd 9/4/34 leaving a wid mbnn; QLF states sol md Judith MOSELEY & dd in NC; QLF from desc Mrs Z W OGLESBY, Quitman, GA. F-S8843 R1537
LEANY, Daniel, esf 1777 in 9th VA Regiment; PN 1818 ae not given, Wheatfield, Indiana Co, PA. F-S40937 R1537
LEAR, Conrad, esf 1775 in VA regiment, Lancaster Co, PA, where b 1738; mvd 3 years after RW to Lincoln Co, NC, where res 14 years, thence Christian Co, KY, for 3 years, thence Logan Co, KY, for 10 years, thence Mecklenburg Co, KY, for 2 years, thence Todd Co, KY, where PN 1833; dd there; d Mary CROUCH & s George, his only surv ch, afp 1852 there for PN due f. F-S31210 R1537
  George, BLW12327 issued 12/9/1793. F-BLW12327 R1537
  William, esf in Colonel George Rogers Clark's Illinois Regiment/o VA troops; dd 2/15/1816; md 1787 Hannah BAILEY (ma-

LEAR (continued)
rriage license 8/8/87) Fauquier Co, VA; wid PN ae 71 there 1838; res there 1848 aec 82. F-W3833 R1537
LEARD, William, esf 1775 Sharpsburg, MD, in 7th MD Regiment; taken POW at Battle of Brandywine, released, & then esf in 6th VA Regiment; PN aec 64 Lancaster Co, PA, 1818; applied 1820 Philadelphia, PA, for replacement of lost PN certificate. F-S40936 R1537
LEASE, John, b 10/8/1770 near Frederick, Frederick Co, MD; esf 1794 Frederick Co, VA in 1st US Regiment & served to 1797; afp ae 63 Hampshire Co, VA, 1833; PAR, svc not in RW. Old War Invalid Rejected File# 15839 R1538
LEATHERS, Paul, b 4/1/1747; esf 1776 Culpeper Co, VA; PN 1832 Scott Co, KY; surname also spelled LEATHERER. F-S16450 R1538
LEATON, Benjamin, see LEETON, Benjamin. F-S41756 R1538
LEAY, William, b Ireland; to America aec 13; esf Rockbridge Co VA, 1775 where res; res VA c30 years, thence NC, thence TN where PN 1819 ae 60-70 Blount Co, having mvd there recently, & had family to support; res there 1821 with Mr BOGLE when had no family to support; QLF states a RW sol William LEE had land grant at Pikeville, TN, dd there, his w Mahala INGRAM dd 1832, Limestone, AL, their ch: John, William, Thomas, Joseph, Allen, Richard, Henry, & others. F-S38910 R1540
LECKIE, William, b 7/9/1764 Port Royal, Caroline Co, VA, where esf 1775 when res Pittsylvania Co, VA; res Hanover Co, VA, after RW, thence Campbell Co, VA, thence Pittsylvania Co, VA; res there 1833, when PN Campbell Co, VA; dd 10/15/42; md 10/20/1790 Elizabeth Straughan LEWIS, Campbell Co, VA, (his surname LECKEY per Co record) at home/o her f; wid PN 1843 Rutherford Co, TN, aec 80; Mrs Martha LEWIS AFF there then ae 79 she witness at wedding of sol; wid res Davidson Co, TN, 1848 ae 81; ch births: Griffin 3/4/1792, Sucky 2/10/94, Lucy Strayer 2/11/1796, Polly 1798 & Sally Sheppard 6/8/1800. F-W25 R1540
LEDBETTER, Richard, b 1738 Brunswick Co, VA; esf 1775 Tryon Co NC, res Mumfords Cove (area later Rutherford Co, NC); mvd back to Brunswick Co, VA, during last years of RW, thence 1790 back to Mumfords Cove; PN 1832 Rutherford Co, NC; after Battle of Blackstocks, his 2 little d's scalped by indians but w & infant escaped; dd 1/22/41 on waters/o Hightower, Lumpkin Co, GA; md 4/24/1822 Elizabeth BERRY/BARRY, Rutherford Co, NC; wid PN 1854 aec 81 McDowell Co, NC when res with Conrad WARD (no kinship given); sol gds Richard O LEDBETTER res 1855 Rutherford Co, NC, when sol s Johnson mentioned; wid gtd BLW29049 in 1855; surname also spelled LEDBITTER; QLF from E B LEDBETTER, Booneville, MS, states her great gdf Isaac (s/o Richard LEDBETTER, Rutherford Co, NC) was f of Elizabeth SITTON, who was gdm of querier. F-26204 R1540
Rowland, b 1764 Brunswick Co, VA; esf c1780 Wake Co, NC, res

LEDBETTER (continued)
there; mvd to Nash Co, NC, thence Marshall Co, TN, where afp 1839, res on waters of Bradshaw Creek; PAR, less than 6 months svc. F-R6237 R1540

LEDLEE, James, esf 1775 in PA regiment; PN ae 67 Brooke Co, VA 1818; res there 1820 ae 69 when had no family; surname also spelled LEDLIE. F-S38133 R1540

LEDWIDGE, William, esf VA; afp 1819 Spotsylvania Co, VA & PAR, too many assets; dd there 10/1827; md there 1814 Rebecca, wid of Thomas OLLIVE; wid mvd 1833 from VA to Fayette Co, KY; afp there 1857 ae 83 when had been boarding with Thomas & Harriet CHRISTIAN (no kinship given) for 20 years; family bible then held by sol d, who then res MO. F-R6239 R1540

LEE, Abner, b 1780 NC; esf 1781 Washington Co, VA, before Battle of Kings Mountain; res there after RW, thence TN where afp 1846 Jackson Co, TN; PAR, insufficient proof of svc; dd 10/7/52 there at home/o d Alsy/Ailcy VAN ZANDT (1855 ae 49); md when a widower 9/12/35 Sally, wid of James MILLER who TN War of 1812 sol; Abner's youngest ch already grown; wid & Abner had s Granville b 5/4/1837 & s Greenwood b 10/1/1840; wid afp ae 60 Jackson Co, TN, 1855 & PAR; also afb for svc of both h's then & BLAR; sol gds John G VAN ZANDT AFF then there ae 27 he res with m when sol dd; Reverend Isaac VAN ZANDT (no kinship given) AFF there 1651; sol d Ailcy VAN ZANDT afp 1853 there as his legal heir, & PAR; QLF 1939 from great great great gdd Mrs J Porter HINES of Bowling Green, KY states sol f William b 1735-40, dd 1810, md Sarah, & their s Abner md Franky McFARLAND, further she has copy of William's LWT. F-R6257 R1541

Daniel, esf in 1st NY Regiment at Elizabethtown, NJ; esf later Valley Forge, PA; PN aec 60 Monongalia Co, Va, 1818. F-S38136 R1541

David, esf VA; afp 1834 & PAR, svc in indian wars only; nothing else in file. F-R6244 R1541

David, b 1/27/1766 NJ; mvd when young with f to Polaw? River thence Salt River, KY Territory, near Beardstown; esf 1781 on Bear Grass Creek above Falls of Ohio River in KY Territory at Sturgess Station; mvd to Salt River, KY Territory, where esf 1782; svc in Indian Wars 1794; mvd from Hamilton Co, OH, 1829 to Tippecanoe Co, IN, where afp 1837, & PAR, less than 6 months RW svc; dd there 1/10/52; md 7/11/1785 Mary OSBORN; wid afp there 1854 ae 89, & her PAR. F-R6256 R1541

Henry, BLW1299 issued 7/3/1789; lieutenant in Lee's Legion; F-BLW1299 R1541

Henry, b Portsmouth, VA; mvd at early ae to Martin Co, NC, & esf there sub for bro mbnn; mvd after RW to Sampson Co, NC thence Edgecombe Co, NC, thence Rowan Co, NC where PN 1832 ae 80, when res there c36 years; QLF 1926 from desc L P HOLLAND, Suffolk, VA; QLF 19-- from desc Mrs Harry L PERRIGO, Alligan, MI. F-S8833 R1541

LEE, James, esf 1777 Fauquier Co, VA; PN ae 57 Pulaski Co, KY, 1818; res there 1821 ae 67 occupation farmer when w Keziah aec 45 & ch Willis Green ae ae 15, John ae 12, Charles Bethel ae 7-8, Polly ae 5, Drewry ae 3, & Anna ae 2 res with him; dd 12/25/36 there; md 1790-1 Keziah MOBLEY/MOBELY/MOBELEY, Madison Co, KY; wid dd 4/12/44 there; s William AFF 1856 birth dates for sol & wid ch: William 3/17/1792, Lewis 1794, Elizabeth 7/11/96, Willis 1899, Benjamin 1804, John 6/15/06, Charles B 3/26/08, James B 3/12/10, Mary 1812, Drury 6/14/14 & Anna 1816; ch decd 1856: Lewis, Willis, Benjamin, & James B; d Elizabeth md Daniel SMITH; d Mary md Gabriel GODBY/GADBY who later md her sis Anna; wid sis/o John MOBELEY; afp 1856 by ch William, John, & Drury, Boone Co, IN, & PAR, proof of parents' marriage and clear contradiction of dates of birth with dates given by sol in 1821; QLF 1933 from desc W Wayne SMITH, professor at University of Idaho, Moscow, ID; QLF 1930 from desc Colonel L O Stephenson, Mayfield, KY. F-R6250 R1542
James, esf 1777 Prince George Co, VA; PN ae 77 Sussex Co, VA & dd there 1/4/34 leaving wid Mary. F-S8828 R1542
James, esf 1776 Stafford Co, VA; PN ae 68 Clark Co, OH 1818; res 1820 Logan Co, OH, with w "somewhat under my age" & s Enoch ae 14. F-S41762 R1542
James, VA sea svc; esf King George Co, VA; dd c1806 Fauquier Co, VA, when youngest ch an infant; md 1st cousin Mary LEE there (MB 2/2/1787), she sis of James LEE who also RW sol; wid mvd 1811-12 to OH, where PN aec 73 Clark Co, 1840; dd Springfield, OH 12/14/43 leaving ch: Sytha w/o John THOMPSON (res MO), James (res IL), Mary wid/o John CONKLIN (res Clark Co, OH), & Lucinda JOHNSON (res Clark Co, OH); surv ch afp due m 1844 Clark Co, OH, which gtd. F-W5466 R1542
John, esf 1777 Greenbrier Co, VA, against indians; later esf Botetourt Co, VA; PN ae 75 Henry Co, IN 1832; sol surname also spelled SEE; QLF 1921 from desc Cora Davy (Mrs E M) SHERBURNE, Knightstown, IN states sol d Mary b 12/25/1787, dd 3/22/1877, md Mr NUGEN & they had d Elizabeth (b Kanawha Co, WV, 11/1/1804, dd 2/10/1891, md Mr HAYES) whose d Mary (b 11/14/1828, dd 3/17/1896, md Mr DAVY) was m/o querier; further sol s of George, further Michael & Charles LEE were either bro's or uncles of sol; QLF 1913 from desc Essie W (Mrs Leroy R) MORRIS of Long Beach, CA; QLF states RW sol Christopher LONG esf Culpeper Co, VA, where b 1746, dd Henry Co, IN, 8/14/1829. F-S17538 R1542
John, b 6/1/1755 PA; mvd ae 13 to Augusta Co, VA, where esf 1781; PN 1832 Montgomery Co, KY. F-S31208 R1542
John, b 11/7/1749; esf VA; dd 3/17/32; md 2/18/1780 Agness JENNINGS, Buckingham Co, VA, who b 9/5/1761; wid PN Cocke Co, TN, 1844; dd 11/22/47 leaving ch: Stephen b 12/2/1780, Nancy FINE b 11/10/82, Polly NETHERTON b 3/14/88, Hiram b 8/20/90, Phebe JOHNSON, & Sarah/Sally LLOYD. F-W380 R1542
Joseph, esf 1778 Hunterdon Co, NJ where b 4/22/1762; res after RW in VA, KY, & IN; PN 1832 Decatur Co, IN; dd 8/24/37

LEE (continued)
   there when res there 15 years; md 11/12/1788 Eleanor DAVI-
   SON/DAVIDSON, Harrison Co, VA; wid dd intestate 10/26/44
   Decatur Co, IN, & never afp; ch births: Andrew 8/28/1789,
   Ann 5/30/90, Hannah 9/2/93, Elizabeth 8/27/96, Rebecca
   9/6/98, Mary 2/15/1801, Joseph 3/12/03, Davison 6/8/05,
   Eleanor 6/16/07, Martha 12/10/10, Susannah 8/4/13, & Perry
   6/20/17; ch liv 1846: Ann, Elizabeth, Rebecca, Mary, Joseph, Davision, Eleanor, Martha, Susannah, & Perry, when
   William RYAN, adm/o sol wid estate, afp, & PAR, ch not entitled PN under current laws; wid d Rebecca RYAN (kinship
   to William not given) AFF 1854 Decatur Co, IN, she one of
   m's heirs; QLF 1934 from great gdd Stella MARLOW, Indianapolis, IN states sol buried Decatur Co, IN. F-R6245 R1542
Joseph, b 9/4/1738 Southampton Co, VA; mvd when very young
   to Cumberland Co, NC, on Deep River, thence Rutherford Co,
   NC, on Bread River where esf 1774; later esf in SC 3rd Regiment; afp 1834 Barren Co, KY; PAR, listed on RW rolls as
   deserter. F-R6252 R1542
Ludwell, esf 1781 Westmoreland Co, VA, s of Richard Henry;
   aide-de-camp to General La Fayette; PN ae 72 Loudoun Co,
   VA 1833; dd 3/23/36; QLF states sol b 10/13/1760 at "Chan-
   tilly", Westmoreland Co, VA, at home of f Richard Henry,
   further sol later member of VA House of Burgesses, US Senator from VA 1792-1800, res Alexandria, VA, on Shuter's
   Hill, mvd to Leesburg, VA, 1801, had elder bro Thomas who
   dd 1803, at Belmont, they nephews of Francis Lightfoot LEE
   who was a signer of Declaration of Independance & who left
   Belmont estate to nephew Thomas. F-S8829 R1542
Philip Richard Francis, esf in VA line; wounded 9/11/1777 at
   Battle of Brandywine & dd of those wounds c2 months later;
   s Philip Thomas only left issue: Sarah Russell (md Richard
   chard Benjamin CONTEE), Margaret Russell (md James Clarke
   LEE), Eleanor (md William DAWSON), & Ann (md William GAM-
   BLE & dd without issue); Sarah Russell CONTEE had ch: Al-
   lice Lee (wid/o Governor KENT), Philip Ashton Lee (dd lea-
   ving minor ch Allice Lee, Philip Ashton & Sally Kent), Ed-
   mund Henry (dd leaving s & only heir Benjamin, of lawful
   age) & Sarah Eleanor (dd intestate without issue); Eleanor
   DAWSON left ch: William, Robert Lee, Frederick, Philip
   Thomas (dd without issue), Mary Ann, Eleanor Georgiana, &
   Frances Laura; Margaret Russell LEE left ch: Eleanor R wid
   of Edward Henry CONTEE, Caroline w of Josias HAWKINS (of
   Chevy Chase, MD), Elizabeth DYSON (wid), & Sarah Emily w/o
   Thomas C FENDALL (of Chevy Chase, MD); Alice L KENT, E R
   CONTEE, Elizabeth DYSON, L E FENDALL, & R CONTEE gave pow-
   er of attorney to agent to afb, & BLW2366 issued to them;
   state/o VA issued BLW for 4000 acres 7/21/1784 to heirs of
   sol. F-BLW2366 R1543
Samuel, b 1763 Richmond, VA; esf 1781 Hardy Co, VA; esf later there sub for f; mvd 1790 to KY where PN 1834 Spencer
   Co; last PN payment in file 1839; QLF states a RW pension-

LEE (continued)
    er Samuel LEE res ae 77 Jackson Co, IN, per 1840 census.
    F-S38738 R1543
    Sinah, former widow of John EUSTACE. (F-W4014)
    William, see LEAY, William. F-S38910 R1543
    William, b 1/24/1754 Albemarle Co (area later Buckingham Co) VA; esf 1778 Buckingham Co, VA; mvd 1788 to Mercer Co, KY, then 1794 Green Co, KY where PN 1832; dd 2/12/35; md 1/24/1783 Drusilla, d of Samuel STAPLES who gave consent (MB 1/13/83), Buckingham Co, VA; wid bc 12/31/1764; ch included Maryan Gresham 6 1/10/1784, Samuel b 5/12/86, William b 2/17/89, Gresham 7/30/1802, & others; wid PN 1839 Green Co, KY, when s Gresham (holder of family bible) AFF there; wid had lost PN certificate replaced there 1852. F-W9117 R1543
    Zachariah, b 1765 Albemarle Co, VA; mvd aec 4 to Rockingham Co, VA, where esf aec 14; afp 1834 Botetourt Co, VA. F-R6260 R1543

LEECH, Burdett, see LEACH, Burdett. F-W3567 R1544

LEEK, William; esf 1775 Shamokin, PA; later esf Long Island, NY, in company which became part/o Colonel Morgan's VA Regiment; PN 1818 Cayuga Co, NY; res there 1820 ae 73 with w ae 72 & gdd Mary ae 13. F-S42853 R1544

LEEPER, James, b 9/1761 Augusta Co, VA; esf 1780 Lincoln Co, NC, where res; mvd after RW to Haywood Co, NC, then to Franklin Co, TN, thence Jackson Co, AL, thence Washington Co, AR, where PN 1833; QLF 1941 from desc D B LEECH of Hot Springs, AR; QLF states sol kin to Hezekiah WEST; QLF says sol dd 1/7/1842 near Fayetteville, AR. F-S31819 R1544

LEETON, Benjamin, b 8/1758; esf 1779 Amelia Co, VA; PN Brown Co, OH, 1819; res there 1820, when had no family liv with him, occupation farmer. F-S41756 R1544

LEFCEY, Shadrach, esf 1776 VA; PN aec 68 Lincoln Co, NC, 1820, occupation farmer, when had w aec 66. F-S41765 R1545

LEFLER, George, esf 1780 VA; PN ae 74 Harrison Co, IN, 1826 when w decd c10 years & ch all md except 2 & none res with him; previous occupation merchant miller; res from time to time with various of his ch. F-S35522 R1545

LEFOE/LEFAE/LEFACE, John, svc with foreign troops; res 1818 NC & no other data in file; PAR; see file of Mary LAFOY, former wid of Jacob WHITE of VA (F-W8056) F-R6269 R1545

LEFTWICH, Augustine (AKA LEFTWITCH, Augustas), b 9/10/1744 Caroline Co, VA; esf 1780 Bedford Co, VA, where res; PN 1833 there; QLF 1931 from Birda BATY, Bessemer, AL, states her great great gdf Micajah STONE came from England, settled in Bedford Co, VA, md Sarah LEFTWICH, niece/o RW sol Colonel Jabez LEFTWICH, & she possibly d/o William, Augustine, or Thomas LEFTWICH, further Micajah & Sarah STONE mvd 1818 to Lincoln Co, TN; QLF 1894 from Mrs Peyton Leftwich TERRY of Roanoke, VA, states sol md (1) 2/12/1765 Mary TURNER, & (2) 9/1821 Mrs Sarah TURNER, further sol bro of Joel, Thomas & William, further a Stephen TERRY of Pittsylvania Co, VA, md Sarah FUQUA, & dd there, & their eldest s William

LEFTWICH (continued)
was captain in VA troops in 1811 & was gdf of querier's h. F-S11364 R1545
Joel, b 11/22/1760; esf 1777 Bedford Co, VA, where res; esf 1780 as orderly sergeant in company/o Captain Thomas LEFTWICH (no kinship given); res Beford Co, VA, after RW, then c1827 to Campbell Co, VA, where PN 1832; dd 4/20/46; bro's & sis's mbnn; QLF states Colonel William LEFTWICH, Colonel Thomas LEFTWICH, Mary Augusta LEFTWICH, Captain Littleberry LEFTWICH, General Jabez LEFTWICH, & General Joel LEFTall of Bedford Co, VA; QLF 1938 from T B LEFTWICH, Globe, AZ, great gds/o RW sol Jabez LEFTWICH, who was bro/o Joel, further querier veteran of Spanish-American War, his eldest s WW1 veteran, & other s John DeVernon presently ser-in US Army artillery; QLF 1938 from Mary S (Mrs F B) HARRINGTON, Los Angeles, CA, whose d desc/o sol who was bro/o Jabez. F-S8830 R1545

LEGG, John, esf 1776 in 3rd VA Regiment; PN ae 63 Champaign Co OH, 1818; res there 1820 ae 65 occupation farmer with w ae 55 & s ae 20. F-S41758 R1545

William, esf 1780 Culpeper Co, VA, but formerly res/o Prince William Co, VA; dd 7/22/1833 leaving no wid but ch: Nancy w/o Frank/Francis BROWN, Hannah, & William; ch afp 1846 Culpeper Co & Prince William Co, VA but no action on afp's indicated; Daniel COLE, b Prince William Co, VA, who esf 1780 with sol, AFF there 1846 aec 82 sol dd Culpeper Co, VA; AFF then by Daniel O'REAR aec 87 he esf Prince William Co, VA, with sol; sol's claim file had been misfiled by PN Office & was found many years later. F-None R1545

LEGON, William, esf 1780 Prince Edward Co, VA, where res; PN ae 77 Smith Co, TN 1832 when John LIGON AFF there (no kinship given); QLF states sol bc 1750 Halifax Co, VA, & dd 1835 TN; QLF states sol b 1756 VA, dd 1838 Smith Co, TN, md Sarah HEWING, mvd 1808 from VA to TN, large family/o ch QLF states sol b Prince Edward Co, VA. F-S1998 R1545

LE GRAND, Paulina, former wid/o Edmund/Edmond READ. (F-W8084)
LEGUE, Edmund, see LEAGUE, Edmond. F-W378 R1545
LEHBERG, John Henry, see LE MOUNTAIN, John Henry. F-S32376 R1546

LEHEW, David, esf 1777 Frederick Co, VA, where b 1775-76 Lehew Township (area later Front Royal); PN 1832 Westmoreland Co PA; res there 1738; surname also spelled LEEYHEW & LEHEU. F-S22355 R1546

LEIDY, Samuel, b 9/1757 Northampton Co, PA; esf 1779 Greenwich Township, Berks Co, PA where res; esf later Shepherdstown, VA; PN 1833 Bedford Co, PA; last PN payment in file 1842. F-S5681 R1546

LEITCH, Andrew, esf Fredericksburg, VA; KIA 9/16/1776 Battle/o Harlem Heights, NY; Fredericksburg clerk of court informed PN Office 1924 that bronze tablet at Columbia University, New York City, lists sol's name as KIA that battle; surv s & heir James Frisbee issued BLW1251 7/5/1799 & also issued

LEITCH (continued)
BLW2708; records lost 1800 Washington, DC, fire; QLF says sol a major in 1st VA Regiment, he having been res of Dumfries, VA; QLF states MD land records list sol ch as James & Sarah. F-BLW1251 R1546

LEMASTER, Joseph, esf 1776 in VA regiment Morgantown, Monongalia Co, VA when res MD; mvd after RW to Abbeville District SC, thence TN, where PN ae 61 Maury Co; res 1823 Williamson Co, TN; dd there 8/1826 while visiting relatives when res Maury Co, TN; md 1791-2 Mary d of John & Mary WADDELL, Abbeville District, SC; wid PN ae 81 Maury Co, TN, 1839, & dd 4/16/45; 5 d's & 2 s's, including John W b 10/21/1793, Mary (1823 ae 24), & Elizabeth (1823 ae 16); s John W md 10/11/1821 Nancey Lee ALMOND, their ch births: Mary Elizabeth 8/29/1822, Marcus Lefayett 12/20/24 (dd 7/25/1825), Saphrona Ann 8/5/27, Charlott Rabakah 3/9/30, John Brown (dd 8/29/1833) & James Knox Polk (dd 5/28/1835); sol son/o Isaac, & bro/o Isaac, Richard, Benjamin, Thomas, Mary, Cathryne, & Charity; sol wid sis of John, William, George, James, Elizabeth & Jane; QLF 1932 from great great gdd Mary Louise HARDISON, Colorado, TX, states sol wid's f Colonel John WADDELL a NC RW sol, res Brunswick Co, NC, & his ch: John, William, George, James, Jane, Elizabeth, & Mary, further querier great great gdd/o NC RW sol William INGRAM F-W797 R1547

LEMASTERS, Benjamin, b 6/15/1756-7; esf 1776 Monongalia Co, VA while res Warm Springs, Berkeley Co, VA; PN 1832 Nicholas Co, VA; md ? when returned home on RW furlough; QLF 1919 from desc Mrs G A MATTHEWS, Charleston, WV, states sol md Miss Martin of MD. F-S18490 R1547

LEMAY, John, esf 1776 near Hampton, VA; esf 1777 Hanover Co, VA, where res; PN ae 73 Granville Co, NC, 1832; dd there 1/5/34; s mbnn 1855 res there; QLF states a sol --- LEMAY of Hanover Co, VA, was probably KIA in RW, left wid Susanna who came 1785 to Granville Co, NC. F-S7147 R1547

LEMEN, William S, b 10/1/1760 Winchester, VA; esf 1777 Point Township, Northumberland Co, PA where res; mvd 1793 to Genesee Co, NY, thence Ontario Co, NY, for c10 years, thence Ossean, Alleghany Co, NY, thence Steuben Co, NY, where PN 1832 res Danville; dd 3/21/45; md (2) Agness EWART at Williamsburg, Ontario Co (later Groveland, Livingston Co), NY on 3/15/1796; wid bc 9/13/1776; PN 1849 Danville, NY; ch included eldest Samuel S b 2/1/1797 who res 1852 Washtenaw Co, MI; sol kin William S LEMEN AFF there, res Green Oak, he witness at sol marriage to Agness; surname also spelled LEMON; QLF states sol middle name Slough; QLF 1926 from great great gdd Gretchen E McCurdy (Mrs Elmer Lewis) MOHN, Elizabeth, NJ, says sol middle name STOUGH. F-W1200 R1547

LEMMON, Jacob, b 5/7/1763 Frederick Co, MD; mvd aec 10 to Augusta Co, VA, where esf 1780; esf 1781 Frederick Co, MD, while visiting relatives there as sub for kin Andrew HULL; returned home to Augusta Co, VA where esf 1782 against in-

LEMMON (continued)
  dians; mvd 8-9 years after RW to Botetourt Co, VA where PN
  1832; dd there 11/9/48; md there 1/3/1797 Jane GILLILAND,
  who b Rockingham Co, VA, & mvd to Botetourt Co, VA, before
  marriage; md at her f's house on James River c22 miles NE
  of Botetourt Co Courthouse; wid PN ae 80 that Co 1852 when
  had 7 children, eldest in his 55 year; wid res there 1855
  when gtd BLW26990. F-W3698 R1547
LEMMONS, John, esf Rockingham Co, VA; VA BLW3383 gtd 8/6/1784;
  mvd to Monroe Co, VA, where dd 2/7/1841; md 1/2/1800 there
  Mary CARR; wid afp there 1855 ae 77, & PAR, insufficient
  proof of svc & proof he same person gtd VA BLW; surname
  also spelled LEMMON; QLF states sol known as John Jr. F-
  R6281 R1547
LEMON, George, esf 1776 Staunton, VA; res Botetourt Co, VA for
  many years, thence Alleghany Co, VA, where PN 1822 ae not
  given; res there 1823 occupation farmer when had no w. F-
  S38137 R1547
  Samuel, BLW12307 issued 3/10/1790. F-BLW12307 R1547
LE MOUNTAIN, John Henry, esf 1777 Berkeley Co, VA; PN aec 70
  Knox Co, IN, when res there c20 years; AFF there then by
  Charles BREWER, formerly of Berkeley Co, VA (b there). F-
  S32376 R1548
LENOIR, William, b 5/8/1751 Brunswick Co, VA; esf 1776 Surry
  Co (area later Wilkes Co), NC; after RW was that Co county
  clerk, member of NC legislature for many years & speaker/o
  NC state senate; commissioned major general/o NC 5th Divi-
  sion of state militia; PN there 1833; dd 5/6/39; gds I/J P
  LENOIR liv 1860. F-S7137 R1548
LENOX, Charles, esf in VA regiment; res 1821 Clark Co, KY when
  requested transfer of PN, having recently mvd from PA; no-
  thing else in file. F-S25629 R1548
LENT, William, esf 1776 Dumfries, Prince William C, VA; mvd to
  PN ae 74 Nelson Co, KY, where PN 1832 res Bardstown; gtd
  BLW by VA; QLF 1919 from desc Mrs J W WILSON, Mayfield, KY
  states sol md VA, dd 1832 Nelson Co, KY. F-S10983 R1548
LEONARD, Frederick, esf 1776 PA in VA regiment; PN ae 68 Sullivan Co, TN, 1829 when just w res with him; dd 1845 Washington Co, VA, when res with s Henry; disposed/o estate to
  ch before dd; surv ch: Elizabeth, Jenny, Mary, Frederick,
  Henry, Michael, George, William, Samuel, Nancy & Margaret;
  William R RHEA & Newell WHICKER AFF 1854 following ch born
  to sol: Elizabeth, Christiana, Mary, Frederick, John, Henry, Michael, George, Gasper, William, Samuel, Nancy & Margaret; d Elizabeth md Mr SOURBEAR & dd leaving ch: Frederick Leonard, Mahala, Thomas J, Elizabeth, George & Catharine; Mahala SOURBEAR md Newell WHICKER, & dd leaving ch:
  Samuel, Zachariah, Sarah E, Malvina, Jane, Thomas P, Louisa & Willis; sol d Christiana md John MALONE & dd leaving
  ch: Elizabeth (w of Zacharia JORDAN) & Dulaney; sol d Mary
  md David HARR; sol d Nancy md John GREEN; sol d Margaret
  md William GREEN; s Henry afp 1854 Washington Co, VA, for

LEONARD (continued)
all sol's heirs. F-S38911 R1549
George, esf 1779 Hudelberg Township, Berks Co, PA where res, as teamster in 1st Regiment/o Light Dragoons/o VA Line; md there Susanna; mvd 1797 to Augusta Co, VA; dd 2/17/1817, leaving money to ch: George, Adam, Susannah HILLEBRANDT, Elizabeth, John, Margaret, Samuel, & Jacob; wid PN ae 79 Augusta Co, VA, 1842; ch births (family bible entries in scribbled German & months difficult to interpret, all surnames spelled LEANER): David 11/23/1784, George 8/17/86, Adam 11/1/88, Elizabeth 11/19/90, Susanna 10/20/92, Daniel 11/19/95, Jacob 2/15/98, Catharina 5/15/1800, Johnann 2/13/02, Margaret 1/27/05, & Samuel 1/6/07; wid res 1848 Augusta Co, VA ae 83. F-W3834 R1549
John, b 4/7/1754 Germany, & raised there; sold into British svc against Americans; deserted them 1st opportunity; esf 1781 Shenandoah Co, VA, in American unit; PN 1823 Hawkins Co, TN; dd 10/7/41; md 6/1796 Edy SCARBOROUGH, Greenbrier Co, VA; wid b 2/22/1771; PN 1850 Hawkins Co, TN; births of ch: David 3/30/1797, Elizabeth 2/14/99, John 2/19/1801, William 2/5/03, Agnes 7/11/05, Jacob 11/12/07, & Edy 3/11/11. F-W1625 R1550
Michael, b Rowan Co, NC; mvd 1779 to Riddle's Station in KY Territory, where esf 1780; settled in Bourbon Co, KY, then 1786 Livingston Co, KY, thence 1797 Scott Co, KY, thence c 1803 Nicholas Co, KY, thence 1808 Scott Co, KY, then 1809 to Grant Co, KY where afp 1835 aec 73 & PAR; PN there 1836 F-S30542 R1550
Robert, BLW12320 issued 5/29/1792. F-BLW12320 R1550
William, b 6/2/1760 Prince George Co, VA; esf 1776 Bute Co, NC; PN 1832 Franklin Co, NC; dd there 4/1/52; md 12/9/1834 there Priscilla D LEONARD; wid PN, & gtd BLW26424 aec 52 there 1855; res there 1867, when PN restored after Civil War; PN increase there 1868 ae 64 res Louisburg. F-W26212 R1550
LERUE, Peter, esf Loudoun Co, VA; dd 12/24/1832 Livingston Co, KY, when w already decd; s David afp ae 48 Greene Co, IN, 1855 for self & other surv siblings: Abner (res Crittenden Co, KY) & Mary w of Abram MAY (res Newton Co, MO) + 4 ch & surv h Rice D LINCHACUM of sol decd d Elizabeth; PAR, less than 6 months svc; QLF 1931 from desc Mrs Charles SYMONS, Plainfield, IN; QLF 1915 from Miss James Morgan LA RUE of Louisville, KY, d/o James Morgan LA RUE, gdd of James Morgan LA RUE, great gdd/o Jacob LA RUE & his 2nd w June MORGAN (mvd 1784-92 to KY), & great great gdd of Isaac LA RUE of Frederick Co, VA. F-R6171 R1551
LESLIE, Alexander, esf 1777-8 Surry Co, VA; settled after this svc Prince George Co, VA; taught school throughout VA before moving to Sullivan Co, TN, 1832 ae 73-74 when blind & deaf. F-S4539 R1551
LESLY, Howel, esf 1778 Sussex Co, VA where b 1761; mvd to Warren Co, NC, where esf c1781; res there 14 years, then mvd

LESLY (continued)
to Wake Co, NC, thence Moore Co, NC where PN 1833 when res there 14 years. F-S8825 R1551
LESSLY, John, esf 1775 PA & PN by that state; PN 1818 Berkeley Co, VA; res there 1820 ae 85 with w Sarah aec 60; sol dd 1/4/25. F-S38139 R1551
LESTER, Alexander, esf 1781 Charlotte Co, VA; esf later 1781 Lunenburg Co, VA, where res with f; res there after RW to 1811, thence Williamson Co, TN, where PN 1832 ae 78. F-S4538 R1552
Thomas, esf 1780 Alexandria, VA; PN 1826 as Thomas Sr ae 69 Gallatin Co, KY, when had w ae 40-50, d ae 18, s aec 16, orphaned gdc ae 4 & 7, & nephew James LESTER liv with him; elder bro John AFF then they served together in RW, & they both wounded at Battle of Guilford Court House. F-S35518 R1552
William, b 10/3/1761; esf 1779 Bedford Co, VA; mvd to Pittsylvania Co, VA, where esf 1781; mvd to Halifax Co, VA, thence Campbell Co, VA, thence Wilson Co, TN, where afp 1837; PAR, less than 6 months svc; QLF 1932 from desc Jessie P DORSEY of Detroit, MI, states sol b VA & dd 1842 TN; QLF 1930 from great great gdd Mrs W Henderson BARTON of Nashville, TN, states sol dd 6/3/1842 & s/o William; QLF 19-- from desc H A ROE, Austin, TX, who also desc of VA RW sol Original WROE. F-R6298 R1552
LESUEUR, Martel (AKA LESEUR, Martil), b 3/8/1758 or 3/8/1761 Manakin, Cumberland Co (area later Powhatan Co), VA; esf latter Co; mvd to Charlotte Co, VA, thence Henry Co, VA, thence Patrick Co, VA, thence Grayson Co, VA, thence Franklin Co, VA, where PN 1832 when res there c18 years; dd 8/10/43; md 6/10/1781 Elizabeth BACON, Chesterfield Co, VA, desc of Nathaniel BACON; wid PN aec 79 Franklin Co, VA, 1844; ch births: Ludwell 12/22/1782, Polly 1/19/84, Patcy 2/18/87, Betcy 3/5/89, Lucy 4/9/92, Moseley/Mosby 10/2/95, James Washington 10/15/98, Catherine Sally 4/8/1800, Dorothea Bacon 10/2/02 & Grandason Bacon 3/7/05; QLF 1932 from desc Mrs James WARTHEN, Jackson, GA. F-W8035 R1552
LETCHWORTH, Benjamin, esf Louisa Co, VA; PN ae 75 Cooper Co, MO, 1832; QLF 1915 from great great gds George B LONGAN, Kansas City, MO. F-S16918 R1552
LEVENS, Henry, b 3/26/1744; esf 1776 at frontier fort on Ohio River c30 miles below Pittsburgh in VA regiment; mvd 1796 to Kaskaskia River in IL, thence 1828 Monroe Co, IL, where PN 1833, when res with s-in-law mbnn; QLF 1935 from desc Mrs Mary J ARTHUR, Los Angeles, CA, d/o Lucretia A LEVENS, states sol dd Monroe Co, IL. F-S32375 R1553
LEVEVER, John, see DEFEVER, John. F-W1834 R1553
LEVI, Isaac, b 2/1749 Hungary; to America aec 17; esf 1780 Lexington, KY Territory, in VA unit; res KY for c40 years, thence OH for 5-6 years, thence IN, where PN 1832 Switzerland Co; dd 9/21/50 Ripley Co, IN; md there 11/14/1841 Mary/Polly, wid of John TUCKER (whom she md 2/1833 Scott Co,

LEVI (continued)
KY, & they mvd to Ripley Co, IN, where he dd 11/14/1840); John TUCKER RW sol from NC & PN 1818 ae 65 Scott Co, KY, & his s by Mary was ae 17 in 1820; Mary afp 3/1853 Jefferson Co, IN, ae 50 for svc/o 2nd h; dd 10/14/53 leaving several ch, some of whom not yet of legal ae; reference made 1854 to 2 of ch/o Mary & John TUCKER; wid's surv ch gtd PN due her. F-W773 R1553

Judah/Judas, esf Fauquer Co, VA; severely wounded at Battle of Waxhaws 1780; PN for disability 1789; dd 6/24/1829; LWT 10/7/1824 Mason Co, KY, listed w Mary; md 10/22/1783 Mary MAGRAW, Fauquier Co, VA; wid b 1/19/1766; PN 1838 Brown Co OH when s Elias res Louisville, KY; wid liv 1847; QLF 1925 from desc Miss Lelah FORMAN, Mays Lick, KY; QLF 1921 from desc Mrs J M JENKINS of Winchester, KY; QLF 1894 from gdd Rebecca J DUNN, Sardinia, Brown Co, OH; QLF states sol dd Maysville, KY. F-W8037 R1553

Rice, b 5/18/1764 s/o Abraham & w Ann, Westmoreland Co (area later King George Co), VA; esf latter Co 1780; mvd 1808 to Knox Co, TN for 7-8 years, thence Anderson Co, TN where PN 1833; dd 2/12/47 there; AKA Rice LEVY; md 8/5/1819 Priscilla HACKNEY (MB 8/5/19), Knox Co, TN; wid PN Hamilton Co TN, 1853 ae 61; gtd BLW26906 there 1855. F-W5314 R1553

LEVISEY, George, b 1765 Ft Bedford, VA; esf 1778 Henry Co, VA; esf 1781 Franklin Co, VA; PN 1832 Hawkins Co, TN; dd 5/19/37 Hancock Co, TN; md Nancy ANDERSON, Franklin Co, VA, who dd 11/21/1843; ch births: James 10/28/1782 (dd 1855 or 4/1856), Elizabeth 9/17/84, Peter 3/13/86, Reachel 2/6/89, Marget 2/18/91, Thomas 2/24/93, George 4/2/94, Mary 8/14/96, Edmon 5/3/99, Jos 5/19/1802, & Enoch 10/28/04; wid never afp; gds John W LIVESAY gtd PN for Mexican War svc, he liv 1855; s Jesse, adm of m's estate, afp 1857 Hancock Co, TN, for self & siblings & PAR; AFF there then by Jesse LIVSAY, s/o sol s Peter; sol d Elizabeth then decd; 2 of sol ch then res Lee Co, VA, 1 res Ashe Co, NC, & rest res Hancock Co, TN. F-R6304 R1553

LEWALLEN, Richard, esf 1781 Prince Edward Co, VA where b 1763; PN Anderson Co, TN, 1832; dd there 5/8/33; md 7/1/1818 Parazeda/Parisida VOWEL there; wid PN there 1853 ae 57; AFF then by Banester VOWELL (no kinship given), witness at sol wedding; wid gtd BLW34923 there 1855 aec 59; large family of ch mbnn; PN restored 1866 ae 73 after Civil War, res near Clinton, Anderson Co, TN. F-W26211 R1553

LEWIS, Ambrose, VA sea svc, free man of color; esf 1776 aboard ship PAGE; esf 1777 Fredericksburg, VA, for svc on DRAGON; PN 1809 for disability from wounds; PN aec 60 Alexandria, VA (then part of DC), 1818; res 1821 ae 68 Washington, DC, occupation barber, family then s aec 10, rest of ch having grown up, & mvd out; bro Charles RW sol from Spotsylvania Co, VA. F-S36041 R1554

Andrew, PN 1793 Mason Co, VA; no other data in file, records lost 1800 & 1814 Washington, DC, fires. F-None R1554

LEWIS, Andrew, b 10/1758; esf 1777 Botetourt Co, VA where res; svd under f General Andrew Lewis; PN 1833 Montgomery Co, VA; dd 9/25/44; md 6/10/1788 Margaret BRIANT, Botetourt Co, VA; wid PN ae 79 Montgomery Co, VA, 1845; QLF states sol b 10/1759 Botetourt Co, VA, md (1) Elnather Strother MADISON who dd before 1788. F-W3431 R1554

Andrew, appointed brigadier general 1776 by Continental Congress to command troops in VA; resigned 1777; dd 1782 VA, place later named Buford Station on TN & VA Railroad, leaving ch: John, Samuel, Thomas, Andrew, William, & Anna (md Captain Rowland MADISON & dd c1798 Mercer Co, KY, her h dd 4-5 years later Warren Co, KY, leaving ch: Eliza/Betsey, John (dd without issue) & Rowland T); Eliza/Betsey MADISON md Edward WORTHINGTON, & had ch: Madison S, John (1858 ae 46), James (1858 ae 52), Rowland M (1858 ae 48), Mary (dd without issue), Edward (dd without issue), Lucy (dd without issue), Patsey & Jane C; Patsey WORTHINGTON md James L ENGLISH & their d Elizabeth 1858 ae 21; Jane C WORTHINGTON md Charles SHACKELFORD & they had ch: Lucy Lewis (1858 ae 14), Edward Worthington (1858 ae 12) & Elizabeth/Eliza Madison (1858 ae 8); Madison S WORTHINGTON md Mary T WORTHINGTON 1824 & they had ch: Margaret W (md J A JUNY) & 3 ch who dd 1837 & 1838; Madison S WORTHINGTON dd 1834 & w Mary T md (2) Dr George VENABLE; Margaret W JUNY afp 1858 ae 30 Hopkinsville, Christian Co, KY where res, for RW svc/o her great great gdf General Andrew LEWIS, & PAR, not entitled under current PN laws; QLF states sol md 1749 Elizabeth, d of Samuel & Sarah GIVENS, Augusta Co, VA, & sol dd Bedford Co, VA 9/26/1781; QLF 1907 from desc Richard McCULLOCH, St Louis, MO, who also desc of sol s Andrew who lieutenant in 7th, 8th, & 13th VA Regiments; QLF states sol bro/o RW sol Major William LEWIS. F-R6308 R1554

Daniel, BLW12305 issued 5/16/1791. F-BLW12305 R1555

Davis, esf Dinwiddie Co, VA, where b 1759; dd 1/2/1831; md there 12/24/1785 Mary FLANDERS; wid afp ae 87 there 1844 & PAR, insufficient proof of svc; dd 10/11/44, leaving ch: Miles bc 1787, John B bc 1802, William, & Dicy (md Grief HARDAWAY & res 1851 GA); sol bro Jesse res 1844 ae 74 Dinwiddie Co, VA; sol bro Raul res Brunswick Co, VA, then ae 87, also RW sol; s's Miles & John afp 1851 Dinwiddie Co, VA, for selves & siblings, & PAR; s Miles liv VA 1860. F-R6323 R1555

Ezekiel, b 1755 Shenandoah Co, VA; esf 1781 Westmoreland Co, PA, where res; res there for 9 years after RW, thence Armstrong Co, PA, where PN 1832 res Sugar Creek Township; referred then to gdf then decd who had res Shenandoah Co, VA & to gdf s Mordecai, also decd, who held family bible; QLF 1908 from desc M B (Mrs Will B) PATTON, Philadelphia, PA. F-S4533 R1555

Feabus/Fabius, esf 1779 in VA regiment; PN ae 75 Fairfax Co, VA, 1820, occupation house plasterer, when had widowed d who had 4 small ch. F-S38135 R1555

LEWIS, George, esf 1781 Accomac Co, VA; PN ae 57 there 1819, when family was Betsey HINMAN & her s John ae 4; dd 5/9/34; md there 11/21/1822 Elizabeth; wid md (2) Richard SUMMERS who dd; wid PN ae 65 there 1853; res there 1866 ae 80 when s mbnn; res there 1869 ae 83, when a John HINMAN (no kinship stated) res there; wid gtd BLW26967 there 1855, & gtd BLW108907 there 1869; PN restored there 1867 after Civil War; QLF 1932 from desc (on m's side) Mrs Nettie L F PUCKETT, Mount Pleasant, Monroe Co, AL. F-W7218 R1556

Henry, VA sea svc, esf VA in army; later esf as marine on a ship; dd 8/23/1799 Caswell Co, NC; md 1777 Polly DOUGLAS, Caroline Co, VA; wid afp 70 Todd Co, KY 1832; dd Henry Co, IA 2/1/41 ae 79; only surv ch Charles afp 1852 ae at least 70; both PAR, insufficient proof of svc. F-R6326 R1556

Herbert, esf 1778 Dinwiddie Co, VA; PN ae 74 Chatham Co, NC, 1833; dd 1/15/41; QLF 1926 from great great gdd Helen Lewis (Mrs Arthur B) SHULTZ, Indianapolis, IN. F-S4529 R1556

Jacob, esf 1775 Berkeley Co, VA, where b 4/15/1755; PN 1833 Tyler Co, VA, where dd 6/23/40 or 6/29/43; md there 12/17/1816 Mary PARKER, wid of William WATSON whom she md 1796-7 Greene Co, PA; William WATSON dd 8/26/1814 while in War of 1812 svc; she afp for War of 1812 svc/o 1st h & PAR (see Old War Widow Rejected File#18831); births/o ch by William WATSON: Frances 6/15/1800, William 8/2/04, David 2/27/06, Nancy 8/11/08, Mary 2/10/10, Prudence 11/18/11, & unnamed male ch 9/10/14; wid PN ae 77 Tyler Co, VA, 1853 for svc/o 1st h when her bro Richard PARKER res there; wid dd 10/29/54; sol bro-in-law James CURTIS AFF ae 80 Ohio Co, VA 1854 he was res Berkeley Co, VA, during RW; QLF states a desc/o sol accepted for membership in DAR. F-W8044 R1556

James, b 4/6/1756 VA; esf 1776 Albemarle Co, VA, sub for neephew William T LEWIS; mvd 1812 to Franklin Co, TN, where PN 1834; P O Address, Winchester, TN, in 1843; dd 2/21/49; md (1) 8/5/1779 ?; md (2) 10/1826 Mary/Polly MARKS (MB 10/17/26), Albemarle Co, VA; wid PN ae 68 Franklin Co, TN, 1853; gtd BLW3067 there 1855; dd 2/1/58. F-W303 R1556

Jesse, esf 1780 Albemarle Co, VA where b 5/13/1763; PN there 1832. F-S5680 R1556

Joel, b Albemarle Co, VA, s of William Terrell Sr; esf 1776 ae 16 VA; mvd c1777 to Surry Co, NC with f & bro's William Terrell Jr, Micajah Green, & James Martin; esf there 1779; mvd 1792 to near Nashville, TN; dd 11/1815 at "Mansfield" near there; md 3/22/1785 Miriam EASTHAM (MB 3/24/86 per Co clerk), Surry Co, NC; 18 ch mbnn; wid md (2) 3/16/16 Colonel Ralph CRABB, Mansfield, TN, & he dd 1/3/36 or 1/5/36; wid res Winchester, TN, until death/o 2nd h, then res with her children in AL & TN; wid PN ae 74 Lauderdale Co, TN, when res with Dr William LEE (no kinship given) at Fulton; AFF then by Dr Wallace ESTILL, s-in-law of her 2nd h; sol uncle James LEWIS (b & raised Albemarle Co, VA) res then Franklin Co, TN, ae 87; sol f KIA in RW skirmish with British just before Battle of Guilford Court House; sol bro

LEWIS (continued)
   William Terrell Jr also RW sol; Maj William B LEWIS & John
   H EATON each md niece of sol wid. F-W780 R1556
John, b 1749 Somerset Co, NJ; esf 1776 Morris Co, NJ, where
   res; 2 years before end of RW mvd to Frederick Co, VA; PN
   there 1833; dd there 3/30/47; md there 8/3/1821 Elizabeth
   TROWBRIDGE; wid gtd BLW61331 there & PN there 1855 ae 84.
   F-18195 R1557
John, BLW12324 issued 12/9/1793. F-BLW12324 R1557
John, esf 1777 Mecklenburg Co, VA, where res; PN ae 74 Halifax Co, VA, 1835. F-S10249 R1557
John, b 6/23/1748; esf 1776 Loudoun Co, VA; mvd west/o Alleghany Mountains & esf Cox's Fort at mouth/o Cross Creek on
   Ohio River above Wheeling; mvd to Washington Co, PA, where
   esf 1780; PN 1833 Rush Co, IN; QLF states a John LEWIS mvd
   from Prince Georges Co, MD, to VA where esf, mvd to KY, md
   (1) Sarah SCEARCE, & (2) Mary KETCHAM, he being buried in
   Liberty Township, Guernsey Co, OH, where s Levi res; QLF
   1938 from DAR agent for sol desc Mrs Verna E CONWAY, Washington, DC; QLF enclosed chart on a LEWIS family of VA as
   follows: William LEWIS emigrated 1650 from WALES, md Elizabeth MARKHAM, Northumberland Co, VA & they had s Vincent
   (b 1707 who mvd to Loudoun Co, VA, & md Ann LONGWORTH) & s
   William who mvd South, further ch of Vincent & Ann Longworth LEWIS were: John md Elizabeth BROWN, Charles md Miss
   HOFFMAN, James md Elizabeth BERKLEY, Joseph md Katherine
   LINTON, George Vincent md Violet GUEST, Sarah md Jonathan
   DAVIS & Ann md Mr JENNINGS, further ch of John & Elizabeth
   Brown LEWIS were: John (b 8/14/1763, dd 8/2/1813) md Hannah LEWIS, Daniel md Susan LEWIS, Vincent md ?, Thomas never md, further ch/o Joseph & Katherine Linton LEWIS were:
   Joseph L md ? late in life, Mary Linton, Hannah E md John
   LEWIS, Susan L md Daniel LEWIS, John md Miss EDWARDS, William Linton md Ann DUNNINGTON of MD, further ch of James &
   Elizabeth Berkley LEWIS were: William B, John, Vincent L,
   Martha I, Nancy L, Susan, Elizabeth B md Mr LESTER, Catherine L md Mr DAME, Jane T md Mr HANCOCK; QLF 1915 from W J
   McILWAIN of Little Rock, AR, whose w desc of sol; QLF 1900
   from great gdd Mrs C W FRY, Huntington, IN, states sol md
   Mary POWER, & they had s Stephen (War of 1812 sol) who had
   d Nancy (md William T GUFFIN), further GUFFIN's had s Walter L (IN Civil War sol) & d Ethel (querier) md Dr FRY who
   was surgeon in Philippine War. F-S16448 R1557
John, esf 1776 VA; mvd to NC where esf under General GREENE;
   PN ae 72 Rutherford Co, NC; mvd 1834 to Anderson District,
   SC; res 1836 Cass Co, GA, where had mvd to res with youngest s mbnn; dd 11/4/40; md 12/22/1784 Ann Berry EARLE, Rutherford Co, NC, at home/o Colonel John EARLE (kinship not
   given); wid PN ae 78 Cass Co, GA, 1845; QLF 1916 from desc
   Mrs Sallie A Lewis FARIS, Clinton, MO, states sol wid was
   sis of General Bayles EARLE, & they both ch of John EARLE.
   F-W3832 R1557

LEWIS, John, esf 1776 as ensign in 9th VA Regiment; dd 6/1823 Sweet Springs, VA, where res; w mbnn dd 1824; ch liv 1832: Mary S w of James L WOODVILLE, Ann M w of John H PEYTON, Margaret Lynn w of John COCHRAN, William Lynn, Sarah E, John Band, Thomas & Pollydora; d Susannah (md Henry MASSIE of Alleghany Co, VA) decd in 1832, & survived by ch: Sarah C w/o Franck STANLEY, Mary P w of John H PLEASANTS, Henry, Eugenia, & Thomas; BLW1864 issued 7/18/1832 to sol heirs; power/o attorney given 1892 to agent in Lawrence Co, OH by E L MITCHELL & Henrietta Matilda Lewis WILLIS (they ch of sol d Henrietta M Lewis MITCHELL) to afb; no action by PN Office indicated on this afb; QLF 1919 from desc Mrs J A HARRISON, Clinton, DE, states sol md Rachel VINEY & buried Lewisburg, Greenbrier Co, WV. F-BLW1864 R1557

Lewis, esf 1776 Shepherdstown, VA; mvd c1797 from Martinsburg, VA, to Fayette Co, PA, where PN 1818 ae 63; dd 3/8/29; md 1785 Sarah who PN ae 79 Fayette Co, PA, 1839 res at Uniontown; ch births: William 10/1/86, Elizabeth 6/16/91, Sarah 11/6/99, Mary 9/16/1802, Lewis 4/24/04, & Richard 5/22/10 or 5/23/10; QLF states sol d Mary md Mr CLEMMER; QLF 1925 from Nancy R (Mrs Sam P) YOKE of Monongahela, PA, great great gdd (on m's side) of VA RW sol Mr LEWIS (not Lewis LEWIS) who b Wales, owned plantation in Culpeper Co, VA, dd there, & his wid Sarah G mvd to Uniontown, PA, (dd there 1829) to res with s William S (dd 1833, md Elizabeth SHANNON, & their ch: Samuel M, Hugh Walker, Eliza, Sarah, & William H, Confederate sol in Civil War). F-W3097 R1557

Matthew, VA Sea Svc, carpenter's mate; dd c7/25/1795 leaving wid Ann & 3 ch: John, Thomas, & Margaret, all under ae 16; md 5/10/1780 Ann, who md (2) c11/23/1819 Robert JAMES, who dd before her; wid gtd VA BLW8247 8/28/1835; dd 9/1836 or 10/36; her sis Mary Ann HOUSE AFF 1837 Elizabeth City Co, VA, that wid ch all since md & decd; Jane, orphaned d of wid s John, chose Thomas PECK as her guardian 1837, Elizabeth City Co, VA; he being adm of sol wid's estate, & had also been guardian of wid d Susan; gdc gtd PN due sol wid. F-W7909 R1558

Ruel, esf Dinwiddie Co, VA, where res; PN ae 73 Brunswick Co VA, 1832. F-S8826 R1558

Samuel, b 7/1756 Highworth, Wiltshire, England; apprenticed to tailor ae 12; came to VA 1774 on ship BRILLIANT; indentured servant to W BALLENTINE, Falls of James River above Richmond, VA; esf 1777 in 5th VA Regiment; serving in NJ when enlistment expired; esf there; res Essex Co, NJ after RW, thence Bergen Co, NJ, where PN 1832. F-S1048 R1558

Solomon, b 1750 Cumberland Co, NC; esf Surry Co, NC, where res; mvd after RW to Henry Co, VA, thence Washington Co, TN, thence Claiborne Co, TN where PN 1832 res near village of Speedwell; dd 3/6/43; md 1/1790 or 1/1792 Catharine who afp ae 84 Claiborne Co, TN, 1843 & PAR, insufficient proof of marriage; dd 8/25/45; Jesse ROGERS adm of wid estate, AFF there 1853 that wid gds mbnn had her family bible; QLF

LEWIS (continued)
1926 from Mrs M L BISHOP Jr, Casper, WY, desc of a RW sol John ROGERS of NC or VA, who PN & dd Claiborne Co, TN, had s Maj David ROGERS (War of 1812 sol of TN, dd 1873 Claiborne Co, TN, md a d of above sol Solomon LEWIS); QLF 1920 from great gds William F ROGERS of National Soldiers Home, Washingon Co, TN, who also great gds of RW sol John ROGERS who served in same unit as Solomon LEWIS. F-R6309 R1559

Spencer, esf 1778 Accomac Co, VA, & served with bro Thomas who 1853 collecting PN for RW svc; afp aec 90 there 1853, & PAR. F-R9978 R1559

Thomas, esf 1776 Augusta Co, VA, where b 1/26/1760; PN 1832 Rockingham Co, VA; bro of Charles (then decd) & Benjamin (then res MO). F-S7138 R1559

Thomas, b 11/18/1764 or 11/20/1764 Caroline Co, VA where esf 1781; res Genesee Co, NY, for 17 years after RW, then to Butler Co, OH, for c3 years, thence 1818 Switzerland Co, IN, where PN 1832; dd there 7/28/32 per wid or 7/28/33 per official papers in claim; md 8/4/1805-6 Sarah CONDLY, Angelica, Allegany Co, NY; wid PN ae 70 Switzerland Co, IN, 1853; gtd BLW27672 there 1855 ae 74; 9 ch mbnn survived f; d Mrs Robert COLLINS res Cincinnati, OH, 1849; QLF states sol res Vevay, Switzerland Co, IN. F-W8032 R1559

Thomas, b 5/3/1755; esf 1776 Washington Co, VA, where res; mvd 1782 to KY where settled on Dick's River, & esf there; PN 1833 Morgan Co, KY; dd 8/9/49; md 3/3/1784 Hannah HOPKINS, Washington Co, VA, who b 3/13/1766; wid PN 1850 Morgan Co, KY; ch births: Francis 3/3/1786, William 9/10/87, John 1/22/89, Mary 8/5/90, Margret 12/12/91, Nancy 4/8/93, Betsey 11/23/94, Hannah 8/17/96, Thomas 7/27/98, Deidamia 2/20/1800, Gardner Hopkins 11/8/01, Edmond P/B 8/5/03, Sarah 4/10/05, Acey 3/4/08, & Belinda 3/14/11; other births (all surname LEWIS): James Cox 11/15/1825, Nancy B 11/1/1827, Henry 3/4/1808, & James C 5/3/1829; QLF 1936 from great gdd Mrs Lawrence M GILLASPIE, Mt Sterling, KY, says sol bro of Asa & Griffith, further sol cemetery headstone in Morgan Co, KY, shows he lived 1755-1849; QLF 1935 from great gdd Nora Johnson (Mrs Frank C) SMITH, East St Louis, IL; QLF 1914 from great gdd (m's side) Mrs Fanny H BOARD, Brandenburg, KY; QLF 1906 from desc Mrs William CAROTHERS, Bardstown, KY, who also desc/o RW sol James COX who served in IL Regiment of Gen George Rogers CLARK. F-W9124 R1559

Thomas, esf 1778 Accomac Co, VA, where b 1759; PN there 1832 & dd there 3/2/51; md there 2/11/1837 Sarah Ann HART; wid PN there 1833 ae 33; gtd BLW26625 there 1855; wid md there (2) 12/31/58 James STEWART, who dd 6/4/60; wid PN restored there 1868 after Civil War; QLF states sol wid dd Accomac Co, VA, 1876, & their s John Denis (b there 2/18/1841) was res Philadelphia, PA, 1918, further sol md (2) Sarah Ann, d/o RW sol John HART (dd ae 106), further Sarah Ann md (2) RW sol James STEWART as his 6th w, & he dd 1860 ae 100. F-W10263 R1559

LEWIS, William, b 10/97/1759 Caroline Co, VA; mvd ae 4 with f
John to Fairfield District, SC; esf there 1776 while res
mouth of Wateree Creek; esf 1779 in company of bro Captain
Charles; afp 1836 Fairfield District, SC & PAR, insuffici-
ent proof of svc; s John then res Alachua Co, FL ae 25-30;
Gray BRIGGS, a gds of sol f, mvd c1806-11 to Natchez, MS;
QLF states sol dd 6/18/41 Fairfield District, SC; QLF 1937
from desc J H MARION, Charlotte, NC, states sol had s John
& s Edward, further sol s-in-law Gladden KING who gtd BLW
in War of 1812 or in one/o later Indian Wars (land near to
Shreveport, LA). F-R6335 R1559
William, BLW12308 issued 11/12/1791; member of Lee's Legion.
F-BLW12323 R1559
William, esf 1780 Pittsylvania Co, VA, where res; mvd c1817
to Surry Co, NC; PN 1832 ae 70 Wilkes Co, NC; dd 6/17/38;
QLF 19-- from desc Mrs A G POINDEXTER, Ft Worth, TX, says
sol s Asa never md & sol s Elias Dodson md Jennie GREEN of
Buncombe Co, NC. F-S7148 R1559
William, esf 1779 Culpeper Co, VA, where b 4/8/1763; PN 1818
there; dd 6/18/51; QLF 1918 from desc Miss Martha S MATH-
EWS, Fulton, MO; QLF 1907 from desc Miss Martha SULLINGER
of Burnsville, NC, states sol dd Culpeper Co, VA. F-S8827
R1559
William, VA Sea Svc; commodore; dd intestate Fredericksburg,
VA, in early 1793 when surveyor of the port of that city,
leaving wid; Robert Lewis McGUIRE, adm of his estate, afp
there 1853, & PAR, sailor not appointed by competent auth-
ority of VA but was sailing master of merchant ship RENOWN
that was impressed into service & paid by Continental Congress, not by VA. F-R62 R1559
William, major in VA Continental Line; BLW1300 issued 8/10/
1789; records lost in Washington, DC, fire; QLF states sol
b 1724 Ireland, 3rd s of John LEWIS & Margaret LYNN, emigrated to America, got medical degree in Philadelphia, PA,
volunteered 1753 in VA, wounded at BRADDOCK'S DEFEAT, was
physician in Augusta Co, VA, commissioned 1776 as colonel
in VA Contintal Line, mvd 1790 to Smith Springs, VA, where
dd 1812, was one of 4 brothers in RW, including Gen Andrew
LEWIS of VA, & their parents were early settlers in Augusta Co, VA. F-BLW1300 R1559
LAYHEW, David, see LEHEW, David. F-S22355 R1560
LIERLY, Zachariah, b 6/20/1755 Culpeper Co, VA; mvd ae 8-10
with parents to Rowan Co, NC where esf 1777 res near Sali-
bury; mvd 1818-19 to Union Co, IL, thence 1822-23 Jackson
Co, IL, where PN 1832; QLF 1920 from desc Mrs Mae Lierle
NATIONS, Augusta, IL; QLF 1938 from gds William H LIRELY,
Campbell Hill, IL, states sol s/o John Christopher LAYRLE,
who s/o Solomon LAYRLE (b 1681 Constance, Germany), further sol b Harpers Ferry, VA, & dd 1843-49, further querier
s/o sol s S P LIRELY. F-S32389 R1562
LIEUZADDER, Abraham, esf 1778 Greene Co, PA, where res, in VA
regiment under Gen George Rogers CLARK; dd Guernsey Co, OH

125

LIEUZADDER (continued)
12/14/1826; md 6/14/1786 Leah, Greene Co, PA who PN aec 78 Guernsey Co, OH, 1845 res Center Township; dd 6/6/50 that Co; ch listed 1852: Elizabeth GROVES ae 64, Mary SMITH (b c1790), Martha/Patty (b 12/17/91 or 12/26/91, md 9/21/1815 Jonathan WARNE, & they had s Thomas b 1816), Nancy aec 58, Rachel BONNEL aec 56, Sally DAUGHERTY aec 54, Isaac aec 52 Leah MARTIN aec 50, & John aec 44; ch who survived m: Elizabeth, Martha/Patty, Leah, John & Isaac; Alexander LUZADDER (kinship not given) & Elijah WARNE (kinship not given) res there 1852; surname also spelled LIEUZADER; QLF 1903 from great gdd Mrs Ferd LUCAS of Greencastle, IN; QLF says sol md Leah HOGUE; QLF 1927 from desc Mrs Lillian MARSHAll of Shoals, IN. F-W24554 R1562

LIGET, John, b 3/1762 Augusta Co, VA; esf 1780 Rockbridge Co, VA, where res; PN 1832 Montgomery Co, IL; res 1836 Washington, AR where mvd to be near children; lost PN certificate replaced there 1841; bro-in-law of Joseph CAMPBELL; surname also spelled LIGGETT, LEGGET; QLF 1894 from W Wirt LEGGETT, Ripley, OH, who desc/o RW sol's Henry FIELD of VA & also of John James LEGGETT or Robert LEGGETT/LIGGETT of VA; QLF 1922 from desc Mrs Richard W HAYNIE of Miami, OH. F-S31816 R1562

LIGHT, Vachal, esf 1780 Halifax Co, VA, where b 1763; PN 1833 Sullivan Co, TN; res 1836 Washington Co, TN; last PN payment in file 1840. F-S1551 R1562

LIGHTBURN, Richard, VA Sea Svc, esf as lieutenant on ship HERO GALLEY; gtd BLW by VA; dd 11/1794 Washington, Mason Co, KY leaving ch: Richard, Lucy & Sarah; s Richard dd 1820 Scott Co, KY, leaving w Temperance & ch: Alvan, Richard P, Martha C, John S, Thomas C, & William L; Temperance res 1834 there & her s Alvan res then Georgetown, that Co; sailor's d Sarah & h John PENCE res 1834 Clay Co, MO; sailor's d Lucy (md Peter JONES) decd in 1834 & survived by d Patsey; sailor's gds Alvan LIGHTBURN afp 1834 for all surv heirs & PAR, sailor resigned from svc before end of RW; Thomas C BURROUGHS of Norfolk, VA, AFF 1852 he one/o sailor's heirs (kinship not given); surname also spelled LIGHTBURNE; QLF states sol md Patsy/Polly. F-R63 R1562

LIGHTFOOT, Philip, esf 1781 VA; LWT of 8/13/1785 probated 6/8/1786 Caroline Co, VA; only s & heir Philip afb 1838 there, & issued BLW2220 6/14/1838; s Philip gtd VA BLW in 1835; sol w kin to John TALIAFERRO. F-BLW2220 R1562

Tapley, esf 1778 Hanover Co, VA, where b 2/15/1761; PN 1833 Williamson Co, TN. F-S4558 R1562

LIGON, Blackman, esf 1776 Halifax Co, VA; PN ae 61 Greenville District, SC 1818; res there 1821 when had s John T ae 29, d Elizabeth ae 25, s Blackman ae 22, gds James B ROSEMAN/ROSAMOND ae 9 & gds Joseph LIGON ae 4; res there 1823 when family w Elizabeth ae 66, d Nancy ae 39, d Elizabeth ae 29 gds James B ROSAMOND ae 13, & gds Joseph LIGON ae 5; dd 5/3/31; md c1780 Elizabeth (b 4/28/1753); wid PN 1841 Green-

LIGON (continued)
ville District, SC; dd 10/15/42; 2nd ch Nancy b 11/1/1784, & md John T MOORE/MOON, they res 1841 Greenville District, SC; sol eldest ch was a d mbnn. F-W9132 R1562
John, b 1761 Chesterfield Co, VA; esf 1780 Halifax Co, VA, where res; mvd 1814 to Smith Co, TN where PN 1832. F-S4555 R1562
Joseph, esf 1781 Halifax Co, VA where res; PN 1807 there for disability from wounds at Battle of Guilford Court House; PN 1833 Montgomery Co, Tn, ae not given; dd 9/21/42; QLF 1926 from desc Katharine K ADAMS, Rogers Park, IL, who also desc/o RW sol's Samuel WILLIAMS, George WRIGHT & Archibald WRIGHT. F-S132 R1562
William, see LEGON, William. F-S1998 R1562
William, esf 1779 Powhatan Co, VA, where b 11/24/1762; res after RW Cumberland Co, VA, thence Prince Edward Co, VA, thence 1816 Owen Co, KY, where PN 1832; last PN payment in file 1841; d Mrs Martha H MORGAN liv 1897 ae 87; QLF says sol md Edith TURNER. F-S13764 R1562
LILBURN, Andrew, esf 1775 VA; PN ae 74 Washington Co, TN, when all ch grown & left, occupation farmer; last PN payment in file 1839. F-S4562 R1563
LILES, David, b VA on Meherrin River; esf Rutherford Co, NC, where res; lived there 25 years, thence Knox Co, TN for c9 years, thence Roane Co, TN where PN 1832 after res there c 27 years. F-S1848 R1563
David, b 8/13/1755 on Meherrin River, VA; mvd when ch with f to Pittsylvania Co (area later Henry Co), VA for 10 years, thence with f to Craven Co, NC for 5 years, thence Rutherford Co, NC, where esf 1776; res there after RW c10 years, thence Jackson Co, TN for 3 years, thence Maury Co, TN for 3 years, thence Carroll Co, TN, where PN 1832; QLF states sol res ae 84 in 11th District of Jackson Co, TN, per 1840 Census, with Joshua DRAPER (kinship not given). F-S4544 R1563
LILLARD, John, esf c1780 Culpeper Co, VA; PN ae 67 there 1832; QLF states sol md Polly SANDRICH; QLF states sol bro Ben RW sol & they both b Culpeper Co, VA; QLF 1919 from great gdd Lena Lillard BLAIR of Ventura, CA, states sol md Polly SANDRICH, & they had 10 ch, further VA RW sol Joseph SPENCER f of querier's great gdm; QLF 1916 from desc F L BURDETTE of Clarksburg, WV; QLF states sol ch: John, Thomas, Ephraim, Joseph, James, Daniel, David, & 3 d's; QLF states Colonel Joseph Dyke SPENCER Sr (f from England) b VA 1739, dd 1831 ae 92, md Nancy MOORE of VA & they had 11 ch, further another Colonel Joseph SPENCER, dd 8/27/1829 ae 74, md Sarah, he afp Pendleton Co, KY, & had s Joseph D who ae 47 at f's death. F-S8860 R1563
LILLISTON, William, esf 1776 Drummondton, Accomac Co, VA; PN there 1818 ae 62; family res with him there 1820 w Elizabeth ae 48 & ch: Sally aec 13, Leah aec 10 & Asa aec 7; dd 1/31/30; QLF 1914 from desc Miss Blanche LILLISTON, Paris,

LILLISTON (continued)
KY; QLF 1939 from desc Mrs Flora Knapp DICKINSON, New York NY, who also desc/o RW sol Richard WIMBROUGH of Accomac Co VA. F-S38141 R1563
LILLY, William, b 1751 Borough Green, Cambridgeshire, England; esf 1777 Fraderick Co, VA where res; afp 1833 Nicholas Co, VA; PAR, sol having dd 9/1834 at ae 65 & not old enough to have served in RW, per the US Attorney/o district. F-R6343 R1563
LIMING, Samuel, esf 1778 in VA Line; PN aec 77 Cincinnati, OH, when res at Colerain, Hamilton Co, OH; last PN payment in file 1834. F-S46390 R1563
LINCOLN, Jacob, esf 1781 in company of Captain Abraham LINCOLN (kinship not given) VA militia; esf 1781 in VA regimet; dd 2/20/1822 Rockingham Co, VA; md 8/1780 Dorcas ROBERTSON, who b 3/15/1763; wid dd 1/25/40 leaving ch: David (b 6/28/1781), Abraham/Abram, Mary/Polly wid/o William HINTON/HENTON, Jacob, Abigail w of Joseph COFFMAN of Rockingham Co, VA, Dorcas w/o John STRAYER of Shenandoah Co, VA, & Rebecca w/o Mathew DYER of Pendleton Co, VA; ch decd on 2/22/37 were John, Elizabeth (left s John CHRESMAN/CHRISMAN), Hannah (left d's Caroline & Josephine EVANS); s Abrah/Abraham afp 1846 for PN due m & PAR, insufficient proof/o svc; QLF 1933 from desc Celia Lincoln SAWYER, Decatur, IL, who great gdd/o sol s David who gtd PN for War of 1812 svc. F-R6347 R1564
LINDSAY, James, 2/20/1755 b Cumberland Co, PA; esf 1780 at Lexington, KY Teritory, in VA unit against indians; afp 1832 Shelby Co, KY, when res Gallatin Co, KY, & PAR; dd there 6/25/33 leaving wid Hetty & 8 ch; wid afp 1834 Gallatin Co KY, & PAR; liv Hancock Co, KY, 1836; decd in 1837; ch mbnn F-R6353 R1566
Lewis, esf 1781 Mecklenburg Co, VA where res; PN ae 78 Charlotte Co, VA, 1833. F-S8862 R1566
William, b 4/15/1760 Chesterfield Co, VA, where esf 1776 in PA regiment; f & 3 uncles served in same regiment; f & uncles taken POW in NY where f & 2 uncles dd; sol mvd after RW to Clarksburg, Harrison Co, VA, for 5-6 years, then to Jefferson Co, KY, thence Shelby Co, KY, where PN 1832 res Vincennes; dd there 10/8/36; md there 4/26/1824 Clarissa PRIOR; wid PN ae 60 Knox Co, IN, 1853; gtd BLW28649 there 1855; res there 1881 ae 90; QLF 1020 from desc Miss Mary BROUILLETTE, Vicennes, IN states sol wid dd 2/19/1883; QLF 1908 from desc Mamie M HOUGH of Effingham, IL, states sol buried Vincennes, IN. F-W553 R1566
LINDSEY, Abraham, esf 1775-6 VA; PN ae 74 Butler Co, KY, 1825, occupation schoolteacher, when res with children mbnn. F-S36043 R1566
Benjamin, b VA; mvd as ch with parents to SC, where esf 1777; PN ae 81 Edgefield District, SC 1834; dd 1841 leaving children mbnn; AFF 1838 by nephew Benjamin LINDSEY Jr (b 12/15/1773) Newberry District, SC. F-S18082 R1566

LINDSEY, Hezekiah, esf Westmoreland Co, PA, in VA regiment; PN ae 71 Clermont, OH, 1818; QLF states sol buried in OH. F-S41770 R1566
James, esf 1775 Frederick Co, VA; PN 1818 Champaign Co, OH, ae 58; res 1820 ae 62 Urbana, OH, occupation farmer, when w ae "50 odd years"; dd there 2/4/24; md 1/1812 Priscilla, wid/o Beverly STUBBLEFIELD (ML 12/20/1812) Winchester, VA; wid md (3) 5/10/1826 John THOMAS who dd 2/19/46; wid PN ae 84 Champaign Co, OH, 1856 res Wayne Township; gtd BLW44933 there 1856; QLF 1911 from desc Carrie PANCOAST of Trenton, MO. F-W25476 R1566
John, b 1759 Baltimore Co, MD; esf 1777 Frederick Co, MD; mvd 1779 to PA, where esf in 1780 near Buffalo Creek (area then claimed by VA & PA) in PA regiment; mvd to Ohio Co, VA, where esf 1781; mvd 1781 to Westmoreland Co, PA, where esf; mvd after RW to KY, where PN 1833 Henry Co; res there 1838 & dd 1838; James E STONE, adm of sol estate, Hancock Co, 1840, when sol s mbnn res there; surname also spelled LINDSAY. F-S30545 R1566
Moses, b Frederick Co, VA; esf 1776 Newberry, SC, where res; esf 1777 in company of uncle Capt James LINDSEY; mvd 1810 to Williamson Co, TN, where PN 1832 ae 70. F-S4551 R1566
Peter, BLW12328 issued 12/9/1793. F-BLW12328 R1566
Walter, esf 1776 in 5th PA Regiment, Chester Co, PA, where res; mvd 1785-6 to Harrison Co, VA where PN 1818 ae 61; dd there 6/28/20; md 2/1781 Mary McCULLOUGH, Chester Co, PA, at home of his bro-in-law John LOUDEN; wid bc 1764 there; PN 1839 Harrison Co, VA; 1st ch, a d, b 6/1782; 2nd ch, a s, b 7/1783; gds's Walter & Levi LINDSAY (brothers) living 1820; wid sis of Catherine (w of David CARPENTER) & of Mrs Martha BLAIR; sol surname also spelled LINSEY & LINDSAY. W8048 R1567
LINE, Adam, b 1737 NJ; esf 1777 Culpeper Co, VA where res; esf 1781 Shenandoah Co, VA where res; PN 1838 ae 100 Hardy Co, VA; w mbnn. F-S7513 R1567
John, esf 1777 in Colonel George Rogers CLARK's VA regiment, near Ten Mile Creek in area later Washington Co, PA; PN ae 74 Shelby Co, OH, 1832; QLF states sol bro Joseph also RW sol. F-S18491 R1567
Joseph, b 5/4/1755 Sussex Co, NJ; esf 1777 Washington Co, PA in Colonel George Rogers CLARK's VA regiment with bro John above; PN 1832 Miami Co, OH; dd 9/4/37; md 1/15/1782 Mary Magdalen HOUST, in PA; wid dd 1/16/42 Shelby Co, OH, leaving ch: (eldest) Catharine JACKSON (1855 aec 71), Abraham (b 11/13/1800), Rebecca KERNS, & Susanna BALL (res 1854 in Auglaize Co, OH); in 1799 sol & w had 9 ch; s Abraham afp 1855 Shelby Co, OH for self & surv siblings; PAR "on technicality", per current PN laws; QLF 1907 from desc Captain Ralph HARRISON, US Army, Chicago, IL. F-R6359 R1567
LINER, Christopher, esf 1780 Augusta Co, VA; mvd after RW to Wilkes Co, GA for c7 years, thence Franklin Co, GA, thence SC for c4 years, thence Habersham Co, GA, thence TN, where

LINER (continued)
  PN ae 69 McMinn Co, 1832; dd 8/3/36 Dobson Co, GA; md 1/5/
  1793, 1/5/1799, or 1/1/1800-01 (all dates given by wid) to
  Anna STOWERS, Franklin Co, GA; wid PN ae 73 Talladega Co,
  AL, 1851; gtd BLW45713 when res Randolph Co, AL, 1855; mvd
  1863 to Decatur Co, GA, where res 1868 Bainbridge when PN
  restored after RW; res there 1869 ae 85-90. F-W3688 R1567
LINEWEAVER, Jacob, b 2/17/1763 PA; mvd as infant with parents
  to Frederick Co, MD, thence ae 11 with parents to Loudoun
  Co, VA, where esf 1780; res there to 1790, thence Shenandoah Co, VA where PN 1833; dd there 8/30/34 at home/o William C LUCKETT (no kinship given); md there 5/6 1792 Margaret PICKLE; wid PN there 1839 ae 73; last PN payment in
  file dated 1841. F-W5325 R1567
LINGENFELTER, Michael, b 11/17/1762 Fredericktown, Frederick
  Co, MD, where esf 1779; res MD after RW, thence VA, thence
  KY, where PN 1822 Gallatin Co when res there 24 years; mvd
  1835 to Indianapolis, IN, to res with 2 s's who res there.
  F-S32379 R1567
LINK, Adam, b 1760 PA; mvd 1775 to Middle Wheeling on Ohio Ri-
  ver; esf 1777 Wheeling or Shepherd's Fort, VA; esf 1779 in
  VA regiment; f killed by indians 1780; res after RW Beaver
  Co, PA, for 7 years, thence OH where PN 1833 Richland Co,
  res Milton Township; s mbnn 1852; gtd BLW26343 Ashland Co,
  OH, 1855; QLF states sol res Sulphur Springs, OH, 1864 ae
  104; QLF states sol dd there 1864; QLF 1927 from desc Mrs
  Grace MILES, Tiffin, OH; QLF states sol one of the last 8
  surv RW sol's. F-S1771 R1568
LINN, Adam, esf 1776 Gettysburg, PA, in 7th PA Regiment; res
  after RW PA, MD, VA, thence 1811 Guernsey Co, OH, where PN
  1832 ae 83; dd there 10/17/34; md 8/17/1780 Ann HEFLY/HEF-
  LEY, Hagerstown, MD; wid PN aec 80 Guernsey Co, OH, res
  Jefferson Township; wid AFF 1846 she res there c34 years &
  res previously Augusta Co, VA; ch births: John 11/20/84,
  Joseph 2/18/87, George 3/2/90, Samuel 9/3/93, Aaren 12/10/
  96 & Andrew (1841 ae 36); QLF states a VA RW sol Adam LINN
  b Ireland, settled Bedford Co, VA where esf, md c1775 Sydney Ann, d of Robert EWING (a JP there); mvd c1788 to TN,
  thence c1800 Trigg Co, KY, where dd c1832, his w dd before
  1787, their d Nancy md Abraham (s/o James BOYD who bc 1738
  Bedford Co, VA, md Martha BURNS, moved before 1775 with
  family to SC & dd in Tory prison, survived by wid Martha).
  F-W5023 R1568
LINOR, Philip, see LYNOR, Philip. F-S38143 R1568
LINTON, William Thomas, b 1/8/1758 Westmoreland Co, VA, s of
  John & Mary Ann; mvd to Halifax Co, VA where esf 1776; res
  for time after 1793 Chester, SC, thence Lancaster District
  SC, thence Union District, SC, then after 3/1800 to Meck-
  lenburg Co, VA, for c10 years, thence Chester District, SC
  for c4 years, thence NC where PN 1818 Iredell Co; res 1824
  Grayson Co, VA; dd there 2/28/27; LWT probated there 4/15/
  1827; md 4/15/1793 Mary Ann, Chester District, SC, who b

LINTON (continued)
12/6/1769; wid PN 1840 Grayson Co, VA; ch births: Mary 11/11/1794, John 7/28/97, Elizabeth 3/12/1800, Margaret Haynes 4/19/02, & Ann Thomas 6/1/08; all these ch listed in 1827 LWT of f except Elizabeth; wid liv 1844. F-W8046 R1569
LINVILL, William, b Frederick Co, VA, where esf 1777 in GA regiment; res after RW Wilkes Co, GA, thence Edgefield & Abbeville Districts, SC, for c12 years, thence Lincoln Co, GA, where PN 1832 ae 75; dd there 11/30/42; md 6/29/1788 Wilkes Co, GA, to Mary d/o Edward MORRIS of Edgefield District, SC & they mvd then to home/o her f; wid b 5/17/1770 & PN 1843 Lincoln Co, GA, 1843; never had ch; her younger bro Thomas was Baptist minister 1845 in Edgefield District SC; sol surname also spelled LINVILLE. F-W5321 R1569
LION, Jacob, see LYON, Jacob. F-S41789 R1569
LIPFORD, Anthony P, b 1755 Dinwiddie Co, VA; esf Cumberland Co VA, where res; mvd 1788 to Pittsylvania Co, VA, where PN 1833; dd there 2/4/41; md there 4/20/1827 Elizabeth FERGUSON (marriage license 4/20/27); wid PN there 1853 ae 63; gtd BLW26966 there 1855; PN restored there 1866 after Civil War; PN increase there 1868; AFF 1833 by Henry LIPFORD (no kinship given) Cumberland Co, VA, he served in RW with sol; sol had s's Amos & David. F-W2623 R1569
Henry, b Dinwiddie Co, VA; mvd aec 5 with parents to Cumberland Co, VA; esf there 1777; PN there 1832 ae 78; P O address 1833 Dickersonville, Powhatan Co, VA. F-S8861 R1569
John, esf 1776 in VA regiment; later 1776 assigned to different VA regiment to serve with 2 bro's mbnn, who had esf Buckingham Co, VA; res after RW Cumberland Co, VA, thence Prince Edward Co, VA, thence Buckingham Co, VA, where PN 1832 ae 77; QLF 1834 from desc C H LIPFORD, Richmond, VA, who also desc/o RW Henry LIPFORD of Cumberland Co, VA. F-S8866 R1569
LIPPINCOTT, Samuel, esf 1779 Shrewsbury Township, Monmouth Co, NY, where b 8/29/1759; res NJ several years after RW, then to PA for over 1 year, thence VA for several years, thence 1803 OH where PN 1833 Clark Co, when res that Co 10 years; QLF states sol dd 9/16/36 Rockfort, Allen Co, OH; QLF says sol s Ephraim mvd to OH, finally settling in Shelby Co, OH F-S4559 R1569
LIPSCOMB, Ambrose, b 1762; esf 1781 Frederick Co, VA, where res; liv there after RW, thence King George Co, VA, thence Randolph Co, VA where PN 1833; dd 5/18/41; md 12/1785 Winny MARDIS, King George Co, VA; wid PN ae 78 Preston Co, VA 1846; ch births: Lucy 12/30/1786, Richard 5/8/88, James 6/28/93, John 11/12/95, Levi 2/4/98, Henry 4/26/---- (year illegible), Fielding 12/29/1802, Eben 8/19/05, & Converse/Catherine (?) 9/18/08; other data in file: Samuel s/o Elisha & Margaret HALL b 11/7/1796, Margaret HALL dd 11/12/1786; s Henry AFF 1846 Preston Co, VA; QLF 1939 from great great gds J Roy LIPSCOMB, Aurora, WV, states sol came 1808

LIPSCOMB (continued)
   to Preston Co, VA; QLF 1935 from great great gdd Vivienne
   LIPSCOMB, Spokane, WA. F-W8252 R1570
Archibald, esf 1779 King William Co, VA, where b; PN aec 74
   Person Co, NC, 1832; dd there 3/22/37; md there 1/1808 Dorothy (d/o Nup PALMER of King William Co, VA), who was wid
   of sol elder bro Thomas whom she had md 12/23/1787 in King
   William Co, VA, (MB 12/20/87 signed by James PALMER, her f
   then decd); Thomas dd 7/22/1807 (also VA RW sol); wid PN
   ae 74 Maury Co, TN 1844 for svc/o 2nd h; wid res then with
   her children; wid 1st ch by Thomas was b 5/1789; wid afp
   for svc of Thomas, but only claim for Archibald's svc was
   allowed; wid gtd BLW5076 Maury Co, TN 1855 ae 83; QLF 1901
   from gds A A LIPSCOMB, Columbia, TN states sol wid dd 1862
   F-W951 R1570
Benoni, esf 1776 King William Co, VA; PN there 1818 aec 62.
   F-S38140 R1570
Henry, BLW12325 issued 5/11/1792. F-BLW12325 R1570
John, esf 1778 King William Co, VA; PN there 1818 ae 67; dd
   9/28/24; md there Elizabeth, d of Ambrose LIPSCOMB; wid PN
   there 1839 ae 78; QLF states sol bro/o William; QLF states
   a RW sol Colonel John LIPSCOMB of Louisa Co, VA, was s of
   Thomas LIPSCOMB of Spotsylvania Co, VA. F-W5323 R1570
Richard, esf 1779 Nottoway Co, VA; PN ae 70 Charlotte Co, VA
   1832; dd there 12/4/38; md 10/9/1806 Mary/Polly COBBS, Halifax, Co, VA; wid PN ae 64 Charlotte Co, VA, 1855; gtd BLW
   43508 near there 1866 when res with d mbnn; res there 1867
   ae 76 when PN restored after Civil War & she signed oath/o
   allegiance; 5 or 6 ch mbnn. F-W8054 R1570
Yancy, N A Account #874; per PN Office "no pension file for
   this soldier." F-None R1570
LISK, John, esf 1779 9th VA Regiment; PN 1818 Monroe Co, OH;
   res there 1820 when family w Elizabeth ae 55 (a cripple) &
   s Nicholas ae 19. F-S41773 R1570
LISTER, Thomas, see LESTER, Thopmas. F-S35518 R1570
LITCHFORD, Arthur, b 1758 Kent Co, England; res James City, Co
   VA, during RW where esf; mvd after RW to Charles City Co,
   VA, thence Campbell Co, VA, where PN 1832 res Russell Parish; last PN payment on file 1838; dd leaving wid mbnn,
   who liv 1841; sol bro mbnn; QLF 1917 from desc Miss Ursula
   M DANIEL, Halifax, NC states sol dd VA; QLF 1917 from desc
   Henry Litchford MARSHALL, Halifax, NC, states sol res 1841
   Lynchburg, VA. F-S7156 R1570
LITLE, Alexander, b 5/5/1748 Charlotte Co (area then part of
   Lunenburg Co), VA; esf 1776 Cumberland Co, PA, res West
   Pennsborough Township; res after RW Carlisle, PA, for 2-3
   years, thence Baltimore, MD for 6-7 years, thence Washington Co, PA, where PN 1832 res Washington; sis Martha IRWIN
   AFF there 1831 ae 84 she res Cumberland Co, PA, during RW;
   surname also spelled LITTLE; QLF states sol dd 1833. F-S4552 R1571
LITTERAL, Richard, esf 1780 in VA 3rd Regiment; PN ae 59 Bote-

LITTERAL (continued)
    tourt Co, VA, 1818; res there 1820 ae 59 when had w & 5 ch
    mbnn; dd there 9/3/40; md (2) 8/26/1830 Jane WELCH, wid of
    George CHAMPE, there in area later Craig Co; wid b former
    Co & res there to 1849, when mvd to Wayne Co, IN; PN ae 62
    Knox Co, TN, 1855 when visiting s mbnn who res there; gtd
    BLW521 then there; wid res 1861 Wayne Co, IN, where some/o
    her ch res. F-W26220 R1571
LITTLE, George, esf Chesterton, PA, in PA regiment; res after
    RW York Co (area later Adams Co), PA; mvd to Hampshire Co,
    VA, c1794 where PN 1832 ae 77; dd there 7/7/44; md c1779
    Elizabeth, Berkeley Co, VA; wid afp there 1845; PAR, proof
    of svc & marriage; res there 1850. S-R6382 R1571
    Jacob, b 3/8/1755 Surry Co, VA; esf 1780 Pitt Co, NC, where
    res; mvd 1795 to Anson Co, NC, where afp 1833; PAR, insuf-
    ficient proof of svc; heirs afp there 1854 & PAR. F-R6383
    R1571
LITTLEPAGE, John, esf 1781 VA Continental Line; VA BLW3987 is-
    sued 10/26/1785; PN 1818 Hopkins Co, KY, ae not given; dd
    3/23/1820; wid Amy adm of his estate then; ch who afb 1843
    as her heirs, Hopkins Co, KY: James, Epps, Richard, John,
    Ellis, Elizabeth w of Alfred HEWLETT, & Polly w of Andrew
    SISK; BLW2037 gtd to heirs. F-S36042 R1572
    John Carter, esf 1775 Hanover Co, VA, where b, kin/o Patrick
    HENRY; acted as guide to Marquis LAFAYETTE 1781; member of
    VA constitutional convention for Hanover Co; PN there 1833
    ae 80. F-S7151 R1572
LITTLETON, Charles, b 1760 Frederick Co, VA; esf 1776 Ninety-
    Six District, SC, where res; mvd to Sumner Co, TN, for 3
    years, thence Giles Co, TN for 12 years, thence Lauderdale
    Co, AL where PN 1833; dd 3/29/48; md 8/1795 Elizabeth HEN-
    DERSON, Newberry Co, SC; wid PN 1850 Lauderdale Co, AL, ae
    80; ch births: Sarah Estes 3/6/1797, David Lee 12/21/98,
    Peter Brazzaman 11/18/1800, Samuel Holbrook 6/13/03, Rubin
    S, Nancy H, Mary M, & John M; wid gtd BLW43506 Lauderdale
    Co, AL, 1856 ae 85; d Mary M WESTMORELAND retained lawyer
    1887 at Florence, AL to query re BLW for f's svc. F-W8255
    R1572
LITTREL, Richard, see LITTERAL, Richard. F-W26220 R1572
LITZENBERGER, George, b Germantown, PA; esf 1780 Chester Co,
    PA; mvd after RW to Winchester, VA, for 13 years, thence
    Greene Co, PA, where afp 1840 ae 82-83; PAR, proof/o mili-
    tary svc (PN Office determined his svc in civilian capaci-
    ty as a guide was not military & his other svc less then 6
    months); children mbnn 1853; QLF states sol f William also
    RW sol. F-R6388 R1572
LIVASAY, George, see LEVISEY, George. F-R6304 R1573
LIVELY, Godrell/Goodwell/Cotrel, esf 1780 Albemarle Co, VA; b
    there 5/16/1763-4; VA BLW4973 issued 12/9/1800; PN Monroe
    Co, VA, 1833; dd 12/2/38 or 12/3/38; md 10/24/1790 Sarah/
    Sally MADDY (MB10/24/90 between Cothel LIVELY & Sally MAD-
    DY) Greenbrier Co, VA; wid b 10/16/1773, dd 9/1/39, 9/3/39

133

LIVELY (continued)
or 9/12/39; ch births: Jane 9/10/1791, Joseph 5/1/93, William 3/19/95, Judith 3/16/97, Cottrel 2/25/99, James 12/20/1802, Thomas 1/20/05, Hemphill 1/21/07, Madison 1/5/09, Mary 1/13/11, Sarah 4/16/13, Wilson 4/12/15, & Lorenzo 4/11/18; boundboy James ELLISON b 11/17/1825; wid never afp; s Wilson adm of m's estate, & afp 1847 Monroe Co, VA, for self & surv siblings: Jane PACK, Joseph, William, Thomas, Judith McGHEE, Salley SMITH, & John; PAR, sol wid not liv 1842 per current PN laws; QLF 1920 from desc Jesse LIVELY, Byer, OH, who s/o sol gds J H LIVELY, further querier f of Mrs L D HANLIN of Lancaster, OH. F-R6389 R1573

Thomas, colored man, esf 1777 Chesterfield Co, VA, in 5th VA Regiment; lost right eye at Battle of Monmouth; PN 1820 ae 84 Chesterfield Co, VA; res there 1820 with d Sally & her h Kit FREMAN & their s James ae 7. F-S38144 R1573

LIVESAY, George, see LEVISEY, George. F-R6304 R1573

LIVINGOOD, Peter, esf 1776 Frederick Co, VA, res Zean's Iron Works; mvd 1784 to Greene Co, PA, where PN 1822 ae 64 when family w ae 64 & ch: Barbary, Mary, Jacob, Catharine, David, Anne, Peter, & Sarah (all over ae 21 & all md except Peter); sol dd 11/14/34; sis Mary HICKMAN AFF 1819 there. F-S4561 R1573

LIVINGSTON, Henry, b 3/1/1764; mvd when infant with f to NC from one of Eastern states; esf 1778 Washington Co, VA, in company/o bro Captain Peter; esf 1779 there as sub for bro Samuel when res on Holston River; mvd 1801 to KY, then to Overton Co, KY, where afp 1832 when res there c30 years; PAR, RW svc of driving pack horses not considered military by PN Office; dd 5/22/34; md 3/21/1793 Susannah CARMACK, Wythe Co, VA; wid afp aec 75 Overton Co, TN 1852; wid PAR; ch births: Polly 3/13/1793, Caty 9/10/96, Sarah 2/21/98, Susanah 12/30/99, Thomas 1/30/1802, Peter 8/13/06, & Nancy 2/19/08; other births in file (all surname CARMACK): Cornelius 1/8/1769, William 1/5/1761, Joseph 4/11/1769, Jane 6/7/1765 & Sarah 8/1797; wid liv 1856, sis/o Jesse CARMACK F-R6394 R1573

John, esf VA; dd 11/16/1826 Blount Co, AL; md 1783 Rachel FREEMAN, Wilkes Co, NC; wid dd 10/7/1845 leaving ch: William, Susan w/o Benjamin JOHNSON, John, Frances w/o Samuel LIVINGSTON, & Elizabeth w/o Joshua ROBERTS; Samuel LIVINGSTON, adm of sol wid estate, afp 1850 Lawrence Co, AL, for wid heirs, & PAR; sol s William AFF ae 67 then there he b Wilkes Co, NC, eldest ch of sol & wid, & he res there when they md. F-R6393 R1573

Justice, VA sea svc, dd 4/1785; PN due sailor paid 1847 to Joseph SEGAR, adm/o his estate, Richmond, VA. F-R64 R1573

Samuel, b 1757 King & Queen Co, VA; esf 1776 Overton Co, NC, area later TN; mvd to Madison Co, AL, thence Morgan Co, AL where PN 1832; dd there 10/16/34 when res there 24 years; md 9/17/1779 or 9/17/1781 Phebe, Washington Co, VA; wid gtd arrears of h PN Morgan Co, AL, 1835; wid PN there 1843

LIVINGSTON (continued)
ae 81; ch: James, Jesse, Anthony, Samuel, William, Joseph, Henry, Susan w/o James KING, & Catherine w/o Ichabod HENSLEY; QLF 1914 from desc Mrs F A COLQUITT, Cordele, GA, who also desc/o Nancy HIGGINS, RW pensioner of Richland Co, SC 1840; QLF 1917 from US Congressman of 19th District of PA of PA for H A LEHMAN, great gds of sol. F-W8050 R1573
LLOYD, George E, esf 1776 Frederick Co, VA; PN ae 71 Fauquier Co, VA, 1829; res 1835 Licking Co, OH, with s-in-law John D SHANK; dd 1/20/53; QLF 1913 from gds T L SCHENK, Oxford, AR states sol dd Harrison Township, Licking Co, OH, & was buried in Edna Township, that Co, further querier a Civil War (Union) sol. F-S41777 R1574
Joseph, esf 1781 VA; mvd 1815 to KY, where PN ae 64 Bullitt Co, occupation schoolmaster, res with w aec 55 & ch: Patty ae 21, Alsey ae 19, Lydia ae 12, John ae 17 & George ae 15; dd 5/11/48; QLF states sol res there 1840 ae 79; QLF states sol md Fanny BROWN, his bro Thomas, b 1744, RW sol, md (1) Patience McCRACKEN, & was VA RW sol, further RW sol Aaron CUPPY, b Morris Co, NJ, or Hampshire Co, VA, md Ruth BUNCH & probably afp Nelson Co, KY, further RW sol Mr WILLIS/WILLS of Culpeper Co, VA, had d Charlotte Elizabeth, who md John SHELBURNE (b 1758) RW sol of Lunenburg Co, VA, who mvd 1803 to Nelson Co, KY where John probably afp. F-S36050 R1574
William, esf Culpeper Co, VA; PN ae 70 Fayette Co, KY, res Jessamine Co, KY; res ae 72 Franklin Co, KY, 1821, occupation tailor, when he & w aec 69 res with one of their sons mbnn. F-S36049 R1574
LOCH, John (AKA HOLE, John), esf 1782 in French artillery unit when res Bucks Co, PA; afp ae 72 Shenandoah Co, VA, 1834 & PAR, service in foreign military unit not covered by US PN laws; QLF 1937 from gdd Mrs C MILLER of Calumet City, IL, states sol b 1752, esf Rockingham Co, VA, & dd 1835 in OH. F-R6396 R1574
LOCHRIDGE, James, b 3/10/1757 Rockbridge Co, VA; mvd when ch with f to Abbeville District, SC, where esf 1774; mvd 1796 to Clarke Co, GA, thence 1807 Maury Co, TN, where PN 1832; dd there 7/28/40; md 8/21/1788 Ann/Anna, Rockbridge Co, VA who b 4/23/1772; ch births: Rebeckah Grimes 4/27/1791, John Weemes 3/8/93, Robert Patton 6/26/95, William 1/2/98, Thomas Messer 10/9/1801, James Hodge 7/3/04 & Samuel 2/14/08; wid PN 1842 Maury Co, TN; surname also spelled LOCKRIDGE. F-W472 R1574
John, b 10/1762 Augusta Co, VA; esf 1781 Rockbridge Co, VA, where res; PN 1832 Montgomery Co, KY; res 1840 Sangamon Co, IL, where had mvd to provide for large family of ch; lost w before move to IL; surname also spelled LOCKRIDGE; QLF states sol b 11/20/1761 Augusta Co, VA; QLF states sol mvd 1835 to Sangamon Co, IL, & dd c1848; QLF states sol dd Chatham, IL & md Margaret HENDERSON of Augusta Co, VA, who dd in Montgomery Co, KY. F-S31218 R1574

LOCK, Charles, b 12/19/1752; esf 1774 Amelia Co, VA; PN Wilson Co, TN, 1832. F-S1683 R1575
  James, b 8/24/1761 Berkeley Co, VA; esf 1779 Augusta Co, VA; mvd 10 years after svc to Mercer Co, KY, for 3 years, then to Barren Co, KY for 3 years, thence Jackson Co, TN, for 5 years, thence Barren Co, KY, for 3 years, thence Smith Co, TN, for 3 years, thence Barren Co, KY, for 3 years, thence Wayne Co, IL where PN 1832; QLF states sol dd Wayne Co, IL F-S31220 R1575
  Richard, b 1/11/1762 Lancaster Co, VA; esf 1778 Lunenburg Co VA, where res; PN 1834 Greenville District, SC; QLF 1928 from desc Margaret Adair CHANDLER of Charlotte, NC, states sol md Mary THACKSTON & mvd 1799 from Lunenburg Co, VA, to Greenville District, SC; QLF states sol res 1840 that district. F-S21351 R1575
LOCKARD, Philip, esf 1780 New Glasgow, Bedford Co, VA; PN 1824 that Co ae 71; dd there 5/3/43; md 1787 Margaret/Peggy GRADY, Amherst Co, VA; wid PN ae 75 Bedford Co, VA, 1843; gtd BLW15432 there 1855 ae 85; ch included Mrs HEATH/KEATH QLF 1927 from desc T O'J WILSON of Bluefield, WV. F-W3836 R1575
  William, esf 1778-9 Amherst Co, VA; PN there 1818 ae 68; res there 1821 ae 70, occupation shoemaker, when w aec 61 & no ch liv with them. F-S38152 R1575
LOCKART, Aaron, esf 1776-7 in 4th PA Regiment; PN 1818 Harrison Co, VA, ae not given; dd Fall 1819; md 1793 w mbnn in NJ, who survived him for 5-6 years; one ch mbnn liv 1851. F-S38146 R1575
LOCKE, Joseph, esf 1717 Lancaster Co, VA; PN there 1818 ae 62 when family s Ludwell ae 26, s Addison ae 14, & d Polly ae 18. F-S38150 R1576
  William, b 3/1/1744 as William STARR; pressed into British army svc at London, England, early in RW; landed at Long Island, NY, where deserted British army & changed surname to LOCKE; esf 1779 American army in Frederick Co, VA where res; PN 1832 Jefferson Co, OH, res Ross Township. F-S8857 R1576
LOCKET, Benjamin, BLW12311 issued 2/10/1796. F-BLW12311 R1576
LOCKETT, Benjamin, b VA; esf VA; PN aec 56 Clark Co, KY, 1818; 3 d's mbnn 1819; res there 1821 with w aec 50, d Polly aec 15, & d Nancy aec 13; res 1835 Franklin Co, OH; surname also spelled LOCKET. F-S41780 R1576
  Edmund/Edmond, esf 1780 Chesterfield Co, VA where b 6/3/1761 s/o Richard & Mary; JP & high sheriff/o Co; PN there 1832; dd there 6/24/34; md 12/8/1785 Sally d/o James & Jane BRYANT (ML 12/3/85), Powhatan Co, VA; wid b 11/5/1762; wid PN Chesterfield Co, VA, 1840 when nephew Edmond A LOCKETT AFF there he b 12/8/1790; other Powhatan Co, VA, marriages in file per that Co clerk: 11/25/1785 John BOATRIGHT to Frances TENLEY, 2/9/1786 Henry HOLEMAN to Elizabeth BRANCH, 2/9/1786 William LOOKADO to Keziah LACY, all couples of that Co. F-W8064 R1576

LOCKETT, James, esf 1776 Cumberland Co, VA where b 11/30/1755; mvd to Johnston Co, NC, where esf 1781; PN 1833 Elbert Co, GA; res 1840 Abbeville District, SC, with s Joel. F-S9374 R1576
Royall, b 8/5/1752; esf 1777 Cumberland Co, VA where res; PN 1833 Mecklenburg Co, VA; dd 7/1/42 leaving children mbnn; QLF 1927 from desc Mrs A B MONTGOMERY, Richmond, VA states sol known as Royall Sr. F-S6799 R1756
LOCKHART, John Sr, b 4/3/1763 Princess Anne Co, VA; mvd with parents to Northampton Co, NC; esf there 1780; mvd several years after RW to VA for c20 years, thence Anson Co, NC, where PN 1832; dd 1/30/35; sol bro Adam res 1832 Anson Co, NC; uncle Captain Samuel LOCKHART RW sol. F-S8850 R1576
John, BLW12306 issued 11/5/1789. F-BLW12306 R1576
William, BLW12310 issued 5/29/1792. F-BLW12310 R1576
William, esf 1777 Staunton, VA; PN 1826 Frederick Co, VA, ae 66 occupation country schoolmaster when had no family. F-S38151 R1576
LOCKHEART, William, b 1759 Chester Co, PA, where esf 1777 when res with f; res after RW Wilmington, DE, then mvd to near Snickers on Shenandoah River in VA, then to Hampshire Co, VA, where afp when res there 26 years; PAR, svc less than 6 months. F-R6400 R1576
LOCKRIDGE, John, see LOCHRIDGE, John. F-S31218 R1576
LODEN, James, esf aec 15 Powhatan Co, VA as fifer; illiterate; afp aec 68 Bledsoe Co, TN, 1833, & PAR, insufficient proof of svc; wid Susan gave power of attorney to agent there in 1851 to afp; gave power of attorney 1860 Cumberland Co, TN to afp; no indication in file on PN Office action on wid's afp's. F-R6406 R1578
William, BLW12317 issued 5/29/1782. F-BLW12317 R1578
LOFTY, William, b 5/10/1761 Chesterfield Co, VA, near Petersburt; mvd ae 6 with f to Dan River, Halifax Co, VA, where esf 1780; mvd ae 36 to Catawba Co, NC, thence Cocke Co, TN where PN 1832. F-S4571 R1578
LOGAN, Alexander, b 10/1761; esf 1780 Fluvanna Co, VA; PN 1832 Amherst Co, Va; last PN payment in file 1839. F-S4571 R1578
John, see LOGGINS, John. F-R6414 R1578
Joseph, see LOGIN, Joseph. F-R6413 R1578
Patrick, esf 1776-7 Redstone, Fayette Co, PA, in 13th VA Regiment; PN 1819 Butler Co, OH; res ae 68 Franklin Co, IN, 1820 occupation weaver, when had no family; QLF 1934 from great great gdd Miss Fay LOGAN, Stockton, CA, states sol b Ulster, Ireland. F-S41778 R1578
Timothy, b Surry Co, NC; esf 1781 Garrard Co, KY Territory, in George Rogers CLARK's regiment; PN aec 74 there 1833; dd 3/21/48; md 10/10/1793 Sarah ALEXANDER, Madison Co, KY; wid PN ae 66 Gerrard Co, KY, 1853; dd there 7/4/53 leaving ch: George (res there then), William, Timothy, Sophia, Margaret SMITH, & Martha MORAN; Hugh LOGAN (no kinship given) adm/o wid estate; Stephen MORAN (no kinship to Martha

137

LOGAN (continued)
  given); QLF 1924 from desc Beulah H (Mrs C D) OSBORNE, Otterville, MO, states sol gdf/o her great gdm, further querier great great gdd of RW sol Richard SHANKLIN (f of Elijah, William & J T) of Hopkinsville, KY area, further querier great gdd of Joel HUBBARD who md Sally ALEXANDER; QLF states sol md 3 times & all 3 wives named Sarah, one being d of Thomas SMITH of Madison Co, KY, who living 1822; QLF states sol probably had s John h/o Mary FINNELL & s Hugh h of Elizabeth LAYER. F-W3700 R1578
William, b 11/11/1748 Spotsylvania Co, VA; esf 1776 York District, SC, where res; esf 1778 Rutherford, NC, where res; mvd back to York District, SC, c1790 where PN 1832; there dd 1/7/33, leaving no wid but ch: Thomas, Elijah, William (decd in 1849), Joseph, John (res there 1848), Mary PACKARD, & Margaret BOWLIN (decd in 1849); QLF states sol md Jane BLACK, & settled Lincoln Co, NC, further sol bro Joseph also NC RW sol, & their bro's John & Thomas fought on side of Tories in RW, all of that Co. F-S18955 R1578
William, esf 1775-6 Augusta Co, VA, where b 6/10/1758; mvd c1796 to Bourbon Co, KY, thence c1822 Nicholas Co, KY where PN 1833; QLF states a RW sol William LOGAN (bro of General Benjamin LOGAN) bc 1750 Augusta Co, VA, md c1775 Agnes McCOWAN, Botetourt Co, VA, later mvd to Lincoln Co, KY where dd c1796. F-S31219 R1578
LOGGINS, John, b 10/11/1733 Orange Co, VA; esf 1777 Halifax Co VA; mvd to Union District, SC, thence Pendleton District, SC, thence 1833 Hall Co, GA where afp 1834 & PAR; s Samuel gave power of attorney there 1853 for afp. F-R6414 R1578
LOGIN, Drury, b 1762 Halifax Co, VA; esf 1776 Tryon, Rutherford Co, NC; PN that Co 1832; dd 10/5/35; md 1783 Sarah, who dd 4/24/40 or 4/26/40; ch who gtd PN due m 1842: Joseph ae 55, Benjamin ae 52 (res Cleveland Co, NC), Levy ae 47, Sarah ae 43, & Anney ae 40; birth data in file: Moses LOGIN 11/10/1784, Susaner LOGIN 4/11/1786, Joseph LOGIN 11/3/1787, & John ROBERTES 6/10/1785 (s/o Mr LOGIN's sis); sol ch PN at Cleveland Co, NC; surname also spelled LOGAN. F-W5464 R1578
Joseph, b 1757 Rockbridge Co, VA; esf 1776 Washington Co, VA where res; mvd 1778 to NC, thence 1799 VA, then 1809 to Morgan Co, KY, where afp 1834; PAR, insufficient proof of svc. F-R6413 R1578
LOGSDON, James V, b 1766 Botetourt Co, VA; esf 1782 Jefferson Co, KY Territory, in VA Line; also served in Indian Wars 1784-1790; PN 1832 Hart Co, KY; dd 3/4/38 leaving wid mbnn who gtd his PN arrears 1839; surname also spelled LOGSDEN. F-S30547 R1579
LOGWOOD, Peggy, former widow of Thomas CRUMP. F-W8058 R1579
LOHR, Peter, b 1757 near Little York, PA; mvd when small ch to MD where esf 1776 Hagerstown; mvd c1790 to Augusta Co, VA, where PN 1832; last PN payment in file 1837. F-S5699 R1579
LONAS, George, b 1764 Philadelphia, PA; mvd to Shenandoah Co,

LONAS (continued)
VA, where esf 1780 Woodstock; PN 1933 Frederick Co, VA. F-S8848 R1579

LONASS, John, esf 1780 in the German Regiment, Frederick Town, MD where res; dd in RW svc; md 2/1779 Mary (b 8/15/1760) & their only ch John b 5/31/1781 (if liv 1837, res OH); wid md (2) Aaron FARDIN/FARDEN (dd 2/21/1834); wid & 2nd h mvd to Berkeley Co (area later Jefferson Co), VA, then to Morgan Co, KY; PN there 1837; decd in 1841. F-W19252 R1579

LONG, Anderson, esf ae 16 Culpeper Co, VA where b 1762; mvd to Shelby Co, KY, thence Mercer Co, KY, thence Warren Co, KY, then to Marion Co, MO, where PN 1832; last PN payment in file 1840. F-S17549 R1580

Benjamin, esf 1780 Caroline Co, VA, where b 1763; PN there 1832. F-S8846 R1580

Benjamin, b 1761 near Winchester, Frederick Co, VA; esf 1778 sub for bro Rosamon, Hampshire Co, VA where res; mvd after RW to Westmoreland Co, PA, thence Co, KY, thence Brown Co, OH, thence Crawford Co, IL, where PN 1835. F-S32383 R1580

Daniel, esf 1778 Culpeper Co, VA, where b 4/11/1756; PN 1833 Madison Co, AL, where dd 5/11/38; wid Martha gtd h PN arrears Huntsville, AL, 1839. F-S13773 R1580

David, b 1758 Bedford Co, VA; esf 1777 Rowan Co, NC, where res; PN 1832 Maury Co, TN; dd 1/24/45 Marshall Co, TN; md 6/28/1787 Mary HOWE, York Co, SC; wid PN ae 82 Marshall Co TN, 1850; ch births: Catsey 2/1788, David 11/17/89, Margret 12/8/90, Mary 4/1793, Martha 11/17/96, Joseph 12/5/97, Jannet 2/1800, Rebecca 3/1802, Esther 6/24/18--, & Elizabeth 4/29/1807. F-W2 R1580

George, b 1763 Conedogwinit, Cumberland Co, PA; esf 1777 in regiment of f Colonel Cookson LONG, res Muncytown, PA; mvd 1781 with f to near Winchester, VA where esf; f dd before 1798 at Falling Springs on Potomac River; sol PN 1833 Warren Co, PA res Brokenstraw Township; dd 3/11/54 Pittsfield Township, that Co; md 8/1792 Isabel McCORMICK, Lycoming Co PA; wid PN ae 78 Warren Co, PA, 1854 res Pittsfield Township 1854; gtd BLW26619 there 1856; dd Fall 1858; many ch mbnn; QLF 1925 from great gdd says sol f Cookson res Martinsburg, WV, & sol bro John also RW sol; QLF 1924 from desc Mrs Charles M ALLEN, Knoxville, TN. F-W9139 R1580

George, esf 1778-9 Shenandoah Co, VA where b 1757-8; PN 1833 Hawkins Co, TN; last PN payment in file 1838. F-S4564 R1580

Henry, esf 1781 Culpeper Co, VA, where b 5/30/1764; PN 1833 Greene Co, TN; dd 1836 TN, leaving wid mbnn who liv 1838. F-S1849 R1580

Jacob, b Chester Co, PA; esf 1775 Tawneytown, Berks Co, PA; PN ae 78 Loudoun Co, VA, 1832; dd 12/22/42; md 9/1794 Eve FUNK of Shelborne Parish (MB 9/8/94), Loudoun Co, VA; wid PN there 1848 ae 70; gtd BLW26907 there 1855 ae 89; QLF states sol s of William, who esf 1780 in 1st VA Regiment. F-W1790 R1580

LONG, John, esf 1776 VA; mvd c10 years after RW to Edgecombe Co, NC, with w's f & family; w's f dd c3 years later; sol PN there 1825 ae 70-75 when w Mary, d mbnn aec 17, & 2 gdc (boy aec 17, girl aec 14) res with him; dd there 10/11/26; md c1783 Mary/Polly ARMSTRONG, Sussex Co, VA; wid PN 1842 aec 80 Edgecombe Co, NC 1842. F-W5029 R1580

John, esf VA; gtd disability PN Spotsylvania Co, VA 1817 because of battle wounds; occupation then manual laborer & unable to sustain himself. F-S25233 R1580

John, esf 1780 Orange Co, VA; PN ae 68 Franklin Co, KY 1819; dd 2/7/20; QLF 1935 from great great gds E A DUNN, Oakland CA, who also great gds/o RW sol James DUNN of VA; QLF says a RW sol John LONG, b 1749 VA, md 1772 Mary HAYNES, Bedford Co, VA, she dd 1825 & he dd 1832 Woodford Co, KY. F-S36047 R1580

John, esf Caroline Co, VA; dd 7/9/1792; md c1782 there Amey GATEWOOD; wid PN there 1840 ae 78; ch births: James 10/27/1783, Reuben 9/12/85 (md Patsey LANDRUM who b 10/5/1791, & their ch: Gabriel R b 9/12/1807, Lavinia b 3/11/10, Elizabeth b 4/26/13, & C Addison 3/6/15); other ch of sol & w mbnn. F-W3433 R1580

John, esf in 8th VA Regiment; PN ae 65 Harrison Co, IN 1819; res 1821 ae 66 Adamson Co, IN, occupation farmer, when res with w Delilah ae 56, s John ae 14, & d Delilah ae 12; dd 5/20/28 Harrison Co, IN; md in VA to Delilah, who PN ae 78 Harrison Co, IN 1842; wid sis-in-law Mildred LONG AFF then there; QLF 1903 from desc Mrs Thomas HICKEY, New Albany, IN, states sol dd Corydon, IN. F-W10200 R1580

John Phillip, esf 1778 NY; later esf in 5th PA Regiment; PN ae 79-80 Pendleton Co, VA, 1830 when occupation "strolling tailor, house to house" when had no family living with him F-S38147 R1580

Jonathan, b 10/16/1758 York Co, PA; esf 1779 Franklin Co, PA where res; mvd to Frederick Co, MD where esf 1781; res after RW in MD, VA, & TN; PN 1833 Hawkins Co, TN; dd there 2/4/41; md 9/1783 or 10/1783 Nancy, Frederick Co, VA who b 4/3/1762; wid PN 1845 Hawkins Co, TN; ch births: John (eldest) 7/5/1784 (md 1/1807 & his 1st ch mbnn b 11/20/1809), David 6/1786, James W 9/1788, Sally 12/1790, Nancy 8/1797, & Mary 3/1800; AFF 1845 by Mordecai Bean ae 73 Hawkins Co, TN, he res 1791-1793 Frederick Co, VA near sol & w; AFF by Mary WRIGHT ae 74 Hawkins Co, TN 1845 she md 3/1789 George WRIGHT, Augusta Co, VA, & they mvd next month to Frederick Co, VA, for c11 years where neighbors to sol & w, & later mvd to Hawkins Co, TN; wid res 1848 there; QLF 1910 from desc Miss Helen Mary LONG of GA states sol ancestors came from Londonderry, Ireland. F-W383 R1580

Levi, esf in VA regiment after Battle of Guilford; afb 1819 Sussex Co, VA; BLW924 issued 7/20/20; QLF states sol maybe f/o Levi LONG who b 1799, dd KY 1882, & md Sarah Dickinson TROWER who b 1798. F-BLW924 R1581

Mathias, esf 1781 Rockingham Co, VA; gave power of attorney

LONG (continued)
  1814 there to agent to afp & afb; no action on claims indicated; per PN Office, sol agent res a pauper in Cumberland, PA 1843 & still held sol power/o attorney paper; sol dd 4/26/16; md 1/31/1792 Mary HUSTAND/HUSTANT (MB 1/26/92) signed by John HUSTAND); wid afp ae 72 Page Co, VA, 1840 & PAR, insufficient proof of svc. F-R6430 R1581
Nicholas, esf 1776 Caroline Co, VA, where b 5/15/1754; lost bro mbnn in Battle of Germantown, where both participated; mvd 1795 to KY where PN 1832 Lexington, Fayette Co; res in 1844 Campbell Co, KY, where dd 10/13/46 leaving no wid (dd before him) but 3 ch: Gabriel (mvd to TX & soon dd there), William (mvd to TX after Gabriel dd & dd there too), & Mary H COLWELL who res with h 1851 Campbell Co, KY; sol res with them at death; sol gds John M COLWELL res 1846 on KY side/o Ohio River; he witness to gdm Mary H COLWELL's signature 1851; near relative of sol, A D SMALLEY, AFF 1846 Newport, KY. F-S31222 R1581
Nicholas, esf 1781 Culpeper Co, VA where b 4/12/1764; mvd c5 years after RW to Botetourt Co, VA, for c20 years, then to Henry Co, VA, for 5 years, then to Greene Co, TN, for c5 years, then to Anderson Co, TN, then to Jefferson Co, TN, thence Knox Co, TN where PN 1833; dd 7/27/39 Jefferson Co, TN; md 11/5/1783 Margaret; wid PN ae 86 Grainger Co, TN, 1844; ch: eldest Betsy (1845 ae 61), William, Joel, Nancy, Sally, Rachel, Hannah, Peggy, Nicholas, Dicey & James; Mary BABB AFF ae 80 Greene Co, TN, 1844 she md (1) 1/15/1787 sol bro John, Botetourt Co, VA, & they had their wedding dinner there at home/o sol & w; QLF 1914 from desc Mrs G S LUSLEY, Fort Scott, KS; QLF 1914 from desc Mrs Martha W J FANCHER, Montrose, MO, states sol 1st ch Elizabeth (called Betsy), further sol s William, b 4/3/1785 & dd 11/15/1849 Iberia, MO, md Ruth GRIMES & their ch: George, Sarah/Sally, Elizabeth/Betsy, Margaret/Peggy, Rachel, Glen, & James (b 4/1/1818 Knox Co, TN), further William's s James (gds/o sol) md 12/6/1849 Harriet Caroline LENNARD, Salem, MO, & their d Martha M (querier) b 4/24/1852 Iberia, MO & she md 5/12/1872 Emmett J FANCHER, further their d Elsie C FANCHER b 4/2/1873 there, & md 5/31/1894 Frank LEMARTY, Montrose, MO, & they had d Violet C LEMARTY b there 4/18/1896. F-W593 R1581
Reuben, b 1758 Halifax Co, VA; esf 1776 as sub for bro John (to finish bro's enlistment) Chatham Co, NC; mvd with f to Broad River in SC, where esf 1780; afp ae 72 Grainger Co, TN, & PAR; res there 1840 ae 81; wid Nancy sent query from Knoxville, TN, to PN Office stating she had given an agent power of attorney to afp & got no response; no action indicated by PN Office on her query. F-R6431 R1581
Reuben, b St Mary's Co, MD; mvd to Culpeper Co, VA where esf 1775 ae 19; BLW480 issued 12/28/1809; PN 1828 Sumter District, SC. F-S46457 R1581
Richard, esf 1775 Culpeper Co, VA where b 9/22/1758; PN 1832

LONG (continued)
  Bedford Co, TN; dd 5/20/48; QLF 1905 from great gdd Mrs Mary Boren PEGUES, Tyler Co, TX. F-S4565 R1581
  Ware, esf Orange Co, VA; dd 9/1808 per wid; md 3/1781 Elizabeth JENNINGS, Orange Co, VA; wid afp ae 92 Greene Co, VA, 1848, & PAR, insufficient proof of svc & marriage; s James AFF 1853 there his f dd Fall 1812; sol eldest s Armistead, b 8/20/1779, AFF there 1853, when m decd, his parents had 4 liv ch then: self, Frances w of Jeremiah BRYANT, James & Richard; adm of wid estate 1853 Robert PRITCHETT. F-R6425 R1581
  William, esf 1780 Culpeper Co, VA, where b 8/20/1760; mvd to Orange Co, after RW, thence Madison Co, VA, for c9 years, thence Orange Co, VA, for 8 years, thence Howard Co, MO, where PN 1832; gtd VA BLW; QLF states sol had s Jacob; QLF states sol md Elizabeth/Betsy WHITLOCK & afp res Fayette, MO. F-S18088 R1581
LONGDON, John, esf 1776 VA in Lee's Legion; BLW423 issued 4/19/1808. F-BLW423 R1582
LONGEST, John, esf 1775 King & Queen Co, VA; afp ae 67 Henrico Co, VA, 1822 occupation farmer when had 4 d's (youngest ae 16) res with him; PAR. F-R6433 R1582
  Richard, esf 1775 in 1st VA Regiment; PN ae 60 King & Queen Co, VA; res there 1820 ae 65 when res with w Elizabeth aec 55 & stepd Elizabeth aec 15; dd 4/20/26; James LONGEST (no kinship given) adm of his estate; sol s Richard made query King & Queen Co, VA, to PN Office 1849 concerning f's PN; QLF 1937 from desc Mrs Mary C HUBBARD, Chicago, IL who also desc of VA RW sol James BLAND. F-S38149 R1582
LONGLEY, William, b 1761 NJ; esf 1780 Loudoun Co, VA, when res there with f; mvd after RW to Shenandoah Co, VA, then to Rockbridge Co, VA, thence Washington Co, VA, then 1800 to Sevier Co, TN, thence McMinn Co, TN, where PN 1833; dd 11/7/41 Polk Co, TN; md 9/1/1784 Mary, Loudoun Co, VA; wid afp ae 78 Polk Co, TN, 1/1844 & dd 6/7/44 or 6/9/44 before afp acted upon, leaving ch: Jonathan (b 1788), Joel (b 6/9/1791), James, Mercy, Sarah, Abigail, & John C (b 1806); s Joel AFF there 1845; s John C afp 1854 Polk Co, TN, for sol surv ch, stating he youngest ch of sol & w; d Abigail & her h William T PATTERSON res then Catoosa Co, GA as was wid sis Mrs Etha BURK then ae 73; ch PAR, sol w not wid in 1838 & dd before 1851, per current PN laws, also insufficient proof of marriage of sol & wid; surname also spelled LONGLY; QLF 1932 from great great gdd Mrs Mary Longley HOOKER of Colorado, TX; QLF 1931 from desc Mrs Katherine Walton MORGAN, Sweetwater, TX, states sol s Joseph b Rockbridge Co, VA, md Priscilla PATERSON, was War of 1812 sol & they had s Campbell b 9/30/1817 Sevier, TN, who was gdf of querier. F-R6435 R1582
LONGWORTH, William, b 5/9/1756 Richmond Co, VA, where esf 1775-1776; mvd c30 years after RW svc to Wilkes Co, NC, thence Stokes Co, NC, where afp 1840; PAR. F-R6437 R1582

LORD, Robinson, esf King William Co, VA where b; VA BLW746 issued 6/5/1783 to sol as Roberson LORD; dd 7/15/1819 Henrico Co, VA; md 11/5/1786 Nancy d/o Sarah DEANE (MB 11/4/85) King William Co, VA; wid b that Co; afp 6/15/1843 aec 76 Henrico Co, VA, & dd there 7/30/43 before claim processed; PN due wid paid to only surv ch Frances D (b 11/3/1786), w of Isham A KING, Henrico Co, VA, 1845. F-W5326 R1586

LORE, Michael, b 10/6/1755 near York, PA; esf 1781 Washington Co, MD, where res; mvd c6 years after RW to Berkeley Co, VA for c7 years, thence Rockingham Co, VA, where PN 1832; QLF states sol surname also spelled LOHR; QLF 1930 from desc Mrs Thorressa Lohr MOORE of London, OH, states sol md Catherine SCHRIVER. F-S5708 R1587

LORTON, Robert, b 2/15/1747; esf 1776 in 4th VA Regiment; PN 1819 St Clair Co, IL; res 1822 Bond Co, IL; d Greene Co, IL, 5/16/33; md 8/15/1779 Tabitha GANNAWAY/GANAWAY, Buckingham Co, VA; wid dd 8/15/1838 Greene Co, IL; ch births (part/o family bible torn & missing): John 10/1780, Robert 9/11/1782, Thomas 12/9/84, William 10/1786, Joseph 4/25/88 Mary/Polly 12/9/90, Henry 8/4/179-, & Sary/Sally 12/11/99; ch who survived m: John, Robert, Thomas, William, Joseph, Mordica D, Henry, Polly NANCE, Sally CHIPMAN, & Susannah PANKY; other births in file (all surname LORTON): Francis 4/24/1794, Martha 5/27/1812, John 11/14/1813, & Elizabeth 12/12/1815; s Robert afp Greene Co, IL, 1844 ae 61 for wid surv ch; PAR, insufficient proof/o sol svc after marriage; QLF 1909 from desc W H LORTON of Springfield, IL; QLF 1908 from desc Tolman T GELDER, Philadelphia, PA, whose m desc of sol; QLF 1928 from great gdd Mrs Lenna Lorton CAMPBELL, East St Louis, IL, who gdd/o sol s Mordica H, further querier's bro Stewart C LORTON was World War II sol. F-R6454 R1587

LOSHIER, Peter, esf in Lee's Legion; BLW13394 issued 4/10/1790 F-BLW13394 R1587

LOT, Levi, esf in Lee's Legion; BLW13393 issued 5/15/1792. F-BLW13393 R1588

LOTT, John, b 10/22/1742 Caroline Co, VA; esf 1778 Albemarle Co, VA where res; mvd 1786 to Fayette Co (area later Woodford Co), KY, thence 1818 Jefferson Co, IN, where PN 1833. F-S18089 R1588

LOUMPKIN, Dickeson, see LUMPKIN, Dickeson. F-R6521 R1589

LOURY/LOWRY, Susan, former wid of Gibson CLUVERIUS. (F-W8061)

LOUTS, Jacob, esf 1778 Stoverstown, Shenandoah Co, VA, where b 12/21/1761; mvd 1783 to Winchester, VA for 3 years, thence Berkeley Co, VA, then to Greenbrier Co, VA, for c6 years, then to Bath Co, VA, then to Gallia Co, OH, where PN 1833, res Wilkesville Township; QLF 1917 from O J ALDRICH, Grand Junction, CO, states sol md Elizabeth WOLF, mvd 1806 to Gallia Co, OH, w dd 1837 & he dd 1839, s Isaac was gdf to querier's w; QLF 1934 from Joseph B LUTZ of Cheyenne, WY, great gds/o Michael LUTZ who appeared in Shenandoah Co, VA & md there 1800. F-S4567 R1589

LOVE, Charles, esf 1777 Philadelphia, PA, in 8th VA Regiment; PN ae 65 Pendleton Co, KY, 1818; QLF 1913 from desc Ethel Brandom (Mrs John J) MORRIS, Carrollton, MO; QLF says sol dd c1818; QLF states a VA RW sol Charles LOVE dd 1824 Cabell Co, VA, leaving w Susannah (nee CHILES) & ch: Daniel, Allen, Agnes ROLFE, William, Mary RUCKER, Susannah HAMPTON & Elizabeth Ann SHORTRIDGE; QLF 1918 from Mrs F H HELSELL, Ft Dodge, IA, desc/o RW sol Charles LOVE who dd Cabell Co, VA. F-S36046 R1590

Elias, b 1750; esf 1777 Southampton Co, VA, where res; PN 1832 there res Nottoway Parish; dd 9/17/36; wid mbnn res 1837 that Co with family; d & 2 sons mbnn. F-S18092 R1590

Henry, esf 1776 Southampton Co, VA, where b 1756; PN there 1832; dd 2/27/40. F-S8856 R1590

James, b 3/10/1762 Augusta Co, VA; mvd ae 12 with f to Montgomery Co, VA, where esf 1779; mvd after RW to Washington Co, TN (area then in NC) for c6 years, thence Buncombe Co, NC, for 5 years, thence Logan Co, KY, for 5 years, thence Williamson Co, TN, for 6 years, thence Maury Co, TN, where PN 1834 when res there c26 years; bro of Robert. F-S21350 R1590

John, b 1762 Brunswick Co, VA; mvd when small ch with f to Charlotte Co, VA, for a few years, thence Wilkes Co, NC, where esf 1780 as sub for f James; moved soon after RW to Stokes Co, NC for 2-3 years, thence back to Wilkes Co, NC, where PN 1832; QLF 1915 from desc Mrs L N COFFMAN, Salem, MO; QLF states sol md 1788 Mary KING & dd 1842 Wilkes Co, NC. F-S8852 R1590

Robert, esf 1780 Caswell Co, NC, where b 12/17/1762; PN 1833 Mason Co, VA; last PN payment in file 1844 in VA. F-S18093 R1590

Robert, b 10/1760 Augusta Co, VA; esf 1776 Montgomery Co, VA where res; mvd 1782 to Washington Co, TN (area then in NC) where commanded regiment/o militia against Chickamauga Indians; PN 1833 Waynesville, Haywood Co, NC; md "present" w 11/11/1783 & had 12 ch by her; NC elector for US president & vice president at every election from the time of Thomas JEFFERSON to Andrew JACKSON; bro James res 1833 Maury Co, TN; bro Thomas AFF then Haywood Co, NC; QLF 1913 from desc Mrs Henry BLACK, Rolla, MO, who also desc/o VA RW sol John CONNELLY (res 1835 ae 74 Bedford C, TN), also of VA RW sol William PAMPHLIN (res 1835 ae 72 Lincoln Co, TN); QLF says sol dd Haywood Co, NC; QLF states sol dd 1845 Waynesville, Haywood Co, NC. F-S8858 R1590

Thomas, b 8/19/1755 Ireland; came to America ae 8; esf 1777 Augusta Co, VA; mvd after RW to Mason Co, VA, then to Letart Township, Meigs Co, OH where PN 1833; dd 12/22/34; md 2/1/1787 Rosanna McCLURE, Rockbridge Co, VA; wid PN 1845 ae 78 Letart Township, Meigs Co, OH. F-W8055 R1590

William, esf Shenandoah Co, VA; BLW12312 issued 5/29/1792; became insane & placed in lunatic asylum 1803 Williamsburg VA, where dd c1811; md 1791 Winford CARNEY, Shenandoah Co,

LOVE (continued)
VA; wid mvd to Harrison Co, VA, thence Lewis Co, VA, then to Upshur Co, VA, where dd 12/27/1847 at res of d Rebecca; eldest ch Samuel afp ae 60 there 1851, & PAR; 2nd ch Charles; another ch Robert AFF then ae 50 Upshur Co, VA, res Meigs Co, OH. F-R6469 R1590

LOVEL, William, b 1/12/1758 Amelia Co, VA; esf 1776 Guilford Co, NC; esf 1781 Surry Co, NC; res after RW Wilkes Co, NC, thence Elbert Co, GA, thence Greenville District, SC, then to Cocke Co, TN, thence Knox Co, TN, thence White Co, TN, thence Overton Co, TN, thence Jackson Co, TN, thence Crawford Co, TN, thence Jackson Co, TN, where afp 1837; PAR, less than 6 months svc. F-R6478 R1591

LOVELACE, Philip, b 1760 Charles Co, MD; esf 1781 Fairfax Co, VA; PN there 1832; dd 3/3/36; md 11/28/1821 Ann FRIZZILE/FRIZLE (ML 11/28/1821), Georgetown, DC; wid PN 1854 aec 54 Fairfax Co, VA; gtd BLW26541 there 1855. F-W12145 R1591

LOVELADY, Thomas, esf Guilford Co, NC, where b 1750; esf 1780 VA; esf 1781 SC; res after RW Washington Co, VA, then to Augusta Co, VA, thence Russell Co, VA, where dd 6/10/1840; md 8/20/1821 Nancy BRIGGS, Floyd Co, KY; wid PN ae 66 Carter Co, KY, 1854. F-W8065 R1591

LOVELESS, George, b 9/5/1760; esf 1777 Holston, VA, as sub for f John who brought family 1778 to Martin's Fort, KY, where indians attacked 1780, & took sol, bro John & their f POW; they exchanged 1784; sol PN 1832 Trumbull Co, OH, res Newton Township; dd 2/26/33, leaving 3 heirs mbnn. F-S4575 R1592

Philip, see LOVELACE, Philip. F-W12145 R1592

LOVELL, Sarah, former wid of William CHANDLEY. (F-W5027)

LOVELY, William L, BLW1302 issued 6/17/1790. F-BLW1302 R1592

LOVEN, James, esf 1780 Amelia Co, VA, where b 1764; PN 1834 Hawkins Co, TN. F-S4572 R1592

LOVERN, Christopher, esf 1780 Caroline Co, VA; PN there 1819 ae 58; res there 1820 with w aec 50 & her d's: Nancy MOORE aec 22, Patsy aec 19, & Elizabeth aec 15; sol dd 6/7/37; adm/o estate Reuben E McDANIEL. F-S8148 R1592

Richard, b 1760 Amelia Co, VA, where esf 1778 as sub for f Moses; esf 1780 Petersburg, VA; mvd after RW to Charlotte Co, VA, for 16 years, thence Halifax Co, VA where PN 1832; dd there 3/2/36; md 12/18/1788 Frances/Fanny BLANKENSHIP, Amelia Co, VA; wid PN ae 69 Halifax Co, VA, 1839; her last PN payment in file 1841. F-W8089 R1592

LOVETT, Joseph, esf 1777 Baltimore, MD, in 16th VA Regiment; PN ae 61 Gulford Co, NC 1818 when res with w & d (other ch having mvd out); res 1827 there occupation farmer when had w Sarah aec 71, d Betsy aec 30 (mentally deranged), & they liv with s Aaron; dd 5/12/33; md 1782 Sarah who dd 11/9/38 leaving ch George, John & Elizabeth; ch births: Mary 12/1/1782, Aaron 11/1/84, Moses 12/1/86, Comfort 9/23/88, Elizabeth 12/3/90, Joseph 6/26/93, John 5/4/96, & George 12/31/97; s George afp 1843 Guilford Co, NC, for self & surv

LOVETT (continued)
   siblings; ch gtd PN due m; surname also spelled LOVET. F-W26804 R1592
LOVING, Christopher, esf 1777 ae 14 in 6th SC Regiment; PN ae 56 Nelson Co, VA, 1819; res there 1820 occupation farmer, when had w ae 45, d ae 19, s ae 19, d ae 17, s ae 15, d ae 13, s ae 11, d ae 9, & s ae 7; dd 9/27/30 Floyd Co, VA, leaving wid Judith; QLF 1921 from desc Frances Claire LOVING, Jacksonville, IL. F-S38153 R1593
   Richard, esf 1777 VA; PN ae 72 Henrico Co, VA 1832; dd 6/24/34 or 6/20/35 Hanover Co, VA; md 12/31/1783 Mary/Polly HARLOW, Henrico Co, VA; wid PN ae 76 Hanover Co, VA, 1840; res 7/1843 Augusta Co, VA; dd 12/21/43; children mbnn; wid bro John res Hanover Co, VA, 1837 ae 67. F-W8033 R1593
LOW, Henry, esf 1777 in 5th Maryland Regiment; PN ae 66 Washington Co, VA 1818; res 1821 there ae 68 occupation farmer with w ae 50, d aec 17, & d aec 10; dd 5/21/45; md (2) 7/21/1836 Eleanor/Ellen KELSOE, Washington Co, VA; wid had family/o infant d's 1852 when she had to work in field gathering corn at 25 cents/day to feed her ch; wid PN there 1853 ae 34-40; gtd BLW8454 there 1855 aec 40 when AFF her h also War of 1812 sol; res there 1865 ae 47 when PN restored after Civil War; last PN payment in file 1890; decd in 1891; surname also spelled LOWE. F-W8259 R1593
LOW, Lott, b 1764 VA; esf 1780 Winton Co (area later Barnwell District), SC; mvd after RW to KY for 15 years, then to Stewart Co, GA, where afp 1835; PAR, insufficient proof of svc. F-R6486 R1594
LOWE, John, b 2/24/1760 St Mary's Co, MD where esf 1778 in 4th MD Regiment; mvd 1785 with f to near Dumfries, Prince William Co, VA; PN there 1839; res there 1843. F-S8859 R1594
   Stephen, esf 1778 Bedford Co, VA, where b 6/1761-2; esf 1780 Orange Co, VA; mvd to Franklin Co, VA, thence Surry Co, NC thence Buncombe Co, NC, where afp 1834 & PAR; dd 6/21/43, leaving wid Sarah who gave power/o attorney to agent there to afp & her PAR; surname also spelled LOW. F-R6189 R1594
   Thomas, b Cumberland Co, VA, where esf 1776 in 10th VA Regiment; PN ae 77 Rockingham Co, NC, 1832; dd there 10/27/35; md 2/20/1783 Mary HOLEMAN, Cumberland Co, VA; wid dd Rockingham Co, NC, 5/13/39; Richard M LOWE (no kinship given) adm of estates of sol & wid afp there 1852 ae 39 for their surv ch: William H (b 11/9/1783), Cynthia WARDLOW (b 2/3/90), Ruth MASSEY (b 11/30/92), John H (b 4/31/97), & Elizabeth WHITSETT (b 3/11/99); PAR, per current PN laws (sol wid dd before 1842); wid bro Yancy res 1852 Rockingham Co, NC, ae 92. F-R6488 R1594
   William, b 2/17/1756 VA; esf 1755 Surry Co, NC, where res; res there c7 years after RW, thence SC on Saluda River for 11 years, thence KY, where PN 1832 Simpson Co; QLF 1934 from great great gdd Mrs Luella R ADAMS, Parowan, Iron Co, UT, states sol md Margaret FAIR/FARR, querier also great great gdd of RW sol William BUTLER who md Phoebe CHILDER/

LOWE (continued)
CHILDERS, querier also great great gdd of RW sol Whittaker REDD Sr who f of Whittaker Jr, William, & Henry. F-S13795 R1594
LOWREY, John, b 4/12/1755 Candle Creek Settlement, Rowan Co, NC; esf NC; mvd 1790 to Elbert Co, GA, for 4-5 years, then to Franklin Co, GA, where dd 9/12/1808; md 3/16/1780 Elender, Rowan Co, NC; wid b 2/22/1762 Frederick Co, VA, & mvd when small ch with f to Rowan Co, NC; res near Beattie's Fort on Catawba River while h in RW svc; ch by sol: James 1/6/1781 (dd before 1840), Ann 1/25/83, Charles 6/27/85, Nathan 11/29/87, Elizabeth 7/15/90, Shadrach 11/5/92, John B 1/1/95 (res 1849 Jackson Co, GA), Middleton 8/12/97, Elender 10/14/1801, & Polly 10/11/03; other file data John D LOWREY b 9/10/1813 (kinship not given); wid md (2) 10/1811 James W COOK, Franklin Co, GA; they mvd 1812 to Jackson Co, GA, where James dd 7/15/33; wid PN 1849 there; sol surname also spelled LOWRY. F-W6709 R1596
Thomas, see LOWRY, Thomas. F-W2139 R1596
LOWRY, John, b 10/1758 Frederick Co, VA; esf 1779 Rowan Co, NC where res; res SC after RW, thence KY, thence TN, where PN 1832 Franklin Co; res 1839 Hamilton Co, IL, when children res IL; Light W LOWRY (no kinship given) AFF then White Co IL. F-S31216 R1596
John, b 3/14/1762 Goochland Co, VA; esf 1780 Bedford Co, VA, where res; f mvd to KY, & took family bible with him; sol PN 1833 Bedford Co, VA. F-S5698 R1596
Susan, former widow of Gibson CLUVERIUS. (F-W8061)
Thomas, b 1760 St Mary's Co, MD; mvd aec 3 to Stafford Co, VA, where esf; mvd c1786 to KY, thence 1816 Clark Co, KY, where PN 1832; dd there 11/21/46; md 10/16/1805 Nancy DEDMAN; wid PN 1853 Clark Co, KY; gtd BLW13444 there 1855 ae 74; William LOWRY (no kinship given) AFF there then; sol bro Moses res 1832 Bath Co, KY. F-W2139 R1596
Thornton, esf 1779 Goochland Co, VA; PN there 1832 ae 71; dd 8/19/43; md 8/1788 Ann THRUSTON (MB 8/5/88 signed by William THRUSTON), Goochland Co, VA; wid PN there 1848 when res there over 80 years. F-W8088 R1596
LOWTHER, Joel, esf 1778 Culpeper Co, VA; esf 1780 Harrison Co, VA; PN ae 62 Athens Co, OH 1818; res there 1820 occupation blacksmith when had w ae 33 & ch: Deidamia ae 13, Elias ae 7, Mary ae 5, & Jackson ae 2; dd 11/12/53 ae 98 near Rutland, OH; md (2) Fall 1812 Nancy DOUGLASS at home of her f in Lee Township, Athens Co, OH, & they had 3 ch; wid PN ae 66 that Co 1853; gtd BLW26844 ae 67 Putnam Co, MO, 1855; William SMITH AFF 1853 ae 57 Athens Co, OH, he md d of sol by 1st w; wid bro David AFF 1854 there ae 51; sol wid dd 5/16/71. F-W4269 R1596
LOYD, James, esf 1777 in VA artillery regiment; PN ae 84 Halifax Co, VA, 1819; res there 1820 occupation farmer when d & her ch mbnn liv with him. F-S38154 R1596
John, b 1763 Cumberland Co, VA; esf Surry Co, NC, where res;

LOYD (continued)
    mvd c1788 from there to Washington Co, VA, where PN 1833.
    F-S8847 R1596.
  Robin (AKA ROBIN, Indian); free man of color; b 1760 Dinwiddie Co, VA, where esf 1778; mvd to NC for 21 years, thence IN Territory, where afp Jennings Co, IN, 1834; afp again 1838 there; PAR both times. F-R6501 R1596
  William, esf Chesterfield Co, VA; PN aec 58 Halifax Co, VA, 1819; res there 1820 when had w aec 40 & 7 ch of which eldest was d ae 21; dd 6/10/35 leaving wid Mary who res 1836 Halifax Co, VA; QLF states a Thomas LOYD settled near Petersburg, VA, & had s's George, Thomas, & William, further s Thomas f/o Daniel & Nancy (md 1st cousin Thomas P LOYD). F-S38145 R1596
LOYDE, George, b Essex Co, VA; esf VA; dd 9/13/1813; md Elizabeth Armstrong WAGGONER (MB 7/23/1793 signed by Benjamin WAGGONER), Essex Co, VA; wid PN there 1843 ae 71. F-W8086 R1596
LOZIER, Hillebrand, BLW13392 issued 2/2/1790. F-BLW13392 R1596
  Jacob, esf 1776 Fort Washington, NY in NJ regiment; esf 1781 VA; PN ae 63 Lyons, Wayne Co, NY, 1823 occupation carpenter when w ae 50, d 17 & s ae 11 res with him; dd 11/16/31 or 11/20/31 or 10/25/32 Royalton, NY; md 1/18/1785 or 1790 Christiana PECK, Wallkill, Orange Co, NY; wid PN 1838 Niagara Co, NY, ae 69; dd 3/27/50; wid sis Jane LOZIER AFF ae 66 Niagara Co, NY, 1838; wid s Israel AFF then ae 27; wid s Ezekiel AFF 1852 ae 54 Orleans Co, NY; s Ezekiel afp for self & surv siblings (Henry, Israel, & William) 1854 Medina, NY, & they gtd PN due m; sol bro Abraham AFF Wayne Co, NY, res Lyons, 1823 ae 70; wid bro Thomas PECK AFF 1854 Onandaga Co, NY, res Syracuse; QLF 1914 from great great gdd Mrs Nellie Wood CUPP, Three Rivers, MI; QLF 1910 from desc Mrs Lilli M SPEER, Springfield, MA. F-W24579 R1596
LUALLEN, Richard, see LEWALLEN, Richard. F-W26211 R1596
LUCADO, Isaac, esf 1776 in 7th VA Regiment; PN ae 62 Fluvanna Co, VA, 1818; res there 1820 occupation farmer when family w aec 52, d ae 30, d ae 27, s aec 17 & s aec 15 + girl (no kin) aec 10; res there 1832. F-S8869 R1596
LUCAS, Basil, esf 1776 MD where b 8/20/1757; PN by state/o MD; PN by US 1833 Berkeley Co, VA, where dd 7/6/41 leaving wid Elizabeth whom md 2/26/1786; wid liv 1843; QLF 1917 from desc U G CRUSE, Houston, TX; QLF states a VA RW sol William LUCAS b 1743 & dd 1814 Lucasville, OH. F-S18097 R1597
  Francis, b 3/10/1753; esf 1775 Culpeper Co, VA; PN 1818 Gibson Co, IN; dropped from PN rolls 1820 by PN Office since he then had too many assets; res there when had w ae 52, & ch: Mary ae 19, Jemima ae 16, William ae 13, & Francis Jr ae 9; res 1830 Princeton, IN; dd 8/18/31 leaving wid & several ch mbnn; QLF 1938 from great great gdd Mrs I J BOWEN of Arkansas City, KS. F-S36687 R1597
  James, esf 1776 Brunswick Co, VA; dd 12/8/1814, leaving wid Mary & 7 ch (eldest Robert ae 35 & youngest a d ae 19); md

LUCAS (continued)
  3/29/1779 Mary d of Captain John LUCAS, Surry Co, VA; wid PN ae 77 Montgomery Co, AL, 1837; her bro Henry AFF there then; wid P O address 1841 Mt Meigs, that Co; QLF states sol dd Hancock Co, GA, further wid res 1840 ae 81 with d Mrs June W FREENEY, also s James dd Hancock Co, GA, also a d md Archibald HUNTER & they lived, dd there; QLF from DAR agent for sol desc Miss A H GEISE of GA; QLF 1916 from sol great gdd Mrs Leola Lucas TINSLEY of Tampa, FL; QLF 1911 from great great great gdd Frances RONEY of Monmouth, IL. F-W12163 R1597
Joel, esf 1776-1777 Pittsylvania Co, VA in 15th VA Regiment; mvd to Yadkin River, NC, thence Union Co, SC for 16 years, thence Blount Co, TN, thence Monroe Co, TN, where afp 1844 ae 88; PAR, insufficient proof of svc. F-R6506 R1597
John, b 7/15/1749; esf 1778 Montgomery Co, VA, where res; PN there 1832; dd 4/19/36; md there 2/15/1777, Mary who b 1/1/1758; wid PN there 1839 when she a great gdm; ch included (all liv 1852): Samuel, Wilson b 11/6/1794, Susan PETUMAN a wid, & Theodicia w/o Lewis WEAVER; surname also spelled LUCASS; QLF 1910 from Mrs Eliza Lucas BROWN of Columbus, OH, states she desc/o a RW sol Captain John LUCAS, b Surry Co, VA, md Mary Rapeler SIMONS, & mvd to GA; QLF 1929 from Miss Mary Kate HUNTER, Palestine, TX, desc of RW sol James HUNTER of Fredericksburg, VA, & Portsmouth, VA, sometimes called James Jr, who md Marianna Russell SPENCE. F-5468 R1597
Nathaniel, esf 1776 in 4th VA Regiment; BLW2636 issued 2/28/1794; dd 5/5/1807 Warren Co, KY; LWT 5/4/1807, probated there 9/1807 lists w & ch: Charles, Robert Wilkins, John, Nancy, Elizabeth, Tabitha, Sarah, & Rebecca; md 1783 Sally d of Robert RIVERS, (MB 4/16/1783 signed by John LUCAS), Greensville Co, VA; LWT of wid f Robert 4/2/1792, probated there 5/24/92, lists w Martha & ch: Polley, Amy, Nancy, Sally LUCAS, Thomas, Robert, Martha w of Benjamin JONES, & Elizabeth w of Nathaniel RIVES; wid Sarah PN ae 84 Warren Co, KY, 1842; QLF 1909 from desc Francis RONEY, Monmouth, IL. F-W442 R1597
Parker, esf 1777 Montgomery Co, VA; PN ae 76 Giles Co, VA, 1832; dd 3/27/35. F-S8868 R1597
Thomas, esf 1775 Philadelphia, PA as marine on ship CABOT of Continental Navy; later commissioned lieutenant in Colonel Daniel MORGAN's VA Regiment; PN 1818 Franklin Co, PA ae 61 when res there 40 years; res there 1820 occupation cooper, when he & w Mary ae 57 res with s John ae 28; other ch liv then: Margaret ae 30, Martha ae 25, Mary ae 22, Eliza ae 19, & Thomas ae 17; sol dd 11/3/23; QLF 1928 from desc Mrs James G BROWN, Montrose, CO; QLF states sol's bro Charles & William served with him in Colonel MORGAN's VA Regiment. F-S40103 R1598
William, b 1754 Frederick Co (area later Montgomery Co), MD; esf 1776 Fredericktown, MD; mvd c1780 to Mecklenburg Co,

LUCAS (continued)
   VA, on Roanoke Rvier where esf 1781; mvd after RW to Rutherford Co, NC where PN 1832; dd 4/6/39; md Summer 1780 Mary; wid PN ae 82 Cleveland Co, NC, 1842; ch births: John 4/25/1781, James Rimer 1/16/84, & Nancy 10/21/91; other births in file: Mimy LUCAS 3/14/1822 & Caty LUCAS 8/26/23. F-W20535 R1598
  William, esf 1777 Gloucester Co, VA; PN there ae not given 1818. F-S38158 R1598
  William, b 7/25/1749 Pittsylvania Co, VA; esf 1772 Botetourt Co, VA, against indians, & again in 1773; esf 1777 Wood's Fort, VA, for RW; afp 1832 Logan Co, VA; PAR, less than 6 months RW svc. F-R6507 R1598
LUCK, John, esf 1778 Pittsylvania Co, VA, where b 6/14/1760; mvd 1825 to Iredell Co, NC, where PN 1833. F-S13635 R1599
LUCUS, William, esf 1774/5 Fairfax Co, VA, in 7th VA Regiment; afp ae 76 Simpson Co, MS, 1832 as William Sr; afp Rankin Co, MS 1835 ae 79; PAR, insufficient proof/o svc. F-R6508 R1599
LUDEMANN, John William, b 5/4/1756 Munden, Hanover Province, Germany, s of Rudolph LUDEMANN & Anna Christine BEURMANN, who md there; esf VA; dd intestate 1786 Richmond, VA without issue; no w mentioned; sis Christine Sophie b Munden, Germany, 7/5/1750, md Franz William HAMPE, & their ch were Anna Christian Hedwig (b 9/13/1774) w/o goldsmith SCHODDE, Henrietta Magdalene (b 5/22/1788) wid/o inspector R REICHARD, Christine Sophie wid of Dr John KAHL, & Franz William (b 4/3/90), all of Munden, Germany; sis Catherine Julianna & sis Anna Christine Hedwid (b there 5/14/1756) survived sol; other siblings dd childless; heirs afp in Germany, & gtd PN due sol. F-R15955 R1599
LUGAR, Adam, b 3/1/1738 Frankfort, Germany; enlisted there ae 33 to serve with British army; deserted in NY, & esf Lancaster, PA, in American unit; later esf NC; PN 1834 Giles Co, VA, where had res 40 years; dd there 3/9/37; md 1777 Margaret CLAP(P), Orange Co, NC; wid PN ae 84 Giles Co, VA 1841 when eldest ch & next to youngest ch Adam res there; dd 2/8/44; QLF 1930 from desc Dolly I Baker BIGLER, Beloit WI. F-W8066 R1600
LUGG, Elizabeth, former wid of Frederick WARNECK. (F-W20540)
LUMBLEY, William, esf 1780 in VA regiment; PN aec 58 Warren Co, TN, 1820 when res McMinnville with w Mary ae 67; mvd to IL, thence AR, thence Barry Co, MO, where res 1837; dd 10/28/43 leaving wid Mary; ch included Washington, who res 1823 McMinnville, TN; QLF states sol buried near Mt Vernon in Dade Co, MO where he mvd to 1839 & built 1st mill there. F-S32000 R1600
LUMKIN, Moore, see LUMPKIN, Moore. F-W8264 R1601
LUMM, Jesse, b 5/12/1764 NC; mvd as infant with m to Loudoun Co VA where his gdf res during RW; esf there 1780; mvd 1818 to Columbiana Co, OH for 14 years, thence Allegheny Co, PA for 2 years, thence Beaver Co, PA where PN 1835. F-S8872 R1601

LUMPKIN, Dickeson, b 1759 King & Queen Co, VA where esf aec 16 sub for f Anthony; mvd after RW to Guilford Co, NC, thence GA, thence TN, where afp 1832 Campbell Co; illiterate; dd there 9/8/51; md 5/22/1820 Susan LUKER, Hall Co, GA; wid afp ae 53 Campbell Co, TN, 1855; both PAR; surname spelled also LUMPKINS & LOUMPKIN. F-R6521 R1601
George, b 9/19/1758 Essex Co, VA;; esf 1777 King & Queen Co, VA, sub for f Anthony; PN 1832 Granville Co, NC. F-S8870 R1601
Moore, esf 1778 Amelia Co, VA; PN 1828 Bedford Co, VA ae not given; mvd to Nottoway Co, VA, thence Pittsylvania Co, VA, where dd 12/8/41; md 12/27/1829 Catharine/Kitty RICHARDSON there at home/o John RICHARDSON (no kinship given); wid PN there 1853 ae 48; gtd BLW12566 there 1855 ae 47; PN reinstated there 1865 ae 57; res there 1869 ae 60; res there 1875 ae 57 (compiler's note: all ages stated by wid during her various court appearances). F-W8264 R1601
Philip, b 1762 King & Queen Co, VA, where esf 1779 as sub for bro Richard; mvd soon after RW to Lincoln Co, KY, for 14 years, thence Burke Co, GA where PN 1833 when res there 32 years; dd there 6/25/37; md (2) c5/21/1827 Nancy LINDSAY, Jefferson Co, GA; wid md (2) John ROGERS who dd Burke Co, GA 4/1/57; wid gtd BLW93548 & gtd PN there 1860 ae 59; dd 8/10/68; her only ch Benjamin F ROGERS afp there 1869 ae 27 for PN due m; AFF by George W EVANS aec 54 Richmond Co, GA, 1860 he md sol gdd; AFF 1833 by sol bro James aec 67, planter of Greene Co, GA, that he res King & Queen Co, VA, when sol esf. F-W10245 R1601
Wilson, esf 1776 in 7th VA Regiment; PN 1828 King & Queen Co VA, ae 74; AFF then there by John LUMPKIN (no kinship given); QLF states sol res 1840 with Susannah WATKINS. F-S38156 R1601
LUMSDEN, Charles, b Prince William Co, VA; esf 1779-1780 Henry Co (area later Franklin Co), VA; PN latter Co 1823 ae 71; dd 2/14/39; md 3/23/1787 Patty RIVES (MB 3/16/87 signed by Jeremiah LUMSDEN), Franklin Co, VA; wid PN there 1843 aec 80; QLF 1924 from desc Sarah R (Mrs Harry Marshall) DIXON, Richland, GA, who also desc of RW sol William JONES Sr of Jasper Co, GA & of RW sol Jeremiah LUMSDEN of VA (later of GA), whose wid Elizabeth Belcher LUMSDEN gtd PN Jasper Co, GA. F-W8067 R1601
John, b 1758 Hanover Co, VA; esf 1778 Louisa Co, VA, where res; mvd 1790 to Fayetteville, Cumberland Co, NC, where PN 1832; QLF 1915 from great gdd (on m's side) Mrs B R DUDLEY of Richmond, VA, states sol w Miss GLASS whose f was also RW sol & res Fayetteville, NC; QLF 1894 from gds J R McDONALD, Memphis, TN whose d was Mrs Clara J RUPPLE; QLF 1939 from great great gdd Bessie M Dudley (Mrs Elmer Ellsworth) BURRUSS, North Garden, VA (d of Mrs B R DUDLEY above). F-S8871 R1601
LUNA, Peter, esf 1779 VA, where res on Holston River; mvd to Davidson Co, TN, thence Sumner Co, TN, then to Lincoln Co,

LUNA (continued)
   TN, where PN 1832 ae 73; res 1846 Marshall Co, TN; b Botetourt Co, VA, 10/1/1760. F-S1554 R1601
LUNSFORD, Mason, esf 1780-81 in General George Rogers CLARK's Regiment of VA troops; PN ae 68 Harrison Co, IN, 1833; res IN 1838. F-S32387 R1601
   Rodham, esf 1779 Fauquier Co, VA; PN ae 70 Lincoln Co, KY, 1832. F-S13803 R1601
LUNTER, Peter, see LANTER, Peter. F-W9114 R1601
LURTY, John, VA sea svc; esf King George Co, VA; lieutenant on board ship DRAGON; purchased ship of own after RW & traded up & down Rappahannock River in VA until appointed to command of reserve cutter at Hampton, VA; dd 5/1795 or 6/1795 while in command of that ship, leaving ch: William, Moore, Robert, & Mary Stevens, per Mason Co, KY, court 1834 they liv then; s William res 1836 Bracken Co, KY; s Moore dd VA leaving ch mbnn; s Robert dd Bracken Co, KY leaving s William & d Elizabeth; d Mary Stevens md Abraham PROCTOR, & dd leaving ch: Notley, Newton, William, George, Larkin, Patsey, Hannah, Fanny STEVENSON, & Lucy Ann w of Baker G WOOD; heirs gtd 1/2 pay PN due sailor 1836. F-R65 R1602
LUSK, Hugh, esf in VA regiment; PN 1829 Hardin Co, KY for disability from wounds at Battle of Guilford; res 1834 Elizabethtown, KY, ae 60-70; QLF states sol md Nancy McMURTRY. F-S25637 R1602
   Joseph, b 3/15/1753 Augusta Co, VA; esf 1776 res at Sycamore Shoals on Watauga River in NC; esf 1777 Washington Co, VA; mvd after RW to TN, thence Buncombe Co, NC, thence McMinn Co, TN, where PN 1832 when res there c13 years; dd 8/15/39 survived by s Joseph Jr; QLF 1934 from great gds Charles S LUSK of Elkins, NM, states sol s Joseph Jr & sol s William (gdf/o querier) both War of 1812 sol's, further querier s of Samuel A J LUSK. F-S4581 R1602
LUTTERELL, Michael, esf 1781 Fauquier Co, VA, where b 10/1751; mvd to KY, then to TN, thence AL, thence IL, where PN 1834 Marion Co; dd 12/19/44; surv ch in 1860: Thomas, James, Alfred, William, & Nancy MATTENLY who all AFF there then; sol bro mbnn res AL 1834; surname also spelled LUTTRELL. F-S32021 R1604
LUTTRELL, James, b 2/12/1755 Westmoreland Co, VA; mvd ae 9 to near Rockfish Creek, Amherst Co, VA, where esf 1780; afp 1837 Knox Co, TN, where res since 1795; PAR, svc less than 6 months; QLF states sol md 1776, & dd 1848 Knox Co, TN. F-R6535 R1604
   Nathan, esf 1780 Fauquier Co, VA, where res; afp ae 80 Weakley Co, TN, 1837, & PAR. F-R6536 R1604
   Rodham, VA sea svc, esf VA; issued VA BLW6948 on 8/22/1831; dd 1/14/32 Owen Co, KY; md 10/1810 Frances ADKINS, Scott Co, KY; wid PN ae 53 Owen Co, KY 1843; gtd BLW71057 there 1857; s John (b 10/25/1811) AFF there then; d Lucy AFF ae 50 there then; s Rodham b 7/13/1818. F-W10206 R1604
LUZADER, Aaron, esf 1776 Somerset Co, NJ, where b 1731; esf

LUZADER (continued)
 1778 Greene Co, PA, where res; mvd 1793 to Monongalia Co, VA, where afp 1833; PAR, insufficient proof of svc; QLF states sol also War of 1812 sol, gtd BLW for land at Grafton, WV. F-R6539 R1604
LYBROOK, Henry, b 4/2/1755 Lancaster Co, PA; esf 1774 at Fincastle (area later Montgomery Co), VA; esf 1776 to fight Cherokee indians; res after RW Giles Co, VA, thence Preble Co, OH, thence Cass Co, MI, where afp; PAR, svc less than 6 months; surname also spelled SYBROOK. F-R10368 R1604
 John, b 11/20/1763 PA; esf 1779, 1780,1781, & 1782 against indians, Botetourt Co, VA; afp 1834 Giles Co, VA; PAR. F-R6540 R1604
LYLE, Margaret, former wid of Samuel LAPSLEY. (F-W9149)
LYNAM, Andrew, b 1/5/1759 Guilford Co, NC; mvd ae 4 with f to VA where f dd & sol orphaned young; esf 1776 Washington Co VA; mvd soon after RW to Garrard Co, KY, thence Bath Co, KY, where PN 1834 when had been minister for 40+ years; dd there 7/3/47; md 1788 Betsy GREENE at home of Francis HOPKINS (no kinship given), Garrard Co, KY; wid PN ae 84 Bath Co, KY, 1849; dd 11/27/51; ch births: Richard 9/11/1789, John 8/26/91, Lee 7/18/93, William Hall 6/6/95, Rachel Green 10/26/98 & Sarah 12/8/1800; s Lee md 1815 Elizabeth; d Rachel (res 1834 Bath Co, KY) md 1/23/1826 Charles RICE, their ch births: William L 10/27/1826, Andrew 7/6/28, & Polly Ann 3/10/30; other LYNAM births: Margaret 1/31/1817, John 2/-/21, Ila 5/10/22, James 8/18/26, William H 6/9/30, & David D 20/22/33; s Richard md Betsey, & they res 1851 Bath Co, KY, & he AFF then there his sis's were Rachel COHEN & Sally RICE. F-9148 R1605
LYNCH, Elijah, esf 1778 Culpeper Co, VA, where res; PN 1832 ae 67 Rockingham Co, NC; dd 12/20/39; md 10/5/1785 Rose CRAWFORD (MB 10/5/85), Culpeper Co, VA; wid dd 6/18/44 leaving ch: Aaron, Elijah, Amy (md Alexander GROGAN), & Sarah (md John WILLSON); s Aaron afp ae 47 Rockingham Co, NC for the surv ch above; ch gtd PN due m. F-W5032 R1606
 Henry, esf 1780-1 VA; PN ae 56 Madison Co, KY 1820; dd 7/12/1849 Macon Co, MO, having mvd there from Howard Co, MO; md 9/22/1789 Sarah/Sally FERRIS/FARISS, Cumberland Co, VA who PN ae 90 Macon Co, MO 1855; gtd BLW43529 there 1856; several ch mbnn; QLF 1934 from desc Helen Myers WARREN, Oceanlake, OR, states her gdm Martha (b 1809 KY) d of sol, further sol res 1800 Henrico Co, VA; QLF states sol & David LYNCH came from Ireland to settle in VA, & city of Lynchburg named for their family; QLF 1915 from gds J H BLACKWELL of Confederate Soldiers Home, Higginsville, MO states sol P O address Bloomington, MO. F-W10210 R1606
 Patrick, b Ireland; esf 1777 Washington Co, MD, where res; mvd 1779 to Bedford Co, VA, where esf; dd there 5/7/1831, 5/7/32, 5/9/32, or 5/7/33; md 11/1780 or Fall 1781 Martha/Patsey WHORLEY/WHERLEY/WHIRLEY near New London, Campbell Co, VA; wid ae 91 in 1839; dd 3/9/43 Bedford Co, VA; s

LYNCH (continued)
    James afp there 1845 ae 64 for self & surv sibling Thomas, their 2 sisters mbnn then decd; ch gtd PN due m; QLF 1930 from great gdd Peytona L HOWELL, New Orleans, LA, says she d of Civil War Confederate sol Peyton B LYNCH, who was s/o sol s Peyton. F-W8071 R1606
LYNOR, Philip, esf 1776 Fauquier Co, VA; PN there 1818 ae 66; res there 1826 aec 70 in Co poorhouse, occupation shoemaker, when ch Polly, Peggy, Nancy, Betsey & Thomas (a millwright) liv far from him & not providing him any support. F-S38143 R1606
LYNOTT, Thomas, DE sea svc, esf Wilmington, DE as cabin boy on ship HOPE; taken POW, escaped, & returned to Wilmington; mvd to Harford Co, MD, thence Harrison Co, VA, where afp 1832 ae 63 when res there 37 years; PAR, svc as cabin boy not covered by current PN laws; surname also spelled SYNOTT. F-R6551 R1606
LYON, Edward, esf 1775 in VA regiment; PN 1818 Abbeville District, SC, when bro-in-law Henry HARPER AFF there; res 1820 there ae 68 with w aec 65 & several ch, including s ae 16 & a d; other ch res in other parts/o the country; QLF 1914 from desc Miss Frances PARKS of Atlantic City, NJ says sol dd 1823, & she also desc of RW sol Christopher TAYLOR who was PN 1833 Washington Co, TN. F-S38920 R1607
    Jacob, s of Alexander; esf 1780 Culpeper Co, VA; PN 1825 ae 63 Wilkes Co, NC; res there 1822 with w Jane aec 63 & ch: Frances ae 32, Ruth ae 21, Austin ae 18, Solomon ae 14, Meredith ae 11, & Jacob ae 8; dd 8/16/40, w having dd earlier; surv ch who afp & afb 1852 Wilkes Co, NC: Frances LION, Rachel w of Atha GENTRY, Valentine LION, James LION, Ruth LION, Elizabeth w/o John GENTRY, Austin LION, Solomon LION, Meredith LION, & Jacob LION; no indication in file/o action on ch claims; surname also spelled LION. F-S41789 R16067
    James, esf 1775-6 Stafford Co, VA; PN ae 60 Fauquier Co, VA, 1818; res there 1820 aec 65 when had no w but ch: John ae 40, James ae 37 & Nancy ae 33; dd there 12/15/36; QLF 1920 from desc Olivetta STRICKLIN of Tonkawa, OK, whose m was a LYONS. F-S38159 R1607
    John, VA sea svc, esf 1777 VA, surgeon's mate on ship HERO; dd between 2/10/1795 & 7/7/1795 Nansemond Co, VA; heirs who gtd 1/2 pay PN 1852: John KEELING of VA, Mary Ann KEELING, Elizabeth SNOW/SNAW, & James SNOW/SNAW; surname also spelled LYONS. F-R66 R1607
    William, b 2/27/1752 Culpeper Co, VA; esf 1781 Wilkes Co, NC where res; mvd after RW to Lawrence Co;, KY where PN 1834; last PN payment in file 1838; QLF 1922 from desc Olivetta (Mrs H M) STRICKLIN, Tonkawa, OK, states sol res 1840 Lawrence Co, KY, further she also desc of RW pensioner Mary Ann SHEPHERD who was res 1840 Mason Co, KY ae 74. F-S8875 R1608
    William, esf Amherst Co, VA; dd 3/30/1811; md 1768 Frances,

LYON (continued)
 who afp ae 89 Nelson Co, VA, 1833, & PAR; James LYON (no kinship given) gave power/o attorney 1854 to agent to afp; his PAR. F-R6554 R1608
MABEN, James; esf VA; stonemason, bricklayer; only bro Andrew, weaver/o Pittessie in parish/o Cules, Fifeshire, Scotland, as sol's heir gave power/o attorney to James LYLE of Chesterfield Co, VA, 1788 to afb; BLW12 gtd to Andrew c1802; surname also spelled MABON & MAVEN. F-BLW12 R1610
MABRY, Braxton, esf 1776 Brunswick Co, VA, where b 5/22/1750; esf 1779 Pittsylvania Co, VA, where res; mvd c1808 to TN, thence Chariton Co, MO, for c3 years, thence Macoupin Co, IL, for c4 years, thence Green Co, MO where afp 1833; PAR, insufficient proof of svc; res 1838 Taney Co, MO, when s James AFF there; one of heirs Reuben CLEVENGER (no kinship given) res 1854 there. F-R6569 R1610
 Mathew, b Bute Co (area later Warren Co), NC; esf 1789 in VA regiment, Northampton Co, VA; PN ae 75 Warren Co, NC, 1834 F-S7174 R1610
MACCOUN, James, esf 1776 Rockbridge Co, VA; PN ae 79 Cumberland Co, KY, 1823 when had w mbnn; surname also spelled MACCONN. F-S36068 R1610
MACE, Isaac, b 7/16/1755 Augusta Co, VA, where esf 1777 as indian spy; hired sub 1781 for army svc; PN 1834 Kanawah Co, VA; name dropped from PN rolls 1835 when PN Office proved he did not render enough svc. F-S8995 R1610
 John, b 3/25/1752 PA; esf 1777 Hampshire Co, VA, where res; PN 1832 Lewis Co, VA; name dropped from PN rolls 1835 when PN Office proved svc not rendered; mvd 1835 to OH to live near sons; res 1837 Vinton Township, Athens Co, OH, with s Paul. F-S13847 R1610
MACHRELL, James, BLW12382 issued 10/6/1792. F-BLW12382 R1610
MACKALL, Benjamin, esf 1782 Fredericktown, MD, in 3rd MD Regiment; PN ae 56 Beaver Co, PA, 1819; res VA 1821-1826, then to PA, where dd 9/5/30 or 9/6/30 Beaver Co; md 12/16/1784 Rebecca; wid PN ae 76 there 1840; dd there 12/13/46; had 6 ch of which eldest Jane b 10/27/1785 who md George DAWSON; sol ch in 1840 were Jane DAWSON (then a wid, res Beaver Co PA), James res there, John res there, Eleanor w of Benoni BLACKMORE & Thomas (res Columbiana Co, OH); 1 ch dd before before sol wid; QLF states sol b 1762 Fredericktown, MD, & md Rebecca DAWSON, who b 1764; QLF 1930 from desc (on m's side) John A CARNAGEY Sr, Madison, IN; QLF 1924 from desc H D McKALL, Toledo, OH, states sol dd near Georgetown, PA. F-W2953 R1611
MACKAY, Walter, esf 1780 Campbell Co, VA; dd Fall 1786; md 1/1776 Catherine McDANIEL, Caroline Co, VA; wid md (2) William ARTHUR, who dd 11/1830; wid afp ae 85 Casey Co, KY, & PAR; children mbnn. F-R270 R1611
MACKEY, Thomas, esf 1777 Annapolis, MD, in 1st MD Regiment; PN ae 75 Washington, DC, 1820; mvd 1826 from Baltimore, MD to VA to reside among friends there; dd 3/16/35; surname also

MACKEY (continued)
spelled MACKAY; QLF states a RW sol Thomas McCOY b VA 1754 near Martinsburg (now WV), res during RW Frederick Co, MD, esf in MD regiment, dd 10/18/1810 Mercer Co, VA, md 1776 Catharine PARK near Martinsburg, WV, his surname spelled also McKOY. F-S38169 R1611

MACKY, Robert, b 3/1756-7; esf 1777 in VA Continental Line as surgeon; killed by lightning 6/8/1805; md 12/6/1789 Ann Elliott BRADLEY, who b 11/10/1766; wid PN 1841 ae 74 Henderson Co, TN, res Jackson, Perry Co, TN; dd 9/30/49 Jackson, TN; ch births: Ann Eliza 6/16/1791, Margaret Burwell 10/8/93, Mary Green 12/20/95, Jane 2/9/98, Robert William 3/6/1800, George Anne Frances 2/4/03, & Elizabeth Susan 12/25/05; Benjamin H GRAVES, adm/o her estate, afp 1853 ae 46 Decatur Co, TN, for her surv ch: Ann Eliza LONGAM, Margaret LASITER, Jane WASHBURN, Robert W, George Anne GRAVES & Elizabeth S HALL; query to PN Office from d Margaret B ADAMS & d George Anne GRAVES 1852 from Decatur Co, TN. F-W1041 R1612

MACLEMORE, John, b 1762 Brunswick Co, VA; esf 1779 Granville Co, NC, where res; mvd 1796 to Montgomery Co, NC, for 8 years, thence Burke Co, NC for 8 years, thence Knox Co, TN where PN 1832; name carried on PN rolls as John McLEMORE; w mbnn; QLF states sol res Knox Co, TN, 1841, & dd there; QLF states sol res 1840 with William McLEMORE (kinship not given). F-S4202 R1612

MACLURG, Walter, VA sea svc, appointed surgeon of hospitals at Hampton, VA, 1777; LWT 12/24/1783, probated 3/25/1784; afp 1799 by James McCLURG (kinship not given) & 1/2 pay PN gtd F-R16117 R1612

MADDEN, William, esf Frederick Co, VA, where b 2/27/1762; PN 1833 Harrison Co, IN, when bro John res there; dd 10/15/34 there; md 5/12/1800 Jane/Jenny HAINEY/HANEY, Frederick Co, VA; wid PN ae 79 Massac Co, IL 1853; gtd BLW26908 when res with children mbnn 1856 Harrison Co, IN. F-W9902 R1613

MADDER, Martin, BLW12378 issued 11/5/1789. F-BLW12378 R1613

MADDING, Chapness, b 8/1763-64 Pittsylvania Co, VA, where esf 1780; PN 1832 Madison Co, TN. F-S4184 R1613

MADDOX, Jacob, b 1/3/1764 Powhatan Co, VA, where esf 1780 sub for f James; mvd to Jefferson Co, TN where PN 1833; dd 12/3/51. F-S1556 R1613

John, esf 1777 Goochland Co, VA, where b; PN ae 71 Ohio Co, KY, 1834; liv 1843. F-S30565 R1613

John, esf 1780 in VA regiment; PN 1818 Fluvanna Co, VA, ae 55; res there 1820 occupation farmer when family w ae 52, s aec 12 & 6 d's (ae of 5 of them 21, 17, 15, 10 & 6); QLF 1921 from great great gdd Mrs Charles CORK of Macon, GA, whose maternal gdf was Alexander Compton MADDOX of Putnam Co, GA. F-S38183 R1613

Matthew, esf 1780 in VA regiment; PN ae 68 Wood Co, VA 1820; dd 1/1/31; QLF states sol dd Wood Co, VA, & was md twice; QLF 1910 from great great gdd Mrs L L HANNUM of Downers

MADDOX (continued)
   Grove, IL, states sol gdf/o her gdm, that sol mvd c1800 to Parkersburg, WV, & buried there in MADDOX Cemetery & had 6 s's & 2 d's. F-S38181 R1613
   Notley, esf VA; dd before 6/7/1832 leaving ch mbnn; BLW12392 issued 1/6/1795; records lost in Washington, DC, fire. F-BLW12392 R1613
   Sherwood, b 12/15/1761 Goochland Co, VA; esf 1779 Powhatan Co, VA, where res; mvd 1793 to Lindsey's Station (area later Scott Co, KY), thence 1805-6 Owen Co, KY where PN 1832 & dd there 3/4/39; md 3/15/1781 Elizabeth FURGERSON, Cumberland Co, VA, at home of William MADDOX (no kinship stated); wid b 12/15/1756 Caroline Co, VA; wid PN 1843 Owen Co, KY, reporting marriage records lost in fire in house/o John FURGERSON (no kinship given), Caroline Co, VA; births of ch: James 6/27/1785 (res 1843 Owen Co, KY), Jacob 2/22/87 (res 1843 Owen Co, KY), Sherwood 11/3/88, Frances 9/30/90, David 8/13/95, Larkin 11/4/98, & Elizabeth 10/30/180-(illegible); other births in file: Granville GARNETT 3/15/1840, Thomas M DANIEL 6/11/1831, Thomas M DANIEL 5/4/1817; AFF 1832 by Susannah GARNETT, Owen Co, KY, she near relative of sol; QLF 1931 from desc Bernard J MADDOX, Charleston, SC who also desc/o RW sol Wilson MADDOX who esf Charlotte Co, VA, & md Delilah who PN Shelby Co, KY; QLF 1913 from desc Virginia Harrison (Mrs Charles B) HOLLISTER, who gdd (on m's side) of War of 1812 sol Sherwood MADDOX, she also gdd (on f's side) of War of 1812 sol John HARRISON of Montgomery Co, VA (bro/o Thomas), she also great great gdd of RW sol Israel LORTON of Augusta Co, VA. F-W2823 R1613
   Wilson, b 9/30/1757; esf 1778 Charlotte Co, VA where res; PN 1832 Shelby Co, KY; dd 6/30/34; md Delilah who b 4/13/1770 & who PN 1839 Shelby Co, KY; ch births: David 1/9/1787 (md 11/1/1810 Polly), John S 3/16/89 (md 7/25/1822 Healthy BRITE), Elijah 1/24/91 (md 3/19/1813 Sally), Wilson 2/15/93 (md 3/12/1812 Prudence), Thomas G 6/18/95 (md 5/7/22 Cynthia), Jenny 12/10/97, Sally 4/17/1800, Elizabeth 9/5/02 (md 3/23/1822 Hiram KERLIN), Patsey 12/20/04, Miles/Myles 8/7/07 (md 10/1/1833 Ellen FRANCIS), Polly 6/14/10 (md 4/9/1829 Melville McCANN), & Delilah/Delia 8/23/13 (md 11/13/1834 Benjamin WARFORD); other family births: Elijah s/o David MADDOX 1/11/1812, Linna d/o Wilson MADDOX 12/20/1812, Henry s of David MADDOX 8/25/1813, Levi s of Elijah MADDOX 8/23/1915, Preston s of Wilson MADDOX 7/20/1815, Guinn s/o David MADDOX 11/7/1815, Levina d/o Wilson MADDOX 7/24/1817, & Sylvester s of Melville & Polly McCANN 3/17/1830. F-W8413 R1613
MADEIRA, Nicholas, esf 1777 Reading, Berks Co, PA, as drummer, where b 12/26/1763; esf later against indians with bro's Michael, Casper & Christian; mvd to Fredericktown, MD, for 6 years, thence Monongalia Co, VA, where afp 1832 res Morgantown when bro Michael res near Reading, PA; sol nephew Nicholas B MADEIRA postmaster then of Morgantown, VA; QLF

MADEIRA (continued)
  states sol md (2) Rebecca RESLER. F-R21798 R1613
MADERA, Christian, b PA; esf 1776 in PA regiment; PN 1818 aec 59 Monongalia Co, VA, occupation wheelwright, blind since 1814; res there 1820 when w aec 65; dd 3/15/22; md 2/23/1779 Anna/Ann BIERLY, Reading, PA; d Elizabeth (wid/o Captain Zacquil MORGAN who dd while serving in 12th US Infantry Regiment) res 1820 in part/o f's home with 6 small ch; sol wid liv 1836 when s mbnn, postmaster/o Morgantown, VA, queried PN Office on m's eligibility for PN; wid not eligible under current PN laws, since she md sol after his RW svc; QLF 1917 from desc Miss Sena K OTTING of Warren, OH. F-S38180 R1613
MADISON, Ambrose, esf 1776 King & Queen Co, VA, where res; PN ae 75 Todd Co, KY, 1832. F-S31229 R1613
  Gabriel, esf in marines 1776 Hanover Co, VA, where res; mvd 1780 to KY Territory where served as colonel under General George Rogers CLARK; dd 4/14/1804 or 4/15/1804 Jessamine Co, KY; md 12/12/1784 or 3/15/1785 (wid gave both dates) Mira/Mirah/Myra in area later Fayette Co, KY; wid PN 1843 ae 80+ Jessamine Co, KY; dd 5/9/45 ae 85, leaving ch: Eliza/Elizabeth L (ae 56 res Jessamine Co, KY), Jane L w/o Dr William ROBERTSON of Woodford Co, KY, Lucy L McMURTRY (a wid), Ann Gabriella w of Strother J HAWKINS, & Martha w/o Charles ALEXANDER (she decd in 1851); other data in file: Francis W ALLEN b 6/30/1779 md 11/24/1804 Eliza L MADISON b 11/4/1788, Madison ALLEN b 7/8/1806, Richard ALLEN b 11/27/1808; sol bro Rowland captain in RW, later Governor of KY, a near relative of President James MADISON; wid niece Mrs Mary Ann TAYLOR AFF 1844 Fayette Co, KY. F-W8418 R1613
  William, esf 1778 VA militia; esf 1781 VA Continental Line; brigadier general, War of 1812; BLW2205 issued 3/29/1838; PN ae 73 Madison Co, VA, by special act of Congress 1838; dd 7/20/1843; LWT probated 8/24/43 Madison Co, VA; md 6/28/1834 Nancy JERALD; wid PN ae 53 Madison Co, VA, 1853; res 1854 Fairfield Co, OH; QLF states sol bro of President James MADISON; QLF 1909 from great great gds James M McGUIRE, New York City, NY, states sol bro/o President MADISON. F-W9944 R1613
  William, b 5/10/1762 Chesterfield Co, VA; esf 1779 Caroline Co, VA, where res; PN there 1833; last PN payment in file 1840. F-S5724 R1613
MAEYER, John, esf in VA regiment; PN aec 65 Shenandoah Co, VA; res 1819 Fairfax Co, VA; res there 1820 when had no family liv with him; res 1822 Washington, DC; res 1824 Stewart Co TN; surname also spelled MAYER & MYER. F-S38954 R1614
MAFFITT, William, esf 1777 Fauquier Co, VA; PN ae 59-60 Spencer Co, KY, 1818; res there 1829 aec 70 when had w Elizabeth ae 60 & ch: William ae 38, Henry ae 27, Peggy ae 22, & Elijah ae 18; dd 6/18/35. F-S36063 R1614
MAGEE, James, esf 1776 Sussex Co, VA, where b 6/12/1762; esf 1780 Caswell Co, NC; PN 1832 as James Sr, Jefferson Co,

MAGEE (continued)
  TN; sol already md at time he esf 1776. F-S1555 R1614
 Ralph, b 6/14/1755 Sussex Co, VA; esf 1777-78 Brunswick Co,
  VA; later esf Sussex Co, VA; PN 1833 Madison Co, KY. F-
  S13894 R1614
MAGERT, Henry, esf 1780-81 Rockingham Co, VA; PN ae 71 Sullivan Co, TN 1832; last PN payment in file 1840 to sol Henry
  Sr. F-S1850 R1614
MAGILL, Andrew, b 1758 near Snow Hill, MD; f dd soon after sol
  birth; esf 1779 Glasgow Co (area later Edgecomb Co), NC as
  teamster; m then still wid; res after RW on Holston River,
  VA, for several years, thence Powell's Valley, VA, for 7
  years, thence Union Co, KY, for 21 years, thence Gallatin
  Co, KY, where afp 1837 when res there 2 years; PAR, svc as
  teamster in state militia not considered true military svc
  F-R6826 R1614
 Charles, esf 1776 Winchester, VA, in 11th VA Regiment; later
  promoted to major & assigned aide-de-camp to General Horatio GATES; gtd BLW by VA; dd 4/2/1827 Winchester, VA; md
  there 5/24/1792 Mary B THRUSTON, who b 7/27/1772; wid PN
  1838 Fauquier Co, VA, when s Augustine res there; res 1845
  Leesburg, VA; res 1848 Frederick Co, VA; s Buckner, Assistant Surgeon of US Navy, dd 1840 southern France; d mbnn
  res 1841 Alexandria, VA. F-W5336 R1614
 James, esf Rockingham Co, VA; PN ae 74 Greene Co, TN, 1832;
  dd 8/24/39; md 3/10/1789 Mary McMEANS, Greene Co, TN; wid
  afp ae 76 Walker Co, GA 1844; PAR, less than 6 months svc;
  ch births: Thomas 12/23/1790, Robert 3/24/92, James 2/2/
  95, Nathaniel 3/28/97, Samuel Wallace 1/17/99, & Hervey 9/
  29/1801; one/o heirs Thomas MAGILL (no kinship given), res
  Sullivan Co, TN, gave power of attorney 1851 to agent to
  afp; QLF 1937 from desc Mrs Mary Magill COPPUS, Boston, MA
  states sol b 1756 Augusta Co, VA & served in 12th VA Regiment; QLF 1922 from desc Miss Bessie MAGILL, Chattanooga,
  TN. F-R6827 R1614
 John, esf 1777 Augusta Co, VA, where esf 1777; mvd 1782 to
  Lincoln Co, KY, thence 1787 Fayette Co, KY, for c2 years,
  thence Bourbon Co, KY, thence 1795 to Franklin Co, KY; PN
  there 1832; last PN payment in file 1839. F-S31230 R1614
MAGINNIS, Daniel, b Allen Township, Northampton Co (or Bucks
  Co), PA; parents b & md in VA; sol esf 1778 in 3rd PA Regiment; BLW1834 gtd for RW svc; esf 1813 Leesburg, VA, for
  War of 1812 & served in 12th US Infantry Regiment; in 1818
  discharged ae 47 from svc by reason/o old ae; gtd BLW11697
  for that svc; dd 1/13/31 Loudoun Co, VA, leaving wid ae 80
  & ch: Daniel (res there 1832), Elizabeth, Sarah NORRIS,
  Susan HILDEBRAND & Margaret LEACH; QLF 1925 from desc Anna
  MAGINNIS, Abington, IL. F-S46323 R1614
MAGWIER, Aleygone, see McGUIRE, Allegany. F-S2797 R1615
MAHAN, James, b 1755 VA between Winchester & the Warm Springs;
  esf 1774 res on Monongahela River, VA, as indian spy; mvd
  to Greene Co, TN, where esf against Cherokee Indians; mvd

MAHAN (continued)
c1798 to Whitley Co, KY, where PN 1833; res 1837 Cole Co, MO, with children mbnn; last PN payment in file 1838. F-S17563 R1615
MAHANES, Tapley, esf 1777 Lancaster Co, VA; PN 1832 Lincoln Co NC, ae 71 when res there c25 years. F-S7187 R1615
MAHER, Patrick, b 3/17/1753, an Irishman; esf 1780-81 Frederickstown, MD, in MD regiment; mvd after RW to area later Adams Co, MD; mvd 1800-02 to Rockbridge Co, VA, where res near Brownsburg when afp 1834; PAR, insufficient proof of svc; surname also spelled MARHAR. F-R6831 R1615
MAHOLLAND, John, b 4/10/1752 Elizabeth City Co, VA; esf 1777 Northampton Co, NC, where res; mvd 1808 to Wilson Co, TN; PN there 1832; dd 8/4/35; md 12/28/1785 Lucy; wid afp 1839 aec 80 Wilson Co, TN & PAR, insufficient proof/o marriage; dd 6/24/40; only surv ch 1852 were William ae 61 & Nancy CRUTCHFIELD, both res Wilson Co, TN; s William adm of m's estate 1855; Nancy also liv then. F-R6832 R1615
MAHONE, Archelaus, b New Kent Co, VA; mvd as ch to Bedford Co, VA, where esf in VA militia; mvd to Rockingham Co, NC, for 2 years, thence Patrick Co, VA, where afp 1833 Patrick Co, VA, & PAR; dd 1/6/42; md 1768 Magdalina BRIDGEMAN; wid afp ae 90 Stokes Co, NC, 1843 & PAR; ch births: William 1769, Micajah 1770, Zachariah 1772, Nancy 1777, Elizabeth 1779, Cecelia 1781, Ann 1783, Fanny 1785, Mary 1787, John 1789, & Archelaus 1791; dd Elizabeth AFF Stokes Co, NC, 1843 ae 64. F-R6833 R1615
MAHONEY, James, BLW12377 issued 5/9/1797. F-BLW12377 R1615
 James, esf Petersburg, VA; PN ae 56 Washington Co, IN, 1819; QLF states sol mvd from KY to Washington Co, IN, 1820. F-S36056 R1615
MAHORNEY, Benjamin, esf 1779 Fauquier Co, VA; PN ae 68 Oldham Co, KY, 1828; res 1833 Marion Township, Putnam Co, IN; dd 12/25/54; s Owen afp as one/o heirs 1855 Putnam Co, IN for PN due f; surname also spelled MAHONEY. F-S32393 R1615
 Thomas, esf 1777 Westmoreland Co, VA; PN ae 85 Prince William Co, VA 1818 occupation farmer, a free man of color; res there 1820 ae 91 when family w Mina & s Jack who both were slaves. F-S38166 R1615
MAIB, John, b Albemarle Co, VA; esf Surry Co, NC, where res in same neighborhood (area later Stokes Co) ever since; PN ae 75 latter Co 1833; dd 7/21/43; md 12/25/1791 Lucinda HYLTON, Surry Co, NC; wid PN ae 83 Stokes Co, NC, 1845; gtd BLW59092 there 1857; eldest s Alexander b there; surname also spelled MAABE & MABE. F-W4f726 R1615
MAID, Thomas, see MEAD, Thomas. F-W9561 R1615
MAIDEN, James, esf 1777 Rockingham Co, VA in 10th VA Regiment; dd c1795; md 8/1775-6 Docia LEE; wid md (2) Bazil HALL who dd 8/1839 Botetourt Co, VA; wid PN aec 90 Rockingham Co, VA, 1843; several ch by sol included eldest Sally, who aec 67-68 in 1845; Jonathan & Zacharias LEE (no kinship given) AFF in behalf/o wid 1844; QLF 1940 from desc Mrs A M BRIT-

MAIDEN (continued)
TON, Touchet, WA, says sol w Theodocia HALL. F-W5098 R1615
MAIGHER, Richard, esf 1775 MA; mvd to Boston, MA, where dd 11/11/1823; md 12/30/1776 Lydia YATES of Bristol; wid mvd after h's death to Norfolk Borough, Norfolk Co, VA, where PN 1842 ae 82; d Catherine RICHMOND (a wid) AFF there then ae 50 she b Bristol, ME; d Ann CARPENTER (a wid) also AFF ae 44 there then she b Bristol, ME; sol surname also spelled MEAGHER. F-W18490 R1615
MAIL, Wilmore, esf 1777 Davis's Marsh, Berkeley Co (area later Jefferson Co), VA, in 12th VA Regiment; PN ae 60 Hampshire Co, VA, a free man/o color; res 1820 Randolph Co, VA ae 66 when w Priscilla ae 59 & s George ae 16 liv with him. F-S38171 R1615
MAIN, Philip, b 1747 Gloucester Co, NJ; esf 1776 in VA regiment, when res on Monongahela River in VA (area later PA); PN 1819 Beaver Co, PA, occupation farmer; referred there 1820 to d ae 17-18; referred there 1821 to 4 s's (all svc War/o 1812 svc) & their families; referred there 1826 to w ae 64, s ae 22-23; dd 4/19/35; surname also spelled MEANS; QLF says sol had d Katherine; QLF 1913 from desc Margaret RAITHEL, Ellwood City, PA; QLF states sol dd North Sewickley Township, Beaver Co, PA. F-S13850 R1616
MAINES, George, esf 1777 Fayette Co, PA, in 10th VA Regiment; PN ae 70 Bracken Co, KY 1818 as George Sr, occupation then cooper; res Mason Co, KY 1822 ae 73 when liv with w aec 64 & d ae 15 (an idiot); res 1824 Bracken Co, KY, when had w aec 66 & large family of ch including d ae 17, s Levi, & s Philip; surname also spelled MAINS; QLF from great gds Edgar Lee MAINES, Rockford, IL, who s of Joseph Harrison who s/o sol s Isaac; QLF says sol dd 11/8/1833 Bracken Co, KY. F-S36080 R1616
MAINS, Francis, BLW12345 issued 7/14/1792. F-BLW12345 R1616
Samuel, b 1760 Lancaster Co, MD; esf Chesterfield Co, VA; afp 1836 Nova Scotia, res Picton District of Halifax Co; PAR. F-R6837 R1616
MAJOR, Samuel, esf 1776 Dinwiddie Co, VA where b 8/10/1760; PN there 1832; dd 6/24/42; md there 3/1800 Nancy PERKINS (MB 3/12/1800 signed by William PERKINS); wid PN there 1853 ae 76; gtd BLW31293 there 1855; numerous ch. F-W8417 R1616
William, b 3/15/1752 Charles City Co, VA; esf 1780 Brunswick Co, VA; where res; mvd to Dinwiddie Co, VA, thence Monroe Co, IN, where PN 1836; AFF there then by Samuel MAJOR (no kinship given) he RW svc with sol & was then RW pensioner; QLF 1936 from desc Mrs Nora M FIELD, Seneca, SC, says sol bro John also VA RW sol; QLF states a William MAJOR b 1748 Culpeper Co, VA, & dd 1840 Paris, MO. F-S15602 R1616
MAJORS, Humphrey, b 1757 Caroline Co, VA; esf 1776-78 Culpeper Co (area later Madison Co), VA, where res; PN 1832 latter Co; family bible then in hands of nephew William MAJORS of Culpeper, VA. F-S5723 R1616
James, BLW12399 issued 3/4/1796. F-BLW12399 R1616

MAJORS, John, b 1760 Baltimore Co, MD; mvd ae 13 with family to Prince Georges Co, MD, thence 3 years later to Alexandria, VA where esf; mvd 1781 to Baltimore, MD where PN 1843 when s Samuel res there. F-S11026 R1616

Thomas, bc 1764 Halifax Co, VA; esf 1779-80 Wilkes Co, NC in NC regiment, where res; mvd to Hawkins Co, TN, thence Madison Co, KY, where PN 1847 when res there c14 years; gtd BLW18210 there 1855; surname also spelled MAGERS; QLF says sol buried Richmond, KY. F-S30564 R1616

MALCOLM, James, VA state navy; captain of ship TEMPEST; taken POW 1781; dd 1811-12; PN gtd 1849 to estate adm Charles H GERKEN for heirs. F-R68 R1617

MALES, John, esf 1777 Hagerstown, MD, in 7th MD Regiment; badly wounded at Battle of Germantown; PN ae 74 Monroe Co, VA 1818; res there 1820 ae 77 when had w, all ch having left home not providing any support to parents. F-S38168 R1617

MALICK, John, b 1/11/1762 Bridgewater Township, Somerset Co, NJ, where esf sub for f; mvd 1787 to Berkeley Co, VA, for c9 years, thence Hampshire Co, VA, where PN 1833; last PN payment in file 1841; QLF states sol res 1840 Hampshire Co VA. F-S7177 R1617

MALLARY, Johin/John, b 5/15/1761 ; esf 1778 Brunswick Co, VA, where res; went to sea after RW until c1837; afp 1839 Hawkins Co, TN, & PAR, insufficient proof of svc; 2nd cousin Robert MALLARY (b 7/1764 Hanover Co, VA) res 1839 Hawkins Co, TN; sol bro mbnn res VA then; cousin Philip MALLARY, a VA RW sol, decd in 1840. F-R6846 R1617

Philip, BLW1502 issued 8/25/1789; Captain in VA Continental Line; records lost in Washington, DC fire 1800; QLF states sol from Fauquier Co, VA. F-BLW1502 R1617

MALLERY, John, esf 1777 Orange Co, VA, where res; PN 1833 ae 74 Limestone Co, AL; dd 11/5/40. F-S16931 R1618

MALLIHAN, John, esf VA; afp 1834 Nicholas Co, VA; witness AFF then there sol aec 58 then, too young to have RW svc; PAR; surname also spelled MALLIHON. F-R6852 R1618

MALLORY, Billy/William, esf Hanover Co, VA, sub for f Charles, when res with him; dd there 11/24/1827; md there 4/10/1796 Catharine L BLUNT at home of Ann BLUNT (no kinship stated) by Reverend Henry MALLORY (no kinship stated); wid PN 1851 there ae 74; children mbnn; sol sis Nancy res there then ae 89; QLF 1932 from Willie Mallory (Mrs Anthony H) HART, Memphis, TN whose f William Barton MALLORY (8/1835-6/1919) captain of Monticello Guards, Charlotteville, VA, esf 1861 for Confederate svc in Civil War, s/o William Wilson (1801 -1875) who s/o William Cole MALLORY, all of Hanover Co, VA W2826 R1618

John, esf 1780 Hanover Co, VA; PN 1818 Goochland Co, VA, ae 57; res there 1820 when family w Elizabeth ae 57 & ch: Rebecca ae 28, Elizabeth ae 24, Sarah ae 20, Pamelia ae 18, Polly ae 16 & William ae 12; QLF 1938 from great great gdd Myrtle Mallory (Mrs F J) FISCHER, Petersburg, VA. F-S38161 R1618

MALLORY, John, b 7/14/1755 near Fork Church, Hampshire Co, VA,
where esf 1775; PN there 1832; dd 3/16/33; md 1788, or 10/
12/1789, or 10/12/1790 Elizabeth DUKE in MD; wid PN 1840
ae 70+ Hanover Co, VA, 1840; res there 1848; ch included s
Clairborne who b before 1793; sol bro's w Catherine AFF ae
61 there 1840. F-W3436 R1618
  John, b 3/11/1759 Orange Co, VA; esf 1781 Louisa Co, VA; mvd
after RW to GA, thence 1831 Benton Co, AL, where afp 1835,
& PAR since PN Office believed then sol identical with sol
John MALLERY, whose name then on PN rolls (see F-S16931);
sol had children mbnn res 1831 Benton Co, AL; sol bro Thomas res 1835 Orange Co, VA. F-R6845 R1618
  Roger, b 5/12/1755 (old style) King William Co, VA; esf 1775
Elizabeth City Co, VA, where res; mvd 1777 to York Co, VA,
where esf; mvd 1779 to King William Co, VA, where esf; mvd
Fall 1779 to Northumberland Co, VA, where esf 1780; mvd
1783 to Frederick Co, VA, for 1 year, thence Rockingham Co
VA, for c31 years, thence Botetourt Co, VA, then 1825 to
Williamson Co, TN where PN 1832; s John AFF there then ae
52 he only s res that Co then; sol bro of James, Francis,
& Philip (latter 2 were officers in RW); QLF states sol dd
1837-8 Williamson Co, TN, & buried there. F-S1684 R1618
  William, b 1/1/1751; esf Louisa Co, VA, where res; PN 1832
Wilson Co, TN; dd 1/3/39. F-S1688 R1618
MALLOW, George, b 3/17/1752 (old style) Lancaster Co, PA; mvd
wih parents to South Branch/o Potomac River (area then Augusta Co, VA, later Rockingham Co, VA), where esf 1778; PN
1832 Greene Co, OH; QLF states sol dd there 1837; QLF 1917
from desc Mrs Charles E. EASTES, Marion, IN; QLF says sol
known as George Sr; QLF says sol dd 4/17/37. F-S2735 R1619
MALLOW, Henry, b 1759 on Mississippi River, his m having been
captured by indians & sold to the French who owned m when
he b; esf 1778 Rockingham Co, VA; PN 1832 Pendleton Co, VA
surname also spelled MALLOWS. F-S45892 R1619
MALONE, Hugh, esf 1779 Harford Co, MD, in 6th MD Regiment; PN
ae 62 Hampshire Co, VA 1818; res there 1820 ae 66 when had
w mbnn ae 76. F-S38167 R1619
  John, esf 1775 Hampshire Co, VA in 2nd VA Regiment; PN ae 64
Woodford Co, KY, 1818 when had no family. F-S36076 R1619
  Thomas, esf 1777 Frederick Co, MD, (area later Montgomery Co
MD); PN aec 76 Monongalia Co, VA, 1820 with w Mary (ae 50-
60), they res on land of s John; other children mbnn; dd
11/27/20. F-S38929 R1619
MALONEY, Archibald, esf 1778 Lancaster, PA in 7th PA Regiment;
PN ae 68 Tazewell Co, VA 1819, occupation farmer; res 1822
there ae 73 when had no family; BLW1707 issued 1/26/31 ae
79 there; dd 2/21/40; md 9/5/1833 Rachel HAWKINS/HANKINS;
wid PN ae 75 Tazewell Co, VA, 1853; gtd BLW158 there 1855.
F-W2219 R1619
  Robert, b Lancaster Co, PA; mvd aec 4 with f to Frederick Co
VA, where esf 1781 when a school boy; PN 1833 Jefferson Co
KY, ae 67 when res KY for 40+ years, having previously res

MALONEY (continued)
  Bullitt Co, KY; dd 3/19/36, leaving wid Nancy. F-S31240 R1619
MALT, Moses, esf VA early in RW; afp ae 80 Scioto Co, OH, 1820 occupation farmer, when had w aec 50 & ch ae 13; PAR, insufficient proof of svc. F-R6856 R1619
MALTSAR, Benjamin, esf in Lee's Legion; BLW12353 issued 9/12/1789. F-BLW12353 R1619
MAN, Abel, esf 1776-7 Amelia Co, VA, where b 1760; mvd 1807 to NC for 2 years, thence TN, thence Franklin Co, IL where PN 1833. F-S32396 R1620
MANARD, James, b 1750 VA; esf Wilkes Co, NC, where res; mvd to Floyd Co, KY, thence Pike Co, KY where PN 1832; res Cabell Co, VA 1841; dd 10/13/52 Wayne Co, VA; md 12/6/1801 Chaney SMITH, Wilkes Co, NC; wid PN ae 77 Wayne Co, VA; gtd there 1857 BLW61200, when Simeon MAINARD (no kinship given) made AFF there; surname also spelled MAINARD/MAINERD/MAYNARD. F-W10212 R1620
MANDERS, Henry, BLW12407 issued 7/5/1794. F-BLW12407 R1620
MANEY, Martin, esf 1775 Washington Co, NC, (area later TN) in 8th VA Regiment; esf there later 9th VA Regiment; PN 1818 ae 69 Blount Co, TN; dd 4/15/30 Buncombe Co, NC; md 9/1781 Keziah VAN/VANN, Washington Co, NC, when her parents living near Jonesboro; wid PN ae 80 Yancey Co, NC 1843; dd there 12/20/49; surname also spelled MANY; ch births (all surname MANY per family bible): Nancy 10/24/1783, John 2/11/85, Martin 10/28/87, William 6/6/95, Elizabeth 3/22/98, & James (date not given); reference made 1821 to s mbnn ae 17; ch who survived m, & gtd PN due m 1851: John (res Yancey, NC), William, James, & Nancy w/o Absolum MEDCALF/MIDCALF of Yancey Co; QLF 1924 from great great gds Howard H ALLEN, Mt Vernon, WA, who gds/o Sarah Maney HOLCOMBE who d of sol s John, further querier great great great gds of NC RW sol George ALLEN, b 1745 Halifax Co, NC, dd 1836 Iredell Co, NC, & buried Rocky Springs, NC. F-W7398 R1621
MANGUM, John, b 1/19/1763 Mecklenburg Co, VA; esf 1779 Newberry District, SC where res; mvd 1805 to Warren Co (area later Clinton Co), OH, thence 1811 Giles Co, TN, thence 1815 St Clair Co, AL, thence 1823-4 Pickens Co, AL, where PN 1832 P O Address Carrollton, AL; dd leaving wid mbnn; final PN payment in file 1841; Rebecca MANGUM (no kinship given) afp 1843 due sol; QLF states sol md Rebecca KNOWLES & sol dd 3/23/32 Fulton, MS. F-S16939 R1621
MANIER, David, see MINEAR, David. F-S15932 R1621
MANIS, Seth, b 1762 Bedford Co, VA; esf 1780 Moore Co, NC; PN PN 1835 Hawkins Co, TN; last PN payment in file 1839. F-S2739 R1621
MANK, Andrew/Henry, esf 1779 Shenandoah Co, VA, where b 1762; PN ae 71 Sullivan Co, TN, 1832; surname also spelled MAUK. F-S1852 R1621
  Henry, esf 1774 Augusta Co, VA, against indians; mvd 7/1780 to Sullivan Co, TN (area earlier in NC), where esf; later

MANK (continued)
   hired subs to take place; afp ae 78 there 1832; PAR, under 6 months svc; surname also spelled MAUK. F-R6863 R1621
Mathias, see MAUK, Mathias. F-R6064 R1621
MANKER, William, b 1/7/1765 MD, c30 miles from Baltimore; esf 1781 Berkeley Co, VA, where res; esf 1790 Redstone Fort (later Brownsville, PA) in General HARMER's Indian WAR; mvd after that svc to Hampshire Co, VA, thence Fayette Co, PA, for 2 years, thence Belmont Co, OH, for 13 years, then to Clinton Co, OH, for 3 years, then to Highland Co, OH, where PN 1833; dd there 4/29/39; md (2) 7/2/1817 Sarah POWERS, Champaign Co, OH; wid PN 1858 Highland Co, OH, aec 73; gtd BLW73506 there then; sol had 24 ch by 2 wives, of which 17 were sons. F-W9942 R1621
MANKINS, William, b 4/5/1760 Charles Co, MD, where esf 1781 as sub for f; mvd to Prince William Co, VA, thence Loudoun Co VA, thence Frederick Co, VA, thence back to Loudoun Co, VA thence Columbiana Co, OH, where PN 1832; QLF states sol dd possibly 1840 ae 101 at or near Lisbon, OH, res Elk Rapids OH. F-S2751 R1621
MANLEY, Ancil, esf 1780 Fluvanna Co, VA; PN ae 69 Anderson Co, TN, 1832; dd 6/22/53; md c11/9/1785 Elizabeth BUTLER, Bedford Co, VA; wid PN ae 86 Anderson Co, TN, 1854; gtd BLW 29024 there 1855 ae 87; res there 1860 ae 92; ch births (all surname MANLY, record torn & smudged): Ann 7/19/178-, Caleb Washington 3/1790, William Woolen 7/11/92, Ann Ducket 9/6/95, Fanney Jackson 2/18/98, Polly Ellender 6/9/1800 Thomas Alexander Butler 3/2/03, John Alexander Butler 3/17/05, Elizabeth Odle 2/266/08, & Ancil Washington Woolen 6/4/12; AFF 1860 by wid neighbors Ancil W MANLEY & Mary BUTLER. F-W959 R1621
   John, esf Elkton, Cecil Co, MD, ae 18 in Lee's Legion; BLW 13525 & BLW39 issued 12/21/1799; dd c2/13/1814 Fairfield Co, OH; md 4/13/1790 Susannah COX, Cecil Co, MD; wid PN ae 74 Fairfield Co, OH 1844 res Walnut Township; res Perry Co OH, 1851; QLF 19-- from desc Mrs Susan E FRAZER of OH; QLF states wid dd 1854 OH; QLF states wid res New Salem, Fairfield Co, OH, & sol middle initial S. F-W5339 R1621
   Micajah, b Cumberland Co, VA; esf 1776 Fluvanna Co, VA where res; PN there 1833 ae 76. F-S13824 R1621
MANLY, George, esf 1780 Lunenburg Co, VA; afp ae 69 Caswell Co NC, 1835 (much of apf illegible), & PAR; d 7/1837; s John (signature witnessed by Thomas & William MANLY, their kinship not stated) gave power/o attorney 1857 Caswell Co, NC to agent to afp, & PAR. F-R6865 R1621
MANN, Benjamin, esf 1761 Louisa Co, VA; PN ae 68 Campbell Co, KY, 1818; res there 1820 when had w mbnn ae 68 & all children of legal age; d mbnn 1825; James MANN (no kinship given) AFF in behalf of sol there 1822. F-S36067 R1622
   Ebenezer, esf 1777 Buckingham Co, VA, in 6th VA Regiment; PN ae 59 Hawkins Co, TN 1818; res there 1820, occupation farmer, with w aec 58, when they dependent on charity of his

MANN (continued)
son. F-S38927 R1622
Francis, esf 1776 Chesterfield Co, VA where b 1/30/1769; mvd to Guildford Co, NC, where esf 1780; mvd to KY after Cornwallis Surrender; PN 1832 Harrison Co, KY, where res since 1792. F-S13826 R1622
Joseph, b 1764 DE; esf 1781 Prince Edward Co, VA, where res; mvd to TN, thence Campbell Co, VA, where PN 1832; dd 1838-39; md Spring 1788 Ann d of William MOORE whose consent to marriage witnessed by John MANN (MB 3/17/88) Prince Edward Co, VA; wid afp ae nearly 80 Hawkins Co, TN 1849; PAR (ineligible per current PN law, sol still liv 1838); dd there c1849; heirs including s William (res 1845 there) afp 1850 res Kingsport, Sullivan Co, TN; PAR, since sol wid had dd before 1850). F-R6870 R1623
Peter, esf c1779 Chesterfield Co, VA, where b 1756; PN there 1832 where always res; dd 3/3/36; md there 1/5/1785 Martha MOORE; wid PN there 1839 ae 75; 3 ch, eldest Agnes who res there 1840 ae over 50; Edward MOORE & Alexander MOORE (ae 70) AFF there 1839 (both b, reared Chesterfield Co, VA, no kinship given) they attended sol wedding. F-W18481 R1623
Robert, b 1/1763; esf 1776 Buckingham Co, VA; PN 1818 Hawkins Co, TN, when res with w (b 10/1764) & they had no living children. F-S38922 R1623
William, b 7/7/1763 Amelia Co (area later Nottoway Co), VA; esf 1777 VA; PN 1833 Nottoway Co, VA; dd there 9/27/38; md Mary HUNDLEY (MB12/30/1787 signed by John HUNDLEY), Amelia Co, VA;wid PN ae 80 Nottoway Co, VA, 1843; 3rd ch Martha W b 3/2/1793; a Martha W PARMER (no kinship given) AFF 1843 Nottoway Co, VA, she had sol family bible for 30+ years; other file data (prepared by James J HUNDLEY, no kinship given): William W HUNDLEY (md 9/22/1811, dd 8/15/1825), Betsey Ann WHITE (b 4/22/1812, dd 9/14/1836), Daniel A BEASLEY b 11/15/1827. F-W7383 R1623
MANNAN, John, esf 1777 King George Co, VA, where b 10/15/1752; res there c15 years after RW, thence Stafford Co, VA for c 10 years, thence Spotsylvania Co, VA, for 8 years, thence 1816 Harrison Co, IN, where PN 1832; dd there 11/10/33; md 4/1776 or 1778 Lettice/Letitia at home of her uncle Moses HOLEY, Lamb's Creek Church, King George Co, VA; wid PN ae 81 Harrison Co, IN 1837; res there 1846 ae 90; dd 10/1851; ch births (1st 4 b dead, & not recorded) surname MANNON in family bible: William 1/4/1785, James 5/13/87, Nancy 8/1/89, John 2/16/91, Sary 3/7/93, Mary 3/14/95 (md Mr CHANDLER), Lucy 12/16/98, Susan/Susannah 12/23/1800 (md Mr KELLY) & Robert 3/16/04; other births: Sarah MANNON 5/9/1838, John Henry MANNON 1/13/1839, & Lisea Jane 5/1842; wid surv ch 1854: Mary CHANDLER & Lucy (both res Harrison Co, IN), William of TX (formerly res Owen Co, KY), & Susan KELLY of Hancock Co, KY; wid sis Mrs Sarah BOWLING AFF ae 80 Harrison Co, IN, she mvd 1829 from VA to IN. F-W9538 R1624
MANNING, Davis, b Buckingham Co, VA; esf 1781 Henry Co, VA; PN

MANNING (continued)
  ae 79 Franklin Co, VA, 1834; afp at home of Peyton ELLISON
  (no kinship given) since he was too infirm to attend court
  F-S16941 R1624
Henry, esf 1776 Little Winchester, MD in 2nd MD Regiment; PN
  ae 77 Augusta Co, VA, 1818; res there 1820 aec 75 when w
  aec 50. F-S38173 R1624
Lawrence, lieutenant in Lee's Legion; BLW 1457 issued 2/16/
  1792; records lost in Washington, DC, fire 1800; QLF 1936
  from Hilda D (Mrs W) BYARGEON of Oak Grove, LA, states sol
  b Ireland, had War of 1812 svc, 1st Adjutant General/o SC,
  md Susan, d of General Richard RICHARDSON, their s James B
  governor/o SC 1802-1804, further querier's gdm Susan MAN-
  NING bc 1775 SC, md Benjamin YOUNGBLOOD. F-BLW1457 R1624
MANNON, Henry, b 10/8/1759 Buckingham Co, VA; esf 1780 Henry
  Co, VA; mvd 1 year after RW to Franklin Co, VA, for 9-10
  years, thence Kanawha Co, VA, for c20 years, thence Lawrence Co, OH, where PN 1833; dd 2/12/38 leaving wid mbnn.
  F-S16187 R1625
John, see MANNAN, John. F-W9538 R1625
MANSFIELD, George, BLW12376 issued 12/9/1793. F-BLW12376 R1626
George, esf 1781 in 1st VA Regiment; PN ae 59 Orange Co, VA,
  1818; res there 1820 ae 61, occupation tailor, when had no
  family. F-S38182 R1626
Robert, esf 1779 Albemarle Co, VA where res; PN ae 70 Orange
  Co, VA, 1832; QLF states sol b 1762, dd 1822, md Mourning
  d/o Micajah CLARK Jr; QLF 1935 from great great gdd Laura
  E CLARK of Boise, ID; QLF 1934 from desc Mrs A V D PIERRE-
  PONT, Petersburg, VA; QLF 1928 from desc Miss Amy BEATTY,
  Crawfordsville, IN, states sol b 12/19/1762, dd 10/1/1833;
  QLF states sol b Albemarle Co, VA, dd Orange Co, VA, & md
  Mourning CLARK; QLF 1905 from great gdd Miss Kate MANS-
  FIELD of Clifton Hills, MO; QLF 1906 from great great gdd
  Helen Fairfax McNAUGHT, Hermiston, OR; QLF 1905 from great
  gdd Mrs J B RANK, Burlingon, IA; QLF 1905 from great great
  gdd Mrs Albert GREENE of Chicago, IL; QLF 1905 from desc
  Carl McNAUGHT, Hermiston, OR; QLF 1905 from great gds Al-
  bert G CLARK, Portland, OR; QLF 1905 from great great gdd
  Mrs Jennie E McNAUGHT, Umatilla, OR. F-S7185 R1626
Thomas, esf c1776 Hampton, VA; afp 1827 Marion Co, TN, aec
  76, occupation farmer, when had w aec 57, s Norman aec 17-
  18, s Thomas 20, s Robert aec 12, d Rebecca ae 30+, d Nancy ae 20+ (res away), & d Betsy ae 8; PAR. F-R6884 R1626
William, b c1745 MD; esf 1780 Bowers Oldfield, Prince Georges Co, MD; dd c4/15/1827 Alexandria, VA; md (1) Lucy at
  Centreville, MD who dd c1806 Oxon Hill, MD; md (2) Kersiah
  LONG, Oxon Hill, MD; wid gtd BLW88030 ae 70 Washington, DC
  1858; PN there 1859 ae 70; sol eldest s William dd ae 66+
  PA 1858; Thomas DONALDSON (res Alexandria, VA, 1815-1824)
  AFF 1858 Washington, DC, sol had s Henry by 1st w; sol s
  s Henry AFF ae 61 Alexandria, VA, that sol 2nd w had s Da-
  vid & s Charles by sol; sol s George res Alexandria, VA,

MANSFIELD (continued)
1859; sol s Henry living 1885.   F-W10211 R1626
MANTLO, John, see MATLO, John.   F-S15934 R1627
MAPENBURG, Alexander, see MASSENBURG, Alexander.   F-R15050 R1627
MAPES, John, esf in Lee's Legion; BLW13529 issued 4/26/1792. F-BLW13529 R1627
MAPP, John, b 1/14/1761; esf 1778-9 Spartanburg District, SC, where f res; mvd 1792 to GA, where dd 3/2/1828 Green Co; md 7/14/1784 Mary,, d of Colonel Henry WHITE, Spartanburg District, SC; wid PN ae 82 Green Co, GA, 1845 when sol bro Robert AFF ae 73 Hancock Co, GA, he 2 years younger than sol; a Molley MAPP b 7/13/1763; wid decd in 1851 when her executor John BONNER AFF Hancock Co, GA; record has newspaper obituary saying sol b VA, mvd with f Littleton to SC about time RW began.   F-W3840 R1628
MARCH, John, esf 1777 Suffolk, Nansemond Co, VA, where res; dd there 4/22/1832; s John A res there 1834 ae 38 when afp & afb for himself & other heirs: David HOWELL Sr, John LANGSTON, Sally BABB, Marian BABB, & John BABB; heirs PAR, not eligible since sol dd before prescribed date; heirs issued BLW7580 on 2/5/34.   F-R6900 R1629
MARCUM, Arthur, see MARKUM, Arthur.   F-R6907 R1629
  Josiah, b 5/2/1769 Chesterfield Co, VA; mvd ae 4-5 to Prince Edward Co, VA, thence when still young to Bedford Co, VA, where esf in VA Regiment as drummer before Gates' Defeat; PN 1832 Lawrence Co, KY; s Stephen 1833 AFF in behalf of f there; sol res OH 1845; QLF states sol dd ae 100-101.   F-S8999 R1629
  Thomas, b 1/4/1752 Caroline Co, VA; mvd aec 12 to Orange Co, NC, where esf 1780-81; PN there 1832; dd there 2/13/39; md 11/30/1773 Fanny; wid PN there 1839 ae 85; ch births (all surname MARCOM in bible record): Meley 9/277/1774, Isaiar 9/5/76, Elisha 11/7/78, Thomas 11/27/81, Polley 3/1/83, Geley 7/28/85, Nancy 12/4/87, Nathan 11/28/90, Betsey 12/15/92, William 12/2/95, Edman 6/3/98, Patcy 3/9/1801, Fanney 9/2/03, & William 8/29/07.   F-W9540 R1629
MARDERS, John, esf 1775 King George Co, VA, where b 1775; PN there 1832 aec 73; AFF there then by James MARDERS, whose kinship not stated.   F-S18500 R1629
MARDIS, William, esf 1777 King George Co, where res; esf 1781 Frederick Co, VA where res; dd 3rd Monday in November 1802 Campbell Co, KY; md 4/1/1779 Elizabeth LIPSCOMB; wid PN ae 82 Campbell Co, KY; dd 4/15/40 ae 83; d Nancy b 7/25/1780, md 10/24/1797 Robert MARSHALL (RW sol from near Hagerstown MD, see F-W2141 for his wid RW PN file) who dd 7/1/1837 Campbell Co (area later Kenton Co) KY; other sol ch births were: Sallie LIPSCOMB 10/29/1781, James 3/3/83, Betsy PERRY 10/15/85, Winne/Wine COOPER 10/31/87, Lucy LIPSCOMB, Polly LIPSCOMB, Stephen, & William; surv ch who gtd PN due m 1851: Nancy MARSHALL, Sallie LIPSCOMB, Betsy PERRY, Winne COOPER, Lucy LIPSCOMB, Stephen & William; QLF 1938 from

MARDIS (continued)
   desc Miss Vivienne LIPSCOMB, Spokane, WA, who also desc of
   VA RW sol Richard LIPSCOMB. F-W8410 R1629
MARICK, John, b 1758 Fredericktown, MD; while bound out there
   to Joseph LOCKER joined troops enroute to Nutter's Fort on
   VA frontier on Monongehela River to fight indians; res af-
   ter RW Mecklenburg Co, VA, then to Wilkes Co, GA, thence
   Washington Co, GA, thence Barnwell District, SC, then to
   Jones Co, GA, thence Dale Co, AL where PN 1833 as John Sr;
   dd c5/10/45 leaving no wid; s John Jr & d Harriet MINSEY/
   MINZEY gtd PN due sol 1851, John Jr then res Dale Co, AL.
   F-S11371 R1630
MARION, Samuel, esf 1776 Goochland Co, VA, where b 1/1750; PN
   1834 Hawkins Co, TN, res Lee Co, VA; living 1843; sis mbnn
   F-S4180 R1630
MARIS, Alexander, see MARS, Alexander. F-R7087 R1630
MARKAM, Lewis, see MARKHAM, Lewis. F-W25669 R1630
MARKER, William, see MANKER, William. F-W9942 R1630
MARKHAM, James, VA state navy, commander of ship TEMPEST which
   captured by British 1780-1 near Richmond, VA; dd 9/1/1816;
   gds Edmund B BARKER, s of William BARKER, gtd 1/2 pay PN;
   gds George B GOOD res 1853 Xenia, OH, 1853; QLF says sail-
   or middle name Luis; QLF states sol s-in-law VA RW sol at
   Yorktown. F-R72 R1630
 John, esf 1779 Prince Edward Co, VA, where b; PN ae 69 Bed-
   ford Co, VA, 1833; QLF 1926 from desc Mary W CASE, Klamath
   Falls, OR, states sol s John was War of 1812 sol from Bed-
   ford Co, VA; QLF states a VA RW sol John MARKHAM md Sallie
   BROWN, & their ch were Major, Marvel, Archibald, Edmund,
   James, Thomas, Josiah, Mary (md c1810 John KELLY/KELLA), &
   Judith. F-S5726 R1630
 Lewis, b 10/7/1763; esf 1780 Fauquier Co, VA, where res; mvd
   to Stafford Co, VA, thence Scott Co, KY, thence Limestone
   Co, AL, thence Lawrence Co, TN, where PN 1833; dd c9/26/46
   Lauderdale Co, AL; md 1/21/1830 Margaret/Peggy SINTER (ML
   1/5/30), Lawrence Co, TN; wid PN 1854 Lauderdale Co, AL;
   gtd BLW39213 there 1855 ae 74, when res Franklin Co, AL;
   sol younger bro William AFF 1832 Fayette Co, KY; QLF 1892
   from James H BRITTON, New York City, NY, whose w d/o James
   Lewis MARKHAM who res Culpeper Co, VA, & dd there c1817, &
   that James Lewis s of VA RW sol (name either James Lewis
   MARKHAM or Alfred MARKHAM who recd BLW), further querier
   mvd 1840 from Culpeper Co, VA, to New York City. F-W25669
   F1630
 Thomas, esf 1776 Prince Edward Co, VA, where b 7/15/57; mvd
   1785 to Bedford Co, VA, where PN 1833 as Thomas Sr; dd 5/
   4/40 there; md there c1786 Nelly WILKERSON, (MB 12/3/1785
   signed by Ranson WILKERSON); wid PN there 1844 aec 80; eldest ch bc 1787. F-W7389 R1630
MARKS, Edward, b 1757; esf 1779 Southampton Co, VA, where res,
   in 4th VA Regiment; mvd 1785 to Surry Co, VA, where PN as
   Edward Sr 1834. F-S11015 R1631

MARKS, Isaiah, esf VA in VA Line; dd 1785 Loudoun Co, VA, never married & without issue; only surv bro Thomas afp 1830 ae 74 Henderson Co, KY, for self & other heirs/o sol; ch/o Thomas were Isaiah, Betsy, Catharine, Deborah, Clementine, & Margaret; sol decd bro Elisha left ch: John, Isaiah, Sarah, George, Mary, Anne, Crissey/Lucretia, all formerly of Loudoun Co, VA; sol decd bro John left ch: John, Benjamin, Elisha, Samuel (res Henderson Co, KY), Jesse (decd & left heirs George & Garland BRADFORD), Sarah OVERFIELD, Margery CREWS, Rachel, Ury RANKINS (she & h decd, left d Ury); sol decd bro Abel left ch: Bennet, Thomas, Abel, Watts, Betsy, Samuel, Mary, Margaret, & Lydia; sol decd sis Ury WILLIAMS left ch: Rachel, Samuel, Elisha, Levi, James, Richard, Leah, Ury, Polly & Milly, all/o VA; sol decd sis Patsey HOWELL left ch Jesse, Abner, & Margaret, all of OH; sol decd sis Mary HUMPHREY left ch: Marcus, Jonah, Nancy YOUNG, & Hanna WILLIAMS, all of Loudoun Co, VA; PN due sol gtd to heirs; BLW1655 issued 7/14/1830 to sol bro Thomas for sol heirs. F-R16055 R1631

John, esf 1777 in VA Line; captain, paymaster, & military clothier; res after RW near Charlottesville, VA; dd 4/1791 Wilkes Co, GA; md 5/13/1780 Lucy, Albemarle Co, VA, wid of RW sol William LEWIS (dd in RW svc 11/14/1779); wid b 2/4/1752; PN 1836 Albemarle Co, VA; dd there 9/8/37; ch/o John MARKS & Lucy: John Hastings & Mary/Polly Garland (md William MOORE of AL); Jane M ANDERSON, d of William LEWIS & Lucy, AFF ae 67 Albemarle Co, VA, 1836 she had bro Reuben LEWIS (dd 2/17/1844 there leaving wid Mildred M but no ch) & bro Merriwether LEWIS (dd without issue); reference made 1791 to Hastings & Peter, sons of sol bro Peter MARKS; QLF 1923 from great great gds John W MARKS, Hartford, KY. F-W4542 R1631

MARKUM, Arthur, esf VA; md 6/26/1794 Anna BRANSGROVE, Washington Co, VA, when she ae 15 & he ae 31; mvd c6 years after RW to Campbell Co, TN, where sol dd 9/25/1832; wid afp ae 78 Scott Co, TN, 1851, & PAR. F-R6907 R1631

MARLAR, John, b Halifax Co, VA; esf 1778-1779 Halifax Co, NC, where res; mvd 1816 to Caswell Co, NC where PN 1833 ae 73-74; dd Surry Co, NC; s Peterson T res Jackson Co, GA, 1853 ae 52. F-S9400 R1631

MARLATT, Abraham, esf Winchester, VA; PN ae 57 Berkeley Co, VA 1818; res 1825 IN; dd 7/23/28 near Crull's Mills, Wayne Co IN; md 8/2/1785 Ann LINDER, Martrinsburg, Berkeley Co, VA, who b 11/8/1767; wid PN 1847 Mercer Co, IL; res 1849 near Covington, IN; eldest s George b 8/13/1786; s Thomas res 1847 ae 54 Washington Township, Wayne Co, IN; d mbnn (bc 1791) md Joseph COWNOVER (b 10/21/1787 Berkeley Co, VA), & they res Washington Township, Wayne Co, IN, 1846; d mbnn 1820 ae 7; wid dd intestate 3/8/1850 Fountain Co, IN; John ALLEN (no kinship given) adm of her estate 1850; QLF 1936 from desc Mrs Mabel MAHIN of Agra, KS; QLF 1921 from great great gdd Mrs Lulu McClure HUNT of Abington, IL says sol s

MARLATT (continued)
   Thomas md Elizabeth BELLAR & they had d Evaline who md Solomon WOLF & they had d Leanna WOLF who md 1872 Warren McCLURE (m maiden name Jane PYLE), & they had d Lulu McCLURE (querier), who md 11/5/1908 James William HUNT; QLF 1919 Mary V L RETECKER, Los Angeles, CA, who great gdd/o Thomas MARLATT, a War of 1812 sol who gtd PN for that svc & mvd c 1820 to Wayne Co, IN; QLF 1916 from desc Maude Davison ERVIN of Hamilton, MO, states her 2nd cousin Walter MARLATT of Kenosha, WI, member of SAR; QLF 1907 from great gds C L MARLATT of Washington, DC. F-W21771 R1631
   Peter, esf 1778 Reading Town, NJ, in 2nd NJ Regiment; PN ae 58 Berkeley Co, VA, 1818; res there 1820 ae 62, occupation farmer, when family w June aec 58, s Jacob aec 12 & d Elizabeth aec 9; surname also spelled MORLATT; QLF 1897 from desc William MARLATT, Cleveland, OH. F-S38177 R1631
MARLE, James, esf 1776 Baltimore, MD as fifer when very young; afp ae 76-77 Loudoun Co, VA 1839 when res there c25 years, & res in Co poor house for past 6 years; PAR, insufficient proof of svc; surname also spelled MARL. F-R6908 R1631
MARNEY, Amos, b 9/1760 Frederick Co, VA; esf 1779 Shenandoah Co, VA where res; res there after RW, thence Rockbridge Co VA for 10 years, thence Roane Co, TN, where PN 1833; there dd 8/22/38 or 8/28/39; md 4/22/1784 Sarah VANCE, Shenandoah Co, VA, who b 5/8/1770; wid PN 1843 Roane Co, TN; gtd BLW34830 there 1855; dd 8/15/58; ch births (family record torn, faded & blotched): Betsey 9/10/1787, David 11/13/89, Amos 1/5/17--, Samuel 2/-/17--, Robert 7/8/95, Sally 2/19/1802, Pheby 9/-/18--, ? -/7/06, & ? -/-/09; other family data: Alizabeth SPENCE b 12/22/1801; David VANCE (no kinship given) AFF ae 76 Blount Co, TN, 1843 he attended wedding of sol; QLF 1936 from desc Mrs J W CROWDER, Kingston, TN; QLF says sol w d/o General Samuel VANCE of Shenandoah Co, VA, who also RW sol; QLF 1919 from great gdd Mrs J R DUNAWAY, Waxahachie, TX. F-W1046 R1631
MARR, John, esf 1781 Orange Co, VA, where res; afp 1840 ae 76 Haywood Co, TN, & PAR, insufficient proof of identity with RW sol/o same name; sol gdd Clara SLOAN, Maury City, Crockett Co, TN, afp for sol svc in both RW & War of 1812; PAR F-R6912 R1631
MARRETT, Larose/Rosey, b 10/19/1749; esf 1777 Winchester, VA; PN 1819 Cabell Co, VA; res 1821 Mason Co, VA, when occupation house carpenter & he had "no family or settled children with whom he could live." F-S38176 R1631
MARRION, Bartholomew, b VA; mvd ae 4 with parents to Granville Co, NC, then to Bute Co, NC, then aec 11 to Surry Co, NC, where he esf 1779; PN there 1832 ae 78. F-S7178 R1631
MARS, Alexander, esf Botetourt Co, VA, where res; dd 5/4/1839 Shelby Co, KY, ae 87, leaving no wid, but ch: Alexander MEIRS, Rachel FERGUS, Shannon MEAIRS, Hannah WALL, John MEAIRS, Margaret MEAIRS, & David MEAIRS (spelling of surnames this way by Co clerk of court); ch living 1855: Ra-

MARS (continued)
  chel FERGUS ae 64, Shannon MEAIRS ae 62, John MEAIRS ae 60, Margaret HALL ae 58 & David MEAIRS ae 56; s David MARS afp 1855 Johnson Co, IN, for self & surv siblings, & PAR, insufficient proof of svc. F-R7087 R1631
MARSH, David, b & raised Amelia Co, VA; esf 1779 VA (area later Russell Co), VA; mvd after RW to Rutherford Co, NC, then to Greenville, SC, for c6 years, then to Campbell Co, TN, for many years, then to McMinn Co, TN, then to Bledsoe Co, TN, thence White Co, TN, thence Wayne Co, KY where afp 1834 ae 75; PAR. F-R6918 R1632
  Henry, b 1761 Amelia Co, VA; esf 1777 Surry Co, VA, res town of Richmond; mvd to Henry Co, VA, where m res & esf there; mvd after RW to Washington Co (area later Russell Co), VA, thence Wayne Co, KY, thence MO Territory, thence McMinn Co TN, then to Bledsoe Co, TN, then to White Co, TN, where PN 1832; gtd BLW26161 there 1855 aec 100; dd there 9/25/59; md c9/6/1816 Phereba HARVEY, Overton Co, TN; wid PN ae 66 White Co, TN, 1860; PN restored there 1866 after Civil War when she signed oath of allegiance; PN increase there 1868 ae 86. F-W9531 R1632
  John, b 10/30/1756 Northumberland Co, VA; esf 1775 Stafford Co, VA, res there; mvd 1777 to Northumberland Co, VA where esf 1778; mvd 1780 to Baltimore, MD, where esf 1780; mvd 1815 to Belmont Co, OH, where afp 1835 res Kirkwood Township; PAR, insufficient proof of svc; QLF 1914 from desc A J SMITH, Chicago, IL. F-R6922 R1632
  Robert, see MURSH, Robert. F-W8416 R1633
  Thomas, esf in 5th VA Regiment; PN 1818 Orange Co, VA, no ae given. F-S38174 R1633
MARSHALL, Benjamin, b 1/22/1759 Charlotte Co, VA, where esf 1780; PN there 1832; QLF states sol md Rebecca JEFFRESS, Prince Edward Co, VA. F-S5728 R1634
  Benjamin, b 1760 Calvert Co, MD; esf 1781 Albemarle Co, VA, where res; PN 1832 Stokes Co, NC; dd 10/28/40 leaving some children mbnn. F-S7176 R1634
  Benjamin, b 1755 Prince Georges Co, MD; esf 1780-1 Hampshire Co, VA, where res; PN 1834 Hardy Co, VA; dd 3/28/34; md c 1775 Elizabeth, Montgomery Co, MD, where they both res at time; wid PN ae 78 Hardy Co, VA, 1838; dd 10/10/45 leaving ch: Hanson/Henson, Mary TUCKER, Samuel (1840 ae 43), Elizabeth, & Emily; s Thomas dd before m. F-W4279 R1634
  Daniel, esf Campbell Co, VA where b & raised; mvd to Rutherford Co, NC where dd 1821 near Murfreesborough; ch who afp 1837: Joseah, William, Robert, Daniel Jr, Walter, George, Polly wid/o James DEJANOTT, Elizabeth w/o John C HALL, Michael w/o Thomas HAMILTON, Martha wid/o Joseph DRAKE, Mildred w of P J CURLE, Isabella w/o Urbelo D EZELL, + Robert M WHITE (s of sol decd d Nancy who md Henry WHITE); heirs PAR, sol dd before PN Law/o 6/7/1832 under which they afp; QLF 1915 from great gdd Mrs M B WHELESS of Birmingham, AL, states her gdm MARSHALL md Mr EZELL & they mvd to TX, fur-

MARSHALL (continued)
ther sol had bro William; QLF from great gdd Mrs Bettie Marshall WHITELEY, Kansas City, MO. F-R6928 R1634

Ezekiel, b 1756-7 Prince George Co, VA; esf 1776 Mecklenburg Co, VA, where res; mvd aec 35 from VA to NC for c14 years, Sumner Co, TN, where PN 1833, when P O Address McCreary's Post Office, Robertson Co, TN; dd 4/3/42; QLF states sol buried Sumner Co, TN. F-S2743 R1634

Francis, b 11/8/1750 Cumberland Co, VA; esf Chesterfield Co, VA, where res; later esf Mecklenburg Co, VA where res; after res there 30 years, mvd to Sumner Co (area later Macon Co), TN, where PN 1832; dd 1/23/36 Sumner Co, TN, at res; md 8/2/1813 Sarah JACOBS, Smith Co, TN; wid PN ae 78 Macon Co, TN, 1853; gtd BLW31331 there 1855; res 1866 for past 5 years with d Sarah H JACOBS on Goose Creek that Co; PN restored there 1867 after Civil War; birth data in file (all surname THOMPSON): Thomas 1/29/1823, Nathaniel 5/29/1824 & James 1/17/1826. F-W6793 R1634

George, esf 1776 Caroline Co, VA; PN 1819 Brown Co, OH, ae 65; res there 1821 ae 67, occupation farmer, with w Rachel ae 46 & ch: Washington ae 1.5 & Marquis de La Fayette ae 5 weeks; dd there 9/5/48 Washington Township; md 2/17/1817 Rachel BOZER, Lewis Co, KY; wid PN 1853 Brown Co, OH, ae 75; AFF then there by sol kinsman William MARSHALL he present at sol marriage to Rachel; sol s Marquis AFF then Ohio Co, VA. F-W304 R1634

Humphrey, b VA; esf 1778 in VA regiment; gtd VA BLW of 4,000 acres; PN 1832 Franklin Co, KY; res there 1835 ae 75; dd 7/3/41; family mbnn; Thomas A MARSHALL (no kinship given) adm of sol estate 1853 Lexington, KY; QLF says sol dd near Lexington, KY, left 2 sons; QLF states sol esf Fauquier Co VA; QLF 1907 from desc J M MARSHALL, Assistant Quartermaster General, US Army, Jeffersonville, IN. F-S31234 R1634

Isaac, esf 1777 in 14th VA Regiment; esf 1778 in 10th VA Regiment; PN ae 60 Iredell Co, NC, 1821, occupation farmer, when had w ae 53 & ch: Jane ae 28, Beheathland ae 24, Eleazar ae 12, & Theophilus ae 10; dd 4/17/39; md 6/17/1785 Mary FOOTE (MB 6/11/85), Warren Co, NC; wid PN ae 74 Iredell Co, NC, 1842; ch births: John F 6/23/1786, Hersey F 12/2/87, William B 7/26/89, Ginsey 4/4/92, Joseph 4/19/93, Margaret 4/-/95, Behethland 5/14/96, G 11/7/98, Richard 10/25/1800, Thomas W 6/15/02, Elizabeth 6/25/04, Eleazar 3/31/08, & Theophilus 12/13/10; wid dd 11/24/49; her LWT probated 2/1850, listing executor s Theophilus & heirs: Theophilus MARSHALL, John F MARSHALL, Margaret MARSHALL, Makethea MARSHALL, June SHOEMAKER, Henry MARSHALL, William MARSHALL, Joseph MARSHALL, Elizabeth MARSHALL, & Eleazar MARSHALL; s Richard afp 1852 Lancaster District, SC for PN due m. F-W3842 R1634

James, captain of VA Line; went to West Indies after RW, but returned to VA 1788 where dd; LWT 2/9/1788 Elizabeth City Co, VA, probated there 9/25/88, listed m Ann, w Eupham, &

MARSHALL (continued)
ch: Ann Armistead, George, Mary, & Jane; all ch dd as minors without issue except (1) Ann who md Charles M COLLIER & (2) Jane who md Walker HAUGHTHAM (MB 11/9/1802); Jane's ch all dd as minors, except Thomas & Frances who md Thomas S YOUNG; afp 1830 Elizabeth City Co, VA, by d Ann COLLIER, Thomas HAUGHTHAM, & Thomas S YOUNG; no action indicated on afp; heirs of sol issued VA BLW for 4,000 acres 12/1830. F-None R1634
James, b 1760; esf 1777 Accomack Co, VA, in 2nd VA Regiment; PN there 1850; dd 1/9/51; md 9/10/1791 Patience; wid PN ae 82 Accomack Co, VA, 1851; eldest ch mbnn ae 60-62 in 1850. F-W7390 R1634
James M, esf 1779 in VA regiment commanded by f Colonel Thomas MARSHALL; PN aec 70 Frederick Co, VA, 1833 res near Front Royal; dd 4/26/48; s James, exec/o sol LWT, afp 1856 for PN due f. F-S7173 R1634
Jenepher/Jenifer, VA sea svc, sailing master of galley ACCOMACK; left svc 1781 & dd 4/1/1792; d Euphemia WALSTON his only heir 1793; PN gtd to adm's of his estate John B AILWORTH & W B H CUSTIS 1846. F-R70 R1635
Jesse, b 11/1765 Brunswick Co, VA, where esf 1781 in company of cousin Captain James MARSHALL; res there c1793, then to Caswell Co, NC, for 3 years, then to Rowan Co, NC, for 9 years, thence Mecklenburg Co, NC, thence Rutherford Co, NC for 2 years, thence Burke Co, NC, where PN 1833; mvd same year to Franklin Co, GA, where dd 2/29/40; md 1782 Nancy INGRAM, Lunenburg Co, VA; wid PN 1843 Franklin Co, GA, ae 70; res there 1845; res 1848 Habersham Co, GA, ae 74; sol AKA Jessy MARSHAL. F-W5350 R1635
John, esf 1775 Fauquier Co, VA, where res, in 11th VA Regiment; PN ae 77 Washington, DC, 1833 when res Richmond, VA; Chief Justice of US Supreme Court; QLF states a John MARSHALL b 3/6/1753, dd 1/21/1819, md Sarah JOYCE, & they res Charlotte Co, VA. F-S5731 R1635
John, esf 1778 Fauquier Co, VA; mvd 1779 to New River (area later Montgomery Co, VA) where esf 1779; mvd 1788 to Licking River (area later Mason Co, KY); PN ae 73 Lawrence Co, KY 1834; dd 9/28/40 & w mbnn dd next day, leaving no children or children's children; Anna PORTER, exec of sol LWT, res 1848 Paintsville, Johnson Co, KY. F-S38162 R1635
Joseph, VA sea svc, sailing master of schooner SCORPION until 1781, when ship captured by British; dd c7/1/1812. F-R69 R1635
Richard, esf 1776 in 1st VA Regiment; BLW12367 issued 3/4/1796; PN 1818 Muskingum Co, OH; res there 1820 ae 63 occupation farmer with w Keziah ae 71, gdc Marshall STUTTS ae 12 & gdd Elizabeth STUTTS ae 9, when gtd BLW961; gdd mbnn w of Samuel STEELE then; dd there 11/4/41 Meigs Township; md Keziah SHERER, Spotsylvania Co, VA 1784-5, who PN ae 90 Guernsey Co, OH, 1847 res Jackson Township; Samuel STEELE AFF then sol wid liv with him & w; wid gtd BLW314 there ae

MARSHALL (continued)
 95 1856; res 1857 Gallia Co, OH; QLF 1895 from desc Lucretia STULTZ, Zanesville, OH; QLF 1913 from desc Miss Elizabeth F MARSHALL, Lynchburg, VA. F-W7391, F-BLW12367 R1635
Samuel, esf 1778 Accomac Co, VA; dd there c2/15/1835 at res Saxis Island; surv ch who afp that Co 1851: Washington, Milly LEWIS, & Elizabeth TYLER; ch gtd PN; James W CUSTIS (no kinship given) adm of sol estate then; QLF 1939 from Mrs Allen T SNODDY, Tulsa, OK, whose gdd mbnn desc of sol. F-S8997 R1635
Thomas, esf 1776 Prince Georges Co, MD where b 2/15/1758; PN 1938 Hardy Co, VA, res Moorefield; last PN payment in file 1841. F-S8992 R1635
Thomas, sergeant of dragoons in VA Line; res 1835 Pittsylvania Co, VA; no other data in file. F-None R1635
Thomas, captain & paymaster in VA artillery regiment; minister in Accomac Co, VA, when dd; exec of estate Thomas MARSHALL (no kinship given) gtd PN due sol 1850 res Mason Co, KY. F-R16057 R1635
William, PA RW sol, not VA; QLF in his file states VA RW sol Reverend William MARSHALL b 1735 Fauquier Co, VA, dd Henry Co, KY, 1808, md 1766 Mary Ann PICKETT in VA & their d Lucy md Edward s/o Richard Marot BOOKER. F-BLW2336 R1635
MARSTON, John, esf c1778 as lieutenant in 1st VA Regiment; LWT 10/25/1797 Surry Co, VA & probated there 3/20/1798, listed w Susanna whose LWT 9/26/1816, witnessed by John MINGE Jr, probated there 5/24/1819, listed kinsman William LIGHTFOOT (ae under 21) & niece Sarah L w of John MINGE; Sarah, w of Robert Buckner BOLLING, only ch of John & Sarah L MINGE; sol heirs Sarah S MINGE, Robert Buckner BOLLING, & Sarah M BOLLING gave power of attorney to agent 1836, Charles City Co, VA, to afp; heirs gtd PN due sol; heirs issued BLW2223 1/29/48. F-R16031 R1636
MARTIN, Adam, b 9//28/1755; esf Augusta Co, VA, where res; dd 4/14/1835 St Louis Co, MO; md 3/16/1778 Mary McMILLIN, who b 3/16/1762; wid dd 4/16/1850 St Louis Co, MO; ch births: Jane 8/30/1780 (dd 4/23/1814), David 9/28/82, Mary M 9/1/84, Nancy A 10/1/87 (md Mr MUSICK & dd 6/27/1814), Elizabeth 2/20/90, Jehoida/Jehoiada P 4/24/94 (dd 11/22/1844), Jonathan P 11/27/99, & Robert N 5/8/1804; s Lewis afp 1852 St Louis Co, MO for self, surv siblings: Elizabeth WHITLEY (AKA Elizabeth HALL), Mary HILDERBRAND, David, Jonathan, & Robert N; ch PAR, insufficient proof/o svc. F-R6961 R1637
Azariah, esf 1780 Amherst Co, VA, in company/o uncle Captain Azariah MARTIN; mvd c1791-2 to KY, where PN ae 68 Clay Co 1834; dd 4/15/34 Rockcastle Co, KY; md 4/1791 Lucy RODES, Amherst Co, VA, at home of her f Charles (MB 4/20/91 listed sol as Azariah Jr, signed by Azariah MARTIN & Azariah MARTIN Jr, & showed consent of Lucy's f); wid PN ae 74 Madison Co, KY, 1840; res there 1843; d Liberty B, b 1812, res there 1843, one of wid's 6 ch; sol bro William res ae 74 there 1840. F-W554 R1637

MARTIN, Benjamin, esf 1781 Cumberland Co, VA; dd 12/16/1814 in Hall Co, GA; md 6/2/1785 Anna, Cumberland Co, VA, who b 6/17/1765; wid afp 1845 Hall Co, GA & PAR; d Lucy DEATON AFF there then ae 40; AFF then by Martin DOWDY ae 79 of Oglethorpe Co, GA, he res Cumberland Co, VA, when sol md Anna; wid ch: Thomas L, Elizabeth, Mary, John, Susannah, Anna, Fanny & Lucy; Stephen MARTIN (no kinship given) gave power of attorney 1853 Hall Co, GA, to agent to afp for sol wid; PAR again. F-R6936 R1637

Benjamin, esf 1775 Fauquier Co, VA where b 7/8/1758 s/o Henry; PN 1833 Barren Co, KY; dd there 9/20/38; md 6/29/1781 Nancy KEMPER, Fauquier Co, VA, who b 3/27/1760; wid afp 2/17/1841 Barren Co, KY & PAR; dd there 6/9/41 or 6/20/41; ch births: Letty 4/4/1782, Nathan 9/3/83, John 11/13/85, Betsey 5/21/88, Mary 9/1/90 (md Mr COLE), Nancy 9/4/92, Rebekah 5/3/98 (md Mr GRIDER), Benjamin H 7/10/1800, & Lucinda 7/6/02; s John AFF Barren Co, KY 1841; s Benjamin H afp there 1852 for himself & surv siblings Mary COLE & Rebekah GRIDER & PAR, sol dd after passage of PN Act of 7/7/1838. F-R6965 R1637

Daniel, esf 1777 NJ in NJ Regiment; BLW8557 issued 9/29/1790 to sol; PN ae 73 Preston Co, VA, 1828, occupation farmer, when res with w Elizabeth ae 69; w Elizabeth dd c6/18/35, & sol md (2) wid woman mbnn, who dd by 1841; sol dd there 10/3/50; md there (3) Eve EVERLY 9/23/1841, who PN there 1853 ae 34; sol s Jacob res there then; wid gtd BLW4 there 1855 ae 36; Elisha LISTON (no kinship given) appointed her guardian by Preston Co, VA, court & some years later Isaac MARTIN (no kinship given) appointed her guardian by 1878; wid dd there 12/4/82; local citizen wrote 1878 PN Office that sol wid was always a bad woman and had 3 ch since her h dd; PN Office replied that bearing/o illegimate children did not affect her drawing of PN. F-W2401 R1638

David, esf 1779-80 Goochland Co, VA, where res; afp 1836 ae 75 Hardin Co, KY, & PAR, insufficient proof of svc; s Moab AFF there 1854 he one of f's heirs. F-R6839 R1638

Elizabeth, former wid of John ARCHER. F-W5348 R1638

George, esf 1778 Orange Co, VA where b 1763; mvd after RW to Albemarle Co, VA, for c14 years, then to Campbell Co, VA, where afp 1833, & PAR, svc as express rider not covered by current PN laws & other RW svc less than 6 months; dd 2/7/34 Lynchburg, VA; md 1783 Elizabeth, d of Thomas JONES (MB 6/14/83), Orange Co, VA; wid mvd after sol dd to Bedford Co, VA, where afp 1844 ae 78 & PAR; eldest s Thomas ae 60-61 then; wid res there 1852 ae 86; res there 1856; QLF 1910 from desc William C SMOCK, Indianapolis, IN. F-R6941 R1638

George, esf c1778 Fairfax Co, VA; severe wounds at Battle of Blufords Defeat disabled him, & caused his early death on 12/1/1805; md 1/15/1775 Mary BAILEY, Fairfax Co, VA who dd 10/22/1843 Pittsylvania Co, VA, leaving ch: Bailey, James, Rebecca, & Sally w/o James M WILLIS; wid sis Martha MARTIN

MARTIN (continued)
  AFF 1841 Patrick Co, VA sol w & ch William & George res at her f's home while sol in svc; AFF then by sol nephew Stephen MARTIN ae 62; wid bro Thomas AFF then Halifax Co, VA, his f Joseph H BAILEY res Loudoun Co, VA, when sol md sis, & that sol & w mvd after RW to Halifax Co, VA, & sol dd in Pittsylvania Co, VA; wid & ch res Aspen Grove when she afp 1843 that Co, but dd before claim acted on; sis Patsy MARTIN AFF 1841 Stokes Co, NC; ch births (bible record badly faded, blotched, & partially illegible): Joel 6/22/1787, Tilly 5/24/91, & Mary 7/11/93; record shows a Sarah BAILEY dd 5/28/1795; surv ch PN 1844 Pittsylvania Co, VA. F-W4543 R1638

Gideon, esf 1780 Amherst Co, VA, in Captain Azariah MARTIN's (no kinship given) company; PN aec 100 Warren Co, KY, 1832 F-S31232 R1638

Hudson, b 5/14/1761 Albemarle Co, VA; esf 1779 Amherst Co, where res, sub for bro William; esf 1781 Fluvanna Co, VA, where res; res after RW Amherst Co, VA, in area later Nelson Co; PN 1832 Nelson Co, VA, when bro William res there. F-S7175 R1638

Hudson, b 7/3/1752 (old style); esf 1776 Albemarle Co, VA, where res; dd 11/28/30 Nelson Co, VA; md 12/2/1778 Jane, d/o Colonel Nicholas LEWIS, Charlottesville, VA; wid b 7/6/1759; PN 1836 Nelson Co, VA; dd there 8/15/38; ch births: Nicholas Lewis 9/20/1779 (dd 8/1/1787), Hudson 7/26/81, John Massie 6/28/83, Molley Walker 6/13/87 (md Mr DICKINSON, & she dd 11/24/1814), Jane Lewis 1/11/90 (md William FABER), Nicholas Lewis 12/11/91, Henry Buck 1/12/94 (dd 1/14/1828), George Washington 2/19/96, & Mildred Harnsley 2/16/1801 (md John F CARR & their s John b 2/25/1819); other bible data: Nicholas LEWIS b 1/19/1734 (dd 12/8/1808), Mary LEWIS b 6/24/1742 (dd 2/9/1824); ch surv m: Hudson, Jane FABER, Nicholas L, George W, Mildred H CARR & John M; sol LWT of 12/27/1830 listed w Jane & ch: Hudson, John M, George W, Nicholas L, Henry (decd), Mary W DICKINSON, Mildred H CARR, & Jane L FABER, + s-in-law William FABER. F-W7394 R1638.

Jacob, b 8/18/1759 Oley, PA; mvd ae 2 with f to Tulpehocken, PA, thence ae 9 to Frederick Co, MD, where esf 1776 in MD regiment, res Fredericktown; mvd 1785 to Loudoun Co, VA, where md (wbnn) for 4 years, thence Bedford Co, PA, for 18-19 years, thence Muskingum Co (area later Perry Co), OH; PN latter Co 1833; dd 6/23/37, leaving children mbnn; bro John decd in 1833. F-S8998 R1639

James, esf Cumberland Co, PA, in 6th PA Regiment; PN 1818 ae 91 Frederick Co, VA. F-S38170 R1639

James, b 8/26/1755 near Watkins Ferry on Potomac River, VA; esf 1775 York District, SC, where res; PN there 1832, & dd there 2/1/0/36, leaving only heir Margaret T CAMPBELL, his only surv ch; she gtd PN due f there 1846. F-S9391 R1639

James, esf 1784 Pittsylvania Co, VA; dd 1/24/1842 Jackson Co

MARTIN (continued)
TN; md 1802 Nancy FARGUSON/FOGGERSON, Pittsylvania Co, VA; wid afp ae 81 Putnam Co, TN, 1855; PAR, sol svc subsequent to RW; ch liv 1855: Gincy ADAMS, Polly, William, Frances RODGERS, & Mary Ann. F-R6966 R1639

James, VA sea svc, esf 1777 as surgeon on ship CASWELL; dd intestate; James P MARTIN, adm/o sailor's estate, gave power of attorney to agent to afp 1850 Norfolk Co, VA; James P MARTIN decd in 1851, when C S MARTIN, adm/o sailor's estate, gave power/o attorney to agent to afp there; heirs/o sailor then: Charles S MARTIN, Nancy MARTIN, Julina WHITE, & H MATTHEWS; heirs gtd 1/2/ pay PN; sailor's bro Luther was f/o Charles S, James, & Nancy; Selden BAILEY (b 1769) AFF 1851 Norfolk Co, VA, his f Ebenezer served with sailor on ship CASWELL. F-R71 R1639

James, b 8/1758 Albemarle Co, VA, where esf 1779 when res with f; mvd from f's home to KY 1784 where fought in Indian Wars; PN 1833 Jessamine Co, KY when line between Jessamine Co & Fayette Co, KY, passed through his property; dd Jessamine Co, KY leaving no wid but ch (all liv 1853): Letitia METCALF, Amanda ARTHURS, Richard, & Lewis Y; QLF's 1904 & 1933 from desc Miss Virginia STEWART, Kansas City, MO; QLF states sol md Miss YOUNG; QLF states sol had 6 ch; QLF 1923 from desc Mrs E S DEWEY, Tulsa, OK, says sol s/o Thomas who came to America when England subdued Ireland, further sol md (1) Judith/Letitia YOUNG of Jessamine Co, KY, & (2) Miss MILLER. F-S31236 R1639

Job, esf 1776 Bedford Co, VA, in 5th VA Regiment; PN 1832 ae 79 Kanawha Co, VA; res there 1834. F-S18496 R1639

John, 1780 Fredericktown, MD; PN 1818 Berkeley Co, VA, aec 63; mvd 1819 to Chambersburg, Franklin Co, PA; res there 1821, when w Catharine aec 74; sol dd there 6/13/24; QLF 1895 from desc James MARTIN of Philadelphia, PA. F-S40123 R1640

John, esf 1776 Augusta Co, VA; PN ae 58 Clark Co, KY, 1818; res there 1820 with w aec 60, unmd d ae 19, & s ae 16; QLF 1939 from Estelle C (Mrs Charles H) WATSON, Evanston, IL, says she desc/o VA RW sol John MARTIN (f John res West Indies before coming to America), who md Sarah JEFFREYS (b 1755, dd 7/13/1830) & they had ch: Enoch, William, Joseph, Jeffreys, Jacob, Elizabeth, & John, further John & Sarah mvd from VA to Shelby Co, KY, then to 1814 Washington Co, IN, further their d Elizabeth md John, s/o VA RW sol Peter MARTIN; QLF states sol dd Clark Co, KY, & w's first name was Rachel. F-S36074 R1640

John, esf 1776 NJ in 4th NJ Regiment; PN ae 77 Tyler Co, VA, 1818; res 1820 Athens Co, OH, ae 81 when res with widowed d Susannah WILSON, other ch having md & mvd away 16+ years before; s Ephraim AFF there 1823 his f & m res VA c1811, & m dd since; sol gave land in OH to gds James WILSON, s of his d Susannah (her h having deserted her); sol also gave land to s Ephraim's s Samuel; sol dd 5/14/37. F-None R1640

MARTIN, John, esf 1779 in SC regiment sub for f (then aec 45); mvd after RW to Hawkins Co, TN, thence c1781 Lee Co, VA, where PN 1823 ae 71; dd 9/15/42 Goochland Co, VA, leaving no wid but ch: Nelson, Judith w/o Benjamin DUVAL, & Nancy w/o William BANKS. F-S15935 R1640
John, BLW12341 & 13389 issued 11/15/1791. F-BLW12341 R1640
John, BLW12389 issued 5/8/1794. F-BLW12389 R1640
John, b 1750 Goochland Co, VA, where esf in VA regiment; PN there 1833, where always lived; QLF states sol md Barbara LEWIS. F-S18104 R1640
John, b 3/1749; esf 1775 Albemarle Co, VA where res; PN 1832 Clark Co, KY; dd 12/3/37; QLF states sol w Elizabeth survived him; QLF states sol b Albemarle Co, VA; QLF states sol md Elizabeth LEWIS, who b 1754; QLF 1919 from desc Mrs C E WAYNE of Kansas City, MO; QLF states sol s of Captain Thomas MARTIN & was 1st cousin to George Rogers CLARK; QLF 1906 from great gds (on m's side) George M JACKSON, Wickliffe, KY, who also great gds of VA RW sol Josiah JACKSON, who was PN 1833 Clark Co, KY. F-S30563 R1640
John, b 2/8/1756; esf 1775 in 2nd VA Regiment; PN 1810 Caroline Co, VA, for disability from wound at Siege of Ninety-Six; mvd 1818 to Wilson Co, TN, where dd 4/10/37; md 4/7/1782 Mary FLIPPO, who b 8/18/1760; wid PN 1839 Wilson Co, TN; births in file (all surname HORNSBY): Maria M 2/29/1820, Elizabeth C 3/8/1822 (dd 6/22/1828), Julia 10/9/1824 Ruth Ann 5/8/1826, & Albert B 4/29/1828; AFF 1839 by May FLIPPO, Caroline Co, VA, bro of sol wid. F-W1443 R1640
John, esf 1781 Fluvanna Co, VA, where res, in 71st VA Regiment; afp ae 70 Greenbrier Co, VA 1834 & PAR; one of heirs Nicholas TINCH gave power of attorney there 1853 to afp, & PAR. F-R6954 R1640
John O F, b 12/5/1764 Halifax Co, VA; esf 1781 Pittsylvania Co, VA; mvd to Augusta Co, VA, where esf 1782; mvd 1807 to KY where PN 1834 Green Co. F-S30569 R1640
Joseph, b 1758 Rocles/Rodes, France; esf 1779-80 in French Army; shipped to Savannah GA, where his unit was repulsed with heavy losses by British; went to Southampton Co, VA, where esf in American regiment; mvd 1782 to Wayne Co, NC, where afp 1832 & PAR, insufficient proof of svc; dd c1835; md Telitha who res Goldsboro, Wayne Co, NC when gave power of attorney 1852 to afp, & her PAR; dd 1859 leaving ch mbnn; QLF 1924 from desc Mrs W H NEWELL Jr of Wilmington, NC states sol md Tillitha BOSWELL of Wilson Co, NC & they res Fremont, NC, querier also desc/o RW sol James HOLLINSWORTH (s/o Henry who md Mary MURRAH of the British Isles) who md Elizabeth MERRIT after RW, & they settled in Sampson Co or Duplin Co, NC, & had d Charity, querier also desc/o RW sol John PERRY (1740-1797, s/o John who md Miss CALDWELL, they both from Wales) who md Nancy MESHAW (1750-1797), & they settled in Bladen Co, NC. F-R6957 R1640
Joseph, esf 1777 Alexandria, VA in 10th VA Regiment; mvd after RW to Loudoun Co, VA, thence Pittsylvania, VA, then to

MARTIN (continued)
Halifax Co, VA, thence NC, thence back to Pittsylvania Co, VA, thence Henry Co, VA, where PN 1818 aec 63; dd 2/14/32 there; md 3/1/? c18 months before end of RW to Patsey BAILEY, Loudoun Co, VA; wid PN aec 79 Rockingham Co, NC 1839; res 1840 Patrick Co, VA; ch births: Stephen 11/28/1779, Susanna 5/8/87, Morning/Moaning 8/1/89; Joseph 9/7/91-92, Thomas 5/26/95, Martha/Patsey 5/27/98 (md John PERDUE); in 1839 ch Stephen, Susanna, Morning & Joseph res Patrick Co, VA; d Patsy then res Rockingham Co, NC; s Thomas then res "somewhere in the West"; QLF 1937 from desc Mrs Bess Hodges LOGAN, Washington, DC, states sol b 1775 VA. F- W9532 R1640

Josiah, BLW12369 issued 3/26/179?. F-BLW12389 R1641

Josiah, esf in VA Continental Line; dd 1814; md 11/1786 Sarah who PN ae 78 King & Queen Co, VA, 1838; AFF there then by William COOKE ae 79 he esf 1779-80 with sol; AFF then there by Ann BROACH ae 74 she at sol wedding; AFF there by Clara COOK (b 2/1765) & Catharine BROOKS (b 10/27/1756) in 1839 they at sol wedding. F-W18485 R1641

Kinchen, esf 1779 Southampton Co, VA, where b 1/6/1762; PN 1832 Anson Co, NC; dd 6/14/41; md 1784 Chloe HOUGH, Northampton Co, NC; wid dd 3/17/45 leaving ch John, William, & Lucy, who gtd PN due m in 1847; s James res 1833 Anson Co, NC, ae 45; AFF there 1846 by wid bro Moody HOUGH that he b 7/2/1771 & sis Chloe b 10/5/1762, & sis md sol in house of their f. F-W5337 R1641

Matt, b 12/26/1763 Charlotte Co, VA; esf 1780 as sub for bro George at Martintown, Ninety-Six District, SC, where res; esf 1780 in GA regiment with 3 bro's; traveled with bro's to Halifax Co, VA, where he esf 1781 as sub for bro-in-law Charles EDWARDS; returned to Ninety-Six District, SC where again esf; res after RW Martintown (area later Edgefield District) SC; mvd 1806 to Bourbon Co, KY, thence same year to Bedford Co, TN, where PN 1833; dd 10/16/46; QLF 1932 from desc Mrs Olin CULBERSON of Austin, TX; QLF 1927 from kin Mrs Luther Wyatt TUCKER, Atlanta, GA, states sol one/o 8 bro's who all RW officers; QLF 1925 from desc Mrs Houston CALDWELL, Nashville, TN; QLF states sol youngest of 8 bro's & md Sallie CLAY, further a VA RW sol Pleasant MARTIN, b 1757 Albemarle Co, VA, & dd 1836 Wilson Co, TN, md Anne MOORMAN; QLF 1912 from desc Mrs Edward SANDERS, Salem VA; QLF 1912 from great gds E M WHITAKER, Midland, TX; QLF states sol s/o Abram. F-S2726 R1641

Moses, b 1/12/1755 Bedford Co, VA; esf 1776 Surry Co, NC res there; mvd c10 years after RW to Knox Co, TN for c7 years, thence Pulaski Co, KY where PN 1833; dd 8/29/37; md 6/1777 Ann HEATH; wid PN ae 79 Wayne Co, KY 1839; ch births: William 4/17/1778, Alex/Alee 8/19/80, John 5/17/84, Matthew 5/2/88, Elizabeth 3/12/91, Mary/Marey 10/18/96, Lois/Loes 12/31/98, Edee/Eda 5/12/1801 (Mrs Edee JONES of Wayne Co, KY 1839), & Moses Tate 1/8/07; other births in file: Mary

MARTIN (continued)
    Ann MARTIN 4/10/1821 & Robert MARTIN (no date); a William HEATH (no kinship given) res 1833 Pulaski Co, KY; QLF 1938 from desc Susie M (Mrs Charles S) PASSMORE, Butte, MT. F-W8415 R1641
Pleasant, esf 1778 Albemarle Co, VA, where b 12/21/1746; mvd c1791 to Amherst Co, VA for c20 years, thence Bedford Co, VA, for c15 years, thence Wilson Co, TN where PN 1832 when res there c6 years; bro Abram Sr res aec 58 Sumner Co, TN, 1833; bro John res ae 74 Clark Co, KY, 1832; George MARTIN (no kinship given) one of 4 heirs of sol; 2 sets of grandchildren mbnn. F-S2729 R1642
Reuben, b 1748 Somerset Co, NJ; esf 1777 Sussex Co, NJ where res; PN 1834 Wayne Co, OH, having previously res Washington Co, PA, & Brooke Co, VA; dd 2/27/44; s Absalom, War of 1812 sol, liv 1834; QLF 1927 from great great gdd Mrs William WESTBROOK, Ashley, OH, states sol buried 2 miles west of Westfield, Morrow Co, OH; QLF 1898 from great gdd Mrs W H TUCK, Piqua, OH, states sol s/o Ephraim & bro/o Absalom, both NJ RW sol's. F-S8989 R1642
Rhodeham, b 1761 Fairfax Co, VA; esf 1781 Guildford Co, NC; PN 1833 Gibson Co, TN where dd 2/13/53; md there 9/30/1840 Jane who PN there 1853 aec 54. F-W9907 R1642
Salathiel, possibly b Amherst Co, VA, since a RW sol David LAWSON AFF 1851 Scott Co, TN, he himself was born there in 1765 & had known Salathiel since infancy; Salathiel esf in 1779 Surry Co, NC where res; sol was 6 feet 9 inches tall; dd 5/6/1827; md 4/3/1782 Mary COOK, Surry Co, NC, who was b 8/23/1763; wid PN 1845 Claiborne Co, TN; dd 3/3/58; ch births (record mutilated & parts of pages missing): David 3/1783, Thomas 2/29/85 (res 1851 Estill Co, KY), Elizabeth 3/27/8-, George Washington 2/11/89 (res 1851 Jefferson Co, IN), William 2/1791, Nancy 5/2/93 (md Mr SHUMATE), Mary 4/9/95, James -/15/96, Wilson 6/17/9-, & Robert -/23/1801; QLF 1931 from desc Blanche B (Mrs Cornelius Rea) AGNEW of New York, NY, states sol name David Salathiel; QLF states sol b 1763; QLF 1914 from great gdd Mrs K BITTERMAN, Lexington, KY. F-W1044 R1642
Samuel, b 1760 esf 1777 Kent Co, MD, in 4th MD Regiment; mvd to PA c1781 for c2 years, then to Berkeley Co, VA, for 5 years, thence Greenbrier Co, VA for 2 years, thence Monroe Co, VA for c30 years, thence Fayette Co, VA where afp 1835 & PAR, insufficient proof of svc; afp 1839 Kanawha Co, VA, & again PAR; illiterate. F-R6971 R1642
Samuel, esf 1776 King & Queen Co, VA, where res; afp 1839 ae 79 Hardeman Co, TN, & PAR, insufficient proof of svc; PN ae 80 there 1840. F-S2728 R1642
Scott, see SCRUGGS, Samuel S. F-S38357 R1642
Thomas, b 5/11/1756 Brunswick Co, VA; esf Chatham Co, NC, at time/o Battle of Cowpens; mvd 1781 to Lincoln Co, NC, then after RW to York District, SC, where PN 1832; dd 5/13/35; md 3/1776 Sabra who b 5/13/1759; wid PN 1840 York District

MARTIN (continued)
SC; ch births: William 12/17/1776, Thomas 12/12/78, John 8/24/81 (dd 3/16/83), John 2/27/84, Elizabeth 1/20/87, & Valentine 3/15/90; other births in file: Sarah MARTIN 2/8/1800, Tinney MARTIN (d of Josiah & Elizabeth) 12/7/1825; births of ch/o Absalom MARTIN: Joab 12/10/1819, Poley S 5/28/21, Valentine 12/16/22, Josiah 2/22/24, Sabra H 11/30/25, & Syrene 2/5/18--; QLF states sol md Rhoda WASHBURN, possibly d/o Gabriel. F-W21740 R1643

Thomas, Captain of 8th VA Regiment; apb 1806 Newport, Campbell Co, KY; BLW236 issued 4/17/1806; QLF states sol also served in 4th VA Regiment, md Ann MOORMAN of Louisa Co, VA & dd c1792; QLF states a VA RW sol Thomas MARTIN of Martinsville, VA, md Hester ROUNDTREE, & they mvd to SC; QLF states sol esf Albemarle Co, VA, dd Newport, KY & md Susan Washington LEADBETTER who survived him. F-BLW236 R1643

William, b 10/10/1763; esf 1779 Lebanon Township, Somerset Co, NJ; mvd 1786 to Harrison Co, VA, where PN 1833; dd 8/25/1851; md 2/23/1815 Jane POWERS (MB 2/22/1815), Harrison Co, VA; wid PN ae 59 there 1853; wid afb 1873 Clarksburg, Harrison Co, VA, stating her name before marriage was Jane CHIDESTER, & gtd BLW113541; dd 4/29/1879; s's & d's mbnn; s-in-law John WILSON; QLF states sol md (1) Susan STOUT; QLF 1900 from gdd Miss May F SHUTTLEWORTH of Baltimore, MD F-W9937 R1643

William, esf Halifax Co, VA in GA regiment; afp aec 63 there 1819, & PAR; AFF 1822 by Nancy & Lucy MARTIN (no kinship given) that sol dd Halifax Co, VA on 5/2/1822 or 5/3/1822. F-R6975 R1643

William, b c1760 Caroline Co, VA; mvd with f 1774 to NC; sol esf 1777 Anson Co, NC where res; PN 1833 Montgomery Co, AL F-S32395 R1643

William, BLW12350 issued 12/31/1791. F-BLW12350 R1643

William, reared Hampshire Co, VA, where res when esf; lost a leg on way home from RW svc when attacked by indians; mvd c1791 to Booth's Creek, Harrison Co, VA, where PN 1832 ae 70; dd 7/3/46; QLF states sol middle name Judgson, md Patricia HAMPTON (dd many years before him), & they had one s Templeton Crim; QLF states sol b 11/30/1762 North River, Hampshire Co, VA (area now Romney, WV), & was s of George. F-S5736 R1643

William, b Albemarle Co, VA; esf 1775 ae 16 Amherst Co, VA, in 7th VA Regiment, where res; mvd after RW to GA, thence Bedford Co, TN, where PN 1834 ae 74; decd in 1842 per AFF then Marshall Co, TN by Benjamin COPLIN & Nancy CARROL; md 11/23/1828 Jane, d/o Benjamin COPLAN; wid applied for h PN arrears 10/12/1842 Connersville, Giles Co, TN. F-S21355 R1643

William, esf 1776 Albemarle Co, VA; PN aec 62 Clark Co, KY, 1818; res there 1832 when had w aec 75 & single d aec 35-40; occupation farmer; bro Austin liv 1818; QLF states sol s of RW sol James (bc 1749, mvd to KY 1780, where dd 1799,

MARTIN (continued)
md Sarah HARRIS, 1746-1804), further sol William md Winifred GENTRY, Albemarle Co, VA, also sol bro Tyre md Mourning JONES there (both b there), they res St Louis, MO, later Boone Co, MO, also sol bro of Azariah. F-S36070 R1463
William, b 1762 Augusta Co, VA; mvd 1780 to Lexington, KY, where esf in VA regiment; mvd to Woodford Co, KY, where PN 1833; dd there 4/13/36; md 4/13/1799 Leticia/Letitia/Letty d/o John McCLANAHAN, Pendleton Co, KY; wid PN aec 79 Woodford Co, KY; dd there 7/8/53 leaving ch Nancy H STOCKDELL, Elia T McAFEE, John, Washington P, Hugh, Elijah, Ann D, Jane, Martha & William; William MARTIN (kinship not given) attorney for sol wid 1849 Versailles, KY; QLF 1929 from great gdd Grace Lee Martin (Mrs Denis) MULLIGAN (d of E L MARTIN) of Lexington, KY. F-W5327 R1643
William, b 11/8/1757; esf 1775-6 Albemarle Co, VA where res; PN 1832 Nelson Co, VA; dd there 12/23/34; md Patsy Key DAVIDSON (MB 12/8/1789 or 12/18/1789), Amherst Co, VA, (area later Nelson Co, VA); wid PN ae 74 Nelson Co, VA 1844; res there 1855 when gtd BLW5080; her m was Miss DAVIDSON, who never md, but had Patsey by a Mr KEY. F-W5342 R1643
William, esf 1779 in 14th VA Regiment; s Samuel afb 1828 for self & other heirs, Bedford Co, VA; BLW1463 issued to them 1828. F-BLW1463 R1643
Zachariah, b 10/4/1761 Halifax Co, VA; esf 1781 Wilkes Co, NC, where res; res there for 10 years after RW, thence Halifax Co, VA, where PN 1833; dd 7/1833; QLF states sol & w Rebeccah sold land in Halifax Co, 1786, further sol md (2) Margaret BRUCE, wid of Colonel John WILSON of Pittsylvania Co, VA, further sol bro/o Reverend James Green MARTIN, who md Susan (BRUCE) LANGLEY of Norfolk, VA, further Reverend James Green MARTIN ancestor of General James Green MARTIN, Mexican War sol, whose descendents later res Pasquotank Co NC. F-S11032 R1463
MARTINDALE, James, b 1754 Bucks Co, PA; esf Union Co, SC where res; mvd after RW to Bedford Co, VA, thence Greenbrier Co, VA, thence c1809 Addison Township, Gallia Co, OH; PN there 1832; dd that Co 7/7/40; md (1) ? who dd Gallia Co, OH; md (2) Mary GILMOUR in NC; wid afp 1844 Gallia Co, OH, when res there c21 years, having previously res VA; wid PAR because h's PN improperly allowed on evidence not considered admissible in 1844, & she failed to furnish more proof of his svc; sol bro William res 1833 Warren Co, OH, ae 80+; QLF states sol dd at Cheshire, OH; QLF 1920 from great gds James A MARTINDALE, Chicago, IL; QLF 19-- from desc Mrs J C ALLEN, Houston, TX; QLF 1917 from desc Mrs A J LINDSTROM of Rock Island, IL. F-R6979 R1644
Samuel, esf 1776 Kent Co, DE, where b 1/14/1752; mvd 1777 to Augusta Co, VA, for several months, thence Duplin Co, NC, where esf 1778; mvd 1792 to Deep River, Moore Co, NC where PN 1832; last PN payment in file 1839. F-S8878 R1644
MASON, Adam, esf Accomac Co, VA, in 2nd VA Regiment; dd there

MASON (continued)
  c11/15/1835 ae 76, leaving no wid but 1 ch William who res there 1850 when gtd PN due f. F-S8996 R1645
Calvert (AKA WOODYARD, Calvert), esf 1782 Charles Co, MD res there; PN ae 74 Rappahannock Co, VA, 1840; AFF there 1841 by Elizabeth WOODYARD aec 50, d/o sol uncle Jeremiah WOODYARD, that sol f Mr MASON & m Miss WOODYARD not md, & sol thus known by either of those two surnames. F-S8956 R1645
David, b 4/2/1757 Hanover Co, VA; mvd when aec 4-5 with parents to Caroline Co, VA where he esf aec 17 in 1st VA Regiment; afp Hawkins Co, TN, 1832; PAR, insufficient proof of svc; afp there 1837 & again PAR. F-R6990 R1645.
Edward, b England; came to America ae 15; to pay for passage was bound out to wid/o Archibald RHEA of Staunton, Augusta Co, VA; esf 1780 Wythe Co, VA, where md & res during RW; mvd several years after RW to Knox Co, TN where PN 1832 ae nearly 90; QLF states sol dd there 8/22/32. F-S4181 R1645
George, b 1757-8 Hampshire Co, VA; esf 1781 Fayette Co, PA, where res; PN 1833 Dearborn Co, IN. F-S33053 R1645
George, esf VA; afp 1832 Caroline Co, VA, too ill to come to courthouse; PAR, insufficient proof/o svc. F-R6995 R1645
James, esf 1777 in 7th VA regiment; later esf Albany, NY, in NY regiment; PN ae 95 Owen Co, KY, when all/o family decd. F-S36064 R1646
John, esf Mecklenburg Co, VA, in GA regiment; PN ae 75 Pickens District, SC, 1832 as John Sr; QLF says sol md Frances BROOKES & dd Campbell Co, VA, further a RW sol Philip MASON md Nancy WALKER & dd c1830 Campbell Co, VA; QLF 1924 from desc Mrs Bessie P LAMB, Enora, SC. F-S9390 R1646
Joseph, esf 1776 in VA regiment; esf 1780 sub for bro William; esf 1781 Botetourt Co, VA; PN ae 75 Breckenridge Co, KY, 1832; QLF states sol may have md Ann TANDY, & their d Ann Tandy md Gabiel KAY. F-30562 R1646
Littleberry, paymaster/o 15th VA Regiment which commanded by his f Colonel David MASON; md 1783 Rebecca BLUNT (MB 1/20/83 signed by William BLUNT) Southampton Co, VA; wid md (2) 8/24/1816 John HARDAWAY (MB 8/22/16), Sussex Co, VA & they had no ch; John dd 9/18/24; wid dd 5/1/45 leaving several ch; s Nathaniel MASON afp ae 51 Sussex Co, VA, as executor of m estate that he & Mary (w/o John SPENCER of Greenville VA) only surv ch of sol & wid; they gtd PN due m; AFF then there by Littleberry W MASON (no kinship given); AFF there then by wid gds A G MASON. F-W23190 R1646
Peter, esf 1776 Prince Edward Co, VA, in 1st GA Regiment; PN ae 68 Lunenburg Co, VA, 1825 w having dd within past year; sol dd 5/13/38; Jacob H FERGUSON (no kinship given) adm of his estate. F-S38172 R1647
Peter, b 8/22/1764 VA; esf 1778 Lancaster Co, VA, where res; after RW went to sea for 7 years, then back to VA for many years, thence KY, where PN 1833 Campbell Co when res there c20 years; mvd 1839 to Jay Co, IN, when w decd & their ch had already mvd there. F-S32394 R1647

MASON, Philip, b 10/26/1752 Amelia Co, VA; esf 1779 Wilkes Co, NC where res; mvd 1785 to Orange Co, NC, thence 1824 Guilford Co, NC, where PN 1834. F-S8994 R1647
Robert, b 4/7/1757; esf 1779 Hampshire Co, VA where res; afp 1837 Knox Co, KY; PAR, insufficient proof of svc; QLF 1930 from desc Eva Mason (Mrs A J) JENKINS, Brazil, IN says sol b England, s of Robert, & dd 1849 Pineville, KY. F-R7001 R1647
Smith, esf 1779 Caroline Co, VA, where b 3/20/1763; esf later there with bro Benjamin; PN 1832 there when bro Benjamin (ae 67) also res there. F-S7180 R1647
Thomas, free man of color, esf 1777 Caswell Co, NC; dd when afp under preparation 10/1832; md 4/1791 free woman of color Elizabeth AILSTOCK, Louisa Co, VA; wid afp ae 90 Campbell Co, VA, 1854, & PAR, insufficient proof of svc & marriage; they had 6 ch; their 1st ch mbnn liv then; 2nd ch Thomas AFF there then ae 57 when he res there 50 years, he having previously res Louisa Co, VA; Elizabeth MERCHANT, gdd/o wid, gave POA 1884 to agent Lynchburg, VA, to afp & afb; PAR, current law did not authorize PN to gdc; BLAR, sol wid then decd. F-R6993 R1647
William, b 1752 Hanover Co, VA; esf 1778 Mecklenburg Co, VA; PN 1832 Iredell Co, NC; dd 10/13/46; md 1/6/1802 Mary/Polly CRITTENDEN, Lunenburg Co, VA; wid PN ae 75 Davie Co, NC 1853; wid gtd BLW26466 there 1855 ae 78. F-W6792 R1647
MASSAY, John, see MASSY, John. F-S1918 R1648
MASSENBURG, Alexander, only record in file is letter 1852 from John GAMMEL, adm/o sol estate, to PN Office which gives no pertinent information; PAR. F-R16060 R1648
MASSENGILL, Henry, b 1758 VA; parents dd when he quite young; esf NC (area later Sullivan Co, TN); PN there 1834, & dd there 9/23/37; md there 8/6/1814 Elizabeth EMMERT; wid PN aec 64 there 1854 when Jacob EMMERT (no kinship given) AFF he had known sol for c50 years & was close neighbor most/o that time; wid gtd BLW26430 there 1855 ae 65; PN restored 1866 after Civil War when res 2 miles west of Union Depot, TN; sol surname also spelled MASSENGELLS & MASENGILL; G D, FD, John T, & J/IT MASSENGILL (no kinship given) all res Sullivan Co, TN, 1868. F-W25681 R1648
MASSEY, Alston S, b VA c25 miles above Halifax; mvd as ch with f to Chesterfield District, SC; esf c1779 SC under General Frances MARION; res that District 45 years after RW, then to GA for 3 years, thence Monroe Co, AL where afp 1848 aec 85; PAR, less than 6 months svc; dd near Monroeville, that Co, 7/17/1753; md 4/14/1820 Emeline ALLEN; wid gtd BLW 87024 Monroe Co, AL, 1855 ae 52. F-R7004 R1648
Caleb, esf Accomac Co, VA in 9th VA Regiment; BLW5205 issued 6/17/1805 by VA Land Office; dd 5/6/1827; md 5/1/1792 Sarah, Worcester Co, MD; wid PN ae 68 Philadelphia, PA 1842; res there 1848; they had no ch. F-W3437 R1648
Edmond, b 1747 Hanover Co, VA; esf Albemarle Co, VA, where res; mvd from Orange Co, VA, to KY where PN 1832 Grant Co;

MASSEY (continued)
    QLF states sol may have md Miss BARRETT & their d Margaret md James RANKIN. F-S16462 R1648
Henry, b 1763 Brunswick Co, VA; mvd 1774 with parents to SC, where esf Waxhaws Settlement (later Lancaster District); PN 1832 Mecklenburg Co, NC, where res since 1800; res 1833 Lancaster District, SC. F-S18103 R1648
John, b 5/30/1765 Hanover Co, VA; esf 1779 Fluvanna Co, VA, where res; res after RW Amherst Co, VA, thence Greene Co, TN, thence Overton Co, TN, thence White Co, TN, where PN 1832 when res there 25+ years; QLF 1937 by US Congressman of TN for constituent Mr O D MASSA of Cookeville, TN, who desc of sol. F-S1918 R1648
John, esf VA; mvd during RW from Albemarle Co, VA to Amherst Co, VA; dd 10/20/1800; md there 1/1/1779 Susannah WRIGHT, who dd 12/1/1847 Nelson Co, VA; ch liv 1853: Edmond, Jesse & Thomas (all res there) + William W, John, & Charles (all res Amherst Co, VA) + Elizabeth GILL & Mary CAMPBELL (both res Rockbridge Co, VA; s Thomas afp then Nelson Co, VA, ae 67 for self & siblings; PAR, PN Office stated it did not appear their f was the person who rendered that RW svc, & there were conflicting claims for sol's of that name, the others being: F-BLW2076 (in which file it was alleged that sol dd King George Co, VA, c1795 leaving ch Lovell & Thomas), & File-W9931 (in which sol wid Judith gtd PN for sol svc, md him 4/13/1792, & he dd 1/29/1829 in AL); QLF says a Charles MASSIE, b 1732, dd 1817, md Mary DAVIS, Hanover Co, VA, purchased Spring Valley Plantation in VA 1768, & they both buried there, & their ch births: John (eldest) c 1760, Thomas 1762, Charles 10/5/1765, Elizabeth 1767, further s John md Miss WRIGHT of Amherst Co, VA, whose ch (1) John b 1790 on Spring Hill Plantation, sol in War of 1812, md 1823 Julier Ann CARTHEY, & dd 10/22/1850 Ozark, AR, (2) William b 1792 VA, (3) Shearwood b 1794 VA, (4) Joseph b 1796 VA, & (5) Martha b 1798 VA. F-R7008 R1648
John, esf VA; dd 1795 King George Co, VA, leaving ch John & Lovell; s Thomas dd intestate, no issue; s Lovell dd Indiantown, King George Co, VA, he f of Robert, Henry, & Susan JACK; Lovell's s Henry dd c1829 leaving ch William & John, both minors in 1834, bound out to Lovell's s Robert by Orphan's Court/o Alexandria to learn tailor trade; sol heirs Robert MASSEY & sis Susan JACK (both ch of sol's s Lovell) afb 1834 Washington, DC, & gtd BLW2076. F-BLW2076 R1648
Lovell, b King George Co, VA, dd after RW leaving wid Sarah & ch Robert, Henry W, & Susan (compiler's note: apparently Lovell, preceding file); s Robert dd 1862 Alexandria, VA; s Henry dd 1820-30 Liberty, OH leaving ch William D & John H; d Susan md Mr JACK & dd before Civil War leaving ch Mary Ann, Sarah, James, & Susan; Mary H WIMSATT (d of sol s Robert) afb 1882 & BLAR, sol's name not in any BLW file of VA or in Historical Register of VA RW sol's. Rejected BLW File #335497 R1648.

MASSEY, Thomas, BLW 12360 issued 1/31/179-. F-BLW12360 R1648
Thomas, see MASSIE, Thomas. F-W7403 R1648
William, esf ae 18 King George Co, VA, in VA regiment; md 1784 Hannah SUTTLES; sol dd 9/10/1837 King George Co, VA, & w dd 1805; they never apf; youngest ch b 8/7/1795 (only surv ch) when he afp 1833 Clark Co, IL 1851 Johnson Co, IN & 1857 there; PAR, insufficient proof of svc. F-R7007 & R7009 (files combined by PN Office) R1648
MASSIE, John, esf in VA regiment; mvd 1818-1819 from New Kent Co, VA, to AL, where dd 1/29/29; md 4/3/1792 Judith MOSS, (MB 4/2/92), New Kent Co, VA; wid PN ae 71 Limestone Co, AL, 1844 when AFF New Kent Co, VA, by Rheuben MOSS (kinship not given); John H MASSIE (kinship not given) signed bond as exec/o LWT/o sol wid 1845 Limestone Co, AL; surety of bond signed by Harriet Ann MASSIE & Mumford J McDANIEL. F-W9931 R1648
Thomas, b 12/26/1759 Buckingham Co, VA; esf 1780 Campbell Co VA, where res; esf 1781 Washington Co, VA; mvd soon after RW to Montgomery Co, VA, thence KY, thence c1827 Sangamon Co, IL, where PN 1832; Joel MASSEY (no kinship given) then res there; QLF states sol dd IL c1835; QLF 1924 from desc Jane Taylor (Mrs G W) JACK, Springfield, IL, states sol dd 8/19/1835 Sangamon Co, IL, buried there, querier also desc of VA RW sol William RALSTON, b 1759, mvd to KY, then 1828 to IL, dd 7/1835 Sangamon Co, IL, & buried there; QLF 1914 from desc Mabel Shields MASON of Colorado Springs, CO says she informed by sol gds M D MASSIE that sol gtd PN for RW svc. F-S31235 R1648
Thomas, b 8/11/1747, old style; esf 1775 in 6th VA Regiment; PN 1833 Nelson Co, VA, as Thomas Sr; dd 2/2/34; LWT 8/22/31 Nelson Co, VA, probated there 2/24/34, listed gdc (parents not stated): Sarah STANLEY, Sarah GOODE, Eugenia MASIE, Mary L PLEASANTS, & Juliet MASSIE + gdc (ch of s Thomas): William, Waller, Patrick, & Paul + gdc (ch of s Henry): Henry & Thomas + gdc (ch of s William): Thomas & Ellen; md 4/11/1781 Sally COCKE; wid PN ae 77 Nelson Co, VA, 1835; dd 4/27/38; ch births: Thomas 10/21/1782, Henry 10/16/84, & William 3/3/95; QLF states sol s/o William of New Kent Co, VA, sol's w of Henrico Co, VA, & one of their descendents was a Judge Thornton L MASSIE. F-W7403 R1648
MASSY, Charles, esf 1780 Prince Edward Co, VA, where b 2/28/1760; esf 1781 there sub for eldest bro Thomas in 4th VA Regiment; f dd 1782; 3 bro's (1 younger & 2 older); both older bro's RW sol's; res after RW Prince Edward Co, VA, for 2 years, then to Amelia Co, VA, for 1 year, then to Prince Edward Co, VA, for c4 years, thence Campbell Co, VA for 4 years, then to Jefferson Co, TN, thence Cocke Co, TN (total of 32 years res TN), thence Orange Co, IN, for c2 years, thence Monroe Co, IN, where PN 1834 when res there over 2 years; dd 1/2/39 there; md 3/3/1789 Elizabeth, d/of William DAVIS (MB 3/5/88) Prince Edward Co, VA; wid PN ae 70 Orange Co, IN 1839; ch liv in 1843: Charles ae 40, John

MASSY (continued)
ae 37-38, Samuel ae 35, Dolley ae 44, Elizabeth ae 42, & Patsey ae 33; ch decd in 1843: James, Peter, Sherrod, Sevier, Enoch, Kitty, & Joanna; surname also spelled MASSEY. F-W9536 R1648

MASTERS, Edward D (AKA DeMASTERS, Edward), esf 1779 VA; res 1820 Nelson Co, VA; gtd BLW1995; PN aec 65 Amherst Co, VA, 1828, when AFF there by John MASTERS/DeMASTERS (no kinship given); dd there 11/24/37; md 8/23/1794 Sally CARTER there who b 8/1775 VA; PN 1848 Nelson Co, VA; ch births: Betsey 9/1797, Nancy 12/1801, Polly 1/1803, John 3/1805, George 4/1805, Wiatt 11/1809, Cornelius 12/1811, Sarah Ann 8/1817 & Elvira 12/1819. F-W2651 R1649

John, esf 1779 near Petersburg, VA; PN 1819 Franklin Co, IN; res there 1820 ae 61 with w ae 65 & s mbnn ae 21; QLF says sol dd IN ae 84; QLF states sol buried near Fairfield, IN, in Fairfield Township. F-S36057 R1649

John, see DeMASTERS, John. F-W3394 R1649

Thomas, esf 1779 Rockbridge Co, VA, in 11th VA Regiment; PN ae 64 Greenville District, SC, 1818; res there 1821 ae 66, occupation farmer, when family s George ae 20, d Margaret ae 17, & d Polly ae 14; dd 8/26/38 there; md 1/1/1822 Elizabeth ROPER there; wid PN ae 75 Forsythe Co, GA 1854; gtd BLW17891 there 1855. F-W13688 R1649

MASTERSON, James, b 4/7/1752 Fairfax Co, VA; esf early in RW when res on Pamlico River in NC; mvd 1770 to KY; settled near Lexington Spring 1780, where esf as indian spy in VA regiment; PN 1833 Fayette Co, KY, where res since RW; dd 12/15/38; md 6/17/1781 Margaret, Fayette Co, KY; wid PN ae 73 there 1838; ch births: Elizabeth 6/11/1782 (dd 7/20/94) William 12/17/83 (dd 7/7/1814), Sarah 8/20/85 (dd 7/29/1814), John 1/21/87, James 10/30/88, Maray 3/15/90 (dd 7/8/1833), Robert 11/20/91 (dd 1/23/1813), Richard 7/25/93, Caleb 1/18/96, Lovet 6/20/97 (dd 1/26/1822), Edward 10/26/98, Peggy 7/1/1802 & Joseph 4/23/07; other births in file: Richard James MASTERSON 1/8/1821, Lovet Ann MASTERSON 5/25/1822, Martin John DAVIS 11/10/1824, Charlton Mersillions METCALF 3/12/1830, Ellenor Masterson METCALF 11/12/1832 (dd 8/26/1834), James William Bradly METCALF 6/12/1835, Joseph Richard Allen METCALF 1/7/1837, & William Ewter HANDCOCK 10/19/1835. F-W8422 R1649

John, esf 1778 Pigeon Creek on Monongahela River, VA (area later Washington Co, PA) in VA Regiment; PN 1832 Nelson Co KY, ae 73. F-S16460 R1649

Patrick, esf 1780 Shenandoah Co, VA; PN ae 82 Morgan Co, KY, 1842; dd 4/10/1855 Owsley Co, KY; md 4/13/1838 Mary SPARKS in Perry Co, KY; wid afp 1856 Owsley Co, KY, & PAR, insufficient proof of marriage & sol svc less than 6 months; in c1858 wid afp again Louisville, KY, & PAR; afp ae 60+ Owsley Co, KY, 1863, & PAR; decd in 1866; wid illiterate. F-R7012 R1649

MATHEW, Isaac, b 1761 Bucks Co, PA; esf 1777 Fauquier Co, VA,

MATHEW (continued)
   where res; res there after RW, then to Culpeper Co, VA,
   thence Monongalia Co, VA, thence Preston Co, VA, where PN
   1832; younger bro Benjamin AFF there then; elder brother
   mbnn; last PN payment in file 1840; surname also spelled
   MATHEWS. F-S9001 R1651
MATHEWS, Benjamin, b 1764 Spotsylvania Co, VA; mvd when ch to
   Caroline Co, VA, where esf 1778-9; mvd to Hanover Co, VA,
   where esf 1780; PN 1832 Jackson Co, AL; dd there 9/2/40;
   md ? there 8/29/1838; wid mbnn gtd there arrears of PN due
   h 1840. F-S32391 R1651
James, esf 1781 Augusta Co, VA; afp ae 79 Boone Co, KY, 1843
   & PAR, less than 6 months svc; AFF then there by sis Elizabeth GAINES ae 68; AFF there then by John P GAINES (kinship not given); QLF 1912 from great gdd Mrs Eva O'DANIEL,
   Brookfield, MO, great great gdd of William MATHEWS who res
   & raised family on Moffett's Branch near Jennings Gap, &
   near Bonds Hill, c10 miles from Staunton, Augusta Co, VA,
   came from Co Armagh, Ireland, & settled there c1720, dd ae
   93 Augusta Co, VA, had w Mary (nee WRIGHT), sons Richard,
   John, Joseph, James, William, Sampson, + d's Mary, Margaret, Jane, Elizabeth, & Kate, querier also great great gdd
   of LeGrand GAINES of Orange Co, VA; QLF 1936 from sol desc
   Miss Edna M DICKEY, Monticello, AR. F-R7021 R1651
Philip, b 1760 Buckingham Co, VA; esf Fairfield District, SC
   1781 where res; afp 1845 Crawford Co, GA, & PAR, svc less
   than 6 months; sons Philip M & James MATTHEWS afp there in
   1852, & PAR: QLF states sol md there. F-R7031 R1652
Philip, esf 1776 Prince Edward Co, VA; PN ae 76 there 1832.
   F-S5729 R1652
Richard, b 2/2/1753 Cumberland Co, PA; esf 1776 Chester Co,
   PA, where res; mvd 1830 to Brooke Co, VA where PN 1833; dd
   3/6/36; wid mbnn dd 8/30/41 leaving only surv ch Elizabeth
   FIGLEY, who afp ae 54 Hancock Co, VA, 1851 for PN due m, &
   PAR, sol md after his last term of svc. F-R7028 R1652
Samuel, esf c1779 Dinwiddie Co, VA, where 4/23/1763; mvd to
   Bedford Co (area later Campbell Co) VA, where esf 1780; PN
   1832 Campbell Co, VA. F-S5732 R1652
Thomas, esf 1776 in VA regiment; dd 2/20/1812 Norfolk, VA;
   md 7/11/1773 Mary/Molly MILLER (MB 7/9/73) Norfolk Co, VA;
   wid PN ae 84 Elizabeth City, Pasquotank Co, NC, 1836; dd
   7/1837; heirs who apf 1850: John M MATHEWS, James NIMMO,
   Claudia H VAUGHAN, Mary L/S BUTLER, M M LEWIS, W P/R MA-
   THEWS, Sarah G E MATHEWS, Ann I NIMMO, John NIMMO, & Clau-
   dia WILEY; heirs PAR; QLF 1936 from desc Mrs ISSA W BURKE,
   Washington, DC; QLF states a Thomas MATHEWS/MATTHEWS b be-
   fore 1750, esf VA, md Eleanor/Elinor BRADSHAW, & their son
   Sampson b 11/1767 (War/o 1812 sol) md 1794 Elizabeth JOHN-
   SON near Salisbury, NC & they mvd 1796 to Robertson Co, TN
   F-W17076 & F-R16019 (combined file) R1652
William, esf 1776 Charlotte Co, VA, in 4th VA Regiment; dd c
   1808 intestate; md 5/20/1780 Mary HUNDLEY near Wylliesburg

MATHEWS (continued)
   VA; wid PN ae 80 Charlotte Co, VA 1838; QLF states sol wid
   listed on 1840 Census of that Co as RW pensioner. F-W5131
   R1652
MATHIOT, George, esf 1777 Lancaster, PA where b 10/3/1759; esf
   1779 there sub for brother Christian; esf 1781 for duty on
   ship OLIVER CROMWELL; PN 1832 Connellsville, Fayette Co,
   PA; md Ruth, who PN 1843 PA, & gtd BLW28553 Monongalia Co,
   VA 1855 aec 84 when s J D res West Fairfield, Westmoreland
   Co, PA; surname also spelled MATHIOTT; QLF 1904 from desc
   Helen F (Mrs H H) KEITH of Topeka, KS; QLF 1921 from desc
   Alice L MATHIOT, Portsmouth, OH, states sol parents Jean &
   Catherine (BERNARD) MATHIOT came to PA from Lorraine Pro-
   vince in Europe; QLF states sol dd 5/4/1840 Connellsville,
   PA, was interpreter for French General Dupretol in RW; QLF
   1893 from great gds Robert M DAVIDSON (major, US Army 17th
   Infantry Regiment), Newark, OH. F-W4486 R1653
MATLO, John, esf 1775 in 1st VA Regiment at Hanovertown, Hano-
   ver Co, VA; PN that Co 1832 ae 78 where had always lived;
   dd 5/30/33 there, leaving no wid but ch: Sarah, Elizabeth
   L, George, & Hezekiah. F-S15934 R1653
MATLOCK, Nathaniel, b 12/1742 Hanover Co, VA; mvd at early age
   to Granville Co, NC where esf early in RW; res after RW in
   East TN, AL & KY; PN 1832 Livingston Co, KY when res there
   c16 years; dd 4/5/38; md 9/1/1769 Martha, who PN ae 92 Livingston Co, KY 1842 when ch: Dolly (eldest, res AL ae 72)
   & Usly (res AL, b before RW); sol & w had 13 ch; surname
   also spelled MEDLOCK. F-W8409 R1653
  Zachariah, esf c1777 in VA regiment; no afp; dd 2/28/1827;
   md 12/7/1780 Lucy WASH, Louisa Co, VA, who b 7/18/1759;
   wid PN 1840 Caldwell Co, KY; res there 1846; dd 4/29/47;
   ch births: Ann 8/25/1784, John 4/6/88, May 2/17/91, Elizabeth 12/15/93, Susanah 2/10/97, Thomas 3/29/1807; other FB
   births: Margaret Melissa POTTS 10/29/1817, William C POTTS
   1/3/1825, Francis W POTTS 6/7/1831, Emily WOOLF 12/7/1814,
   William Harrison WOOLF 12/21/1815, Perry WOOLF 12/19/1817,
   Carvin WOOLF 10/9/1620, Lucy Ann WOOLF 3/19/1823, David B
   MICHEL 7/25/1827, & James P MICHEL 3/15/1830; FB marriages
   (record badly smudged): Ridden (?) & Elizabeth WOOLF 2/11/
   181-, John MATLOCK & Susanah W ROBERTSON 2/17/1820, Thomas
   W MATLOCK & Jane E WHITE 12/18/1834; Thomas W MATLOCK, adm
   of sol wid estate, afp 1848 Caldwell Co, KY, for following
   heirs of wid: self, John MATLOCK, Charles J WHITE, John C
   WHITE, John C PRINCE, & H H PRINCE, all res Princeton, KY;
   AFF 1840 Caldwell Co, KY, by Mrs Sally PORTER ae 76-77 (b
   Amelia Co, VA, & raised Louisa Co, VA) that her h also RW
   sol & she present at marriage of Zachariah & Lucy MATLOCK.
   F-W8420 R1653
MATTHEWS, Francis, esf 1779 Old Town, MD; PN aec 60 Augusta Co
   VA; res there 1820 with w aec 59; ch mbnn. F-S38178 R1654
  George, esf 1780 Accomac Co, VA in 1st VA Regiment; PN there
   1818 ae 57; res there 1820 with w Esther aec 50, d Mahala

MATTHEWS (continued)
   aec 15, d Rosey aec 9, d Ruby aec 7 & houseboy Custis VES-
   SELS aec 16. F-S38179 R1654
George, BLW1497 issued 8/17/1789. F-BLW1497 R1654
Giles, b 1754 King & Queen Co, VA; mvd to Hertford Co, NC,
   where esf in 2nd NC Regiment; mvd to Pitt Co, NC, where PN
   1833. F-S8993 R1654
Isaac, b 2/13/1762 Mecklenburg Co, VA; mvd to Edgefield District, SC, where esf; mvd 1801 to Jackson Co, GA, where PN
   1832; surname also spelled MATHEWS; QLF states sol was res
   Jackson Co, GA, 1840. F-S31843 R1654
Jeremiah, b 12/29/1759 VA; esf 1777 Cumberland Co, NC, where
   res; mvd 1783 to Oglethorpe Co, GA, thence Clark Co, GA,
   thence 1828 Newton Co, GA, where PN 1835; dd there 8/5/42;
   LWT probated 9/5/42 there; md 1782 Sarah JOHNSON, Johnson
   Co, NC; wid PN ae 78 Newton Co, GA, 1843; dd 12/16/50 leaving 8 surv ch; ch births (part of record badly blotched):
   Burrel/Burwell 6/29/1784, William 2/24/87, Mary/Polly G
   10/7/89, Albert/Elbert 3/7/92, Jeremiah 1/26/95, Cade/Cady
   12/27/97, Cary I 10/21/1800, Sarah V 4/4/03, Louis M, Elijah W; other births: George (negro) 5/3/1801, Phillis (negro) 1/5/1796, Mingo (negro) 8/7/1802; Nicholas H BACON, b
   3/13/1801, md sol d Sarah V 12/20/1820, & their ch births:
   Durliner Pope 7/3/1822, Sturlin Theophilus 5/14/24, Sarrah
   Agnes 9/6/26, Ofielder Ann Henretter 10/7/28, Eliza Anter-
   nitt 11/15/30, Mary Frances 6/15/33, Nicholas Hobson 5/24/
   35, & Everlin King 7/26/37; marriage dates: Perliner P BA-
   CON 7/4/1843, Sterlin T BACON 3/17/44, Ofielder H BACON
   7/23/48, Henry J BACON 8/5/1850, & Sarah A BACON 2/2/51;
   Henrietta BACON dd 4/17/1847; Sarah A WOODS dd 12/20/1853;
   afp 1854 Fulton Co, GA, by sol s-in-law Nicholas H BACON,
   res there, adm/o sol estate, for PN due sol wid; AFF 1843
   Oglethorpe Co, GA by wid bro Cary JOHNSON; sol surname also spelled MATHEWS; QLF 1916 from great gdd Miss Mary MA-
   THEWS, Thomaston, GA, states sol md Sarah BRINKLEY & was s
   of James. F-W4488 R1654
Jesse, esf 1775 Isle of Wight Co, VA, ae 15; PN there 1832
   ae 73. F-S5735 R1654
John, esf 1775 Prince William Co, VA, as minuteman, where b
   1/2/1754; later esf there in 3rd VA Regiment, & wounded in
   both legs at Battle of Brandywine; mvd c1789 to Wilkes Co
   (area later Lincoln Co), GA; afp 1832 latter Co, & PAR,
   insufficient proof of svc; res there 1840; brother Newman
   res 1832 Lincoln Co, GA; QLF states sol md c1785 Nancy DI-
   CKINSON, & they had ch Willis D, George, & Mary, further
   sol w d/o John DICKINSON & w Miss PRENDERGAST, whose other
   ch were John & Charles. F-R7023 R1654
Littleberry (AKA MATHEWS, Littlebury), esf 1775 Caroline Co,
   VA; afp aec 70 Surry Co, NC, 1821 when had w & d Betsey;
   PAR, svc not in continental establishment; afp there 1822,
   occupation farmer, aec 77 & PAR again; dd 3/10/33, leaving
   wid Sally who dd 10/7/46, leaving d Nancy JOYNER (1851 aec

MATTHEWS (continued)
   70), s Bradley (1851 ae 55), & d Susan ROSE (twin to Bradley); s Bradley gave power/o attorney 1853 Surry Co, NC to agent afp; PAR. F-R7027 & F-R7026 (files combined) R1654
Thomas, esf 1781 Charles City Co, VA where b 12/30/1763; mvd 1798 to Edgecomb Co, NC, thence 1818 Brunswick Co, VA; afp there 1837; PAR, insufficient proof/o svc; AFF then by bro William B of Prince George Co, VA; bro mbnn then res Nottoway Co, VA. F-R7032 R1654
William, b 4/10/1763 Mecklenburg Co, VA; esf 1777 Lincoln Co NC, where res; res after RW Pendleton District, SC, thence Edgefield District, SC, thence c1799 Jackson Co, GA, where PN 1832; gtd BLW30911 there 1855. F-S31842 R1654
William, b 1753 Spotsylvania Co, VA; esf 177- Caroline Co, VA; (record badly blurred & illegible in places); mvd to Granville Co, NC for c12 years, thence KY, thence TN where PN Warren Co 1832. F-S2745 R1654
MATTINGLY, James, esf 1780 Alexandria, VA, in 3rd VA Regiment; PN ae 55 there 1818 (area then in DC); res 1820 Fairfax Co VA, ae 60, occupation farmer, when had w Elizabeth aec 58, d Nancy aec 34, d Massie aec 40 & s Lewis aec 28; res 1841 DC, where had mvd to be near children who then res Georgetown; md 1784 Elizabeth who survived him; sol younger bro Thomas res Washington, DC; surname also spelled MATTINGLEY F-S36055 R1655
John, esf 1776 Prince William Co, VA; PN there 1819 ae 58; res 1820 Occoquan, VA, occupation keeping toll bridge, family liv with him then only w Dykeander (b 11/1760); dd 2/23/24; md 3/6/1781 Dykeander BOSWELL/BOZEL; wid PN ae 77 Prince William Co, VA, 1838; res 1843 with s-in-law Samuel H FISHER; wid dd 2/28/44; Samuel H FISHER gtd PN due her 1846 Occoquan, VA. F-W5346 R1655
MATTOCKS, Richard, b 3/1763 VA; esf 1775 Sunbury, Northumberland Co, PA; res there after RW for number/o years, thence Fayette Co, PA, thence Crawford Co, PA, for 20 years, then to Mercer Co, PA, where PN 1833 Pymatuning Township when res there 10 years; s Jacob AFF there then; sol bro Peter AFF then ae 73 res Crawford Co, PA; bro Joseph res Mercer Co, PA, then; QLF 1898 from desc Henry N MILLER, Chicago, IL. F-S16185 R1655
MATTOX, John, BLW12374 issued 7/14/1702. F-BLW12374 R1655
MAUK, Andrew/Henry, see MANK, Andrew/Henry. F-S1852 R1655
Mathias, esf Winchester, VA, where res, in VA militia or in State Line; dd near there 7/22/1802 aec 51; md c1779 Anna CRUMB at her f's home on the Long Marsh, Frederick Co, VA; wid md (2) 10/1803 Frederick KYLE, that Co, who dd 1820 in Hardy Co, VA; wid mvd 1823 from Frederick Co, VA to Newton township, Muskingum Co, OH, where afp 1848 ae 86; PAR, insufficient proof of svc; s Anthony res there then ae 65; AFF then there by Christian & Henry CRUMB (no kinship to wid stated) they svd in RW same time as her h; 1st ch mbnn of sol & wid b before surrender/o CORNWALLIS; surname also

MAUK (continued)
spelled MANK; QLF says a Matthias MAUCK came from Germany 1747 to Frederick Co, VA, was RW sol there. F-R6064 R1655

MAUPIN, Cornelius, b 2/3/1758 Albemarle Co, VA where esf 1778; afp there 1832; PAR, less than 6 months svc; QLF 1925 from desc Jennie L GRAYSON, Charlottesville, VA, states sol md Mourning HARRIS & they had s Bernard; QLF says sol dd Howard Co, MO where had mvd from Madison Co, KY, further sol s/o John & Frances (DABNEY) MAUPIN whose s's Daniel & William also RW sol's, further sol Cornelius md (1) Mourning HARRIS, (2) Miss TOMLIN, (3) Miss PAUL, (4) Miss ELLIS, & (5) Ann BRATTON; QLF 1916 from desc Mrs A P MARKLAND, Armstrong, MO. F-R7041 R1655

Daniel, esf 1776 Albemarle Co, VA where b 9/16/1756 on Moormans River; PN that Co 1832; QLF 1918 from desc Mrs Jessie SCHLEICHHARDT, Ft Dodge, IA, states her gdf Henry C MAUPIN was s/o Thomas who was s/o Daniel who was gds/o Daniel who was s of French Huguenot emigrant Gabriel MAUPIN; QLF 1932 from great gdd Mrs Annie Maupin (Dr Hugh B) KINCAID, Knoxville, TN. F-S5733 R1655

Daniel, esf 1780 Albemarle Co, VA, where res; dd 8/29/1832 Madison Co, KY, aec 70; md 6/16/1805 there Margaret/Peggy McWILLIAMS (MB 6/10/1805 signed by John C McWILLIAMS); wid PN aec 73 there 1853; gtd BLW26486 there 1855; had "number of children"; s George W res there 1832. F-W556 R1655

Gabriel, esf 1776 near Williamsburg, VA, serving as captain, keeper of magazines (ammunition) for whole RW; VA gtd him BLW3773 on 3/10/1785; George W O MAUPIN, adm/o sol estate, afp Norfolk Co, VA, for self & other heirs, & PAR, svc not within provisions of current PN laws; QLF 1939 from desc Mrs Harry McPHERON, Charleston, IL. F-R16058 R1655

Thomas, esf Albemarle Co, VA; dd 1/23/1828 leaving wid & many ch; md 6/17/1784 Ann/Anna who PN ae 72 Albemarle Co, VA 1838; res there 1844 ae 78 when her AFF witnessed by Clifton & Elizabeth MAUPIN (no kinship stated). F-W7402 R1655

Thomas, esf 1780 Albemarle Co, VA, sub for f; PN ae 68 Madison Co, KY 1832 when res there 35 years; dd there 2/25/55; md 7/10/1825 Margaret BURNSIDE(S) there; wid PN there 1856 ae 56; gtd BLW40708 there then; res 1871 Richmond, that Co ae 73; Jesse R & Clay MAUPIN (no kinship given) mentioned; QLF says sol md (1) Elizabeth/Nancy MICHIE, or Judith COOK & (2) Margaret BURNSIDES. F-W9920 R1655

William, esf 1778 Albemarle Co, VA, where b 11/19/1759; PN there 1822; QLF states sol res Fredericksville Parish, Albemarle Co, VA, 1840 as William Sr with s William Jr; QLF states sol md Jane JAMESON, & they had ch Synthia E, Tilman J, Waller C, William O, Albert A, Polly J, Frances, & Logan J, further sol nickname was "Mountain Billy"; QLF 1916 from desc Mrs Eva Maupin RANSDELL of Washington, DC. F-S13851 R1655

MAURY, Abraham, esf 1776 Albemarle Co, VA; PN ae 60 Stafford Co, VA, 1818; res 1820 ae 62 Spotsylvania Co, VA, occupa-

MAURY (continued)
tion formerly merchant/farmer but now blind & living among friends; dd 3/23/33 Fredericksburg, VA, leaving no wid but ch: Willia G GREGORY, James F, Catherine M HAY, Abraham Jr & Elizabeth B VASS (a wid); d Elizabeth afp 1833 for self & siblings at Fredericksburg, VA, stating sol res Spotsylvania Co, VA, for c20 years before death, having previously res Madison Co, VA; ch gtd PN due f; sol bro Fontaine AFF 1818 when res Washington, DC. F-S5730 R1655

William, b 3/3/1762 MD c10 miles from Baltimore; mvd when ch with f to Pittsylvania Co, VA, where esf 1781; mvd c1787 to Halifax Co, VA, for c15 years, then to Wilson Co, TN, where PN 1832. F-S2000 R1655

MAUZY, Peter, b 3/1757 Fauquier Co, VA; esf 1777 Stafford Co, VA; PN 1832 Fleming Co, KY; QLF states sol md Sarah HUGHES & he dd 1841; QLF states sol res Sherbourn, KY; QLF states sol md Sarah HUGHES at Norfolk, VA & dd in Fleming Co, KY; QLF 1922 from desc Miss Annie INGRAM, Louisiana, MO, who also desc of RW sol Jeremiah INGRAM of Greene Co, KY; QLF 1903 from great gdd Barbara R FOUCHE, Mount Pleasant, IA. F-S11031 R1656

William, esf 1779 Stafford Co, VA; PN 1832 Rush Co, IN, ae 79, res Noble Township; QLF states sol a Baptist minister, who dd 1835 at Rushville, IN; QLF 1916 from desc Mrs Lulu Carr (Mrs J A) DICK, Oak Park, IL, states sol b 12/27/1755 Stafford Co, VA, md 7/20/1772 Ursula ARNOLD, mvd 1792 to KY, thence 1829 Rush Co, IN where dd 4/5/1837, also querier gdf John Arnold MAUZY a War of 1812 sol; QLF 1924 from desc Mrs Frederick WEAR of San Angelo, TX; QLF 1913 from desc Mrs John A JAY of Kokomo, IN, whose m was gdd of sol; QLF 1924 from desc Miss Annie INGRAM of Bowling Green, MO, says sol d Polly md 1797 querier's ancestor Edwin PORTER; QLF 1909 from desc P F McCLURE, Pierre, SD; QLF 1887 from gds J H MAUZY, Rushville, IN, who also gds/o PA RW sol Robert CALDWELL, both buried near Rushville. F-S16184 R1656

MAXCY, Joel, b 1762 Prince Edward Co, VA where esf 1780 in 2nd VA Regiment; mvd to Logan Co, KY, for c35 years, then mvd to Butler Co, IL, thence Sangamon Co, IL where PN 1832; dd there 12/27/44; md 2/17/1815 Betsey Ann, Warren Co, KY who PN ae 62 Sangamon Co, IL 1853; gtd BLW26968 there 1855; dd 2/18/56; QLF 19-- from desc Miss Beulah MAXEY, New Berlin, IL, states sol md (1) Mrs Susan HILL & (2) Mrs Betsy A HOWARD; QLF 1903 from gds J H MAXEY, Pasfield, IL, who gds/o sol & 2nd w Betsey Ann. F-W5331 R1656

MAXEY, Horatio, b 4/28/1764 Powhatan Co, VA where esf 1781 sub for f John; mvd 1804 to Greene Co, OH, where afp 1832, res Xenia Township; PAR, under 6 months svc. F-R7043 R1656

John, esf 1756 Buckingham Co, VA, where b 1756, & PN there 1841; AFF then there by Edward MAXEY ae 63 & William MAXEY (no kinship given); QLF states sol md Miss MAXEY; QLF 1917 from desc Mrs M S MEISNER of Atlanta, MO, states sol dd c 1850 & md Miss Mary MAXEY. F-S8991 R1656

MAXEY, John, esf 1781 Prince Edward Co, VA, where b 6/1764 or 7/1764; later esf sub for md bro Shadrach; mvd shortly after RW to Powhatan Co, VA, where PN 1832; dd there 1/4/40; md there 7/23/1792 Ann/Nancy LANGSDON by Parson Elisha MAXEY (no kinship given); wid PN there 1843 ae 78; gtd BLW 40002 there 1856; s Elisha AFF there 1855, res Sublett's Tavern; QLF 1934 from desc Miss Kate M WHITE of Knoxville, TN; QLF 1911 from desc R J MAXEY of Madison Barracks, NY, says sol md Mary Anne & they had s Elisha. F-W5351 R1656

William, b 2/11/1759 s/o Radford Sr & w Elizabeth; esf Halifax Co, VA; later esf as sub for bro Josiah; dd 5/27/1833 Monroe Co, KY, where settled 1806; md 9/9/1784 Anna/Nancy, Halifax Co, VA who b 10/4/1764 Lunenburg Co, VA, d/o James & Anne WILLIAMS; wid PN 1846 Monroe Co, KY; ch births: (FB record partly illegible): Radford (1849 ae 63), John 12/8/1787, Edward (5th ch), Robert C 10/2/96, Rice 7/23/1800, & Nancy 1/17/18--; other data: James W MAXEY & Anne md 8/29/1811, Varney ANDREWs & Mary W MAXEY md 9/10/1826 (first ch William Allen b 9/30/1827, dd 10/20/1827); QLF states sol wid dd 1850 & sol b VA; QLF gives more MAXEY data from old family history: (1) RW sol Edward MAXEY of Buckingham Co, VA, md Judith FORD, (2) RW sol Nathaniel MAXEY b 1757-58, (3) RW sol Joel FORD of Buckingham Co, VA, md Mary GARRETT & (4) RW sol Peter FORD b 1754-55 Buckingham Co, A, md Judith MAXEY, & mvd to KY 1777-1781, & (5) RW sol Peter FORD of Buckingham Co, VA, md Miss BONDURANT. F-W8412 R1656

MAXFIELD, William, BLW12409 issued 5/11/1792. F-BLW12409 R1656

MAXWELL, James, VA sea svc, commander/o ship CORMORANT, a trading vessel, about end of RW; later Commissioner of the VA Navy & superintendent of shipyards; gtd special VA BLW by Governor of VA; William MAXWELL, adm of sailor's estate, afp 1845, & gtd PN arrears due sailor; heirs applied for additional BLW, but PN Office stated sailor not entitled to another BLW. F-R73 R1657

Nathaniel, b Ireland; came to America ae 8 with widowed m, & settled Chester Co, PA, where esf early in RW; mvd 1791 to Washington Co, VA, where PN 1833 ae 91; dd 1/22/34; md 12/16/1770 Esther, Philadelphia, PA; wid PN ae 90 Washington Co, VA, 1844; ch births: Thomas 6/5/1774 (mvd to MO, where dd, had s Nathaniel V), John 2/24/76, William 3/9/78, Jane 1/9/80, & Alexander 11/16/83; gds Wallace MAXWELL res 1845 Abingdon, VA ae 38; gds John V MAXWELL res 1845 Caledonia, MO; s-in-law mbnn 1845; QLF 1913 from desc Jessie L MAXWELL, Spring Lake, NJ; QLF states sol md Esther CARSON, & they had s Nathaniel, s John, s William & gds Nelson, further a VA RW sol Thomas MAXWELL dd 9/5/1826, md 6/5/1774 Jane WILLOUGHBY, further a James MAXWELL b 3/23/1814, s of a VA RW sol, md Margaret CARTY, Washington Co, VA, mvd to Potosi, Washington Co, MO, thence Carthage, MO, & their ch were: George William (md 1st Miss CARSON, then Louisa SATER, & res Weiser, ID), Venie (md Mr STEELMAN), Laverda (md Mr DREISBACH), & John. F-W5132 R1657

MAXWELL, Thomas, very little data in file; sol esf VA; afp IN, & PAR, insufficient proof of svc; withdrew afp; QLF 1902 from great gds F W MAXWELL of Springfield, IL, states sol served in VA regiment. F-R7048 R1657

MAY, Abram, b 1762 in lower part of VA, age registered in German language in bible now in hands of bro mbnn; esf c1779 when res Tigers Valley (area later Harrison Co), VA; esf 1781 Hampshire Co, VA; mvd after RW to NC for 20 years, thence KY for 15 years, thence IL for 4 years, thence TN for 2 years, thence IN where PN 1832 Green Co when there 4 years; sol bro William AFF then there ae 62, who not RW veteran; AFF there then by John MAY (no kinship stated); sol dd leaving wid Martha, who apf 1844 stating she md sol 1786-87; her afp sent to PN Office by her Congressman, but no action then indicated on afp; PAR. F-S17562 R1658

Charles, esf 1781 with General George Rogers CLARK troops; dd 2/7/1832 Fayette Co, PA, leaving wid, 3 s's, & 2 d's; md 9/30/1782-3 Mary PARKESON; wid afp ae 79 Fayette Co, PA 1840; PAR, less than 6 months svc. F-R7055 R1658

David, esf Pittsylvania Co, VA; afp ae 70 Perry Co, KY, 1834 & PAR, less than 6 months svc. F-R7052 R1658

Edmond/Edmund, esf 1777 Charlotte Co, VA; PN 1819 Maury Co, TN, ae 47; res there 1821, occupation farmer, ae 59 with w Martha ae 36-37, & ch: David Hary ae 14, Stephen ae 11, James W ae 9, Matilda ae 4, & Edmund ae 2. F-S38923 R1658

George, came ae 11 from Germany to VA with f & rest of family; esf 1776 Loudoun Co, VA, where res; PN 1818 Jefferson Co, TN; res there 1821 ae 79 with w Rachel ae 36 & ch: George ae 18, James ae 16, Martin ae 14, Stacy ae 10, Jane ae 8, Rachel ae 7, & Moses ae 3. F-S38928 R1658

Humphrey, esf 1776 Charlotte Co, VA, where res; mvd 1780 to KY Territory where esf 1782 with General CLARK; PN 1833 ae 75 Mercer Co, KY, 1833; dd 2/14/38; md 12/19/1797 Susannah COULTER/COULLER, Mercer Co, KY; wid PN there 1838 ae 64; s William W b 8/1800; QLF say sol b Maysville, VA, (town no longer in existence) & md Susannah COULTER. F-W8408 R1658

John, est 1776 Buckingham Co, VA where b 2/27/1757; mvd 1780 to Guilford Co, NC, where esf 1781; res there (area later Rockingham Co) after RW; mvd to Campbell Co, VA, 1830-31, thence back to Rockingham Co, NC, where PN 1832; dd 3/20/44; md 4/21/1779 Elizabeth HUNTER, Bedford Co, VA, who b 11/12/1761 there d/o John Sr who gave consent to marriage; her bro John Jr signed MB 4/19/1779; wid PN 1845 Rockingham Co, NC; dd 7/17/48; surv ch Alexander, Charles, & Robert gtd PN due m there 1851; ch births: John Hunter (eldest) 7/5/1782 (dd 12/10/1786), Charles 9/14/84, Booker 9/6/87, Alexander 7/16/90, Rachel McFd MAY 11/13/92, Powhatan 6/26/95, John Wesley Jr 3/10/1800, James Hunter 1/29/02 & Robert B (no date given); QLF 1928 from desc Mrs Haller W REID, Wentworth, NC. F-W18476 R1658

John, b 11/1760 Essex Co, VA; esf 1777 Henry Co, VA, where res; mvd after RW to Buncombe Co, NC, thence Blount Co, TN

MAY (continued)
  thence 1820 McMinn Co, TN, where PN 1832; dd 12/28/39; md c1780 Charity TAYLOR, Henry Co, VA, who dd 12/27/1842 leaving ch: Leroy, William, George, Peter, Phalby MARKRUM, Elender ROGERS, Escheler HARRIS, & Marry HAWKINS; ch afp Polk Co, TN, 1844, & PAR, proof of marriage of parents before 1794; in 1834 William MAY Sr (no kinship given) AFF McMinn Co, TN he served in RW with sol; in 1844 Daniel MAY AFF ae 58, Polk Co, TN, his f William bro/o sol; AFF then there by Rhoda MAY ae 78 she md sol bro William in 1783, & sol md Charity c3 years earlier; James HAWKINS, s-in-law/o sol, AFF ae 47 then there; in 1846 Mrs Moly HAWKINS (no kinship given) AFF she had d b 2/1/1780. F-R7051 R1658
John, esf ae 17 Martinsburg, Berkeley Co, VA; dd 1/23/1813 Floyd Co, KY; md 3/1780-1 Sarah, & they mvd c1789 from VA to Pike Co, KY; wid Sarah afp ae 86 there 1845; PAR, insufficient proof of svc & marriage; s Thesolard (named after s/o Hercules from Homer's works) b 7/26/1805; s Samuel of legal ae when AFF res 1845 P O address Prestonburg, KY; QLF 1939 from DAR agent, Long Beach, CA, for sol desc Mrs Mable Bertha May Winn, states sol bc 1760 near Baltimore, MD, esf 1777 when res with aunt, md Sarah PHILLIPS, Martinsburg, VA, who b 1759, & dd 1845 Pike Co, KY; QLF says sol w d of RW sol Colonel Thomas PHILLIPS who md Miss POLLARD. F-R7056 R1658
Mary, former wid of William BRABSTON. (F-W960)
Thomas, b 1755 Caroline Co, VA; mvd to Grayson Co, VA, then to Surry Co, NC, where esf 1780; afp 1836 Fayette Co, AL & PAR, less than 6 months svc. F-R7057 R1658
Thomas, BLW12364 issued 3/26/1792. F-BLW12364 R1658
Thomas, esf 1779 in 7th VA Regiment; PN ae 58 Caroline Co, VA 1818; res there 1820 ae 75 when a cripple for 15 years, & res with d ae 32 & s aec 18; res aec 60 Caroline Co, VA; dd 5/14/1830. F-S38175 R1658
William, b 5/3/1764 Essex Co, VA; esf 1779-80 Henry Co, VA, where res; mvd c8 years after RW to Union Co, SC, for c6 years, thence Buncombe Co, NC, thence Blount Co, TN, then to Hiwassee RivEr in the Cherokee Nation, then to Chattahoochee River (area later Murray Co) GA, where res when PN 1833 when afp McMinn Co, TN; dd 3/4/44; md 7/1783 Rhoda, who b 2/3/1765; wid PN 1844 Polk Co, TN; liv 1849 DeKalb Co, GA, when res there for 2 years; ch births: Orpah 5/6/1784, John 1/13/86, Daniel 4/16/88, William 1/11/90, Ruth 10/8/92, Mary Ann 2/8/95, Asa 10/29/97 (line drawn through name & date of birth), & James 4/29/1800. F-W5335 R1658
MAYBERRY, Frederick, b VA; esf 1781 Bedford Co, VA, where res; mvd after RW to Cocke Co, TN, then to Henderson Co, KY, thence Hamilton Co, IL, where afp 1834 ae 78, & PAR, less than 6 months svc; QLF states sol dd 1828, buried Big Hill Cemetery, Hamilton Co, IL. F-R6567 R1659
George, b 10/1760 NJ; esf 1779 Bedford Co, VA where res; mvd c6 years after RW to Hancock Co, TN, then to Perry Co, AL,

MAYBERRY (continued)
  where PN 1832 when res there c12 years; QLF states sol res
  Bibb Co, GA 1840; QLF 1936 from desc Mrs Edythe E WHITLEY,
  Nashville, TN. F-S11030 R1659
 William, esf 1776 as marine on ship EFFINGHAM; esf 1778 in
  4th PA Artillery Regiment; PN 1810 Wood Co, VA; res there
  1820 ae 82 with w ae 63, their only ch having mvd away c25
  to 30 years earlier; William MAYBERRY Jr AFF 1819 there he
  svd in RW with sol; sol bro George AFF there 1820; sol res
  1824 Muskingum Co, OH, where had mvd from VA; QLF says sol
  dd there bet 1820 & 1830. F-S41819 R1659
MAYE, William, b 1/26/1747 Princess Anne Co, VA; mvd 1771 to
  Martin Co, NC, where esf at beginning of RW; PN 1833 Hyde
  Co, NC; dd 1/4/34. F-S7188 R1659
MAYER, John, see MAEYER, John. F-S38954 R1659
MAYES, Benjamin, see MAYS, Benjamin. F-R7054 R1659
 William, esf 1777 in VA regiment; PN 1832 Lincoln Co, NC, ae
  73 when had w ae 65, d Susanah ae 25-26,   d Nancy aec 24,
  d Martha aec 20, & s Thomas L. F-S41799 R1659
MAYFIELD, Abraham, b Culpeper Co, VA; mvd aec 2 with f to Bute
  Co (area later Warren Co) NC; esf 1780 Bute Co, NC; mvd to
  SC, where afp ae 66 Greenville District, when res there 46
  years; PAR, less than 6 months svc. F-R7060 R1659
 Elijah, b 6/10/1762 Amherst Co, VA; mvd ae 12 with parents
  to Montgomery Co, VA, where esf 1776; taken POW 1780; escaped 1782, returned to VA for 1-2 years where md, then to
  Jefferson Co, KY, for c16 years, thence Hickman Co, TN; PN
  there 1834; P O Address there 1837 Palestine; sol bro Mi-
  cajah res 1835 Sullivan Co, IN. F-S2754 R1659
 Micajah, esf 1779 VA; mvd c1822 from KY to Sullivan Co, IN,
  where PN 1828 ae 79. F-S36692 R1659
MAYHEW, John, b 2/13/1758 Prince Georges Co, MD; esf Loudoun
  Co, VA, where res; PN 1832 Iredell Co, NC, when res there
  30 years; dd 4/2/38, leaving wid mbnn; QLF 1931 from desc
  Mrs Thomas MILWEE of Charlotte, NC, states sol buried Ire-
  dell Co, NC. F-S9401 R1659
 William, b 1759-60 VA on James River; esf 1781 Lincoln Co,
  NC, where res; mvd c1782 to Rutherford Co, NC, where PN
  1832. F-S7184 R1659
MAYNARD, Richard, b 10/17/1750; esf 1775 Amelia Co, VA; mvd to
  GA, then to SC, then to c1817 Henry Co, KY, where PN 1832.
  F-S13828 R1660
MAYNER, Richard T, esf VA; afp 1834 KY; claim suspended for
  further proof of svc; papers sent to U S Congress & lost;
  dd Warren Co, KY; PN Office sent letter 1852 to sol d Mrs
  Mary Mayner LEWIS, Bowling Green, KY, reporting sol's afp
  never acted on. F-R22014 R1661
MAYO, Benjamin, esf 1777 in 14th VA Regiment; PN ae 63 Fluvan-
  na Co, VA, 1819; 3 s's (ae 10,16, & 13) res with him 1820;
  dd 1/22/26; md 5/7/1800 Judith L HUNT, Fluvanna Co, VA who
  PN there 1853 ae 80; AFF then there by Landy L, John H, &
  Richardson MAYO (no kinship given) in support/o wid claim;

MAYO (continued)
wid gtd BLW28528 in 1855. F-W5341 R1661
Stephen, esf 1776 Albemarle Co, VA as minuteman; esf 1777 in 14th VA Regiment; PN ae 75 Fluvanna Co, VA, 1832; dd there 3/16/47; md there 11/24/1834 Rebecca DAWSON (ML 11/24/34); wid mvd c1849 to Pulaski Co, VA, where PN 1854 ae 39; gtd BLW17884 there 1855, when AFF there by Lanty MAYO (no kinship given) who res there; still res there 1867 ae 55 with d mbnn when PN restored after RW; John W MAYO (no kinship given) AFF there then; res there 1903 with d (a wid ae 70) when 2 gdd's helping support her; per special act of Congress (she one of only two surv Revolutionary War widows) gtd increase of PN to $25 per month 4/8/1904; dd 3/6/1904 ae over 90 Mewbern, Pulaski Co, VA, the next-to-last surv Revolutionary War widow; other ML's listed in Fluvanna Co, VA, co clerk's written report to court: Lewis N JOHNSON & Mary A CLEMENTS 1/31/1835, John M BRYAN & Mary Ann BUGG 12/28/1834, & Stephen CLEMENTS & Dolley B TRICE 1/6/1835; QLF states Rebecca DAWSON was sol's 3rd w; QLF 1913 from great gdd Pearl MAYO (Mrs J W) YOST of Glen Alum, Mingo Co WV, who desc of sol & w Rebecca DAWSON; QLF states sol had several children by his 1st 2 wives. F-W25680 R1661
MAYS, Benjamin, b 1757 Stafford Co, VA; esf 1777 Amherst Co, VA; had a family during RW; mvd c1799 to Iredell Co, NC, where PN 1832; md Leutitia/Lutitia, who afp 1844 Franklin Co, NC, but apparently afp not received by PN Office; gave power of attorney 1851, Davidson Co, NC, to agent to afp; PAR, insufficient proof/o svc; QLF 1906 from desc F P MAYS of Oakland, CA who also desc/o RW sol Joel DIXON; QLF says sol md Lutitia in 1776, mvd 1800 to Statesville, NC, where he PN & dd. F-R7054 R1661
William, VA sea svc, esf 1776 aboard ship TARTAR as marine & carpenter; dd intestate 11/26/1831 Charlotte Co, VA leaving no wid but ch: Nancy CHAFFIN, Sarah, Elizabeth CHAFFIN, Prudence F, Jane W DENTON, & Tabitha W GREEN, all res Charlotte Co, VA, except Elizabeth & Jane res in West; ch afp 1838 Charlotte Co, VA, & gtd PN due m. F-W18491 R1661
MAYSE, Charles, esf 1779-80 Amherst Co, VA, where b 5/22/1763; PN there 1833 where always res; children mbnn; AFF then by Elijah MAYES (no kinship given) there. F-S8879 R1661
MAZARETT, John, esf in VA artillery;   dd Westmoreland Co, VA, between 7/5/1793 (date of LWT) & 7/29/1794 (date LWT probated); adm of estate then Robert HILL of that Co; PN gtd 1845 to Henry NORTHROP, adm/o sol estate. F-R16059 R1661
MAZE, James, b1764 Albemarle Co, VA; esf 1782 as indian spy, Greenbrier Co, VA, where res; afp 1833 Lewis Co, VA & PAR, svc not as RW sol. F-R7066 R1661
McADAM, John, surgeon of VA Line;   dd St Stephens Parish; LWT probated 12/13/1784 Northumberland Co, VA lists f & m mbnn both liv, sis Janet BROWN (m of Amy), bro George Thomas, sis Charlotte, other md sisters mbnn, kin Tommy & Charles McADAM; Thomas TAYLOR, Lancaster Co, VA, adm/o sol estate,

McADAM (continued)
   sold in 1807 300 acres awarded sol for RW svc; one/o heirs Thomas BROWN res 1823 Northumberland Co, VA; in behalf of sol heir Martha C TAYLOR (w/o Thomas C TAYLOR) BLW1088 issued 5/14/1824 to J. Taliaferro; QLF states sol gtd VA BLW in 1784, having served 7 years in 8th VA Regiment. F-BLW 1088 R1661

McALEXANDER, Alexander, b 5/1/1756 Albemarle Co, VA; esf 1778 Amherst Co, VA, where res; PN 1834 Nelson Co (area formerly Albemarle Co), VA; elder bro John mentioned then; dd 1/30/40; md 5/2/1786 Martha/Patsey BURNETT (MB 2/27/86) Amherst Co, VA; wid PN 1844 Nelson Co, VA ae 75; res there 1849 when s David R res Lovingston, VA; ch births: Jane 1/14/1787, William 1/1/89, John 4/24/91, James 11/23/93, Edmund Tucker 2/22/96, Alexander Waugh 7/28/98, Patsy Burnett 11/8/1800, Amelia Carlisle 12/28/02, Samuel Ramsey 4/5/04; David Robinson 12/6/06, & Joseph Roberts 5/1/09; Lucinda McALEXANDER (no kinship given) AFF 1844 Nelson Co, VA. F-W5339 R1662

McALISTER, Joseph, esf 1776 Botetourt Co, VA where res, in 7th VA Regiment; PN ae 78 Pulaski Co, KY as Joseph McALLISTER; dd there 7/27/33, leaving no wid but ch: Robert, John, George, Adam W, & Harvey; other ch then decd: James & Martha JAMES. F-S31241 R1662

McALLESTER, Daniel, b 11/13/1760 King William Co, VA; mvd when quite young with f to Hanover Co, VA; esf there 1776; mvd 1785 to Oldham Co, KY, thence Shelby Co, KY where PN 1833; dd 8/21/46; surname listed on PN rolls as McCALISTER, but signed afp McALLESTER; heirs 1857 Lucy CARSON & Nancy HARRES (both kinship not given); QLF states sol res Shelby Co KY, as Daniel McCALLISTER Sr. F-S31245 R1662

McALLISTER, Joseph, see McALISTER, Joseph. F-S31241 R1662

McAMISH, Thomas, see McCAMISH, Thomas. F-W6800 R1662

McANALLY, David, esf 1780 Albemarle Co (area later Amherst Co) VA, where b 8/5/1748 (old style); mvd 1791 to Hawkins Co, TN, thence 1796 Grainger Co, TN, where PN 1833; AFF there then by sons John ae 64 & Charles ae 59; dd 12/24/34/35; md (1) 3/1/1768 Patty PANNELL, (b 3/2/1748, dd 3/29/1789) leaving children; md (2) 3/18/1790 Nancy KYLE, Amherst Co, VA, who b 3/15/1765; wid PN 1840 Grainger Co, TN where res still 1848. F-W966 R1662

McANELLY, Peter, esf 1781 Louisa Co, VA, where b; res there to c1790; PN ae 74 Knox Co, TN, 1832 when res there over 20 years; QLF states sol listed on 1840 Census, Knox Co, TN, as Peter McNELLY ae 85. F-S16467 R1662

McBEE, Isaac, b 2/13/1764 Halifax Co, VA; esf c1780 Greene Co, NC; mvd to Washington Co, NC, thence Hawkins Co, TN, then 1803 to Cumberland Co, TN, where afp 1840, & PAR. F-R6587 R1662

   Israel, b 1761 Pittsylvania Co, VA; mvd during RW with f to Washington Co, NC, (area later TN); esf 1778 Pittsylvania Co, VA, while visiting relatives; PN 1838 Grainger Co, TN,

McBEE (continued)
& res there 1844; gtd BLW26413 there 1855; QLF 1905 from desc Lockie BALL, Batesville, AR; QLF states sol dd c1856 Union Co, TN; QLF 1914 from desc Esther M MOONEY, Heyworth IL, who also desc of RW sol Captain Daniel HUDDLESTON. F-S2784 R1662

Silas, b VA; mvd ae 1 with f to Spartanburg District, SC, & esf there 1781; PN ae 68 Lowndes Co, MS, 1833; dd 1/8/45, leaving wid mbnn; QLF states sol b 11/24/1765; QLF 1937 from desc Mrs William B BENJAMIN of Lake Providence, LA, states sol md in KY & buried Pontotoc, MS. F-S7202 R1662

McBRAYER, Hugh, mvd 1779 with f from Botetourt Co, VA, to KY Territory, where sol esf 1781 ae 13 with bro mbnn against indians; taken POW, & held until 1783; afp aec 67 Anderson Co, KY, 1835; PAR. F-R6588 R1662

McBRIDE, Hugh, b 9/1762 York Co, PA; esf 1780 Loudoun Co, VA; afp 1832 Spartanburg District, SC; PAR, less than 6 months svc; QLF 1929 from desc Miss Florence CRAIG of New Albany, MS, states sol md Martha, & they res Cedar Springs, Abbeville District, SC, after his RW svc. F-R6589 R1663

Stephen, esf 1778 aec 20 Hampshire Co, VA; dd 3/1837 Columbiana, OH; s Jeremiah afp ae 67 Martin Co, IN, for himself & other heirs of sol 1855; PAR, sol never got a PN & there no provision under current PN laws for ch to receive PN of f; QLF states sol md Miss SMITH, & their ch: John, James, Jeremiah, Andrew, Evan, Abram, Ann, Hannah, & Betsy; QLF 1933 from desc Halene C (Mrs H F) PINNELL, Omaha, NE, says sol bc1761, dd 3/8/1837, buried Hanoverton, Columbiana Co, OH, querier also desc of NC RW sol Samuel SULLIVAN/SILLIVEN; QLF 1928 from great great gdd Emily M STREET, Pasadena, CA, says sol b 2/10/1754, & md Hannah SMITH, who b 3/31/1761. F-R6591 R1663

William, b 8/16/1756 Somerset Co, NJ; esf 1781 Fauquier Co, VA, where res; PN 1832 Union District, SC, when res there c40 years. F-S9425 R1663

McCABE, Hugh, esf Amherst Co, VA where res; PN aec 75 Maury Co TN, 1832. F-S2005 R1663

McCAIN, Hance, b 6/11/1763 PA; esf 1780 Henry Co, VA; mvd after RW to TN, thence KY, thence TN, thence AL, thence MS, thence AL, where afp 1830 Fayette Co; afp there 1833; afp 1839 Choctaw Co, MS; all PAR. F-R6594 R1663

Hugh, very little data in file; afp 1834 Lewis Co, VA; PAR, by evidence/o true age (ae 53 in 1834 per court witnesses) being too young to have been RW sol. F-R6596 R1663

William, esf 1776 in VA company which went to Canada; later esf 1778 NY; wid Charlotte afp Orange Co, NY (no date stated); claim forwarded to US Congress, which never returned to PN Office; PAR, defective proof of svc; 4th ch b 1784; little data in file; QLF 1907 from gdd Mrs Theresa McCain DURLAND, Brooklyn, NY, states sol esf with 5 bro's, querier also desc of NY RW sol Jeremiah CURTISS; QLF 1919 from great gds Frederick E McCAIN, Detroit, MI, who also great

McCAIN (continued)
  gds of NY RW sol Samuel FERGUSON. F-R6592 R1663
McALESTER, Daniel, see McALLESTER, Daniel. F-S31245 R1663
McCALLEY, James, esf 1776 in 3rd VA Regiment; PN ae 62 Montgomery Co, KY, 1818; surname also spelled McCALLY, F-S36095 R1664
  Campbell, see McCAULEY, Campbell. F-W8444 R1664
McCAMISH, Thomas, esf 1780 Bedford Co, VA, where res; PN ae 73 Greene Co, TN 1832; dd there 1/4/40; md 9/18/1810 or 9/19/1810 Jinney/Jenney WILSON (MB 9/18/10 between Thomas McCAMISH Sr & Jinney WILSON signed by Thomas McCAMISH who s of William) Greene Co, TN; wid PN there 1853, res near Greenville; gtd BLW12574 there 1855; res there 1866 ae 86 when PN restored after Civil War; nephew Thomas McAMIS/McCAMISH res there 1853 ae 67. F-W6805 R1664
McCAMPBELL, Andrew, esf 1781 Rockbridge Co, VA, where res; dd 1/28/1825; md 4/12/1781 Mary ANDERSON, Rockbridge Co, VA; wid afp 1838; PAR, svc less than 6 months; dd 5/4/38; afp 1853 Knox Co, TN, by s Andrew & he PAR; QLF states a VA RW sol Andrew McCAMPBELL md Ann GILMORE. F-R6607 R1664
  James, esf Rockbridge Co, VA against indians & later against British; dd 5/18/1809; md 12/22/1774 Martha ANDERSON, that Co; wid afp 1836 Knox Co, TN, & PAR; Mary McCAMPBELL (no kinship stated) AFF there then she present at sol wedding; Nancy ANDERSON (no kinship given) AFF there then. F-R6606 R1664
  Solomon, b 8/17/1753 County Down, or County Antrim, Ireland; esf 1776 Rockbridge Co, VA, where res; PN 1832 Knox Co, TN F-S1694 R1664
McCAN, Patrick, esf in PA regiment; PN 1818 Lewis Co, VA ae 33 but name dropped from PN rolls 1835 for fraud, when PN Office determined he too young to have served in RW (ae 12-13 in 1785); sol an Irishman, who had bro KIA in RW; QLF 1915 from great gds Joseph M KELLOGG, Urbanna, IL, states his gdm Mary McCAN (d/o sol) was b 6/22/1788 Lewis Co, VA, & was not sol's eldest ch, further querier had spoken with Mrs Mary Bennett HAGLER, Milton, IA, who recalled that sol had res at her m's home in Randolph Co, VA 1850-55 when he ae over 90 (Mrs HAGLER being great gdd/o sol), further sol had s Patrick, & PN Office may have confused sol with that s; PN Office reply to this query was that it was too late to change their decision, because original witnesses were all decd. F-S18502 R1664
McCANDLESS, John, esf 1775 in 9th VA Regiment; esf 1777 in 4th VA Regiment; PN ae 63 Hardin Co, KY 1818; dd there 2/2/27; md 4/5/1785 Jane/Jinney MASON, Greenbrier Co, VA, who b 5/3/1764; wid PN 1839 Hardin Co, KY; res 1843 Larue Co (area formerly in Hardin Co) KY; ch births: Polly 9/3/1785, Alexander 11/7/89 (res 1853 Hodgenville, KY), William 2/21/92 & Cynthia (res 1839 ae 33 Hardin Co, KY); wid had other children mbnn, & 1st 3 listed above were the eldest; wid sis Mrs Frank BURKS ae 69 & bro John MASON ae 68 res Har-

McCANDLESS (continued)
 din Co, KY, 1839; QLF states sol res Pennsylvania Line, KY
 when PN 1818 Hardin Co, KY. F-W8441 R1664
McCANN, Hugh, see McCAIN, Hugh. F-R6596 R1664
 John, esf Amherst Co, VA; mvd to SC near Kings Mountain; esf
 there 1780; PN ae 75 Lawrence Co, TN, 1832; dd there 2/3/
 41; md 11/1/1811 Biddy HOLLAND, White Co, TN; wid had md
 (1) Mr BELCHER; wid PN ae 66 McNairy Co, TN, 1853; gtd BLW
 29050 there 1855 ae 65; PN restored there 1869 after Civil
 War when she signed oath of allegiance. F-W5361 R1664
McCANNON, Christopher, sergeant-major/o VA regiment; wounds at
 Battle of Guilford in 1781 almost deprived him of use of
 right arm; PN for disability soon after; BLW12373 issued
 5/17/1792. F-BLW12373 R1664
McCANT, James, esf 1780 in 1st VA Regiment; PN ae 65 Spotsyl-
 vania Co, VA 1823, occupation laborer, when had d Susan ae
 22 & d Elizabeth ae 17; dd 7/1828; md 11/20/1795 Elizabeth
 RAMSEY (MB 11/21/95 between James McKENT & Betsey RAMSEY),
 Spotsylvania Co, VA; wid PN aec 79 Sumner Co, TN, 1849; d
 Elizabeth AFF then there her m mvd 1833 from Spotsylvania
 Co, VA, to Sumner Co, TN; ch/o sol & w: Joseph, James, Su-
 san, & Elizabeth. F-W1909 R1664
McCARGO, Radford, esf 1779 Cumberland Co, VA where b 1762; mvd
 1781 to Prince Edward Co, VA, where f res; PN 1834 Fayette
 Co, KY; res 1838 Boone Co, MO, where s-in-law mbnn living;
 last PN payment in file 1839; QLF states sol buried Boone
 Co, MO, & gravestone placed there by DAR. F-S16955 R1664
 Stephen, esf in VA regiment; dd soon after RW having had no
 w or ch, leaving bro David as only heir; David gave power
 of attorney 1837 res Campbell Co, (res formerly Cumberland
 land Co) VA to agent to afb; gtd BLW2200. F-BLW2200 R1664
McCARMICK, George, esf 1776 VA when raised company of soldiers
 & was their captain; PN 1818 ae not stated Mercer Co, KY;
 dd there 1/21/20; LWT dated 1/20/20, probated there 4/1820
 listed ch: Abraham, William, Isaac, Hetty, Polly McGORHAM,
 Comfort GOODNIGHT, James, Andrew, Elizabeth CREWSON & Sally CROTHER/CRETHEN; ch George & John not mentioned in LWT;
 d Comfort w/o Michael GOODNIGHT/GOODKNIGHT wrote letter to
 PN Office 1834 from Harrodsburg, KY; d Polly McGORHAN then
 res Mercer Co, KY; s Abraham C AFF 1856 Georgetown, Pettis
 Co, MO; sol heirs afp & PAR; QLF 1924 from great great gdd
 Mamie McCORMICK, Bowling Green, KY; QLF states sol b 4/6/
 1742, dd 1/21/1820, md Mary/Polly; QLF 1922 from desc Mrs
 D L SHUMATE of Kansas City, MO, states sol esf in 13th VA
 Regiment & dd 1/30/1820. F-S36105 R1664
McCARMISH, Thomas, see McCAMISH, Thomas. F-W6805 R1664
McCARNEY, Peter, BLW12344 issued 11/6/1789. F-BLW12344 R1664
McCARNISH, Thomas, see McCAMISH, Thomas. F-W6805 R1664
McCARTER, James (AKA CARTER, James M), b 1/5/1761; esf 1777
 Mecklenburg Co, VA; PN there 1832; dd there 4/16/40; md
 1782 Nancy JONES who dd there 1/27/1841; d Nancy w/o James
 HENDRICK afp due m there 1855; AFF there 1858 by William

McCARTER (continued)
    MALLETT (b there 8/3/1776) that sol & w eloped & then came to live on farm of MALLETT's f. F-S7216 R1665
McCARTNEY, Peter, esf 1777 in 1st VA Regiment; dd c1809 Crawford Co, PA, never having apf or afb; d & heir-at-law Catherine MOUNT afb 1837 Washington Co, OH & gtd BLW2184 res Zanesville, OH. F-BLW2184 R1665
McCARTY, Andrew, esf 1778 in 2nd PA Regiment; PN ae 68 Jefferson Co, VA, 1818. F-S38194 R1665
    Daniel, esf 1779 Loudoun Co, VA, where res; PN 1811 for disability from wounds at Battle of Buford's Defeat; res 1833 Montgomery Co, KY, ae 79; dd there 1/8/48 leaving no minor children; md there 1/29/1837 Mary DEBARD; wid PN 1854 Carter Co, KY, ae 78 res Oak Hill; gtd BLW11165 there in 1855 F-W8225 R1665
    Daniel, esf Fauquier Co, VA, early in RW in 3rd VA Regiment; dd 9/1781; md 3/1778 Jemima ELLSMORE, Fauquier Co, VA; wid md (2) 10/1783 William KIRK who dd 7/16/1834; wid afp 1844 Rockbridge Co, VA, ae 92; PAR, proof of marriage. F-R5988 R1665
    Thomas, esf 1776 Pittsburgh, PA in VA regiment; PN 1818 Henry Co (area later Oldham Co), KY when res there 7-8 years, having previously res Jefferson Co, KY; res there 1821 ae 84; dd 11/15/22 or 11/28/23 or 11/16/23; md 11/1773 or 9/11/1/1774 Ann/Anna/Anne SCOTT, Monongahela District, PA; wid PN ae 82 Washington Co, IN, 1832; res 1841 Oldham Co, Co, KY; ch births: 1st 12/8/1775 (dd 2/1776), 2nd 9/2/1776 (dd 9/19/1776), 3rd 9/21/78 (decd), William 2/8/80, Sarah 5/9/82 (md Thomas ANDERSON), Anne 3/27/84, Mary 11/10/86, Margaret 11/14/88 & Nicholas 10/22/91 (res 1832 Washington Co, IN); gdd Evi ANDERSON, d of Sarah, res 1843 Oldham Co, Co, KY & res 1854 Kelly's Landing, KY; gds Thomas ANDERSON s/o Sally, AFF 1842 Oldham Co, KY. F-W8424 R1665
McCARY, Richard, esf 1778-9 Amherst Co, VA; PN ae 56 Edgefield District, SC 1818; res there 1820 with w mbnn & ch: Louisa aec 16, William ae 15, Kitty ae 13, Richard aec 11, & Benjamin ae 9; w dd before he mvd c1827 to Bibb Co, AL, to be near children who had mvd there; dd Mobile, AL before 1855 F-S38187 R1666
McCASLAND, John, b 6/1/1760 Cumberland Co, PA, where esf 1776 in PA regiment; esf there 1778 sub for bro William; mvd in 1780 to Falls of the Ohio where esf in General Clarke's VA troops; mvd 1801 from KY to Davidson Co, TN, where PN 1832 when had children ae 50+ & great grandchildren "old enough to go to the mill". F-S4197 R1666
    William, b 3/8/1758 Chester Co, PA; reared Cumberland Co, PA where esf 1776; mvd after RW to Augusta Co, VA, res for 17 years there, thence Henry Co, KY for 7 years, thence Jefferson Co, IN, where PN 1833; dd 5/3/39; md 3/30/1781 Eleanor, Franklin Co, PA; wid PN 1839 Jefferson Co, IN, where still res 1844 ae 83; res 1846 Morgan Co, IL where had mvd to live with youngest s James H; res 1848 Sangamon Co, IL,

McCASLAND (continued)
  when her signature witnessed by s James H & J I McCASLAND; ch births: John 2/14/1782, Dorathia 2/17/84, Susana 5/27/86, John 7/27/88, Mary 9/13/90, Elener 12/23/93, Sarah 2/10/96, William D 4/24/97, Pheby 7/13/1800, Lovina 4/28/02, & James H 4/19/04. F-W21790 R1666
McCAULEY, Campbell, esf ae 15 VA & fought through RW receiving 22 wounds; sent letter 1810 from Botetourt Co, VA to state legislature requesting PN, since he unable to work because of disability from wounds; gtd PN by VA, & dd 5/1814 Montgomery Co, VA; md Mary HARNESS (MB 11/1/1787), Botetourt Co, VA; wid PN aec 90 Rockcastle, KY, 1843 when res with s mbnn; AFF 1843 there by David HARNESS aec 62, s/o sol wid, that he aec 4 when sol md his m; AFF there then by Elizabeth HARNESS aec 57 (no kinship given); wid res there 1844 F-W8444 R1666
  John, B 12/1756 New Castle Co, DE; mvd quite young with f to York Co, PA, thence Loudoun Co, VA, for 3 years, then to Bedford Co (area later Cambpell Co), VA, where esf 1776; mvd 1779 to Washington Co, VA where PN 1832. F-S7207 R1666
  Thomas, esf near Ellicott Mills, MD in VA regiment; mvd 1818 to Harrison Co, KY, where PN 1833 ae 75. F-S31248 R1666
McCAUSLAND, Andrew, b 7/14/1757 Chester Co, PA; esf 1776 Augusta Co, VA; PN 1833 Bath Co, VA. F-S5751 R1666
  Andrew, esf 1777 in 6th VA Regiment; PN ae 62 Washington, DC 1819, res of GA; res ae 65 Henrico Co, VA 1820 when stated then no family, & esf in 10th PA Regiment. F-S38199 R1666
McCAWLEY, Campbell, see McCAULEY, Campbell. F-W8444 R1666
McCHISICK, Rachel, former wid of John MORRIS. (F-R6772)
McCHRISTY, James, esf 1780 in VA regiment, res near Pittsburgh PA, area later Westmoreland Co, or Fayette Co, PA; PN ae 62 Estill Co, KY, 1822 when w decd, & ch were Polly ae 26, John ae 24, William ae 22, Sally ae 18, Jesse aec 15, Isaac aec 12, & James aec 7; in 1827 bro William res Preble Co, OH, & bro Charles res Warren Co, OH. F-S36094 R1666
McCLAIN, Abijah, b 9/2/1754 Monmouth Co, NJ, or Middlesex Co, NJ; esf 1778 Ohio Co, VA, where res; PN 1832 Greene Co, PA res Cumberland Township; dd 7/11/48; md 2/1836 Lydia WAY, Jefferson Township, Greene Co, PA; wid PN ae 80, that Co, 1854; gtd BLW17584 there 1855; QLF says sol md Lydia WAY, nee CLARK. F-W7408 R1667
  John, b 2/3/1761; esf 1776 Ohio Co, VA, where res; mvd 1777 with f's family to PA where esf 1778; esf 1779 sub for bro Abijah; PN 1832 Mercer Co, PA, when res there 25 years; dd 11/9/38; w & children mbnn; QLF 1903 from desc J S DuSHANE of New Castle, PA. F-S2775 R1667
McCLAIN, John, see McLAIN, John. F-S5744 R1667
  Laughlin, see McLAIN, Laughlin. F-BLW12346 R1667
McCLALON, Joseph, esf 1780 Botetourt Co, VA, where b 12/1764; PN 1832 Harrison Co, IN; res 1844 Lauderdale Co, TN, where had lately mvd from IN after w dd & children had mvd away, & wanted to res with his d Mrs John NEVILL there; res 1850

McCLALON (continued)
    McCracken Co, KY. F-S31846 R1667
McCLANAHAN, Alexander, b 2/20/1755 s of William who res Culpeper Co, VA during RW; reared Fauquier Co & Culpeper Co, VA & esf Botetourt Co, VA after 1778; dd 5/25/1824 Morgan Co, AL; md 5/6/1788 Sarah MOORE (MB 5/5/88 between Sarah MOORE & Alexander McCLENAHAN) Botetourt Co, VA, who b 2/20/1760; wid afp ae 88 Morgan Co, AL 1856 & PAR; gtd BLW47511 then; ch births: John 2/20/1789, Elisabeth 12/22/90, James 12/26/92 (dd 5/20/1825 Morgan Co, AL), Mary 2/8/95, William 4/12/97 (dd 8/18/1827 Morgan Co, AL), Alexander 4/10/99, Elijah 9/14/1800, & Peggy Ann 8/20/02; marriages: John McCLANAHAN & Elisabeth 4/22/1810, Andrew NEELEY & Elisabeth McCLANAHAN 5/1/1813, Elisha MOORE & Mary McCLANAHAN 3/5/1815, William McCLANAHAN & Jane CHILDERS 8/28/1823, Elijah McCLANAHAN & Marjory CHILDERS no date given, V L DENTON & Margaret A McCLANAHAN 2/26/1837; John D McCLANAHAN, Hartselle, Morgan Co, AL, gave power of attorney 1891 as heir of sol to agent to request duplicate/o BLW47511 gtd to sol wid, which had been lost. F-R6617 R1667
    Thomas, b 1753 Westmoreland Co, VA; reared Fauquier Co, VA & Culpeper Co, VA; s of William who res Culpeper Co, VA, during RW; esf 1775 there; esf after 1778 Botetourt Co, VA, where res; mvd 1788 from Montgomery Co, VA, to Bourbon Co, KY, where esf against indians; PN 1832 Simpson Co, KY & dd there 10/15/45; md (1) 1778 sister of John GREEN, Culpeper Co, VA; md (2) 3/1/1817 Tabitha WILLIAMS, Logan Co, KY who PN ae 64 Simpson Co, KY 1853; gtd BLW33771 there 1855; sol had 7 ch res with him in 1832, & had total of 20 ch by two wives; QLF states sol middle name Strother. F-W1052 R1667
    William, b 7/25/1762; esf Culpeper Co, VA, in VA regiment; res there during RW with parents; at Battle of Bufords Defeat suffered 13 wounds; PN 1808 for wound disability; res 1832 Fauquier Co, VA; dd 2/8/42 leaving w Sarah who liv in 1844; large family of ch; sol bro James res 1840 Fauquier Co, VA; QLF states 2 of sol's d's still liv in 1906; QLF 1939 from desc Mrs Katherine WALSH of Savannah, GA, states sol w maiden name may have been SPENCE; QLF 1927 from desc J E BIRD; QLF 1940 from Mrs J Q McDOWELL, Albuquerque, NM, great great great gdf of VA RW sol William McCLANAHAN from Augusta Co, VA, b 1733-1740 (s of Elijah who bro/o James, Blair, & Robert, & uncle of Colonel Alexander McCLANAHAN), who md Sarah NEELEY, & they settled 1780 at Big Lick (now Roanoke), VA, also querier great great great gdd VA RW sol John DICKSON (f/o Joseph) from Greenbrier Co, VA, further querier desc/o RW sol Archibald McDOWELL of Greenbrier Co, VA, also her h great great great gds/o RW sol Williams ERWIN of Augusta Co, VA. F-S5742 R1667
McCLARREN, Daniel, see McLARREN, Daniel. F-R6776 R1667
McCLELLAN, Joseph, see McCLALON, Joseph. F-S31846 R1668
McCLEMAN, John, esf in VA regiment; 1st PN for disability from wounds by VA; later PN by US for total disability 1814 res

McCLEMAN (continued)
near Norfolk, VA. F-S25267 R1668
McCLENAHAN, Alexander, see McCLANAHAN, Alexander. F-R6617 R1668
McCLESKEY, James, b 1755 PA; esf 1776 NC when res VA; esf 1777 VA at that res; mvd 1778 to SC, where again esf; PN 1832 Hall Co, GA; res there 1833. F-S16475 R1668
McCLINTIC, William, esf 1778 Bath Co, VA, where res; dd 9/13/1786 from effects of wound received at Battle of Guilford; md 3/4/1782 Alice; wid PN by VA until she md (2) 5/14/1804 William H CAVENDISH, who dd 8/14/1818; wid afp ae 86 Bath Co, VA, 1848 when res on Jackson River; PAR, insufficient proof of svc & marriage; s Colonel William McCLINTIC res 1854 Bath Co, VA; QLF states sol md Alice MANN; QLF states sol b 1759; QLF states sol served in 8th VA Regiment; QLF 1936 from Edith (Mrs Eldo W) WOOD, Huntingburg, IN, desc/o VA RW sol Robert McCLINTIC who b 1760 Bath Co, VA, dd 1844 Greenbrier Co, VA, & md Jane MANN of Alleghany Co, VA. F-R1819 R1668
McCLINTICK, Joseph, b Ireland; came to America 1763; settled 1774 VA location, where esf 1774 for Battle of Point Pleasant; drafted 1782 in KY Territory & hired sub to take his place; later fought there against indians; afp 1835 ae 83-84 at VA location where settled 1774; little data in file; parts of file illegible. F-R6623 R1668
McCLINTOCK, Samuel, esf 1781 Augusta Co, VA, where b 1763; mvd 1835 to Tazewell Co, IL, where afp 1840; PAR, insufficient proof of svc; his only surv ch Adam referred to 1854. F-R6624 R1668
McCLOUD, John, b 3/16/1741 Piscataway Co, MD; esf Fairfax Co, VA, where res; mvd to Loudoun Co, VA, where esf; PN 1832 Bourbon Co, KY. F-S13883 R1668
McCLUNG, Archibald, esf 1780 Rockbridge Co, VA, where b 3/25/1764; mvd to Botetourt Co, VA, where PN 1844 res there 40 years; AFF then by bro Joseph of Rockbridge Co, VA, ae almost 70 that Archibald served in RW with their f, & Joseph then had family bible; AFF then there by James McCLUNG (no kinship given) age nearly 78; AFF there by sol sis Elizabeth STUART then who b 3/15/1768. F-S9010 R1668
William, esf 1778 Rockbridge Co, VA; afp ae 76 Blount Co, TN 1836; PAR, insufficient proof of svc; QLF 1912 from desc Miss Fannie McGUIRE, Bronwood, GA. F-R6628 R1668
McCLURE, Alexander, esf 1780 Rockbridge Co, VA, where b 8/1/1763; PN 1842 Franklin Co, KY; dd 7/6/42; children mbnn in 1843; QLF 1912 from desc Miss Addie M POTTER, Waucoma, IA; QLF 1927 from desc Mrs Charles A SEMLER, Benton Harbor, MI F-S30575 R1669
John, b 4/15/1760, 2nd s/o John by his 2nd w; esf 1776 Botetourt Co, VA, where res; esf 1788 Russell Co, VA where res as indian spy; esf for War of 1812 Pendleton District, SC, where res; mvd 1829 to Rabun Co, GA, where afp 1844; PAR, insufficient proof of svc; md (1) w mbnn 1790 Russell Co,

McCLURE (continued)
   VA; md (2) 12/6/1829 Margaret McCLAIN; sol res 1855 Habersham Co, GA; dd there 5/24/58, leaving wid Margaret; QLF 1940 from desc Martha H (Mrs George S) SWEZEY, Wayneston, VA, who also desc/o VA RW sol William PORTER Sr of Fincastle, Botetourt Co, VA, whose w was Mary. F-R6632 R1669
Nancy, former wid of James FOSTER. (F-W7409)
Samuel, b 5/16/1748 Augusta Co, VA; esf 1774 & 1775 against indians; esf 1781 in VA regiment; res after RW for 1 year in TN, thence Fayette Co, KY for 17 years, thence Clark Co IL, where PN 1833; QLF 1930 from desc Mabel Milligan SEMLER, Benton Harbor, MI; QLF 1931 from desc Mrs H H MURRAY, Riverton, NJ, states sol md (1) Sarah ALLEN, & (2) Elizabeth Gould RUTAN. F-S33079 R1669
Thomas, esf c1780 VA; dd 11/10/1818; md 3/30/1778 Janet, Botetourt Co, VA; wid PN ae 85 Scott Co, KY, 1836; 1st ch dd in infancy; other ch births: John 8/10/1780, Caty 1/24/83, Nathaniel 11/8/84, Nancy 9/16/86, Jinny 5/12/88, Betty 2/11/90, William 9/6/92, & Peggy 1/6/96. F-W8429 R1669
William, esf Rockbridge Co, VA, for RW in VA Line; esf Washington Co, VA, for War of 1812; dd 1814 Norfolk, VA; md 9/12/1789 Mary, & they had 6 ch; wid md (2) Adam SURBER, who dd 4/10/1833; wid afp ae 69 Pulaski Co, KY, 1844; PAR, insufficient proof of svc; sol 6th ch William AFF there then ae 43-44; Thomas SURBER (no kinship given) gave 1852 there power of attorney to agent to prosecute claim of Mary SURBER; QLF states sol md 1/20/1790 Mary SHIELDS, d of a wid Mrs SHIELDS, sol KIA at Norfolk, VA, his wid then mvd to Leesburg, TN, thence 1821 Pulaski Co, KY where she dd, her ch by sol were: Mary, Elizabeth, Jemima, Sallie, Jane, Levisa, Robert, William, David, & John Shields (b 1811), wid md (2) Dr SURBER; QLF 1915 from desc Miss Annie L SNORF of Roswell, NM; QLF states another VA RW sol William McCLURE/MACCLURE, res probably Henry Co, VA, where esf 1776, dd c 1800, md Mary CLATON/CLAYTON. F-R10313 R1669
McCLURG, James, surgeon in RW; no PN record available. F-None R1669
McCOLLOCH, Abraham, esf 1777-8 in VA regiment; PN 1833 Ohio Co VA, ae not given; dd 5/5/39 there near Wheeling leaving no wid but ch: Samuel, Elizabeth wid of William SMITH, Sarah, Ebenezer, Abram, Rebecca wid of Joseph WILSON, James, William, Margaret w/o Edward MORGAN, & John; PN Office examined sol claim 1835, & determined svc less than 6 months, & dropped his name from PN rolls; s Samuel afp 1860 Ohio Co, VA, as adm/o f's estate, for all sol heirs; PAR. F-S15534 R1669.
McCOMAS, John, b 10/15/1757 NC; esf 1778 Augusta Co, VA, where res; esf 1780 Rockingham Co, VA where res; mvd after RW to Montgomery Co, VA, then to Kanawha Co (area later Cabell Co), VA; PN 1832 latter Co when res on Guyandotte River 35 years; dd 3/31/37; md 2/1786 Catharine d/o Andrew HATFIELD (MB 2/21/86 signed by Isaac HATFIELD), Montgomery Co, VA;

McCOMAS (continued)
    wid PN ae 81 Cabell Co, VA 1840; sol sis Catherine McCOMAS
    AFF then there she b 4/7/1772 Shenandoah Co, VA; sol bro
    Jesse AFF then there sol eldest ch Isaac aec 53 in 12/1839
    F-W18496 R1670
McCOMB, William, esf 1777 Augusta Co, VA, where b 5/20/1750;
    mvd 1783 to KY, thence 1810 to Clark Co, IN, where PN 1832
    F-S16198 R1670
McCONIHEY, John, b 4/15/1752 Bucks Co, PA; mvd ae 10 to Loudoun Co, VA, where esf 1780; mvd 1801-2 to Bedford Co, VA, where PN 1833; PN suspended 1836 when PN Office determined sol svc less than 6 months; QLF 1929 from gdd Mrs E C ANDERSON, ae 82, Charleston, WV, d of sol s John who was War of 1812 sol; surname also spelled McCONAHEY & McCONNELEY; QLF 1931 from great great gdd (on f's side) Mrs Ernest H SMITH of Norfolk, VA; QLF states sol dd 1846 & married Mary DAVIS. F-S16953 R1670
McCONKEY, David, b 1759 Baltimore, MD, where esf to guard western frontier of MD; afp ae 74 Tyler Co, VA, 1833, & PAR; surname also spelled McKONKEY. F-R6744 R1670
McCONNELEY, John, see McCONIHEY, John. F-S16953 R1670
McCONNELL, Abram, esf c1777 Berkeley Co, VA, where res; mvd c 1793 to Washington Co, VA; dd there 8/7/1830; md 3/3/1780 Rosanna FRYATT, Berkeley Co, VA; wid dd 5/8/1846 Washington Co, VA, leaving ch: Abram, James S, Thomas, & William; sons Abram, James S, & Thomas res there 1855, but William then decd (left heirs); s James S apf there 1856 as adm of f's estate & PAR, insufficient proof/o svc. F-R6643 R1670
    Hugh, b 1756 New Castle, DE; esf 1776 Ohio Co, VA, res Grove Street Station; afp 1834 Fountain Co, IN; PAR, insufficient proof/o svc; QLF states sol dd 1835 at or near Covington, IN, & he md Elizabeth JOLLY who dd 1842 Benton Co, IN F-R6641 R1670
    Robert, esf 1777 in 4th PA Artillery Regiment; dd 1786 at sea; md 2/20/1781 Jane McCLURE, Philadelphia, PA; wid b PA & md (2) John DUNN of Philadelphia, PA, who dd 1820; wid PN aec 79 Richmond, Henrico Co, VA, 1837 where res, having previously res Fluvanna Co, VA; her ch by sol: Mary Reding b 4/8/1782 & Ann Maria b 7/17/1783; those ch gtd BLW276 in 1806 for f's svc; d Mary Reding md William WEAVER, & dd 7/22/1822; d Ann Maria md 2/15/1810 Benjamin SEAY (res 1837 Fluvanna Co, VA, when w Ann Maria decd); wid had 8 ch by 2nd h John DUNN, all decd in 1837 except 1 mbnn; Elizabeth FORBES, wid of Richmond lawyer John FORBES, AFF then Richmond, VA, she b 3/19/1782 & lived as neighbor of sol wid in Fluvanna Co, VA, when wid sis Miss Ann McCLURE res with Mrs FORBES; Julia L DUNN, gdd/o sol wid, liv 1850 w/o William F JOHNSTON whose uncle Andrew JOHNSTON res then Richmond, VA; sol bro James M dd leaving his estate to sol's 2 d's Mary & Ann; QLF 1940 from desc Mrs Henry C MORRIS of Washington, DC. F-W7050 R1670
McCORD, John, b 11/25/1763 Albemarle Co, VA; esf 1775 Ninety-

McCORD (continued)
Six District, SC, where afp, & PAR; bro Charles, res there then, had family bible. F-R6646 R1670
Samuel, BLW12349 issued 5/29/1792. F-BLW12349 R1670
William, b 1762 Frederick Co, VA, where esf 1780-81 Winchester; mvd 1792 to Laurens Co, SC, for c17 years, thence OH for c2 years, thence Knox Co, IN, where PN 1832; last PN payment in file 1839; QLF states sol listed on 1840 Census of IN as RW pensioner. F-S16194 R1670
McCORKEL, Robert, esf 1776 Staunton, Augusta Co, VA, where b near that city; PN ae 72 Lawrence Co, OH, 1832 res Union Township; dd 3/10/33; QLF 1917 from desc Miss Estelle R MORRISON of Omaha, NE, states sol md Elizabeth FORREST. F-S9430 R1671
McCORKLE, Samuel, esf 1777 Augusta Co, VA; PN ae 72 Green Co, Co, 1832. F-S30956 R1671
NcCORMACK, Adam, BLW12406 issued 7/14/179-. F-BLW12406 R1671
Joseph, see McCORMICK, Joseph. F-R6648.5 R1671
William, esf Berkeley Co, VA, for RW; esf 1781 & 1792 Sullivan Co, TN against indians; dd 1818-19 "some distance from home"; md 2/14/1782 or 2/10/1783 Nancy, Berkeley Co, VA; wid afp ae 78 Overton Co, TN 1844; PAR, insufficient proof of 6 months svc & marriage; afp again there 1852 & PAR; 12 ch mbnn; power/o attorney 1857 Adamsville, GA, to agent by s Alexander to prosecute interest in m's claim; QLF 1926 from great gdd Myrtle McCORMICK, Shoals, IN. F-R6648 R1671
McCORMICK, Francis, esf 1780 Frederick Co, VA, where b 1764; res there after RW for 13 years, then to Hamilton Co, OH, where PN 1832 res Anderson Township. F-S3783 R1671
George, see McCARMICK, George. F-S36105 R1671
John, b 8/30/1754 near Winchester, VA; esf 1776 res on Holston River, VA, in VA regiment; esf 1780 Bedford Co, PA, in PA regiment; PN 1832 Fayette Co, IN res Harrison Township; dd there 4/18/37; md 3/24/1785 Catharine DRENNING, Friends Cove, Bedford Co, PA; wid PN ae 75 Fayette Co, IN, 1844; large family of ch including Lewis W who res 1848 Connersville, IN, where m gtd BLW33748 1855; QLF 1917 from great gdd Gertrude Kirkwood IVES, New Castle, IN, says sol d Catherine KIRKWOOD was a charter member of Indianapolis, IN, DAR Chapter; QLF 1940 from desc Gertrude V IVES, New Castle, IN; QLF 1906 from the McCORMICK brothers (merchants of Verona, IL), who desc of sol; QLF 19-- from desc Altie G (Mrs H H) WHEELER, Indianapolis, IN, says sol wid dd 2/22/1862; QLF 1899 from desc L A KIRKWOOD of Muncie, IN; QLF 1922 from desc Ralph H BRILES, Indianapolis, IN, says sol md Catherine DRENNEN, who b 1/25/1769, & dd 2/22/1862; QLF says sol & w had 14 ch. F-W9557 R1671
Joseph, b 1762 VA; esf 1781 McCormicks Garrison, KY Territory (area later Lincoln Co, KY) in VA troops as indian spy; Emmett McCORMACK, (legal representative/o sol & w Margaret who both then decd) gave power/o attorney 1854 Lincoln Co, KY, to agent to afp; George L LEE, executive of sol LWT,

McCORMICK (continued)
    afp 1854 Boyle Co, KY; both PAR. F-R6648.5 R1671
  William, see McCORMACK, William. F-R6648 R1671
McCOWAN, James, esf 1776 in 4th VA Regiment; PN ae not given, Logan Co, KY, 1818. F-S36101 R1671
  Patrick, esf 1776 in 13th PA Regiment; PN 1818 Bath Co, VA; res there 1820 ae 67, occupation laborer, no family living with him. F-S38195 R1671
McCOY, Daniel, b 7/1750 Sutherland Shire, Scotland; esf 1779 Albemarle Co, VA, where res; mvd after RW to Amherst Co, thence c1813 Franklin Co, TN where PN 1832 ae 82. F-S4195 R1672
  Daniel, esf 1779 Fauquer Co, VA, where PN 1818 when res Garrard Co, KY; res 1823 latter Co with w Agnes ae 58, 3 d's & s ae 17; 10 ch; mvd 1834 to Adams Co, IL, as all ch had left KY; res 1835 that Co, when had 4 s's & 1 d res Clayton, IL; s James Moody then res that Co; QLF states sol b 10/15/1761 Scotland, dd 2/23/1836, & buried at Clayton, IL F-S36083 R1672
  Eneas, BLW12343 issued 5/12/1792. F-BLW12343 R1672
  John, esf 1782 Frederick Co, VA, where res; esf 1786 against indians when res Hawkins Co, TN; after 8 years in TN, mvd to KY for 25 years, thence 1826 Hendricks Co, IN where afp 1833 ae 68; PAR, less than 6 months svc in RW; heir-at-law George McCOY (no kinship given) gave power/o attorney 1854 there to agent to afp, & PAR. F-R6663 R1672
  Robert, esf 1778 Augusta Co, VA, where b 11/26/1761 s/o Captain John who also RW sol; res after RW Pendleton Co (area formerly Augusta Co) VA; mvd 1806 to Knox Co, IN, where PN 1832; s General William res then Pendleton Co, VA, when a William McCOY Jr (no kinship given) JP there; last PN payment in file 1840. F-S16197 R1672
  Samuel, esf 1776 Isle of Wight Co, VA in 4th VA Regiment; PN there 1818; res there 1821 ae 66 occupation cooper with s-in-law Cartwright PRICE, when sol had 2 young ch. F-38196 R1672
  William, b 9/15/1760; esf 1778 Fauquier Co, VA, in 13th VA Regiment; PN 1832 Decatur Co, IN; dd 2/10/42 Louisville, Jefferson Co, KY; md there 1/1838 Susan HANNEN & had no ch by her; wid PN there 1863 ae 84 when steps Jesse (s/o sol) ae 47 AFF for her there; AFF then there by sol gds Daniel Jefferson LITTRELL; wid dd 7/17/1863 at home/o steps Jesse & was buried Eastern Cemetery, Louisville, KY; wid had afb just before dd, & her LWT 6/5/63 left that BLW to Jesse as her sole devisee; since wid dd before receipt of BLW, PN Office ruled survivors not authorized BLW. F-W9991 R1672
  William, esf 1778 in 3rd VA Regiment; PN 1818 Woodford Co, KY; res there 1825 aec 66, occupation originally a tailor, but not then employed; never md. F-S36098 R1672
McCRARY, John, b 1752; esf 1775 Mecklenburg Co, NC, where res; esf 1780 Rowan Co, NC, where res; PN ae 80 Franklin Co, TN 1832; res 1839 Jackson Co, AL with d mbnn; surname spelled

McCRARY (continued)
  McCRAVEY. (Compiler's note: Although file heading and National Archives book listing RW sol's show sol as being VA RW sol, file indicates that sol served only in NC units, & was not res of VA). F-R16947 R1673
McCRAW, Francis, BLW12372 issued 5/11/1792. F-BLW12372 R1673
  Francis, esf 1780-81 Henry Co, VA; gtd BLW73; PN ae 58 Grayson Co, VA, 1818; dd 1/2/39; md 1786 Sally BURRUSS, Surry Co, NC; wid PN ae over 80 Grayson Co, VA, 1842; dd 9/27/43 Carroll Co, VA, leaving ch William, Martha, Francis, & George; ch gtd PN due m there 1846. F-W7410 R1673
  Francis, esf 1777 Powhatan Co, VA where b 5/9/1760 s/o Francis; mvd to Buckingham Co, VA, where PN 1833; dd 9/28/1834 there; md there 2/7/1795 Mary Harrison WORD, d of Thomas & Lockey WORD; PN ae 80 Prince Edward Co, VA, 1848; births/o ch: Lockey Harrison 11/15/1795 (md 1st 10/30/1818 James B WOODSON & 2nd 11/26/1823 John W REDD), Thomas Word 5/18/97 (md 6/5/1822 Martha A BONDURANT), Mary Alice 12/26/98, Cary Harrison 10/6/1800 (md 12/17/23 Susanna HIX), Ann Word 6/30/02 (md 5/9/25 William H RANSEN), Francis Dancy 7/16/04 (res 1849 Buckingham Co, VA), & Miller Woodson 9/5/07; other birth: Lewis Booker 8/29/1819 s of James B & Lockey H WOODSON; births of ch of Benjamin H WORD & w Sally: William H 12/25/1804, Dashwood 11/6/06, Sarah 5/10/10, Benjamin H 8/31/08, Quin Morton 5/22/12, Susanna Martha McCraw 12/28/15; other birth: Lavinia Martha M 7/31/1816 d/o John FLOOD & w Fedners; QLF 1909 from desc Mrs Leonidas CAIN of St Matthews, SC; QLF 1928 from gds Timothy Logan McCRAW of Dobson, NC. F-W2406 R1673
McCREARY, George, b 1752 Armagh, Ireland; esf 1776 York Co, PA where res; res there for c11 years after RW, then to Washington Co, PA, for c9 years, then to Ohio Co, VA, for c5 years, thence Licking Co, OH, thence 1832 Knox Co, OH; PN there 1832, res Chester Township; last PN payment in file 1837; QLF says sol dd 1842 Knox Co, OH; QLF 1924 from desc D M LADD, Los Angeles, CA; QLF says sol buried near Chesterville, OH, in Old Chester Burying Ground, & gravestone says dd 2/26/1842. F-S8883 R1673
McCROSKEY, John, esf 1776 Rockbridge Co, VA where b 9/26/1757; mvd to Washington Co, VA, where esf 1779; PN 1832 Sevier Co, TN; surname also spelled McCROSKY; QLF 1931 from great great gdd Mrs T C YOUNG, Birmingham, AL. F-S2781 R1673
  John, b 1763-4 Augusta Co, VA; esf Washington Co, VA, where res; dd 2/10/1850 Habersham Co, GA; md 4/14/1790 Margaret, Washington Co, VA; wid afp ae 76 Lumpkin Co, GA 1851; PAR, insufficient proof of 6 months svc; gds James M HUGHES of Clarksville, GA, AFF 1851 Lumpkin Co, GA, that sol 3rd ch John D b 7/1796. F-R6656 R1673
McCROSKY, James, esf 1780 Rockbridge Co, VA where b 11/1/1860; PN 1832 Scott Co, KY; dd 10/25/35; s William res 1854 Livingston Co, KY when gave power/o attorney to agent to afp F-S11050 R1673

McCRUM, Michael, BLW13527 issued 3/27/1793. F-BLW13527 R1673
McCUBBIN, Nicholas, b 1/8/1769 near Sandy Creek, Pittsylvania Co, VA; esf 1779 Guilford Co (area later Rockingham Co) NC where res; PN 1832 latter Co where res since RW except for 3 years in Pittsylvania Co, VA; dd 2/20/46 Rockingham Co, NC; md 12/22/1798 Nancy JONES, Halifax Co, VA; wid dd 11/29/52 Rockingham Co, NC; only surv ch John afp 1854 there & gtd PN due m; sol bro Zachariah res 1833 Beans Station, Tazewell Co, VA. F-W3574 R1674
McCUIN, Patrick, see McEWING, Patrick. F-R16267 R1674
McCULLOCH, John, see McCULLOCK, John. F-S7204 R1674
William, esf 1776 Augusta Co, VA; PN 1827 White Co, TN, aec 82, occupation farmer, res with w aec 63, s Thomas aec 22, d Catarver aec 23, & d Kizia aec 33; had 7 d's & 7 s's. F-S38936 R1674
McCULLOCK, John, b Albemarle Co, VA; mvd 1769 with f to Washington Co, VA, where esf 1777 while res with f; esf 1777 there in f Lt Thomas McCULLOCK's company; f died 10/12/80 as result of wounds from Battle of King's Mountain; sol PN ae 70 Washington Co, VA, 1832; dd there 4/29/38; no children by 1st w who mbnn; md (2) Elizabeth, & he survived by their ch Thomas I/J b 8/4/1835 & Sarah Ann W b 4/6/37; wid md (2) 12/25/38 Augustin R MALLICOTE; they res 1856 Washington Co, VA, when Jacob LYNCH of Abingdon, VA, & Tobias SMYTH of that Co, as guardians for sol childen, afb, & BLW 47666 gtd to ch Thomas I/J & Sarah Ann W; Robert McCULLOCH (no kinship given) AFF there then. F-S7204 R1674
McCULLOUGH, James, esf 1776 Stafford Co, VA; PN 1818 Montgomery Co, KY; dd 12/17/1818. F-S36106 R1674
William, b 12/18/1759 Greenwich Township, Warren Co, NJ, s/o Benjamin; esf 1776 that Co in f Lt Benjamin's company; PN 1832 Asbury, Mansfield Township, that Co; dd 2/9/40 that Co; md (2) 7/18/1824 Mary, who dd 1849 Cincinnati, OH, who had no ch by sol; ch who survived sol: Lititia w of Israel DISOWAY, Jane Van ANTWERP (dd Fall 1840), Benjamin (dd Fall 1849), & William B (res 1851 Dearborn Co, IN); s William adm/o f's estate 1851; AFF 1850 by Andrew Kevan MAYER (no kinship given) Petersburg, VA, provided above data on sol's ch; AFF witnessed by Dinwiddie Co, VA, court clerk David M BERNARD. F-S7204 R1674
McCULLUM, James, esf 1781 Redstone (later Brownsville, PA) in area then disputed between VA & PA; b 8/25/1761 near there on Monongahela River; mvd after RW to Nelson Co, KY, then to Hardin Co, KY, where PN 1833. F-S30579 R1675
McCUNE, Peter, b 11/1748; esf 1777 in VA regiment; PN 1818 Lewis Co, VA; res 1820 Weston, that Co; dd 1/15/31-2; md 1/13/1781 Christiana OBRIAN/OBRIEN, Ft Richard, near Clarksburg, Monongalia Co (area later Harrison Co) VA; wid PN ae 72 Kanawha Co, VA 1839 when res there with s-in-law BARNABAS COCK, JP & minister; sol & w had 10 ch. F-W7412 R1675
Samuel, esf 1776 Augusta Co, VA, where b 1755; PN there 1832 F-S11042 R1675

McCUTCHAN, John, b 8/13/1750 Little Calfpastures, Augusta Co, VA; esf that Co 1777; PN there 1832 as John Sr; QLF states w dd before sol; QLF states sol dd 4/17/1842 Rockbridge Co VA, & w Elizabeth HODGES dd 8/1833; QLF 1933 from great great gds Purdon G BLACK, St Louis, MO, states sol md Elizabeth HODGE, querier also great gds/o James BLACK, War of 1812 sol, s/o VA RW sol Samuel BLACK. F-S13886 R1675

John, esf 1781 Augusta Co, VA where b 1753; PN 1832 Davidson Co, TN; s J B mentioned 1837; surname also spelled McCUTCHEN; QLF says sol mvd from Augusta Co, VA, to Washington Co, VA, thence 1789 TN, where dd, md c1769 Elizabeth WEAR/WARE. F-S21369 R1675

William, b 11/17/1758 or 11/27/1758; esf 1778 Staunton, VA; res 1780 Waynesboro, VA, when esf in company/o kin Captain Samuel McCUTCHEON; PN 1833 Augusta Co, VA; dd there 6/29/48; md 5/20/1794 Jean FINLEY/FINELY d/o Robert (MB 5/13/94 between William McCUTCHEM & Jane FINLY), Augusta Co, VA; wid PN there 1849 ae 79; QLF 1916 from great gdd Miss Ada C MEEK, Greenville, VA, states sol s of Samuel (VA RW sol, who came from Scotland, md 6/27/1753 Elizabeth FULTON, & they both liv 1807), querier now res in house built by sol 1795. F-W1888 R1675

McDADE, James, esf 1777 Hampshire Co, VA, where res; PN ae 69 Mason Co, VA 1818; res there 1820 with w, s ae 20, s ae 16 & d ae 14; dd 6/30/33. F-S38193 R1675

John, b 1748 Chester Co, PA; esf 1775 Berkeley Co, VA, where res; mvd to Greenville District, SC, then to Gwinnett Co, GA, where PN 1833; QLF 1924 from great great gdd Dora (Mrs C F) McKENZIE, Augusta, GA. F-S31856 R1675

McDANAL, John, b 11/4/1758 VA; esf 1776 Orangeburg District, SC where res; mvd c1827 to Jefferson Co, AL where afp 1847 & PAR; dd 11/16/50; surv ch who gave power/o attorney 1856 to agent there to afp: William, Jeremiah, Nathan, Phebe, Lucretia WALDROP, Nancy STRINGFELLOW & Mary PEARSON; surname also spelled McDANIEL. F-R6674 R1676

McDANIEL, Clement/Clemont, esf 1776 Halifax Co, VA where b 12/19/1759; PN 1832 Shelby Co, TN; dd 9/25/36; md 10/20/1779 Elizabeth, Pittsylvania Co, VA; wid PN ae 77 Shelby Co, TN 1839; dd 9/23/40 leaving children mbnn; ch births: Sarah Watson 8/15/1780, Anne Smith 2/23/83 (dd 11/12/1834), Stephen Coleman 6/23/85 (dd 7/1834), Livingston 5/25/1804 (dd 4/20/1834), & Emily Virginia 7/31/07 (dd 7/16/1834); John RALSTON (no kinship given) wrote letter 1839 to PN Office from Big Creek, Shelby Co, VA, reporting that sol wid then res with him. F-W7419 R1676

Henry, b 11/1763 Pittsylvania Co, VA; esf 1779 Bedford Co, VA; mvd 1781 to Greenbrier Co, VA, where parents had mvd c 1780; res there to 1810, thence Walnut Township, Gallia Co OH, where PN 1832; dd that Co 9/28/38; md 5/15/1788 Hannah BRYAN, Greenbrier Co, VA; wid dd 5/5/41; s Alexander, adm of m's estate, afp 1853 Gallia Co, OH, for self & rest of surv siblings: John, Caleb, Icher, Sarah BOGGS, Benjamin,

McDANIEL (continued)
   Ephraim, & Celia SHUMATE; ch PAR; QLF 1938 from desc Clyde
   E McDOWELL, Elvins,MO, gds of sol gdd; QLF 1910 from great
   gds Guy McDANIEL of Oak Hill, OH; QLF 1916 from great gdd
   Jesta McDaniel RICHARDS, Salisbury, NC; QLF says sol eld-
   est s was John; QLF 1927 from desc H B MADDY, Huntington,
   WV. F-R6678 R1676
   James, b 12/26/1755-6 Halifax Co, VA; esf 1777 Bedford Co,
   VA, where res; mvd to Greenbrier Co, VA, where res 1790-92
   against indians; afp 1845 Jackson Co, OH; PAR, insuffici-
   ent proof/o svc; QLF states sol dd 1847 Jackson CO, OH, ae
   98 years & 8 months. F-R6680 R1676
   John, b 1741 VA; esf 1776 Guilford, NC, where res; afp Rhea
   Co, TN, 1832 & PAR; dd 4/27/33; md 11/1/1786 Margaret WAT-
   KINS (MB 12/20/1788 his name given as John McDONALD) Botetourt Co, VA; wid dd 8/7/49; liv ch 1857: Mary LOUDERBACH
   ae 70, Margaret WOLF ae 58, & James ae 50; other ch: John
   dd ae 68, Daniel dd ae 66, Anny dd ae 64, Thomas dd ae 62,
   Edward dd ae 60, Elizabeth COFFEE dd ae 56, Catharine TAY-
   LOR dd ae 54, & Nancy JACKSON dd ae 52; s James adm of m's
   estate afp 1857 & PAR. F-R6681 R1676
   John, esf Orange Co, VA, early in RW; dd 1811; md 2-3 years
   after RW to Elizabeth CRAWFORD d/o Martin (MB 11/1786, his
   name given as John McDONALD), Rockingham Co, VA; wio PN ae
   79 there 1840, when AFF there by Zachariah CRAWFORD ae 65-
   66 (no kinship given); AFF there then by James MEADOWS ae
   78 that sol esf with affiant's bro Francis; AFF then there
   by Absolom ROACH ae 80; AFF then there by John DAVIS ae
   80; wid res there 1843 ae 78. F-W3845 R1676
   John, see McDONOUGH, John. F-R6690 R1676
   Mathias, esf 1780 Culpeper Co, VA where b 3/1/1749; PN ae 83
   Robertson Co, TN, 1832. F-S2796 R1676
   Thomas, esf 1776 in 3rd NC Regiment; PN ae 69 Monroe Co, VA,
   1832; dd 12/17/34; 3 ch mbnn. F-S38192 R1676
   Valentine, b 1/11/1760 on South Branch of Potomac River, VA;
   mvd very young with f to Baltimore Co, MD, then to West-
   moreland Co, PA, where esf 1777; mvd to Mason Co, KY, then
   to Clermont (later Brown Co), OH; PN 1833 latter Co, when
   res there c20 years; dd there 1/13/45 (per wid); dd 1/30/
   45 (per official record); md 10/15/1798 Sarah JONES, Mason
   Co, KY; wid PN aec 75 Brown Co, OH 1853; gtd BLW58688 that
   Co 1857. F-W25691 R1676
   Walter, b 1747 Anne Arundel Co, MD; esf 1776 Prince Georges
   Co, MD where res; mvd after RW to VA, thence Brown Co, OH,
   where PN 1833. F-S18505 R1676
   William, esf 1776 Calvert Co, MD where res; afp ae 81+ Clinton Co, OH, 1835 when P O address Wilmington, OH; PAR, insufficient proof/o 6 months svc; bro Walter res Prince Georges Co, MD, 1776 & res Brown Co, OH 1835; QLF states sol
   b 6/1754, dd 12/24/36 Clinton Co, OH, res Berkeley Co, VA,
   before mvd to OH, one of sol d's b 1784 Berkeley Co, VA, &
   he came to OH 1811-13 with her & her h. F-R6683 R1676

McDANIEL, William, esf 1780 Halifax Co, VA; mvd c1813 to TN, & dd there c1820 ae 62 Sumner Co; md c1784 Martha d of Colonel Joseph WINSTON (also RW sol) of NC; Robert WILLIAMS, a cousin to sol w & an elder bro of Colonel John WILLIAMS of East TN (now decd) accompanied newlywed sol & w to VA; sol wid dd 1834 ae 66 in Western District of TN, leaving ch: Joseph, Alfred W, Winston, Samuel, Fountain J, & Ann PUGH; sol bro Clement, also an RW sol, dd c1834; wid sis Elizabeth md Robert WILLIAMS, Governor of MS Territory; sol s Alfred W res 1854 Natchez, MS when sol s Samuel res O'Brien Co, TN; sol s Winston decd then; sol d Mrs HALLY & sol s Fountain J then res Sumner Co, TN; sol d Mrs Ann PUGH then res Halifax Co, VA; sol heirs afp 1857 then, & PAR. F-R6684 R1676

McDEARMAN, Thomas, b 1758 Prince Edward Co, VA, where esf 1775 in 1st VA Regiment; mvd to Amelia Co, VA where esf 1780 in f Lieutenant Dudley's company; PN 1832 Charlotte Co, VA; dd 5/24/38 survived by children mbnn. F-S5749 R1676

McDERMENT, Joseph, b 10/3/1756 or 10/23/1756 Bucks Co, PA; esf Fairfax Co, VA, in NC regiment; res Fairfax Co, VA, until after end RW; mvd to Fairfield District, SC, thence Wilkes Co, GA, thence Jackson Co, GA, thence Madison Co, GA, then to Clark Co, GA, where PN 1833; res 1842 Jackson Co, GA, with one of sons mbnn; res 1834 Blount Co, AL, with s Joseph, Jr. F-S16472 R1676

McDERMID, Francis, see McDURMID, Francis. F-R6686 R1676

McDONALD, Archibald, esf 1777 in 1st PA Regiment; PN 1828 Ohio Co, VA; dd 3/12/38; QLF states sol b 1760; QLF says sol dd Ohio Co, VA, buried there, md Elizabeth BROWNLEE, Washington Co, PA, & mvd 1811 to Ohio Co, VA; QLF 1902 from great gdd Miss Anne M CARTER, Wheeling, WV, sis/o Mrs John T FARIS, Philadelphia, PA; QLF 1936 from desc Emma Carter (Mrs A J) HOLSOM, Wink, TX; QLF 1913 from great gds H P FARIS, Clinton, MO; QLF 1909 from desc Mrs Margaret C HOLLIDY of Canonsburg, PA. F-S889.5 R1677

Archibald, b 12/25/1752; esf Alexandria, VA; PN 1821 Winchester, Frederick Co, VA, when had w ae 65 & gdc aec 12 res with him; dd 8/27/39. F-S38190 R1677

Charles, esf 1777-8; dd 4/2/1821 Fayette Co, KY; md Hannah, who PN Montgomery Co, OH, 1846, having previously res Warren Co, OH, when res with d Jane & her h Thomas WESTLAKE; they all mvd 1847 to Tippecanoe Co, IN, where wid dd 1/8/48 at home of Jane & Thomas, leaving ch: John (res Warren Co, OH), Jane, Margaret FOSTER (res Butler Co, OH), Francis B (res Carroll Co, KY), & Charles C (res Jennings Co, OH); s Charles C afb & gtd BLW2438 Jennings Co, OH, 7/1849 & wrote to PN Office 1851 when res Thorntown, Boone Co, IN asking how to get the land; Charles C in 1848 had collected PN due m but never gave it to her; Thomas WESTLAKE (he ae 41 & w Jane ae 43) complained to PN Office 1850 when he res Tippecanoe Co, IN, his bro-in-law Charles C McDONALD was a profligate, who never shared BLW2438 with siblings,

McDONALD (continued)
& whose own m never had trusted him, that Charles had never cared for his m like the WESTLAKE's with whom sol wid had lived for many years, further court had appointed Thomas WESTLAKE as adm of estate of sol wid; surety bond for adm signed by James WESTLAKE (no kinship given); Charles C wrote 1852, res Crawfordsville, IN, to PN Office complaining some of PN originally due f should be sent to Charles, who then in dire financial straits, further Charles' w was d/o Captain Samuel CAMPBELL, War of 1812 sol, & also gdd/o Judge PRATHER. F-W7421 R1677

Edward, BLW12347 issued 5/29/1792. F-BLW12347 R1677

John, b 1753 King George Co, VA; esf 1781 Bedford Co, VA res there; PN 1832 Henry Co, IN; res 1839 Des Moines Co, IA, where had mvd to res with s mbnn. F-S16951 R1677

John, esf 1780 Culpeper Co, VA, where b 12/26/1764 s/o John; mvd to Scott Co, KY, for 1 years, thence 1805 to Franklin Co, KY, where PN 1833; dd there 1/5/43; md 8/15/1831 Mary WISE, Lawrenceburg, Anderson Co, KY; wid PN ae 68 Franklin Co, KY, 1857; gtd BLW73644 there then; dd 10/10/57; s Elijah & her gds Ezekiel McDONALD ae 43 mentioned 1857; Susana, Ellen, & Eliza McDONALD (all kinship not given) mentioned then. F-W9186 R1677

John, see McDONOUGH, John. F-R6690 R1677

Peter, b Cape May, NJ; f dd when sol a boy & m md (2) Mr McLAUGHLIN, & they settled in Berkeley Co, VA; sol esf there 1777; mvd 1790 to Jefferson Co, KY, then to 1794 Clark Co, IN; dd there 3/5/1825 or 3/18/1825; md 4/1/1782 Katharine/Catherine WISE, Berkeley Co, VA; wid dd 1/14/41 Clark Co, IN; ch births: Mary 1/6/1784, John 10/25/85, Sarah 9/28/87 (md Andrew MITCHELL), James 11/13/89, Catharine 8/29/91, Daniel 9/6/93 (dd before m), Elisabeth/Elizabeth 8/20/95 (md ? & dd before m), Rachel 4/14/98 (md ?, dd before m), Permely/Permelia 9/15/1800 (w/o James KING 1846, w/o David COPPLE 1852), David 4/18/03 & Peter 2/18/06 (dd before m); part/o birth data illegible; Lucindy, d/o James & Mary McDONALD, b 12/17/1815; Kity MITCHELL b 7/21/1812; Andrew MITCHELL ae 72 AFF Berkeley Co, VA 1846, adm/o wid estate; s James afp 1852 for self & surv siblings: Mary, John, Sarah MITCHELL, & Permeley COPPLE; ch gtd PN due m; QLF says sol esf ae 18; QLF 1930 from desc Miss Edith WOOD, Elkhart IN, states sol esf in 8th VA Regiment F-W9554 R1677

Terence, esf 1778 Richmond, VA; PN ae 60 Henrico Co, VA 1821 when had no family. F-S38191 R1677

William, esf 1776 Wilmington, DE, in 2nd DE Regiment; afp ae 93 Ohio Co, VA, 1852; PAR, insufficient proof of svc. F-R6689 R1677

William, member of Lee's Legion; BLW13528 issued 2/19/1790. F-BLW13528 R1677

McDONNALD, John, see McDONALD, John. F-W9186 R1678

McDONOUGH, John, esf Frederick Co, VA; md Spring 1783 Margaret there & they mvd to Hawkins Co, TN, where he dd 4/14/1833;

McDONOUGH (continued)
   wid afp there 1834 ae 67, & PAR, insufficient proof/o svc; had 2 s's, 1 War of 1812 sol; s-in-law mbnn. F-R6690 R1678
Redmont, esf Perth Valley, Cumberland Co, PA in 6th VA Regiment; PN 1818 Ridgeville, OH; res 1820 ae 75 Lebanon, Warren Co, OH, occupation farmer with w Jane ae 60. F-S41852 R1678
McDORMAN, Daniel, esf in VA regiment; d Nancy TAIT & only heir gtd BLW8084 by VA 12/13/1834; gave power of attorney 1845 Norfolk, VA to afb; BLW2381 gtd her 1845. F-BLW2381 R1678
David, esf in VA Line; PN 1829 Spotsylvania Co, VA; PN claim adjudicated by US Treasury Department & his PN certificate Number 951, thus no data in PN Office files. F-None R1678
David, BLW12404 issued 7/7/1792. F-BLW12404 R1678
McDOWELL, Daniel, esf 1777 Greenbrier Co, VA; PN ae 80 Bourbon Co, KY 1832; QLF says sol b 1751 VA, his LWT of 1834 probated 1836 Bourbon Co, KY. F-S1231 R1678
James, esf 1777 Rockbridge Co, VA, where b 4/29/1760 s/o Samuel; PN 1832 Fayette Co, KY; dd 12/31/43 Mason Co, KY; md 9/22/1780 Mary d of John LYLE & w Elizabeth PAXTON, (MB 9/21/1780 signed by John LYLE), Rockbridge Co, VA; wid b 11/18/1763; PN 1844 Mason Co, KY; ch births: Isabella 8/11/1781, Salley 4/24/83, Samuel 7/23/85, Juliette 10/9/87, Polley 2/2/90, Magdalene 4/23/92, John L 8/24/94, James E 1/31/97, & Hester 4/27/99; s James E AFF 1844 Mason Co, VA F-W8430 R1678
John, esf 1776 in VA regiment; mvd soon after RW from Rockbridge Co, VA, to KY, where PN ae 73 Fayette Co 1831; gtd BLW1749 there then; dd there 7/18/35 leaving wid Jane, who gtd his PN arrears; s William liv 1844; QLF 1914 from desc Mrs Charles RATLIFF, Texarkana, TX; QLF 1937 from Mrs W S DOZIER, Dawson, GA, who desc of a VA RW sol John McDOWELL, b 1758-9 VA, dd 1828-30 Hardin Co, VA, his ch deaths: Nancy 1/11/1845, John Jr 3/11/1840, Mary 2/2/1850, William Allen 2/14/1850 & Swepson 11/17/1877 (b 1795, md Elizabeth CARMAN, who b 1802 & dd 12/13/1856); QLF 1920 from great great gdd Mrs Jane LEIGHTON, Iowa City, IA, states sol & s William among early settlers/o land on White River between Terre Haute & Indianapolis, IN. F-W30578 R1678
John, esf 1775 Amelia Co, VA, in 11th VA Regiment; afp ae 87 Larue Co, KY 1845; PAR, insufficient proof/o svc. F-R6694 R1678
Michael, esf 1777 Bedford Co, VA; PN ae 85 Claiborne Co, TN, 1832. F-S1690 R1678
William, b 1761 MD; esf 1780 Loudoun Co, VA, where res; mvd soon after RW to Fairfax Co, VA, thence back to Loudoun Co VA, then 1809 to Fayette Co, KY, then 1826 to Gallatin Co, KY where PN 1833; QLF 1929 from Frank M HARADON, Marshalltown, IA, whose w Lola B desc of sol, & her cousin Mrs George FALK also desc of sol. F-S30580 R1678
McDURMID, Francis, esf 1780 VA; afp ae 66 Fleming Co, KY, 1823 former occupation carpenter but lost sight/o one eye & now

McDURMID (continued)
  unable to follow that trade, res with w ae 52, s Orlesto aec 14, s Jason ae nearly 12 & d Asenath ae nearly 11; PAR insufficient proof of svc; dd 4/23/33 Maysville, KY; md 5/16/1792 Margaret RIDDIN/REDDEN, Mason Co, KY; wid afp 1863 there ae 85, & PAR; AFF then there by William WILLIAMS ae 79, res Nicholas Co, KY, who came from VA 1793 with f & m, & they settled Mason Co, KY, near town of Washington; sol sis Catharine WILLIAMS AFF 1853 Greenup Co, KY, she about 2 years younger than sol, their f mvd from Prince William Co, VA, to Lexington, KY, where she md Charles WILLIAMS in Fall 1783; AFF 1854 Greenup Co, KY by John YOUNG ae 90 who mvd from VA to KY 1787. F-R6686 R1679
McELHANEY, John, captain of VA troops; dd 1/1/1806 leaving wid (decd in 1832) & 7 ch: Sophy (decd before 1832), Betsy (decd before 1832), Strother L, Polly, Peggy, Jane w/o David McCAMPBELL, & Ann; this data given by AFF 1832 by John Mc CAMPBELL ae 62-63 Rockbridge Co, VA; AFF then there by VA RW sol John WILEY ae 71; sol surv ch then authorized William WILLSON, adm of sol estate, to afp; PAR, for evidence of places of res of surv ch, & their assent to payment to sol estate adm, & for copy/o sol LWT or proof that sol dd intestate; data furnished to PN Office, & ch gtd PN due f; s Strother L liv 1843. F-R16313 R1679
McELHANY, Samuel, b Lunenburg Co, VA; esf 1777 Chester District, SC, in NC regiment; PN there 1832 aec 64, res York District, SC; dd 7/26/46; md 4/16/1792 Elizabeth; wid PN ae 74 York District, SC 1846; ch births: Rachel 3/28/1793, James 3/1/95, & Elizabeth 7/1/97; birth record faded badly partly illegible; other births: Elizabeth HOOD 5/6/1797, E McELHANEY 5/5/1805. F-W12455 R1679
McELHENEY, William, b c1759 Lunenburg Co, VA; esf 1779 Chester District (area later Craven Co), SC; res after RW Richland District, SC, thence Edgefield District, SC, then to Abbeville District, SC, thence 1825 to Jasper Co, GA where afp & PAR, insufficient proof of svc; AFF 1834 by Stephen McELHENEY (no kinship given); surname also spelled McELHENNY F-R6697 R1679
McELHENNY, Stephen, b 1759-60 Lunenburg Co, VA; esf 1776 Craven Co, SC; PN 1832 Chester District, SC; listed as reference Samuel McELHENNY (no kinship given). F-S21368 R1679
McELWEE, James, b 8/19/1758 VA; mvd as youth to York District, SC, where esf 1774-75 in SC regiment; esf 1781 Washington Co, VA; returned to York Co, SC, where esf 1782; mvd 1832 to Pike Co, MO, where PN then; dd there 1/13/34; md Fall/o 1793 Rhoda BLACK, Abbeville, SC, who b 3/1777; wid afp 4/1848 Cuivre Township, Pike Co, MO but dd 8/23/48 before PN gtd; her PN then allowed to surv ch: Dan, James, Ross, Abner, Mary, Elizabeth, Ann HENRY & Rhoda GIVENS; ch births: Ann 4/1/1795 (md 1822 Josiah HENRY, York District, SC), James 9/17/1802, Dan 5/2/06, Rhoda 6/8/08 (md 5/14/1840 John GIVENS, Pike Co, MO), Ross 5/29/09, Mary 7/9/12, Ab-

McELWEE (continued)
ner 1/6/14, & Elizabeth 10/1/17; sol gds J J McELWEE postmaster, Sulphur Lick, Lincoln Co, MO 1877 when his f & all uncles decd but aunts Rhoda GIVENS & Elizabeth McELWEE res then Louisiana, MO; QLF 1894 from great gds Dr L C McELWEE of St Louis, MO; QLF 1907 from great gds William C SHELLEY of Washington, DC states sol f James also RW sol. F-W9553 R1679

McELYEA, Patrick, b 1751 York Co, PA; esf 1776 Caswell Co, NC, where res; mvd to Washington Co, VA where esf 1781; mvd to Montgomery Co, VA, thence Surry Co, NC, thence Grayson Co, VA, thence Carter Co, TN, thence Montgomery Co, TN, thence Davidson Co, TN, then to Dixon Co, TN, then to Jackson Co, AL, c1825 where PN 1834; last PN payment in file 1841. F-S2789 R1679

McENTIRE, John, esf 1777 in 3rd VA Regiment; PN ae 66 Anderson Co, TN, 1818; res there 1820 with w ae 78 mbnn. F-S38935 R1680

McEWIN, Patrick, see McEWING, Patrick. F-R16267 R1680

McEVER, Angus, esf 1777 in 12th PA Regiment; gtd BLW299 & disability PN in VA 1805; dd 8/15/37 Berkeley Co, VA; md 9/4/1783 Catharine; wid PN ae 81 Berkeley Co, VA, 1839 when s John mentioned; wid res there 1844 ae 86; surname spelled also McKEEVER & McIVER. F-W5355 R1680

McEWING, Patrick, esf 1777 Prince William Co, VA; PN 1818 ae 70 there; res there ae 88 in 1831; dd there 1845, & children mbnn gtd PN due f; Polly McEWING afp aec 70 there 1859 as sol wid, alleging she md sol 1839; PAR, PN Office determined she never md sol, but only lived with him as his cook. F-R16267 R1680

McFADDEN, John, esf 1776 Hagerstown, MD, in 6th MD Regiment, when res near there; b 9/15/1760 c9 miles from Hagerstown; mvd 1784 to Augusta Co, VA, where PN 1832, when res near Staunton; bro James AFF there then aec 66. F-S7193 R1680

McFALL, Cornelius, b8/1734 Co Antrim, Ireland; landed 1775 at port of Hampton, VA; settled Augusta Co, VA, where md; mvd to Albemarle Co, VA, where esf; PN there 1832; occupation weaver; dd c1883 there leaving wid mbnn. F-S5753 R1680

McFALLS, Arthur, b 5/22/1751 Bedford Co, VA where esf just before RW against indians; mvd to NC where esf 1776 Burke Co NC res there; gtd BLW18136 Yancey Co, NC, 1836; dd 4/9/39; md 5/2/1814 Emzay HOLLYFIELD (MB 5/12/1814 signed by Duram McFALLS); wid PN ae 66 Yancey Co, NC, 1851; res there 1856 ae 67; sol surname also spelled McFAULS. F-W9187 R1680

McFARLAND, Robert, b 3/15/1759 Orange Co, VA; mvd aec 8 with f to Bedford Co, VA, for c4 years, thence Botetourt Co, VA, where esf 1776; mvd to Washington Co, VA, where esf 1779; md there mbnn; mvd to Jefferson Co, TN, where PN 1832 as Robert Sr when a Robert McFARLAND Jr was presiding justice of Court of Pleas & Quarter Sessions; reference made 12/5/1837 to death of Colonel Robert McFARLAND Sr and to his s Carl Robert; QLF states sol dd 1834 Jefferson Co, TN; QLF

McFARLAND (continued)
   states sol also War of 1812 svc; QLF states sol dd 5/20/1834, md Margaret McNUTT of Jefferson Co, TN, & s Robert b 4/17/1791 (dd 8/11/1844, md (1) Hannah BARTON, (2) Mary Ann SCOTT, & was War of 1812 sol). F-S2004 R1681

McFARLING, John Bennett, esf 1777 Alexandria, VA, in 3rd VA Regiment ; PN there 1818 aec 59; AFF there then by John HUGHES ae 63 that sol md John's sis; sol res there 1820 with family mbnn which included crippled bro ae 75; sol dd 10/15/1822. F-S36086 R1681

McFERRAN, Samuel, esf 1778-79 Botetourt Co, VA, where b 4/29/1761; mvd 1792 to Lincoln Co, KY, then to Mercer Co, KY, then to Clark Co, KY, then to Adair Co, KY, then 1804 to Smith Co, TN, then to 1830 Hardin Co, TN, where PN 1833; last PN payment in file 1838; surname also spelled McFARRAN. F-S1691 R1682

McFERREN, John, b Ireland, to VA 1772; settled Greenbrier Co, VA 1775 where esf; afp there 1835; PAR, insufficient proof of svc. F-R6712 R1682

William, b 1755 York Co, PA; mvd with f to Augusta Co, VA, where esf 1776; mvd 1777 with f to Washington Co, VA where esf; res near Abingdon, VA, for c35 years, thence Rutherford Co, TN; mvd 1832 to Tipton Co, TN, where PN 1833; md 2/1780 mbnn; res 1833 with s-in-law mbnn; last PN payment in file 1841; surname also spelled McFERRIN; QLF says sol dd 1845 Marshall Co, TN; QLF states sol md Jane BERRY; QLF 1922 from desc John B McFERRIN, Collierville, TN. F-S2791 R1682

McGANNON, Darby, esf 1777 Culpeper Co, VA; PN ae 62 Gallatin Co, KY, 1818; res 1825 Jennings Co, IN, with w mbnn, s Alexander ae 19, d Jane ae 18, twins Salley & Aylesey ae 15, & s Hugh ae 12, + other children mbnn; QLF 1928 from desc Elizabth GOTTBERG, Seymour, IN; QLF 19-- from desc Frances C GREEN, Huron, SD, states sol b Belfast, Ireland & had ch Thomas, Zachariah, John, Reuben, Alexander, Hugh, Jane, Sally, Mary DAMSEL, & Alice; QLF 1901 from great gdd Mrs W A GUTHRIE, Washington, DC. F-S36104 R1682)

McGAUGHY, Samuel, b 7/15/1763 York Co, PA; mvd ae 9 with f to Washington, Co, VA, on Holston River where res when RW began; esf 1778 Sullivan Co, NC, sub for f; mvd to Greene Co (state not stated) for 44 years, thence settled on French Broad River to 1818, thence Lawrence Co, AL where PN 1833; dd there 1/5/1840-41; md 2/24/1784 Jane LAUGHFLAND, Sullivan Co, NC; wid PN ae 78 Lawrence Co, AL, 1842; dd 4/1/47; children mbnn; sol younger sis Agnes ALEXANDER AFF there; Jeremiah ALEXANDER (NKG) AFF there then he in RW svc with sol; sol surname also spelled McGAUGHEY; QLF 1936 from desc Mrs Edward H PATTERSON, Fort Smith, AR. F-W9981 R1682

McGAVOCK, Hugh, b 9/1761; esf 1779 Montgomery Co, VA, where res (area later Wythe Co, VA), PN 1834 Wythe Co, VA; res 1835 on Reed Creek there; dd there 4/2/44; w dd before him; 10 ch; s James dd before sol leaving wid & children mbnn; in

McGAVOCK (continued)
1844 other 9 ch who afp: Joseph, Jacob, Robert, Hugh, Randal (res there ae 43, P O address 1850 Wytheville, VA), Sally, Polly w/o Thomas CLOYD (she dd before 1850), Eliza w/o Andrew B EWING & Margaret w of Samuel H McNUTT (she dd before 8/25/1845 leaving h & several ch mbnn); one/o sol s md d/o US Senator Felix GRUNDY who in 1835 gave AFF Davidson Co, TN, that he & one of sol bro's md sisters; sol's youngest bro David res Davidson Co, TN, 1835 aec 72; sol bro-in-law Joseph KENT res 1832 Wythe Co, VA, & in 1835 JP for that Co ae 70, he having md sol sis c50 years before, & was nephew of Colonel Joseph CROCKETT. F-S16948 R1682

McGEE, Herman/Harmon, esf 1776 Sussex Co, VA where b 7/7/1760; mvd 1800 to Rockingham Co, NC, for 2 years, then to Guilford Co, NC, for 6 years, then to Stokes Co, NC, where PN 1832. F-S7194 R1683

John, esf 1778 Rockbridge Co, VA, where res, in 12th VA Regiment; mvd after RW to TN, where res Warren Co 1818; dd there 1/24/1820; md 1792 Esther CLENDENNING, Sevier Co, TN who dd 3/1846 Warren Co, TN, leaving ch: Jane wid of James HENNESSEE, Polly w/o of Ezekiel McGREGOR, John, Sally, Samuel, & James L; Charles M FORREST, adm of wid estate, afp 1852 for her ch; PAR, insufficient proof of her marriage. F-R6717 R1683

Ralph, see MAGEE, Ralph. F-S13894 R1683

Samuel, b 3/1/1750 (old style) New Kent Co, VA; esf 1776 Pittsylvania Co, VA, where res; mvd after RW to TN for 4 years, then to SC for 4 years, then to KY, where settled Woodford Co; PN there 1832; dd 12/27/34; QLF says sol s/o Edward & w Elizabeth (nee DeJARNETTE), sol f s of Thomas McGEE (to VA from Scotland, md Ann BAYTOP of Kent County, England), sol md Olivia MEURE/MUSE; QLF states sol md 10/19/1778 Olive MUSE & he was bro/o Micajah. F-S31249 R1683

Thomas, b 2/17/1749 RAndolph Co, NC; mvd to Pittsylvania Co, VA; went 1777 on business to Baltimore, MD, where esf in 4th GA battalion; esf c1779 Burke Co, NC; later esf Wilkes Co, NC; returned to Pittsylvania Co, VA, after RW, then to Stokes Co, NC where md mbnn, thence c1784 TN where PN 1833 Humpreys Co when res there c10 years. F-S4194 R1683

Thomas, b 3/11/1767 Cumberland Co, NJ where esf near Bridgetown while res c45 miles from Philadelphia, PA; mvd after RW to Monongalia Co, VA, then to Preston Co, VA, where PN 1833; QLF 1924 from desc Dora McGEE (Mrs John T) FOWLER of Columbus, OH, whose gdf b Kingwood, WV; QLF 1907 from desc Miss Estelle L McGEE, Muncie, IN through sol s William who had s Wesley who had s Jackson; QLF 1894 from gds Rev N M WATERS of Dubuque, IA, states sol dd 7/1849 ae 93, further sol P O address then Evansville, Preston Co, WV; QLF 1937 from desc Mrs Chester KIRK, Sheridan, WY, who gdd/o Thomas McGEE (b Preston Co, WV) s of William McGEE. F-5753 R1683

Thomas, esf 1775 Bedford, PA; PN ae 65 Fayette Co, OH, 1819; res 1821 Washington Co, VA, ae 66 where had lived over 40

MCGEE (continued)
    years; decd in 1853, when afp there by ch Thomas, Hannah, John, Mary, Elizabeth, Sally, & Edward. F-S38202 R1683
McGEHE, William, b 1755 New Kent Co, VA; esf 1777 Pittsylvania Co, VA; PN 1833 Jackson Co, AL; dd 5/1/36; his PN arrears paid to wid mbnn F-S32399 R1683
McGEORGE, Thomas, b 1/23/1758 Hanover Co, VA; esf 1778 Botetourt Co, VA, where res; mvd 1816 to Knox Co, KY, for 6 years, thence Warren Co, TN, having res short time Blount Co, AL, & Franklin Co, TN; PN 1833 Warren Co, TN; dd 4/27/34. F-S2801 R1683
    William, esf 1778 King William Co, VA; PN there 1819 ae 63; dd there 11/26/22, leaving wid Elizabeth; wid & s W E res there 1844. F-S38201 R1683
McGHEE, William, b 1761-62 Louisa Co, VA; esf 1777-78 Mecklenburg Co, NC, where res near Charlotte; mvd aec 45 to TN, thence Christiana Co, KY, for 8 years, thence White Co, IL for 11 years, thence McLean Co, IL where PN 1833; QLF 1915 from desc Mrs Elizabeth McGhee BREAZEALE, Mount Olive, NC. F-S33068 R1683
McGINNIS, Andrew, esf 1775 Halifax Co, VA, where b 2/14/1756; mvd to Patrick Co, VA, thence Stokes Co, NC, thence Barren Co, KY where PN 1833; dd there 11/23/37; md 80/20/1782 Anna, Halifax Co, VA; wid b 3/21/1761 Lunenburg Co, VA; her f mvd family to Halifax Co, VA; wid PN Barren Co, KY 1839; Mary FRANCIS AFF there then ae 75 she present at sol marriage; wid AFF there 1840 her eldest s William b 7/4/1783 Halifax Co, VA, & he res then Barren Co, KY; wid res there 1843 F-W8426 R1684
McGLASSON, John, esf 1780 Buckingham Co, VA where res; PN 1830 Campbell Co, VA, for disability from wound recd at Battle of Ninety-Six; dd 10/13/1832 Campbell Co, VA; md Nancy in Buckingham Co, VA, 8/27/1785; wid PN ae 72 Campbell Co, VA 1839 when surv ch: Juda/Judah w of Alexander DOYLE/DOYAL, Patsey w of Telmon/Tilmon DIXON, Nancy w of Benjamin CROOK, Elizabeth w of Calvin W HULL, William, & James; AFF then by Mary HAMILTON ae 88 there she res Buckingham Co, VA, when sol md; AFF 1839 Boone Co, KY, by Rebecca McNEAL ae 66 she present at sol marriage & that sol & w had total of 10 ch. F-W8440 R1684
    Matthew, esf 1778 Buckingham Co, VA where b 1/3/1756; mvd to Amelia Co;, VA, where esf 1780; mvd back to Buckingham Co, VA, where esf 1781; mvd soon after RW to Charlotte Co, VA, thence Campbell Co, VA, thence Cumberland Co, KY; PN 1832 Adair Co, KY; w mbnn. F-S15530 R1684
McGLOGHLIN, Hugh, see McLOUGHLIN, Hugh. F-W6537 R1684
McGLOUGHLIN, John, esf 1781 Augusta Co, VA, where b 5/26/1764 (area later in Rockingham Co, VA); PN 1833 Bath Co, VA; dd 3/19/38; md 11/9/1790 Ann/Anne WILEY; wid PN ae 72 Bath Co VA, 1841 when res on Jackson River; s John mentioned 1843; QLF 1929 from desc Mrs C R SWISSHELM of Jamestown, NY. F-W18494 R1684

McGUIRE, Allegany, esf Cumberland Co, VA, where b 8/6/1757 on Willis Creek; f mvd to Henry Co, VA, where sol esf again; esf once for uncle Stanard RICHARDSON; mvd after RW to Elbert Co, GA, then to TN, where PN 1833 Maury Co when res there c25 years; mvd 1843 to McNairy Co, TN, to res with s mbnn; AKA Aleygone MAGWIER. F-S2797 R1685
Elijah, b 1/17/1757 Cumberland Co, VA; esf 1777 SC in 3rd SC Regiment; PN 1827 Tuscaloosa, AL, where dd 12/31/43; md 1784-85 Everet who dd there 7/17/1848; sol & wid buried at John THOMAS's on Byler's Road, 16 miles north/o Tuscaloosa AL; ch in 1856: John (res Tuscaloosa, AL, ae 70), Elijah Jr (aec 67 there), Amos (bc 1791, res Chicasaw Co, MS, but decd in 2/1856), Merry (res Tuscaloosa Co, AL, aec 62), Williams (res Choctaw Co, MS, aec 59), Polly (res Fayette Co, AL w/o John SPEARS), Moses (res Tuscaloosa Co, AL, aec 53, where judge/o probate court) & Rhoda WHATLEY (res Tuscaloosa Co, AL, aec 50); ch afp then & gtd PN due m; QLF 1939 from desc Connie M COLLINS of Montgomery, AL, through sol ch Merry. F-W8274 R1685
James, esf 1776 Botetourt Co, VA; mvd to KY 1783 where took part in General George Rogers CLARK's campaign against indians; PN 1820 Franklin Co, KY; res Anderson Co, KY, 1832 ae 85 (area was formerly part of Franklin Co); dd 8/28/38. F-S13896 R1685
John, esf 1776 Little Fork, PA, in 4th PA Regiment; esf 1780 in 5th VA Regiment, later transferred to 2nd PA Regiment; PN 1818 Sussex Co, VA, ae 76 when already receiving small PN from PA; res ae 84 Newton Township, Sussex Co, VA, 1820 formerly res/o Hardiston Township, that Co; family in 1820 was w Lidea aec 60. F-S34426 R1685
John, b 4/22/1756 Ireland; esf 1780 Mercer Co, VA where res; PN 1832 Morgan Co, KY, where had res since RW; dd 4/10/37; only child mbnn 1853; QLF states sol & w Nancy buried at Bloomington Blockhouse, Magoffin Co, KY. F-S31244 R1685
Joseph, b 7/24/1752 Easton, PA; esf 1779 Bedford Co, VA; mvd after RW to KY; PN 1832 Henry Co, KY, res there 36 years; w Ann; s James P gave power of attorney 1855 to agent Lawrence Co, IL, to afp when f decd. F-13892 R1685
William, esf VA; lieutenant; gtd PN 1781 for disability from wound recd at Battle of Eutaw Springs; PN 1801 by VA; res 1808 Winchester, VA; AFF then by Sigismund STRIBLING there he served with sol at Eutaw Springs in 1st VA Artillery Regiment; BLW1522 issued 8/25/1789. F-BLW1522 R1685
William, b1757-58; esf 1776 Greenbrier Co, VA; PN 1832 Tazewell Co, VA; d 3/5/37. F-S5746 R1685
McGUY, Bennet, BLW12394 issued 2/24/1794. F-BLW12394 R1685
McHANEY, Terry, esf 1776 Bedford Co, VA with GA troops; PN aec 64 Pittsylvania Co, VA, 1821 when had w Sarah aec 60 & d Fanny ae 20-21; dd 7/2/38 leaving 3 ch mbnn; QLF 1913 from great gdd Mrs Anna Ware TAGGART, Kansas City, MO, who also great gdd of VA RW sol John WARE; QLF states sol 1st name was Terence; QLF 1927 from desc Lena W VARNEY of Genoa, NE

McHANEY (continued)
F-S38185 R1685
McHENRY, Isaac, b 12/27/1763 Hampshire Co, VA; esf 1780 Mononganlia Co, VA, (area later Randolph Co) as indian spy in VA militia; mvd 1786 to Green Co, KY, thence 1807 Pickaway Co OH, thence 1830 Putnam Co, OH, where afp 1835; afp 1837 Allen Co, OH; PAR both times. F-R6732 R1686
McHONE, Archibald, b1745 New Kent Co, VA; mvd aec 2 with m & f to Bedford Co, VA, where esf 1780; mvd after RW to Stokes Co, NC, thence 1836 Patrick Co, VA, where afp 1833; PAR, less than 6 months svc. F-R6733 R1686
McILHANEY, John, see McELHANY, John. R16313 R1686
McILHANEY, James, see McILHENY, James. F-S38188 R1686
McILHANY, James, see McILHENY, James. F-S38188 R1686
McILHANY, James, esf VA; dd 9/16/1804, leaving wid Margaret & ch Mary, Cecelia, James, Louisa, & Mortimer; md 12/25/1778 to 12/31/1778 a wid Margaret WILLIAMS (MB 12/21/1778) Loudoun Co, VA, they both of Shelburne Parish there; wid afp ae 76 that Co 1836, & PR, md after sol left svc; sol sis Hannah PARKER AFF there then ae 75; wid dd 3/1837; sol s James res Purcell's Store, that Co when he sent query letter 1846 to PN Office. F-R6734 R1686
McILHENY, James, esf in 3rd year of RW in 12th VA Regiment; PN ae 64 Huntsville, AL, 1818; illiterate; res there 1819; dd c1823; s Moses res Huntsville, AL, 1861. F-S38188 R1686
McINLIN, Mary, former wid of William KEATH. (F-W21650)
McINTIRE, James, esf 1778 VA; one of heirs s James afb Bedford Co, VA, 1828; BLW1431 issued to heirs. F-BLW1431 R1687
Robert, b 1/1/1761 Frederick Co, MD; esf 1778 Yohogania Co, VA (area later Fayette Co, PA); PN ae 71 Brooke Co, VA, 1832; res there 1835 when res there 50+ years; later dropped from PN rolls, when PN Office determined his svc less than 6 months; QLF 1932 from desc Mrs T B PENNYBACKER of Parkersburg, WV, says sol md Anne HYATT & they had d Nancy F-S5743 R1687
William, esf 1775 Caroline Co;, VA; PN ae 65 Gallatin Co, KY 1818; res there 1821 when had no wife or ch to assist him; res there 1826 ae 72; occupation farmer. F-S36113 R1687
McINTOSH, Alexander, BLW12342 issued 6/20/1789. F-BLW12342 R1687
Charles, b 1759-60 Culpeper Co, VA; esf 1780 Caswell Co, NC, where res; res there after svc 10 years, thence Robertson Co, TN, where PN 1832 when bro Nimrod res there; dd there 9/9/1836 or 9/19/1836; md 1792 (per wid AFF) Candace/Candis McAELHANY, Montgomery Co, TN; record states marriage 1795; wid PN there 1850 ae 74; res 1852 ae 78 P O address Barren Plains, TN; dd 11/13/1854; youngest ch Sena b 9/7/ 9/27/1816; other ch: John, Alexander, Margaret, Elijah, Julia, & Anderson. F-W3704 R1687
Francis, esf 1781 Prince William Co, VA where b 1764-65; mvd c1807 to NC for 4 years, thence East TN for several years, thence KY for c12 years, thence Decatur Co, IN, where afp

McINTOSH (continued)
  1837; PAR, less than 6 months svc. F-R6741.5 R1687
Thomas, b Fairfax Co, VA; esf 1776 Dumfries, Prince William Co, VA, in 1st VA Cavalry Regiment; mvd after RW to Oldham Co, KY; gtd BLW8133; PN 1836 Washington, DC; res KY 1837; QLF states a RW pensioner, Thomas McINTOSH, listed in 1840 census of Trimble Co, KY ae 83 res with James JOHNSON. F-S30573 R1687
Thomas, b 12/4/1754 Culpeper Co, VA, on Rappahannock River; mvd to Caswell Co, NC where esf 1777; mvd c1802 to Robertson Co, TN, for c12 years, thence Stewart Co, TN, where PN 1832 ae 78; bro of Charles & Nimrod who res Robertson Co, TN, 1833. F-S1563 R1687
William, BLW12380 issued 5/5/1790. F-BLW12380 R1687
William, esf in VA regiment; wounded 3/15/1781 at Battle of Guilford Courthouse; gtd disability PN 1790 when res Richmond, VA; decd when family mbnn afp, but their claim not approved by supreme court; no official papers in file. F-None R1687
William, b Prince William Co, VA, where esf Dumfries, VA; PN ae 62 Dumfries, VA; res 1832 Anderson District, SC; res 1839 Noxubee Co, MS, with d Nancy LIDDELL, he having lately mvd there from SC; AFF then by James LIDDELL (NKG) Noxubee Co, MS; sol dd 1846 there; w dd before him; sol survived by d Elizabeth HAMMILL (a wid res Fredericksburg, VA 1850) & d Nancy LIDDELL; James McINTOSH (NKG) AFF Prince William Co, VA, 1850 he b & reared there; Davie PERRY AFF Fredericksburg, VA then his w near relative/o sol; sol gds Stephen HAMMILL liv 1854. F-S47469 R1687
McJUTTY, Samuel, see McQUIETY, Samuel. F-R6812 R1688
McKAMEY, John, esf 1781 Pendleton Co, SC; dd 1/1/1834 ae 70; md 11/5/1795 Mary at home of William McKAMEY, Augusta Co, VA; wid afp ae 78 Roane Co, TN, 1854; PAR, insufficient proof of svc; ch births: Anna 11/23/1797, Ischela 6/21/99, Margret 1801, Malinda 1/24/03, Sarah 3/24/04, Sinthy 2/1/07, John 12/3/09, William 4/24/12/, Robert Harvey 12/15/15 Pamela Jane 3/15/18, Mary/Polly Minerva 2/1/20, & Nancy Eleanor 1/22/24; AFF 1852 Roane Co, TN by Eleanor C MARTIN aec 66 she present at sol marriage. F-R6743 R1688
McKAMY, James, b 1/19/1753 Augusta Co, VA; esf 1776 Rockbridge Co, VA, where res; PN 1832 Blount Co, TN; last PN payment in file 1837; s mbnn 1838; surname also spelled McKARNY; QLF states sol md Agnes TELFORD. F-S2811 R1688
McKANNON, Christopher, see McCANNON, Christopher. F-None R1688
McKAY, Robert, esf 1779 Shenandoah Co, VA, where b 2/12/1760; mvd c1810 to IN where PN 1833 Jefferson Co. F-S16956 R1688
William, b 7/23/1759 Scotland; to NC c1772-73 with parents; esf 1776 Bladen Co, NC, where res, in 6th NC Regiment; esf 1780 Rowan Co, NC, where res; mvd to Iredell Co, NC, then to Richmond Co, NC, then to Chesterfield Co, SC, then to Ohio Co, VA, (area later Tyler Co); PN 1833 Tyler Co, VA; dd 10/6/36; md 2/1787 Nancy McKAY/MacKAY; wid PN ae 69 Ty-

McKAY (continued)
: ler Co, VA; wid stated when she mvd to VA in 1785 she had 4 ch including Nell (b 4/19/1788) & Isabella; wid bro Hugh (res 1819 Richmond Co, NC, md d of Hugh McLEAN & they had ch John, Nancy, Daniel, Hugh, Catherine, George, & Lochland) AFF his f dd 4/4/1802, m dd 1/1813; wid sis Isabella dd GA 8/24/1811 leaving ch Nancy, Peggy, John, Neily, Daniel, & 1 mbnn & those ch res 1816 with f mbnn in Jones Co GA on Ocamulgee River near Ft Hawkins; wid bro John dd 11/11/1795 Goochland Co, VA; wid sis Catherine dd unmd 8/15/1814; wid bro Adam res Robeson Co, NC, md 8/31/1815 Catherine (d/o Manassah HENDERSON) & in 1819 they had a s & had lost a d; wid sis Margaret md 2/9/1809 John (s/o Alexander GORDON) & they had ch Alexander, Isabella, Effey, William & 1 d mbnn, Margaret's h John GORDON having dd 5/1/1818, or 5/2/1818; wid bro William, a merchant, res 1816 in Wilmington, NC, md c1818 Anny D BERRY; wid bro Alexander, a bachelor 1819; QLF 1917 from desc Mrs E K PERKINS of Doss NC; QLF 19-- from great gdd N Elena (Mrs W H) COLLINGE of Muses Bottom, Jackson Co, WV, states sol dd Tyler Co, WV; QLF 1917 from desc Emma P PERKINS of Ravenswood, WV; QLF 1934 from great gds A W McKAY, Middleport, OH, states sol & w both b Scotland. F-W7429 R1688

McKEE, James, b 3/14/1752 PA; mvd 1774 with bro mbnn to Rockbridge Co, VA, settling on Kerr's Creek; esf there 1776 as sub for bro William; dd there 8/4/1832; wid Nancy dd there 2/5/35 leaving s John T & d Mary Jane T w/o Andrew BRATTON who afp there 1835; ch gtd PN due m; sol bro William, who also VA RW sol, res there then; QLF 1929 from desc Mrs Charles R BROCK of Denver, CO, states sol md Esther/Nannie HOUSTON, an aunt of Colonel Samuel HOUSTON of TX; QLF 1915 from Walter H DUNLAP, Washington, DC, desc of RW sol James Logan McKEE, whose wid Nancy Scott McKEE gtd PN; QLF 1927 from desc W A BRATTON, Madison, WV. F-S16854 R1688

: Samuel, not RW sol but veteran of Indian Wars 1792-1794; esf 1792 VA in 1st Sublegion/o US Riflemen against indians; PN 1822 Detroit, MI, for disability from 2 battle wounds; Old War Inv File #2520 R1688

: Samuel, b 7/3/1764 Augusta Co, VA; esf 1780 Rockbridge Co, VA, where res; mvd 1782 to Mercer Co, KY, where esf in Gen George Rogers CLARK's expedition against indians; res Lincoln Co, KY, to 1795, then to Clark Co, KY, for c10 years, thence Montgomery Co, KY where PN 1837 when s mbnn living; QLF 1915 says sol s of James & Lydia (TODD) McKEE, further a RW sol James COCKRAN md (1) Mary McATTENCE, & he buried Fleming Co, KY; QLF 1923 from desc Mrs M C BURWAUGH, Chicago, IL, says sol md Betsy LOWRY & dd 1842 Montgomery Co, KY. F-S30574 R1688

McKELVY, William, b 1744 Ireland; brought as small ch to Charleston, SC, where res when esf 1777; mvd after RW to one/o "northern states" for a few years, then to VA for several years, thence Smith Co, TN, thence KY, thence Giles Co, TN

McKELVY (continued)
thence Rutherford Co, TN, where PN 1832; dd there 8/11/34; md 1/1789 or 2/1789 Mary MASON, Cumberland Co, VA; wid PN ae 75 Gibson Co, TN, 1848; ch births: Elizabeth 2/5/1791, John 8/17/93, William 1/20/96, Katharine 8/15/99, Willis W 2/27/1801, Mary 8/12/03, James 2/26/05, & Hugh 11/4/08; s Hugh AFF 1848 Gibson Co, TN, he had family bible; s John War of 1812 svc at Battle of New Orleans; sol wid res 1852 Gibson Co, TN; QLF 1928 from great gdd Mrs Louis W CAMPBELL, Pelham, NY. F-W3 R1689

McKEMY, Samuel, esf 1780 Rockbridge Co, VA, where b 1759; PN 1833 Green Co, TN, where dd 8/23/34; md 9/12/1783 Sarah DIXON who dd 12/9/41; ch births: Rebecka 12/19/1783, Robert 1/4/87, Anna 3/9/89, Elender 3/22/91, Alexander 7/3/93, Jinny 4/22/96, Samuel 10/9/99, Jane 7/5/1806, John 7/4/09, Rebeckah 7/19/11, Samuel 3/24/14, Poley 12/17/19, & Hugh w/29/24; s Robert md 10/1/1805 Elizabeth PORTER; s Alexander md 3/26/1818 Malinda BORDEN; s Samuel md 12/5/1825 Polly GABELL; s Robert McKEMY md (2) 3/21/1839 Nancy GRAGG; s Robert afb 1844 Green Co, TN for self & surv siblings: Alexander, Rebecca COOK, Elender OTTINGER, & Jane BORDEN, & they gtd PN due m. F-W126 R1689

McKENNAN, William, son of Presbyterian minister, esf DE at beginning of RW; md 1785 Elizabeth, Redlion Hundred, Newcastle Co, DE, who b there 4/18/1761 d/o John & Dorothea (McKEAN) THOMPSON who md 10/17/1758 Philadelphia, PA; sol & w mvd after marriage to farm owned by her f in Newcastle Co, DE, thence 1797 after her f dd to Brooke Co, VA, then to Washington Co, PA, where sol dd 1/14/1810, leaving w Elizabth & 6 ch mbnn; sol issued BLW1471 5/30/1789; wid PN 1838 when res with s Th M T in borough of Washington, Washington Co, PA; wid dd 4/16/39. F-W3104 R1689

McKENNEY, Charles, b Buckingham Co, VA; esf 1776 Bedford Co, VA, where res; mvd 2-3 years after RW to Wilkes Co, GA, thence Jackson Co, GA, where PN 1822 ae 79 when res there 30 years; res 1833 Hurricane Shoal, that Co; dd 2/27/34; QLF says sol known as Charles Sr, was survived by w Elizabeth & ch Rachel WEBB, Sarah HAMPTON, Milly JOHNSON, Betsy HEARN, Wilson, & Samuel. F-S16477 R1689

John, b 12/15/1759 Amelia Co, VA; esf 1777 Burke Co, GA, res there; mvd with f to Richmond Co (area later Columbia Co), GA, where esf 1778; mvd 1781 to Wilkes Co, GA (area later Lincoln Co), where esf against Cherokee indians; PN 1832 as John Sr, Lincoln Co, GA; dd 8/25/37. F-S31848 R1689

Tully, see McKINNEY, Tully. F-R6752 R1689

McKENT, James, see McCANT, James. F-W1909 R1689

McKENZIE, Alexander, BLW12358 issued 11/26/1792. F-BLW12358 R1690

Alexander, see McKINZIE, Alexander. F-W8439 R1690

John, b 9/17/1757 Albemarle Co, VA; esf 1776 Halifax Co, VA, where res; esf 1778 in SC regiment; esf later in NC regiment; PN 1833 Carroll Co, TN, where dd 11/5/42; md 12/20/

McKENZIE (continued)
1792 Martha/Patsey BONNER, Washington Co, GA, who b 1/8/1775; wid PN 1843 Carroll Co, TN, when had s Jeremiah (b 11/6/1793) & s Alexander A ae 44; wid liv 1851; QLF 1910 from desc Mrs John FITE of Jackson, TN; QLF 1919 from desc Miss Louise SCATES, Memphis, TN. F-W1049 R1690

McKEY, Bennett, esf 1777 Westmoreland Co, VA, in 15th VA Regiment; PN there 1818; res there 1820 ae 64 when family ch ae 12 & ch ae 10 mbnn. F-S38197 R1690

McKIE, Daniel, esf 1779 Luneburg Co, VA, where b 5/6/1758; PN 1832 Maury Co, TN, as Daniel Sr; dd 11/16/1839 Lafayette Co, MS; md 3/18/1794 Fanny HERNDON, Newberry Dist, SC, who b 12/2/1876; wid afp 1848 Marshall Co, MS; PAR, proof of marriage; gtd BLW49264 Lafayette Co, MS, 1855; ch births: Elizabeth 1/24/1795 (dd ae 9 months), Polly Wiley 11/10/96 (dd 9/28/1848), Herndon 12/4/98 (dd 6/24/1832), Daniel Pines/Piner 9/21/1800 (dd 1846), Green 9/2/02, twins Frances Susannah & Sarah Ann 9/4/05, Michael Jefferson 8/20/07 James M 11/24/09, Benjamin F 10/1/11 (dd 9/9/1852), Stephen R 9/6/13, Washington 10/5/15 (dd ae 8 weeks), & William 5/31/20 (dd ae 2 weeks); wid dd 9/5/1855; ch marriages: Frances Susanah 10/6/1822 to Andrew MATHURST, Daniel Pines to Nancy MILLS, Sarah Ann 12/16/1823 to Thomas DAVIS, James M 11/11/1842 to Juliett FONDREN & Stephen R 1/9/1844 to Martha A ROGERS; QLF 1902 from desc Irene McKIE, Holly Springs, MS, d/o G W McKIE who s/o sol Daniel McKIE of SC, also querier maternal great great gdd of RW sol Adam ALEXANDER of NC who signer of Mecklenburg Declaration of Independence; QLF 1932 from great great gdd Louise E MAGRUDER, Annapolis, MD, d/o Reverend James Mitchell MAGRUDER who md 1/17/1894 Margaret McKie MOSBY, d of Lt William John MOSBY of CSA who md Mariah Louisa McKIE, d of sol s Michael Jefferson McKIE, further siblings of querier were James Mosby MAGRUDER & William Howard MAGRUDER, further Michael Jefferson McKIE md 3/20/1828 Margaret WILLIAMS (b12/20/1811), dd 8/29/1878 & w dd after him, their ch: (1) Nancy Edmondson b 12/28/1828, md 12/5/1848 E M FLY, (2) Frances Herndon b 9/3/1832, md 9/28/1851 Columbus READ, (3) John William b 1/14/1834, md 11/10/1855 Sarah M MOORE, he sol from MS in CSA, wounded Battle of Fredericksburg, dd 5/24/1863, (4) Martha Ann King b3/7/1836, dd 4/3/1867, md 2/10/1857 James R BARNETT, (5) Mary Elizabeth b & dd 1838, (6) Margaret Eugenia b 9/2/18--, dd 5/30/1853, her twin (7) Sarah Caroline dd unmd 1928, (8) Maria Louise b 12/19/1843, dd 9/1918, md 11/19/1868 John MOSBY, their ch: Margaret McKIE & William John, (9) Nathan Whitehead b 7/4/1849, dd 8/19/1878, (10) Michael Jefferson b 1851, dd 1852, (11) Zoradia R b 8/28/1852, dd 9/1/1878, (12) James Denes b 5/4/1856, & (13) Joe Davis b 11/30/1858). F-R6750 R1690

McKINNEY, Charles, esf 1780 where b 3/9/1763; esf 1781 sub for bro Thomas; res there after RW except for 3 years in NC, thence 1826 Limestone Co, AL, where PN 1833; QLF says sol

MCKINNEY (continued)
   mvd to AL to be near his children. F-S31852 R1691
David, esf 1780 Augusta Co, VA where res; dd 5/7/1822 Orange
   Co, IN, or Washington Co, IN; md 9/25/1785 Margaret WALL-
   ACE; wid afp ae 85 Washington Co, IN, 1851; PAR, insuffi-
   cient proof of svc & marriage; children mbnn; sol cousin
   res Fulton Co , IL, 1851 ae 75. F-R6766 R1691
Dennis/Denis, esf 1777-78 Staunton, VA; PN ae 60 Lincoln Co,
   KY, 1818; res there 1820 when said he never md. F-S36110
   R1691
John, b 4/2/1757 Frederick Co, VA; mvd ae 7-8 with f to Cam-
   den District, SC where esf 1774, 1775, 1776, 1777, 1778, &
   1779; mvd 1781 to Hanging Fork of Deck's River, Lincoln Co
   KY Territory where esf 1782 in Gen George Rogers Clark's
   troops; mvd 1785 to Jessamine Co, KY; PN 1833 Versailles,
   Woodford Co, KY, when res there since 1819; dd 8/24/1837;
   md 1781 Hannah/Anna EVINS (MB 8/7/1781 signed by Nathaniel
   EVINS) Rockbridge Co, VA; wid PN ae 77 Versailles, KY 1838
   dd 12/16/1845; children mbnn; John McKINNEY (NKG) co clerk
   of Woodford Co, KY 1833; QLF 1939 from Mrs William J JOHN-
   SON of Campobello, SC, states a John McKINNEY (bc 1735 VA)
   md Elizabeth McDOWELL, & their d Rebecca (b 6/15/1760) was
   great great gdm of querier, their d Jane b 9/11/1779 Ches-
   ter Co (area then Craven Co), SC, & they mvd to Jessamine
   Co, KY, before 1802, where John dd c1811, their 2 sons-in-
   law Ray MOSS & John G BROWN; QLF 1902 from desc C L JESTER
   Corsicana, TX; QLF 19-- from desc Mrs Katie B COOKE, Wash-
   ington, DC, niece of Mrs Mary H LETCHER. F-W558 R1691
John, BLW12385 issued 3/26/1792. F-BLW12385 R1691
John, esf Augusta Co, VA; gtd disability PN by VA 1786 & by
   US 1817 for disability from wound recd at Battle of Point
   Pleasant 1774; dd 9/27/1825 Bourbon Co, KY; md 9/13/1785
   Polley TRIMBLE, Augusta Co, VA; wid afp 1841 Bourbon Co,
   KY, ae 81; PAR, sol svc before commencement of RW; James
   WALLACE AFF ae 70 Fayette Co, KY where res, 1841 he cousin
   to sol, their m's being sis's, also he & sol mvd 1785 to
   KY; QLF states Mary/Polly TRIMBLE sol's 2nd w; QLF states
   sol 1st w Elizabeth COLEMAN; QLF 1832 from desc Mrs S H
   WELCH of Lansing, MI, states sol had bro David; QLF 1925
   from desc Isabel Routh (Mrs Lee) BOYER, Deadwood, SD, says
   sol dd near Clintonville, KY. F-R6768 R1691
Nevin, esf VA; dd 2/13/1809 Halifax Co, VA; md 12/20/1785
   Sarah WADE, Prince Edward Co, VA; wid PN ae 84 Halifax Co,
   VA, 1844; John S PLEASANTS AFF there then ae 85 he served
   with sol in RW; AFF there then by RW pensioner George ES-
   TES he served with sol in RW; AFF then by James CASADAY ae
   85, Charlotte Co, VA, he served with sol in RW. F-W7431
   R1691
Robertson/Robert, esf Westmoreland Co, VA in VA state artil-
   lery; dd c1820; md 1791 Mary SUTHENFIELD (MB 10/6/1791 be-
   tween Robinson McKINNEY & Mary SUTHENFIELD), Campbell Co,
   VA; wid b 5/4/1772; md (2) c1830 Charles BETTISWORTH, who

MCKINNEY (continued)
    dd 6/12/1843; wid afp 1846 Adair Co, KY, & PAR. F-R873 R1691
  Thomas, esf 1777 VA; PN ae 58 Jefferson Co, KY, 1818; res there 1823 when had w mbnn ae 46 & ch: William ae 16, Lucinda ae 13, Sarah Ann ae 7, & 1 ch mbnn; dd 12/10/1823. F-S36088 R1691
  Tully, esf Berkeley Co, VA; dd 8/7/1807; LWT dated 7/22/1807 Jefferson Co, VA, probated there 9/9/1807, listed w Polly, & ch: Francis, Nancy, Polly, Caty, & Jenny, witnessed by James HITE, Edward VIOLETT, & James COYLE; T A MOORE then county clerk; md 1785 Mary THOMAS (ML 10/21/1786), Berkeley Co, VA; wid dd 1/18/1852; surv ch who afp 1856 Jefferson Co, VA: Francis aec 70, Mary aec 66, Catherine CATRO aec 64, & Jane SULLIVAN aec 56; AFF then by Edward V COYLE ae 56 of Berkeley Co, VA, William HURST ae 63 of Jefferson Co, VA, James G COYLE (s/o James who halfbro/o sol & younger than sol), Thomas HITE (s of decd James), Braxton DAVENPORT aec 65, Charles CATRO (h/o sol d Catherine), Samuel SULLIVAN (h/o sol d Jane) & Fannie DAWES (d/o sol halfbro James COYLE; children PAR; surname also spelled McKENNY & McKENNEY. F-R6752 R1691
  William, esf 1776 Charlotte Co, VA, where res; went to GA & esf with GA troops; PN ae 74 Adair Co, KY, 1832; QLF says sol dd KY. F-S16470 R1691
  William, b 1764 Sussex Co, VA, s/o Daniel; esf 1782 Franklin Co, NC, where res, in 10th NC Regiment; mvd after RW to York District, SC, then to Sandyland, Rutherford Co, NC, where PN 1832; gtd BLW26891 there 1855; dd 10/31/57; gds David W McKINNEY res 1859 Yanceyville, NC. F-S9017 R1691
McKINNON, Lathlin, b Scotland; came ae 13 to PA 1771 where esf 1776 in 7th or 8th PA Regiment; settled after RW in Sussex Co, VA, where afp 1832 ae 74; PAR. F-R6753 R1691
McKINNY, Michael, b 1760 MD; mvd 1775 to western VA (area later Harrison Co) where esf 1777 as indian spy; afp rejected for fraud, details not given. F-R6767 R1691
McKINSEY, Alexander, see McKINZIE, Alexander. F-W8439 R1691
  Moses, esf 1778 Frederick, MD, as drummer; BLW11514 issued 4/8/1796; PN 1818 ae 58 Allegany Co, MD; res there 1820 when had w aec 56, s ae 18, d ae 16, & 2 gds ae 7; dd 3/3/1824; md 12/1784 Sarah McKENZIE, Hampshire Co, VA; wid PN ae 76 Allegany Co, MD 1841; AFF then there by Lucy McVICKER ae 59 she present when sol & w md by Catholic priest; AFF 1842 Knox Co, OH, by John DURBIN he witnessed sol wedding at res of Jacob SLAGLE, Hampshire Co, VA; wid res ae 79 Cresaptown, MD, 1844; she & h both illiterate; wid decd in 1851; QLF 1920 from desc Mrs Ella Porter GLOVER, Kahoka MO, whose great gdm d of sol; QLF states Moses, Joshua, & Jesse McKENZIE all esf together Frederick Co, MD, in 7th MD Regiment, & Jesse md Catherine JONES. F-W4288 R1691
McKINZIE, Alexander, esf Albemarle Co, VA, early in RW; afp KY 1820-21 but dd 9/17/1821 before afp acted upon; md 3/13/

MCKINZIE (continued)
- 1786 Tabitha B HILL (MB 3/29/1786 per Co clerk), Albemarle Co, VA; wid PN ae 70 Lincoln Co, KY 1840; AFF then by Jesse LEWIS ae 77 Albemarle Co, VA, he esf with sol & sol & w had 5-6 ch; wid res 1843 Lincoln Co, KY when children mbnn F-W8439 R1692
- Isaac, esf 1777 Montgomery Co, VA; PN ae 70 Morgan Co, KY, 1833. F-S30571 R1692

McKISSICK, Rachel former widow of John MORRIS. (F-R6772)

McKITTRICK, John Sr, esf 1777 Augusta Co, VA where b; mvd 1793 to Washington Co, KY, where PN 1832 ae 72; AFF then Mercer Co, KY, by John MAGILL Sr & Richard HOLMAN they served in RW with sol; sol dd 2/1/39; s Thomas afp for arrears due f 1853; surname also spelled McKITRICK; QLF says sol b 7/3/17--, dd & buried at Mackville, KY; QLF 1926 from desc Mrs Samuel PENDLETON, Independence, MO. F-S13647 R1692

McKIZICK, Ann, former widow of John BURNS. (F-R6770)

McKNIGHT, Benjamin, esf 1776 Shepherdstown, VA in 7th VA Regiment; PN ae 62 Frederick Co, VA; res 1820 Fauquier Co, VA, ae 64 when had no family & res at home of bro mbnn recently decd; occupation laborer. F-S38176 R1692
- Eli, b 10/12/1760 DE; mvd aec 2 with f to Loudoun Co, VA, where esf 1780; PN there 1832; AFF then there by Rufus UPDIKE ae 79 he served in RW with sol. F-S2710 R1692
- Michael, BLW12401 issued 3/1/1793. F-BLW12401 R1692
- Michael, esf 1776 Moorefield, VA; PN ae 71 Hardy Co, VA 1820 occupation farmer when had no family whatsoever. F-S38200 R1692

McKOWN, James, b 9/2/1758; esf 1776 Berkeley Co, VA where res; esf 1781 Hampshire Co, VA; res after RW in PA, VA & OH; PN 1833 Knox Co, OH, res Milford Township; dd 1/9/1845 Jackson Co, VA; md c1782 Phebe CASTO, Winchester, VA; wid PN ae 95 Jackson Co, VA, 1850, when her sis Sarah WRIGHT AFF there; s Gilbert McKOWN AFF there then; wid res there 1852 when Elias McKOWN (NKG) Co JP; wid dd 1/2/55; ch included Sarah, Isaac, Mary/Polly & Gilbert (b 1787 Greene Co, PA), QFL 1929 from desc Mrs Ora Gerhart BEATTY, Centerburg, OH. F-W7430 R1692

McKOY, James, b 4/10/1760 St Marys Co, MD; mvd ae 8 with f to Westmoreland Co, VA; where esf 1778; PN there 1833; AFF by Benedict LAMKIN there then he esf with sol; sol m & bro's unable to read. F-S5750 R1692

McLAIN, Henry, b 5/10/1750 Lancaster Co, PA; esf Amherst Co, VA, where res; f living during RW; PN 1832 Nelson Co (area previously Amherst Co), VA; bro James RW sol who also esf Amherst Co, VA; QLF 1900 from great gdd Olive McClain OSTIEN, St Paul, NE, says sol dd 1839-41; QLF 1924 from desc Mrs Grace McClain ROPER of Chicago, IL; QLF from desc Mrs Bessie M DENNIS, Deer Lodge, MT, says sol dd 1841 & md Esther HENDERSON. F-S7196 R1693
- John, esf 1778 Greenbrier Co, VA, where res; PN 1832 Rockbridge Co VA, ae not given; AFF then there by RW sol John

McLAIN (continued)
  DAVIDSON ae 75 sol served in RW with DAVIDSON's bro; William MOORE, Rockbridge Co, VA JP, AFF then ae 84 he served with sol in RW; sol dd 12/23/34. F-5744 R1693
Laughlin, esf VA; s & heir-at-law John gtd BLW12346 issued 1789; s John liv 1823; QLF 1914 from desc Mrs Allen T SNODDY of Stratford, OK; QLF states a Laughlan McLEAN, s/o Allen or Neal McLEAN who were RW sol's, md Flora McLEAN & they came to CT, then to Robeson Co, NC. F-BLW12346 R1693
Thomas, b 1759 Fauquier Co, VA; esf 1778 Pittsylvania Co, VA where res; mvd c1782 to GA, where PN 1832 Newton Co. F-S31851 R1693
McLANAHAN, Thomas, see McCLANAHAN, Thomas. F-W1052 R1693
McLANE, Allen, captain in Lee's Legion; BLW1474 issued 7/25/1787; records lost in 1800 Washington, DC fire. F-BLW1474 R1693
Laughlin, see McLAIN, Laughlin. F-BLW12346 R1693
McLARDY, Alexander, esf 1776 in 1st VA Regiment; PN 1818 Logan Co, VA, ae not given. F-S36092 R1693
McLARREN, Daniel, esf 1777 VA; esf 1818 Chesterfield Co, VA, occupation farmer when w ae 64 & s Daniel ae 28; afp there 1832 ae 70; PAR both times; LWT dated 2/20/1827, probated there 6/11/1832, lists w Susana, d Jane w of Benjamin KENT (+ their ch Susana & John), s Daniel Jr, gdd Jane Harrison McLARREN, gdd Susana KENT, gds John KENT, & gdc --- KENT; LWT witnessed by Robert BELDEN, Henry McLARREN, Judson ANDREWS, & John DYSON; co clerk then Parker POINDEXTER; co clerk/o court then Silas CHEATHAM; sol dd leaving ch: Harrison, Jane/Jency KENT, & Daniel Jr, per co clerk; wid dd 9/28/32; d Jane KENT then decd, having left d Susana (dd without issue) & d Julian, who md her own uncle Daniel McLARREN Jr (both liv 1861); sol s Harrison res, if alive, in GA, but not heard of in many years; sol s Daniel Jr afp 1860 Petersburg, VA when executor/o f's LWT. F-R6776 R1693
McLAUGHLIN, Jacob, esf Mecklenburg Co, NC, with bro Stephen; f mvd family to Rogers Fort, GA, where sol esf in GA state legion; mvd c1801 with w to Russell Co, VA, where afp 1818 & PAR; dd there 1/22/31; md Mary on Catawba River, SC, she having been b there; wid afp 1846 Russell Co, VA, when sol bro John AFF ae 87 Tazewell Co, VA, that sol eldest of parents' ch, & he & sol both illiterate, & that he also RW sol, & that he mvd c1816 to Tazewell Co, VA; AFF 1846 Russell Co, VA, by Johnson HOWARD ae 63 that sol s Neeley bc 1802 there & presently neighbor to deponent & that sol eldest ch Davis L now ae 30; sol wid PAR. F-R6778 R1693
John, b 1/26/1757; esf 1778-79 Mecklenburg Co, NC; mvd after svc to Cumberland Co, NC, for 3-4 years, then to Randolph Co, NC, for several years, then to Patrick Co, VA, then to Tazewell Co, VA, where PN 1832; AFF then there by John PRUIT who served with sol in RW; dd there 2/17/1848; md c 4/1/1785 Judith/Judy LEATHERS in SC; wid PN ae 95 Tazewell Co, VA, 1858; 3rd ch Jacob AFF there then ae 67 that f & m

McLAUGHLIN (continued)
   had 13 ch (eldest, if liv would now be ae 83) & that m now res with her children; wid gtd BLW84064 there then; AFF by George STEELE ae 76 there then, & by John BROWN ae 77. F-7436 R1693
John, esf 1775 Bedford Co, VA, in 5th VA Regiment; PN ae 64 Caldwell Co, KY, 1819; res there 1820, occupation farmer, when family w aec 64 & some young gdc; mvd to MO in early 1828 where dd 7/17/1828. F-S34987 R1693
John, see McGLOUGHLIN, John. F-W18494 R1693
Stephen, b 9/3/1759 on head of Eddisto River; mvd as infant with f to Mecklenburg Co, NC, where esf 1777 with eldest bro Jacob who dd in VA; later sol esf GA; res after RW NC, thence VA, thence Jefferson Co, TN where PN 1833; dd 3/26/46; md 10/11/1792 Nancy TAIT, Patrick Co, VA; ch births: Willis 5/9/1794, John 8/16/96, Appy 3/11/98, Ephraim 3/4/1800, Mary 1/30/02, Archibald 3/24/05, Nancy 4/13/07, Samuel 3/26/09, Stephen 1/22/11, Jacob 2/10/13, Alfred 3/6/15, & Wilson 4/25/17; wid PN ae 71 Jefferson Co, TN, 1846; res 1848 Green Co, TN. F-W963 R1693
William, b 12/19/1757 Bedford Co, VA, where esf 1775-76 in 5th VA Regiment; res after RW Botetourt Co, VA, for 6-7 years, thence Bedford Co, VA, for 4-5 years, then to Botetourt Co, VA, for several years, then to Wythe Co, VA, for 2 years, then to Rockbridge Co, VA, where PN 1832; last PN payment in file 1840. F-S18121 R1693
McLAURINE, James, esf 1777 Cumberland Co, VA, in 7th VA Regiment; afp there 1843 ae 84; PAR, less than 6 months svc; QLF 1908 from great gdd (on m's side) Mrs N E BOGGESS, Waco, TX, says sol s of Episcopalian minister who buried beneath chancel in old Peterville Church, also querier desc of RW sol Samuel WOODFIN of Powhatan Co, VA. F-R6780 R1694
William, esf 1780 Powhatan Co, VA; PN there 1843 ae 81 when bro James AFF there. F-S9015 R1694
McLOUGHLIN, Hugh, esf 1777 Augusta Co, VA; dd 6/5/1798 Bath Co VA; md 8/18/1789 Agnes/Ann/Nanny, d of David GURN/GWINN, Pendleton Co, VA; wid b 8/18/1770; md (2) 1/1810 James WILEY on plantation of her f, where she b; 2h dd 7/14/1838; sol d Jane KIRKPATRICK gtd BLW by VA; wid PN 1845 Bath Co VA; QLF states several of sol ch mvd to OH. F-W6537 R1694
McLURE, Abdiel, esf 1776 Cumberland Co, PA; res 1818 Wheeling, WV, where dd 1828; md 1/3/1771 Mary, Shippensburg, PA; wid PN ae 90 Wheeling, WV, 1836; dd 4/25/37 or 4/27/37; had 8 ch: Andrew bc 1771, Ann, Mary dd before 1836, John ae 56 in 1836 res Wheeling, WV, Keziah, Jane, James, & Robert b 7/18/1790; QLF 1909 from great great gds A M LAZIER of Jamestown, NY; QLF states sol dd 6/11/1828; QLF states sol b 6/8/1751 & dd 6/11/1828. F-W7434 R1695
McMAHAN, Andrew, esf 1776 King & Queen Co, VA; esf 1779 Alexandria, VA; PN aec 58 Wilson Co, TN, 1818 when res with 2 unmd d's on land of s William (ae 29); d Polly ae 22-23 in 1820; sol bro mbnn; QLF 1927 from great gdd Miss Nan WICK-

McMAHAN (continued)
ERSHAM, Tacoma, WA, states RW sol Andrew W McMAHAN md 2/3/ 1786 Mary DILLON, Halifax Co, VA, & their ch: Thomas b2/2/ 1787, Elizabeth, William, Lucy, Henry, Polly, & Nancy, his w dd 1818, he md (2) 1820 Oney JOHNSON, Wilson Co, TN, his surname before RW was McHANEY, & he dd 1827 TN ae 66 (querier has 140- year-old family bible to prove above data). F-S38931 R1695
John, esf 1777 Augusta Co, VA, where b 1755; mvd to Sevier Co, TN, for several years, then to McMinn Co, TN, where PN 1833 when res there 12 years. F-S2808 R1695
John, esf 1775 Prince Edward Co, VA where b; PN 1832 Laurens District, SC; dd 10/16/35. F-S18110 R1695
Joseph, b 5/1761; esf 1777 near Pittsburgh, PA, as fifer and drummer in VA Regiment; PN 1828 Adams Co, OH; mvd to Scioto Co, OH, thence 1837 Whiteside Co, IL; dd 4/1838 Cincinnati, OH, in steamboat explosion; md 3/1792 Mary, Pittsburgh, PA; wid PN ae 79 Albany, IL; gtd BLW39530 there in 1855 ae 88; ch births: John (eldest) 4/22/1793, Elizabeth 12/30/95, James 1/15/98, Joseph 5/22/1802 (dd 12/16/1814) Robert 8/5/04, Sarah 5/1/07 (dd 4/12/1835), Abner 6/2/09 (dd 2/20/1832), May 8/22/11 (dd 9/4/1823), Phebe 2/11/14 (md Jonpathan DAVIS who AFF 1853 Whiteside, IL), Gregory/ Gregg 5/2/16 (part owner of store in Albany, IL, also captain of steamboat, dd 12/26/1852 St Louis, MO, at home of bro-in-law Mr ANDERSON), & Oliver 8/4/18; surname spelled also McMAHON; QLF says sol md Mary SCHRYHAUSER; QLF 1907 from gds C L McMAHAN, Chicago, IL; QLF 1923 from desc Miss Alice M BOOTH of Clinton, IA. F-W23941 R1695
Robert, esf 1780 Augusta Co, VA; dd Madison Co, IL, 1823; md 1795 Nancy KESTER, St Clair Co, IL; wid afp ae 80 Madison Co, IL, & PAR; liv 1860. F-R16357 R1695
William, esf 1789 in Washington Co, VA, militia, where res, per AFF by former neighbor & company commander Alexander BARNETT; gtd license to preach as Methodist minister 1797 Rowan Co, NC; dd ae 55 Batavia Township, Clermont Co, OH 1814; md 3/29/1790 Rebecca FOSTER (MB 9/23/1790 as William McMAHON), Rowan Co, NC; wid b 1/8/1769 there; afp 1855 Clermont Co, OH & PAR, insufficient proof of svc; AFF then there by Susanna DIAL, d of sol sis. F-R6786 R1695
McMAHON, Andrew, BLW12340 issued 2/15/1799. F-BLW12340 R1695
Peter, esf 1776 Loudon Co, VA; PN ae 65 Allegany Co, MD; res there 1820 ae 67 occupation weaver, when had w ae 50-60, s William, s Thomas, & gdc ae 6-7 liv with him; res Cumberland, MD, 1834. F-34981 R1695
McMANNERS, William, esf 1779 Albemarle Co, VA, with bro Charles; sol badly wounded 1780 & had to leave svc; mvd to KY after RW, where afp ae 95 Garrard Co 1853, when blind. F-R6789 R1695
McMANNES, Charles, b 1762 York Co, PA; sol & family driven by indians 9/1776 from their home on frontier settlement of western PA, & took shelter at Ligonier Garrison, Westmore-

McMANNES (continued)
  land Co, PA; esf there 1780 with bro James in VA regiment; PN 1832 Brown Co, OH, res Jackson Township; bro James res there then; QLF states sol md Ellen, mvd c1815 to Brown Co OH, & dd near Winchester, OH, & their s Joseph b 1796 PA; QLF states sol buried Cherry Fork, OH. F-S2807 R1696
McMANNIS, Charles, esf 1777 Staunton, VA, in VA regiment when res Albemarle Co, VA; PN ae 52+ Bullitt Co, KY, 1819; res there 1820, occupation farmer, when family w aec 45 mbnn & ch: Thomas aec 14, Nancy aec 16, Polly aec 13, William aec 10, Felix ae 8-9, Margaret aec 5, Sally aec 3, & Fielding aec 1.5; surname also spelled McMANUS. F-S36107 R1696
  John, b 1760 Chester Co, PA; esf 1778 Wheeling, VA, in Colonel George Rogers CLARK's regiment; res after RW KY, OH, & IN; PN 1832 Pike Co, IN; dd 12/31/42 Boone Co, IN, leaving 4 ch including John (res 1843 Royalton that Co). F-S17574 R1696
McMASTERS, Michael, b Ireland; esf 1777 in 16th VA Regiment; PN ae 78 Spencer Co, KY, 1828. F-S36093 R1696
McMEANS, James, esf 1779-80 Falls of the Ohio in VA regiment; esf KY Territory when res on Salt River; mvd after RW to IL, thence 1815 MO, where afp 1835 St Louis ae 70; PAR, less than 6 months svc; surname also spelled McMEINs. F-R6793 R1696
McMEEKIN, Robert, esf 1777 Fauquier Co, VA in 3rd VA Regiment; PN ae 73 Fayette Co, KY, 1834;   dd 3/18/1836; md Martha, Fauquier Co, VA, during RW; had several ch by 1792; wid PN aec 85 Fayette Co, KY, 1838 when s James AFF he b 10/15/ 1792 in KY; AFF then there by s Samuel & s James they had bro William (now decd) who b 1785; surname also spelled McMICKIN & McMECKIN. F-W8442 R1696
McMILLAN, Joseph, see McMILLIAN, Joseph. F-S18116 R1697
  Thomas, esf in VA regiment; never afp because/o too many assets; dd 6/8/1831; md 1787 Mary YOUNG, Allegheny Co, PA; wid PN ae 73 there 1839 when bro John YOUNG AFF Pittsburgh PA he res there c40 years; wid res Robison Township, Allegheny Co, PA, 1844 having res there for 50 years; surname also spelled McMILLIN. F-W2830 R1697
McMILLEN, Robert, b York Co, PA; esf 1777 Chester Co, PA, in PA regiment, when res Toughkenamon Township; mvd to York Co, PA, thence Westmoreland Co, PA, where esf 1781; mvd to Preston Co, PA, where PN 1832 when res there c45 years; dd 10/16/1834; md 8/22/1785 Mary near Fort Pitt, PA; her two bro's mbnn present at her wedding; wid PN ae 79 Preston Co VA 1845; ch including s mbnn; Sabina/Salina McMILLEN (NKG) AFF then she res in sol home when he dd; wid res Preston Co, VA 1848; surname also spelled McMILLAN; QLF states sol md Mary WHITE who bc 1766 & dd after 1845. F-W7426 R1697
McMILLIAN, Joseph, b 19/15/1763 Loudoun Co, VA, or Fauquier Co VA, s of Martha; esf 1781 Fauquier Co, VA, where res; PN 1833 Greenbrier Co, VA; later dropped from PN rolls when PN Office determined his svc less than 6 months; dd 7/9/55

McMILLIAN (continued)
Greenbrier Co, VA; md 7/22/1791 Jane HANNA(H) there; wid gtd BLW47425 there 1856 ae 70. F-S18116 R1697

McMILLION, John, b 1760 Caswell Co, NC; esf 1777 Pittsylvania Co, VA, where res; mvd 1814-15 to Stokes Co, NC, then to Franklin Co, GA, where PN 1833; AFF then there by William RAMSEY & Jeremiah McMILLIAN (NKG) they knew sol during RW; sol gtd BWL28535 there 1855; QLF states RW sol John R drew land in Cherokee Land Lottery in GA. F-S16463 R1697

Joseph, see McMILLIAN, Joseph. F-S18116 R1697

McMILLON, John, see McMILLION, John. F-S16463 R1697

McMONAGILL, Charles, esf Lee's Legion; BLW12351 & 12352 issued 9/2/1789. F-BLW12351 R1697

McMULLEN, Alexander, b 6/15/1745; esf 1777 Baltimore, MD; mvd to Berkeley Co, VA, thence Frederick Co, VA where PN 1818; res there 1820, occupation laborer, when w Hannah (ae 80 & crippled) but no children liv with them. F-S38198 R1697

McNABB, David, esf 1780 Washington Co, NC; dd there 5/3/1826; md 1778 Elizabeth TAYLOR, Augusta Co, VA, in Stone Meeting House; her younger bro Andrew res there & soon after sis's marriage mvd to NC, where settled near her; wid PN ae 79 McMinn Co, TN, 1837; her bro Andrew res Washington Co, TN, then ae 76; Dr Isaac McNABB (NKG) AFF there then; wid dd 6/20/38 near Jonesborough, TN; s mbnn 1838 res near there; James McNABB (NKG) made inquiry 1854 to PN Office about sol wid PN. F-W7438 R1698

McNATT, John, b 1/1/1763 VA; esf 1779-80 Marlboro, SC; f liv during RW; PN 1832 Roane Co, TN; dd there 1848; md 3/1816 Lucretia there; wid PN there 1853 ae 60; gtd BLW1968 1855 there; QLF states sol s of Richard MacNATT, who came from Scotland & settled in Penn's Colony. F-W2655 R1698

McNEELY, David, esf 1777 in 7th VA Regiment; PN aec 73 Pope Co IL, 1826. F-S35524 R1698

David, b 10/15/1758 Augusta Co, VA; esf ae 18 in 14th VA Regiment; PN 1832 Madison Co, AL, where dd 7/19/36; md 2/23/1789 Rebecca DICKEY, Madison Co, KY; date of marriage per Co clerk was 5/7/1789; wid dd ae 85-86 there 9/19/1852 at home of d Nancy BARNETT, leaving ch Nancy, Martha CULVER, George, & William, all res there; d Nancy b 3/4/1790, md 6/23/1808 Hugh BARNETT (b 4/24/1790, decd in 1854); HUGH BARNETT family records: James Porter BARNETT b 1/22/1818, David Price BARNETT b2/12/20, Martha BARNETT b 12/10/21, Lucy BARNETT b 12/27/23 (dd 7/17/29), Enos Henderson BARNETT b 12/30/25, Louisa BARNETT b 4/16/1829, Louisa SIMPSON dd 6/11/1853, Robert BARNETT b 1/3/1832, Sary Ann BARNETT dd 4/22/1852 ae 31, Wesley Hoes BARNETT dd 10/10/1852 James BARNETT (f of Hugh) dd 3/4/1816 ae 48, Jane BARNETT dd 10/26/1836 ae 70 & 6 months, William A COMBS dd 9/30/1846, John COOMBS dd 5/15/1847 aec 57, & John W BARNETT (s of David & Sary) dd 12/3/1849 ae 3; in 1854 Robert BARNETT (NKG) res Madison Co, TN, ae 22; John S BARNETT (NKG) res there then ae 45; James F BARNETT (NKG) res there then;

MCNEELY (continued)
  sol surname also spelled McNEELEY. F-W1051 R1698
McNEES, James, b 1750 Charlotte Co, VA; esf 1775 Lawrence Co, NC, where res; mvd to York Co, SC, thence 1806 Jackson Co, GA, where afp 1832; dd there 5/1833 before afp acted upon; PN Office determined sol svc less than 6 months & PAR; wid mbnn 1834. F-R6802 R1699
McNEIL, Jacob, b 6/1759 VA; esf 1776 as indian spy & ranger when res on VA frontier; mvd after RW to Franklin Co, VA, where PN 1832 as Jacob Sr; Gabriel McNEIL (NKG) mentioned then; QLF 1936 from great great gds Robert O McNIEL, Roanoke, VA, states sol b Pocahontas Co, VA, & was stepson of Mr IRESON. F-S5745 R1699
McNELLY, Michael, b 2/12/1759; esf 1775 Winchester, VA; PN Blount Co, TN; res there 1820, occupation tailor, when had d Mary ae 37 liv with him; res there 1831. F-S38943 R1699
McNERNAR, George, esf VA; afp aec 70 Lewis Co, VA, 1834; witness AFF sol then only ae 50-60 & was too young to have RW svc; sol PAR; surname also spelled McNEMAR & McVERNARS. F-R6807 R1699
McNICKLE, John, VA sea svc, surgeon in VA navy; had kin in NY; went there after RW, & never returned; dd intestate 1817; bro of Neale; William SCOTT, adm/o sailor's estate, gtd PN due sailor 1836; heirs included sis Mrs BARD + other sis's & nephews of NY. F-R74 R1699
McPHEETERS, John, esf 1780 Augusta Co, VA; PN ae 71 Washington Co, IN, 1833 when signed name as John McPHEETRS; QLF says sol dd 7/10/1839 & buried near Blue River, Washington Co, IN, 3.5 miles from Fredericksburg; QLF 1937 from great great gdd Mrs Louis F JAUSSAUD of Walla Walla, WA says sol buried in Palymaria Cemetery in IN; QLF says sol d Margaret dd in OR. F-S17576 R1699
McPHERSON, Barten, esf 1780 Botetourt Co, VA, where res; dd 5/5/1836; md 5/5/1788 Elizabeth, Botetourt Co, VA; wid afp ae 75 McMinn Co, TN 1844; PAR, less than 6 months svc; Daniel McPHERSON (NKG) AFF then ae 88 Roane Co, TN where res he saw sol in Botetourt Co, VA, after sol RW svc; AFF then by Maximillian PROCTOR/McPROCTOR ae 86 & w Mary ae 83 they witnessed sol marriage in Botetourt Co, VA; QLF 1939 from desc Guy H WELLS, president of Georgia State College for Women, Milledgeville, GA, states sol dd Rhea Co, TN, & sol bro Daniel dd there too. F-R6810 R1700
  James, esf SC; dd 1789; md 3/1/1785 Nancy SPAULDING in SC, her parents having mvd soon after RW to near Columbia, SC, from VA; wid md (2) 9/9/1790 Roger CANNON, Richland District, SC, & they mvd to Sumter District, SC, where he dd 1805-6; only ch of sol & wid: Thomas b 4/17/1786 & James b 1/20/1790; wid PN ae 84 Walton Co, GA, 1851; AFF then by Thomas McPHERSON ae 80+, Richland District, SC, he younger bro/o sol who dd at home of their m. F-W5896 R1700
  William, esf West End, VA, c18 months before end of RW; dd c 1804; md 1791/1793 Linda SMITHERMAN, Colchester, Fairfax

McPHERSON (continued)
   Co, VA; AFF 1851 Fairfax Co, VA, by Franky BARKER & Thomas HALL; wid afb ae 84 Fairfax Co, VA, 1855; BLAR, no proof that wid's h was the William McPHERSON who was VA RW sol; wid referred to as Sinny Ann then by person whom she gave power of attorney to afb. BLW Rejected File #75166 R1700

McPIKE, John, b 9/7/1750 Chester Co, PA; esf 1775 York Co, PA, where res; mvd 1792 to VA, thence 1823 Adams Co, OH, where PN 1832; res 1839 Brown Co, OH. F-S2810 R1700

McQUADY, John, b 3/22/1760 Culpeper Co, VA; mvd ae 5 with f to Spotsylvania Co, VA, where esf 1776; PN 1833 Woodford Co, KY, where dd 12/24/41; md there 12/5/1838 Susan HANKS, wid of James D SMITH; wid md (3) 4/9/1846 Jesse GRADDY, who dd 8/19/51; wid PN ae 55 there 1853; res ae 70 Versailles, KY 1868; sol surname also spelled McQUADDY & McQUIDDY; QLF 1928 from desc Miss/Mrs Alpha B NASH of Sarasota, FL. F-W7603 R1700

McQUAY, William, see McQUIE, William. F-S16952 R1700

McQUEEN, Alexander, esf 1775 Culpeper Co, VA where b 3/17/1751 mvd 1829 to Muskingum Co, OH where PN 1832; AFF then by David JAMISON, Culpeper Co, VA, ae 81 he esf with sol in RW; AFF then by Benjamin HUMPHREY, Culpeper Co, VA he esf with sol in RW, sol now res with children in OH. F-S5075 R1700

   Joshua, esf 1777 Holliday's Cove, VA, in 13th VA Regiment; PN 1819 Madison Co, KY, aec 63, where res since 1795; gtd BLW6578 by VA 9/18/1823; res ae 76 Fayette Co, KY, 1832 when gtd BLW1883; QLF 1919 from gdd Mrs Willshire RILEY of Atlanta, GA, who also gdd of RW sol William SHARP of Fayette Co, KY. F-S36102 R1700

   Thomas, b 12/1761 Baltimore, MD; esf 1782 near Mingo Bottom on Ohio River, Ohio Co, VA, in VA regiment; bro of Joshua; PN 1832 Bartholomew Co, IN; dd 1838 leaving wid & 11 ch; md w mbnn c1801; wid dd 1839; s-in-law Moses JOINER res in Randolph Co, MO, 1851; Elizabeth, w/o sol bro Joshua & d/o Captain George BROWN, AFF 1832 Bartholomew Co, IN, her h & sol esf together; QLF 1909 from great gdd Mrs W M ALEXANDER, Rushville, IN, states sol f Uriah also RW sol, further querier gdd (on m's side) of RW sol William WALKER; QLF 1913 from great gds Harry Groll NEWTON, Vincennes, IN, s/o Madison NEWTON & Nancy STOUGHTON (whose m was sol d Elizabeth McQUEEN), F-33080 R1700

McQUIDDY, John, see McQUADY, John. F-W7603 R1700

McQUIE, William, b 5/1758 Amelia Co, VA; esf 1775 Mecklenburg Co, VA; mvd 1790 to KY, thence 1830 Pike Co, MO, where PN 1833; QLF says sol buried Bowling Green, MO; QLF 1919 from great great gdd Madeline Shwimmer (Mrs E O) HIND, Indianapolis, IN. F-S16952 R1700

McQUIETY, Samuel, b 1751 Co Antrim, Ireland; esf 1778 Loudoun Co, VA, where res; mvd several years after RW to Mason Co, KY, thence Highland Co, OH, where afp 1833; PAR, insufficient proof/o svc; surname also spelled McQUITTY & McJUTTY F-R6812 R1700

MCQUINN, John, esf VA; PN ae 81 Fayette Co, VA, 1822 when no fixed place/o res but went around area chopping wood, etc; ch: William aec 33, Timothy aec 25 & Polly aec 23, all of them extremely poor. F-S40141 R1700
McQUOWN, John, esf 1776 Fauquier Co, VA; PN 1818 Licking Co, OH; res there 1820 ae 70 when had w Mary ae 64 & gds Solomon McQUOWN living with him; dd 3/1828 leaving no wid but children mbnn; QLF 1933 from desc Richard Sherman BENNETT, Chicago, IL. F-S41821 R1700
McREE, William, b 1756 Ireland; esf 1778 near Chambersburg, PA in NJ Line, where res; PN 1833 Harrison Co, VA; QLF 1927 from great great gds C R BOYLES, Morgantown, WV, says sol surname also spelled McCRAY. F-S5754 R1700
McROBERTS, James, b 5/22/1763; esf 1779 Washington Co, PA; esf later West Liberty, VA; esf 1781 Pittsburgh, PA; mvd 1786 to IL Territory; PN 1828 Monroe Co, IL; dd 2/10/44; md 5/25/1792 Mary HARRIS (MB 5/24/1782), Montgomery Co, TN; wid b 3/22/1776; wid PN 1850 Monroe Co, IL; ch births: Catherine 4/14/1794, Charlotte 5/9/96, Samuel 2/8/99, Thomas 2/24/1801, Sarah 3/16/03, Elizabeth 4/3/05, James 7/19/07, Anna 4/4/11, Mary 3/11/14, & Josiah 6/12/16; wid gtd BLW 26888 Monroe Co, IL, 1856. F-W2225 R1700
John, esf 1781 Augusta Co, VA; afp ae 92 Lincoln Co, KY 1832 PAR, less than 6 months svc. F-R8872 R1700
McSPADDEN, Archibald, see McSPEDEN, Archibald. F-S4204 R1701
Samuel, b 1756 Rockbridge Co, VA where esf 1775 res near Lexington; mvd after RW to near Abingdon, VA, thence Jefferson Co, TN, where PN 1834; QLF 1898 from desc Mrs James R GRAY, Atlanta, GA, states sol res Dandridge, TN, & dd 8/4/ 1844, further he manufactured powder for US for use in War of 1812 Battle of New Orleans, querier also desc of VA RW sol Abednego INMAN who md Mary RITCHIE, lived in Dandridge TN, dd 2/2/1831, & his wid dd 6/23/1836; QLF states sol md 1780 Susannah EGLE or Elizabeth EDLE; QLF 1918 from desc Louise Wilson REYNOLDS, Vienna, VA, says sol md Polly BERRY who survived him. F-S4203 R1701
McSPEDDIN, Thomas, bc 3/12/1748 Augusta Co, VA; esf 1777 when res on Laurel Fork of Holston River at Edmondson Settlement, VA; mvd 1785 to Davidson Co, TN, thence 1809-10 Wilson Co, TN where PN 1832; dd there 5/11/33 leaving wid Mary; Thomas C McSPEDDEN (NKG) res there then. F-S2813 R1701
McSPEDEN, Archibald, b 1750 Rockbridge Co, VA; esf 1778 when res on Holston River in area later Washington, Co, VA; mvd a few years after RW to Jefferson Co, TN, thence 1818-19 Monroe Co, TN, where PN 1833. F-S4204 R1701
McSWAIN, Edward, BLW12393 issued 5/29/1792. F-BLW12393 R1701
McUIN, Patrick, see McEWING, Patrick. F-R16267 R1701
McVANY, Christopher, b 1757 PA; esf 1777 Frederick Co, VA; mvd after RW to Hardy Co, VA, thence Frederick Co, VA, then to Augusta Co, VA, thence Rockingham Co, VA, thence Pendleton Co, VA, then to Bath Co, VA, then to Harrison Co, VA (area later Lewis Co); PN 1832 Lewis Co, VA; dd 6/30/1853 Upshur

McVANY (continued)
   Co, VA; md 10/1796 Mary PUSSE/PUSIE/PASEL; wid afp 1854, & PAR; afb ae 80 Upshur Co, VA, 1860 & BLAR; sol PN had been suspended by PN Office, when witness AFF sol was deserter; Margaret MEANS AFF ae 78 Lewis Co, VA 1836 sol was RW sol; wid PAR & BLAR, insufficient proof of svc; surname spelled also McVANEY. F-S15533 R1701
McVAY, Daniel, esf in 12th VA Regiment; later esf Shenandoah Co in 8th VA Regiment; PN 1818 KY ae 71 when poor & crippled; no family & no occupation 1821; res Fayette Co, KY, 1825, when requested replacement of lost PN certificate. F-S36108 R1701
McVERNARS, George, see McNERNAR, George. F-R6807 R1701
McWHIRTER, James, b on Rockfish Creek, VA; mvd aec 8 to Union District, SC, where esf 1778; PN there 1834 ae 74; decd in 1843. F-S7199 R1701
McWHORTER, George, b 2/8/1762 VA; esf 1780 Mecklenburg, NC, where res; PN there 1833; dd 2/14/41 leaving 1 ch Samuel, who res Union Co, NC, 1852; QLF states sol bro of William. F-S9011 R1701
   Henry, b 11/13/1760 NJ; esf 1776 Orange Co, NY where res, in NY regiment; esf 1778 Northumberland Co, PA, in PA company against indians; md in Bucks Co, PA, & mvd 1786 from there to Harrison Co, VA; PN 1832 Lewis Co, VA; John McWHORTER (NKG) then JP there; last PN payment in file 1833; QLF states sol dd 1848 Harrison Co, VA, was bro/o James & Thomas, & they all esf Orange Co, NY; QLF 1897 from great gds H C McWHORTER, Charleston, WV, a judge of WV Supreme Court of Appeals. F-S7210 R1701
   John, b 1749 Albemarle Co, VA; esf 1778 Union District, SC; PN 1832 Casey Co, KY; dd 6/7/33; md (1) Miss JASPER, md (2) 4/14/1784 Elizabeth, Union District, SC; wid PN ae 76 Casey Co, KY, when d Sally PIGG ae 53; s Robert mentioned then; mvd 1840 to MO to be with her 2 s's & 2 d's mbnn; dd c1841 Hay Co, MO; a Lewis PIGG (NKG) res there 1840; QLF 1923 from kin E L PIGG, Missouri City, MO. F-W9560 R1701
McWILLIAMS, James, esf 1782 in Armand's Legion; afb 1834 Rockingham Co, VA; BLW2022 issued 11/13/1834. F-BLW2022 R1701
   James, s/o Hugh of Henry Co, VA; esf 1778 Orange Co, NC, res there, in NC regiment; esf 1781 Henry Co, VA, in VA regiment; PN ae 71 Hardin Co, KY, 1842, where res since 1801; dd there 8/26/43 at res on Mill Creek; md 1/1/1780 Martha JAMESON, Henry Co, VA; wid PN ae 82 Hardin Co, KY, 1848; had 10 ch: Mary/Polly, Jane, Samuel, Hannah, Elizabeth, James, Martha, Sarah, & 2 Anna's (1st dd young); s-in-law Washington SMITH res Hardin Co, VA, 1848 ae 61; QLF 1929 from great great gdd Lucinda A (Mrs N A) LILJA of Madison, WI; QLF 1923 from desc Mrs Edwin H JOLLY, Paducah, KY; QLF 1902 from desc Miss Ida BRIDWELL, Charleston, MO. F-W3026 R1701
   John, b 6/14/1760 Somerset Co, NJ; esf 1776 Shepherdstown, Berkeley Co, VA; PN 1832 Augusta Co, VA; dd Fall 1852 lea-

McWILLIAMS (continued)
 ving heirs mbnn; QLF says sol md Maggie FISHER; QLF 1914 from desc Mrs Jessie Berry (Mrs Hubert) WEBSTER, Greencastle, IN, says sol b Ireland & came to America quite young. FS9005 R1701
 Joshua, VA sea svc, midshipman in VA navy; VA BLW issued him 7/15/1783; dd c1796; only ch Miss McWILLIAMS of Charlotte Hall, St Marys Co, MD, res 1852 there with family of N F D BROWNE, sent query then to PN office concerning afp & afb; no action on query in file. F-R75 R1701
 William, b 1759 Co Down, Ireland; esf 1777 Washington Co, PA where res; mvd 1785 with family to Ohio Co, VA, then 1800 to Belmont Co, OH; PN 1832 Knox Co, OH, res Clay Township, when liv there 8 years; dd 4/21/40 that Co; md 3/5/1793 or 3/6/1793 Mary MERRITT, Washington Co, PA; wid PN ae 71 Knox Co, OH, res Clay Township; res there 1849; s John, b 1/31/1797, was eldest s alive when res 1846 that Co; other children mbnn; QLF 1917 from great great gdd Miss Lizzie McWILLIAMS, Sigourney, IA, states sol came from Ireland c 1775, settled Wheeling, WV, querier was great gdd of sol s John; QLF states sol dd Martinsburg, OH. F-W4289 R1701
 William, esf 1777 Spotsylvania Co, VA, res near Fredericksburg; dd 4/17/1801 Pittsylvania Co, VA; md 4/6/1782 Dorothea Braym, orphan d of John BRENGER, Spotsylvania Co, VA; wid b 3/1/1765; wid md (2) George BUCKNER who dd 11/18/28 Caroline Co, VA; wid afp 1838 there, & PAR; dd there 8/26/39 leaving several gdc; her LWT listed heirs William G MINOR, Robert D MINOR, & Ann B WALKER; gds Robert D MINOR of Washington, DC, gave power of attorney 1852 to agent to afb, & PAR; wid f John BRENGER had only 2 d's, Dorothea & & Ann Braym, who 2/26/1780 md George FRENCH; executors of John BRENGER's LWT were George FRENCH & Andrew BUCHANAN. F-R1410 R1701
MEACHAM, Joseph, b 2/25/1761; esf 1781 Chatham Co, NC, where res; PN 1832 Christian Co, KY; QLF 1915 from Anna Meacham (Mrs George T) DINSMORE of Lyons, KS, states sol dd 9/1838 Christian Co, KY. F-S11062 R1702
 Richard, b 1760 Caroline Co, VA; esf c1777 Chatham Co, NC; mvd to Morgan Co, GA, thence 1810 Clark Co, AL, thence Washington Co, thence Green Co, thence 1833 Perry Co, AL, where afp 1835, & PAR. F-R7071 R1702
MEACHUM, Ichabod, esf 1775 in MA regiment; esf 1777 aboard MA ship TRUMBULL; PN ae 59 Montgomery Co, VA, 1818; res there 1820 ae 61 when no children res with him; surname spelled also MEACHAM; QLF says sol dd VA. F-S38204 R1702
MEAD, John, esf 1775 Winchester, VA; esf 1776 Frederick Co, VA in 11th VA Regiment; PN aec 64 Henry Co, KY, 1818; living there 1820 when had s (had w & 5 ch) & d Mrs WILSON (had 5 ch); QLF 1901 from desc Miss Augusta GLENN, Indianapolis IN. F-S36125 R1703
 John, esf 1775 in 14th VA Regiment; PN ae 65 Augusta Co, VA, 1818; res there 1820 aec 68, occupation welldigger, when w

MEAD (continued)
& ch all decd. F-S38210 R1703
Minor, b 1763 Spotsylvania Co, VA; esf 1779 Louisa Co, VA; later esf Mecklenburg Co, VA, where res; PN 1832 Carroll Co, GA; dd there 3/25/37; md 1/6/1793 Jane PRYOR, Columbia Co, GA; wid PN ae 73 Carroll Co, GA, 1849; wid gtd BLW2187 there 1855 ae 79; res 1861 Haralson Go, GA where mvd c1856 QLF 1901 from relative Mrs Dora Glenn GANO of Indianapolis IN, who great gdd of sol sis Patsy Meade GLENN. F-W5369 R1703
Thomas, b 1754 Frederick Co, VA; esf 1776 Pittsylvania Co, VA, where res; PN 1833 Pike Co, IN; dd there 1/14/35; md after Battle of Guilford Courthouse to Sarah DAVIS (MB 11/16/1781 between Thomas MAID & Sarah DAVIS, signed by Benjamin DAVIS) Pittysylvania Co, VA; wd PN ae 90 Pike Co, IN 1842 when AFF there by d-in-law Polly MEAD. F-W9561 R1703
William, esf 1776 Hanover Co, VA; PN ae 62 Roane Co, TN 1819 & res there 1826 ae 68, occupation farmer, when w ae 66; s William AFF there then; dd 3/1831; md 1789 Sarah, who dd 3/1835 leaving s's William M, Minor, & John (gave power of attorney 1833 Roane Co, TN, as adm of f's estate, to agent to afp). F-S38942 R1703
MEADE, Everard, esf 1776, captain in VA Line; LWT as Everard Sr dated 1/13/1801 Amelia Co, VA, probated there 4/28/1803 listed w Mary, s's David, Richard E, Seth, Hodijah, Benjamin, & Lincoln, & d Sally; LWT executives were w Mary, Joseph EGGLESTON & Richard EGGLESTON; LWT witnesses were Mary G LUSH, Daniel HARDAWAY, William T EGGLESTON, Eliza ARCHER, & Jane S COCKE; wid Mary LWT dated 9/1/1830 there, probated there 9/26/1833 listed her 1st h Benjamin L WARD, s Hodijah, s Benjamin L, d Maria WARD w/o Mr RANDOLPH, gds Edwin RANDOLPH, gds Edmund RANDOLPH, gdd Charlotte RANDOLPH, d Sallie R MEADE, gdd Mariann, & Peyton RANDOLPH (decd, NKG); s Hodijah & s Benjamin L afb there 1834 & gtd BLW2063. F-BLW2063 R1703
Thornton, esf c1788 Louisa Co, VA; PN there 1818 ae 59; res there 1820, occupation farmer, when had w Mary aec 57 & s mbnn ae over 21 liv with him; AFF then there by David BULLOCK he served with sol in RW; sol dd 12/31/33; md 1/24/1788 Mary GARLAND (MB 1/18/1788, signed by William MEADE), Louisa Co, VA; wid dd 8/5/1838; only liv ch Madison afp ae 46 there 1844 for PN due m, stating his 2 siblings dd unmd & without issue; AFF 1846 by Lewis D ROBERTSON there that he built coffin for sol wid, & she buried 8/6/38; s Madison gtd PN due m; in 1820 John POINDEXTER Louisa Co clerk of court, Peter CRAWFORD chief magistrate. F-W18506 R1703
William, b 8/22/1762 Frederick Co, VA; esf 1778 Wilkes Co, NC, where res; mvd 1792 to Washington Co, VA, thence Greenup Co, KY, thence Logan Co, VA, where PN 1833; mvd 1836 to Jennings Co, IN, to res with s mbnn, P O address there Ely, IN; AFF then there by Samuel MEADE (NKG); AFF 1832 by sol sis Elizabeth COOPER, Greenup Co, KY; sol dd 21/1841;

MEADE (continued)
  only s Samuel appointed adm of f's estate 1841 by Logan Co
  VA court; Samuel gtd PN arrears due f 1841; surname also
  spelled MEAD. F-S19394 R1703
MEADEN, Andrew, b 4/4/1755 Shenandoah Co, VA; mvd as small boy
  with f to near Hillsborough, NC, then 10 years later with
  f to Yadkin River, Rowan Co, NC, where esf 1776 against
  Cherokee Indians; thence sol mvd ae 22 to Guilford Co, NC,
  for 2 years, where esf 1780, thence on Yadkin River to end
  of RW; mvd after RW to New River, VA, for 1 year, thence
  Washington Co, VA, then to NC for 13 years, thence Jefferson Co, TN, where PN 1834 when res near Morristown; last
  PN payment in file 1840. F-S4188 R1704
MEADOR, Benjamin, esf 1780-1 Amelia Co, VA, where b 8/18/1763;
  esf 1781 sub for f Benjamin MEADOR/MEADOWS, who res there
  during RW; mvd to Bedford Co, VA where PN 1833 when living
  there 40 years; bro Hezekiah res there then 1862. F-S9405
  R1704
 Isham, esf 1781 Bedford Co, VA, where b 3/20/1762; PN 1832
  Smith Co, TN; dd 3/2/40; md (2) 5/9/1817 Mrs Martha SULLIVAN, SmithCo, TN (area later Macon Co); wid PN ae 74 Macon
  Co, TN, 1853; sol s Jobe, by 1st w, res ae 69 Jackson Co,
  TN, 1854; sol s Jesse, by 1st w, res ae 55 Macon Co, TN,
  1854; sol nephew Banister MEADER res Macon Co, TN, 1854 ae
  54; sol wid gtn BLW40693 there 1855 aec 75; QLF 1925 from
  desc Mrs Sterling CARRINGTON, Belmont, MA; QLF states sol
  md (1) Betty BRADSHAW. F-W25697 R1704
 Joel, esf 1779 Bedford Co, VA, where b 3/8/1760; mvd 1800 to
  Smith Co, TN, where PN 1832; dd 4/7/34 or 4/8/34; md 6/13/
  1780 Sally MEADOR, Bedford Co (area later Franklin Co), VA
  wid b 3/1762; PN 1837 Smith Co, TN; ch: Ann b 8/1781, Lydia, Jeptha, Milley, Sally, Bennet, Banister b 1794, Ruth,
  & Joseph; sol bro Isham then ae 71 & sol bro Jonas then ae
  75 both res there & both in RW svc with bro Joel; sol bro
  Job AFF there 1837 aec 73; s Bennet AFF there then; QLF
  1939 from grandnephew Monroe MEADOR, Green Bottom, Cabell
  Co VA. F-W7445 R1704
 Jonas, esf 1781 Bedford Co, VA, where b 2/3/1758; served in
  same RW company with bro's Isham & Joel; mvd 1809 to Smith
  Co, TN, where afp 1832; PAR, less than 6 months svc; QLF
  1919 from Susie Meador (Mrs E F) WALDEN, Morehouse, MO, b
  Cumberland Co, VA, d/o Merritt Singleton MEADOR, s/o Jonas
  MEADOR who s/o William MEADOR who s/o John MEADOR who s of
  Jonas MEADOR who s of Jehu MEADOR Sr, further LWT of Jehu
  MEADOR Jr made 1820 Cumberland Co, VA. F-R7081 R1704
MEADOWS, Josiah, b 2/1758 Bedford Co, VA; mvd to Botetourt Co,
  VA where esf; PN 1832 Giles Co, VA; minister; surname also
  spelled MEADOW; Banister MEADOW/MEADER (NKG) res Giles Co,
  VA 1832; last PN payment in file 1841; Jacob MEADOWS (NKG)
  mentioned; QLF 1938 from desc Mrs Virginia Meador WARD of
  Bluefield, WV. F-S7225 R1704
 Francis, esf 1777 Augusta Co, VA in 10th VA Regiment; PN aec

MEADOWS (continued)
64 Monroe Co, VA, 1818, when res there c9 years; in 1820 had 16 ch mbnn of whom 12 were s's & 6 of ch under ae 14; dd there 11/20/36; md Fall 1790-91 Frances BUSH, Rockingham Co, VA; wid PN aec 70 Monroe Co, VA 1841; surname also spelled MEDOWS. F-W5367 R1704

Israel, esf 1776 Sweet Springs, VA; mvd 1800 to Madison Co, KY, thence Estill Co, KY, where PN 1818 ae 62; dd 9/30/27 there; md 7/8/1778 Barbara GREEN in Botetourt Co, VA, when they both res of Greenbrier Co, VA; 1st ch Nancy b Spring 1779, md Zachariah PHILLIPS (b1783) who AFF 1838 Estill Co KY, when w Nancy decd; sol eldest s William ae 58 in 1839; sol d Elizabeth b 12/1786 md Mr COLE, & she AFF Fayette Co KY, 1839; sol 7th ch Jacob b 11/8/1792 & res 1839 IN; sol 10th & last ch Rebecca b 7/18/1799. F-W8451 R1704

Jacob, esf 1781 Rockingham Co, VA, where res; PN ae 69 Giles Co, VA, 1832; last PN payment in file 1838. F-S9412 R1704

James, bc 1755 Halifax Co, VA; esf 1778 Rowan Co, NC, where res with f during RW; mvd with f after RW to Burke Co, NC, thence 1795 Clark Co, KY, thence 1819 Wayne Co, KY, thence 1833 Warren Co, IL, where PN 1835 when blind; dd 5/9/38 there; md 12/19/1787 Jane; wid afp ae 77 Warren Co, IL, 1843; PAR, insufficient proof/o svc & marriage; PO address 1844 Monmouth, IL, care of Henry MEADOWS (NKG). F-R7082 R1704

James, b Orange Co, VA; mvd as small ch with m & f to Rockingham Co, VA, where esf c1779; PN there 1832 ae 72; last PN payment in file 1838. F-S8895 R1704

William, esf Bedford Co, VA; dd 10/18/1831 Stratton Township Edgar Co, IL, leaving no wid but s Jubal, who afp there 1860 ae 60; PAR, no current law authorizing PN to ch of RW sol's; QLF 1908 from great gds J R MEADOWS, Vermilion, IL, states sol surname also spelled MEADOW; QLF states sol mvd to KY shortly after RW & ch included Sarah & William; QLF states sol mvd to KY c1807 with ch: Elizabeth (bc 1784, dd 1856, md 4/2/1806 Jesse COLE), Mary (bc 1789, dd 1849, md 12/30/1806 William S CHAMBERS), & Sarah (b 8/20/1796, dd 8/5/1877, md 1814 David CHAMBERS), all these ch dd Monroe Co, IN; QLF 1938 from desc Esthel MEADOWS, Huntington, WV; QLF 1919 from desc Mrs Ella M HONNOLD of Kansas, IL. F-F-R16416 R1704

MEAIRS, Alexander, see MARS, Alexander. F-R7087 R1704

MEALEY, James, esf 1781 Goochland Co, VA; PN ae 68-69 there 1832. F-S9408 R1704

MEALLY, Charles, b 1763-64 King George Co, VA; esf 1779 Johnson Co, NC; mvd (all NC) to Warren Co, thence Halifax Co, thence Roberson Co, thence Bladen Co, thence Cumberland Co where afp 1834; PAR. F-R7083 R1704

MEAN, Robert, came to America from Ireland; esf VA; afp ae 72 Lewis Co, VA, 1834; PAR, less than 6 months svc. F-R7084 R1704

MEANLY, John, esf 1780 Chesterfield Co, VA; PN aec 53 King &

MEANLY (continued)
Queen Co, VA, 1818; AFF then by neighbors John KIDD, Thomas KIDD, Roderick STARLING, & Dr Moore G FAUNTLEROY; res there 1820 ae 57 when family w Philadelphia ae 41 & ch Mary Ann ae 11, John ae 9, James ae 7, & Sarah ae 1; dd 1/8/21; md 9/17/1807 Philadelphia WALKER (MB 9/7/1807, signed by James NUNN, witnessed by Robert POLLARD), King & Queen Co, VA; wid PN ae 75 Richmond, VA 1853; afb & gtd BLW30942 there 1855 when witness Emeline H MEANLEY (NKG); clerk of court there then James O POLLARD; dd there 3/8/64; only surv ch John F afp there 1868 for PN due m which had been stopped during Civil War, & he gtd PN money; letter to PN Office 1868 from wid gds George L MEANLEY, Tappahannock, VA, states sol wid dd leaving 2 ch, which were his f & his uncle John F, George being the eldest son of his f who had dd in early 1868; surname also spelled MEANLEY. F-W9948 R1704
MEANS, Philip, see MAIN, Philip. F-S13850 R1705
William, b 5/3/1765 near Staunton, Augusta Co, VA; mvd when infant with f to settle on branch of Tyger River, SC (area later Fair Forest, Union Co, SC) where res during RW; esf there 1781; mvd to GA 12-15 years after RW, then to Adams Co, OH, for c23 years, thence Edgar Co, IL, where PN 1833; dd there 6/11/48; md (2) 4/18/1811 Susan, wid of John CHENOWETH, Adams Co, OH; wid PN ae 67 Edgar Co, IL, 1853, res Paris, IL; gtd BLW28635 there 1855; QLF says sol dd Paris, IL; QLF states sol md (1) Nancy SIMONTON & they had s John who SC War of 1812 sol; QLF 1924 from desc Mrs P E RITZ of Waterloo, IA, states sol of Scottish anc. F-W5368 R1705
MEARES, Joel, esf 1780 Dobbs Co, NC, where b 5/1754; mvd 1780 to Cumberland Co, NC, then to Henry Co, VA, for 20 years, thence Hawkins Co, TN, thence Buncombe Co, NC, thence Warren Co, TN, where PN 1835 when res there 25 years; dd 12/21/35 leaving wid mbnn; surname also spelled MEARS. F-S2816 R1705
MEARS, Alexander, see MARS, Alexander. F-R7087 R1705
Hilary/Hillary, bc 1765; esf in 9th VA Regiment; PN ae 73 Accomac Co, VA, 1832; AFF then by neighbors Houston KELLAM ae 74 & John HARMAN ae 69; sol dd c4/1/36, leaving no wid but ch: William B, Jesse, Nancy (md John TURLINGTON), George, & Elizabeth (md Mr TURLINGTON); d Elizabeth was decd in 1850 having left ch: William T, Nathaniel, Elizabeth A, & John, their guardian being Peter TURLINGTON (NKG); sol s William B was decd in 1850 having left ch: David P, Jesse, & Thomas; above named living descendants of sol listed as his heirs by Accomac, VA, court in 1850. F-S18508 R1705
MEDARIS, Massy C, b Essex Co, VA; mvd when quite young with older bro mbnn after death of f to Chatham Co, NC, where esf 1780; mvd c7 years after RW to Guilford Co NC where PN ae 77 in 1832. F-S9410 R1705
MEDCALF, John, see MEDKIFF, John. F-W3852 R1705
MEDEARIS, John Washington, b 2/22/1744 Essex Co, VA, between

MEDEARIS (continued)
Rappahannock & Dragon Rivers, s/o John MEDEARIS & w Rachel DAVIS; esf 1776 NC; PN 1828 Bedford Co, TN; md 12/20/1780 Sarah (wid of Thomas BELL) who dd before him; sol dd 3/21/34 or 3/3/34; ch: Benjamin, B W H, Polly (only surv ch in 1854) & Washington Davis (b 9/20/1783, md 6/1809 Elizabeth S d/o Thomas WOODWARD of Amelia Co, VA); births of ch of s Washington Davis: Rachel 3/10/1811 (md 5/14/1829 David, s of Thomas & Sarah YOUNG of GA), Sarah H 12/24/1813 (md 8/8/1835 James D LLOYD), Margaret B 2/10/1816 (md 8/6/1835 Henry S BLACKMAN), Polly 5/23/1818, Christian L 8/1/1820, George Washington 3/15/1823, William Green 8/10/1825, Elizabeth S 6/2/1830, Martha Frances 10/6/1832 & Wily W 3/28/1836; a Mary MEADEARIS (NKG) md 1/26/1839 W R YOWELL; Samuel ARNOLD AFF 1857 Shelbyville, TN, his w Elizabeth d of sol s Benjamin MEDEARIS; Davidson M SMITH, adm of sol estate, & John M SMITH (NKG) both res Bedford Co, TN, 1853; sol surname also spelled MEDEASIS; QLF 1908 from great gdd Mrs Rosa May O'NEAL of Huntsville, AL; QLF 1915 from great great gdd Mrs F F REHFELDT, Asylum, MI; QLF 1925 from desc T M COOPER, Fort Worth, TX; QLF 1835 from great great gdd Miss Margaret PHILLIPS, Yazoo City, MS. F-S2823 R1706

MEDKIFF, John, esf 1780 Pittsylvania Co, VA where b 3/11/1761; PN 1832 Patrick Co, VA; dd 7/18/39; md 9/10/1782 Mary d of Joseph PARSONS, Pittsylvania Co, VA; wid PN ae 77 Patrick Co, VA, 1841; surname also spelled MIDKIFF & MEDCALF; QLF 1907 from great great gdd Mrs C J CONWAY, Chicago, IL. F-W3852 R1706

MEDLAR, Boston, b 5/9/1763; esf 1777 Hagerstown, MD where res, in 7th MD Regiment; PN 1818 Jefferson Co, VA; w mbnn liv 1820 ae 43; sol dd 8/19/32; children mbnn 1849. F-S38212 R1706

MEDLEY, Bryant, b 1748-49 Dinwiddie Co, VA; mvd ae 5 to Dobbs Co, NC, where esf; esf 1778 Lenoir Co, NC, where res; mvd 1823 to Stokes Co, NC, where PN 1833 when had children res KY; QLF 1930 from desc Faye Medley (Mrs J F) SCHWEIBLE of Minneapolis, MN. F-S8894 R1706

John, b 2/26/1746 Frederick Co, MD; esf Fauquier Co, VA, res there; PN 1833 White Co, TN; QLF 1930 from Faye Medley (Mrs J F) SCHWEIBLE, Minneapolis, MN, says she gdd of Sauel MEDLEY who b 6/2/1793. F-S1698 R1706

MEDOWS, Francis, see MEADOWS, Francis. F-W5367 R1706

MEEK, Alexander, b 12/14/1764 Cumberland Co, MD; esf 1779 Washington Co, VA; PN 1832 Lincoln Co, TN; res 1843 Marshall Co, MS where had md children mbnn; gtd BLW34827 there 1855 F-S7218 R1706

Bazil, b 1740 MD; esf 1777 Frederick Co, VA, where res; PN 1834 Henry Co, TN when res there 25 years; dd 1/18/40; QLF states sol bro John also RW sol; QLF 1923 from DAR agent Mrs Elizabeth REYNOLDS of Abingdon, IL, who gdd of RW sol Bazel MEEK b 3/7/1763 Hagerstown, MD, dd 1/12/1844 near Eureka, IL, md (2) 1843 Salina DOLPH, he sometimes called

MEEK (continued)
  Benjamin. F-S15521 R1706
  Jacob, b 3/17/1755 on Elkridge near Baltimore, MD; esf 1776 Westmoreland Co, PA, where res; later 1776 esf in VA militia company; mvd after RW to KY, for 18-19 years in Shelby Co & Henry Co; PN 1832 Wayne Co, IN; last PN payment in file 1840; QLF states sol dd 1843 & buried near Boston, IN F-S18480 R1706
  Samuel, esf VA; dd 7/9/1812 Cedarville, VA, near Abingdon; w Elizabeth dd there 5/21/1831; d Mary A HOPKINS afp 1856 Grainger Co, TN & PAR, no current law authorized PN to her QLF 1925 from desc Georgia May L V MEEK, Springfield, MO, states sol bc 1760 s/o Samuel, came to America c1770, settled in MC c1784, mvd to Brooke Co, VA, where dd, wid Pallie WELLS md again after h death, sol s Robert of PA & OH md Esther McCOMB. F-R7094 R1706
MEEKS, Austin, esf VA early in RW; PN ae 75 Fluvanna Co, VA, 1818. F-S38211 R1707
  John, esf 1780 Hanover Co, VA; PN 1818 Louisa Co, VA; res ae 59 there as John Sr 1820 with w Elizabeth ae 58, s Charles ae 22, d Nancy ae 18, s James ae 14, & s William ae 2; QLF states sol liv 1839-40 aec 78. F-S38207 R1707
MEFFORD, John, esf 1781 Rockingham Co, VA, sub for f Gasper; afp ae 76 Logan Co, KY, 1840; PAR, less than 6 months svc; surname also spelled MEFFERD. F-R7097 R1707
MELAM, John, see MILAM, John. F-W9951 R1708
MELSON, Charles, esf 1776 Bedford Co, VA; PN there 1818 ae 67. F-S38209 R1709
  William, PN sea svc, b 1749 or 1754 Accomac Co, VA; esf as privateer aboard ship THE THREE BROTHERS, Philadelphia, PA where res; taken POW, released, then esf aboard ship RAINBOW, Philadelphia, PA; mvd to SC where esf 1777 in army; mvd to Yancey Co, TN, where afp 1836 ae 82; PAR, svc not truly military. F-R7112 R1709
MELTON, Benjamin, b Albemarle Co, VA; esf 1776 Caswell Co, NC, where res; res there after RW, thence Warren Co, KY, then 1820 to Lawrence Co, IL where PN as Benjamin MILTON ae 66; dd there 9/6/43; md there 10/17/1833 Elizabeth FOWLER; wid PN ae 52 there 1853; gtd BLW26773 there 1855; John MELTON (NKG) res there 1833. F-W2227 R1709
  Charles, esf 1777 Loudoun Co, VA; PN ae 61 Hardin Co, KY; res there 1820 with w Tebbie ae 54. F-S36123 R1709
  Isham, esf 1778 in VA regiment; PN 1818 Edgefield District, SC; res there 1821 ae 61 with w Sarah ae 60, d Betsey ae 16 & d Nancy 13; other children mbnn. F-S38944 R1709
  Pearce W, esf 1780 Fluvanna Co, VA where b 3/8/1763; PN 1833 there; AFF there then by John HAISLIP, Daniel THACkER, & John BARSHAW they served in RW with sol; AFF there then by Austin SEAY, Walker TIMBERLAKE (clergyman), James STRATTON & Benjamin WOODY. F-S11065 R1709
MELTON, Thomas, esf Loudoun Co, VA; PN aec 68 Clark Co, KY, 1819; res 1820 Fayette Co, KY, occupation farmer, when he

MELTON (continued)
& w aec 60 res with children mbnn. F-S36116 R1709
   William, esf 1776 NC; PN ae 63 Lawrence Co, IL, 1821; bro of
   Benjamin above who AFF there 1821; res there 1825 ae 68,
   occupation tailor, with w ae over 80; they had no children
   F-S36117 R1709
MENALLY, Michael, see McNELLY, Michael. F-S38943 R1710
MENEFEE, Henry, esf 1779 Culpeper Co, VA; dd 8/26/1831; md
   2/13/1786 Mary ROBERTS; wid PN ae 79 Rappahannock Co, VA,
   1840; dd 9/22/40; 8 children mbnn; QLF 1921 from Mrs W W
   GRAVES, Jefferson City, MO, desc of another Henry MENEFEE,
   b 2/28/1754, esf 1777 with above sol, md 11/19/1773 Sarah
   DOLLINS. F-W18504 R1710
   Spencer, esf 1779 Culpeper Co, VA, where b 1762; mvd after
   RW to KY, thence c1827 Decatur Co, IN, where PN 1832. F-
   S16191 R1710
MENTER, Barker, see MINTER, Barker. F-BLW2187 R1710
MENZIES, Samuel P, see MINZIES, Samuel P. F-W25713 R1710
MERCER, Hugh, brigadier general of VA troops; BLW1527 issued
   7/5/1791 to his only surv ch William, John, George, & Lucy
   PATTEN; record lost in Washington, DC, fire 1800; QLF says
   sol came from another country to Spotsylvania Co, VA; QLF
   1938 from desc Mildred M HINER, Canton, OH; QLF states sol
   dd 1/12/1777; QLF 1921 from desc A L MERCER, New York, NY.
   F-BLW1527 R1710
   Isaac, VA sea svc, master of galley SAFEGUARD, which ship
   dismantled 1779; recd full pay 1786 for service prior to
   1782; very little data in file. F-R76 R1710
MEREDETH, David, esf VA; dd 12/24/1814-15 Amelia Co, VA; md
   there 6/3/1796-97 Elizabeth WASHAM; wid afp ae 82 Rockcastle Co, KY 1850; PAR, insufficient proof/o svc & marriage;
   d Keziah A KING AFF there then she b 10/24/1796 Amelia Co,
   VA; Andrew KING (NKG) res 1853 Rockcastle Co, VA; QLF says
   a VA RW sol David/Davis MEREDITH md Elizabeth WINFIELD, &
   they had d Elizabeth who md Robert ROSE (b Westmoreland Co
   VA); QLF 1936 from desc Mrs James E JOHNSTON Jr, Ft Worth,
   TX. F-R7118 R1711
MEREDITH, James, b 9/8/1762; esf 1779 Chesterfield Co, VA, res
   there; occupation millwright 1781-1792; settled 1792 Hanover Co, VA, where PN 1833; dd 3/20/40; md 12/27/1792 Mee-
   cha/Mercha HOOPER, Hanover Co, VA, neither having been md
   before; MB 12/19/1792 signed by Richard HOOPER there; wid
   PN there 1843 aec 68; res 1848 Henrico Co, VA ae 72; dd
   7/5/52; QLF 1939 from Rosella Meredith (Mrs H J) DUTTON,
   Lindsay, CA, desc of RW sol James MEREDITH, who md Mary
   CREWS, & their s David md Miss FARMINGTON; QLF 1935 from
   desc Mildred C HORNOR, Chicago, IL. F-W3849 R1711
   Jesse, esf 1776 Brunswick Co, VA, in 4th VA Regiment; PN ae
   67 Smith Co, TN, 1819; res 1821 ae 67 Dallas Co, AL, when
   applied for transfer/o PN; dd there 2/22/34 when w already
   decd; surv ch Jesse & James gave power of attorney Claiborne Co, LA, 1860 to agent to claim f's PN arrears; sol

MEREDITH (continued)
   surname also spelled MEREDETH. F-S38205 R1711
Samuel, member of Lee's Legion; BLW 12354 issued 9/2/1789.
   F-BLW12354 R1711
William, captain of 1st VA Artillery Regiment; POW 1780-83;
   BLW1519 issued 2/18/1793; PN 1828 Harrison Co, KY; dd 2/
   20/33; QLF 1933 from desc L E BLACK of Portland, OR, says
   sol came from Wales to America in early 1760's. F-S46393
   R1711
MEREWETHER, James, see MERIWETHER, James. F-R16407 R1711
James, see MERIWETHER, James. F-R16407.5 R1711
Valentine, esf VA; dd 8/15/1832; md 12 27/1790 Priscilla
   POLLARD, Fairfax Co, VA; wid PN ae 67 Henry Co, KY, 1838;
   wid sis Frances/Fanny POLLARD AFF then there ae 70+; wid
   sis Mrs Sally WOOLFOLK AFF then there ae 70+; wid gtd BLW
   26099 Jefferson Co, KY, 1855 ae 83-84; res Henry Co, KY,
   1857 ae 85; liv 1858; ch: Thomas H, William C, David C,
   George, Mildred A, Martha, & Priscilla all res 1834 Oldham
   Co, KY. F-W8454 R1711
William, see MERIWETHER, William. F-S47954 R1711
MERIDETH, Jesse, see MEREDETH, Jesse. F-S38205 R1711
MERIFIELD, John, b 1759 Winchester, VA; esf 1776 VA; res c40
   years in KY (Christian & Logan Co's), thence Macoupin Co,
   IL, where afp 1834 ae 74; PAR, less than 6 months service.
   F-R7119 R1711
MERITT, James, b 3/1/1755 Essex Co, VA; esf Surry Co, NC where
   res, in NC regiment; PN 1833 Anderson District, SC; QLF
   1917 from desc Grace YOUNGBLOOD, Republic, MO, states sol
   md Nancy COGGIN, querier also desc of RW sol's (NC or SC)
   Richard RAGSDALE who md Rebecca MITCHELL & John RAGSDALE
   who md Amy MOLDING. F-S21883 R1711
MERIWETHER, James, esf 1777 in VA Line; BLW1509 issued 7/28/
   1790; dd 3/18/1803; LWT dated 9/8/1802 Jefferson Co, GA,
   probated there 4/4/1803, lists bro Thomas, niece Susanna
   PATTERSON, niece Jane PATTERSON, & niece Elizabeth CASON;
   LWT executrix Susanna PATTERSON gave power of attorney to
   agent 1834 Putnam Co, GA, to afp; sol estate adm Alexander
   MERIWETHER (NKG) afp 1857 Pulaski Co, GA; they both PAR.
   F-R16407 R1711
James, esf VA, where lieutenant 3 years in VA Line; gtd BLW
   2326 for land in KY 1784; dd there 1801; PN Office allowed
   commutation for svc, & mistakenly paid it to wid of James
   of GA, above; afterwards that wid opted for the allowance
   due her own h. F-R16407.5 R1711
Thomas, major of 1st VA Regiment; LWT dated 9/8/1802 Jefferson Co, GA, probated there 4/4/1803, lists niece Susanna
   PATTERSON, niece Elizabeth CASON (niece of Jane M PATTERSON), Julia Maria d/o friend John BERRIEN who sol LWT executor; sol great niece Jane Louisa EARLY (d/o Jane PATTERSON & h Eleazer EARLY) liv FL 1853; LWT 11/30/1825 of sol
   niece Jane M P EARLY, Chatham, GA, lists niece Jane Louisa
   (EARLY) STURGES; this LWT probated 6/26/1829 there when

MERIWETHER (continued)
 Jane M P's h Eleazar EARLY res Brunswick, GA; Jane L HAWKINS afb Jackson Co, FL, & gtd BLW1820. F-BLW1920 R1711
 William, esf 1776 VA; in 1781 sol bro James, a lieutenant in a VA Regiment, resigned to join another unit & William was appointed to take his place; sol mvd to KY, where PN 1832 Jefferson Co ae 74; gtd BLW7608 by VA 1834; dd 2/10/42 there; bro James mvd to KY c1787 & dd Fall 1801; sol s David res 1851 Jefferson Co, KY, & was US senator in 1852; sol s's Albert G & Thomas W res 1851 Hickman Co, KY; sol d Catherine R md William R DAVIS, & she res 1851 near New Madrid, MO; Mildred E, d of sol decd s James B & w of Martin D McHENRY, res 1851 Shelby Co, KY; Emily A, d of sol decd s James B & w of William H MERIWETHER, res 1851 Jefferson Co, KY; QLF states sol b Goochland Co, VA, md possibly Elizabeth WINSLOW; QLF 1937 from Helen (Mrs William S) McGILL, Elsinore, CA, states her ancestor Thomas MERIWETHER b 12/25/1730 Goochland Co, VA, md Martha COX there & dd 1790 Jefferson Co, KY. F-S47954 R1711
MERRELL, Andrew, esf 1775 Morris Co, NJ, where b 5/8/1757 Roxbury Township; mvd 1783 to Loudoun Co, VA, for c2 years, thence Washington Co, MD, for c2 years, thence Loudoun Co, VA, & Hampshire Co, VA, for c10 years, thence 1797-8 Estill Co, KY, thence Clark Co, KY where PN 1833; dd 5/29/35 surname also spelled MERRILL; QLF says sol w Elizabeth res res Princeton, NJ; QLF 1934 from desc Clyde W KURTZ, Reliance, WY. F-S31253 R1712
MERRIMAN, Francis, esf 1776 Powhatan Co, VA, in 2nd VA Regiment; PN ae 68 Knox Co, TN 1820 when w & s aec 18 res with him; dd 8/19/22; md 7/28/1791 Martha AMMONETT, Powhatan Co VA; wid dd 7/5/1844 leaving ch: Martha, Phebe PORTER (a wid), & Dicy w of Michael BRADBERY (he afp ae 54 Davidson Co, TN, 1845 for wid heirs; ch gtd PN due m. F-W157 R1715
MERRITT, Archelaus, esf 1781 Chesterfield Co, VA; PN 1821 Jefferson Co, KY, aec 61, occupation farmer, when had w ae 48 (md 28 years, & she liv & not res with him then), 3 s's & 4 d's, none of which res with parents then; QLF 1901 from desc Miss Carrie E SMITH, Philadelphia, PA. F-S36124 R1715
 Daniel, b 12/12/1761 East Chester Co, NY; mvd with f 1763 to NC (area later Caswell Co); esf 1778 in NC unit when res Washington Co, VA; esf 1779 Caswell Co, NC, where res; PN there 1832; dd 12/22/33; md 1/27/1782 Nancy; wid PN ae 78 Caswell Co, NC, 1840; ch births (family bible blotched, partly illegible): --- 12/8/1782, Saley D 12/17/83, Lavoiney 10/27/87, Laney 9/23/90, Poley 5/28/91, Nancy 10/28/93, Daniel 11/19/95, Lucy M 3/22/98, ---tey 1/4/1801, Susanna 7/8/180-, Benjamin 9/17/04, & Sidney S 9/25/07 (he res 1840 Caswell Co, NC); surname also spelled MERRIT. F-W7441 R1715
 Levi, esf 1781 Burlington Co, NJ; PN ae 62 Greene Co, PA, 1838 Marshall Co, VA, having recently mvd there from PA; dd 4/28/38; surname also spelled MERRIT. F-S38208 R1715

MERRITT, Major, private in VA unit; BLW12368 issued 5/7/1793.
F-BLW12368 R1715
MERRITT, Major, esf 1779 Essex Co, VA; PN ae 60 Bedford Co, VA
1819; res 1820 Henrico Co, VA, occupation carpenter, with
w aec 63; dd c1826; w Happey dd c1829; heirs mbnn afp 1853
Lynchburg, VA; no action on afp indicated. F-S38213 R1715
Samuel, esf 1777 in 2nd VA Regiment; PN 1818 Botetourt Co,
VA; res there 1920 ae 62, occupation laborer, when had w &
ch: Washington ae 14, David ae 11, Pallman ae 7, Samuel ae
4, James ae 1; surname also spelled MERRIT. F-S38206 R1715
William, b 12/20/1762 Essex Co, VA; esf 1780 Surry Co (area
later Stokes Co), NC, where res; PN 1833 Stokes Co, NC; dd
5/22/41 leaving wid mbnn; wid gtd PN arrears due h 1843 NC
F-S2821 R1715
MERRIWETHER, David, BLW1511 issued 6/19/1795. F-BLW1511 R1716
James, see MERIWETHER, James. F-R16407 R1716
Thomas, see MERIWETHER, Thomas. F-BLW1920 R716
Valentine, see MEREWETHER, Valentine. F-W8454 R1716
MERRY, Philip, b Kilkenny, Ireland; to America 1769; esf 1776
Falmouth, Stafford Co, VA; PN aec 84 Fauquier Co, VA 1833;
dd 9/6/1837; md 12/20/1789 Rose WHARTON, King George Co,
VA; wid PN ae 74 Fauquier Co, VA, 1839; res there 1843 ae
79 with nephew Samuel WHARTON; dd 2/29/44. F-W7440 R1716
MERRYMAN, Thomas, esf 1776 Williamsburg, VA in 2nd VA Regiment
PN as Thomas Sr ae 65 Cumberland Co, VA, 1827. F-S38203
R1716
MERSHON, Titus, esf 1776 Hunterdon Co, NJ, where b 1755; mvd
after RW to Morgantown, WV, thence KY where PN 1834 Laurel
Co; dd there 4/11/41; md there 3/16/1832 Elizabeth HUGHS,
whose 1st h William DAVIS dd TN; wid b 4/14/1798; wid md
(3) 11/3/45 William HUBBARD who dd 1/2/55 Clay Co, KY; wid
PN there 1836; res Manchester there 1872; Joseph HUBBARD,
s of wid 3rd h, res 1859 Clay Co, KY. F-W10137 R1716
MERYMAN, William, b 1754 Bedford Co, VA; esf 1780 Granville Co
NC; mvd to SC, thence GA where afp Carroll Co 1834, & PAR;
decd in 1846 when 1 d mbnn. F-R7136 R1716
MESSENGER, Abner, esf 1778 Simsbury Township, Hartford, CT; PN
ae 74 Preston Co, VA, 1832; QLF states sol b 1760, & dd
1845 Preston Co, VA. F-S9022 R1717
MESSHEW, Jesse, b 1756 Goochland Co, VA; esf 1776 Georgetown
District, SC; mvd after RW to KY for 15 years, then to
Jackson Co, TN, for 1.5 years, then to Henderson Co, KY,
thence Hickman Co, KY, where PN 1834; surname also spelled
MESSHEU. F-S15523 R1717
METCALF, Danza, b on Roanoke River in VA; esf Rutherford Co,
NC, where res during RW; also served with GA troops; PN ae
73 Rutherford Co, NC, 1832; dd there 3/9/39; md there 9/2/
1792, or 8/3/1792, Mary BRADLEY; wid PN ae 65 there 1840;
res there 1844 ae 70; sol bro Warner also gtd RW PN. F-
F-W4280 R1718
Vachel, esf 1780 Berkeley Co, VA where b 9/22/1760; afp 1836
Cross Creek Township, Washington Co, PA; PAR, less than 6

METCALF (continued)
  months svc. F-R7148 R1718
 Walter, esf in 8th VA Regiment; BLW410 issued 4/22/1808 to
  Isaac DIX (NKG), Accomac Co, VA, when sol decd. F-BLW410
  R1718
 William, b 1764 VA; esf Rutherford Co, NC where res, serving
  with 3 bro's in company in which f Anthony a lieutenant; 1
  bro decd & other 2 res there 1832; mvd after RW to Jefferson Co, TN, then to Knox Co, TN, then to Claiborne Co, TN,
  then to White Co, TN, then to Marion Co, TN, where PN 1832
  when res there 7-8 years. F-S2820 R1718
METHANY, William, esf 1777 Berkeley Co, VA, res on Shenandoah
  River, in 16th VA Regiment; PN ae 73 Augusta Co, VA, 1832;
  liv 1836. F-S18122 R1719
METHEANY, Luke, esf 1777 Berkeley Co, VA; PN ae 64 Overton Co,
  TN, 1818; res there 1820, occupation house carpenter, when
  had w aec 63 almost blind, d Emillia ae 22, s William aec
  20, & crippled s Joshua ae 14 liv with them; mvd 1828 to
  Monroe Co, KY where dd 8/4/39 or 8/5/39; md 12/25/1781 El-
  ender ORR, Frederick Co, VA; ch births: John 11/25/1783,
  Anne 11/15/85, Sary 10/1/87, Margaret 1/15/90, Mary 2/2/92
  Luke 5/2/94, Moly 9/6/96, Mily 1/2/99, William 12/22/1800,
  & Joshua 9/16/05; wid afp ae 80 Monroe Co, KY, 1840; PAR,
  she not a wid at time/o pertinent PN Act; AFF then by Mary
  FULKS there she b 1772 Loudoun Co, VA, her f mvd 1778 to
  Frederick Co, VA, where her bro John FULKS b 1778, her
  youngest sis b there 1781, further that sol's bro's Archibald & Daniel (both decd 1840) came to her house to report
  sol & Elender ORR md Christmas Day; sol s Joshua AFF Monroe Co, KY, 1843 his m dd 5/15/1842, leaving ch: John, Sarah, Polly, Margaret, Luke, Ellender, Milley, William, &
  Joshua. F-R7149 R1719
MICHAEL, Jacob, esf York, PA; mvd c1800 to Henry Co, VA; dd
  12/26/1813; md 1782 Catharine GOODE, Little York, PA, when
  present were her bro David GOODE, sol sis Elizabeth & her
  h William YOUNG; wid afp ae 85 Henry Co, VA, 1845, & PAR;
  afp presented by her to US Congress 1850 & again PAR; her
  bro David GOODE res 1846 Franklin Co, PA; s-in-law Solomon ALLICE of West Columbia, VA, wrote query to PN Office
  1860 about PN for sol wid; sol d Elizabeth also sent query
  then, & was informed no PN authorized for ch of RW sol & w
  under current laws; QLF 1891 by gdd Sarah COOPER, Redmond,
  Mason Co, WV. F-R7152 R1719
MICHELL, Reaps, see MITCHELL, Reaps. F-BLW2335 R1719
MICHIE, George, s/o James; esf 1777 Fredericksburg, VA; afp ae
  68 Wayne Co, TN 1827, occupation farmer, when had w Judith
  (his 2nd w nee FLOOD aec 60), d Lucy ae 25, d Betsey aec
  23; PAR. F-R7153 R1719
MICOU, Henry, esf 1776 in 3rd VA Regiment; PN 1818 King George
  Co, VA, ae 69; res there 1820 ae 71 when had w Nancy aec
  61, single d's Anna ae 26, Evelin ae 24, & Jane ae 18, + d
  Melissa (a wid with 4 small ch). F-S38218 R1719

MIDCAP, John, b 11/15/1763-5-6 (all 3 years given by sol), Alexandria, VA; m & f dd when he infant; esf 1780 Fauquier Co, VA, where res; esf 1790 Nelson Co, KY against indians; afp 1835 Jefferson Co, IN; PAR, less than 6 months svc. F-R7155 R1719

MIDDLEBROOK, John, esf 1777 in 6th VA Regiment; res after RW Hanover Co, VA, thence Caroline Co, VA where res 1810; AFF then there by James WILSON, who served with sol in RW in 6th VA Regiment; gtd BLW565; dd 5/9/1815; md 6/9/1785 Lucy TURNER, Caroline Co, VA; wid PN ae 69 St Margaret's Parish there 1839 had 7 ch of which 3 decd & 4 liv 1840 including Sally who b there 10/1792; AFF 1841 there by Jonathan DICKERSON his d Nancy b 10/22/1792 there; wid gtd BLW38535 there 1855; AFF there then by Josephus GATEWOOD & Mary J MIDDLEBROOK (NKG); John S PENDLETON then Co clerk of court there; AFF 1838 there by Smith MASON ae 76, Robert SATTERWHITE ae ae 85 (RW svc with sol), Agness YARBROUGH ae 76, William GATEWOOD ae 76, & by Augustine GATEWOOD ae 64.   F-W3443 R1719

MIDDLESWART, Jacob, b 10/61 Monmouth Co, NJ; reared in PA; esf 1779 Washington Co PA; esf 1782 in VA regiment; mvd c1809 from PA to Brown Co, OH, where PN 1834; dd there 5/1/37; md 2/22/1787 Jane near Pittsburgh, PA; wid PN ae 73 Brown Co, OH 1838; res there 1843 ae 74 Jackson Township; births of 1st 5 ch: James Martin 3/16/1788, Mary 12/25/89, Sarah 1/15/92, Elizabeth 2/24/94, & Hannah 6/8/96; surname also spelled MIDDLESWORT. F-W4034 R1719

MIDDLETON, Basil, esf 1777 as surgeon in VA regiment; gtd BLW 358 in 1807; dd 1809 Prince George Co, VA; md 9/1788 Mary BELCHERS/BELSCHER of Southampton Co, VA; wid dd 9/15/1841 at home of Mr & Mrs John CARGILL, Sussex Co, VA; 1st ch dd ae 4 months; 2nd ch Benjamin dd Petersburg, VA, leaving no wid or ch; s George dd without heirs; s Aubin dd leaving s Arthur & s George; their guardian Nathaniel Thomas WILLIAMS afp 1843 Southampton Co, VA, & ch gtd PN due gdm; Margaret, w/o John CARGILL, AFF then Sussex Co, VA she cousin to sol wid; AFF then by her h John CARGILL; sis/o Margaret CARGILL, Mrs SHORE md 11/1788.   FW18522 R1720

John, member of Lee's Legion; BLW2705 & BLW1468 issued to s & heir John 3/2/1799; records lost in Washington, DC, fire F-BLW2705 R1720

John, b 4/24/1764 Lancaster Co, PA; esf 1777 Shenandoah Co, VA; mvd 1813 to Highland Co, OH, where PN 1833; last PN in file 1840. F-S2847 R1720

John, esf 1780 Loudoun Co, VA, where b 11/20/1761; mvd 1796 to Harrison Co, VA, where PN 1832; dd there 1/31/37; md 3/28/1797 Eleanor HARDY, Winchester, VA; wid PN ae 78 Harrison Co, VA, 1837; children mbnn then; res there 1857 when wid gtd BLW28594; surname also spelled MIDETON; QLF 1933 from great great gds (on m side) Dorsey BARTLETT, Clarksburg, WV, states sol wid dd 6/26/1864, sol s of John who also RW sol, & they kin to Arthur MIDDLETON, who signer of

MIDDLETON (continued)
   Declaration of Independence. F-W7464 R1720
MIDKIFF, Isaiah, b 12/18/1760 Halifax Co, VA; esf 1777 Henry
   Co, VA; mvd later 1777 to Surry Co, NC, where esf 1780; PN
   1832 Grainger Co, TN; AFF there then by John MAY that he
   esf 1777 Henry Co, VA, with sol. F-S1700 R1720
   John, see MEDKIFF, John. F-W3852 R1720
MILAM, John, b 6/12/1753 Brunswick Co, VA; mvd with f to Halifax Co, VA, where res during RW; esf there 1775 in 7th VA
   Regiment; mvd to Laurens District, SC, thence c1819 to Madison Co, AL, where PN 1832; dd there 10/19/38 or 10/26/38
   md 1813 Polly ALLISON, Laurens District, SC; wid PN ae 75
   Monroe Co, MS, 1858. F-W9951 R1720
   Jordon, b 2/26/1750; esf 1781 Henry Co, VA, where res; PN
   1832 Hickman Co, TN; P O address 1837 Centerville, TN; mvd
   10/1851 to Carroll Co, AR, where dd 12/23/51 at home/o Samuel MILUM (NKG); md 8/2/1792 Mary PEACOCK, Abbeville District, SC, who b 12/23/1773; gtd BLW82517 when res Marion
   Co, AR 7/1855; PN 10/1855 Carroll Co, AR; ch included Henry & Edward, both res 1858 Marion Co, AR. F-W25709 R1720
   Rush, b 1759 Culpeper Co, VA; mvd ae 2 with m & f to Bedford
   Co, VA; esf there 1781; mvd 1786 to Botetourt Co, VA, then
   1812 to Kanawha Co, VA where PN 1833; name dropped from PN
   rolls 1835 by PN Office when proof/o 6 months of svc found
   insufficient; surname also spelled MILLAM. F-S7943 R1720
MILBOURN, Andrew, b 1763 NJ; raised Loudoun Co, VA, where esf
   1780 Leesburg; mvd 1789 to Campbell Co, VA, for 10 years,
   thence Columbiana Co, OH where PN 1832; last PN payment in
   file 1839; surname also spelled MILBURN. F-S2845 R1720
   Thomas, b 1742-43 VA; raised in Stafford Co, VA, where esf
   1780; mvd to Brunswick Co, VA, thence 1784 Caswell Co, NC,
   for 14 years, thence Rockingham Co, NC, thence 1826 Sumner
   Co, TN, where PN 1833. F-S2846 R1720
MILBURN, William, esf 1781 Prince William Co, VA when res Frederick Co, VA; PN ae 69 Greene Co, TN, 1832; dd 2/11/1835
   there; md 6/1787 Bethea HUTCHISON, Loudoun Co, VA; wid PN
   ae 77 Greene Co, TN, 1843; gtd BLW26856 there 1855;   dd
   there 11/14/62; ch births: David 3/15/1789, Elizabeth 12/
   23/94 (md Mr GASS), William 2/7/98, Nancy A 2/14/99 (md Mr
   BALES), Mary/Polly H 5/8/1801, Rachel 7/3/03 (md Mr HIGH),
   Beca 11/6/07, & Bethire 1/19/09 (md Mr HOPE); adm of wid's
   estate James A BALES 1869, when her heirs were: William G
   ROBERTS, John MAHONEY, Malinda P MILBURN, Sarah A MILBURN,
   L K COX, Samuel BABB, Nancy A BALES, Mary H MILBURN, Rachel HIGH, Elizabeth GASS, & Bethia HOPE; wid dd 11/4/62;
   her PN cut off during RW, & her adm James A BALES applied
   1870 ae 34 Greene Co, TN, for PN arrears due her; PAR, wid
   dd without having reestablished PN claim; her ch res 1870:
   Nancy A BALES, Mary H MILBURN, Rachel HIGH, all Greene Co,
   TN, & Bethia HOPE, Bradley Co, TN. F-W51 R1720
MILES, Charles, b 3/8/1756 Culpeper Co, VA, where esf 1775 res
   Great Bridge; PN there 1832; dd there 1/4/38; md 6/17/1779

255

MILES (continued)
   Patty/Patsey, d of William VAUGHAN; wid PN ae 76 Culpeper
   Co, VA 1838 res Stevensburg; wid sis Almond VAUGHAN AFF ae
   82+ then Culpeper Co, VA; wid res 1844 Covington, KY, with
   dd mbnn; d Sarah AFF then Kenton Co, KY. F-W8455 R1721
Jesse, b 7/1/1763 Prince Georges Co, MD, s of Richard; esf
   Berkeley Co, VA, where res, sub for f; res there after RW,
   mvd c1793 to Nelson Co, KY; PN 1833 Bullitt Co (area formerly in Nelson Co), KY; dd 4/11/38. F-S1235 R1721
John, esf 1776 Amelia Co, VA; PN ae 73 Prince Edward Co, VA,
   1829, occupation planter, when family res with him: w Ann
   aec 60, d Frances aec 30, d Elizabeth aec 25, gds Filmor
   aec 18, & gds Frank aec 7. F-S38219 R1721
John, esf 1777 Fauquier Co, VA in 10th VA Regiment; PN ae 79
   Clermont Co, OH, 1818; dd 1/8/33 Williamsville, OH; md 11/
   15/1789 Mary BEASLEY, Loudoun Co, VA, when she ae 25; wid
   PN aec 80 Clermont Co, OH 1846; gtd BLW13902 there 1855 ae
   90; d Hannah WALKER, b 11/10/1790, AFF 1845 there she res
   there 1814-15 & had then ch aec 3; wid sis Alice CHALMERS,
   (twin to bro Silas, 2-3 years younger than wid), md 1785,
   had s William CHALMERS b 1794, & she res 1849 Clermont Co,
   OH. F-W2682 R1721
John, esf 1777 Culpeper Co, VA in VA regiment; PN ae 59 Henry Co, KY, 1818; dd there 10/9/28; md 1/1/1784 Mary/Polly
   DUVALL, Culpeper Co, VA; wid mvd soon after h dd to Montgomery Co, IN, where PN 1839 ae 73; res there 1851; dd 6/
   30/55; ch births: William 9/3/1784, Elizabeth 10/14/86,
   Benjamin 11/28/88, Ames 11/11/90, John 1/23/92, Wats 2/14/
   94, Alice 2/25/96, Ann 12/3/99, twins Jefferson & Thomas
   6/28/03 or 6/28/05 & George 11/10/07; s John res 1839 Henry Co, KY; s Jefferson res 1839 Montgomery Co, IN; Reuben
   MILES (NKG) AFF 1839 Shelby Co, KY, he b 7/26/1765, & witnessed marriage of sol & w Polly; QLF 1915 from great gdd
   Mrs Jane Miles JARVIE of Sigourney, IA, states sol wid dd
   1855 Montgomery Co, IN. F-W9567 R1721
Michael, esf 1780 in VA regiment; dd c1795 French Broad; md
   md 12/1781 or 1/1782, or 2/1782 Mary HARRISON who res with
   her f at fort at Falls of the Ohio; wid mvd to where now
   Bardstown, KY, to live at home of her bro-in-law, Captain
   Philemon WATERS; wid PN ae 83 Washington Co, KY, 1840 when
   res there c48 years; her bro Thomas res then Marion Co, KY
   ae 70, & AFF his f & family mvd to Falls of the Ohio in
   Spring 1780; wid dd 9/9/1854; only ch mbnn. F-W8456 R1721
Thomas, b Charles City Co, VA; mvd when boy with stepfather
   to Cumberland Co, VA, thence Caswell Co, NC, where sol esf
   1776-77; mvd 1798 to Davidson Co, TN, thence 1804 Williamson Co, TN, for c10 years, then to Wilson Co, TN, where PN
   1832 aec 80; dd 9/15/38; md 2/1773 Ann, who PN ae 89 Rutherford Co, TN, 1840; ch births: Heartwell/Hartwell 4/1774,
   John 177-, Ann 6/4/78, Thomas 7/20/80, Betsey 9/9/82, Byrd
   4/4/85, Phanny 1/28/88 & Patterson 3/11/90 or 3/14/90; QLF
   1914 from great great gds Clifford LOVE, Murfreesboro, TN,

MILES (continued)
   states sol wid res with s Patterson near Florence in Rutherford Co, TN. F-W8457 R1721
Thomas, b11/10/1760 Spotsylvania Co, VA; esf 1779-80 Caswell Co, NC; afp 1833 Baldwin Co, GA; PAR, insufficient proof/o svc; dd 11/23/44 Russell Co, AL; w dd before him; d & only ch Louisa P (w of John CROWELL) res 1853 Oswichee, Russell Co, AL, had children mbnn, & her d's h Methodist minister, who res Glenville, AL, 1857, afp there for sol d, & PAR. F-R7168 R1721
Thomas, b 2/1761 MD; esf 1781 Albemarle Co, VA; PN ae 73 Amherst Co, VA 1833; last PN payment in file 1841. F-S15939 R1721
William, esf 1777 Culpeper Co, VA; PN ae 65 Fayette Co, KY, 1818; QLF states sol dd c1824. F-S36142 R1721
MILIRONS, William, esf 1777 in 12th VA Regiment; PN 1818 Warren Co, GA, ae not given. F-S38222 R1722
MILKOLLIN, Jonathan, b Loudoun Co, VA; esf 1781 Botetourt Co, VA; mvd 1788 to OH, thence 1800 Hambleton Co (area later Clark Co); PN ae 67-68 Clark Co, OH, 1818. F-S16977 R1722
MILLAR, George, esf 1780 Shenandoah Co, VA, where b 5/24/1762; mvd 1794 to Clark Co, KY where PN 1832; last PN payment in file 1841; QLF 1931 from Charles A WHITE of Danville, IN, whose w great gdd of sol; QLF 1925 from desc Frank W GARDNER, Columbus, OH, says sol bro/o William who dd 1827; QLF 1918 from desc Geraldine W (Mrs E M) BLESSING of Danville, IN, states sol s Martin res Sharpsburg, KY, later res Cincinnati, OH, md Deborah STEVENSON/STINSON who survived him & afp for Martin's War of 1812 svc, & they had ch Taliaferro & Matilda CASKEY. F-S16486 R1722
MILLBANK, John, esf in VA Line; mvd to KY c1806 where sol dd c 1827 Scott Co; AFF then there by Akilles STAPP (NKG); md 4/10/1773 Mary, Culpeper Co, VA; wid afp ae 86 Scott Co, KY, 1836; PAR, insufficient proof of svc; res there 1842 when gave power of attorney to afb; PAR again; ch births: Elender 4/16/1774, Elizabeth 4/23/77, Charles 5/26/78, Anny 11/22/79, Mary 11/1781 & Sally 5/29/83; Ann STAPP (NKG) afp there 1852, & PAR. F-R7163 R1722
MILLBURN, William, see MILBURN, William. F-W51 R1722
MILLEGAN, John, BLW12383 issued 5/9/1797. F-BLW12383 R1722
MILLER, Andrew, b 2/25/1760 Rosenfelt, Germany; came to America when infant with f & they settled Philadelphia, PA; mvd to Hampshire Co, VA, where sol esf 1777 in area later Hardy Co, VA; mvd 1787 to Randolph Co, VA, where esf 1833, & PAR. F-R7176 R1723
Barney, b near Josephstown, PA; mvd aec 10 to Berkeley Co, VA where esf 1781; res there 17 years, thence Breckenridge Co, KY, where PN 1832 ae 68; res 1836 as Barney Sr, Spencer Co, IN, when had 2 d's & 2 s's res there; his application for PN transfer there witnessed by Nicholas MILLER & Barney MILLER Jr; sol liv 1839; QLF 1913 from desc Margaret Karney MORROW, Upland, CA, states sol w Tissue drew PN

MILLER (continued)
S-16973 R1723
Benjamin, esf 1781 near Romney, Hampshire Co, VA, where res; afp ae 71 Wayne Co, OH, 1833 res Canaan Township; PAR, under 6 months svc; QLF 1922 from gdd Eliza Melissa BROWNING of Chicago, IL; QLF 1908 from great gds James F BROWNING, Chicago, IL, states sol had older bro's Isaac & Henry, who also esf Hampshire Co, VA, mvd to OH, settled near Canton in Stark Co & dd there, further sol md 1784 Elizabeth PARKER, Hampshire Co, VA who had 3 bro's also RW sol's including Henry PARKER, further sol gdd Mrs David RITTERSBACH res Akron, OH, 1908; QLF 1930 from great great gds C O Van METER, Wooster, OH, states he has copy/o sol notebook containing family births as follows: sol b 3/14/1762 & dd 3/28/1841, sol w Elizabeth PARKER b 12/8/1766 & dd 3/21/1851 their ch births: Isaac 3/14/1785, Sarah 12/21/86 (md Abraham Van METER), Luke 12/9/88, John 1/15/91 (twin Susannah dd 1795), Abraham 3/28/93, Jonathan 7/15/96, Elizabeth 9/22/98, Jacob 9/15/1801, twins Joseph & Benjamin 6/4/02, James 9/12/04, Susannah 10/11/06, & Myrtilla 4/8/09; further sol & w res Wooster, OH, when last ch b, having previously res near Wellsville or Steubenville, OH; QLF 1922 from great gdd Arletta (Mrs E A) MANSFIELD of Buffalo, NY.
F-R7178 R1723
Christian, esf 1780 Shenandoah Co, VA, where b near Woodstock; PN ae 88 there 1832; dd 4/28/36; md 1770 Catharine WISMAN; wid PN ae 83 there 1837; dd 2/2/39; ch births: Philip 9/29/1772, Jacob 4/8/75, Catharine 8/2/78, John 5/3/81, Mary 8/19/83, Joseph 2/5/86, Henry 3/27/88, Barbary 12/11/90, & Elizabeth 1/25/94; AFF 1837 there by Jacob W MILLER (NKG) ae? & Christian MILLER (NKG) ae 78 in behalf of sol wid; George WISMAN (NKG) AFf then there he witnessed sol marriage; QLF 1914 from desc Mrs Major J B DOWNING of Middleport, OH, d of William Clendennin MILLER who s of sol s Henry, says sol b 1744 Shenandoah Co, VA, s of Jacob who came to Valley of VA c1740, further sol md Catherine WEISMAN; QLF 1914 from great great gdd Mrs P G JONES, Alameda, CA; QLF 1895 from A F ASBURY, Higginsville, MO, says his children desc of VA RW sol Christopher MILLER of Woodstock, Shenandoah Co, VA. F-W18515 R1723
Daniel, b 12/1747; esf 1775-78 Augusta Co, VA; PN 1832 Montgomery Co, VA, as Daniel Sr; dd 2/28/40 leaving wid mbnn.
F-S5762 R1724
Daniel, esf 1778 Winchester, VA; PN ae 64 Fayette Co, PA, 1819 res Uniontown; res there 1820 occupation tailor, when liv with w Barbara ae 61 & widowed d & her 4 small ch; mvd back to Winchester, VA where dd 11/24/1825; md right after RW Barbara, Winchester, VA; wid PN there 1838 ae 81 when eldest s Presley ae 54; John CROCKWELL AFF there then he & sol boys together there; William SEEMER (b 7/1783) AFF there 1839 he h of sol d Elizabeth (b 10/1/1804); AFF then there by Elizabeth BALL ae 72 that sol was apprentice wor-

MILLER (continued)
  king for her f when md Barbara, Winchester, VA. F-W18512
  R1724
David, esf 1779 in 3rd VA Regiment;   dd 7/1798; md c12/1780
  Ann CRAIG, Williamsburg, VA;   wid PN there 1837 ae 73;   dd
  12/17/44; sol niece Martha BASKERVILLE w/o Ezekiel F EAST-
  MAN res 1828 Chillicothe, OH; sol niece Mary K BASKERVILLE
  res then Fayette Co, OH; these nieces gtd BLW1328; Colonel
  Burwell BASSETT AFF 1837 New Kent Co, VA, he knew sol wid
  before her marriage, & he mvd from Williamsburg, VA, 1779,
  he former US congressman from VA; QLF says a VA RW sol David MILLER had d Isabella who md 1794 Baldwin HARLE, Maryville, TN. F-W18516 R1724
Edward, b 1/3/1746; esf 1775 Henrico Co, VA, where res;   PN
  1832 Spencer Co, KY. F-S16484 R1724
Edward, b Shenandoah Co, VA; esf 1779 Augusta Co, VA, where
  res; res after RW Millerstown, Shenandoah Co, VA, thence
  1799 to Gallia Co, OH, thence Lawrence Co, OH, then c1826
  to Shelby Co, IN, where PN 1832 aec 79, res Henricks Township; dd that Co 1/26/36; md 9/1/1787 Rebecca, Stoverstown
  Shenandoah Co, VA; wid PN ae 68 Shelby Co, IN, 1839 when
  res with s Edward; ch births (all liv 1839): William 7/12/
  1788, Catharine 1/12/90, Christina 10/-/91, Polly 3/1/93,
  John 2/-/95, Jacob 11/-/96, Rebecca 7/24/98, Henry 3/1/
  1801, Alexander 5/19/03, Andrew 3/4/05, Isaac 7/14/07,
  Elizabeth 8/28/09, & Edward 4/2/13; sol nephew John ELLIN-
  GER res 1839 Shelby Co, IN; QLF states a VA RW sol Edward
  MILLER b 1737 VA, & md Miss LEE; QLF 1925 from gds James/
  Jap MILLER, Morristown, NJ. F-W9571 R1724
Francis, BLW12356 issued 10/22/1791. F-BLW12356 R1724
Francis, esf 1780 Culpeper Co, VA, where res; mvd 1795 to
  Jessamine Co, KY, where PN 1833 ae 85+; dd 10/19/39; md c
  1782 Elizabeth FREEMAN who b 4/28/1761; wid PN 1843 Jessa-
  mine Co, KY; youngest ch Merriman F AFF there then he b 8/
  29/1804, & his parents had 12 ch: eldest ch Polly ae 58-59
  then if liv, 3rd ch Elizabeth b 1/27/1787, Cathy b 2/28/97
  Mason b 10/27/98, Patsey b 9/27/1802, William b 6/23/03,
  & Merriman 8/29/04, others not named; Rebekah FREEMAN AFF
  1843 Laurel Co, KY, she md c1791 to wid bro John FREEMAN.
  F-W8459 R1724
Francis, b & raised Kingston Parish, Gloucester Co, VA where
  esf 1776; dd 3/8/1781 leaving w & 3 small ch mbnn; md 10/
  1776 there Averilla DIGGS, who also b there (area later in
  in Mathews Co, VA); wid md (2) 9/1796 Thomas OWENS, who dd
  12/24/1821; wid PN ae 79 Mathews Co, VA, 1837; AFF then
  there by sol bro Gabriel MILLER, b 1781 & raised Kingston
  Parish, Gloucester Co, VA; AFF 1837 Mathews Co, VA, by Josiah PUGH ae 76 who also b Kingston Parish, Gloucester Co,
  VA; QLF says sol wid res 1840 ae 74 with James D OWEN, Mathews Co, VA. F-W19951 R1724
Frederic(k), b PA; ae 10 when f killed by indians; mvd with
  m then to Shenandoah River in PA, thence Buckingham Co, VA

MILLER (continued)
   where esf 1780; res there c20 years, thence Wilkes Co, NC, for c18 years, thence Bedford Co, TN, for 1 year, then to Wayne Co, KY, where PN 1832 ae "80 odd years plus", res at Wayne. F-S30589 R1724
Frederick, b 8/8/1760 Augusta Co (area later Rockingham Co), VA; esf 1778 Rockingham Co, VA, where res; PN 1832 Preble Co, OH; QLF 1929 from great gdd Leila Miller SMITH, Ligonier, IN, states sol f also RW sol; QLF states sol dd 1835 Preble Co, OH, & had desc Jacob F MILLER; QLF says sol mvd c1790 to Hawkins Co, TN, thence 1795 Anderson Co, TN, then 1803 to Preble Co, OH, where dd near West Alexandria. F-S2831 R1724
George, esf 1776 Carlisle, PA in company which joined 6th VA Regiment; transferred to 4th MD Regiment; PN Baltimore, MD 1818; res there 1820 ae 69 when w Margaret ae 50; dd 4/26/28. F-S35001 R1725
George, see MILLAR, George. F-S16486 R1725
Henry, esf 1776 York Co, PA in PA regiment, where b 10/1755; PN 1833 Somerset Co, PA, res Petersburg; res 1837 Preston Co, VA; dd 4/2/42; md 11/25/1781 Mary Ann LINARD who PN ae 86 Preston Co, VA 1846; eldest d Elizabeth PAUL then ae 65 & 2nd d Mrs ALBRIGHT mentioned then; QLF 1925 from great great gdd Alice Paul (Mrs Charles Howard) SMOAT, Camden on Gauley, WV, states her gdf s of sol d Elizabeth; QLF 1925 from Marcia O STEPHENSON, Independence, IA, desc of RW sol John Henry MILLER, who md Ann Mary LININGER/SININGER, mvd to Hanover Co, PA, thence Pres Co, VA, & they had d Margaret; QLF 1924 from Miss Margaret B STEPHENSON of Independence, IA, who also desc of RW sol John Henry MILLER. F-W7458 R1725
Henry, b 6/10/1758 Germany; came to America 1771 with f, & settled at Olney, Reading Co, PA where esf 1776 in 9th PA Regiment; esf 1779 Hampshire Co, VA; PN 1832 Franklin Co, OH, res Clinton Township; last PN payment in file 1838. F-S2830 R1725
Henry, b 12/6/1759 Augusta Co, VA; mvd to Bedford Co, VA, where esf 1776; mvd 1783 to KY, thence 1829 Tippecanoe Co, IN, where PN 1832; dd 11/18/46; QLF 1909 from great gds Reverend John H FAZEL, Topeka, KS; QLF 1938 from desc Mrs J O BIRDSALL, Spencer, IA; QLF 1937 from desc Ruth M WILSON, Tulsa, OK, states sol md Sarah PERCY & was of German descent. F-S16481 R1725
Henry, esf 1781 Rockingham Co, VA, where b 7/14/1764; afp there, & PAR, less than 6 months svc; nephew of RW sol Michael COGER; QLF 1912 from desc Mrs Claud S SANFORD of Greenville, SC, states sol f Henry also RW sol who b 1743 Rockingham Co, VA, md Elizabeth KOOGER, & their s Henry md Mary PRICE & dd 9/18/1850, also both Henry's b & dd Elkton VA. F-R7196 R1725
Jacob, esf 1780-81 Shenandoah Co, VA, where b 8/12/1760; mvd 1816 to KY, where PN 1833 Harrison Co; QLF 1918 from desc

MILLER (continued)
  Mrs Ella SEACHREST of Chicago, IL; QLF states sol res 1840
    Cynthiana, KY, w maiden name maybe BACON. F-S31258 R1726
  Jacob, esf 1777 Loudoun Co, VA; mvd 1795 from Winchester, VA
    to KY, where PN 1818 ae 64 Jefferson Co; in 1820 sol had 5
    ch res with him: George ae 29, Isaac ae 22, Mary ae 25, d
    Teny ae 18, & Eliza ae 13; mvd c1824 to IN; dd 7/25/39 at
    Crawfordsville, IN; md 4/1782-87 Margaret DICK near Winch-
    ester, VA; wid b 1762-68; PN 1840 Montgomery Co, IN; eld-
    est s John b 1-2 years after marriage & was decd in 1844;
    s George dd 7/14/1846 Crawfordsville, IN, per headstone
    erected by relative Mrs Maria GIBSON; QLF 1931 from great
    great gdd Mabel J FUNDERBURG, Denver, CO, says sol wid dd
    1/22/1863 ae 97, querier being great gdd of sol s William
    who buried by his f. F-W9569 R1726
  Jacob, b 10/1763 Lancaster Co, PA; esf 1781 Loudoun Co, VA,
    where res; afp 1837 Bedford Co, VA; PAR, under six months
    svc. F-R7200 R1726
  James, b 8/12/1748 Baltimore Co, MD; esf 1780 Shenandoah Co,
    VA, where res; mvd from VA to TN, & leaving military dis-
    charge paper with widowed m; PN 1834 Claiborne Co, TN; dd
    8/26/41 leaving wid mbnn. F-S4210 R1726
  James, esf in 10th VA Regiment; PN 1819 Patrick Co, VA; res
    there 1820 aec 64 with w mbnn; Benjamin SHINAULT & John
    HUGHES AFF there then they in RW svc with sol. F-S38230
    R1726
  Javan, lieutenant in VA unit; nephew & heir Abijah PARSONS
    gtd BLW1871 Princess Anne Co, VA, 1832. F-BLW1871 R1726
  John, b 1765 Washington Co, MD where esf in MD regiment; mvd
    with f after RW to PA, then to Shenandoah Co, VA, then to
    Botetourt Co, VA, thence Grainger Co, TN, thence White Co,
    TN, where PN 1834 when res there 24 years; dd there 11/4/
    46; md 7/5/1787 Mary DOTSON, Shenandoah Co, VA; wid PN ae
    81 White Co, Tn, 1849; AFF 1846 by Hiram DODSON (NKG) & by
    Valentin DODSON (NKG). F-W47 R1727
  John, esf Botetourt Co, VA, where reared; PN ae 71 Carter Co
    TN, 1832. F-S1921 R1728
  John, esf 1778 Berkeley Co, VA, where b 2/1/1759 near Keys
    Ferry; PN 1833 Morgan Co, VA. F-S9026 R1728
  John, esf 1778 in 1st VA Regiment; PN 1821 Adair Co, KY, ae
    63 when had no w or ch res with him; mvd c1826 to Russell
    Co, KY, where res 7 years; last PN payment in file 1833.
    F-36136 R1728
  John, b 1750 Germany; to America ae 10; esf 1780 Berkeley Co
    VA; res Botetourt Co, VA, when esf last time; res there
    until 1800, when mvd to KY, where PN 1833 Bullitt Co. F-
    S38223 R1728
  John, b 3/8/1761 Caroline Co, VA; esf 1778 Bedford Co, VA;
    BLW10629 issued 1/5/1782; PN 1832 Sumner Co, TN; dd 6/16/
    48; md 8/26/1841 Lucy HICKMAN, Davidson Co, TN; wid PN
    there 1853 ae 67; wid gtd BLW14517 there 1855 ae 70. F-
    W5380 R1728

MILLER, John, esf VA; dd 8/25/1832 Knox Co, TN; md 1776 Eve
WHITENER; wid afp ae 100 & 6 months on 7/31/1851 there, &
PAR, insufficient proof/o svc; dd 8/2/53; ch: eldest Polly
(ae 69 if liv 1852), Jacob, Isaac, Nancy LOY, Elizabeth
GRAVES, & Rachel COX; all survived m except Polly, & they
res 1854 Knox Co, TN & Anderson Co, TN; Jacob MILLER (NKG)
JP/o Knox Co, TN, 1851; Lewis MILLER (NKG) res Anderson Co
TN, 1852 aec 55; QLF 1935 from desc Miss Lisselle Eunice
CALE, Clarinda, IA, says sol md Eve WAGGONER, who b 1749 &
dd 1853; QLF 1836 from desc Mrs D Clay SWISHER, Clarinda,
IA; QLF states sol md Eve WHITENER/WAGGONER & some/o their
ch were John, Louis, Emanuel, & George, further sol buried
Maynardville, TN. F-R7187 R1728

John, esf c1780 Albemarle Co, VA, where b 1/1/1750; dd 8/8/
1808 Madison Co, KY; md 3/28/1774 Jane DELANEY, Orange Co,
VA (area later Madison Co); wid dd 3/13/44 Madison Co, KY;
ch births: Robert 3/1/1775, William 6/19/76, Anna 11/3/71,
Thomas 3/30/79, John 9/30/80, Elizabeth 3/20/82, Delaney
12/13/83, Joseph 5/15/86, Gerard/Garand B 17--, Jane 4/18/
92, & Frances S 6/18/94; s Robert afp 1853 Madison Co, KY,
for self & surv siblings Joseph & Jane LACKEY; PAR, insufficient proof of 6 months svc; QLF states sol's bro's Robert (b 5/5/1734, RW sol in 14th VA Regiment, of Orange Co
VA) & Thomas (b3/20/1750, also RW sol). F-R7203 R1728

John, raised at Warm Springs, VA; esf VA early in RW; mvd c
1800 to Washington Co, PA, for c19 years, thence OH, where
dd 7/6/55 Salem Township, Meigs Co, leaving no wid, but
youngest dd Catherine CLOUSE; she afp ae 67 Gallia Co, OH,
1857 as only surv ch, & PAR. F-R7208 R1728

John A, b 5/29/1758 Bucks Co, PA; esf 1775 Hampshire Co, VA,
where res; mvd after RW to KY for 20 years, thence IN for
12-14 years, thence Greene Co IL, where afp 1833; PAR, under 6 months svc. F-R7211 R1728

John H, b 1735 Amity Township, Berks Co, PA; esf 1778 Henrico Co, VA; PN 1832 Knox Co, TN. F-S2829 R1728

Joseph, b 7/29/1753 Amherst Co, VA; esf 1775 Botetourt Co,
VA, where res; PN 1832 Adair Co, KY; dd 6/11/37; QLF 1939
from great great gds Eugene BURTON, Hayward, WI, says sol
buried Smith's Burial Ground, Columbia, KY; QLF 1928 from
desc E C BROCKMAN of St Louis, MO; QLF 1927 from gdd Mrs
Charles W HENRY, Wynnewood, OK; QLF 1922 from desc Charles
G ALLEN, Keokuk, IA, states sol b Ireland & md 1774-5 Miss
MONTGOMERY in VA. F-S13943 R1728

Lawrence/Lorentz, volunteer in Lancaster Co, PA, before RW;
esf VA; gtd disability PN 1783-85; mvd then to KY, then to
Natchez, MS, thence LA; PN ae 82 St Helena Parish, LA 1832
F-S31257 R1728

Lewis, esf 1777 Winchester, VA; PN ae 64 Shenandoah Co, VA;
res there 1820 when had d's ae 19,14, & 10, + 2 s's ae not
given; w decd in 1823 when sol had mvd to Gallia Co, OH;
he & d Ann aec 16 res 1824 with s-in-law Benjamin THOMPSON
there when rest of ch all md except Polly ae 19; s Lewis &

MILLER (continued)
  s Daniel res 1826 Luray, Shenandoah Co, VA, Lewis Jr & his youngest d & children, having returned there to live with s-in-law John WILLIAMS & family; sol res 1830 Shenandoah Co, VA, with P O address Luray, & dd 6/10/31; Valentine MILLER AFF 1818 & William MILLER AFF 1819 Shenandoah Co, VA, both NKG. F-S38225 R1728
  Michael, b 2/28/1760; esf 1781 Hardy Co, VA; PN 1832 Monroe Co, IL; bro William AFF then St Clair Co, IL, formerly res Hardy Co, VA. F-S33103 R1729
  Peter, b 5/15/1759 Woodridge, NJ; mvd to Highland, Orange Co NY; esf 1776 in NY regiment; esf 1777 Chester, NJ; mvd c 1796 to Monongalia Co, VA, where PN 1832; dd 4/20/38; md 2/5/1785 Mary, Goshen, NY; wid PN ae 82 Marion Co (area formerly Monongalia Co), VA, 1845; John MILLER (NKG) AFF there then; wid sis Ann CARPENTER AFF there then ae 75 she raised in NJ & mvd to Monongalia Co, VA, c1805, she only sibling of sol wid now liv; AFF then there by Mathew FLEMING he neighbor to sol & w there 30 years; QLF 1831 from desc Mrs Lottie Jackson PATTERSON, Oberlin, OH, states sol dd Middletown (now Fairmont), WV, also sol md Mary MILLER (not related), querier also desc/o RW sol William FLEMMING who b Scotland 1/5/1717 & came to DE 1741; QLF 1900 from great gds Frank E NICHOLS of Fairmont, WV; QLF 1910 from great gds Francis E NICHOLS, Fairmont, WV. F-W7456 R1730
  Philip, b 3/10/1759; esf 1776 Berkeley Co, VA, where he & parents res on Sleepy Creek; PN 1823 Washington Co, PA; dd 6/4/52 Tyler Co, VA; md 9/13/1785 Lois BENJAMIN; wid PN ae 87 there 1852; AFF then there by Joshua RUSSELL he neighbor of sol & wid since 1832; wid gtd BLW40691 Pleasants Co, VA 1855 aec 95; QLF 1832 from desc Helen Rice (Mrs E M) MONTGOMERY, Detroit, MI. F-W3707 R1730
  Robert, esf 1777 in 14th VA Regiment; PN 1818 Pendleton District, SC ae 61; res there 1820 when w Annis ae 57 & youngest s Squire ae 17; QLF 1896 from great great gds George S POWELL, Asheville, NC; QLF 1915 from great gds Lewis M PEEPLES, Cartersville, GA. F-S47514 R1730
  Robert, esf 1777 Augusta Co, VA, sub for f Patrick; dd 2/18/1828; md 7/17/1793 Jane YOWEL, Augusta Co, VA; wid dd 9/17/1839 Greenbrier Co, VA; s John afp 1847 there for self & other surv siblings: William, John, Alexander, Elizabeth, Jane ALEXANDER, & Margaret GEORGE, all res there, + Mary FERRY & Robert, all res Daviess Co, MO; sol bro John ae 75 & sol sis Mary BENSTON ae 85 both res then Monroe Co VA; ch PAR, insufficient proof of svc. F-R7205 R1730
  Samuel, esf 1775 Kent Co, MD, where b 1/6/1755; PN Brooke Co VA, 1833 where mvd 1797; AFF 1832 by Rebekah BECK (NKG) ae 70 Ohio Co, VA, she knew sol for as along as she could recollect. F-S15940 R1730
  Thomas, b Cecil Co, MD, s/o Samuel who dd there; esf 1777 in 8th VA Regiment; PN ae 58 Franklin Co, OH, 1818; dd 7/16/1821 or 7/17/1821 Chillicothe, OH; md 8/7/1784 Ann/Nancy d

MILLER (continued)
of James & Susan BALL (MB 8/6/1784), Chesterfield Co, VA; wid PN ae 71-72 Pittsylvania Co, VA 1838; sol bro John M & sol sis Agnes WILLIAMS & sol sis Deborah res then Cecil Co MD; sol s Samuel T AFF 1825 Pittsylvania Co, VA, he nephew of William MILLER of Cecil Co, MD, & that sol dd at home/o Stephen C CISSNA (NKG), Chillicothe, OH; AFF 1838 by Isham BALL, Powhatan Co, VA, he youngest of ch of James & Susan BALL of Chesterfield Co, VA, sol wid 4th ch of parents, & that all siblings decd then except sol wid, himself, & Archer (mentally incompetent); QLF 1897 from gds Thomas Cecil MILLER, Lynchburg, VA states sol wid dd 1840; QLF 1920 from great gdd Miss Virginia A SPURR, Aurora, IL. F-W7454 R1731

Valentine, esf 1776 Loudoun Co, VA, where b 1/12/1762; afp 1842 Monroe Co, VA; PAR, insufficient proof of svc; md d/o Philip ENSMINGER of Rockbridge Co, VA; sol d Catharine FINK AFF 1842 Monroe Co, VA, her f res Rockbridge Co, VA, over 40 years ago when she ae 12-13; AFF 1842 by wid sis Mary VANCE, Monroe Co, VA, that John NOLAND, b & raised in same neighborhood as sol in Loudoun Co, VA, esf with sol, & dd Gallia Co, OH. F-R7227 R1731

William, esf 1776 Amherst Co, VA where b 1756; mvd to Wilkes Co, NC, where esf; mvd after RW to Wilkes Co, GA for 12-13 years, thence Madison Co, KY for 4-5 years, then to Davidson Co TN, thence 1820, thence Ray Co, MO, where afp 1836 & PAR. F-R7229 R1731

William, esf 1776 in 8th PA Regiment; later esf in VA regiment; PN ae 62 Fleming Co, KY, 1818; res there 1830 when name dropped from PN rolls for having too many assets; res 1835 Marion Co, IN, having recently mvd there from KY to be with children; res 1838 ae 71 Fleming Co, KY, when had w aec 67 & 1 d mbnn liv with him. F-S16203 R1731

William, b 3/1/1757 PA near MD border; esf 1780 Rockbridge Co, VA, when res there 13-14 years; PN there 1832; last PN payment in file 1838; QLF 1930 from great gdd E Frances WHELON, Minneapolis, MN, states sol buried at Cheviett, OH near Cincinnati; QLF states sol b 3/1/1757 Lancaster Co, PA, s of Henry MILLER & w Rebecca BOGGS, mvd with parents to Rockbridge Co, VA, 1770, md there 1785 Elizabeth, d/o Thomas LACKEY & w Agnes LEECH, sol dd there 11/7/1840, w dd 8/6/1834, their ch: Henry, James, Thomas L, Nancy, Agnes, William, Nathan, Ichabod, & Martha; QLF 1920 from desc Mrs F H GLENN, Stuttgart, AR. F-S5764 R1731

William, lieutenant in VA Line; BLW1520 issued 7/5/1799 to Henry GARNET, executive of sol LWT. F-BLW1520 R1731

William Heath, esf 1778 Goochland Co, VA where always lived; dd 5/23/1815 there; md there 3/19/1772 Joanna LEPRADE of that Co; wid PN there 1838 ae 89; dd 2/27/39 leaving no ch but 6 gdc & 1 great gdc; ch: John b 5/1/1773, John b 3/10/1775, & Betsy b 7/8/1776; gds William H FORD adm/o her estate there 1852; AFF 1838 there by David ROYSTER ae 78,

MILLER (continued)
    who served in RW with sol; AFF then Albemarle Co, VA, by
    James H TERRELL ae 54, gds of RW sol William DOUGLAS of
    Goochland Co, VA; AFF then by RW pensioner Archelaus PER-
    KINS ae 78 Goochland Co, VA; AFF then there by RW sol John
    RICHARDS ae 85; AFF then there by RW sol John MARTIN ae 85
    who esf 1781 in company commanded by sol; AFF then there
    by RW sol Henry ISBEL ae 78 who served in sol company; AFF
    then there by John SALMON ae 85, neighbor of sol all their
    lives, who served in sol's company; AFF then there by John
    CLEMENTS ae 81, RW pensioner, who served in sol's company;
    QLF states a RW sol William MILLER of Goochland Co md 1743
    Mary HEATH & their ch included John. F-W7451 R1731
MILLERWAY, Isaac, esf 177- Dover, Kent Co, DE, in DE regiment;
    PN ae 67 Albemarle Co, VA, 1819; res 1820 there occupation
    farmer when had w aec 53, s aec 15, d aec 13, & d aec 11;
    in 1833 heir-at-law George MILLOWAY afb there & gtd BLW
    1998; in 1838 court action there declared following to be
    sol heirs; w Susan & ch: George, William S, Isaac, Patsy
    MAHANY, Susan, Nancy SIMS, & John W. F-S38227 R1732
MILLIGAN, Hugh, esf 1776 in PA regiment; PN ae 85 Hardy Co, VA
    1820 occupation farmer, when had no family whatsoever. F-
    38232 R1732
  John, b 8/1751 Co Down, Ireland; came to America ae 19, lan-
    ding at New Castle, PA; esf 1775 in PA regiment; mvd after
    2 years to Berkeley, VA, where esf 1778; mvd 1793 to Ohio
    Co, VA, where PN 1833; dd 2/5/38; QLF 1919 from desc Mrs
    Robert M WILSON, Indiana, PA; QLF 1929 from desc Margaret
    KINNEY, Demson, IA, states sol res near Carlisle, Chester
    Co, PA, when esf, was from Ayrshire, Scotland, & md Mary
    ADAMS. F-S13939 R1732
  John, esf 1775 in 12th VA Regiment; PN ae 80 Scott Co, KY,
    1818 when blind & supported by Co, formerly a blacksmith;
    res there 1820 when had no family. F-S36130 R1732
MILLIKEN, James, b 8/19/1754 on ship enroute from Londonderry,
    Ireland, to New Castle, DE; esf 1776 Rockbridge Co, VA,
    where res; esf 1780 Washingotn Co, NC, where res; esf 1788
    against Cherokee Indians in area later Blount Co, TN; PN
    1832 Cocke Co, TN. F-S3609 R1733
MILLION, John, esd 1781 Stafford Co, VA where b 5/10/1763; mvd
    1783 to Madison Co, KY, where afp, all ch having left home
    & PAR; sis Sarah Ann COMBS AFF Edgar Co, IL, then ae 91,
    sol her eldest bro & she had s William COMBS Jr b Stafford
    Co, VA, c1776. F-R7242 R1733
MILLIWAY, Isaac, see MILLERWAY, Isaac. F-S38227 R1733
MILLNER, Luke, b 9/20/1750 Richmond Co, Va; esf before 1781 in
    Halifax Co, VA where res; mvd 1790 to Lincoln Co, KY, then
    to Harrison Co, KY, where PN 1833; dd 12/25/35. F-S31259
    R1733
MILLOWAY, Isaac, see MILLERWAY, Isaac. F-S38227 R1733
MILLS, Francis, esf 1776 in 1st VA Regiment; PN ae 60 Scott Co
    VA, 1818; res there 1821 as Francis Sr, when had w Agness

MILLS (continued)
ae 63, & ch: Ann I/J ae 40, Sarah A ae 33, Mary ae 29, Agness ae 24, Jane ae 22, & Francis ae 31. F-S38229 R1734

George, esf 1777 Prince William Co VA; PN there 1832 ae 76; dd 5/27/38; md 3/9/1785 Lydia CALVERT, wid/o Obed COOKSEY; ch births: John Dyson 12/20/1785, Caty 9/17/89, & Ann 8/8/95; wid PN ae 88 Prince William Co, VA, 1838; AFF 1839 by wid sis Margaret MILLS there; wid dd 3/20/44; s John Dyson & d Ann w/o John WOODYARD afp there 1852 as legal heirs to m; sol d Caty md Mr RUSSELL; AFF 1853 Fairfax Co, VA, by Thomas SELECMAN ae 73 & William DAVIS ae 70 they went to same school with sol s John in 1785; AFF by sol s John Dyson, Prince William Co, 1854 he then res on his farm where he b 3 miles from Occoquan; AFF then there by William DAVIS ae 46 he lived whole life near home/o sol, & William's s Peter b 3/20/1844, & William's f Henry still liv there; AFF then Fairfax Co, VA, by Tapley & Mary BEACH they lived near sol wid when she dd. F-W7449 R1734

Isaac, private in Lee's Legion; BLW issued 3/5/1792. F-BLW 1792 R1734

James, esf 1781 Prince William Co, VA, where b 1759, in 3rd VA Regiment; mvd 1796 to Nelson Co, KY, thence c1840 Spencer Co, KY, where afp 1845 ae 86, & PAR; dd there 2/23/53; md 8/18/1836 Nancy HANSBOROUGH/HANSBERRY, Jefferson Co, KY who afp there 1857 ae 70, & PAR; gtd BLW73537 there then. F-R7247 R1734

John, esf 1775 Henrico Co, VA, near Richmond, where res; dd 1818 Halifax Co, VA; md 1772 Sarah, Henrico Co, VA; wid PN ae 71 Halifax Co, VA, 1845; dd there 6/10/48, leaving ch: John (b 1774), Samuel, James, Hezekiah, Elizabeth HARPER, & Nancy TUCK, who all liv 1850. F-W4550 R1735

John, esf in 7th VA Regiment; PN 1828 Ohio Co, VA ae not given; dd 11/23/33; md 9/13/1785 Ruth d of David SHEPHERD, Ohio Co, VA; wid PN ae 71 there 1838; d Ruth w of Francis WOOD mentioned 1834; AFF then by Lydia S CRUGER ae 69 Ohio Co, VA, where res 57 years, she present at sol wedding to Ruth, sis of Lydia's decd h Moses SHEPHERD; AFF there 1839 by Archibald WOOD, who res there since 1784; memo in file says 1840 William MILLS of AL, s/o sol, claimed John MILLS of Ohio Co, VA, fraudulently got PN by impersonating John MILLS, who did the RW svc & dd 1811-12 in GA; no PN Office action indicated in file on that claim; AFF 1843 by Jacob GOODING & John THORNBURY there; QLF 1917 from desc Mrs S C WOLF, Excelsior Springs, MO. F-W5378 R1735

Menan/Menam, b 1750 Caroline Co, VA; esf 1776 Albemarle Co, VA, where res; mvd to KY 1811 where PN 1833 Anderson Co, res Lawrenceburg; s J J T res there 1834; sol res 1835 Fayette Co, KY, when requested replacement of lost PN certicate; AFF then there by RW pensioner John PARKER who served with sol; QLF 1932 from desc Grace C (Mrs George R) DAVIS, Miami, FL, states sol b 1753, md Frances JOUETT, dd 1838 Montgomery Co, OH when res with s Reverend J J T; QLF

MILLS (continued)
   states sol dd Dayton, OH. F-S31245 R1735
  Moses, esf 1776 Halifax Co, VA in 14th VA Regiment; PN ae 85 Fayette Co, GA 1832; dd 7/3/33; md 12/8/1787 Keron Happach /Happoch d/o James & Lucy RATHER, then both decd (MB 12/3/ 1787, signed by Francis CLARK, & witnessed by George WATKINS), Charlotte Co, VA; Winslow ROBINSON court clerk of that Co 1839; wid PN ae 75 Fayette Co, GA, 1839; res there 1843. F-W3853 R1735
  Thomas, b 5/5/1761 Baltimore, MD; esf 1777 in VA regiment, res near Fort Shepard, which near mouth of Wheeling Creek; esf 1779 Redstone Fort (now Brownsville, PA); mvd after RW to Fayette Co, KY, for 1 year, thence Mason Co, KY, for 20 years, thence IL where PN Lawrence Co; res there 1835. F-S33101 R1736
  Thomas, b 8/1765 near head of the Elk, MD; esf res 1781 Ohio Co, VA; wounded 8 times by indians 1782; esf 1791-93 in VA ranger company against indians at Kirkwood's Blockhouse; PN 1833 Ohio Co, VA when res Tyler Co, VA; res 1834 Monroe Co, OH, where had moved to be near children mbnn; last PN payment in file 1839; QLF states sol md Mattie PHILLIPS, & they had s Jacob. F-S16200 R1736
  Wyatt, esf Charlottesville, VA; dd 1/1808; md 12/1785 Sally STARKE, Hanover Co, VA; md 1/24/1786 per certificate of Co clerk of court Philip B WINSTON 1842; wid PN ae 73 Albemarle Co, VA 1842; AFF then there by Joseph MILLS (NKG) ae 83; AFF then by Edmund J DAVIS ae 66 neighbor of sol wid; AFF then there by Richard SNOW ae 88; sol wid decd in 1846 when PN due her paid to her adm/o estate to date 12/22/44. F-W5381 R1736
  Zachariah, esf 1781 Albemarle Co, VA; dd there 8/1822; md there 12/16/1808 Mary CATLING (MB 12/6/1808), who b 12/21/ 1781; wid PN there 1857 when Co clerk/o court Ira GARRETT; wid gtd BLW71135 there then; res there when PN restored to her 1865 after she gave oath of allegiance. F-W9195 R1736
MILNER, Amos, esf Monongalia Co, VA;; esf after RW against indians; James SIGMAN & Samuel FOSTER AFF 1836 Union Co, IN, when sol ae 77; no afp or afb in file for sol; QLF states sol from Fayette Co, VA. F-R7252.5 R1737
  Luke, see MILLNER, Luke. F-S31259 R1737
MILOY, John R, esf 1776 NJ in 3rd MA Regiment; PN 1819 Harrison Co, VA; res there 1820 ae 58; dd 11/14/32; QLF 1907 from gdd Mrs Martha E HEWITT, Riverside, CA, says sol recd BLW for land in present site/o Macomb, IL. F-S38224 R1737
MILSTEAD, Zelus, esf Amherst Co, VA where b 1756; mvd to Spartanburg Co, SC, thence Hancock Co, GA for 15 years, thence Logan Co, KY, then to Williamson Co, TN, then to Muscle Shoals, Maury Co, TN, thence Lincoln Co, TN where PN 1832; QLF 1930 from desc Miss Mary Emma DUNN of Owensboro, KY, says sol res Lincoln Co, TN, 1835. F-S1857 R1737
MILTEAR, William, b 4/9/1732 Nansemond Co, VA, where esf c1778 when had w & 4 small ch; PN ae 100 there 1833 when blind;

MILTEAR (continued)
AFF then there by Reverend John HARRELL & John GOODMAN; Co clerk of court then John T KILBY; sol res there 1834. F-S16966 R1737
MILTON, Elijah, esf 1775 & 1776 Prince William Co, VA, where b 12/23/1755; md 1/29/1794 Kitty, who dd 7/29/1828 Fayette Co, KY; PN 1833 Fayette Co, KY, where dd 10/15/33, leaving ch: Caroline T (b 12/2/1794, md Mr WATKINS), Ebin (b 5/8/97), John (b 3/24/1802), Bushrod I (b11/10/09) & William E (b 7/21/11); sol LWT dated there 7/24/1833, probated there 11/1833 listed ch: William E, Bushrod I, Caroline, Ebin, & John. F-S30588 R1737
Thomas, see MELTON, Thomas. F-S36116 R1737
MILUM, Jordan, see MILAM, Jordan. F-W25709 R1737
MIMS, Robert, esf 1778 Goochland Co, VA; PN ae 76 Pike Co, KY, 1834. F-S30590 R1737
MINEAR, David, b 1755 Bucks Co, PA; esf 1779 Monongalia Co, VA & his bro Jonathan served with him 1780; f killed by indians 4/1781; bro Jonathan killed by indians 4/16/1783; sol PN 1833 Randolph Co, VA; dd 10/20/1834; PN due him paid to ch Enoch, Elizabeth BONNIFIELD, & Mary MILLER 1861; QLF 1912 from desc Franklin MAXWELL, Dallas, TX; QLF 1925 from desc Mrs Grant PARSONS of Omaha, NE, states sol s of John. F-S15932 R1737
MINES, Peter, esf 1777 Rockbridge Co, VA; PN ae 67 Augusta Co, VA, 1818; res there 1820 when had w & d mbnn; dd 9/30/25; QLF 1914 from desc Wilbur C MORRISON, Clarksburg, WV. F-S38214 R1739
MINIX, Margaret, former widow of Andrew PITMAN. F-W9998 R1739
MINNIS, Calohill, BLW1507 issued 7/14/1792. F-BLW1507 R1739
Francis, BLW1525 issued 11/17/1791. F-BLW1525 R1739
Holman, BLW1506 issued 7/5/1794; Calohill MINNIX (NKG) executor of his estate. F-BLW1506 R1739
John, b 2/11/1755, VA; mvd to Orange Co, NC, 1763 where esf 1775 Hillsboro; PN ae 81 Orange Co, NC, 1836 as John Sr. F-S9413 R1739
John, BLW12397 issued 7/14/1792. F-BLW12397 R1739
MINNIX, Margaret, former widow/o Andrew PITMAN. F-W9998 R1739
MINOR, Jacob, esf 1780 in VA Line; PN 1829 Casey Co, KY, aec 70 occupation farmer; w dd before then & children md many years, & had left home; AFF then Greene Co, KY, by Larkin MINOR (NKG) he knew sol during RW; QLF 1909 from gds William MINOR ae 73, Parksville, KY, says sol prob b Mecklinburg Co, VA, esf there, & dd KY. F-S36143 R1739
Jeremiah, esf 1775 Orange Co, VA, where res; PN ae 87 Scott Co, KY, 1833; res there 1837 ae 90. F-S2843 R1739
John, b 1/5/1747 Winchester, VA; mvd to MD, thence PA, where esf 1777 on Whitely Creek, Washington Co, PA, in PA regiment; PN 1833 Greensboro, PA; dd 12/5/33; surname spelled also MINER; QLF 1912 from Mrs Ellen Gatewood SUTTON, Baltimore, MD, d of William Town GATEWOOD, who s of William Kemper GATEWOOD & w Barbara, d of RW sol Major John MINOR

MINOR (continued)
  of Louisa Co, VA; further m of William Kemper GATEWOOD was
  Miss DANDRIDGE; QLF says sol md Casandra WILLIAMS. F-S2840
  R1739
Joseph, esf 1776 King & Queen Co, VA, where b 9/1760; mvd
  1802 to Fayette Co, KY, for c7 years, thence Scott Co, KY,
  for 4 years, thence Owen Co, KY, where PN 1833; AFF there
  then by James HOSKINS ae 75 who b & raised King & Queen Co
  VA, & lived 6 miles from sol there, & they esf together;
  Nancy, w of above James HOSKINS, AFF then there ae 72 she
  too b King & Queen Co, VA near sol's res & knew his sis's;
  sol dd 11/19/35; md 1780 Mary HOSKINS at house of her f in
  King & Queen Co, VA; wid afp aec 80 Owen Co, KY 1837; PAR,
  proof/o marriage (King & Queen Co public records destroyed
  in fire 1828); AFF 1837 Henry Co, KY by wid bro Joseph HO-
  SKINS; wid dd 10/18/1838; s Joseph afp ae 56 Owen Co, KY,
  1851 for self & siblings George (eldest aec 79 then), Thomas, & Edward; PAR, proof of parents' marriage; sol bro
  Reuben KIA in RW at Lindley Mills, NC. F-R7260 R1789
Larkin, esf 1780 in VA regiment; PN ae 55 Green Co, KY 1818;
  res there 1829, when had w ae 57 (b 7/1772), 3 unmd d's, &
  s ae 17; QLF 1909 from H A SCOMP, Parksville, KY, says sol
  bro Jacob also RW sol, both b Mecklenburg Co, VA, they bro
  of Reuben, who esf Charleston, SC (KIA 1781 in NC), also
  they bro of George, John, & Thomas (gdf of querier); QLF
  1932 from great great gds Ralph B TETER of Greenview, IL,
  says sol middle initial M. F-S36150 R1739
Peter, captain in VA line; decd in 1789; BLW344 issued to
  Erasmus GILL (NKG), adm of sol estate, Dinwiddie Co, VA.
  F-BLW344 R1739
Reuben, esf in 2nd VA Regiment; dd 1/20/1832 King & Queen Co
  VA; md 9/11/1799 Mary, who afp ae 74 Caroline Co, VA, when
  res King & Queen Co, VA, 1854, & PAR; AFF then by Joseph
  GREENSTREET ae 76 & John G CALE ae 63 (both NKG), Caroline
  Co, VA; AFF there by sol bro Coleman of King & Queen Co he
  b & raised latter Co; Robin POLLARD clerk/o court for King
  & Queen Co, VA, then. F-R7261 R1739
Thomas, esf 1775 Leesburg, VA, in 5th VA Regiment; PN ae 68
  Jefferson Co, OH, 1821 occupation farmer when had w ae 63,
  d Rebecca ae 38, & d Ann ae 12; Charles ESKRIDGE was Loudon Co, VA, Co court clerk in 1781, still same job in 1839;
  AFF 1822 Jefferson Co, OH by William WATSON that he neighbor of sol when sol esf; AFF 1824 there by Stacy McDONALD
  he esf with sol 1777 Loudoun Co, VA, in 5th VA Regiment;
  AFF then by George FLETCHER, Jefferson Co, OH, he esf with
  sol & Stacy McDONALD; sol dd 6/11/34; md c3/14/1781 Ann/
  Nancy JENNINGS of Cameron Parish (MB 3/4/81, signed by Daniel JENNINGS), Loudoun Co, VA; wid b 10/15/1761; wid PN
  aec 78 Jefferson Co, OH, 1840 res Salem Township; AFF then
  there by Rebecca MINOR (NKG); ch births: Daniel Jennings
  6/2/1782, Rebeccah 9/5/84, Elizabeth 1/1/86 Robert 1/25/89
  Spence 11/23/91, Thomas Eskridge 5/16/94, Peggy 12/25/96,

MINOR (continued)
John 9/6/99, Thomas Jefferson 12/16/1802, Ann Williams 4/9/06, & Marthy Jennings 11/29/09; James SINCLAIR was magistrate in Loudoun Co, VA, 1839. F-W4494 R1739

Thomas, esf 1777 in VA regiment; BLW1679 gtd sol; PN ae 77 Spotsylvania Co, VA 1830; Stapleton CRUTCHFIELD then clerk of court that Co; AFF then there by Richard PEACOCK, also RW sol from there; sol dd 7/21/34; md 1780 Elizabeth, d of Colonel James TAYLOR, Caroline Co, VA; wid dd 12/7/36; afp then by s Hubbard, adm of her estate, & her surv ch gtd PN due her; her ch: Patsey T (md Henry T CHIVIS), Malinda (md George BUCKNER), Sarah Ann (md Addison M LEWIS), Elizabeth (md William JACKSON), Nancy, James, Lucy, twins Thomas & John, Jefferson, Hubbard T (b 8/1/1795), Alice T & Ann Maria (md Francis W SCOTT); wid ch liv 1848: Malinda, Sarah Ann, Elizabeth, James, Jefferson, Hubbard T, Alice, & Ann Maria; d Patsey T CHIVIS dd before f leaving ch: Thomas M, John M, Mrs Sarah HALYARD, Elizabeth T (md John/James SPENCER), Ann H (md Bruton R HAMM), & Mary E (md Alfred CLARK/CLARKE); AFF 1848 by Martha BULLOCK ae 85 Spotsylvania, VA, neighbor of sol w when sol md; AFF 1848 by George THORNTON, Green Co, VA, he b & raised Caroline Co, VA, & mvd 1782 to Green Co, AFF witnessed by JP Anthony THORNTON (NKG); AFF then by VA RW sol Benjamin TRUSLOW; John PENDLETON clerk of court of Caroline Co, VA, 1850; QLF 1921 from desc Mrs John T WATSON of Walla Walla, WA. F-W5374 R1739

Threesivelus, b 2/28/1759 Essex Co, VA; mvd to King & Queen Co, VA, where esf 1777-78 in VA regiment; mvd after RW to King William Co, VA, then to 1785 Bedford Co, VA, where PN 1834; AFF there then by sol bro William; AFF then by Ephraim MINOR ae 54 s of John MINOR (NKG) of King & Queen Co, VA; sol mvd 1842 to Saline Co, MO; last PN payment in file 1841; QLF 1938 from desc Stella Minor (Mrs Leon S) BARNES, Northwood, IA. F-S16968 R1739

Vivion, b 11/4/1750 s of John & Sarah; esf 1775 Caroline Co, VA, where res, in 3rd VA Regiment; dd 9/29/1791; md (1) 6/15/1773 Barbara (b 2/11/1752, d of David & Mary COSBY) who dd 9/21/1778; md (2) 3/31/1780 Elizabeth (b 1/12/1760, d/o Reverend Archibald DICK & w Sarah) at Reverend DICK's home & Reverend performed ceremony in Caroline Co, VA; wid f dd 11/11/1811 ae 87 & his wid dd 9/26/1824 aec 90; sol wid PN 1838 there, & dd 4/1/46; births of sol & 1st w: George 5/1/1774, Mary Overton 8/19/75 & Annie 3/10/77 (dd 8/10/77); births of sol & 2nd w: Archibald 5/12/1781 (dd 7/3/1827), Joseph 11/15/82 (dd 9/1/1827) & Alfred 6/1/1784 (dd 12/16/1835); wid survived by d Matilda w of Robert COLEMAN & Susan wid/o William S WYATT, & by gdd Eliza (w/o Edwin HILL) d/o wid decd s Archibald; wid bro Archibald DICK res Caroline Co, VA, 1838 ae 75; wid gds John V WYATT res Hanover Co, state not given, & was executive of her LWT; William B WYATT (NKG) res 1838 Caroline Co, VA; Lewis MINOR (NKG) dd

MINOR (continued)
10/12/1819 of yellow fever near St Stephens, AL when ae 30 years, 9 months & 27 days; Eldred MINOR (NKG) dd 6/6/1822; Thomas Vivion COLEMAN (NKG) dd 9/28/1811 when ae 8 months 7 days; Thomas B COLEMAN (NKG) dd 3/21/1821; Susanna WEST (NKG) dd 4/15/1808; George S MINOR (NKG) dd 5/8/1833 of cholera aec 24 Vicksburg, MS; AFF 1809 by James BRAXTON, Caroline Co, VA, a RW sol who esf there 1778-77; QLF lists following VA RW sol's: John MINOR (b 11/18/1735, dd 3/21/1800, md Elizabeth COSBY), Thomas MINOR (b 8/5/1740, dd 2/16/1816, md Mary DABNEY), Garrit MINOR (b 3/14/1744, dd 6/25/1799, md Mary D TERRELL), James MINOR (b 2/28/1745, dd 6/9/1791, md Mary CARR), Dabney MINOR (b 6/11/1749, dd 11/7/1799, md Ann ANDERSON). F-W23992 R1739

William, b 8/29/1752 King & Queen Co, VA; mvd c1775 to King William Co, VA, where esf 1777; mvd 1789 to Bedford Co, VA where PN 1834; bro of Threesivolius who also RW sol. F-S11070 R1739

MINTER, Barker, esf Chesterfield Co, VA in 2nd VA Regiment; dd intestate; AFF 1836 by Bartlet BRIZENDINE who served with sol; afb Essex Co, VA, 1837 by Richard & Ann SHEARWOOD, Margaret & Mary MINTER, who all minors & wards/o Catherine MINTER, & she in her own right, all heirs/o sol; heirs gtd BLW2187; Robert SHEARWOOD AFF there 1834; James Roy MICOU Sr then Co clerk of court there. F-BLW2187 R1740

John, b 1755 Culpeper Co, VA; mvd 1770 to Connellsville, PA, where res near when esf c1776 Westmoreland Co, PA; mvd after RW to Harrison Co, KY, for 20 years, thence 1808 Delaware Co, OH, where PN 1832, res Radnor Township. F-S9027 R1740

John, esf Kingston Parish, Gloucester Co (later Mathews Co), VA, where b; dd 1810 Mathews Co, VA; md 1777 Johanna WILLIAMS, when sol in RW svc, Gloucester Co, VA; wid ae 74 Mathews Co, VA, 1836; 1st ch b 1781 dd young; 2nd ch b1783 + several more mbnn; Mathews Co court clerk 1836 Shepard G MILLER; AFF there 1837 by Josiah PUGH ae 75 & Isaac SMITH ae 74 they b & raised Kingston Parish, Gloucester Co, VA, sol esf with them; AFF then by Mathias GAYLE & John CHRISTIAN, Mathews Co, VA, they served in RW with sol; AFF then there by sol sis Joice HUDGINS. F-W18513 R1740

MINTON, Ebenezer, esf 1777 Pattonsburg, VA in 3rd VA Regiment; BLW12361 issued 12/27/1794; PN ae 59 Lee Co, VA, 1819; res there 1820 when liv with w Elizabeth aec 55 & ch: Isaac ae 17, Ebenezer ae 15, Liddie ae 13, Betsey ae 11, & Vardeman ae 9 + 2 orphan gdc (Washington MINTON ae 7 & Preston MINTON ae 5); Charles CARTER then co clerk/o court there; sol res 1826 Blount Co, TN with children including Ebenezer Jr QLF 1823 from desc Mrs Elizabeth Cargan MILLER of East St Louis, IL. F-S38949 R1740

John, b 3/1754; esf 1775 Cumberland Co, VA; res VA after RW with w; mvd to GA where PN 1812 Wilkes Co; res there 1820 when w ae 45 & no ch liv with them; dd 3/22/1821; QLF 1932

MINTON (continued)
   from desc Mrs Ponder S CARTER of El Paso, TX. F-S36156 R1740
   John, esf 1781 Stafford Co, VA where b 1761; mvd 1806 to Fayette Co, KY, thence Henry Co, KY where PN 1836; dd 11/20/38; md 12/18/1781 Jane who b 5/1763-64; wid afp 1839 Harrison Co, KY, & PAR, sol dd after passage/o PN Act of 7/7/1838; 3rd ch Fanny HILL/BELL AFF 1839 there she b 5/18/1796 & had s Jackson G/Y. F-R7263 R1740
MINZIES, Samuel P, esf Northumberland Co, VA; PN ae 74 Wood Co KY 1832; dd there 2/23/33; md there 5/16/1821 Hannah HUNT; wid PN ae 74 there 1855; gtd BLW30926 there then. F-W25713 R1740
MITCHEL, John, b 5/1/1763 Dawston, Lancastershire, England; to America 8/1774 landing at Yorktown, VA; settled 1775 Hampshire Co, VA, where esf 1780; PN 1832 Lewis Co, VA, as Reverend; dd 4/29/40 leaving wid mbnn; QLF states sol dd Lewis Co, VA; QLF 1907 from great gdd Mary E Cook HAGLER of Milton, IA, states sol ran away at VA port from captain of ship SORTOR to whom he bound as sailor, settled 1808 on his farm, preached gospel for 40 years, buried in Harmony Churchyard at Jane Lew, WV, & his tombstone reads dd ae 78 years, 11 months & 26 days; QLF says sol esf Romney, Hampshire Co, VA, & mvd to Lewis Co, VA, 1808; QLF states sol a pioneer Methodist preacher. F-S5761 R1740
MITCHELL, Adam, esf 1781 Campbell Co, VA, where b; mvd 1791-92 to Green Co, KY, where afp 1833; PAR, less than 6 months svc; AFF there then by William STEARMAN (b 10/9/1755) that sol md William's sis, Campbell Co, VA; QLF 1917 from desc Charles R DAVIS; QLF 1908 from desc William H MARTIN, Parsons, KS. F-R7265 R1741
   Amasa, esf 1779 near West Point, NY in MA regiment as fifer; BLW4647 issued 1/13/1799; PN ae 69 Kanawaha Co, VA, 1821 occupation laborer; when had w mbnn & ch: John ae 19, Lucy ae 17, James ae 14, Harvey ae 10, & Eliza ae 6; res 1839 Scott Co, IN, where mvd to be near children; last PN payment in file 1848; surname also spelled MITCHEL; QLF 1918 states sol b 1761, md Mary FRYMIER, dd 1851, & buried in Friendship Cemetery, Scott Co, IN. F-S36699 R1741
   Archelaus, esf 1776 Louisa Co, VA, in 3rd VA Regiment; PN ae 64 Amherst Co, VA, 1818; res there 1820 no children or family liv with him except 2nd w ae 50 mbnn; AFF there then by Philip THURMOND & John EUBANK; AFF then by John SHELFATHAM, Nelson Co, VA, who also RW sol. F-S38226 R1741
   Charles, VA sea svc, b 1759 Goochland Co, VA; esf 1780 New Kent Co, VA, aboard ship BETSY & PEGGY; esf 1781 in VA Regiment; mvd after RW to Fluvanna Co, VA, thence 1795 Fayette Co, KY for 1 year, thence Frankfort, KY, thence Woodford Co, KY, thence 1803 Shelby Co, KY where PN 1833; last PN payment in file 1838. F-S31261 R1741
   Cheney/Chaney, esf 1776 Brunswick Co, VA in 3rd GA Regiment; PN ae 80 Greensville Co, VA, 1823, when had no land or in-

MITCHELL (continued)
come. F-S38228 R1741

Edward, esf 1775-76 Hanover Co, VA, where b 8/3/1760; mvd in 1778 with f to Botetourt Co, VA where esf against indians; mvd 1784 to MD for 5-6 years; left Botetourt Co, VA, 1818 & mvd to St Clair Co, IL, where PN 1835 as Reverend; bro Reverend Samuel AFF there then he ae 12 in 1776; AFF 1834 by Samuel KENNERLY, Botetourt Co, VA, that he served with sol in RW; sol dd at home there 12/3/1837, c5 miles from Belleville, IL; md 8/26/1784 Ann/Nancy HAILY, Charleston, MD, who b 9/21/1763; wid PN 1849 St Clair Co, IL; sol bro Samuel AFF then Grant Co, WI, he witnessed sol's marriage; AFF then by sol s James of Belleville, IL, his sis & bro-in-law mbnn res nearby; QLF says sol & bro Samuel sons of James of SC, who mvd to VA; QLF says sol bro James also RW sol, who dd of camp fever 8/20/1781 at Jamestown, VA; QLF 1901 from great gdd Sophie G M STOCKTON, St Louis, MO; QLF 1896 from Miss J S MITCHELL, San Francisco, CA, great gdd of sol & bro Samuel in that sol f of her gdf & sol bro Samuel (also RW sol) gdf of her gdm, her grandparents thus being cousins. F-W23991 R1741

Elijah, b 3/6/1761 VA; esf 1779 Mecklenburg Co, NC; PN 1832 Preble Co, OH, when res there c25 years; res 1845 Huntington Co, IN, P O address Warren, IN; dd 8/1/47; reference made to Reverend Samuel MITCHELL (NKG) res Preble Co, OH, 1832 & to Fleming MITCHELL (NKG) res 1845 Warren, IN; QLF 1900 from kin Mrs Addie CLEVELAND of Huntington, IN; QLF 1923 from desc Mrs W A CORYEA, The Dalles, OR, states sol res New Paris, OH 1832 when PN; QLF 1928 from desc (on f's side) Miss Ruth M HAMMON, Vincennes, IN, says sol dd Warren, IN. F-S2838 R1741

Flud, b 2/10/1757 Brunswick Co, VA; esf 1775 Ninety-Six District, SC, where res, in SC regiment; mvd after RW service to Brunswick Co, VA, thence 1 year after RW ended to Edgefield District, SC, for 1-2 years, thence Burke Co, GA for 2 years, thence Edgefield District, SC, thence 1809 Madison Co, MS Territory, which became Limestone Co, AL, where PN 1832; QLF states sol 1st name also spelled FLOODDE & w named Sarah. F-S16970 R1741

George, b 3/16/1763; esf 1781 Richmond Co, VA, in 8th VA Regiment; PN 1832 Henry Co, KY; sometimes signed name as George K; mvd 1843 to Jackson Co, MO, for 2 years, then to Platte Co, MO, where dd 3/5/48; md Elizabeth WATTS, Woodford Co, KY, 6/17/1790; wid PN ae 80 Platte Co, MO, 1853. F-W9574 R1741

Henry, esf 1779 Brunswick Co, VA; mvd after RW to Mecklenburg Co, VA, thence 1797 Franklin Co, VA where PN 1833 aec 70. F-S5768 R1741

James, b Yorktown, VA; bound & apprenticed ae 15 to f James then master of ship BALTIMORE & served 4.5 years; then esf aboard frigate TRUMBULL on which wounded 1779, & taken POW; released & esf Boston, MA, aboard frigate DEAN for 2 years;

MITCHELL (continued)
  served on several other ships, again taken POW by British
  ship, on which became master's mate for over 1 year; came
  back to Baltimore, MD, 1796; master of brig WEXFORD 1800,
  captured by Spanish ship, which ship soon captured by privateer & sol freed to bring his ship back to US; last sea
  svc on US frigate UNITED STATES; afp 1802 Alexandria, VA;
  no action on afp indicated in file. F-R671 R1742
James, b 11/1754; esf 1776 Bedford Co, VA, in 14th VA Regiment, when res in house of John RODGERS (NKG); mvd 1781 to
  Mercer Co, KY, where fought against indians; mvd 1807 to
  Robertson Co, TN where PN 1832; AFF then by Henry AYRES he
  RW sol in 5th VA Regiment & was neighbor of sol in VA; AFF
  there then by Nathaniel TERRY, who served in RW with sol;
  QLF states sol b Bedford Co, VA, dd 5/18/1835 Robertson Co
  TN, md Elizabeth BRUMFIELD, their d Martha b 1780 & she md
  Green CATO; QLF 1916 from desc Miss Rosalie A COCKE, Mont-
  vale, VA, states sol was minister, also querier desc of RW
  sol's; (1) John IRVIN, Campbell Co, VA, s of John who set-
  tled at Hat Creek there during administration/o GOV GOOCH,
  (2) Reverend William IRVIN, also s of John, (3) Colonel
  HOLT of Bedford Co, VA, through 2 of his d's, (4) Reverend
  David RICE/o Bedford Co, VA who b Hanover Co, VA; QLF says
  sol gtd BLW land in Robertson Co, TN. F-S2836 R1742
James, esf 1782-83 Ohio Co, VA, against indians; mvd 1798-99
  to Green Co, KY, where dd 8/7/1830; md c3/1/1791 Elizabeth
  YATES, Ohio Co, VA; wid afp aec 80 Green Co, KY & PAR. F-
  R7270 R1742
Jesse, b 6/1760 Brunswick Co, VA, where esf 1776 in 3rd VA
  Regiment; mvd to Chatham Co, NC, where esf 1780 in NC re-
  giment; mvd after RW to Martin Co, NC, thence 1808 Wilson
  Co, TN, then to Rutherford Co, TN, thence 1818 Madison Co,
  TN, thence Limestone Co, AL, where PN 1832; mvd 1842 to De
  Soto Co, MS to live near children; last PN payment in file
  1842; s Drewry/Drury gave power of attorney 1852 Limestone
  Co, AL, to agent to claim PN arrears due decd f. F-S7232
  R1742
John, see MITCHEL, John. F-S5761 R1742
John, esf in GA Line; heir-at-law Joseph A W WHITE (NKG) afb
  Bibb Co, GA, 1852; clerk of court of Liberty Co, GA, AFF
  then Joseph A WHITE of Bibb Co, GA, his sis Arabella THOM-
  SON of Bibb Co, GA, William B JACKSON of Chatham Co, GA, +
  descendents of John MITCHELL the Younger (if any) were all
  heirs/o sol; BLW2464 issued 4/27/1852 to heirs; QLF states
  sol served in 3rd GA Regiment & he md Sarah THWEATT of VA.
  F-BLW2464 R1742
John, esf 1776 Morristown, NJ where b 1759; mvd 1800 to Har-
  rison Co, VA, where res when afp ae 74 Lewis Co, VA, 1833;
  PAR. F-R7274 R1742
John, esf 1776 Amelia Co, VA; PN 1832 Montgomery Co, VA, ae
  72. F-S5763 R1742
John, esf 1781 Bedford Co, VA, where b 11/3/1761; PN there

MITCHELL (continued)
   1833; AFF then there by Samuel WILLIS ae 69 & George SWAIN ae 74 they served in RW with sol; AFF by Mrs Ellender ROSS there 1836 she neighbor of sol during RW; AFF then by Thomas PAYNE there; AFF there then by Pleasant PRESTON ae 63, who knew sol during RW; AFF there then by Bowker PRESTON, JP of Co, he storekeeper there 1797-1808; QLF 1927 from desc Mrs J H GILLESPIE, Chattanooga, TN. F-S5767 R1742
John, b 12/1765 Rowan Co, NC; esf 1780 in General George Rogers CLARK's regiment of Bryant Station, KY Territory; mvd 1784 to Woodford Co, KY, where PN 1832; dd 8/5/41; last PN payment in file 1842. F-S16485 R1742
Mark, esf 1777 Culpeper Co, VA; PN 1818 Warren Co, TN ae 63-64; res there 1820, when family w mbnn ae 47, d ae 14, ch ae 11, s James ae 6, & s Isaac ae 2; res there 1836; dd 4/18/38; surname also spelled MITCHEL; QLF says sol b London, England, landed in Philadelphia, PA 1774, md after RW Mary/Polly RIDER/RYDER, Washington Co, VA, near Abingdon, mvd c1793 to Warren Co, TN, where dd on Rocky River ae 89; QLF 1934 from great great gds W C KENNADAMER, Yonkers, NY, says sol buried in old Baptist graveyard in Rocky River, near the bridge on Spence Road, 10 miles from McMinnville, TN, & headstone indicates he RW sol. F-S38947 R1743
Nathaniel, esf 1776 in VA regiment where sergeant major; esf DE later in DE Line where major; dd c2/23/1814 leaving wid since decd, & following s's: Absolute, William J, Alfred, Theodore, & Dagworthy (dd Philadelphia 2/1832), + d's Deborah, Mary Ann, & Elizabeth; d Deborah md Whiting SANFORD & they decd leaving d Deborah; d Mary Ann md John KING, & they dd Washington, DC leaving only ch Nathaniel; d Elizabeth (dd unmd); s Theodore res Laurel, DE, s Alfred res at Trenton, NJ, when s William J gave power of attorney 1832 Washington, DC, to agent to afb; sol surv children gtd BLW 1868 issued 8/2/1832; QLF 1910 from Miss W E McCULLOUGH of Davenport, IA, states her great gdf Nathaniel MITCHELL who b Albemarle Co (area later Nelson Co), VA, was colonel in War of 1812, & possibly was s of RW sol Nathaniel. F-BLW 1868 R1743
Reaps, esf in VA regiment; LWT dated 2/28/1803, probated 8/4/1803 Sussex Co, VA, listed w Susannah, s Paul, d Martha TURNER, s Thomas Branch, s Henry, & d Peggy, executor Benjamin TURNER, witnesses William RIVES, Jones MITCHELL, James MITCHELL & Miles TURNER; sol d Martha wid/o Benjamin TURNER, gave power/o attorney 1844 Sussex Co, VA, to agent to afb; sol s Paul then decd; sol s Thomas & s Henry not heard from in many years & presumed decd; sol d Peggy w of William ELDEN then; sol d's Martha & Peggy gtd BLW2335 issued 1844 as sol's only heirs. F-BLW2335 R1743
Reuben, esf 1777 Mecklenburg, VA, in GA regiment; mvd soon after RW to NC, where PN Chatham Co 1818 aec 65; dd 2/11/1826; md 4/2/1731 Ann PENNINGTON, Mecklenburg Co, VA whose m cousin to Pres George WASHINGTON; wid PN ae 77 Martha's

MITCHELL (continued)
Vineyard, Chatham Co, NC, having res that Co for 53 years; dd there 9/4/43; ch births: Ned 6/2/1784 (eldest, decd for many years in 1841), Lucy BAILEY 2/24/86, Sarah/Salley/Sary 2/12/90, Benjamin 7/11/92, Henry 3/1/94, & Rheuben/Reuben 5/24/98-9 (res 1848 Chatham Co, NC); all ch survived m except Ned; Robert PENNINGTON (NKG) AFF 1818 NC. F-W5373 R1743

Richard, b f8/12/1762 Culpeper Co, VA; esf 1776-7 Spotsylvania Co, VA, where res; mvd to Caroline Co, VA, where esf 1781 in VA regiment; PN 1833 Fayette Co, KY. F-S1234 R1743

Robert, esf 1777 Lunenburg Co, VA, in VA regiment; PN 1819 Charlotte Co, VA; res Lunenburg Co, VA, 1829 ae 72 where dd 12/30/46; md 12/25/1788 Letitia/Letty at home of her f William REN Sr (MB 12/23/1788) Lunenburg Co, VA; wid PN ae 70 there 1847 where res 20 years; large family of ch mbnn; wid liv 1850. F-W3441 R1743

Robert, b 9/6/1741; esf 1775 Winchester, VA where res; taken POW & returned there; esf 1776 there in 11th VA Regiment; mvd c1790 to Warm Springs, VA, for several years; res 1811 Morristown, Belmont Co, OH, when PN 1818; res there 1823; res 1826 Ohio Co, VA; dd 6/1827; md 7/1773 Eve, Winchester VA, who PN aec 84 Belmont Co, OH, 1839; res Union Township there 1848; ch included Mary BRAMHALL (md 1803) who res ae 55 there 1839. F-W7459 R1743

Samuel, b 4/1751 Co Derry, Ireland; to America 1772, settled in Cumberland Co, PA, where esf 1776 in PA regiment; mvd 1781 to York Co, PA, for 2 years, thence Ohio Co, VA, near Wheeling, thence 1813 Mill Creek, Hamilton Co, OH, thence 1814 Preble Co, OH, where PN 1832 when 2 of ch res Greene Co, OH; md ? 1781; QLF 1909 from great gdd Mrs W O ORR of Bellefontaine, OH, states sol dd 1837 Preble Co, OH, had 2 ch, w dd before him; QLF 1916 from great gds A T BREWER of Cleveland, OH. F-S2837 R1744

Samuel, esf 1779 Bedford Co, VA, where b 11/5/1759; PN there 1833 res Russell Parish; dd that Co 3/25/35; md 9/6/1791 there Margaret/Peggy C CLAYTOR; wid PN there 1839 ae 66; Reverend C MITCHELL (NKG) res there 1832; Robert C MITCHELL (NKG) co clerk of court & Samuel P MITCHELL (NKG) JP there 1833; QLF 1909 from great great gdd Mary McCONNELL, Bellefontaine, OH; QLF 1915 from Marie FLOYD of Galveston, TX, says a RW sol Major Samuel MITCHELL of Bedford Co, VA, s/o Labin & Mary (nee ENNES). F-W3851 R1744

Samuel, b 3/15/1760 below Fredericksburg in King William Co, VA; esf 1775 Montgomery Co, VA, where res; mvd 1818 to OH, where PN ae 73 Miami Co 1832 res Bethel Township; dd 4/25/40 that Co; md 7/7/1780 Malinda CECIL, Montgomery Co, VA, who b 4/15/1760; wid PN 1849 Miami Co, OH; s George AFF there then; William CECIL (NKG) AFF then there he b VA & res in same VA neighborhood as sol; John CECIL (NKG) AFF there then he b VA & knew sol there; sol & w had several ch, the eldest ae 65-70 in 1849; QLF says sol res New Car-

MITCHELL (continued)
lisle, OH; QLF states sol dd near Troy, OH. F-W4030 R1744
Samuel, b 3/25/1764 Louisa Co, VA; mvd 1774 with f to Botetourt Co, VA, where esf 1780; mvd 1817 to St Clair Co, IL, where afp 1834; PAR, less than 6 months svc; Reverend Edward MITCHELL (NKG) AFF there, res Belleville, who also RW svc; sol an ordained minister for 40 years in 1834; visited s John T at Urbana, IL, 1853; res of "Elm Wood", Salina Co, IL, 1854. F-R7283 R1744
Thomas, esf 1780 in VA regiment; PN ae 63 Charlotte Co, VA, 1818; res there 1820 occupation planter, when had w Nancy ae 55, s Claiborne ae 16, & s Samuel ae 12; QLF states sol md either Nancy RUMSEY or Nancy LOONY. F-S38231 R1744
Thomas, VA state navy, esf 1778 Lancaster Co, VA aboard ship DRAGON; PN ae 74 Frederick Co, Va, 1832; dd there 1/24/35, leaving no wid but 10 ch: Mary w/o John SMITH, Deborah w/o Henry SMITH, Eliza w/o Lewis RATHBONE, Sally Ann w of John S CRAWFORD, Grace w of Hiram MURPHY, Isaac, Peyton R, William (dd IL c1845-6, leaving several ch mbnn), Thomas (dd PA 1841-3 leaving 2 ch mbnn) & John (dd 1847 Mexico unmd); afp 1851 by Hiram MURPHY, executive/o sol LWT, Fredericksburg, VA; QLF says sol md Deborah PERKINS. F-S5766 R1744
William, b4/1/1761 VA; esf 1780 Union District, SC, where res; mvd c1821 to Franklin Co, GA, where PN 1832; dd there 2/22/43; md 9/6/1786 Eleanor CALDWELL, Union District, SC; wid PN ae 76 Franklin Co, GA, 1843; res 1856 Hart Co, GA, when gtd BLW38520; ch births: Henry 12/26/1788, Sarah 4/29/93, Nanny 10/25/95 & Winny 12/22/98; in 1843 Henry MITCHELL (NKG) AFF Franklin Co, GA he present at sol wedding; QLF 1914 from desc Miss Bessie Mae DANIEL of Eastman, GA, states sol known as William Sr, was res Willis, Franklin Co, GA, querier also desc of RW sol Baker AYRES of Whitehead, Habersham Co, GA; QLF 1923 from desc Hilda MEADOW of Washington, DC, who also desc/o RW sol Giles LETCHER of VA F-W5379 R1744
William, b 1764 Chester Co, PA; esf 1780 Rockingham Co, VA, where res; res after RW in NC, KY, TN, IN, IL, & MO; PN 1832 Franklin Co, MO; last PN payment in file 1838 when known as William Sr, res Washington Co, OH. F-S16967 R1744
William, esf 1778 Amelia Co, VA, in VA regiment, where b 4/15/1759; mvd 1797 to Union District, SC where PN 1832. F-S21374 R1744
William, esf 1777 in VA regiment; PN 1824 Morgan Co, AL, ae 68 when w decd & all ch had moved away; sometimes res with one of sons; dd 9/18/40; QLF 1920 from desc Kathryn Kennelly (Mrs K W) BULLION, El Dorado, AR, states sol res 1840 Lawrence Co, AL, querier also desc/o RW sol Kichen/Kinchen PENNINGTON of Montgomery Co, NC; QLF says sol res Lawrence Co, AL, with A MITCHELL. F-S38216 R1744
William, esf 1776 Hobs Hale, VA, in 1st VA Regiment; esf as marine aboard ship MOSQUITO c1778; gtd VA BLW 6/22/1810; PN ae 78 Spotsylvania Co, VA, 1825. F-S38221 R1744

MITCHELL, William, b 10/20/1746 Essex Co, VA; esf 1778 Amelia Co, VA, where res; sol mvd to KY, thence IN, where PN 1832 Parke Co, res Reserve Township; dd 7/8/36 or 8/28/36; md 12/5/1776 Chloe Nancey, who b 1/23/1755; wid afp 8/12/1842 Morgan Co, IN & dd 8/28/42 before afp acted upon, survived by ch: Mrs Oliva BULLINGTON (wid of John), William (aec 60 Clay Co, MO), Giles of Morgan Co, IN, James (aec 56 of McLean Co, IL), Frederick (dd aec 68 Dixon Springs, TN, leaving ch Philip & Polly) & Mrs Ann SPARKS (w of Wesley, she dd aec 43, leaving ch: Thomas, Wesley, Mary, Billey & others mbnn) of Parke Co, IN; ch Ann & Frederick decd in 1852 ch Oliva (eldest, ae 74) & Giles ae 64 afp 1852 for heirs of m, & PAR, proof of her marriage to sol; in 1853 clerk/o court of Morgan Co, IN, certified sol wid survived by ch: Oliva BULLLINGTON, William, Giles, James, Polly BURTON, & Elizabeth ELLIS; s Giles adm of m's estate; QLF states sol dd Carbon, IN. F-R7269 R1744

MITCHEN, Benjamin, esf 1780 Bedford Co, VA; dd 3/20/1829; md 10/1771 Isabella; they had 5 ch before end of RW; wid afp there 1844 ae 89; AFF then there by John ARTHUR in support of widow's claim; PAR for further proof; dd 8/19/44; s Samuel gave power of attorney to agent there 1854 to afp, & PAR again. F-R7284 R1745

MITCHUM, Collin, esf 1776 Woodstock, VA, in 8th VA Regiment; later esf in 5th SC Regiment; PN by VA for disability from wound; PN aec 65 Shenandoah Co, VA, 1825 occupation laborer, when no family except d mbnn & her 5 small ch res with him; AFF then by Joseph EVANS, co JP; surname also spelled MITCHIAM & MICHUM. F-S38215 R1745

MIZE, Shepherd, esf 1780 Lunenburg Co, VA, in VA regiment; afp ae 71 Newton Co, GA, 1832; PAR, less than 6 months svc; dd 1836 DeKalb Co, GA; s Wiley AFF 1856 Randolph Co, AL, f md in Lunenburg, VA, to m mbnn who dd 1802 Union District, SC F-R7287 R1745

MOBLEY, Clement (AKA MOBLY, Clemmant), b 10/4/1746 Bedford Co, VA; esf 1775 SC; res 1778 Camden District, SC; mvd after RW to Madison Co, KY, then to Warren Co, KY, then 1831 to Crawford Co, AR Territory, where PN 1834 when w Sibella res with him (her given name not shown in file, but shown in PN record of sol bro Isaiah who b 1754-5 SC, F-S31864); F-S31866 R1746

MODERELL, Adam, b 7/5/1755 Lancaster Co, PA; f Robert mvd when sol small ch to York Co, PA; sol mvd ae 20 to Mecklenburg Co, NC, for c3 years, thence Lincoln Co, KY, for 2 months, thence Jefferson Co (area later Nelson Co), KY, where esf 1781 in KY militia against indians; mvd after RW to Augusta Co, VA, for 10 years, then to Pulaski Co, KY, for 20 years, thence Owen Co, IN, where PN 1832. F-S31869 R1746

MOFFETT, Jesse, esf 1777 Fauquier Co, VA, where b 1759; PN there 1832; dd there 12/6/36; md there 12/27/1782 Elizabeth; wid PN there 1839 ae 79; wid sis Hannah LEAR AFF she md c4 years after Elizabeth to William LEAR (decd 1839), &

MOFFETT (continued)
   sis Elizabeth already had 4 ch by then; Hannah LEAR gtd PN Fall 1838 for decd h RW svc; Aaron BISE AFF 1839 there he b 1/15/1784, was neighbor/o sol, grew up with sol d Hannah (aec 55 then, md Mr BRAG & mvd to Western country), sol & w had other ch than Hannah, 1 of them md halfbro of Aaron; Fauquier Co clerk of court A J MARSHALL AFF then he unable to find record/o sol & w marriage there; AFF 1832 there by James BURDETT & John MURPHY they served with sol; wid res 1848 there aec 88 when gtd PN increase; s John res 1843 Warrenton, VA; QLF 1800 by SAR agent for sol desc T F Van NATTA of St Joseph, MO. F-W3446 R1746
MOFFITT, William, see MAFFITT, William. F-S36063 R1746
MOHON, John, b 10/1760 Chesterfield Co, VA, where esf 1780 in 5th VA Regiment; mvd 1780 to Lunenburg Co, VA, thence 1781 Prince Edward Co, VA, where esf, thence Guilford Co, NC, thence Lunenburg Co, VA, where PN 1833; attached to NC regiment during Battle of Guilford Court House, NC; AFF 1833 Chesterfield Co, VA, by Ezekiel PERKINSON he esf 1778 with sol in Lunenburg Co, VA. F-S5781 R1746
MOLER, Gasper, bc 1759 near Harpers Ferry, VA, on Potomac River; esf 1778 Berkeley Co, VA, where res, sub for bro Jacob, in VA regiment; mvd after RW to Bedford Co, PA, for c 14 years, then to Washington Co, PA, for c18 years, thence Pittsburgh, PA, for c8 years, then to Morgan Co, OH, where PN 1832; dd 2/17/45; md 4 or 5 times after return from RW svc, none of wives named. F-S2874 R1746
MOLLEHON, John, esf VA; afp before 1/13/1835 Greenbrier Co or Nicholas Co, VA; claim papers sent to US District Attorney to reexamine & never returned; they determined he res when boy in Greenbrier Co, VA & was too young to have served in RW; PAR; surname also spelled MOLLIHON; QLF 1939 from desc Mary FRAME, Arlington, MA, who also desc of RW sol Francis BOGGS of Nicholas Co, VA. F-R7295 R1746
MOLSBEY, William, esf 1775 Philadelphia, PA, in VA regiment; esf 1780 in 9th PA Regiment, when res Chesterfield Co, PA; PN ae 73 Hawkins Co, TN, 1832; dd 12/10/1840; md 5/1792 Nancy GROVES at her f's home, Hawkins Co, TN, when her bro John present; wid PN ae 85 there 1844; AFF then there by wid halfsis Elizabeth Groves HORN ae 72; wid bro John AFF there then ae 84; wid dd there 10/22/1847 leaving ch: John STOKELEY (by 1st h John Sr), David MOLSBEY, Polly Molsbey BOWMAN wid/o Jacob, both/o Hawkins Co, TN, & William MOLSBEY Jr of KY or IN; ch births by sol: David 2/1/1794, William 3/-/1795 & Polley 5/29/99; s William Jr's w Elizabeth b 2/28/1794; wid s John STOKELY res near Madisonville, TN, 1846 ae 62 when bro Christopher STOKELY decd; wid s David md Marget; ch gtd PN due m; surname also spelled MOLSBE & MOLSBEE. F-W1061 R1746
MONDAY, Aaron, see MUNDAY, Aaron. F-W1634 R1747
   Edward, BLW12370 issued 12/13/1791. F-BLW12370 R1747
MONK, Joseph, esf 1778 Botetourt Co, VA; lost eye at Battle of

MONK (continued)
Guilford Court House; PN ae 70 Chesterfield Co, VA, 1819; res there 1820, occupation teacher, blind for many years, when family d ae 40 & gdd ae 11 mbnn. F-S38237 R1747

MONROE, Alexander, esf 1777 Fauquier Co, VA; PN ae 61 Pendleton Co, KY, when Baptist minister; res there 1820 when had w Elizabeth ae 56, d ae 15, gds ae 10, & gdd ae 7 res with him; s George T res there 1821; res 1838 Marion Co, IN; dd 11/20/42 leaving no wid; QLF says sol res 1840 ae 85 Perry Township, Marion Co, IN, with Joseph WALLACE (NKG); QLF 1938 from Lillian Monroe (Mrs Norman W) BOWMAN, Vanceburg, KY, desc of VA RW sol Alexander MONROE who came from Edinburgh, Scotland to Fauquier Co, VA, where settled, md Margaret LONG; QLF states sol res with Captain Joseph WALLACE 1840 at Southport, IN; QLF says sol bro of VA sol John who later PN & res KY. F-S16984 R1747

George, esf Fairfax Co, VA, early in RW, where b 1760; later esf in 7th VA Regiment; mvd c1790 to Montgomery Co, NC, thence 1798 Rowan Co, NC where PN 1832; QLF 1933 from desc Mrs M N HOYLE, Salisbury, NC, says sol LWT lists m-in-law Elizabeth FORREST (had land in Montgomery Co, NC) & his ch John, Forest, Woodson, Sally HAMPTON, Nancy PINKSTON,, & Polly, + gdc George, Fanny, & Polly OWEN. F-S7241 R1747

George, b 1762 Fauquier Co, VA; esf 1780 in VA regiment; PN there 1832 where always res; QLF says sol dd 8/31/32, was bro of James (b Fauquier Co, VA, dd Hampshire Co, VA), & John (physician & preacher who b 4/10/1750 Fauquier Co, VA & dd 8/17/1824 Hampshire Co, VA). F-S46060 R1747

George, surgeon in RW; BLW1523 issued 5/20/1789. F-BLW1523 R1747

James, 5th Pres of US; esf 1775 in 3rd VA Regiment; BLW2368 issued on 2/2/1784 by VA for svc as major; dd 7/4/1831; PN due wid gtd to only surv ch: Maria H (w/o Samuel L GOVERNEUR, who AFF 1844) & Eliza K HAY (decd & adm/o her estate 1844 was Richard SMITH). F-W26271 R1747

John, esf 1775 Westmoreland Co, VA, where b 11/10/1749; mvd 1798 to King George Co, VA, then 1801 back to Westmoreland Co, VA, thence 1807 Woodford Co, KY for short time, thence Scott Co, KY, thence 1816 back to Woodford Co, KY, thence 1832 Ohio Co, KY, where PN same year; dd 5/25/37 leaving children mbnn; QLF 1919 from great great gdd Mary Anna DUNN of Owensboro, KY, says sol dd Woodford Co, KY, md 12/17/1778 Winifred BERRYMAN (b 9/16/1757, dd 1/24/1798) & ch births: William 9/16/1779 (dd 10/21/1833), Waters 10/17/80 dd same day), Rebekah 3/28/82 (dd 8/13/1805), Elizabeth Newton 1/18/84 (dd 1/1836), Mary Ann 8/24/86 (dd 7/8/1870) Winifred Berryman 4/11/89 (dd 9/13/1792), Elenor 9/23/92 (dd 7/25/1837), & Andrew Pinkney 11/25/94 (dd 4/1862); QLF 1922 from Mrs M H GRASSLY, Springfield, MA, whose children desc/o sol, says sol probably md (2) 1799 Betsey TRIPLETT. F-S31267 R1748

John, esf 1776 in 5th VA Regiment; PN 1818 Cumberland Co, KY

MONROE (continued)
    1818; res there 1820 ae 65 when family w Rachel & ch: Fanny, Mary, Betsy, Andrew, & John; dd there 3/22/35; md 4/8/1784 Rachel at Round Hill Church, Westmoreland Co, VA, or King George Co, VA; sol res 1799 to c1803 Amherst Co, VA; wid PN ae 80 Cumberland Co, KY, 1839; res there 1844 when John P MONROE (NKG) JP of co; AFF then by Elihu BECK that he knew sol & w in Amherst Co, VA; ch births: Susannah 2/21/1785, Fanny 2/9/87, Ann 10/8/89 (dd 1/5/--) Lucy 10/10/91 (dd 10/25/1793), Sally 9/1/93, Mary 4/18/96, Andrew 1/22/99, Jeney 8/23/1800, Elizabeth 5/4/02, & John 7/2/04. F-W8468 R1748
    Spencer, b 1760 Fairfax Co, VA, where esf 1780 in VA Regiment; esf 1781 Colchester, Fairfax Co; mvd c1819 to Loudoun Co, VA, where PN 1832; eldest bro William mentioned. F-S8900 R1748
    William, b Westmoreland Co, VA, where res till ae 17; esf 1777 in VA regiment; PN ae 72 Frederick Co, VA, 1832; QLF states sol dd 1844 leaving w Ann. F-S5784 R1748
MONTAGUE, Peter, esf 1777 in 2nd VA Regiment; PN ae 85 Orange Co, VA, 1818; surname also spelled MONTACUE; QLF 1920 from desc Mary Marshall Daniel (Mrs A M) SCOTT, Baltimore, MD, who also desc of RW sol's Peter M DANIEL (b 1763, dd 1856, esf 1779 Louisa Co, VA), Stephen GOOCH of Prince William Co, VA, Thomas MARSHALL (dd 1793 Culpeper Co, VA) & John R JONES of Albemarle Co, VA. F-S38239 R1748
    Rice D, esf 1780 Cumberland Co, VA, where res, sub for bro Thomas; PN ae 66 there 1832; mvd 1833 to Montgomery Co, VA where dd 4/3/49; md 10/1830 Ann ADAMS (MB 10/5/30) Cumberland Co, VA; wid PN ae 70 Montgomery Co, VA, 1853; gtd BLW 30935 there 1855; PN restored there 1866 after Civil War when had widowed d mbnn; s Rice D res 1885 Christiansburg, WV when he Montgomery Co clerk/o court; QLF 1925 from desc Miss Lelia Montague HICKOK, Christiansburg, VA, states sol middle name Daniel, querier also desc/o VA RW sol's Brigadier General Andrew LEWIS & Captain William McCLANAHAN. F-W2416 R1748
    Richard, VA sea svc, VA BLW1432 issued 5/2/1783; LWT dated 9/3/1789 South Farnham Parish, Essex Co, VA, probated that Co at Tappahannock, left all assets to w Charlotte & listed his bro's William & Philip, witnesssed by John SADLER, Henry VASS Jr, & W MONTAGUE; wid Charlotte's LWT dated 8/14/1802 Essex Co, VA, & probated that Co at Tappanannock 12/20/1802 listed s Abraham to whom she left all assets, + her bro-in-law Thomas MONTAGUE's ch Katherine & Sarah S, + her bro-in-law William MONTAGUE's ch Clarasa, Katherine, & William + her bro Robert SEMPLE (executor), witnessed by John CLARK, Charles LEE & Jacob MONTAGUE; s Abraham dd, & Philip T MONTAGUE adm/o his estate; Middlesex Co, VA court ruled 1831 sailor's only lineal descendants then Augustus H MONTAGUE, Richard D MONTAGUE, Philip H MONTAGUE, & Jane MONTAGUE (her guardian then Philip T MONTAGUE), Erastus T

MONTAGUE (continued)
   MONTAGUE guardian of Richard D & Philip T MONTAGUE; desc's gtd PN due sailor's wid. F-R77 R1748
Thomas, esf 1775 Cumberland Co, VA where b; PN there 1832 ae 78; bro Rice D AFF there then he served in RW with Thomas; sol dd c9/4/39; Randolph MONTAGUE (NKG) res 1834 Cartersville, VA; sol wid gtd PN arrears due h 1841; QLF states a VA RW sol Thomas MONTAGUE of Orange, Louisa, or Cumberland Co, VA, dd in RW svc/o small pox 1777-8, buried at the old quarry on old stage road from Cumberland Court House & his w Jane DANIEL dd 1811-12, their ch: John, Catherine, Jane (md Mr NETHERLAND), Thomas, Rice Daniel, Peter, Mickelbrough, & William. F-S5775 R1748
MONTGOMERY, Alexander, esf 1777 Washington Co, VA, in VA regiment; PN ae 77 Morgan Co, KY, 1832 when occupation blacksmith, & no family to support; AFF then by Benjamin WAGES, Floyd Co, KY who served in RW with sol & wounded at Battle of Eutaw Springs; AFF there then by Peter SULLIVAN who also served with sol; QLF states sol may have had d Jane who md Edward MAXWELL. F-S36172 R1749
Hugh, esf 1776 in 4th VA Regiment; PN aec 70 Isle of Wight Co, VA, 1832. F-S38245 R1749
Hugh, b 2/25/1755 or 2/25/1752; esf 1777 Pittsburgh, PA, in VA regiment; esf 1812 Butler Co, OH, for War of 1812, & s Henry served with him in same company, & Henry gtd BLW for svc; PN 1819 Butler Co, OH; res 1820 Decatur Co, IN, occupation farmer, w Eve aec 62 & 1 boy liv with him; res 1825 there; dd there 5/20/30; md c8/1784 Eve HARTMAN at or near Gettysburg, PA, & she dd c8 years before him; sol never md again; ch: Mary (eldest, b 6/14/1785, decd in 1855), Henry (b4/29/90 Beaver Co, PA), Hugh, George, Robert, Margaret w of Benjamin KIRCHEVALL & Sarah MARTIN; s Henry afp Decatur Co, IN, 1855, & PAR, per F-R7318; PN files S35525 & R7318 consolidated by PN OFFICE in 1939. F-S35525 R1749
James, esf c1776 VA; John MONTGOMERY (NKG), adm of sol esAFF 1844 KY & gtd PN due sol; PN Office stated sol drowned 1784; QLF (date illegible) from sol great gds James MONTGOMERY, Greenfield, IN, states sol s/o Hugh of Shrewsbury, Kanawaha Co, VA, & dd in RW svc at Battle of White Plains, NJ, leaving wid Martha (nee SHERRY), s James (gdf of querier) & d Peggy. F-R16521 R1749
John, MD sea svc; b 1760 Calvert Co, MD; esf 1777 Westmoreland Co, VA, where reared, aboard ship DEFENCE; esf 1781 in VA regiment; mvd to MD 1782 where PN 1832 Frederick Co; dd 3/2/46 leaving ch: John, James & Isabella BRIAN (dd before 1853 leaving no ch); s's John & James gtd f's PN arrears 1853 Urbana, MD, where res; QLF says sailor b 6/18/ 1760 & dd Urbana, MD; QLF says a John MONTGOMERY, dd 1791, md 1759 Janet COOK, they res Westmoreland Co, VA, & had s John who RW sol. F-S8901 R1749
John, b 4/3/1762; esf 1779 Amherst Co, VA, where res; mvd to KY 1789, where PN 1833 Adair Co; last PN payment in file

MONTGOMERY (continued)
1839; QLF states sol res ae 78 Adair Co, KY, 1840 with Robert MONTGOMERY per KY 1840 census. F-S30593 R1749

John, b 8/1764; esf 1777 Moore's Fort, Washington Co, VA, where res, in VA regiment; PN 1832 Parke Co, IN, formerly res Franklin Co, IN; bro James mentioned then; family res with him 1826: w aec 53, d aec 14, & d aec 11; Alexander MONTGOMERY (NKG) AFF Floyd Co, KY, 1830; MIchael MONTGOMERY (NKG) AFF Parke Co, IN, 1830; last PN payment in file 1838 when sol res Peoria Co, IL; 3 of ch, including youngest, res 1839 IL; bro of sol mbnn in RW svc with him. F-S33124 R1749

John, b 1756 Stafford Co, VA; esf 1781 Bedford Co, VA; mvd after RW to Guilford Co, NC, where PN 1832; dd 5/13/40; md 8/7/1819 Nancy BUSICK, Rockingham Co, NC; wid md (2) Zebulon PRITCHET (dd before 5/176/1853); wid PN ae 58 Guilford Co, NC, 1853; gtd BLW15175 there 1855 ae 62; PN increased there 1868 ae 73 when P O address McLeansville; her PN restored (stopped during Civil War) there 1867 ae 72 after signed oath of allegiance. F-W980 R1749

John, lieutenant colonel/o Illinois Regiment/o VA State Line 1778; killed by indians while hunting 12/31/1796, when res Clarksville, TN; sol s William dd Livingston Co, KY, leaving ch: Joseph B, John S, James M, Margaret, William, David, Jonah & Elizabeth; s Joseph dd IL, leaving ch Joseph & Elizabeth; Jonah H MONTGOMERY, only surv gdc of sol, appointed 1849 by court of Fulton Co, KY, guardian for Margaret, James, & William (they orphans of William A/W MONTGOMERY decd of Livingston Co, KY); Jonah H also appointed by same court guardian of William & Alexander (ch of A A CALHOON & w Margaret decd, who formerly Margaret C MONTGOMERY); Jonah H & wards only liv heirs of sol 1849, & they gtd 1/2 pay PN due sol; QLF 1929 from great great great gdd Mrs Ethel G WOCKENPUSS, Baltimore, MD; QLF states sol slain by indians 11/27/1794 on TN frontier, md Janet COOK, founded city of Clarksville, TN, was member of NC legislature & NC constitutional convention, & TN county named after him. F-R16522 R1749

Richard, esf York Co, PA, where b & raised, in PA regiment; PN ae 75 Washington Co, VA 1833 where mvd to 1793 from PA; Henry MONTGOMERY (NKG) AFF there then that he res York Co, PA, when sol esf; sol dd there 2/8/40; md Elizabeth McCALL 1787 York Co, PA; Isaiah LYNCH, clerk of court of Washington Co, VA, AFF 1853 sol wid Elizabeth then insane & sol s Richard Jr appointed her guardian as nearest/o kin; wid PN there then; gtd BLW26383 there 1855; John MONTGOMERY (NKG) AFF there 1854 ae 96 he came from PA aec 66 to there with sol & w & res with them to c1818, thence res nearby; AFF 1854 by John SPEER aec 70 Johnson Co, TN he b & reared Washington Co, VA near sol home & went to school with 2 or 3 of sol ch; AFF 1854 by John LARIMER ae 80 there he worked ae 20 as carpenter on sol farm; sol s John gtd BLW there

MONTGOMERY (continued)
   1851 for his War of 1812 svc. F-W7485 R1749
  Thomas, esf 1776 in 8th PA Regiment; transferred 1777 to VA
    regiment; PN ae 82 Nelson Co, KY, 1832; dd 9/24/1833 (per
    wid claim) Washington Co, KY; md 7/26/1787 Frances/Fanny
    POLLARD, Amherst Co, VA; wid PN ae 86 Washington Co, KY,
    1851; gtd BLW17729 in 1855; dd 2/19/57; s Thomas Jr AFF
    1834 Nelson Co, KY, his f still liv ae 83; US Treasury De-
    partment reported sol dd 8/30/1834, & last PN payment made
    to s John as executor; QLF 1922 from great gdd Mrs Jessie
    Montgomery CLARK, Chicago, IL, states sol came to US 1769
    & settled near Philadelphia, PA. F-W8474 R1749
  William, esf 1776 Amherst Co, VA, in VA regiment; PN ae 75
    Marion Co, MO 1832; dd 11/22/32; w dd before him; s Jordan
    adm/o f's estate AFF 1843 Palmyra, MO, f's heirs scattered
    about the country. F-S16981 R1749
MONTH, Ambrose, esf c1780 Spotsylvania Co, where b 3/4/1764-5
   at the Hayfields, of mixed blood being part Shawnee Indian
   & part negro, but was born free; mvd several years after
   RW to Person Co, NC, thence Grainger Co, TN, for 4-5 years
   thence Knox Co, TN, where PN 1834; illiterate; dd 6/8/42;
   md 1/12/1833 Daphne, a free negro, Knox Co, TN, where she
   PN 1853; gtd BLW26159 there 1856; dd 7/27/64; Charles BUR-
   GER adm/o her estate 1866 ae 50 when her heirs were: Maha-
   la McDONALD, Agnes HARBISON, & Mary SAWYER, her only surv
   children, all res there; they gtd PN due m. F-W7477 R1750
MOODY, Banks, name on VA pensioner list 1835; papers lost 1814
   Washington, DC, fire; no other data in file. F-None R1750
  Edmund/Edmond, b 9/18/1755 Albemarle Co, VA; esf 1778 Char-
    lottesville, VA, where res, in VA regiment; res Albemarle
    Co, VA after RW, thence Fluvanna Co, VA, thence c1803 Cum-
    berland Co, KY, thence 1830 Morgan Co, IL, where res when
    PN 1831 Sangamon Co, IL; family then w Sarah/Sally, s Jef-
    ferson ae 11, s Washington ae 6, d Halley ae 8, d Char-
    lotte ae 4, & d Elsada ae 2; dd c9/10/1838-9 Morgan Co, IL
    (several witnesses state dd 1838); md (2) 2/1821 Sarah HA-
    MILTON, Monroe Co, KY; wid PN ae 52 Mason Co, IL, 1855, &
    gtd BLW85081 then; res 1868 Logan Co, IL, P O address Lin-
    coln, IL when Alfred MOODY (NKG) witness to her signature;
    last known address Hopkins, MO 1880; dd 12/8/81 per report
    to PN Office by s-in-law Wiley TRACY of Skidmore, MO after
    query to him by postmaster; postmaster also queried Willi-
    am GRAY, Clearmont, MO, but no response in file. F-W25726
    R1750
  Edward, b 1766 Albemarle Co (area later Fluvanna Co) VA; esf
    1780 Amherst Co, VA; PN ae 64 Ashe Co, NC, 1821 occupation
    farmer, when had w & ch: Katey ae 25, Polly ae 23, Billy
    aec 21, David ae 19, Annie ae 17, Cely ae 15, Nancey ae 13
    Phoebe ae 11, Levi ae 9, Franky ae 7 & Joel ae 5; dd there
    1/1/38; md c3/17/1794 Frances/Fanny CARTER, Botetourt Co,
    VA; wid PN 1846 ae 73 Watauga Co (area earlier Ashe Co),
    NC; s David AFF then Carter Co, TN, he b 7/1802, 4th ch of

MOODY (continued)
  parents & older siblings births: William 1800, Polly 1798, Catherine 1796 & Sally 1794; MB 3/17/1794 Botetourt Co, VA for sol & w signed by Joseph WILLIAMS, per report by that Co clerk of courts Ferdinand WOLTZ 1846; AFF then by wid bro William CARTER ae 68 Carter Co, TN, that sol w b Shenandoah Co, VA, where their f dd, & m md (2) John MILLER, with whom sol w res Botetourt Co, when affiant informed m of marriage/o sis; m & stepf rushed to church to stop marriage but too late, & that marriage before 1/1/1794 (sol wid earlier afp had been rejected because marriage indicated to be before 1/1/1794, per current PN law); AFF 1846 Carter Co, TN, by Hannah HENDRIX ae 87 she b 1/3/1759 Frederick Co, VA, & md h John there 2/22/1781, their 7th ch b 8/18/1793, & sol & w md before then; AFF 1820 by Charles KINNEY ae 59 Augusta Co, VA, AFF certified by that co JP David W PATTERSON; AFF 1821 by physicians, William BOYS & Edmund EDRINGTON, of Staunton, VA, they examined wounds of sol recd at Battle of Ninety-Six; QLF states sol youngest ch Joel dd Winter 1908-09 & number/o sol gdc res near Foscoe, NC. F-W2158 R1750

  Jinnie, former widow of John GRAFTON. (F-W5391)

  John, esf 1776 PA; afp ae 68 Henrico Co, VA, 1826, res Richmond; PAR, his svc not in Continental Line, per current PN laws. F-R7303 R1750

  Thomas, esf 1780 Cumberland Co, VA, where b 6/18/1762; mvd 1785 to Oglethorpe Co, GA where PN 1832; dd here 11/10/36; md there 12/29/1830 Selah/Celia GOOLSBY (ML 12/29/30); wid PN there 1855 ae 70; gtd BLW40506 there 1856. F-W25732 R1751

  Thomas, b 11/9/1759 Cumberland Co, VA; esf 1776 Lunenburg Co VA, where res, owner of wagon team & pressed into svc with Southern Army & was forage wagon driver part of svc time; mvd 1793 to Surry Co, NC, thence Craven Co, NC, then 1816 to Warren Co, TN, thence 1829 Clarke Co, AL where afp 1833 PAR, insufficient proof of svc; John MOODY (NKG) AFF 1834 Oglethorpe Co, GA, he res 1776 ae 23 Lunenburg Co, VA near sol; sol 1852 ae 94 gave power of attorney to agent Clarke Co, AL, to afp, & PAR again. F-R7304 R1751

  William, BLW12400 issued 7/5/1794. F-BLW12400 R1751

  William, esf 1778 in 1st VA Regiment; PN ae 56 Fluvanna Co, VA, 1818 when Co clerk of court John TIMBERLAKE; res there 1820 ae 59, occupation millworker, when no person res with him; dd 12/30/36. F-S38233 R1751

  William, esf 1775 Martinsburg, VA, in 8th VA Regiment; esf 1777 Fredericksburg, VA; PN 1818 Rockbridge Co, VA; res 1820 there ae 71, occupation laborer, when had w aec 63 & no ch liv with them. F-S38246 R 1751

MOON, Jacob, esf Bedford Co, VA, in VA regiment; KIA 3/15/1781 Battle of Guilford Courthouse; md Fall 1778 Ann/Nancy AMMON of New Kent Co, VA, who bc 1750; they had s Christopher & ch mbnn (b after death of f & dd in infancy); wid md

MOON (continued)
  (2) VA RW sol Samuel HANCOCK, who dd 4/14/1837, & she gtd PN for his svc (see Samuel HANCOCK file on Reel 1178, data extracted in Volume 2 of this series); wid dd 5/22/41 Bedford Co, VA; s Christopher afp there 1842 ae 63 for PN due m for f svc & gtd; Ammon HANCOCK (NKG) attorney for Christopher then; Christopher res there 1845. F-W4691 R1751
MOONEY, Briant/Bryant, esf early in RW with VA troops, serving to end of RW, per wid; she later claimed he esf 1776 Oglethorpe Co, GA in 3rd GA Regiment; sol never afp, mvd c1804 to IL Territory, area later Edwardsville, Madison Co, IL; res 1826 St Clair Co, IL, where dd 6/12/26 or 6/12/27 at Lebanon; md 3/7/1793 Margaret GILLIAM, Oglethorpe Co, GA, who b SC; wid afp 1834 Adams Co, IL, & PAR, insufficient proof/o svc; d Edith May b Winter 1804-5 near Edwardsville IL, md Thomas STANLEY, & they res 1850 Highland, IL, where her m (then ae 81) res; d Mary Malinda, b Summer 1809 Edwardsvile, IL, res 1852 near Quincy, IL, when m res with her part of time. F-R7310 R1751
  Martin, b 7/1752; esf c1775 Albemarle Co, VA, in 14th VA Regiment; PN 1818 there; res there 1820 with w Patsy ae 58, & s ae 15; res there 1824 when he had no occupation, & w Patsy ae 65. F-S38234 R1751
  Richard, esf 1779 Albemarle Co, VA, in VA regiment; PN there 1816 ae 57; res there 1819 ae 61 when w Milly ae 55; res there 1820 when ch res with him: Richard ae 16, Anderson ae 13, John ae 11 & Thomas ae 9; dd 1818 per wid (date obviously an error, per PN Office, since sol last PN payment in file dated 1822); md 12/25/1788 Mildred/Milly CARROLL there; wid PN there 1841 ae 68 where always res; dd 8/5/51 there; Patsey MOONEY (NKG) there 1850. F-W3855 R1751
MOORE, Abraham, b 9/1/1758 Lancaster Co, PA; esf 1775 Berkeley Co, VA; esf 1777 Frederick Co, MD; PN 1833 Shelby Co, KY; QLF 1912 from great gds David STROUSE, Rockville, IN; QLF 1913 from desc Miss Nellie D WHITE of Rockville, IN; QLF 1920 from desc Mrs G W RANSOM of Tulsa, OK; QLF 1921 from great great gdd Mrs H B JONES of Fairfield, VA; QLF 1925 from great gds Isaac R STROUSE of Rockville, IN. F-S2846 R1753
  Alexander, b 4/22/1756 on Ridley Creek, New Castle Co, DE, where esf in VA regiment; res 1820 VA; mvd 1820 to Philadelpia, PA, where PN 1832 ae 78; res there 1834 when partially paralyzed. F-S5773 R1753
  Alexander, esf 1776 Pittsburgh, PA, in 8th VA Regiment; PN aec 55 Philadelphia, PA, 1818; res there 1820, occupation weaver, when only family w mbnn, they both afflicted with rheumatism. F-S41893 R1753
  Alexander, esf 1780 Spotsylvania Co, VA, where b 2/4/1762; PN there 1833 where always lived; AFF there then by Reverend Philip PENDLETON (RW sol ae 74) & Joshua LONG; sol dd there 2/4/34; md 2/1785 Mary PEARCE/PEIRCE/PEARSE/PIERCE there 2/1785 (MB 2/5/85, signed by Martin FINE); wid dd

MOORE (continued)
  there 4/26/41 leaving no living ch; before md sol wid had
  an illegitimate son James PEARCE who dd 9/9/1838 leaving 5
  legitimate ch: John, James Washington, Nancy, Lucy w/o Horace HALL, & Philadelphia wid/o George STEWART, all ch res
  Philadelphia, PA, except Philadelphia STEWART who res KY;
  John PEARCE Sr, adm of sol wid estate, afp 1842 ae 79, for
  wid heirs, & PAR, wid left no legitimate children by sol.
  F-R7346 R1753
Amos L, b 5/13/1747 Albemarle Co, VA; esf Goochland Co, VA,
  where res, in VA regiment; PN ae 85 there 1832; nearest
  neighbors then: Charles ROGERS, Robert PLEASANTS, Charles
  HATCHER, Samuel N CRAGWELL, Major Peter GUERRANT, Dr William M ANDERSON, John MARSTON, Dr Thomas P WATKINS, Colo-
  nel Benjamin ANDERSON, William MILLER (Co clerk of court),
  Robert REDFORD, Francis M ROYSTER, Colonel John GUERRANT,
  Dr Thomas WOOD, John WATKINS, David ROYSTER, & George WIL-
  LIAMS; James H TERRELL AFF 1841 Albemarle Co, VA, he held
  manuscript volume/o Parish Register of Goochland Co, begun
  in 1756 by Parson William DOUGLAS, minister/o parish & gdf
  of affiant, which listed marriage of sol Amos Lad MOORE &
  Ann ROGERS of that parish on 12/21/1775; Alonzo GOOCH then
  JP of Albemarle Co, VA, & Ira GARRETT then clerk of court;
  sol dd 3/7/36; md Ann ROGERS, who PN aec 85 Goochland Co,
  VA, 1841; ch births: (record badly faded & partially illegible): ? 17--, John 17--, Judith 5/11/1778 & Amos Ladd 3/
  20/1780. F-W5145 R1753
Andrew, b 6/9/1758 York Co, PA; res during RW Bedford Co, PA
  when esf 1776 in PA regiment; esf 1780 Ohio Co, VA; mvd
  1788 to that Co, then 1795 to Mason Co, KY, then 1797 to
  Northwest Territory to that part now in OH; mvd from Brown
  Co, OH, 1819 to Bond Co, IL, then to Putnam Co, IL, where
  afp 1836; PAR, insufficient proof/o 6 months svc; dd 4/20/
  1845; md Fall 1793 Elizabeth, West Liberty, Ohio Co, VA;
  wid afp 1855 ae 80 Putnam Co, IL, & PAR; afb there then &
  gtd BLW139857. F-R7313 R1753
Andrew, esf 1775 Augusta Co, VA, where res, in 9th VA Regiment; referred to in 1809 as general but no explanation of
  that title: dd 5/14/1821; md 3/31/1795 Sarah/Sally d/o Andrew REID, Rockbridge Co, VA, by Reverend William GRAHAM;
  wid PN there 1848 ae 71; s S McD AFF Lexington, VA, where
  Co clerk of court then, his f gtd BLW for land in OH 3/13/
  1809; AFF there then by Hugh BARCLAY, Co JP; AFF by John
  ALEXANDER & Margaret GRAHAM there then they present at sol
  marriage; William WHITE JP/o that Co 1856 when sol wid gtd
  BLW 38539; s S McD res then Lexington, VA; Charles CHAPIN
  clerk of court there then. F-W1454 R1753
Asa, nothing in file except statement he res/o VA; apparently file lost. F-R7314 R1753
Charles, b 4/15/1761 Rockbridge Co, VA, where res when esf
  1776 in NC regiment; mvd to NC, then to Fayette Co, KY,
  thence Adair Co, KY, where PN 1832. F-S30599 R1753

MOORE, Charles, b 1/11/1763 Hanover Co, VA; esf 1779 Rowan Co, NC, where res, in NC regiment; mvd after RW to Cocke Co, TN, then to Warren Co, OH, then to McLean Co, IL, where PN 1833; dd 9/19/39; md 4/2/1793 or 4/12/1793 Martha near Salisbury, Rowan Co, NC; wid PN ae 69 Woodford Co, KY, 1843; res 1849 Tazewell Co, IL, when Martha Jane MOORE (NKG) res there; ch births: William C 2/3/1794, John A 3/18/96, Alice C 6/3/99, Prescilla 2/2/1802, Mary 2/4/05, Hugh C 3/18/08, Josiah 4/15/10, Alfred 4/27/13, & Sarah 1/11/17; other births in file: Alexander McKEE 8/30/1838 & Marthy McKEE 6/3/1840; s William C AFF Woodford Co, IL, 1844; sol eldest bro mbnn mvd to AL many years before 1833; QLF says sol md Martha CUNNINGHAM. F-W24005 R1753

Daniel, b 12/12/1764 Albemarle Co, VA; esf 1781 in 10th NC Regiment, when res Globe Settlement on Johns River, Burke Co, NC; PN that Co 1833 as Daniel Sr; QLF says sol md Rachel STONE; QLF 1939 from desc Florence P (Mrs Henry E) HACKMAN, Peru, IL, says sol dd 11/12/1842. F-S7249 R1753

David, esf 1776 in VA regiment; PN ae 66 Jessamine Co, KY, 1818; res there 1821, occupation farmer for another man, when had w aec 70 & gdd aec 28 (had d Sally aec 5 & Betsey aec 2); dd there 7/1839 leaving no wid; wid Nancy afp 1853 Mercer Co, KY, when had eldest gdd (b 11/16/1839) res with her; wid maiden name Nancy GRAHAM & claimed she md sol c 1815 near Fredericksburg, VA; eldest ch liv 1853 ae 36; wid afp again ae 65-70 Mercer Co, KY, 1861 claiming she md in Spotsylvania Co, VA; ch by sol: Sarah, Betsy, David, John, Jane, & Matilda, with eldest ae 44 in 1861; d Betsy md c1835 Jessamine Co, KY, to Stephen THOMAS; wid claimed sol previously md & had s James & s John when she md sol; wid gtd BLW316256 in 1861; AFF then Mercer Co, KY, by wid d Betsy (md 2nd Mr WISLER) ae 42 & wid s Daniel ae 37-40, they both res Boyle Co, KY; PN Office surmised that claimant Martha was actually gdd of sol, whom they believed dd leaving no wid & that Martha falsely claimed to be his wid to get PN & sol 2 great gdd's, Sally & Betsy, mentioned by sol 1821, were gdd mbnn's ch then; wid PAR both times, for PN record shows sol had no wid when dd, & his PN arrears then paid to his estate adm; file mns MB between Elizabeth MOORE & Stephen THOMAS 1/1/1838 Jessamine Co, KY with consent of her f David MOORE & m Nancy MOORE. F-R7349 R1753

David, b 11/20/1783 Amelia Co, VA; esf 1780 Lunenburg Co, VA where res, sub for f Robert; mvd after RW to Surry Co, NC, for many years, then to KY, then to Cole Co, MO, where PN 1832, when res there for 13 years; dd 4/30/40; Jesse MOORE (NKG) adm of sol estate. F-S16980 R1753

David, b 1758; esf c1776 Staunton, VA, in VA regiment; dd 12/2/1831; md 8/17/1788 Jane DuPRIEST, Augusta Co, VA; wid b 5/5/1770; PN 1840 Bedford Co, TN, when res Marshall Co, TN; AFF then by s William, Bedford Co, TN, that eldest sis Anne b 7/17/1789; AFF then there by George CAMPBELL aec 71 he knew sol when sol esf with affiant's bro John CAMPBELL;

MOORE (continued)
   AFF then there by wid sis Ann CAMPBELL their m res Amherst
   Co, VA, when sol came to get consent to marriage, sis Jane
   then res with uncle James ELLIOTT, Augusta Co, VA; births
   of sol & wid ch (family bible record torn & partially il-
   legible): Anne 7/17/1789, William 2/7/92, & Levi 5/-/--;
   other bible data: Truman & Mary BIVENS md 2/5/1803, Watson
   & Polley GILLISPIE md 12/24/1812, David D MOORE & Rebecca
   --- md 7/22/1820, George W --- md Rhody R MOORE 2/-/----
   F-W1456 R1753
Enoch, b 6/18/1758 NJ; mvd when ch with m & f to Allegany Co
   MD, where esf 1778 in MD regiment; mvd 1791 to Harrison Co
   VA, where PN 1832; Daniel MORRIS & James BURKETT AFF there
   then when Co clerk of court David DAVISSON; liv 1834; last
   PN payment in file 3/4/34; name dropped from PN rolls 1835
   by PN Office who determined sol was early settler, who was
   an indian fighter & his svc not covered in pertinent RW PN
   laws. F-S5785 R1754
George, b 10/1749 Frederick Co, MD, s/o George & Phoebe; esf
   Old Town of Skipton, MD, in MD regiment; esf 1778 Washington Co, MD, where res, sub for bro-in-law Obediah FORSHAY,
   in MD regiment; esf 1779 Fort Frederick, MD, sub for bro
   William; later esf sub there for bro John; mvd 1791 to location not given, thence 1793 KY, where settled near Washington, Mason Co; mvd 1806 to Champaign Co, OH; res 1826
   Logan Co, OH; mvd 1842 with s William to Jasper Co, IN,
   where PN 1848; dd there 7/18/48; md 10/24/1780 Ann/Nancy
   BALL (ae 72 in 1826); they had 21 ch, including William
   (res 1848 Jasper Co, IN), George (dd 6/17/1855), John (dd
   2/1855), Mahala (md John WOODFIELD, & dd c2/28/1854), Nancy DOWDEN, Phebe (dd without issue), & Mary STANDAGE; surv
   ch 7/20/55 Nancy DOWDEN & William; gds George FITCH ae 15
   in 1826; d Mary STANDAGE had ch George & Nancy; QLF states
   sol w dd VA, s William War of 1812 sol, res with f Shelby
   Co, OH, & dd Jasper Co, IN, also sol great gds George MOR-
   GAN res Renselaer, IN 1934 ae 86 & was Civil War sol, also
   sol tombstone reads, "dd 7/18/1848 ae 98 years, 9 months,
   & 8 days, a veteran of 1776" F-33116 R1754
George, esf 1780 Charlotte Co, VA, where esf 1780; mvd 1796
   to Green Co, KY, then to 1816 Howard Co, MO, then to Boone
   Co, MO, where PN 1833. F-S17593 R1754
Jacob, b Huntington, NJ; mvd to VA where esf 1775 Loudoun Co
   in 3rd VA Regiment; gtd BLW by VA 9/5/1811; PN ae 72 Scioto Co, OH, res Portsmouth, occupation blacksmith & shoemaker, when had no family. F-S40167 R1755
James, b 2/20/1760 York Co, PA; esf 1777 Bedford Co, PA, res
   there; mvd after RW to Brooke Co, VA, thence Brown Co, OH,
   where afp 1837 when res there 37 years; PAR, insufficient
   proof of 6 months svc. F-R7331 R1755
James, b 3/1/1749 Lunenburg Co, VA; esf 1781 Mecklenburg Co,
   VA; res after RW Amelia Co, VA; mvd to Caswell Co, NC,
   thence Montgomery Co, TN, then to Dickson Co, TN, where PN

MOORE (continued)
   1832; res Charlotte, TN 1836; last PN payment in file 1839
   F-S4227 R1755
James, esf 1776 Dinwiddie Co, VA, in 6th VA Regiment; PN ae
   82 Pendleton Co, KY. F-S11104 R1755
James, esf 1780 Albemarle Co, VA, in VA regiment; PN ae 79
   Jasper Co, GA, 1832; res 1836 Simpson Co, KY, with d Polly
   (Mrs Edward L) GAINES when w decd & ch all grown & md; QLF
   from desc Mrs Rosa Thornton LANE, Atlanta, GA, also desc/o
   VA RW sol William DAVIS, who PN Wilkes Co, GA. F-S30592
   R1755
James, esf 1776 Westmoreland Co, VA, where res; afp 1839 ae
   86 Roane Co, TN, when res there 25-30 years, & PAR; dd 2/
   11/49 leaving wid Agnes who dd 3/10/1849, leaving 7 ch all
   liv 1851: William, David, Edward, John, Winney, Elizabeth,
   & Mary Ann; s David afp ae 48 White Co, TN, 1851 for self
   & siblings, & PAR. F-R7332 R1755
Jesse, esf 1777 in VA regiment; PN ae 68 Surry Co, VA, 1818;
   res there 1827 ae 78, occupation farmer, when had w Nancy
   ae 54 & d ae 14 liv with him; assessors of his assets then
   there Richard H COCKE, August W HUNNIWELL, William JONES,
   Joseph BARSHAM, Edwin EDWARDS, & John C CRESAP, witnessed
   by Butler COCKE; last PN payment in file 1831. F-S38242
   R1755
John, b 11/19/1754 Brunwick Co, VA; mvd aec 18 to Orange Co,
   NC where esf 1780; mvd to Rowan Co, NC, for c4 years, then
   to Rutherford TN, NC, for c20 years, thence York District,
   SC, where PN 1833; QLF states sol md Mary/Polly BOLES. F-
   S18133 R1756
John, b 9/5/1761 Louisa Co, VA; esf 1780 Rowan Co, NC; mvd
   1811 to Bedford Co, TN, where PN as John Sr 1832; dd there
   1/6/42; md Fall 1787 Elenor MARBREY, Rowan Co, NC, who PN
   ae 80 Bedford Co, TN 1843; AFF there then by Luke MARBERRY
   (NKG), who witnessed sol marriage & burial; wid res there
   1848 ae 85; QLF 1908 from desc Miss Nell MOORE of Shelbyville, TN; QLF 1912 from great great gdd Mrs Emma Ward
   TALLEY of Oklahoma City, OK, through sol d Eleanor, who md
   Morgan SMITH, their d Frances Eleanor SMITH md Isaac WEBB,
   their d Tabitha WEBB md J H WARD, they parents of querier.
   F-W40 R1756
John, b 1750 Culpeper Co, VA; mvd with m & stepf John LUCAS
   to Halifax Co, NC where stepf dd; sol bound out there 1774
   as apprentice carpenter; esf 1781 there in NC regiment;
   mvd to Madison Co, KY, then to Caldwell Co, KY, then to
   Scott Co, MO, where afp 1834 ae 83 res Moreland Township;
   PAR; dd 9/11/34 MO leaving wid Mildred; md 10/3/1789 Mildred Lucas BELL, Sussex Co, VA, at her m's house (m wid of
   James BELL) by Baptist minister John McGLAMERY; wid afp
   aec 75 Caldwell Co, KY 1843, & PAR; dd there 7/20/44, leaving ch: James B (b 4/2/1791, res there 1852), Mary (ae 58
   w/o Joseph WHITE), John ae 56, Hannah (aec 55 w/o Meredith
   GIBSON), Morris aec 53, Andromache (aec 47 w/o Samuel WIL-

MOORE (continued)
    LIAMS), & Rebecca (aec 45 w of William TERRY). F-R7340 &
    F-R7348 (consolidated) R1756
John, b Frederick Co, MD; f mvd family to western PA on Middle Creek (that area then in dispute with VA), c10 miles from Redstone (area now Brownsville, PA), where esf 1777; later esf in General George Rogers CLARK IL regiment to fight indians; bro Thomas served with him; mvd 1783 to KY, where PN ae 75 Mercer Co 1832; bro Thomas AFF then there; QLF 1903 from great gds B O HANGER. F-S11106 R1756
John, VA sea svc, esf 1776 Accomac Co, VA, where res, aboard ship HORNET (captain then Richard PAYTON); later master of galley LEWIS; later master of ship GLOSTER; BLW1854 issued 11/4/1783; dd Accomac Co, VA early in 1798 leaving only ch who md Shadrack W OUTTEN of Accocmac Co, VA, who res 1846 Elizabeth City Co, VA; they had ch: Elizabeth w of John BAYNES, Mary unmd, Powell G, Margaret w of Charles BRYAN, Augustus, John & Martha Jane (last 3 under ae 21 in 1846); Shradrack W OUTTEN then afp for his ch as adm of sailor's estate; Wishwood ARMISTEAD then clerk/o court of Co, & J M WILLIS then Co JP; sailor's gdc gtd 1/2 PN due gdf; QLF 1905 from George R WOOD, Hampton, VA, his w's m gdd/o sailor. F-R78 R1756
John, VA sea svc; esf Lancaster Co, VA as sailing master; dd 1802 leaving ch: (1) Ann, md James BOWEN, & dd leaving s William liv 1850, (2) Judith who md William DAWSON of Lancaster Co, VA (they both decd 1850 having left 5 ch: John, William, Lewis, Ann, & Alice, all liv 1850, except Ann who md Beverly KIRK, & dd leaving only ch Francis, liv 1850); Edward CUMEE appointed sailor's adm of estate 1802 by justices Martin SHEARMAN, William KIRK, William YERBY, & Joseph CARTER; John MOORE (NKG) of Rockbridge Co, VA, gave power of attorney 1807 to agent to afp & afb; sailor shipmates, Luke ASHBURN & Lewis HINTON, AFF 1835 Lancaster Co, VA; AFF 1850 there by Susan ASHBURN taken at home of her s William G ASHBURN before Co JP James W GRESHAM, that she b & raised there & now aec 74; John M DAWSON, adm of estate of sailor 1852 there, when Robert T DUNAWAY was Co clerk/o court & Warner EUBANK was deputy Co clerk; John M DAWSON had given 1850 power of attorney to Reuben SAUNDERS to afp & afb; John M DAWSON also gave bond, signed by Samuel C TAPSCOTE & Richard B MITCHELL for inventory/o sailor's estate; file contains many arguments that PN paid to heirs/o John MOORE of F-R78 above wrongfully & should lawfully go to John MOORE of this file; no action by PN Office on this claim indicated. F-R78.5 R1756
Jonathan, esf 1775 in NY regiment; esf 1776 in NJ regiment; transferred 1777 to Gen George WASHINGTON bodyguards; BLW 8595 issued 10/29/1789; PN ae 61 Warren Co, OH, 1818; res there 1820 when had s Jonathan ae 11; mvd 1839 to Warren Co, IN to live near s mbnn; dd 9/23/53 Bartholomew Co, IN; md Elizabeth LONG (MB 7/8/1790) Berkeley Co, VA, which Co

MOORE (continued)
   clerk/o court Ephraim G ALBURTIS certified 1856 that MB in
   Co records; wid gtd BLW349 Bartholomew Co, IN, 1853, & her
   afb witnessed by Jonathan & Barbara MOORE (NKG);   PN ae 95
   there 1856; BLW15419 issued 2/11/1856 to wid but later was
   cancelled she having dd before receipt; QLF states following data on sol tombstone: b 8/2/1754 & dd ae 99 years, 1
   month, & 23 days. F-W4743 R1757
Lambeth, b 6/15/1755 near King & Queen Co, VA, Court House;
   esf 1780 Richmond, VA, in VA regiment; returned to m res
   in King & Queen Co, VA, then to Yorktown, VA, where esf in
   VA regiment; afp 1835 & 1837 Hamilton Co, OH res Coleraine
   Township; PAR both times; one of heirs Robert MOORE gave
   power of attorney 1854 Hamilton Co, OH, to agent to afp,
   & PAR; sol w Frances then decd. F-R7343 R1757
Mark, see F-W7471, record of Martha MOORE/MORE, former wid/o
   Ephraim ELDER.
Michael, esf 1777 Berkeley Co, VA, in 12th VA Regiment; PN
   1818 Bath Co, VA; res there 1820 ae 60, occupation farmer,
   when had w ae 53, d Louisa ae 15, & s Sila ae 3; surname
   also spelled MOOR; QLF 1903 from great gdd Mrs Elizabeth R
   JACKSON, Silver City, NM. F-S36165 R1757
Nicholas, esf 1781 in 4th VA Regiment, & disabled by wounds;
   PN ae 69 Montgomery Co, KY 1818; res 1820, occupation wea-
   ver, Winchester, KY, ae 71, when w decd & children grown &
   left home. F-S36179 R1757
Peter, res Westmoreland Co, VA, long before RW, but esf 1775
   Fauquier Co, VA, in 3rd VA Regiment; AFF 1793 by Colonel
   Thomas MARSHALL, commander/o 3rd VA Regiment in RW; sol dd
   7/1/1818; md (2) 1805 Margaret LOVE, Fayette Co, KY; ch:
   Mary, Thomas L, Robert H, William S, Nancy, & Blackwell;
   wid PN 1853 there ae 71 when ch liv: Mary BARTON, Thomas L
   & Robert H; AFF 1855 Bourbon Co, KY, by George MOORE, s of
   sol by 1st w who dd c1804, that he witnessed f's marriage
   to 2nd w; wid gtd BLW11159 Fayette Co, KY, 1856; QLF 1916
   from great gdd Alta Love Moore (Mrs L W) DAVIS of Everett,
   WA, d/o George Peter MOORE, s/o Thomas Love MOORE, s/o sol
   QLF 1919 from desc Mrs H E ENGEL of Everett, WA. F-W25716
   R1758
Reuben, esf 1777 Culpeper Co, VA, where b 1754; PN there
   1832; AFF then there by Almond & Thomas VAUGHAN they knew
   sol during RW; AFF then by Robert POLLARD, then res Richmond, VA, he former res of Culpeper Co, VA & knew sol from
   youth; Thomas T LIGHTFOOT Culpeper Co court clerk in 1832;
   sol dd 6/27/1839; md there 9/26/1804 Elizabeth W STEWART
   (ML 5/26/1804 per Fayette MAUZY, Co court clerk 1853); wid
   PN there 1853 ae 90; QLF 1912 from desc Miss Bernice Hol-
   loway KENT, Washington, DC. F-W8466 R1758
Robert, b 5/5/1751 Charlotte Co, VA where esf 1776 in VA regiment; mvd 1797 to Bedford Co, VA, where PN 1832; sis-in-
   law mbnn res Charlotte Co, VA, 1832. F-S5790 R1758
Robert, esf 1777 Williamsburg, VA, in VA regiment; afp 1824

MOORE (continued)
  Cocke Co, TN, ae 78, occupation farmer, when w Nancy ae 60
  & s Drury/Densy ae 21 res with him, & PAR; surname also
  spelled MOOR. F-R7352 R1758
Samuel, b 7/14/1761 Staunton, VA; esf 1781 Greenbrier Co, VA
  where res; res there after RW, thence KY, thence IN, where
  PN 1832 Putnam Co. F-S16983 R1759
Stephen, VA sea svc, esf Accomac Co, VA, aboard ship ACCOMAC
  & DILIGENCE; gtd VA BLW there; dd there 1816; md 1/24/1782
  Catharine BOGGS; ch births: Levi 1782, John 8/26/86, Rachel 8/23/94, Catherine 11/25/97 & Sukey 1/28/1801; wid dd
  8/25/1838 leaving ch: Levi, John, Rachel, Caty CROCKETT, &
  Sukey SCOTT, all liv 1853, except John who dd 1841; s Levi
  afp 1853 Accomac Co, VA, for self & siblings; William P
  MOORE(NKG) JP, John W GILLET co clerk of court there then;
  Delaney KINNSHAW & Robert HICKMAN witnesses there then; ch
  gtd PN due m then; Scearbrough BLOXSOM AFF 1833 there he
  served aboard ACCOMAC with sailor; John BULL Sr AFF there
  he served aboard DILIGENCE with sailor. F-W9577 R1759
Thomas, esf 1777 Pittsburgh, PA, in VA regiment; later esf
  in Gen Anthony WAYNE's troops against indians; PN 1818 ae
  57 Bracken Co, KY; res there 1820 when had w ae 59 & twin
  sons David & Jonathan ae 15; dd 8/18/25; QLF states a RW
  sol Thomas MOORE b Co Tyrone, Ireland, esf Westmoreland Co
  PA, in VA regiment, mvd after RW to Columbiana Co, OH, PN
  1819 & dd c1825. F-S36169 R1759
Thomas, BLW12348 issued 2/23/1792. F-BLW12348 R1759
Thomas, esf 1780 Buckingham Co, VA, where b 11/24/1760; PN
  1834 Macoupin Co, IL; QLF 1911 from great gds Robert C
  MOORE, Carlinsville, IL. F-S33137 R1759
Thomas, b Frederick Co, MD; esf 1776 in VA regiment when res
  on Monongahela River near old Fort Red Stone; later esf in
  Gen George Rogers Clark IL Regiment; PN ae 77 Mercer Co,
  KY, res near Shawnee River Ferry; dd 2/25/35; md 3/25/1882
  or 3/25/1883 Elizabeth HARBERSON at Harberson's Station;
  wid b 8/1766; PN 1835 Mercer Co, KY; their 8th ch, Senator
  Thomas H, AFF there 1838 he b 8/12/1796. F-W564 R1759
Thomas, esf 1779 Chesterfield Co, VA where b & raised, in VA
  regiment; res after RW there, thence 1788 Campbell Co, VA,
  where PN 1832 ae 83; dd 11/3/34; md 5/22/1785 Sarah/Sally
  ANGEL (MB 5/19/1785 signed by Henry MOORE) Powhatan Co, VA
  whose clerk of court Richard J GRAVES certified MB in that
  Co records 1839; wid PN 1840 Campbell Co, VA, when Jesse
  BURTON JP & William A CLEMENT clerk of court there; AFF by
  Joicy STORER there then ae 83, who knew sol wid since 1788
  when sol & s had 1 ch; James MOORE (NKG) "an aged and respectable citizen" AFF there 1833 he knew sol all his life;
  Reverend Henry BROWN AFF there then; AFF then by Allan L
  WYLLIE he neighbor of sol in Chesterfield Co, VA, when sol
  esf; sol res ae 78 Campbell Co, VA, 1843, when gtd PN in-
  crease; Thomas FOX JP there then. F-W5388 R1759
Thomas, esf 1776 in 9th VA Regiment; PN ae 79 Accomac Co, VA

MOORE (continued)
1819; Co clerk of court there then Richard D BAYLY; George PARKER JP there then; sol res there 1821 ae 80, occupation blacksmith, when had w Tabitha aec 60; dd 12/31/24; md 4/8/1792 Tabitha SHREWS/SHREVES there; wid PN there 1844 ae 81; Colonel Thomas H/K KILLIAM AFF then sol eldest ch Hancock b 4/20/1793, AFF witness William MOORE Sr (NKG); AFF there then by Margaret HAMMEL; sol wid res there 1848 when her PN increase claim witnessed by Rachel L JESTER & Susan BRADFORD; JP then William Pollard SMITH; a Thomas S ROGERS s/o Mager & Elisbeth ROGERS b1798. F-W5390 R1759

William, b 1754 Botetourt Co, VA; esf 1780 Randolph Co, NC, where res, in NC regiment; res after RW Moore Co, NC, then 1808 to IN Territory; PN 1832 Orange Co, IN; dd 4/15/33; QLF states sol b 12/16/1754 & dd 4/15/1832, per his tombstone in old cemetery a few miles east of Paoli, IN, other members of family buried there, also his w Rachel b 1762 & dd 5/19/1829, ch included Henry Reed & Polly Ann; QLF says sol served in 3rd NC Regiment. F-S17592 R1760

William, b 1759 Berkeley Co, VA; esf 1776 when res at headwaters of Holston River in Montgomery Co, VA; mvd 1777 to Holichucky River in what now Washington Co, TN, where esf; esf 1780 in Colonel SEVIER's NC Regiment against indians; PN 1832 Monroe Co, TN. F-S2858 R1760

William, b 1758 MD; esf 1777-8 Rowan Co, NC, in NC regiment; esf 1780 in VA regiment against indians; PN 1832 Monroe Co IN having mvd there from KY; dd 7/15/44 Washington Co, IN; md (2) 4/20/1800 Ann INYART (MB 4/19/1800 signed by Jonathan MOORE), Lincoln Co, KY; sol s William res ae 46 Lincoln Co, TN, 1846; sol wid PN ae 71 Orange Co, IN, 1853; res 1855 Lawrence Co, IN, when gtd BLW26485; Silas MOORE (NKG) res there then; QLF says sol md Olivia FRU & dd Livonia, IN; QLF 1912 from desc Mrs Bertha F CRILEY, Ottumwa IA. F-W2152 R1760

William, esf 1781 Rockbridge Co, VA, where res during RW, in VA regiment; PN there 1832 ae not given. F-S5787 R1760

William, esf 1776 Buckingham Co, VA, where res, in VA regiment; PN ae 76 Jackson Co, MO, 1833; QLF 1927 from DAR agent, Independence, MO, for sol desc Mrs A J HININGER. F-S16982 R1760

William, esf VA; lost leg at Battle of Kings Mountain; PN 1789 for wound disability, when res Washington Co, VA; QLF states sol had w & dd c1827; QLF states sol dd 1826 & had son who md Elizabeth STEELE. F-25312 R1760

William, esf 1776 Fredericksburg, VA; taken POW & released; esf 1779 in VA regiment; PN aec 62 Rockcastle Co, KY 1818; res there 1820 when w Franky aec 50 & ch James ae 20, John ae 19, William aec 15, Marshal aec 12, Polly aec 10 & Elizabeth aec 7 liv with him; dd 3/3/1835. F-36166 R1760

William, esf Loudoun Co, VA; dd 1/29/1816; md 3/2/1786 Dianna/Dianah STONE, Lunenburg Co, VA; wid afp ae 76 Henry Co, KY, 1840; s Jeremiah AFF there then he b 1789; AFF there

MOORE (continued)
  then by Elijah POLLARD ae 68 that he knew sol in Lunenburg
  Co, VA; Henry FARMER AFF there then ae over 47 he neighbor
  of sol in Lunenburg Co, VA; sol wid dd 5/8/1842 Henry Co,
  KY, leaving ch Betsy, Sally & Nancy HUEY; d Sarah gave power of attorney 1853 there to agent to afp; all PAR; list
  of marriages in Lunenburg Co, VA, performed by Baptist minister Thomas CRYMNS included that of sol & w plus following: Freeman QUIMBY & Anny STANLEY 11/9/1785, Pitman SMITH
  & Hannah HAMLET 1/26/1786, John WHITLOCK & Christian BEAS-
  LEY 1/12/86, Giles TAYLOR & Sine STOKES 7/6/1786, Samuel
  SANDS & Margaret CRAGHEAD 7/20/1786, & Richard CLAIBORN &
  Mary COOK 9/9/1786; William TAYLOR clerk of court there
  1849. F-R7315 R1760
  William Daniel, esf 1777 in 15th VA Regiment; PN ae 74 Ches-
  terfield Co, VA, 1830; res there then, occupation farmer,
  when had w & gdd Mary MOORE aec 12; Parke POINDEXTER then
  Co court clerk; AFF there then by neighbor Lucy ELAM; also
  AFF there then by Richard ELAM, Aaron HASKINS, James ELAM
  & John CONDREY. F-S38241 R1760
  Wilson, b c1760 VA; esf 1776 Lunenburg Co, VA, where res, in
  VA regiment; PN aec 74 Allen Co, KY 1832; dd 12/21/37 lea-
  ving children mbnn; QLF 1931 from desc George S MOORE, New
  York, NY. F-S31262 R1760
MOOREHEAD, Charles, private in Lee's Legion; BLW12355 & 13964
  issued 2/18/1793. F-BLW12355 R1761
MOORLAND, Charles, see MORELAND, Charles. F-S1920 R1761
  Thomas, esf 1776 Goochland Co, VA, where b 3/1753; PN 1833
  Monroe Co, TN. F-S2876 R1761
MOORMAN, Robert, decd in 1859 when heirs afp; sol had afp se-
  veral times in lifetime & PAR, res then SC; file apparent-
  ly lost when sent to U S Congress. F-R7359 R1761
MORCHESON, John, see MURCHESON, John. F-R7362 R1761
MORE, Martha, former widow of Ephraim ELDER. (F-W7471)
  Thomas, see MOORE, Thomas. F-W5388 R1761
MOREHEAD, Charles, esf 1780 Fauquier Co, VA, in Lee's Legion,
  while res with f; mvd to Logan Co, KY, where senator in KY
  legislature 1808-09; PN there 1828 ae not given; sol sis
  Mrs K DONALDSON AFF then Warren Co, KY, she next oldest ch
  to sol; QLF states sol b 1762 Fauquier Co, VA, & dd 1828
  Logan Co, KY. F-46363 R1761
  John, b 6/1750 Hunterdon Co, NJ; f dd Fall 1764; esf 1775
  Loudoun Co, VA; PN 1832 Union Co, KY; QLF 1914 from desc
  Mrs F L GIBBS, Vandalia, MO; QLF states sol md Ann MOFFETT
  F-S30600 R1761
MORELAND, Charles, b 9/8/1764; esf 1781 Goochland Co, VA, where
  res; PN 1832 Carter Co, TN. F-S1920 R1762
  Dudley/Dudly, b 4/4/1762; esf 1778 Goochland Co, VA in VA re-
  giment, where res; mvd c1802 to Carter Co, TN, thence c1821
  Wayne Co, KY, where PN 1832; illiterate; dd 2/13/39; md 4/
  4/1784 Elizabeth by publication of church banns, Goochland
  Co, VA; wid afp ae 78 Wayne Co, KY,1839; PAR, insufficient

MORELAND (continued)
proof of marriage, & sol dd after 1838 per current PN law; afp ae 82 there 1843 & PAR; afp ae 83 there 1845 & PAR; dd 3/10/46 there at home/o d Elizabeth leaving ch: John (b 6/11/1790), Mary WHALEY, Anne BRUMMIT, Winney HOLLEY, & Elizabeth WOODLY/WOODBY; s John, adm of m's estate, afp then Clinton Co, KY, stating his bro William then decd, & John younger than sis's Mary & Anne, also he mvd c1840 to Monticello, Wayne Co, KY, then early 1846 to Clinton Co, KY; John & sis' PAR; William MILLER, clerk of court of Goochland Co, VA, certified 1845 that sol & w marriage not listed in that Co records. F-R7368 R1762

John, b 10/1/1752 VA; esf 1776 Hampton, VA, in VA regiment; PN 1818 Clark Co, OH; res there 1820, occupation farmer, with w Catherine aec 65 when s-in-law mbnn providing their support; QLF 1927 from great great gdd Mary E TELFORD of Pipestone, MN says sol d md Mr CUNNINGHAM, they had d Temperance who md James WADDELL, they querier's grandparents, also an Alexander WADDELL res Bath Co, VA, during RW, mvd to Gallia Co, OH where his naturalization papers signed by John HANCOCK. F-S40170 R1762

Vincent, esf 1780 Sugarland District, near Potomac River, in MD or VA troops; dd 6/7/1838 Henderson Co, TN; md 4/1789 Mary, Rowan Co, NC; wid afp ae 84 Henderson Co, TN 1853, & PAR, insufficient proof of svc; eldest ch Malinda then aec 63; 4th ch Samuel AFF there then ae 57 his m res with him. F-R7369 R1762

MOREY, Peter, b 9/15/1760 Philadelphia, PA; mvd when ch to Augusta Co, VA, where esf 1780 in VA regiment; res there after RW for 10-12 years, thence Sullivan Co, TN for 1 year, thence Knox Co, TN, where PN 1833; signed afp as MOREY but PN as MOWRY. F-S1568 R1763

MORGAN, Benjamin, b 10/10/1762 Fauquier Co, VA; esf 1781 in VA regiment when res Culpeper Co, VA; mvd 1791 from Fauquier Co, VA to Mecklenburg Co, VA, thence 1798 back to Fauquier Co, VA, for 2 years, then to Culpeper Co, VA, for 5 years, thence SC for c18 years, thence Madison Co, AL, where res with children mbnn when w dd, thence Davidson Co, TN where PN 1832; dd 9/29/41; QLF 1920 from kin Miss Sarah P MORGAN of Union Co, SC; QLF 1906 from L A CAMP, whose w great gdd of sol, says sol dd & buried Davidson Co, TN; QLF says sol md 1782 Elizabeth KEMPER, Fauquier Co, VA, & she dd Union District, SC; QLF 1934 from great great gdd Mrs Clyde Carrington BOGGAN of Knoxville, TN says sol d Elizabeth Fishback PETTY b 5/17/1793 Fauquier Co, VA, & was great gdm of querier who holds Elizabeth's family bible, further one of Elizabeth's gdd's mbnn then liv. F-S2860 R1764

Benjamin, b 12/24/1760 Philadelphia Co, PA; esf 1779 Berkeley Co, VA in VA regiment; PN 1832 Monroe Co, VA; dd 2/24/36; md 7/18/1783 Ann ELLIS, Hagerstown, MD who b 1/4/1766; wid PN 1842 Monroe Co, VA; ch births: John 11/11/1784, Phebe 8/26/86, Moses 8/16/88, Aaron 8/26/90, Jesse 10/20/

MORGAN (continued)
92, Elizabeth 12/13/98, Nancy 6/15/1801, Eleanor 6/9/04, Benjamin 12/29/05, James R 3/21/09, & Hannah 4/16/11; Henry ALEXANDER AFF 1832, 1842 Monroe Co, VA; John HUTCHINSON AFF there 1832 & 1842 (then Co court clerk); William VASS AFF there 1847 when res 40 years; M McDANIEL then JP; Samuel CLARK AFF there then when res 30 years; Henry FRANCIS AFF there then when res 51 years; George FOSTER AFF there then ae 80; QLF says sol wid dd 8/31/1852; QLF 1908 from Dr I R LeSAGE, Huntington, WV, his w desc of sol. F-W3854 F-R1764

Charles, private in VA Line; BLW12352 issued 4/6/1790; QLF 1937 from desc Mrs Mildred Ervin HICKS, Lafayette, IN says sol s of Captain Charles MORGAN (tax collector for George WASHINGTON), & b VA in area later PA, esf 1777 in 13th VA Regiment; QLF states sol dd 10/25/1808 ae 65 Allegheny Co, PA, Moon Township. F-BLW12352 R1764

Daniel, brigadier general, BLW1496 issued 8/25/1789 for 850 acres; Daniel MORGAN of Shullsburgh, WI, afb 1885 for self & family as sol desc's, saying sol b 1736 near Draperstown Co Derry, Ireland, came to America with f, served 1755 in French & Indian War with Gen BRADDOCK, fought at Battle of Bunker Hill in RW; desc's BLAR, since sol gtd all land due him in 1789; QLF from Mrs H C HARGIS, Pawhuska, OK, desc/o sol s William, says sol dd 1802 VA. F-BLW1496 R1764

Evan, b 3/1/1754 Town Creek, Allegheny Co, PA; mvd when infant with f David to Frederick Co, VA; mvd 1774 to Monongalia Co, VA, where esf then against indians; esf 1776 in PA regiment; esf 1777 in company/o bro Captain Morgan MORGAN; commissioned ensign 1780-81 by GOV/o VA & served with VA troops; PN 1832 Monongalia Co, VA when s mbnn; Thomas P RAY then Co court clerk; sol bro Zacquil also RW sol; Dudley EVANS AFF there 1833 he knew sol since 1779; Reverend Joseph A SHACKELFORD AFF there 1833; AFF then there by David R MORGAN (NKG) he JP there 1827-28, that Joseph BURNER served in RW with sol; PN Office reported that sol s Evan Stephen dd 8/26/1814 in War of 1812 svc, & Evan Stephen's wid Elizabeth md (2) 5/25/1817 Henry DENNIE (dd 10/5/1835 Middletown, OH), & she gtd PN for 1st h War of 1812 svc, & dd 7/4/1879 St Marys, OH; QLF states sol dd 1851 ae 105 & his s Evan S dd/o measles during War of 1812 svc; QLF 19-- from US Congressman for sol relative Mrs H W STONE of Wilder, ID; QLF says sol dd ae 100 years & 12 days. F-S11098 R1764

Haynes, esf 1776 as colonel in VA Line; gtd VA BLW 1784; dd 3/1795 Pittsylvania Co, VA; LWT recorded there 1795 listed his w Mary, William TERRY, & Joshua STONE as executors; md 10/29/1774 Mary d/o William THOMPSON, Halifax Co, VA while sol res there; wid mvd 1817-18 to Rowan Co (area later Davis Co), NC, where PN 1837 ae 87; dd 5/16/40; ch births: Mary 1775 (dd 1775), Haynes 6/27/78, Mary Thompson 1781, & Elizabeth Lawrance 12/17/87; wid sis Susannah TERRY AFF

MORGAN (continued)
1837 Halifax Co, VA she md & had ch before her sis md sol; William TERRY (NKG) mentioned then; AFF there then by William BUFORD, Pittsylvania Co, VA, he knew sol's children; AFF then there by Armistead SHELTON he knew sol & w; AFF there then at home of Co JP Samuel FITZGERALD by Edmund FITZGERALD (NKG) he knew sol & w & was res Halifax Co, VA, when they md; AFF then by William HALL ae 69 Pittsylvania Co, VA, he b & raised Halifax Co, VA near res of sol wid f William THOMPSON Sr; AFF then Pittsylvania Co VA by Johanna LOVELL, who knew sol wid & her f; AFF Grayson Co, VA, then by Samuel McCAMANT, member of VA senate; James ANDERSON then clerk of court, James ANDERSON Jr (NKG) was JP; William TUNSTALL then clerk/o court/o Pittsylvania Co, VA, & JPs were Jeduthan CARTER, Vincent WITCHER & John A CLARK AFF there 1833 by RW sol's Jesse GWINN, Robert FERGUSON, & David IRBY; J M WILLIAMS, Samuel POINTER & William PANNILL all JP there then; John ARRINGTON AFF there then he served in sol's regiment in RW; AFF there 1834 by RW sol's Hampton WHITE & John ARRINGTON; AFF 1838 Davis Co, NC, by sol d Elizabeth Laurance & h Henry R SHELTON. F-W17157 R1765

Henry, b 12/7/1758 Rowan Co/Guilford Co, NC; esf 1779 latter Co in NC regiment; esf 1780 Montgomery Co, VA, where res, in VA regiment; res there after RW svc 18 years, then to Grainger Co, TN, for 11 years, thence Warren Co, TN, for 4 years, thence Logan Co, KY, for 5 years, then to White Co, TN where PN 1832; dd there 2/22/49; md 9/1785 Susan/Susanna POE, Montgomery Co, VA; wid PN ae 86 White Co, IL 1851; d Susan AFF there 1851 aec 54; other children mbnn. F-W3709 R1765

James, b 4/1/1758 Anson Co, NC; esf 1777-78 Mecklenburg Co, NC, in NC regiment; mvd to Caswell Co, NC, thence Washington Co, VA, thence Lee Co, VA, thence Knoxville, TN, then to Pulaski Co, KY, thence White Co, TN, thence Franklin Co TN, then to Marion Co, TN where PN 1836; referred then to large family/o girls & to s-in-law mbnn who had dd leaving large family; res 1844 Coffee Co, TN, when children res in Middle TN; sol had s & some d's liv 1848 & eldest s KIA in Florida War; sol dd 10/12/51 Tippah Co, MS; md 1806 Naomi, near Monticello, KY; wid PN aec 67 Tippah Co, MS 1858 when gtd BLW94517; dd there 12/31/65 at home of d Nancy who w/o William KINCAID/KINCADE; they res there 1876 when Nancy m's only legal heir & she gtd PN arrears due m (PN stopped during Civil War); sol bro of John & Mark. F-W25729 R1765

James, b 4/5/1748 Frederick Co, VA; esf 1778 Monongalia Co, VA, where res, in VA regiment; res there to 1820, then mvd to IL, where PN 1835 Vermillion Co; children mbnn; Zacquil MORGAN ae 81 & Evan MORGAN ae 81 (both NKG) AFF Monongalia Co, VA, 1834 they knew sol; sol dd 3/1/40; QLF says sol md c1786 Margaret JOLIFF; QLF 1914 from DAR agent, Effingham, IL for sol great great gdd Miss Bessie S PARRISH; QLF says

MORGAN (continued)
  sol buried Wauwatosa near Milwaukee, WI; QLF states sol dd Valparaiso, IN & buried Wayne Co, OH, md Hannah COX who dd 1839 Valparaiso, IN; QLF states sol dd Milwaukee, WI; QLF states sol d Sarah b 12/7/1785, & md Jonathan BUTLER. F-S33138 R1765
James, b 3/9/1760 on James River, VA; esf 1776 Fairfield Co, SC, where res, in SC regiment; mvd to Warren Co, GA, then to Franklin Co, TN, thence Perry Co, AL where PN 1833; mvd c1842 to McNairy Co, TN to res with children mbnn; James H MORGAN (NKG) AFF there then; QLF states sol had s Nathan b 1798, s William, & d Ritta; QLF 1940 from great great gdd Mrs Ruby GEUPEL, Evansville, IN, who also great great gdd of RW sol --- TUCKER who had ch: Gabriel, Ethel, Robert, Daniel, Reuben, Eppes, Susan, & Frances (PN Office identified this 2nd RW ancestor as Herbert T TUCKER, who recd PN in GA). F-S1704 R1765
James, esf 1780 Gloucester Co, VA; dd 3/6/1830; bro William AFF Mathews Co, VA, then he recd RW PN & esf with James, & he attended marriage/o James 9/16/1790 to Ann/Anne FOREST, Gloucester Co, VA; Richard B BRAMLEY JP of Mathews Co, VA, 1839; sol wid PN ae 71 Mathews Co, VA, 1839; AFF then by George CALLIS who served in RW with sol; Co clerk of court then Shepard G MILLER; Co JP then William M BROWNLY; wid res ae 83 there 1848. F-W7468 R1765
John, b & raised Mecklenburg, Co, VA, where esf in VA regiment; PN there 1833 ae 75; Joseph BUTLER Sr & James JONES AFF there then, Daniel S HICKS then Co JP & John G BAPTIST then Co clerk/o court; AFF there then by Bartlett COX, who esf with sol, & lost leg at Battle of Guilford Courthouse; sol md 4/1803 Sarah CHAMBLIN (MB signed by Nathaniel MOSS) Mecklenburg Co, VA; marriage performed by Reverend William CREATH, whose other marriages performed that year were as follows: Robert COLE & Mary STEWART 1/1803, Herman COX & Priscilla SMITH 3/1803, Bines JACKSON & Polly TURNER 4/1803, William LOVE & Susanna BRAME 5/1803, Benjamin FREEMAN & Sarah BOOKER 5/1803, Thomas McCARTER & Caty BOWEN 6/1803, Daniel HAZLEWOOD & Lucy WALLACE 8/1803, Elisha BOWEN & Magdala SALLEY 8/1803, Francis MANHALL & Jane HESTER 11/1803, William HUDSON & Jane PURYEAR 11/1803, Willis JONES & Polly STONE 11/1803, Jesse SEE & Betsy NORTHINGTON 12/1803, Thomas SAUNDERS & Polley MORRIS 12/1803, Banister COX & Rebecca BURRUSS 12/1803; wid PN there 1853 ae 70; JP there then John H McKINNEY & Richard B BAPTIST Co clerk of court; George MILLS ae 37, Emily MILLS ae 35 (NKG) witness to wid signature, when wid gtd BLW27675 there 1855; agent for afp & afb was John James DALY; Albert COLEY AFF there 1854. F-W25725 R1765
John, s/o William (by 1st w) who res Fauquier Co, VA, during RW; sol esf 1775, & KIA at storming of Quebec; elder bro Charles mvd 1783 from Fauquier Co, VA to Muhlenburg Co, KY where dd 1822; ch of Charles: Willis res KY 1831, Eliza-

MORGAN (continued)O
Elizabeth (md Mr MORTON), Anne (md Armistead MOREHEAD), John, Rosanna (md Mr TAPP), Lucinda (md Mr TARNES), & William (4 ch & w in 1822); heirs of sol bro Charles gtd BLW 2049 in 1834: (1) Willis MORGAN, (2) John MORGAN, (3) Lucinda (Morgan) TARNES, (4) John, Willis, & James MORTON + Lucinda FRAIL, all heirs/o Elizabeth (Morgan) MORTON decd, (5) Charles, Alfred, Susanna WATKINS, & Julia EDWARDS, all ch/o Anne (Morgan) MOREHEAD decd, (6) Charles & Cythea Ann HUGHES, heirs of Polly HUGHES decd, (7) Elizabeth Ann, Robert, Mary, Susan, & John Willis, all heirs of John MOREHEAD decd, who heir of Anne (Morgan) MOREHEAD decd, & (8) Susan Eliza, & Rosanna, ch of Rosanna (Morgan) TAPP decd; Daniel MORGAN AFF 1832 Mason Co, KY, that he s of Charles, who s of Simon of Fauquier Co, VA, & Charles had bro John who served in War of 1812 & the families were cousins; Susanna CLARKE AFF 1831 Fauquier Co, VA, she sis/o Charles & John MORGAN, sons of Simon, & her two cousins, Charles & John, were the only 2 sons of William MORGAN by his 1st w; E CLARKE (NKG) res there then; BLW2049 issued 7/10/34. F-BLW2049 R1765

Jonas, esf c1778 Shenandoah Co, VA, in VA regiment; date of death not given; md 1774 Susannah HARDIN & they had 3-4 ch before he esf; wid PN ae 102 Warren Co, VA, 1837; AFF then there by Moses HENRY ae 80 & Robert RUSSELL ae 80; Co JP there then Abner SMITH, & Robert TURNER Co clerk of court; wid decd in 1846. F-W7480 R1766

Morgan, b 8/24/1760 Lancaster Co, PA, s of Nathaniel; mvd as young ch with f to Montgomery Co, VA where esf 1776 as sub for f; mvd several years after RW to Wythe Co, VA, thence 1795 Fayette Co, KY, thence 1802 Cumberland Co, KY, where PN 1833; QLF 1928 from desc Mrs Albert BOLAND of Cleveland OH says sol md Drucilla PRICKETT; QLF says a Morgan MORGAN md Jane, d/o Squire BOONE Jr, in KY. F-S31265 R1766

Nathan, b 10/2/1752 DE; esf 1777 VA, where res, in VA regiment; res VA after RW for 2 years, then to GA for c8 years then to SC for 3 years, then to KY for 2 years, then to IN where PN 1832 Switzerland Co, when res IN for c20 years; QLF 1926 from desc Cadence Guernsey (Mrs Charles W) WOODS, St Louis, MO, states sol b 10/21/1752 near Lynchburg, VA, & buried Vevay, IN; QLF 1926 from great gdd Miss Nell MORGAN of Henryville, IN. F-S16985 R1766

Raleigh/Rawleigh, no RW svc; esf 1791 ae 18 at Shepherdstown Jefferson Co, VA, in WAYNE's Indian War, as lieutenant and aide-de-camp; dd 6/28/1824 Bedford Springs, PA, from effects of 3 wounds recd at St Clair's Defeat; md 2/20/1807 Elizabeth RICHARDS (ML 2/20/07), Culpeper Co, VA; wid afb ae 60 Shepherdstown, VA, 1850; BLW12346 issued 12/31/51; res there 1855; children mbnn; witnesses to afb Jacob MORGAN (NKG) & Walter B SELBY; Thomas A MOORE court clerk & Charles HARPER JP there then; Fayette MAUZY court clerk of Culpeper Co, VA, 1853; QLF states following VA men had War

MORGAN (continued)
of 1812 svc: (1) Raleigh MORGAN, b 1757 Berkeley/Jefferson Co, VA, md 1790 Lydia SWARINGEN, (2) William PORTERFIELD, b1745 Berkeley or Jefferson Co, VA, dd 1821, md 1774 Mary Paud --- & their s (3) William PORTERFIELD b 1787, dd 1837 who md Mary Ann WILLIAMSON, (4) Aaron SMITH, b 1751 Harrison Co, VA, dd 1826, md Sarah ALLEN, & their s (5) Joshua SMITH b 1776, dd 1850, md 1799 Mary WALMSLEY & (6) Charles B WILLIAMS, b 1792 Berkeley/Jefferson Co, VA, dd 1855 & md Drusilla MORGAN. Old War Widow File 10531 R1766

Reece, esf 1774 Bedford Co, VA in VA regiment; dd there 1817 md there 1777-78 Mary HOOD; wid PN ae 83 Franklin Co, VA, 1839; s-in-law mbnn then; James M HOLLAND Jr, Co JP, AFF there then sol wid res with him "as one of his family"; Co JP there then Matthew PATE; M G CARPER then Co court clerk there; AFF there then by John BUFORD & Joseph HUNDLEY who both had RW svc with sol; Patience HUNDLEY (NKG) AFF there then she res near sol & w in Bedford Co, VA; Martin DOODY AFF there then he neighbor/o sol & w in Bedford Co, VA for 5 years; AFF 1840 by Jemima CUNDIFF, Bedford Co, VA, her s Isom/Isham b 8/24/1779 & sol & w md before then; AFF there 1840 there by Jemima's h Elijah that sol carried wounded neighbor Isaac REEDY off battlefield during RW; JP's there then William W REECE (NKG) & N R ROBERTSON. F-W4297 R1766

Simon, esf early in RW as captain of infantry; BLW issued 4/16/1794; PN 1808 for disability from wound at Battle of Eutaw Springs; dd 7/8/1810 Fauquier Co, VA, when adjutant general of state of VA; md there 3/28/786 Elizabeth, d of Captain William PICKETT; wid PN ae 73 Fleming Co, KY, 1839 when res with s Colonel D MORGAN who was then member of KY state senate; s Charles then Captain in US Navy; William HELM, Fauquier Co, VA, JP, AFF then sol wid was sis of his m; wid res 1843 Fleming Co, KY, when Daniel MORGAN (NKG) was Co magistrate; QLF 1900 from gdd Mrs John McMULLIN of San Francisco, CA; QLF states sol wid d of Captain William PICKETT (b 1742) & w Lucy BLACKWELL. F-W8475 R1767

Thomas, b Bedford Co, VA; esf 1778 Botetourt Co, VA, in VA regiment when res there; PN ae 82 Greene Co, TN 1833; last PN payment in file 1839. F-S2862 R1767

Thomas, esf 1779 Williamsburg, VA, in VA regiment when res/o Baltimore Co, MD; PN ae 80 Harrison Co, OH, 1833. F-S2861 R1767

William, esf 1776 Cumberland Co, VA, in VA regiment, where b 5/10/1757; esf 1777-78 Powhatan Co, VA in VA regiment; esf 1781 Prince Edward Co, VA, where res; PN there 1832 ae 75 res/o St Patrick's Parish; AFF there then by Jehue SIMMONS & Robert MORGAN (NKG); Co clerk there then Branch J WORSHAM; AFF there 1833 by clergyman William JOHNSON; mvd to Shelby Co, KY, then to IN, then 1837 back to Shelby Co, KY to res near children. F-S5782 R1767

William, b 1762 Kingston Parish, Gloucester Co, VA; esf 1777 there sub for f; later esf there sub for bro James; PN Ma-

MORGAN (continued)
thews Co, VA, 1832; dd there 5/18/40; bro James decd in 1839 having left wid Ann; ages of sol & John MORGAN (NKG) recorded in same book; Thomas HUDGINS Co JP when John MORGAN & Gabriel HUGHES AFF there 1832; Shepard G MILLER then Co court clerk. F-S7246 R1767

William, esf 1777-78 Fredericksburg, VA, in VA regiment when res Culpeper Co, VA; taken POW at Charleston, SC, brought to Jamaica, where released after peace treaty ratified; PN ae 60 Shelby Co, KY, 1819; res there 1820 when family liv with him was w, 5 single d's (ae's 16-10) & md d who had 3 small ch (deserted by h); res 1828 Shelbyville, KY; BLW 1944 issued 5/24/1833; mvd to IN but returned to Shelby Co KY 1837. F-S18985 R1767

Zackquil, b 9/8/1758 Frederick Co, VA; esf 1778 Monongalia Co, VA, in VA regiment; PN there 1832 when bro Evan ae 79 res there; Co court clerk then Thomas P RAY; Stephen MORGAN (NKG) & Reverend Joseph A SHACKELFORD AFF there 1833; dd 2/27/34; md there 9/18/1794 Sina/Cina WEST, who b 11/1/1777; ch births: Stephen H 12/1/1797, Sally 2/22/1800, Mary 11/20/02, Melinda 2/22/05, Katharine 7/8/07, Rebecca 7/16/10, John Parimount 10/-/12, David James 1/17/15, Samuel Moran 1/16/17, & Elizabeth 3/20/20; wid PN 1849 Marion Co, VA, when s Stephen H AFF there; Thomas S BOGGESS Co clerk of court then; Alexander NEWMAN, then member/o US Congress elect of 15th VA District, AFF there; Joseph HARTLEY AFF then Monongalia Co, VA he himself md there 11/13/1794; sol nephew James MORGAN ae 69, AFF there then he attended sol wedding; Co JP there then Thomas S HAYMOND; wid res Marion Co, VA, 1851; QLF 1919 from great gdd Mrs Rolfe M HITE of Fairmont, WV; QLF says a Colonel Zackwell MORGAN was comander of VA minutemen & he md Drusilla SPRINGER, also Colonel Morgan MORGAN of Berkeley Co, VA, md Catherine GARRETSON; QLF states sol bro/o David & James. F-W1912 R1767

MORGERT, Peter, b 4/18/11758 Sussex, NJ; esf 1777 Loudoun Co, VA, where res, in VA regiment; mvd 1782 to Bedford Co, PA, where PN 1833 res Colerain Township; dd 11/6/1846 Bedford Co, PA. F-S4591 R1768

MORIN, Edward, esf 1775 King George Co, VA, where res, in VA regiment; mvd to Fauquier Co, VA where esf in VA regiment; PN ae 87 Campbell Co, KY, 1832; dd 10/9/41; QLF states sol dd at Flat Springs, KY; QLF 1939 from great great gdd Adelaide Morin MATHEWS, Chicago, IL, says sol b 1745 VA; QLF 1893 from great gdd Mrs LeMaire RAMSEY of Newport, KY says sol b Culpeper Co, VA, dd ae 97 years, 6 months, & 23 days at res of s-in-law Henry SPILMAN, Alexandria, KY, & one of sol's d's liv in 1898; QLF 1920 from James M OGDEN, Indianapolis, IN, whose w desc of sol, states sol dd Campbellsburg, KY; QLF 1926 from desc Carrie L (Mrs M Bryant) GRIFFITH, Columbus, OH. F-S16489 R1768

MORING, John, esf 1781 Surry Co, VA, where b 1764, in VA regiment; mvd 1805 to Chatham Co, NC where PN 1832; sis Eliza-

MORING (continued)
beth COCKS AFF Surry Co, VA then; John COCKS (NKG) AFF also there then; AFF then there by Tobias PRICE he served in RW with sol; sol dd 9/21/1844; QLF says sol known in 1840 as John Sr. F-S7239 R1768

MORIS, Thomas, see MORRIS, Thomas. F-W8465 R1768

MORRELL, John, b 1/7/1759 Yorktown, VA; esf 1775 in 4th VA regiment; mvd after RW to NC for 4 years, then to TN for c19 years, thence IL where afp Fayette Co 1833 ae 74; PN claim suspended for reason not given; w dd 1807 Roane Co, TN; sol dd 5/1846 leaving ch John, Ann, Susan, & Polly; s John afp 1853 ae 60 Warren Co, TN, as adm/o f's estate for self & siblings Ann ae 58 w of George GRAHAM, Susan ae 55 w of Thomas KEEF & Polly w/o John MONROE, & PAR. F-R7396 R1768

MORRIS, Amos, b 8/25/1758 or 8/25/1760 Berkeley Co, VA, near Winchester, VA, on Apple Pie Ridge; mvd aec 10 with f to Yohogania Co, VA, area later Greene Co, PA; esf 1778 in VA regiment when res Jarrett's Fort on "Big Whitely"; PN 1832 Monongalia Co, VA when res there c12 years; AFF there then by Samuel MINER & William STILES; AFF there then by Henry YOHO ae 80, George WADE ae 72, & James TROY ae 73 they all served in RW with sol; sol liv there 1836; QLF says sol md Rebecca TYLER who kin to Pres John TYLER, further sol son Amos Jr (b VA 3/30/1789 & dd 7/25/1878 Lyndon, KS) md 1810 Joana LANTZ (adopted into family of Andrew LANTZ) who b 5/25/1792 Greene Co, PA, & dd 1/9/1878 Oquawka, KS, their ch births: Margaret May 5/10/1811, Andrew 1812, Rebecca 1814, Lucretia 1815, Melinda 2/7/16, George W 1819, Theodore 1820, Isaac 1823, Peria Ann 1825, Susan 1826, Amos Tyler 1828, Joanna 1830, Lot 1831, Sarah Jane 1833, James 1835 & Huston 1836; QLF says a VA RW sol James MORRIS res Blackville, Monongalia Co, VA, where PN & mvd to Wetzel Co, VA, where dd c1834; QLF states sol dd c1847 Monongalia Co, VA; QLF 1938 from great gdd Mary Isgrigg (Mrs Frank) HAMILTON, Terre Haute, IN, says sol md Rebecca TYLER & their ch were Isaac (md Matilda FITZGERALD), Hannah (md Lewis CONGER), Rebecca (md Mr JONES), Lucretia (md Mr McQUAY/McCRAY), George md (Nancy FITZGERALD), Amos (md Ann NEWBERRY/LAWRENCE), Levi, & James. F-S7244 R1770

Bazil, b 3/2/1760 Hampshire Co, VA; esf 1778 Ten Mile Level; esf 1780 sub for Archibald MORRIS (NKG); res after RW Ohio Co, VA, thence Belmont Co, OH, thence Monroe Co, OH, where PN 1832 res Center Township; dd 1/4/41 leaving no wid but children mbnn; heir Sarah YOHO mentioned 1841; QLF states sol res 1840 Monroe Co, OH, with Robert MORRIS (NKG). F-S5103 R1770

Benjamin, b 6/4/1763 Spotsylvania Co, VA; esf 1780 Botetourt Co, VA, where res; res after RW Rockbridge Co, VA, thence 1808 to place on Scioto River in OH, c20 miles below Chillicothe, thence Mad River for 1 year, thence Miami Co, OH, where PN 1832 res Monroe Township; last PN payment in file dated 1839. F-S2863 R1770

MORRIS, George, b 3/29/1763 Hanover Co, VA; esf ae c16 Louisa
   Co, VA, where f then lived; PN 1834 Orange Co, VA when res
   there c25 years; co clerk then Reynolds CHAPMAN; dd there
   5/15/1853; LWT written that date, & witnessed by Richard G
   BIBB, James ROBERTSON, Benjamin F DUNN; LWT listed w Mary,
   d Polly MUSGROVE, d Sarah BIBB, s Richard G, d Ann CHILES,
   d Susan B HORD, & children mbnn of decd s Dabney; s Tandy
   cut off for "bad conduct" & other children mbnn who joined
   him also cut off from LWT; LWT executor William CHILES; md
   (2) 3/5/1847 Mary HEASTERN/HEASTIN (ML 3/5/47), Orange Co,
   VA; wid PN ae 49 there 1856; gtd BLW53757 there then. F-
   W27804 R1770
Isaac, BLW12398 issued 7/15/1789. F-BLW12398 R1770
Isaac, b 1760 Hano Co, VA, where esf 1775; mvd soon after to
   Louisa Co, VA, with f, where esf again; PN 1832 Perry Co,
   AL; QLF 1913 from great great gdd Mrs Z H LANE, Sylacauga,
   AL, whose great gdf John was s/o sol. F-S13965 R1770
James, esf 1781 Berkeley Co, VA, where b 1757; PN 1832 Fair-
   field Co, OH, res Amanda Township. F-S2865 R1771
James, esf in VA regiment; dd 4/1838 Roane Co, TN; md 5/1790
   Darcas MORGAN, Sullivan Co, TN; wid afb 1839 Roane Co, TN,
   & BLAR, insufficient proof of svc. BLW Rejected File No.
   298867 R1771
Jesse, b 3/7/1757 Fairfax Co, VA; mvd to Surry Co, NC, where
   esf in NC regiment; PN 1834 Green Co, KY; QLF 1913 from
   desc Mrs. William J McCARROLL, Fulton, MO. F-S38236 R1771
John, b 8/31/1764 Halifax Co, NC; esf 1781 Rowan Co, NC; res
   after RW Montgomery Co, VA, Edgefield District, SC, Jackson Co, GA, Wilson Co, TN, Lincoln Co, TN, Franklin Co, TN
   thence Jackson Co, AL, where PN 1832 as John Sr; last PN
   payment in file 1838; decd in 1844 when kin John MORRIS
   afp there as adm of estate of sol. F-31868 R1771
John, BLW12387 issued 10/22/1791. F-BLW12387 R1771
John, esf 1776 in 15th VA Regiment; PN 1818 Westmoreland Co,
   VA, ae over 60; Samuel TEMPLEMAN then co JP, & Joseph FOX
   co court clerk; res there 1820 occupation farmer with no w
   but 7 ch (girls ae 19,17,15,13, 10, & 4, & boy ae 11); res
   there 1823 ae 70, with ch Christianna ae 20, Elizabeth ae
   18, Angelia ae 16, William ae 14, Catey ae 12, Polley ae
   10, & Sally ae 7. F-S38235 R1771
John, b King & Queen Co, VA; mvd when small ch with parents
   to Hanover Co, VA, where f soon dd & m dd c6 months later;
   esf there 1779 in VA regiment; PN 1832 ae 70 Louisa Co, VA
   & dd 12/29/34; md 2/3/1791 Lucy WALKER (MB 2/3/1791 signed
   by Thomas DUN, & witnessed by John POINDEXTER Jr), Louisa
   Co, VA; wid PN there 1840 ae 74, when Co clk John HUNTER;
   AFF then there by Mary BURCH she present at that marriage.
   F-W18530 R1771
John, esf in VA regiment; dd 2/18/1807; md 8/5/1783 Rachel
   DAVIS, Rutherford Co, NC; wid md (2) Daniel McCHISICK/Mc-
   KISSICK (dd 2/18/1826); wid afp ae 86 Union District, SC,
   1849; PAR, insufficient proof of svc; eldest ch b 5/11/

MORRIS (continued)
   1784; eldest s William gave power of attorney 1820 Bertie
   Co, NC, witnessed by Mylls MORRIS (NKG) to agent to afp, &
   PAR; sol wid dd Union District, SC 3/4/1852 leaving d Polly MOTT, s James MORRIS, & d Elizabeth MORRIS; d Elizabeth
   MORRIS gave POA 1853 there to agent to afp & PAR; d Polly
   MOTT AFF ae 64 there 1851, when res Spartanburg District,
   she had bro Thomas; sol bro Micajah dd Rutherford Co, NC,
   a RW pensioner; James FOSTER AFF ae 68 Union District, SC,
   1851 he b & raised in VA, mvd from Charlotte Co, VA, when
   ae 13 with f Francis to Union District, SC, that f esf VA
   & served as wagoner with sol John MORRIS, also that James'
   f-in-law Joshua FOSTER was RW pensioner, also James' bro
   Robert came to SC with sol John MORRIS. F-R6772 R1771
   John, esf 1777 Orange Co, VA, aec 16 in 2nd VA Regiment; mvd
   after RW to Campbell Co, VA, then to Franklin Co, VA, then
   to Sumner Co, TN, thence Murray Co, TN, thence Wayne Co,
   TN, where afp 1836 ae 76; PAR. F-R16548 R1771
   Jonathan, b 6/15/1753 VA; mvd ae 10-12 with f Joseph to Mud-
   dy Creek Settlement, Greene Co, PA, thence Garrett's Fort,
   where esf as indian spy & scout; PN 1834 Greene Co, PA res
   Dunkard Township; bro mbnn; QLF states sol had bro George;
   QLF 1936 from desc James S SELLERS, Kahoka, MO, states sol
   dd 3/20/41, querier also desc of RW sol Reverend John GAR-
   RARD who b VA & had s Justice, querier also desc of RW sol
   Reverend John CORBLY, b 1735 England, came ae 14 to America, md Abigail BULL of Winchester, VA, & served in RW from
   KY. F-S7247 R1771
   Lester, b 7/5/1750; esf 1779 Brunswick Co, VA, where res, in
   1st VA Regiment; PN 1818 Giles Co, TN; res there 1826 with
   w Frances ae 65, d Lucy ae 18 & d Martha (wid with ch Sally, Rebecca & Susan); QLF states sol living 1841; QLF 1908
   from great gdd Miss Annie PEPPER of Athens, AL, states sol
   listed on 1840 census of TN. F-S2003 R1771
   Micajah, esf 1776 in VA regiment; PN ae 74 Rutherford Co, NC
   1830; dd 12/25/39; md 1790 Sally MOORE (MB 2/2/1790) Rutherford Co, TN; wid PN there 1843; gtd BLW34917 ae 86 Macon
   Co, NC, 1855; 1st s William b 1791; 2nd s Aaron b 1793.
   F-W4036 R1771
   Nathaniel, b 6/26/1756; esf 1775 Brunswick Co, VA where res;
   PN 1833 Jones Co, GA. F-S31871 R1772
   Nathaniel G, esf 1775 in 9th VA Regiment; md shortly after
   Battle of Monmouth to mbnn; PN 1818 ae 70 Bracken Co, KY,
   when widower without ch; res there 1820 when had neither
   ch nor kin in US; dd 9/15/24. F-S36178 R1772
   Reuben, esf 1776 in 1st VA Regiment; esf 1777 as marine on
   privateer ship; esf later 1777 in 2nd VA Regiment; PN 1832
   Warren Co, OH, ae 76. F-S9036 R1772
   Samuel, BLW214 issued 10/16/1805; esf 1779 in 18th VA Regi-
   ment. F-BLW214 R1772
   Thomas, b 1/16/1761 Prince William Co, VA; esf 1780 Surry Co
   NC, where res; mvd 1781 to KY, where esf against indians;

MORRIS (continued)
PN 1835 Madison Co, KY, where dd 8/4/42; md 1/6/1787 Susan d/o John APPLETON, Surry Co, NC; wid PN ae 75 Madison Co, KY, 1844; 9 ch: Eleanor (b 9/1787, md 2/7/1805 Elias PINKSTON, Madison Co, KY & they had s mbnn who ae 44 in 1849), Lewis, Simpson, Patsy (md Mr MORBERLY), Margaret (md Mr EASTERS), Mary (b 2/28/1800, md Jesse FRANKLIN), Jane (b 8/1805 md Mr GOODRIDGE), Ennis (youngest s, ae 32 in 1845) & ch mbnn; d Eleanor PINKSTON AFF 1845, 1848, & 1849 Madison Co, KY; wid gtd BLW28526 in 1855; surname also spelled MORIS; QLF says sol d Sarah md c1800 to Thomas MONTGOMERY, Madison Co, KY. F-W8465 R1772

Thomas, esf 1779 Augusta Co, VA, in VA Regiment; PN 1818 Nicholas Co, KY; res there 1820 ae 67 with w Mary aec 50, & ch: William ae 11, Ann ae 9, Jane ae 6, twins Lucinda & Harry ae 5 & Barton ae 2; res 1838 Fulton Township, Hamilton Co, OH where had mvd to be with children; dd 11/18/39; wid dd 1856; s Harry H res 1856 Fulton, OH; QLF 1929 from desc Elizabeth Morris WHITECOTTON of Kansas City, MO. F-S41015 R1772

Travis, b 6/12/1758 Richmond Co, VA; esf 1777 Prince William Co, VA, where res, in VA regiment; mvd with f to Surry Co, NC, where again esf; res after RW NC, GA, thence Alexander Co, IL, where res when PN 1833 Union Co, IL; dd 9/12/1841, leaving children mbnn. F-S33123 R1772

William, esf 1781 NC in NC regiment; mvd c1805 to Jackson Co GA, thence Gwinnett Co, GA where PN 1821 ae 63; dd 8/8/24; md Spring 1785 Betsey McGINNIS, Halifax Co, VA, her cousin Methodist minister William MOORE officiating; wid PN ae 73 Gwinnett Co, GA, 1840; in 1820 sol had d Betsy ae 16 & gdd Peggy MORRIS aec 12 liv with him & w. F-W5147 R1772

William, esf 1777 Peachbottom Ferry, PA, in PA regiment; svc in War of 1812 also; PN ae 57 Loudoun Co, VA, res Leesburg 1818; res there 1820 with w mbnn ae 53, d Kittura ae 20, s Britton O, d Louisa ae 14, s Thomas ae 12, & d Janetta ae 9; res 1823 Muskingum Co, OH; dd OH; wid dd OH c1852. F-S40173 R1772

Zadoc/Zadock, b Fall 1761 DE, where esf 1777 in DE regiment; PN 1818 Monongalia Co, VA, when stated had 14 children by 2 wives; res there 1820 with w Elizabeth aec 50, s aec 13, s aec 14, & twins (s & d Elizabeth) who b 1/1809; 2 s mbnn had War of 1812 svc; s Richard living 1823; QLF 1825 from desc H F MORRIS, Charleston, WV. F-S38247 R1772

MORRISON, Andrew, b 10/24/1754 NY; mvd when ch with f to Berkeley Co, VA; mvd 1779 to Greenbrier Co (area then Pocahontas Co), VA where esf 1779 against indians; afp there 1835 & PAR, insufficient proof/o svc; QLF states sol dd 9/15/45 Greenbrier Co, VA, near Martinsburg. F-R7474 R1773

Ezra, b 1756 Amherst Co, VA, where esf 1776 in 2nd VA Regiment; PN 1832 Lincoln Co, KY; dd 11/1/44 leaving only surviving ch Elizabeth BRIGHT. F-S13956 R1773

Hugh, esf 1775 in 1st VA Regiment; esf 1776 in 2nd VA Regi-

MORRISON (continued)
  ment; PN ae 66 Allen Co, KY, 1820, occupation farmer, when res with d Sally HAWKINS & her h Thomas; Christopher TOMPKINS AFF there then he esf with sol. F-S36180 R1773
James, b 1744 near Durham Iron Works, Bucks Co, PA; esf 1775 Cumberland Co, PA, where res; mvd 1785 to Lycoming Co, PA, thence 1800 Warren Co, PA, where PN 1833 res Kinzua Township; md 1770-1774 in Loudoun Co, VA, w mbnn; last PN payment in file 1838; QLF 1911 from great gdd Miss Maude M MORRISON of Cornplanter, PA, states sol dd 1839 Kinzua, PA on an island in the Alleghany River that bore his name, md Martha Griffin BACON; QLF 1931 from desc Mrs John M HALT, Quaker Bridge, NY. F-S23816 R1773
James, esf 1776 Pittsylvania Co, VA, in 6th VA Regiment; PN ae 74 Hawkins Co, TN, 1832; dd there 3/3/42 leaving no wid but ch John, Anna, David, Polly, Betsy, James, Nelly, William, Jane, Rhoda, & Rachel; s James afp there 1855 giving following data on siblings: Anna (md Lewis DALTON, both dd there leaving 5 ch none of which res there), David blind & res there 1855, Polly (res Greene Co, TN, 1855), Betsy (md Abner DEATHERAGE & res Roane Co, TN 1855), Nelly (md James HALL & res Greene Co, TN 1855), William (res Greene Co, TN 1855), Jane (md John LIGHT & res Hawkins Co, TN, 1855), Rhoda (md Stacy LIGHT & res Hawkins Co, TN, 1855), Rachel (md Jonathan LIGHT & res Washington Co, TN 1855). F-S2869 R1773
James, b & raised Prince Edward Co, VA, where esf 1776 in VA regiment; mvd 1797 to Mercer Co, KY, thence 1800 Henderson Co (later Union Co), KY; PN ae 78 Union Co, KY, 1833. F-S31269 R1773
James, see MORRISTON, James. F-S40183 R1773
James, b 1761 Berkeley Co, VA; esf 1779, 1780 & 1781 Augusta Co, VA where res, against indians; mvd 1784 to Berkeley Co VA, thence 1787 Augusta Co (area later Greenbrier Co), VA; afp ae 73 Pocahontas Co, VA, 1834; PAR, insufficient proof of svc; clergyman Robert BURNSIDE, S D HOPKINS, & Thomas HILL (co JP) AFF there then. F-R7421 R1773
John, esf 1776 Frederick Co, VA, in VA regiment; PN 1832 ae 75 Greene Co, TN; dd 12/12/42. F-S45874 R1773
John, b 5/1/1765 Orange Co, VA, where esf 1781 in VA regiment; res there 31-32 years, thence Goochland Co, VA, then 1821 to Louisa Co, VA, where PN 1834; dd there 8/20/49; md there 1/18/1839 Polley THOMASSON when known as Major John; wid afp there early 1853 ae 71; PAR, insufficient proof of being wid of sol; dd there 9/1853 when David HUNTER was Co court clerk; sol bro George AFF 1834 Henry Co, VA when res Louisa Co, VA; George GRAVELY Co JP, & Anthony M DUPUY Co court clerk/o Henry Co, VA, then; AFF 1832 Louisa Co, VA, by Jesse SANDERS he esf with sol, per Louisa Co JP William C NELSON; Robert CLARK AFF 1832 Orange Co, VA, he served in RW with sol, per that Co JP Lawrence T DADE; Reynolds CHAPMAN then Orange Co court clerk. F-R7424 R1773

MORRISON, Joseph, b 11/30/1759; esf Martinsburg, Berkeley Co, VA, where res; f living during RW; PN 1832 Marion Co, IL, res Salem; dd 8/23/35 or 8/25/35 leaving wid Elizabeth who gtd his PN arrears; QLF 1920 from gds Obadiah F EVANS, Salem, IL, s/o d of sol, states sol came from TN to IL 1826, sol wid dd 1845, also querier served in Civil War in 40th IL Infantry Regiment Volunteers; QLF 1923 from great gdd Minnie MARCH, Centralia, IL, states sol wid dd 8/11/1844; QLF 1928 from desc Mrs W F PERIMAN, Chicago, IL, says sol b Martinsburg, WV. F-S31268 R1773

Samuel, b c1776 near Hagerstown, MD; esf 1792 Wheeling, WV, where res, against indians; mvd 1845 to Knox Co, OH, from Holmes Co, OH, where had res for 25 years; afp ae 71 Knox Co, OH, 1846 when res with s mbnn; PAR; AFF 1845 there by Sarah WADDLE ae 80 that her h Robert WADDLE (dd c1830) in svc with sol & had known sol since boyhood; Joseph SLOAN AFF Knox Co, OH, 1846, res Monroe Township, who knew sol since sol infancy. F-R7428 R1774

MORRISS, Claiborne, b 3/8/1752 Louisa Co, VA; esf 1777 King William Co, VA, where res; PN there 1832; Robert POLLARD Co court clerk & Thomas DABNEY Co JP there then; sol dd 1/6/39. F-S5776 R1774

MORRISSON, Edward, b 4/1758 NJ; esf 1777 Fauquier Co, VA, in VA regiment; PN there 1832; following AFF there then they had known sol for 15-20 years: Daniel S PAYNE, John PAYNE Jr, James PAYNE, J MARSHALL & Thomas HILLARY; A J MARSHALL Co court clerk then, & Robert BRENT then Co court justice. F-S5780 R1774

MORRISTON, James, esf 1777 Pittsylvania Co, VA, in 5th VA Regiment; PN aec 65 Hawkins Co, TN, 1818. F-S40183 R1774

MORROW, Robert, BLW 1508 issued 7/5/17899 to David MORROW, only surv bro & heir of sol; records lost in Washington, DC, fire 1800; QLF states sol officer in 3rd VA Regiment, & md Jane PEDEN, wid of Mr MOXTON. F-BLW1508 R1774

MORS, Alexander, b 2/22/1750 PA; esf 1777 Montgomery Co, VA, in VA regiment; mvd 1817 to Shelby Co, KY where PN 1834 as Alexander MORSE. F-S38240 R1775

MORSE, Ebenezer, esf 1779 in 3rd VA Regiment; PN aec 55 Westmoreland Co, VA 1818; res there 1820 aec 57 when physically unable to pursue former occupation of blacksmith; family then 2nd w aec 25, no children. Bennett McKAY AFF 1819 there he served with sol in 3rd VA Regiment; William MIDDLETON then Co JP, & Joseph FOX then Co court clerk there. F-S38243 R1775

MORTIMER, Famous, b 1763 Loudoun Co, VA, where esf 1781 in VA regiment; mvd 6 years after RW to Fleming Co, KY, where PN 1834; dd there 5/15/51; md there 10/13/1816 Mary BLUE; wid md (2) 12/18/1855 Joseph FAGAN, Parke Co, IN; wid afp 1858 ae 65 McLean Co, IL, res Old Town; PAR, not a wid then because 2nd h still liv; David BLUE (NKG) AFF 1834 Fleming Co, KY, where res; Leonard BEAN AFF 1849 Mason Co, KY, he served with sol in same regiment; QLF 1937 from desc Hazel

MORTIMER (continued)
   MORTIMER, Rockford, IL, states her gdf Emanuel MORTIMER, s
   of sol & bro to Famous MORTIMER Jr who f of Mrs Elvira La-
   ton PAYNE who joined DAR on sol's RW svc, also sol surname
   sometimes spelled MORTIMORE, also sol w Mary BLUE b1793 &
   dd 1866, also sol had bro William & a sis, & their m was
   Sarah. F-R3418 R1778
James, esf 1778-9 New Windsor, NY in NY artillery unit, when
   res NY; PN ae 76 Grayson Co, VA, 1832; Co court clerk then
   Martin DICKINSON. F-S5774 R1778
MORTON, Edward, b 3/1763-4; esf Augusta Co, VA, where res on
   Bull Pasture waters; PN 1832 Pendleton Co, VA; Zebulon DY-
   ER then Co court clerk; Edward STEWART Sr AFF then Bath Co
   VA, he esf with sol; Charles STEWART then that Co JP; sol
   illiterate & dd 2/20/52; QLF says sol b Rockingham Co, VA;
   QLF 1821 from desc Miss Mayme MORTON, Sutton, WV; QLF 1922
   from great gdd Mrs Abbie Morton COMPTON, Camden on Gauley,
   WV. F-S5778 R1778
Hezekiah, esf in 6th VA Regiment; gave power/o attorney 1801
   to John WATTS, Prince Edward Co, VA, to afb; WATTS autho-
   rized attorney John FIGG to claim BLW for sol; Co JP then
   Archer ALLIN; Co court clerk then Francis WATKINS; sol gtd
   BLW69; sol PN 1829, & dd 6/30/31; PN Office reports no PN
   records for sol found; QLF 1906 from desc Mrs Emmet L WIL-
   LIAMSON, Martinsville, VA. F-BLW69 R1778
James, esf 1777 in 4th VA Regiment; BLW1614 issued 4/26/1798
   PN 1828 Prince Edward Co, VA, res Willington, VA; res 1843
   ae 87 Cumberland Co, VA, where had res 7-8 years with s Dr
   William S MORTON; Co JP then Allen WILSON; QLF 1916 from
   desc Mrs Robert Leslie GOAD, Hazard, KY, states sol f John
   also RW sol & was captain in 4th, 8th & 12th VA Regiments,
   querier also desc of VA RW sol Richard Sandburne WOOD who
   md Elizabeth MICHAUX (her parents res 1st/o Manakin Town,
   area then in Stafford Co, VA). F-S9035 R1778
Josiah, b 12/26/1760 Prince Edward Co, VA, where esf 1779-80
   in VA regiment; res there c20 years after RW, thence Caswell Co, NC, where PN 1833; last PN payment in file 1843;
   decd in 1844 when only ch mbnn living. F-S8898 R1778
Samuel, b 9/23/1745 Prince Edward Co, VA; esf 1775-6 Halifax
   Co, VA, where res, in VA regiment; mvd 1794 to Clark Co,
   KY, thence 1832 Madison Co, KY, where PN 6/1834; dd 7/19/
   34; mention made of s mbnn 1845; Richard MORTON (NKG) res
   1851 Lancaster, MO; QLF 1911 from desc Mrs William WIDDI-
   COMB Jr, Grand Rapids, MI, states sol b Richmond, VA, & dd
   Madison Co, KY. F-S38238 R1778
Thomas, b 8/29/1752 Chester Co, PA; esf 1775 Cumberland Co,
   PA, in PA regiment; mvd 1780 to Jefferson Co, KY Territory
   where esf 1781 in General George Rogers CLARK VA regiment;
   commissioned captain in Nelson Co, VA, militia 1786, lieu-
   tenant colonel 1790; appointed associate judge/o Perry Co,
   IN, 1814; PN 1832 Vermilion Co, IL. F-S32411 R1778
William, esf 1779 Charlotte Co, VA where res; PN 1832 aec 72

MORTON (continued)
  Gibson Co, TN; QLF says a VA RW sol William MORTON b 3/28/ 1743 Prince Edward Co, VA, esf Charlotte Co, VA, & md Susannah WATKINS. F-S2007 R1778
MOSBY, Hezekiah, see MOSLEY, Hezekiah. F-S13959 R1779
  Joseph, b 1/28/1758 Goochland Co, VA; mvd 1766 with f to Rowan Co, NC (that Co divided, & area became Surry Co); sol esf 1776 Surry Co, NC, in Samuel MOSBY (NKG) company of NC regiment; esf 1780 in NC company where bro Daniel was ensign; mvd 1782 to Mercer Co, KY, then to Lincoln Co, KY, where esf in General George Rogers CLARK regiment against indians; PN 1834 Fayette Co, KY; last PN payment in file 1845; QLF 1933 from great grandniece Betty G (Mrs G S) MADDOX, St Louis, MO, states sol dd 1848 Fayette Co, KY. F-S15539 R1779
  Littleberry, esf in 2nd GA Regiment; taken POW, released, & furloughed home to VA; esf there in VA regiment; apb 1803 Powhatan Co, VA as Littleberry Jr; BLW64 issued 9/16/1803; QLF says sol s of Benjamin MOSBY & Mary POINDEXTER. F-BLW 64 R1779
  Robert, esf VA in company of Captain John MOSBY (NKG) & went to GA where served under Captain Littleberry MOSBY; taken POW there; dd 8/9/1798; LWT 8/10/1798 Powhatan Co, VA, & probated there 8/15/1798 lists w & eldest s John, appoints John ROBINSON & Wade MOSBY executors, witnessed by William MARTIN, James TAYLOR, & John SWANN Jr; Abner CRUMP then Co court clerk; md there 10/1785 Susanna ROBERTSON (MB 10/13/ 85 signed by James TAYLOR); wid gtd BLW2382 there 1832; PN aec 72 there 1838; Thomas MILLER Co JP there 1832; Benjamin MOSBY (NKG) & Judith M SMITH AFF there 1838 that sol & w had 3 or 4 ch before 1794, that sol bro/o Captain John & Captain Littleberry MOSBY; court record there 1830 listed ch of sol & w: Jacob, Charles W, Clarissa (w/o Joseph MOSBY), Susanna (w/o Isaac A ALLIN), Elbert (then decd without issue), & John (mvd away from Co over 7 years before & whereabouts unknown); Joseph MOSBY & w Clarissa res Buckingham Co, VA, 1846 when gave power/o attorney to agent to apb; Rolfe ELDRIDGE then Co clerk of court there. F-W7478 R1779
  Wade, b Cumberland Co (area later Powhatan Co), VA; esf 1777 Prince Edward Co, VA, when student at Hampton Sidney Academy; esf 1779-80 as 2nd lieutenant in company of bro Captain Littleberry Jr; later esf in company of bro-in-law Captain Robert HUGHES; later raised company under bro Major Littleberry Jr; later esf under f Colonel Littleberry Sr, who was Commandant of Militia of Cumberland Co, VA; PN ae 72 Powhatan Co, VA, 1832; dd 6/1/34; md 1785 Susanna TRUEHEART (MB 4/13/1785) Hanover Co, VA; wid PN ae 71 Powhatan Co, VA 1838; res 1848 Richmond, VA; res 1850 Henrico Co, VA, when PN increased; ch included John G, Mary G MORRISON, & Littleberry H, all b before 1794. F-W3856 R1779
  William, esf 1778-79 in 7th VA Regiment; PN aec 64 Adair Co,

MOSBY (continued)
  KY, 1818; res there 1820 ae 66, occupation farmer, when w
  Dianna ae 56, s Jesse ae 20, d Elizabeth aec 16, & d Nancy
  ae 14 res with him; res there 1834 ae 76 when gtd BLW1612;
  dd 7/15/43; md 10/5/1786 Dianna JESSE (MB 9/27/1786 signed
  by Thomas JESSE, witnessed by Abner CRUMP) Powhatan Co, VA
  wid Dianna/Diana PN ae 78 Adair Co, KY, 1843; had "large,
  respectable family of children"; PN increased there 1845
  when res at home of William JESSEE (NKG); wid bro Lazarus
  AFF there 1843 he present at her marriage. F-W8469 R1779
MOSELEY, Arthur, esf 1781 Powhatan Co, VA, where b; PN there
  1832 aec 70. F-S7240 R1779
  Arthur, esf 1781 Buckingham Co, VA; dd 8/31/1829; md there
  Sally PERKINS 12/1788; wid PN there 1846; sol sis Judith
  COURTNEY AFF there then ae 78 she herself md 10/1792; John
  PATTISON, surveyor, AFF then ae 62 he esf with sol; David
  PATTESON AFF there then ae 88 per Co JP J M PATTESON; Ed-
  mond GLOVER also Co JP then; sol wid gtd BLW26542 when she
  res Wheatland, that Co, 1855 with s Dr William P; Rolfe
  ELDRIDGE then Co court clerk; sol bro of David. F-W74581
  R1779
  Benjamin, esf 1779 in VA Line; gtd VA BLW1468; dd 7/26/1799
  Buckingham Co, VA, leaving wid Mary & ch William, Mary (md
  Rolfe ELDRIDGE), Lucy (md Dr James AUSTIN & she dd before
  1849), Margaret (md James JONES & she dd before 1849), &
  Matthew (dd without issue); sol md 12/25/1783 Mary, d of
  Mrs Ridley BRANCH, Chesterfield Co, VA; wid PN ae 74+ Buc-
  kingham Co, VA, 1839; gtd BLW2436 there then; ch of Dr
  James AUSTIN & w Lucy: Lucy Ann (md Austin MORGAN), Thomas
  A, Mary/Maria Agness, & James; ch/o James JONES & w Marga-
  ret: Ann (md John MAY), Amanda, Lucy, Virginia, James,
  William W, & Margaret; sol wid gtd PN increase Buckingham
  Co, VA, 1843; power of attorney given there 1849 by James
  AUSTIN Jr to apb; John HILL AFF there 1855 his w gdd/o sol
  F-W5387 R1779
  Benjamin, esf VA; apb 1833 Powhatan Co, VA, by Mary WATKINS,
  Ann B JONES (both ch of decd sol), & ch of sol decd d Eli-
  za BRANCH (Eppes, Ann Jones, Frances, & Benjamin); Samuel
  JONES (NKG to Ann B), s of Samuel, recd BLW1832 there for
  sol heirs & stated he soon heading West; QLF 19-- from sol
  great gds C H ROBERTSON, Hillsboro, NC, says sol LWT probated 5/19/1791 Powhatan Co, VA. F-BLW1932 R1779
  James, b 12/24/1756 Brunswick Co, VA; esf Union District, SC
  1776 in SC regiment; PN there 1832; dd there 5/19/40; md
  before 1830 (2) Mrs Martha PICKENS, who dd 10/2/39; their
  only ch Jane b 12/31/35 there & md there ae 16 to Shelton
  M McWHIRTER; Jane McWHIRTER afb there 1855 ae 20 & gtd BLW
  40688; sol had children mbnn by 1st marriage who all over
  ae 21 in 1855; sol 2nd w by her 1st h had s John PICKENS,
  who survived her; surname also spelled MOSELY; QLF states
  sol md (1) Nancy JASPER & (2) Patty PICKENS. F-S9421 R1779
  Joseph, esf 1781 Chesterfield Co, where b 1/1/1765; PN 1832

MOSELEY (continued)
  Abbyville District, SC, as Joseph Sr. F-S21981 R1779
Leonard, esf 1779 Henrico Co, VA, in VA regiment; PN 1818 ae 67 Fayette Co, KY when res Woodford Co, KY; res there 1821 ae 69, occupation farmer, with w aec 70 & s aec 22; surname also spelled MOSELY. F-S36173 R1779
Peter, b 4/4/1763; esf 1781 Powhatan Co, VA, in VA regiment; PN Chesterfield Co, VA, 1833; Co court clerk then Parke POINDEXTER; George W CALE & William LIGON both then Co JP; Seth HUTCHENS AFF then there he served in RW with sol; Goode GILL & Thomas WILSON AFF there then for sol; surname also spelled MOSELY; QLF 1922 from desc Miss Ann MOSELEY, Dallas, TX, who also desc of VA RW sols Tulley MOSELEY & Burwell P MOSELEY, both of Norfolk, VA.. F-S9037 R1779
Thomas, b 1/7/1759 Powhatan Co, VA, where esf 1780 in VA regiment; mvd c1794 to KY, where PN 1834 Montgomery Co, when he judge of Superior Court there; dd there 1835; s Daniel P res 1852 Greenup Co, KY, when he claimed PN arrears/o f; QLF states a Thomas MOSELEY md 12/4/1759 Jane STONER, Cumberland Co, VA. F-S15337 R1779
William, esf 1776 Powhatan Co, VA; brigadier general of VA & state treasurer after RW; gtd VA BLW115 in 1783, BLW4728 in 1796, & BLW536 in 1807; dd 9/1808, leaving wid Nancy, s William J, & Elizabeth (md William RADFORD); sol md 12/3/1784 Nancy IRVINE, Bedford Co, VA; wid PN there 1838 ae 74 when Dosha HARRIS AFF there ae 75; Co JP then James A MERIWETHER, & Co clerk/o court Robert C MITCHELL; John WATTS AFF 1826 Campbell Co, VA, he VA RW officer & served with sol, & that sol s William J res 1826 Pennsylvania hospital for insane persons; John ALEXANDER then Co court clerk, & Richard PERKINS Co JP; BLW1189 issued 10/13/26 to Elizabeth RADFORD for sol s William J; William DANIEL AFF 1838 Campbell Co, VA, one/o judges/o General Court of VA; James BENAGH then court clerk/o Lynchburg, & David Russell SYMAN alderman & JP there; QLF 1923 from desc Mrs Anne W CLEMENTS, Radford, VA; QLF 1930 from great gdd Mrs J W WHITTLE, Columbia, MO, states sol s of Francis, & sol s William had War of 1812 svc. F-W5385 R1779
MOSELY, James, see MOZLEY, James. F-W25721 R1779
MOSLEY, Hezekiah, b 1/12/1760 Powhatan Co, VA, where esf 1781 in VA regiment; PN there 1832; Bartlett COX AFF there then when Robert R DABNEY Co JP; AFF there then by Thomas TUCKER he esf with sol; Francis S SAMPSON Co JP there then; sol mvd 1838 with his slaves to Erie Co, NY, to free them there & to see them provided for. F-S13959 R1781
Thomas, see MOSELEY, Thomas. F-S15357 R1781
MOSS, Henry, BLW1504 issued 5/29/1792; captain in VA Line; records lost in Washington, DC, fire 1800. F-BLW1504 R1781
James, 9/6/1760 Cumberland Co, VA; esf 1778 Powhatan Co, VA, in VA regiment; mvd to Buckingham Co, VA, then to Prince Edward Co, VA, where PN 1833 when res there 30+ years; AFF by Charles WOODSON when Branch J WORSHAM Co clerk/o court;

MOSS (continued)
  clergyman Charles VENABLE AFF there then sol of good character; John THOMPSON AFF 1833 Campbell Co, VA, he served with sol in RW; Paulett CLARK AFF there then; John TANEY AFF there then he served with sol at Battle of Guilford Court House; John ALEXANDER Co court clerk 1833 Campbell Co, VA, when Samuel DRAKE Co JP; QLF says sol middle name Bennett; QLF 1927 from desc Mrs F E RICHARDSON, Oak PARK, IL, says sol dd 1846 Prince Edward Co, VA, his LWT dated 1837 & probated there 1846. F-S18515 R1781
John, b 8/1762 Prince William Co, VA; mvd to Fauquier Co, VA then to Loudoun Co, VA, where esf 1781 in VA regiment; mvd to Fauquier Co, VA, for 4-5 years, thence back to Loudoun Co, VA, for 2 years, thence back to Loudoun Co, VA, thence 1794 Madison Co, KY, then to Clark Co, KY, then to Montgomery Co, KY where PN 1832; AFF there then by John BERRY he served in RW with sol; William B MOSS (NKG) AFF 1832 Fleming Co, KY, where res; QLF states sol md Miss FORSYTHE, & his LWT probated 1837 Green Co, KY. F-S16488 R1781
Moses, b Loudoun Co, VA; esf 1780 in VA regiment while res Nolachucky, VA; PN ae 77 Fleming Co, KY, 1835; QLF 1905 from gdd Mrs D S P GRAY, Chrisman, IL, says sol dd Fleming Co, KY; QLF 1911 from desc Mrs Margaret Gray BUCK, Bloomington, IL, says her m Mrs Isabelle Moss GRAY of Chrisman, IL, desc of sol; QLF states sol md Lucretia WILLIAMS; QLF 1927 from great great gds Reverend A H HORD of Germantown, Philadelpia, PA. F-S30598 R1781
Samuel, esf 1781 New Kent Co, VA, where b 5/23/1764, s/o Samuel & w Elizabeth; PN there 1833; clergyman James CLOPTON AFF there then sol of good character; William LADD & James WILLIAMS AFF there then for sol; presiding judge then William H MACON & John D CHRISTIAN Co clerk/o court; RW sols Beverly CRUMP, John Augustine TAYLOR, Thomas H MACON, William H MACON, & Thomas H TERRELL AFF then there for sol; sol dd 9/24/43 leaving wid mbnn; QLF 1938 from desc Mrs F M WARD, Victoria, TX, states sol res 1840 New Kent Co, VA, with Samuel MOSS (NKG), she also desc of RW sol James MOSS who res 1840 ae 80 with James MOSS (NKG) Prince Edward Co, VA. F-8988 R1781
Wilkins, his d Priscilla COMBS gave power/o attorney 1855 to agent to afp, Washington Co, VA, witnessed by Hugh & William JOHNSTON; BLAR; Co JP there then John W HAMES & Jacob LYNCH Co court clerk; d Priscilla COMBS afb there 1855 reporting sol w dd 3/1826, & he dd 2/6/1836, leaving ch Priscilla, William, Helms, & Jackson; Priscilla did not know which state sol served from; PAR, insufficient proof/o svc F-R7460 R1781
Zeally, esf 1777 Loudoun Co, VA, where res, as an assistant quartermaster; in 1783 was building forts in KY & defending against indians; PN ae 79 Switzerland Co, IN, 1834; dd 10/31/39 Peoria Co, IL; md 10/28/1790 Jenny/Jennett/Jane GLASCOCK, Fauquier Co, VA; wid PN 1851 Peoria Co, IL, ae

MOSS (continued)
81; had 2 s, including William S; QLF states sol f William who also VA RW sol & was military chaplain; QLF 1831 from desc Rudolph H MEREDITH, Chicago, IL, states sol res 1834 Vevay, IN, she also desc/o VA RW sol Gregory GLASCOCK. F-W24184 R1781

MOSSER, John, esf 1781 Shenandoah Co, VA in VA regiment; PN ae 74 Smyth Co, VA, 1832; last PN payment in file 1840. F-S5786 R1782

MOSSOM, David, esf as captain of VA Line; dd leaving no issue; surname also spelled MOSSUM; had one sis Nelly who md William Roe CUNNINGHAM & she dd before sol, leaving ch James, David, William Roe, & John, all of whom dd without issue except John who liv 1831 & decd in 1841; sol aunt Mary ROE md James CUNNINGHAM, they both decd in 1841 leaving ch (1) Elizabeth Roe (md John WEBB, they dd leaving s James), (2) William Roe (dd intestate, leaving ch James, David Roe, & John who all dd without issue, except John who dd leaving d Mary who md John PUCKINGTON/PINKINGTON, & she dd, but he liv 1841, their other ch John, Thomas, William, James, Ann who md Jeremiah CAIN, & Catharine), (3) Mary (md James LATIMER, & they dd leaving ch Roe who dd leaving ch Mary, who md Josiah SHELTON, James, Amelia, Barbara, & Pascow), data per Elizabeth City Co clerk of court Samuel S HOWARD; AFF then there by James WEBB; BLW9036 & 9037 issued 11/10/1843 to Mary WEBB; BLW9038 & 9039 issued then to Mary SHELTON, James LATIMER, & Amelia LATIMER; BLW9040 & 9041 issued then to Pascow LATIMER; BLW9042 & 9043 issued then to John & Thomas CUNNINGHAM, Ann CAIN, & Mary PINKINGTON; BLW9044 & 9045 issued then to Catharine CUNNINGHAM; heirs afp 1841 & PAR. F-R16608 R1782

MOTHERSHEAD, Nathaniel, b 3/1754 Westmoreland Co, VA; esf 1775 Orange Co, VA, where res, in VA regiment; PN 1828 Scott Co KY, for disability from wound at Battle of Brandywine; dd 12/29/1834 Scott Co, KY; md 8/27/1781 Ruth, Orange Co, VA, who b 11/2/1763; wid PN 1836 Scott Co, KY; ch: Elizabeth (w of James GREER), Alvan, Tabitha (w of Walker CHAMBERS), Sally (w of John CHINN), M B, Barzilla, Polly (w of Samuel ROSS) & John L; ch/o sol in 1845: Elizabeth GREER (res Marion Co, IN), Alvan (res Owen Co, KY), Tabitha CHAMBERS (res Montgomery Co, KY), Sally CHINN (res Marion Co, IN), M B (res Scott Co, KY), Barzilla (res Madison, IN), Polly ROSS (res St Louis, MO), & John L (res Indianapolis, IN); wid sis Martha GIPSON AFF Scott Co, KY; Moses B MOTHERSHEAD (NKG) AFF there then; sol surname also spelled MOTHERSHED; QLF says sol middle initial G; QLF 1936 from great gds James H TAYLOR, Los Angeles, CA, says sol w d/o either John & Elizabeth BURT, or Moses BURT & w Hannah GREEN. F-W8472 R1782

MOUNT, Ezekiel, b 11/22/1758 Amwell Township, NJ, where esf in Flying Camp Corps; mvd 1780 to Loudon Co, VA, where esf in VA regiment 1781; PN there 1833; sol neighbors Hannah MAD-

MOUNT (continued)
   DUX, Peyton POWELL, & Daniel L REES AFF there then; Co JP then William BENTON; Charles BINNS then Co clerk of court; QLF 1912 from desc Ida Helen McCARTY of Pennsville, IN. F-S11117 R1784
   Matthias, esf 1776 Shepherdstown, Berkeley Co (area later in Jefferson Co), VA; res 1787 NJ; res 1828 Lansing, Tompkins Co, NY, where PN 1829; res 1830 Danby, that Co, where dd 6/11/47; md 5/27/1820 Dinah FORTNER, Lansing, NY; wid PN ae 66 Danby, NY 1853; gtd BLW33749 there 1855 ae 68; Lewis FORTNER (NKG) res there 1853; sol first name also spelled Mather & Mathew; QLF 1937 from great great gdd Mrs E S ATKINSON, Houston, TX, whose great gdf was s/o sol, says sol esf in 12th VA Regiment. F-W8470 R1784
MOUNTJOY, Alvin, b 1/28/1747; esf 1775 Stafford Co, VA, in 3rd VA Regiment, in company led by bro 1st Lieutenant William; mvd 1784 from Stafford Co, VA, to Pendleton Co, KY, where he PN 1818; dd 11/3/27 near Falmouth, that Co; md 9/2/1777 Mary, Stafford Co, VA; wid b 7/13/1760; PN 1837 Pendleton Co, KY; ch births: ? b 1779 (dd aec 4), Thomas L 11/6/1781 (dd 10/1826), William A 12/18/83 (dd 1834), Mary W 5/13/87 (md Mr BEST), Sarah C 3/17/89 (md Mr FRAZER), Alvin Jr 1/20/92 (dd 1793), Richard (dd as infant), Alvin Jr 12/7/94 (dd 11/1834), & Elizabeth 1797 (dd 1797); d Mary W BEST AFF 1837 Pendleton Co, KY; d Sarah C FRAZER AFF there then she md (1) Alexander MONROE (dd 1814) & they had s Sidney H b 12/29/10; all of wid ch dd childless except Mary BEST & Sarah FRAZER, they both widows in 1837; sol wid then res with d Sarah; d Mary BEST res nearby then; AFF then by Maria LAWSON there her f bro of sol; AFF there then by Hannah COPPAGE ae 61 she b Stafford Co, VA, mvd 1800 to KY, & she now wid; AFF then there by Samuel PURDY ae 53 he knew sol & family when they res Bourbon Co, KY & Samuel associated with sol s Thomas L when young man; Amos PETTIT AFF there then ae 71 he knew sol s Captain Thomas L, d Nancy, & s Alvin, now all decd; sol wid dd 3/16/39, & her surv ch Mary BEST & Sarah FRAZER gtd PN due m. F-W8471 R1784
   John, esf 1777 in 10th VA Regiment; bro of RW sol Alvin who dd Pendleton Co, KY; BLW1355 & BLW2492 issued 2/26/1793; PN ae 75 Pendleton Co, KY, 1818; dd there c2/28/26; d Mrs GRIGG res KY 1848. F-S36175 R1784
MOUNTS, Thomas, b 7/8/1764 near Fort Cumberland; esf 1779 Westmoreland Co, PA, where res, in PA regiment of Colonel Caleb MOUNTS (NKG); esf 1780 in PA regiment of Colonel Providence MOUNTS (NKG); res 27 years in PA, then to KY for 15 years, thence IN where PN 1832 Switzerland Co, IN; QLF says sol b VA, md Nancy (1767-1842) d of Colonel William CRAWFORD who burned at stake 1783 Sandusky, OH, also sol & w dd Switzerland Co, IN, buried near Grants Creek Church, ch Polly, Nancy, Rachel, Jessica, & others. F-S17594 R1784
MOURNING, Christopher, esf VA; PN 1809 for disability; res MO 1817 having mvd there from NC; records lost in Washington,

MOURNING (continued)
   DC, fire 1814; QLF states sol esf in 4th VA Regiment; QLF states sol PN 1809 Scott Co, MO, having mvd from NC that year. F-S24746 R1784
MOUTRY, Joseph, esf 1778 Caroline Co, VA, where b 17607; res NC after RW, then 1820 to MO where PN 1834 Washington Co, res Crawford Co, which recently formed from Washington Co; dd 1/25/46 Crawford Co, MO; md 1781 Lucy, Chatham Co, NC; wid afp ae 90 Washington Co, MO, 1852 when res Crawford Co MO, & PAR. F-R7474 R1784
MOWRY, Peter, see MOREY, Peter. F-S1568 R1785
MOXLEY, Jeremiah, esf Westmoreland Co, VA; dd 5/23/1798; md 5/23/1798 Hannah ROBINSON (MB 5/23/1796, signed by Solomon ROBINSON, witnessed by James BLANDY), Westmoreland Co, VA, per that Co court clerk J Warren HUTT report in 1852; wid md (2) Mr STRINGFELLOW; wid gave power of attorney 1853 to agent Simon T TAYLOR, witnessed by Nathaniel W POPE, Fauquier Co, VA, to afp; PAR, insufficient proof of svc; QLF 1924 from desc Mrs Arthur NICHOLS, St Louis, MO, who great great gdd/o RW sol James VERDIER who dd 9/1785 Martinsburg VA, whose w Susannah dd there 2/20/1807, both buried there & their s James b 2/1764 Sharpsburg, VA, md Mary SNODGRASS 1795 & mvd to MO 1836. F-R10269 R1785
   Rhodam/Rhoadham/Rodeham, lieutenant/o VA Line; KIA 7/29/1780 at Battle of Buford's Defeat, SC; Daniel McCARTY AFF 1811 Fairfax Co, VA he fought in that battle, his AFF witnessed by James COLEMAN & Spencer JACKSON; John POWELL AFF then Fairfax Co, VA, he served in same company as sol & wounded in same battle, his AFF witnessed by George SUMMERS & David STEWART; AFF then there also by John COLEMAN & William GUNNELL Jr; Co clerk of court then William MOSS; Joseph & William MOXLEY, heirs to William MOXLEY (NKG) gave power/o attorney then to William B HARRISON of Loudoun Co, VA, to afb, witnessed by Samuel MURREY (Co JP) & John ROSE; Charles BINNS then Co court clerk; POA given there 1811 by Adam POFF & George SAVAGE to William B HARRISON to afb; AFF there then by Edward RINKER & Samuel DUNLAP; BLW597 issued 9/11/1812 to Joseph & William MOXLEY. F-BLW597 R1785
MOYER, Michael, b 9/27/1745 Northampton Co, PA; mvd aec 7 with f to near Millerstown (later called Woodstock), Shenandoah Co, VA; esf Rockingham Co, VA, in VA regiment; res there 1833 when PN; AFF there 1834 by Henry WHETZELL ae 76 he in RW svc with Michael; Co JP then Christian HORN. F-S18107 R1785
MOYERS, Adam, esf VA in 3rd VA Regiment; dd 1842 Greene Co, PA & wid dd there 4/15/1848, leaving 4 ch; youngest ch Peter afp 1856 aec 64 Union Co, TN, as only surv ch, & PAR; AFF there then by Israel MACBEE aec 94 he served in 3rd VA Regiment with sol. F-R7477 R1785
MOZE, James, see MAZE, James. F-R7066 R1785
MOZINGO, George, esf 1779 Culpeper Co, VA, in VA regiment; PN there 1832 ae 72; Francis F LIGHTFOOT then Co court clerk;

MOZINGO (continued)
QLF says sol listed on 1840 VA census ae 79, res Rappahannock Co, VA; QLF says MOZINGO family came from France c 1760; QLF from desc Mrs Daisy McKENZIE, Lowswille, KY. F-S5783 R1785

MOZLEY, James, esf 1775 in VA regiment; PN 1822 Bedford Co, Co TN, ae 62 occupation farmer; dd 9/25/35-6 Marshall Co, TN; md 3/27/1821-2 Martha TRAMMEL, Bedford Co, TN; wid PN 1853 Dickson Co, TN ae 68; ch in 1822: Mary ae 12, Maria ae 10, William ae 8, Jane ae 6, Dixon ae 4, & Daniel Seaborn ae 6 weeks; wid gtd BLW1855 as Martha MOSELY, Hickman Co, TN, ae 69. F-W25721 R1785

MUCKLEVAINE, Tunis, b 8/18/1759 Rockingham Co, VA; res during RW Pendleton Co, VA, where esf 1776 in VA regiment; PN ae 74 Kanawha Co, VA, 1833; AFF then there by Daniel B HARDAWAY & Jacob MUCKLEVAINE per Co JP Barnabas COOK; Co court clerk then Alexander W QUARRIER; dropped 1834 from PN list when PN Office found his ae only 61 then, & therefore was not old enough to have served in RW; this result of AFF by Philip STATZER & John SUTTON there then that sol ae only 61 then; surname also spelled MUCKLEWAINE. F-S9043 R1786

MUHLENBERG, Peter, brigadier general of VA troops; BLW1495 issued 5/18/1789; records lost in Washington, DC, fire 1800; QLF says sol colonel of 8th VA Regiment. F-BLW1495 R1786

MUIR, Francis, MD sea svc & Continental Line of VA; esf in MD Navy on ship DEFENCE before 1776; esf 1777 in VA regiment where captain; gave power/o attorney 1805 Dinwiddie Co, VA to agent to apb, witnessed by Nathniel MANSON & John BOOTH when John PEGRAM Jr Co JP, John NICHOLAS Co clerk/o court; sol gtd BLW237. F-BLW237 R1786

MUIRHEAD, Henry, b 10/5/1763 Loudoun Co, VA, where esf as sub for bro Andrew; mvd after RW to Shenandoah Co, VA, then to Greenbriar Co, VA, then to Montgomery Co, VA, thence Hickman Co, TN, thence Holmes Co, MS, where PN 1842, res near Lexington. F-S30609 R1786

MULBERRY, John, esf 1775 Stafford Co, VA, in 2nd VA Regiment; PN 1818 Bath Co, KY; res there 1820 ae 65 with w Elizabeth & d's Fanny aec 26, Cela aec 23, & Mary aec 20; a md d liv elsewhere; mvd 1837 to Scott Co, IN, to live near Thomas SPILLAR/SPILLERS, who s of w by her 1st marriage; dd there 4/13/38 at house of Thomas SPILLAR; md 8/22/1792 Elizabeth SPILLERS, Scott Co, KY; wid dd 11/25/42 Scott Co, IN, leaving her s Thomas + ch by sol: Fanny DRAIN & Mary HOPKINS, both liv 1850, when Thomas SPILLAR AFF Lawrence Co, IL, he present at m's marriage to sol; Fanny DRAIN & Mary HOPKINS gtd PN due m 1850 Lexington, Scott Co, IN. F-W9584 R1786

MULLEN, Anthony, esf 1777 Fredericksburg, VA, in VA regiment; gtd BLW11 & BLW198; PN ae 77 Lincoln Co, TN, 1828 when had w, 4 s's (eldest ae 17), & 4 d's liv with him; 18 ch altogether; dd there 11/3/26; md (2) 11/1818 Sarah RAMBLES, Albemarle Co, VA; wid PN ae 74 Lincoln Co, TN, 1854; sol s William aec 66 & sol s Andrew aec 55 AFF there then their

MULLEN (continued)
   m was 1st w of sol; surname also spelled MULLENS & MULLINS
   F-W8280 R1786
MULLENS, John, esf 1779 in 1st VA Regiment; taken POW at Siege
   of Charleston & to England for several years; PN Floyd Co,
   KY 1833 ae 60; res there 1823, occupation farmer, when had
   w Nancy aec 57, s John ae 15, d Betsy ae 11, & s Joshua ae
   8; AFF there then by bro Joshua aec 63; AFF there then by
   Silas P WOOTON who served in RW with sol; dd 2/25/38 Perry
   Co, KY; md 6/8/1792 Nancy GENTRY, Halifax Co, VA; wid PN
   ae 65 Perry Co, KY, 1839; res 1848 Letcher Co, KY; gtd BLW
   34839 there 1855 ae 80; ch: John b 7/30/1794, Mary b 6/25/
   96, Daniel b 7/14/99 (res 1839 Perry Co, KY), John (ae 15
   in 1823), Betsey (ae 11 in 1823), & Joshua ae 8 in 1823;
   s Daniel AFF 1839 Perry Co, KY, he 3rd ch of sol; Joseph
   MULLENS (NKG) res Letcher Co, KY 1855; John MULLENS (NKG)
   JP there then; sol surname also spelled MULLINS; QLF says
   one/o soldier's d's md John ADAMS, & they res Perry Co, KY.
   F-W3032 R1787.
   Joshua, esf Pittsylvania Co in VA regiment; PN aec 70 Perry
   Co, KY, 1828; had 12 ch, 9 then alive, 7 of them liv with
   with him, eldest/o those 7 ae 18-19, & youngest was d ae 4
   months; dd 2/8/51 Knox Co, KY; md 1798 Anna ROBINSON/RO-
   BERTSON, Carter Co, TN; wid PN ae 72 Knox Co, KY 1853; gtd
   BLW26635 Laurel Co, KY 1858; sol surname also spelled MUL-
   LEN & MULLINS. F-W25671 R1787.
   William, esf Washington Co, VA, where res, in VA regiment to
   fight indians & guard frontiers; mvd to Powells Valley, VA
   thence Wayne Co, KY, thence Madison Co, AL, then to Franklin Co, AL, where afp 1842 ae near 80; PAR, svc not considered truly military; surname also spelled MULLINS; QLF
   says sol s of Matthew MULLINS & Mary MAUPIN who also f & m
   of Matthew & Gabriel. F-R7489 R1787.
MULLIKIN, John, esf 1776 Spotsylvania Co, VA, in 6th VA Regiment; PN ae 67 Shelby Co, KY, 1818; res there 1820 with w
   aec 70; had 6 sons in War of 1812 where 1 KIA & others all
   wounded; QLF says sol b Montgomery Co, MD; QLF 19-- from
   desc Mrs Doris A ELLIOTT, Washington, DC. F-S35529 R1787.
MULLINGS, James, b 11/17/1751 King William Co, VA; esf 1776
   Charlotte Co, VA, in VA regiment; PN there 1832; res there
   1834 with w Agnes ae 84 & ch: Amey ae 48, Frances ae 44, &
   Latitia ae 42 (all unmd); several gdc mbnn; clergyman Abner W CLOPTON & Elisha COLLINS AFF there 1832; Co clerk of
   court then Winslow ROBINSON; John FRAM AFF then Lunenburg
   Co, VA, he served in RW with sol per Co JP George L BAYN,
   when William H TAYLOR Co court clerk; AFF 1834 Charlotte
   Co, VA, by James CRUTCHER, Seth FARLEY, & William CRAWLEY
   that sol then deaf & a cripple; AFF there then by Richard
   COREY, Richard COLLINS, & Grandison COLLINS per that Co JP
   Joseph FAISON; Thomas PETTUS AFF ae 74 there 1833 he esf
   with sol, per Co JP William B MATHEWS; AFF there then by
   by John D RICHARDSON & Joseph WYATT, per Co JP Anderson C

MULLINGS (continued)
  MORTON; sol surname also spelled MULLINS. F-S10251 R1787
MULLINS, Ambrus, esf 1780 Franklin Co, VA, where b 1757; had
  w & 2 ch then; 1st 2 times drafted paid for substitute but
  3rd time went into svc; mvd to Green River, SC, thence NC,
  then to Russell Co, VA, where afp 1835; PAR, less than 6
  months svc; Co JP then Reuben STEELE, & Co clerk of court
  James P CARRELL; Richard STANLEY AFF then there he served
  in RW with sol, per Co JP Zachariah FUGATE. F- R7484 R1787
  Charles, b 7/18/1749 PA, but principally raised in VA; mvd
  during RW to NC & settled on Broad River in Rutherford Co,
  where esf in NC regiment; res NC after RW for c30 years,
  thence Calloway Co, KY, where PN 1832. F-S30610 R1787
  Gabrel/Gabriel, b 3/22/1758 Albemarle Co, VA where esf in VA
  VA regiment 1776-77; mvd c6 years after RW to Madison Co,
  KY, where PN 1833; AFF by Humphrey BECKETT ae 76 Pendleton
  Co, KY res Pickaway Co, OH, he served with sol from Albemarle Co, VA; sol dd c1842; heirs mbnn 1869 from IN queried PN Office, whose response not shown in records; QLF
  says desc Margaret HUSSMAN of AR applied 1917 to join DAR
  based upon sol's svc, reported sol dd 1841 Pendleton Co,
  KY; QLF 1916 from desc Opal WINDOFFER of Kokomo, IN. F-
  30608 R1787
  James, b 3/26/1747; esf 1778 Charlotte Co, VA, where res; dd
  4/5/1827 Mercer Co, KY; md 12/26/1764 Mary; wid afp 1842
  Edgar Co, IL, & PAR, insufficient proof/o 6 months svc; ch
  births: Nancy 1765, Martha 1766, Sarah 4/13/1768, Ephraim
  1769, Coleman 12/25/73, Jane 12/1775 (md Daniel CASSADAY),
  Stephen 6/1777, Susannah 8/1779 (md Abraham OWEN), Paul
  12/1781, s mnbnn (dd as infant 1783) & Polly 9/1785; d Sarah AFF ae 66 Mercer Co, KY, 1837; wid dd 3/15/45, leaving
  ch Stephen, Jane, Paul, & Susannah; s Stephen gave power/o
  attorney 1854 Edgar Co, IL to agent to afp for self & siblings Paul, Jane & Susannah; they PAR; sol surname spelled
  also MULLINGS; QLF 1910 from great gds O B LESTER of Washington, DC. F-R7488 R1787
  Joseph, b 3/2/1739 Prince Edward Co, VA; esf 1781 Halifax Co
  VA, where res, in VA regiment; mvd many years after RW to
  Henry Co, VA, thence Pittsylvania Co, VA, then to Grainger
  Co, TN, then to Jefferson Co, TN, then to Bedford Co, TN,
  where PN 1832; surname also spelled MULLENS. F-S4238 R1787
  Matthew, b 6/17/1764 Albemarle Co, VA, where esf in VA regi-
  ment; mvd 1794 to Madison Co, KY, where PN 1832; AFF there
  then by Benjamin CLARK (b 12/13/1759) he knew sol from in-
  fancy in same VA neighborhood; sol dd 12/6/35; QLF 1926
  from desc Dr H E MONROE, Shelbyville, IL, who also desc of
  VA RW sol John MONROE, who b 4/10/1760 Cartersrun Valley,
  Fauquier Co, VA & dd 8/17/1824; QLF says sol had s William
  F-S31271 R1787
  Stephen, b 10/31/1763; esf 1779 Charlotte Co, VA, where res,
  in VA regiment; PN 1832 Blount Co, AL; dd 5/17/33; sol md
  4/1782 Dorcas, Lawrence Co, SC, at her f's house; Dorcas b

MULLINS (continued)
    4/12/1775; ch births: Samuel 12/22/1792, Hosea 5/19/95, Nancy 2/17/97, James G 12/2/98 (dd 7/19/1829), Mary S 11/12/1800, Dianna 8/15/02, Mandlin 4/5/04, Elizabeth 11/26/06, Martha 4/1/10, & Julia H 5/25/13; wid PN 1833 Blount Co, AL; dd 8/25/42; s Samuel afp 1854 Blount Co, AL, when all siblings alive except James & Nancy; ch gtd PN due m then; AFF then by sol wid's sis Mrs Rody HUGHS ae 84 Marshall Co, AL, she present at sol wedding, & Rody's 3rd ch William b soon thereafter; AFF then there by William HUGHS (NKG) ae 61. F-W10546 R1787
MUMMY, Christopher, b 4/2/1753 Germantown, PA; esf 1779 Brooke Co, VA, where res, in VA regiment; res after RW Washington Co, PA, thence Brooke Co, VA, thence Harrison Co, OH, then to Morgan Co, OH, where PN 1832; AFF then there by Charles D WELLS he esf 1779 with sol in same VA unit; QLF says sol surname also spelled MUMMA, MOOMAW, & MOOMAH; QLF says sol dd Morgan Co, OH. F-S4247 R1788
MUNDAY, Aaron, esf 1779 Stafford Co, VA, where b 3/7/1762; res there 8-10 years after RW, then to Fairfax Co, VA, for c2 years, thence Loudoun Co, VA where PN 1832; AFF then there by Sanford J RAINEY & Thomas R SAUNDERS; sol dd there 9/8/34; md 11/17/1798 Ann SINCLAIR, Prince William Co, VA, per certification 1848 from that Co court clerk John WILLIAMS; wid PN ae 81 Loudoun Co, VA 1848; that Co court clerk then Charles G ESKRIDGE & Co JP Joshua PUSEY; AFF then there by Elizabeth HOWELL & Rosannah MUNDAY (NKG); wid gtd BLW16386 there 1855 ae 87; witness to her afb then John J JOHNSON & Joseph BARNHOUSE; Co JP then Noble S BRADEN. F-W1634 R1788
    Benjamin H, b 7/14/1763; esf 1781 Essex Co, VA, in VA regiment, sub for Robert BEVERLEY; PN there 1835; Robert HILL & clergyman Philip MONTAGUE AFF there then; Co court clerk then James Roy MICOU & Co JP Thomas C GORDON; last PN payment in file 1838. F-S10250 R1788
    Jeremiah, esf 1779 Essex Co, VA, in VA regiment; PN ae 55 Lincoln Co, NC 1818; res there 1827 aec 67 occupation farmer, when liv with w aec 50 & ch: Osbourn ae 20, Patsey ae 18, Jeremiah ae 14, Spencer ae 12, Fletcher ae 10, Chloe ae 8, Monroe ae 5 & infant Elizabeth; dd there 9/12/35; md 11/1798 Chloe SHELTON, Pittsylvania Co, VA; wid PN Lincoln Co, NC 1848; gtd BLW17886 there 1855 ae 76 when had 10-11 ch, most/o whom res NC; family bible excerpt blotched, faded, & partly illegible gave birth data: James FLEMING 3/16/1793, Spencer MUNDY 7/24/1814, Fletcher MUNDY 1817, Chloe MUNDY 9/1819, & Monroe MUNDY 1822. F-W2636 R1788
    Jonathan, b 1756 Albemarle Co, VA , where esf 1775 in VA regiment; PN there 1832 when Ira GARRETT Co court clerk; AFF then by James DUNN & Richard SNOW they served in RW with sol; dd 6/11/33; QLF 1936 from desc Mrs R C OMOHUNDRO of Fork Union, VA; QLF says MUNDAYs came from Staffordshire, England & settled in Spotsylvania Co, VA, where a Jonathan MUNDAY witnessed a LWT 1665, & one of his descendants was

MUNDAY (continued)
Samuel MUNDAY whose LWT was probated 1792 & listed his ch: (1) Jonathan, above sol, who md Matilda BEAVER & their ch Matilda, Nancy, Charles, Walker, & Thomas whose ch were: Evana, Civil War sol Clark, & Isabella, (2) Reuben, (3) Abraham, (4) Samuel, (5) Jane, & (6) Mary, further a Jonathan MUNDAY md 1820 Mary EDWARDS, further a John MUNDY, s John & s William, all b Staffordshire, England, settled in Culpeper Co, VA, where either s John or s William md Lady ELGIN, & Reuben, s/o either John or William, md Nancy ASHFORD, & Reuben's descendants included following brothers: Reuben Henley MUNDY, Colonel Man MUNDY a lawyer, Dr James Drake MUNDY, Dr Isaac Foster MUNDY & William Harrison MUNDY. F-S5795 R1788

Samuel, esf 1779 Albemarle Co, VA, in VA regiment; PN there 1820 ae 60 when Alexander GARRETT Co court clerk; witness to sol afp: John WATSON, Martin DAWSON, William WOODS, & Frank CARR; sol 1820 occupation farmer liv with w 3 months older than he, & s & d both grown up. F-S38248 R1788

MUNDELL, John, b 5/5/1760 Southampton Co, VA where esf 1778 in VA regiment; afp 1832 Northampton Co, NC when res there 10 years; PAR, insufficient proof of 6 months svc; legal heir d Mrs Charlotte REESE res 1853 Pleasant Hill, Northampton Co, NC; George R REESE (NKG) then that Co JP; sol surname also spelled MUNDLE; QLF says sol w Virginia & they had ch Fanny, Charlotte, William, & Thomas, further sol & bro Joseph came to VA from Spain or France. F-R7490 R1788

MUNFORD, James H, b 9/14/1760; mvd ae 10 from NC to Nottoway Co, VA, where esf 1777 ae 16; later ensign in company company commanded by f who captain; PN 1832 Nottoway Co, VA; witness to afp John H KNIGHT, William HARPER & Austin WATKINS; George KIDD AFF there then he served in same company with sol & sol f; Frances FITZGERALD then Co court clerk, Hezekiah R ANDERSON then Co JP; sol dd there 6/10/38; md there 9/30/1807 Elizabeth R POWER (MB 9/29/07, signed by Thomas POWER), Warren Co, NC; wid gtd PN ae 68 Nottoway Co VA, 1854 when Co presiding justice Thomas M ROWLETT & Richard EPES Co court clerk; witness to her afp then Thomas S MUNFORD (NKG) & David C JONES; gtd BLW51758 there 1856; Co JP then Alexander MCQUIE, & J P STITH Co court clerk; QLF states sol middle name Hall, & his w dd 1861. F-W8478 R1789

William Green, power/o attorney given 1833 Gloucester Co, VA to agent Robert H ARMSTEAD of Williamsburg, VA, by a John SINCLAIR to claim any PN due his w who was gdd/o sol Colonel William Green MUNFORD; Arthur L DAVIS then Gloucester Co court clerk & William K PERRIN Co JP; records contains no action by PN Office on claim. F-R15597 R1789

MUNN, James, esf 1776 in MD Flying Camp troops; esf 1782 under uncle Colonel William CRAWFORD of MD against indians where that uncle KIA & sol wounded; later sol in VA unit which guarded Mason-Dixon Line surveyors; PN 1809 Scioto Co, OH,

MUNN (continued)
　　for wound disability; dd there 3/11/39; w Azuba dd 4/16/40 there leaving ch: William (res there 1853), John, Mary (md Mr OLIVER), Hannah (md Mr BURT), Eleanor (md Mr MARSHALL), & Solomon; s William, adm/o m's estate, afp there 1853 for self & above listed siblings, & PAR; QLF 1917 from great gdd Alice Munn (Mrs Martin W) MILLER, Kansas City, MO; QLF 1911 from great gds F M BURT, Vancouver, WA; QLF 1902 from great gds George MUNN, Scioto Co, OH. F-R7492 R1789
MUNROE, William H, bc 1760 Fairfax Co, VA, where esf 1780 in VA regiment; PN there 1833; reared 8 ch including an only d; Spencer MUNROE (NKG) AFF there then ae 73 he knew sol since boyhood & esf with him in RW; neighbor John G HUNTER AFF then he knew sol since 1776; William MOSS Co clerk of court & Robert RATCLIFFE Co JP; QLF 1919 from desc Paul A KLAYDER, Armstrong, MO, who also desc of VA RW sol Philip MERRY of Fairfax Co, VA; QLF 1935 from Mrs Bernyce Monroe FRIDGE, Tallulah, LA, says her great gdf Joseph B MONROE b VA c1820. F-S9433 R1791
MURCER, James, b 6/1762 Amelia Co, VA, & was left orphan; esf 1780 Chester District, SC, where res, in SC regiment; esf 1781 Rowan Co, NC where res, in NC regiment; afp 1842 Talladega Co, AL, & PAR, insufficient proof of svc; surname also spelled MERCER; QLF says sol had sons Silas, Herman, Daniel & Joshua. F-R7502 R1792
MURCHESON, John, b 10/2/1764 Caroline Co, VA; mvd 1779 to Bedford Co (area later Campbell Co), VA; esf 1781 Bedford Co, VA, in VA regiment; afp 1832 Campbell Co, VA, & PAR, less than 6 months svc; AFF then there by clergyman Henry BROWN & John PRIBBLE; Co court clerk there then John ALEXANDER. F-R7362 R1792
MURDEN, Mary, former widow of Anthony MURPHY. F-R7503 R1792
MURDOCHS, John, b 6/22/1742 Balanalack, County Armagh, Ireland esf 1778 in 12th VA Regiment; PN 1818 Washington Co, VA, when Co court clerk Andrew RUSSELL & judge was Peter JOHNSTON; sol res there 1820 ae 78 occupation farmer with w ae 65 & 2 orphan gdc ae 4 & 5; dd there 7/19/1828 leaving ch: Joseph, Jane w/o J BRADY, Mary w/o Anderson KELLY, Robert, James G, John, & Nathan; Peter J BRANCH then Co clerk of court; sol md in PA 1779 Margaret FORAN, who b 1775 near Little Brandeewind, PA & dd 9/16/42; s Joseph gave power/o attorney 1854 Washington Co, VA, to John W STEVENS to afp for self & surv siblings John & Nathan, & they gtd PN due m; AFF then there by Jacob TOOLE. who made coffin for sol wid; her neighbor John THOMPSON AFF per Co JP Conrad FUDGE then there; George W HOPKINS judge then, & Jacob LYNCH Co court clerk; surname also spelled MURDOCH & MURDOCK. F-W9582 R1792
MURFREE, George, esf 1780 in VA regiment; PN 1818 aec 64 Isle of Wight Co, VA; Co court clerk then Nathaniel YOUNG; Richard E PARKER then Co JP; sol res there 1821 when had w & 3 ch mbnn to support. F-S38252 R1793

MURPHEY, Charles, esf 1777 in 10th VA Regiment; PN 1818 Orange Co, VA, ae 76; res there 1820 ae 79 occupation cooper with w Mary aec 75, d Lucy aec 50, d Salley aec 30, d Polly aec 28, & d Eveline aec 21; dd 2/2/38; ch mbnn gtd PN arrears. F-S38251 R1793

Edward, b 12/25/1742 York Co, PA; esf 1774 Rockbridge Co, VA in VA regiment; mvd 1777 to Botetourt Co, VA, where again esf; mvd after RW to Greene Co, TN, then to Sevier Co, TN, then to McMinn Co, TN, where PN 1832 when res there for 13 years; David CALDWELL & James CALDWELL AFF then there they served in RW with sol. F-S1569 R1793

Gabriel, b c1756 1756; esf place not given; dd 1818 Russell Co, VA; md 1771 Clarissa HARNDON, Caswell Co, NC, who dd VA 12/28/1842; s John afp ae 44 Logan Co, VA, 1858 & PAR; AFF then there by John BUCHANAN; William TILLER then Co JP & William STRATON Co court clerk. F-R7509 R1793

James, esf in VA regiment; PN 1786 for disability; res Wythe Co, VA, 1823 when John JOHNSTON Co JP & Co clerk of court John P MAYHEW; sol surname spelled also MURPHY. F-S25317 R1793

John, b 1733 Dublin, Ireland; esf 1780 Fauquier Co, VA where PN 1832; AFF then there by Jesse MOFFETT he esf 1781 there & served with sol; Co court clerk there 1832 Alexander J MARSHALL, & Co JP William HORNER; sol dd 5/17/38; QLF says sol md Elizabeth MALING of England, & their ch Alexander, Nancy, & Travis. F-S5798 R1793

John, b 7/1750; esf 1777 in 12th VA Regiment; gtd BLW564, which sold in 1811; Jonathan CLARK, lieutenant colonel of 8th VA Regiment (later brigadier general) AFF then; sol PN aec 68 Ross Co, OH; res 1820 Fairfield Co, OH, occupation farmer, with w Elizabeth aec 46. F-S40191 R1793

Leander, esf 1776 Prince William Co, VA; PN ae 72 Spencer Co KY, 1832. F-S11126 R1793

MURPHREY, George, see MURFREE, George. F-S38252 R1793

MURPHY, Anthony, esf 1781 as captain/o VA militia; dd Princess Anne Co, VA, c11/2/1799; inventory of estate made 12/1799 there witnessed by John WHITEHEAD, John WRIGHT & John HARNESS; md there 8/27/1787 Mary WEST (MB that date signed by Simon MARVAUTT) per certificate/o that Co court clerk John J BURROUGHS 1849; wid md there (2) 1807 William PORTLOCK (MB 5/4/1807 signed by William WEST & witnessed by E H MOSELEY), who dd 1813; wid md (3) James MURDEN, who dd 1844; wid gave power of attorney Norfolk, VA, 1849 ae 78 as Polly MURDEN to agent to afp; city clerk of court there then John WILLIAMS; wid s James PORTLOCK res then Princess Anne Co, VA; clergyman William W STRAWHAND AFF there then; John H DAY then Co JP; sol bro James AFF Norfolk, VA then ae 82 sol dd aec 50, AFF witnessed by clergyman John E EDWARDS; city JP then Charles H SHEILD & Edwin P HATCHER then notary public; Thomas CAMPBELL AFF then Princess Anne Co, VA, he esf with sol, AFF witnessed by clergyman David RIGGS; Swepson A BROCK AFF then there his decd f was adm/o estate

MURPHY (continued)
  of Jesse MORRIS who was adm/o estate of sol; wid res there 1852 when gave power/o attorney to agent to afp; PAR both times for insufficient proof of svc; Co JP then Jonathan HUNTER; wid liv 1854 aec 94. F-R7503 R1793
Arthur, b 1762 Franklin Co, NC, or Sussex Co, VA; esf 1778 Bute Co, NC, in NC regiment; esf Franklin Co, NC, when later res there; mvd ae 40-45 to Logan Co, KY, for 2 years, then to near Red Banks, Henderson Co, KY, then to Johnson Co, IL, then to Lawrence Co, AR, where PN 1833 when res there 6 years; dd 4/6/35. F-S31872 R1793
Gabriel, b 1/1760; esf 1778 Hampshire Co, VA, in 1st VA Regiment; later esf in 7th VA regiment; PN 1819 Nelson Co, KY, when res there over 27 years; res there 1820 when had w aec 57, 2 d's, & gdc aec 4; res there 1840; surname also spelled MURPHEY. F-S35531 R1793
Hezekiah, esf 1781 Montgomery Co, MD, where b 1763-4; moved 1788 to Loudoun Co, VA, thence 1793 back to Montgomery Co, MD, thence with f to Nelson Co, KY, thence 1831 Lincoln Co MO, where res when PN 1832 Nelson Co, KY; dd 7/31/42; md 4/17/1794 Sary COTTON, Nelson Co, KY; wid PN ae 74 Lincoln Co, MO, 1850; gtd BLW26974 there 1855 ae 78; surname also spelled MURPHEY. F-W5395 R1794
James, esf in 1st MD Regiment; leg shot off at Battle/o Long Island; gave power of attorney 1789 Montgomery Co, MD, to agent to afb; decd in 1791; md Mary CRADICK; s William AFF 1802; Charles CRADICK (NKG) AFF 1803 Loudoun Co, VA, sol's ch then liv were Ann, William, Samuel, Oratia, & Benjamin; AFF witnessed by James McILHANY; ch gtd BLW105. F-BLW105 R1794
James Jeffrey, esf 1776 in VA regiment; PN ae 66 Orange Co, IN, 1819; res there 1822 ae 75 with w ae 67; QLF 1935 from great gds John D WELMAN, Evansville, IN, says sol b c1751 VA, md 9/5/1786 (1) Magdalin NEWLIN/NEWLAND who dd, md (2) Margaret, & they came from Shenandoah Co, VA, to IN Territory c1811, settling on land 1814 which later Township of Stampers Creek, Orange Co, IN, & sol dd there c1826, where buried in cemetery now owned by querier. F-S35532 R1794
John, esf 1779 in Illinois Regiment of VA State Line; PN ae 69 Jefferson Co, KY, 1832. F-S13998 R1794
John, b 7/31/1763 Princess Anne Co, VA, where esf 1779 when he & bro James res Kempsville, that Co; res there after RW thence 1790 Borough of Norfolk, VA, where afp 1840, & PAR; bro James AFF then Princess Anne Co, VA, to judge Tazewell TAYLOR; Simon STUBBS of Norfolk, VA, attorney for sol heir-at-law Ann CLARKE, queried PN Office 1853 for any PN due sol. F-R7514 R1794
Joseph, b 1761 Pittsylvania Co, VA; esf 1781 Henry Co, VA; mvd after RW to TN, thence NC, then to MO where res for 31 years when PN 1832 St Francois Co; dd there 2/10/34; md 1/12/1797 Sarah, Greenbrier, SC; wid PN ae 77 St Francois Co MO 1853; wid gtd BLW26636 there 1857 when nephew Henderson

MURPHY (continued)
MURPHY AFF there; wid res there 1858; ch births: Kasiah 10/21/1796, John 2/22/98, Sarah 1/28/1801, Joseph 11/10/03 Millie 1/3/05, Lewis 1/5/07, Tampfrey 12/26/08, Cynthia 4/3/11, ch unnamed 12/12/13 (dd age 1 month), Rachel 5/4/16, Mariney 10/3/18, Matilda 9/6/21, & James 4/2/23; surname also spelled MURPHEY. F-W25737 R1794

Martin, BLW12384 issued 7/14/179-. F-BLW12384 R1794

Michael, esf 1777 in 6th VA Regiment; s John certified 1828 as one of heirs/o sol by Bedford Co, VA, court, per deputy Co court clerk Gustavus A WINGFIELD; s John afb then Campbell Co, VA; BLW1425 issued 12/19/1828. F-BLW1425 R1794

Owen, esf 1776 Martinsburg, Berkeley Co, VA, in 12th VA Regiment; PN 1818 Alleghany Co, PA; AFF then by Presley NEVILL, Clermont Co, OH, he served in RW with sol; sol res there 1820 ae 76 occupation farmer with w ae 68 & s ae 26; QLF states sol lived to be over 90; QLF 1922 from desc Albert J MURPHY, Detroit, MI. F-S41908 R1794

Patrick, esf 1777 in 6th VA Regiment; sol nephew John MURPHY certified 1828 by Bedford Co, VA, court as one of heirs of sol; that nephew afb then Campbell Co, VA; BLW1430 issued 12/6/1828 to heirs of sol; QLF 1932 from great great gdd Mrs A T LeCHIEN, Williamsburg, KS, says sol b Dublin, Ireland, also svc in French & Indian War, & his s John settled in Braxton Co, WV, where querier gdm Susan MURPHY born; QLF 1936 from desc Mabel J MURPHY, Elgin, IL, says sol res most/o life in Braxton Co, WV, md Nancy JAMES, & dd c1821. F-BLW1430 R1794

Samuel, b 5/12/1758 Frederick Co, VA; esf 1775, while res on Jacobs Creek, Bedford Co, VA, in 8th VA Regiment; esf 1777 in 13th VA Regiment; esf 1781 in regiment of George Rogers CLARK, was wounded, captured by indians, taken to Detroit, where sold to British; escaped 1782; PN 1832 Armstrong Co, PA; QLF 1937 from desc Neal THOMAS, Ply, OH, says sol res Freeport, Armstrong Co, PA. F-S22413 R1794

William, b 3/12/1759 Pittsylvania Co, VA; esf 1776 Bedford Co, WV, where res; esf 1778 Washington Co, NC, in NC regiment; esf 1780 in VA regiment; esf 1782 in NC regiment; PN 5/1833 St Francois Co, MO; dd there 11/2/33; md 1/26/1782 Rachel HENDERSON on Nolichucky River (area later in Greene Co), NC; wid b 11/15/1764; PN 1841 St Francois Co, MO; ch births: John Croford 10/16/1782, Mary Hodges 6/22/84, Martha Hodges 5/29/86 (dd 10/26/1803), Elizabeth Barton 4/16/88, William Eccles 5/8/90 (dd 8/29/1810), Delilah Sarah 5/14/92, James Henderson 5/19/94, Keturah Beavers 4/9/96, Francis Menifee 5/23/98 (dd 5/1/1808), Sarah Barton 1/4/1800, David Henderson 6/12/02, Henderson 9/1/0-, & youngest ch mbnn 5/6/06; Joseph MURPHY (NKG) AFF 1833 ae 72 St Francois Co, MO, he res with sol during RW; William MURPHY Jr (NKG) JP of St Francois Co, MO & David MURPHY (NKG) AFF then there; sol halfbro David MURPHY, who b 4/23/1770, AFF there 1842 for sol wid; her s Henderson MURPHY AFF then

MURPHY (continued)
there; surname also spelled MURPHEY; QLF states a William MURPHY, & sons Joseph & William esf VA, elder William dd 1799 on way home to TN from MO, his wid Sarah coming to MO 1803, where she dd 1817 Murphy Settlement (now called Farmington), MO, & their sons all mvd to MO; QLF says sol dd Farmington, MO. F-W9580 R1794

MURRAH, Joshua, b 3/15/1764 Pittsylvania Co, VA; esf Burke Co, NC, where res, in NC unit; later esf in SC regiment; mvd after RW to Wilkes Co, NC, for c25 years, thence Logan Co, KY, where PN 1832; dd 7/12/36; md 11/29/1786 Lucy, who b 6/19/1771; PN 1839 Robertson Co, TN; ch births: Williams 9/5/1787, Nancy 2/20/88, Margaret E 1/9/90, Sally 12/15/91 Joshua 9/21/93; All 12/2/95, Jane 9/19/98, Emanuel 3/14/99 Joseph 1/28/1801, Jeremiah 2/13/03, John B 4/25/05, Abraham 3/30/07, Light 12/29/08, Lucy 3/29/10, Robert J M 3/29/12; births of gdc: Robert MURRAH 3/21/1828 & Light MURRAH 1/19/1829; wid res ae 77 Logan Co, KY; s Light AFF Robertson Co, TN, 1839; s John B res 1860 Springfield, TN. F-W1063 R1795

MURRAY, Charles, esf 1775 Berkeley Co, VA; esf 1776 PA in Flying Camp Company of PA; PN ae 70 Fairfax Co, VA, 1818 when Thomas MOSS Co JP & William MOSS Co court clerk; res there 1820 ae 84 (as stated) with w ae 78, d ae 40 & s-in-law ae 50; dd c1821 survived by s James (liv 1837); surname also spelled MURRY; QLF 1926 from agent for sol desc Mrs Zachariah Demenieu BLACKISTACE of Washington, DC, says sol came from Scotland to Fairfax Co, VA; QLF 1934 from desc Mrs Blanche W SHAFER of Cincinnati, OH; QLF 1911 from desc Mrs J S Spencer THORNE of Falls Church, VA says sol b 1/3/1742 Scotland, came to America 1764, md Elizabeth, who b 3/4/1749, querier being d/o Mildred MURRAY who d/o Mary MURRAY who d/o James MURRAY who s/o sol. F-S38249 R1795

James, b 7/7/1755 or 7/9/1755 VA; esf 1775-6 Ninety-Six District, SC, in SC Regiment; PN 1832 Franklin Co, NC; res 1838 with s James H, Pickens Co, AL; res 1837 with youngest s F D, Montgomery Co, TN; d 9/17/40 leaving wid mbnn. F-S1922 R1795

James, esf 1781 Culpeper Co, VA; dd there 3/1813; md there 1779 Susannah AYLOR (MB 3/23/1779 signed by Henry AYLOR); wid dd there 7/1841 at home of Jacob AYLOR (NKG); neither she or h afp; AFF 1841 there by William HITT ae 62, per Co JP Armistead BROWN; AFF then by William LEWIS ae 86 & John CREAL they esf 1781 with sol, per Co JP James M BROADUS; Polly, w/o Lewis HITT & d of Jacob AYLOR (Jacob then decd) AFF there 1846; Co court clerk Madison Co, VA, 1846 Belfield CAVE, magistrate Francis H HILL & Co JP Elliot BLANKENBECKER; Benjamin HOFFMAN ae 88 & Cornelius CARPENTER AFF then they esf with sol; Co JP then William L FOUSHEE; only surv ch Simeon afp ae 62 Madison Co, VA, 1848, & PAR. F-R7526 R1795

Mark, b & raised Caroline Co, VA, where esf 1777 in VA regi-

MURRAY(continued)
ment; mvd to Hanover Co, VA, where esf; mvd c1782 to Halifax Co, VA, where afp 1832 aec 72; Samuel WILLIAMS then Co court clerk there; sol afp there 1834 ae over 80 (as stated) when Co JP John S VAUGHAN; AFF then there by Richard CARTER Sr & Isaac SATTERFIELD; William HOLT then Co court clerk; sol PAR both times; surname also spelled MURRY. F-R7522 R1796

Reuben, esf VA; res 1838 Fauquier Co, VA; PAR, less than 6 months svc; records sent to Congress, never returned to PN Office; QLF 1914 from desc Ida Murray (Mrs J C) CARMICHAEL of Pike Co, MO. F-R7524 R1796

Richard, esf 1776 Winchester, Winchester Co, VA, in 8th VA Regiment; PN 1820 Frederick Co, VA, occupation common laborer, blind in one eye, when had w ae 53-4 & d Lucinda ae 12; res there 1822 ae 67; AFF then there by William KINGREE & George SYFFERT, witnessed by Co JP David MEADE; sol mvd 1837 to Belmont Co, OH, to live with 2 sons, when sol petitioned George DUTTY, magistrate of nearby Ohio Co, VA, to get change/o PN address; Thomas DUTTY of latter Co witnessed petition, & John McCOLLOCH Co clerk of court; AFF then there by Edwin G & Charles L HAFF. F-S38253 R1796

Thomas, esf 1776 Becford Co, VA, in VA regiment; PN 1832 ae 74 Columbus Co, GA; bro David AFF then Lincoln Co, GA; sol dd there 1836; surv s David S gave power of attorney there 1850 to agent to afp. F-S31874 R1796

MURRELL, Benjamin, b 1760 Lunenburg Co, VA; esf 1780 Henry Co, VA, aec 20; mvd 1781 to Washington Co, NC (area later TN), where esf in NC regiment against indians; mvd 1784 to Hawkins Co, TN, then 1788 to Jefferson Co, TN, for 17 years, thence Lincoln Co, AL, for c20 years, then to Hardeman Co, TN, for c4 years, thence Weakley Co, TN, where PN 1832; dd there 5/25/35, leaving LWT which named s William as one of execs; md 9/30/1783 Mary SIMS, Hawkins Co, TN who b 11/30/1764; wid afp 1841 Weakley Co, TN & PAR; dd there 7/26/43; ch births: Betsey 10/30/1784, Jefferson 11/23/86, Richard 11/15/88 or 12/15/88, Isaac 4/29/89, Nancy 4/26/92, Sarah 12/28/93, Mary 12/22/95, John Sims 2/13/98, Matilda 11/17/99, Charlotte 10/26/1801, Lucy 6/1/04, Gemimy 3/10/05, Lemuel 1/31/07, & William 4/2/09; other births in file: Richard Decatur MURRELL 12/30/18, Thomas Jefferson MURRELL 11/1820, & Artemicy Francis MURRELL 2/10/22; marriages: Betsy MURRELL & Joseph ROUTH 11/1804, Richard MURRELL (s/o sol) & Rachel HODGES 6/22/1809, John S MURRELL (s/o sol) & Sarah BLACK 4/16/1818, Lemuel MURRELL (s/o sol) & Alis 11/5/1828, William MURRELL & Nancy 10/22/1829; deaths: Rachel (w of Richard MURRELL) 10/21/1816 & Sarah (w/o John S MURRELL) 6/14/1823; s William afp Hardeman Co, TN 1853 & 1854 & PAR; sol ch living 1854: William of Hardeman Co, Co, TN, Jeffrey of Fayette Co, TN, Richard of Weakley Co, TN, John S of Weakley Co, TN, Lemuel of MO, Nancy SLAUGHTER of Tipton Co, TN, Mary GRAGG of Washington Co, AR, Charlotte of

MURRELL (continued)
  Weakley Co, TN, Lucy CUNNINGHAM of MO, & Jemimah HYDE of Limestone Co, AL; sol ch decd 1854: Isaac, Matilda SLAUGHTER, Elizabeth ROUTH, & Sarah SMITH; Granville P MURRELL afp Weakley Co, TN, as adm/o estate of sol wid; wid s William WEAKLEY AFF then Hardeman Co, TN, he had no known relative named Granville P MURRELL, William then res Bolivar TN; record gives no resolution of this situation. F-R7527 R1796
  Samuel, b5/24/1756 Albemarle Co, VA where esf 1778 in VA regiment; mvd 1806 to Barren Co, KY, where PN 1832 as Samuel Jr; dd there 9/8/36; md 6/1/1784 Susannah PURYEAR, Goochland Co, VA; wid b 3/12/1766; PN 1839 Barren Co, KY; ch births (surname in bible MURELL): Polley 4/9/1785; George 10/24/86, William 9/18/88, Samuel 11/17/90, Jenney 11/21/92, Hezekiah 1/21/95, Betsy 4/16/97, James 6/10/99, Susannah 5/9/1802, Schuyler 3/11/05, & Robert 9/1/09; in 1840 Robert MURRELL & Co JP James MURRELL AFF on family/o sol & w; wid res there 1843; QLF says sol wid lived Glasgow, KY; QLF states sol dd Glasgow, KY, & w dd there 1852. R-W3031 R1796
MURRY, Daniel, esf 1780 in 14th VA Regiment; gtd BLW1575 Bedford Co, VA 11/23/1829 ae 74; AFF then there by James HAMBLETON ae 75, per Co JP N ROBERTSON; Co clerk/o court then Robert C MITCHELL; AFF there then by James COTTRIL ae 76, who served in RW with sol; QLF says sol had s who md Mary KENTON, d/o the famed scout. F-BLW1575 R1796
  James, esf in General WAYNE's force against indians; dd 6/2/1840; md 2/14/1836 Sany; wid md (2) 2/14/42 Abraham GISH, who dd 3/15/58; wid afp then ae 58 Franklin Co, VA, & PAR, svc not in RW; AFF then by John BONSACK, Roanoke Co, VA, he witnessed sol marriage to Sany; AFF then there by Jacob BONSACK (NKG). F-R4052 R1796
  Mark, see MURRAY, Mark. F-R7522 R1796
MURSH, Robert, esf 1776 in 15th VA Regiment; PN ae 60+ York Co SC, 1818; res there 1820 ae 62 with w Elizabeth aec 59 & ch: Sally ae 28, Elizabeth ae 32, Rhody ae 20, & 7 gdc ae 8 to 1 (Philadelphia, Nancy, Alsey, Joseph, John, Miranda, & Fanny); dd 12/7/37; md 10/1/782 Elizabeth, King William Co, VA, in form & solemnity of Pamunky Indian tribe, they both being members; per indian custom, they lived together as man & w for 2 years before being married, per Christian custom, sol having become a Baptist preacher; wid PN there 1843 ae 80; ch births: Kitty 8/16/1784, John 5/6/86, Robert A 3/24/88, Sarah 3/29/90, James 3/13/92, Philadelphia 2/5/94, Betsey 11/14/96, Patsey 2/28/98 & Rhoda 2/21/1800; births/o ch/o John & Betsy HOUGHLAND: John 5/16/1822, Elijah 3/8/23, Stephen F 11/16/24, Mary H 72/27, Vina P 3/13/29, Robert A 11/25/30, Catey Van Winkle 6/9/32, & Nancy Elizabeth 1/2/34; James, s/o John MURSH, b 2/24/1806; sol wid res 1847 York Co, SC, when d Rhoda AFF there; d Sarah BROWN AFF there 1849. F-W8416 R1797

MURTLE, Benjamin, b 2/1763 Culpeper Co, VA, where esf 1780 in VA regiment; PN there 1832; AFF then there by William BROWN; AFF then by Mason NEWMAN & John BREEDLOVE (ae 80), Madison Co, VA, before magistrate Charles R GIBBS, witness Jonathan C GIBSON, a practicing attorney; QLF 1939 from desc Mrs E B MILLER, West Point, MS, says sol had s John. F-S5799 R1797

MURVIN, Patrick, esf 1776 Loudoun Co, VA in VA regiment; PN ae 73 Hardin Co, KY 1832; AFF then there by James WILLIAMS ae 70 res Loudoun Co, VA, he knew sol & Isaac SKINNER since youth; Isaac SKINNER AFF then Bullitt Co, KY, he served in RW with sol; record contains copy of newspaper obituary on sol, published 4/1/1845 Elizabethtown, KY, reporting sol b Loudoun Co, VA, dd ae 86 Elizabethtown, KY, 1845, when res there over 40 years as farmer, w blind for last 20 years & survived sol only a few days; sol left 3 ch. F-S1239 R1797

MUSE, Fauntley, b 1/17/1757 near Winchester, VA; while res c16 miles from Pittsburgh, PA, esf 1776 in PA regiment; PN Allegheny Co, PA, 1832; dd 9/12/40 while on visit to s James who res near McKeesport, PA; md 9/7/1820 Margaret MENTO, Salem Township, Mercer Co, PA, who wid/o Nathan PATTERSON; wid PN there 1853 ae 73; mvd 1854 to Clark Co, IL, having res Mercer Co, PA, for c47 years; sol s James then res IN; Sarah J MATHEWS (NKG) & Sarah STINSON (NKG) AFF then they lived on farm with sol wid for c40 years; sol wid gtd BLW 26831 in 1855; QLF says sol res Fredericksburg, VA for many years before moving to McKeesport, PA, also sol s John res latter city 1900; QLF 1939 from DAR agent for sol desc Mrs L C MOOK of PA. F-W8480 R1797

George, b 7/23/1754; esf Hampshire Co, VA, in 12th VA Regiment; PN 1818 Fleming Co, KY; res there 1821 with w whose ae near his; AFF 1818 there by John COLLINS he also RW sol & lived in same house with sol during RW; QLF 1933 from E E TASSEY of Pittsburgh, PA, states sol bro of her ancestor Fauntley MUSE & that George's LWT 1826 listed w Mary who b 1755, further Fauntley's m was Elizabeth FAUNTLEROY, & he named after her family. F-S35526 R1797

Richard, b 1752 Lancaster Co, VA; esf 1775 Wythe Co, VA, res there, in VA regiment; PN 1839 Pulaski Co, KY, where moved to 1805; Robert SAYERS AFF there 1839 ae 87 he res Fincastle Co, VA, when sol esf & he knew sol when they in RW svc F-S30612 R1797

MUSGROVE, Samuel, b 6/27/1760 Loudoun Co, VA where esf 1776 in VA regiment; PN 1832 Parke Co, IN, res Sugar Creek Township; dd that Co 4/3/47; md 5/20/1790 Elizabeth, area later Hawkins Co, TN; wid b 1/11/1771; PN 1847 Parke Co, IN; family birth record badly blotched & many parts illegible; 3rd ch John b 10/16/1796; 4th ch Samuel b 7/6/1800; these sons AFF 1847 Parke Co, IN. F-W9583 R1797

William, esf 1777 in 13th VA regiment; PN ae 59 Loudoun Co, VA, 1819; res there 1820 occupation laborer with w Abigail ae 55, d Sidney ae 12 & s Ephraim ae 10; AFF 1819 by Uriah

MUSGROVE (continued)
SPRINGER, Fayette Co, PA, captain/o 13th VA Regiment in RW he knew sol in RW svc; sol mvd 1826 to Belmont Co, OH to live near children. F-40190 R1797
MUSH, Robert, BLW12408 issued 7/14/1792. F-BLW12408 R1797
MUSICK, David, b 3/13/1763 c3 miles from Charlottesville, Albemarle Co, VA, his birth recorded by gdf David LEWIS, & that book in possession of William MUSICK of St Louis, MO, 1834; sol mvd aec 13 with f Abraham to Rutherford Co, NC; esf there in NC regiment, & served several tours with bro Captain Lewis who KIA 1781 by indians; mvd 1791 to Fayette Co, KY, for 1 year, then to Bourbon Co, KY, where res with bro Obadiah until 1794, when mvd to Whiteside's Station, IL; mvd 1795 across Mississippi River to Upper LA & settling in area later St Louis Co, MO; captain in War of 1812; PN there 1834; dd 11/19/37 & left wid mbnn; QLF 1930 from desc J A HANLEY of Washington, DC, states sol bro Abraham also RW sol & fought beside w in Battle of Cowpens, querier also desc/o VA RW sol's Alexander & Samuel HANLEY/HANDLEY from Botetourt Co, VA, querier also desc/o RW sol Colonel William WALTON who settled in St Louis Co, MO, after RW. F-S16988 R1797
Thomas R, b 10/26/1757 Spotsylvania Co, VA, where esf 1775; mvd 1776 to Albemarle Co, VA, where esf; mvd 1778 to Rutherford Co, NC, where esf in NC regiment; md there, w mbnn; later esf in SC regiment against Tories; mvd 1798 to Lincoln Co, KY for 2 years, thence Barren Co, KY, thence 1803 Province of LA & settled near village/o St Ferdinand, area later in St Louis Co, MO; PN there 1834; last PN payment in file 1840; QLF 1936 from great great gdd Mrs Margaret R TEAGUE, Dayton, OH, says sol s-in-law of RW sol James NEVILL; QLF says sol middle name Roy; QLF 1911 from desc Mrs Henry WOOD, Rolla, MO, who also desc of VA RW sol Ephraim MUSICK. F-S1687 R1797
MUSSER, John, see MOSSER, John. F-S5786 R1797
MUSTAIN, Avery, b 2/26/1756 Pittsylvania Co, VA where esf 1776 in VA unit; PN there 1832 res Camden Parish; David H CLARK then Co clerk of court, court members being Coleman D BENNETT, John A CLARK & William S PANNILL; clergyman Griffith DICKENSON & William DOVE AFF there then for sol; sol dd 8/31/33; md 3/1783 Mary BARBER who b & raised same neighborhood as h; wid PN ae 74 there 1839 when William H TUNSTALL Co court clerk, court members were William A ANTHONY, William H FITZGERALD, James NANCE, & William S PANNILL; John NEAL AFF there then he served in RW with sol; AFF then by Samuel SHELTON there he neighbor/o sol since before RW; ch births (record badly faded, blurred, torn, & partly illegible): Drury 3/17/1783, Joel 2/1785, Seludy 3/31/87, --- 5/6/89, Shadrack 7/11/92, Molley 8/21/94, ---wood 9/27/96, ---as 12/29/98, & ---abeth 3/17/1801; other birth data in file: Clark H MOORE 2/7/1807 + ch of Samuel & Saluda DALTON (Polly 2/12/1810, Avery 12/9/11, & Elizabeth 7/25/13);

MUSTAIN (continued)
   wid apf 1843 there ae 78 for PN increase, witnessed by J BRUMFIELD & James G ROYALL; she & sol md there; file contains War of 1812 record saying John MUSTAIN (NKG) who esf Pittsylvania Co, VA, in VA company, gtd BLW8889 McDonough Co, IL, 1855 ae 69. F-W7488 R1797
MUTERSPAW, Philip, b c1744 Germany; to America ae 1 or 2 with parents; esf 1776-7 Cumberland Co, PA, when res near Shippensburg; mvd to Washington Co, MD, where res near Hagerstown when esf 1781 in MD regiment; mvd after RW to Rockingham Co, VA where PN 1833; Co court clerk there then Samuel McD REID; Daniel AYERS & clergyman Andrew B DAVIDSON AFF then there for sol. F-S9435 R1797
MYER, John, see MAEYER, John. F-S38954 R1798
MYERS, Adam, b 3/25/1755 Fort Town on South Branch of Potomac River, VA, s/o Henry MOYER Sr; esf Uniontown, VA, area later PA, in VA unit; later esf in unit in which bro Frederick was ensign; PN 1832 Huron Co, OH, res Ridgfield Township; dd 1/2/15/44; md 8/2/1779 Mary, d/o Christian & Elizabeth WIEDMAN; wid b 2/1/1762 at South Branch, VA; PN Huron Co, OH, 1845; ch births: Barbara 7/2/1780, John 4/11/82, Jacob 8/13/84, George 12/3/86, Isaac 10/8/89, Elizabeth 1/26/91, Hanah 9/6/93, Adam 12/23/95, Sarah 7/10/1800 & Silas 2/13/02; surname also spelled MOYER; QLF 1908 from desc Mrs Herman STOCKER of Macomb, IL, who also desc of PA RW sol Michael EVERLY. F-W10552 R1798
   Christopher, b 3/1759 Frederick Co, MD, where esf 1781 in MD regiment; res there after RW, thence VA where res c5 miles from Winchester, thence Muskingum Co, OH, thence 1832 Knox Co, OH, where PN 1832 res Wayne Township; QLF says sol dd Knox Co, OH. F-S2890 R1798
   Henry, b 1756 on South Branch of Potomac River, VA; esf 1778 Montgomery Co, PA where res, as sub for bro Frederick; mvd after RW to mouth/o Muskingum River, OH, thence KY, thence to home of s in Ripley Co, IN; PN there 1834; dd 12/20/42; QLF says sol buried Cross Plains, Ripley Co, IN. F-31876 R1798
   Henry, b 3/15/1756 Berkeley Co, VA; esf 1776 Yorktown, York Co, PA, where res, in PA unit; res Berkeley Co, VA, since RW, where PN 1832; bro's Peter & John AFF there then; presiding justice there then Charles ORRICK; Co clerk/o court Harrison WAITE; sol AFF 1834 Seneca Co, OH, when res Crawford Co, OH; d Priscilla HART afp that Co when sol & w Susannah decd, & PAR. F-R7544 R1798
MYRES, William, b 1/11/1756 Kent Co, MD, where esf early in RW as marine aboard PA sloop CONGRESS; esf there 2 years later in MD regiment; mvd to Monongalia Co, VA, then to Territory of MO, thence IL, where afp Clinton Co, when res c 22 years there; PAR, less than 6 months svc; ship CONGRESS was a privateer ship, & that svc not covered by current PN laws; surname also spelled MYERS. F-R7545 R1799

INDEX

This index lists women with their married names and their maiden names, when known, and the men who are not the subject of an entry. Children are also included.

ABBOTT, Chloe 89
ADAIR, Margaret 136
ADAMS, Ann 281 EE 57 Gincy 178 John 318 Katharine 127 Luella 146 Margaret 156 Mary 265 Nancy 18
ADDISON, Arthur 12 Elizabeth 12 Robert 12 Rosey 12 Wallace 12 William 12
ADKINS, Frances 152
ADKISSON, Sally 58
AGNEW, Blanche 181 Cornelius 181
ARMS, Mary 21
AILSTOCK, Elizabeth 185
AILWORTH, John 174
ALBERTIS, Ephriam 292
ALDRICH, O J 143
ALEXANDER, Adam 229 Agnes 221 Charles 158 Henry 297 Jane 263 Jeremiah 221 John 287 312 313 322 Martha 158 Sally 137 Sarah 138 W M 239
ALFORD, Mary 93 William 93
ALFRED, Susannah 65 Thomas 65
ALLEN, Charles 139 262 Effey 85 Effie 85 Eliza 158 Emeline 185 Francis 158 George 164 Howard 164 J C 183 John 85 170 Nancy 26 Sarah 208 301 Ursula 26
ALLICE, Solomon 253
ALLIN, Archer 309 Isaac 310 Susanna 310
ALLISON, Polly 255
ALMOND, Nancy 115
ALSOP, Jane 20
AMMON, Ann 285 Nancy 285
AMMONET, Martha 251
AMOS, Anne 43 Nicholas 43
ANDERSON, A L 68 Ann 271 Benjamin 28 287 E C 209 Elizabeth 28 Evi 204 Hezekiah 321 James 298 Jane 170 MC 13 Martha 202 Mary 202 Nancy

ANDERSON (continued) 119 202 Sarah 204 Thomas 202 William 287
ANDREWS, Eliza 9 Judson 233 Mary 195 Varney 195 William 195
ANTHONY, Rachel 95 William 330
APPLETON, John 306 Susan 306
ARCHER, Elizabeth 176 243 John 176
ARMISTEAD, Wishwood 291
ARMSTEAD, Robert 321
ARMSTRONG, B 63 Betsy 85 Caroline 63 David 63 Eleanor 63 John 85 Mary 140 Polly 140 Roberta 63
ARNOLD, Elizabeth 247 Mary 105 Samuel 247 Ursula 194
ARRINGTON, John 296
ARTHUR, Catherine 155 John 278 Mary 118 William 178
ARTHURS, Amanda 178
ASBURY, A F 258
ASHBURN, Luke 291 Susan 291 William 291
ASHFORD, Nancy 321
ATCHISON, W A 67
ATKINSON, E S 315 Sally 58
AURNER, Elizabeth 37
AUSTIN, James 311 Lucy 311 Maria 311 Mary 311 N E 44 Thomas 311
AVERETT, T H 15
AYCOCK, Eula 9
AYERS, Daniel 331
AYLOR, Henry 326 Jacob 326 Polly 326 Susannah 326
AYRES, Baker 277 Henry 274
BABB, John 168 Marian 168 Mary 141 Sally 168 Samuel 255
BACON, Durliner 191 Eliza 291 Elizabeth 118 Everlin 191 Henrietta 191 Henry 191 Martha 307 Mary 191 Nathaniel 118 Nicholas 191 Ofielder

BACON (continued)
  191 Perliner 191 Sarah 191
  Sarrah 191 Sterlin 191 Sturlin 191
BAILEY, Ebenezer 178 Hannah
  108 Jane 7 Joseph 177 Lucy
  276 Martha 176 Mary 176 Patsey 180 Sarah 177 Selden 178
  Thomas 177
BAKER, Butler 42 Cyntha 23
  Dolly 150 George 47 Glenna
  104 Horace 194 Joseph 43 Leanah 47 Susanna 104 T H 20
BALCH, Amos 61 James 61 John
  61 Margaret 60 Stephen 61
  Thomas 61 William 61
BALES, James 255 Nancy 255
BALL, Ann 263 264 289 Archer
  Elizabeth 258 Isham 264
  James 264 Lockie 201 Nancy
  263 264 289 Susan 264 Susanna 129
BALLARD, Dilly 15
BALLEW, John 102 Joseph 102
  Lucinda 102 Lucy 102
BALLINGER, Ollie 20
BANKS, Nancy 179 William 179
BAPTIST, John 299 Richard 299
BARBEE, Anna 51
BARBER, Mary 330
BARCLAY, Hugh 287
BARKER, Edmund 169 Elizabeth
  53 Franky 238 Mary 83 Molly
  83 Sarah 53 William 53 169
BARNES, Ayvrilla 103 Francis
  103 John 103 Leon 270 Sally
  103 Stella 270
BARNETT, Alexander 235 David
  237 Enos 237 Hugh 237 James
  229 237 Jane 237 John 237
  Louis 8 Louisa 237 Lucy 237
  Martha 229 237 Nancy 237 Robert 237 Sary 237 Wesley 237
BARNHOUSE, Joseph 320
BARNS, Francis 103
BARRERE, Elizabeth 4 Virginia
  3 4
BARRY, Elizabeth 109 William
  98
BARSHAM, Joseph 290
BARSHAW, John 248
BARTHOLD, Oscar 87

BARTLETT, Dorsey 254
BARTON, Hannah 221 Mary 292
  Pattie 42 W Henderson 118
BASKERVILLE, Martha 259 Mary
  250 Samuel 97
BASSETT, Burwell 259
BATY, Birda 113
BAUM, Michael 72 Nancy 72
BAYLY, Richard 294
BAYN, George 318
BAYNES, Elizabeth 291 John 291
BAYTOP, Ann 222
BEACH, Mary 266 Tapley 266
BEADLE, John 108 Mary 108
BEALE, Catharine 50 Robert 86
BEALL, Elizabeth 63 Henry 63
BEAN, Leonard 308 Mordecai 308
BEARD, James 27 Margaret 27
  Susannah 81
BEASLEY, Alice 256 Christian
  295 Daniel 166 Mary 256
BEATTY, Amy 167 Ora 232
BEAVER, Matilda 321
BECK, Elihu 281 Mary 45 Rebecca 263
BECKETT, Humphrey 319
BEEL, James 290 Mildred 290
  Peggy 12 Sally 71
BELCHER, Biddy 203 Elizabeth
  151
BELCHERS, Mary 254
BELDEN, Robert 233
BELL, Elizabeth 93 Fanny 272
  Joseph 93 N J 58 Nancy 93
BELLAR, Elizabeth 171
BELSCHER, Mary 254
BELVILL, Margaret 24
BENAGH, James 312
BENJAMIN, Lois 263 William 201
BENNETT, Coleman 330 Mary 202
  Nancy 81 Richard 240
BENSTON, Mary 263
BENTON, William 315
BERKLEY, Elizabeth 122
BERNARD, Ann 34 Catherine 190
  David 213 John 34
BERRIEN, John 250 Julia 250
BERRY, Anny 227 Archibald 80
  Benjamin 80 Catharine 80 Catherine 80 David 80 Elizabeth 2 80 109 Ellen 80 George 80 Henry 80 Jessie 252

BERRY (continued)
  John 34 80 313 Margaret 80
  Mary 2 34 Matilda 34 McKinley 80 Phebe 80 Pliny 2 Polly 240 Rebecca 96 Rhoda 80
  Tabitha 2 3 Thomas 34
BERRYMAN, Thomas 39 Winifred 280
BESS, Rebecca 76
BEST, Mary 315
BESTOR, George 75
BETHSWORTH, Charles 230 Mary 230
BEURMAN, Anna 150
BEVERLEY, Robert 320
BIBB, Richard 304 Sarah 304
BICKLY, Frances 101
BIER, Betty 98 Robert 98
BIERLY, Ann 158 Anna 158
BIGBEE, Ann 107
BIGBY, Nancy 107
BIGELOW, Agnes 61 Nancy 61 Robert 61
BIGGS, D E 54
BIGLER, Dolly 150
BINNS, Charles 315
BIRDSALL, J O 260
BISE, Aaron 278
BISHOP, M L 124
BITTERMAN, K 181
BITTERS, Albert 28 Emma 28
BIVENS, Mary 289 Truman 289
BLACK, Henry 144 James 214 Jane 138 L E 250 Rhoda 219 Samuel 214 Sarah 327
BLACKISTACE, Zachariah 326
BLACKMAN, Henry 247 Margaret 247
BLACKMORE, Benoni 155 Eleanor 155
BLACKWELL, J H 153 John 56 Judith 56 Lucy 301
BLADES, John 91 Sarah 91 Zadock 91
BLAIR, Henningham 35 Lena 127 Louisa 35 Martha 129 Walter 35
BLAKE, Harold 11
BLAKELEY, William 94
BLANDY, James 316
BLANKENBECKER, Elliot 326
BLESSING, E M 257 Geraldine

BLESSING (continued)
  257
BLOXSOM, Scearbrough 293
BLUE, David 308 Mary 308 309
BLUNT, Ann 162 Catharine 162 Rebecca 184 William 184
BOARD, Fanny 124
BOATWRIGHT, Frances 136 John 136
BOGGAN, Clyde 296
BOGGESS, N E 234 Thomas 302
BOGGS, Catharine 293 Francis 279 Rebecca 264 Sarah 214
BOHN, Delilah 105 Polly 93 Sally 93
BOLAND, Albert 300
BOLES, Elizabeth 106 Mary 290 Polly 290
BOLLING, Robert 175 Sarah 175
BONAR, Helen 44
BOND, Mary 53
BONDURANT, Martha 212
BONNEL, Rachel 126
BONNER, John 168 Lucy 79 Martha 229 Patsy 229
BONSACK, Jacob 328 John 328
BOOKER, Edward 175 Lucy 175 Richard 175 Sarah 299
BOONE, Jane 300 Squire 300
BOOTH, Alice 235 John 317
BOOTON, Rutha 54 Travis 54
BORAN, Mary 30 Polly 30, William 30
BORDEN, Jane 228 Malinda 228
BOREN, Mary 142
BOSWELL, Dykeander 192 Telitha 179
BOWEN, Ann 291 Caty 299 Elisha 299 I J 148 James 291 Magdala 299 William 291
BOWLES, Elizabeth 106 James 106
BOWLIN, Margaret 138
BOWLING, Mary 76 Priscilla 76 Sarah 166
BOWMAN, Bersheba 96 Lillian 280 Norman 280 Polly 279 Rebecca 95
BOXELL, J W 55
BOYD, Abraham 130 James 130 John 3 Lucinda 4 Martha 130 Maud 38 Nancy 130

BOYER, Isabel 230 Lee 230
BOYLES, C R 240
BOYS, William 285
BOZEL, Dykeander 192
BOZER, Rachel 173
BRABSTON, Mary 197 William 197
BRADBERY, Dicy 251 Michael 251
BRADEN, Noble 320
BRADFORD, Betsy 15 Clara 12 Elizabeth 15 Garland 170 Henry 15 James 15 Susan 294 Vance 15
BRADLEY, Ann 156 Mary 252
BRADSHAW, Betty 244 Eleanor 189 Elinor 189 Honor 52
BRADY, J 322 Jane 322
BRAG, Hannah 279
BRAKE, Winifred 7
BRAME, Susanna 299
BRAMHALL, Mary 276
BRANCH, Ann 311 Benjamin 311 Eliza 311 Elizabeth 136 Eppes 311 Frances 311 Peter 322 Ridley 311
BRAND, Martin 103
BRANDOM, Ethel 144
BRANDON, Nancy 12
BRANSGROVE, Anna 170
BRATCHER, Honor 52
BRATTON, Andrew 227 Ann 193 Mary 227 W A 227
BRAXTON, James 271
BRAY, Elizabeth 29
BREAZEALE, Elizabeth 223
BREEDLOVE, John 329
BRENGER, Ann 242 Dorothea 242 John 242
BRENT, Robert 308
BREWER, A T 276
BRIAN, Isabella 282
BRIANT, Margaret 120 Nancy 32
BRIBE, Mary 25
BRIDGEMAN, Magdalina 160
BRIDWELL, Ida 241
BRIGGS, Gray 125
BRILES, Ralph 210
BRINCKLEY, Elizabeth 72 Robert 72
BRINKER, Abraham 63 Elizabeth 63
BRINKLEY, Sarah 191
BRINTLE, Eliza 100 Oliver 100

BRITT, Culliver 86 Frances 86
BRITTON, A M 160 James 169
BRIZENDINE, Bartlet 271
BROACH, Ann 180
BROADUS, James 326
BROCK, Charles 227 Stephen 323
BROCKMAN, E C 262
BROOKES, Frances 184
BROOKS, Catharine 180 Susannah 86
BROUILLETTE, Mary 128
BROWN, Allie 76 Amy 199 Armistead 326 Eliza 149 Elizabeth 79 122 239 Fanny 135 Francis 114 Frank 114 George 239 Henry 293 322 James 149 Janet 199 John 230 234 Lemuel 50 Nancy 114 N F 242 Patsy 50 Sallie 169 Sally 40 Sarah 40 100 328 Temperance 50 William 329
BROWNING, Dolly 72 Eliza 258 James 258
BROWNLEE, Elizabeth 216
BROWNLY, William 299
BRUCE, Margaret 183 Susan 183
BRUMFIELD, Elizabeth 274 J 331
BRUMLEY, Betsy 43 David 43 Sally 43 William 43
BRUMMIT, Anne 296
BRUSTAN, John 45 Levina 45
BRYAN, Charles 291 Hannah 214 John 199 Margaret 291 Mary 199 Nancy 24
BRYANT, Frances 142 James 136 Jane 136 Jeremiah 142 Sally 136
BUCHANAN, Andrew 242 Jane 87 John 323 Josiah 87 Robert 87 Samuel 87
BUCK, Margaret 313
BUCKLEY, J L 108
BUCKNER, Dorothea 242 Elizabeth 42 George 242 279 Malinda 270
BUFORD, John 8 301 William 298
BUGG, Mary 199
BULL, Abigail 305
BULLINGTON, John 278 Oliva 278
BULLION, K W 277 Kathryn 277
BULLOCK, David 243 Martha 270
BUNCH, Isabella 80 Ruth 135

BUNTIN, Andrew 97
BURCH, Mary 304
BURDETT, James 279
BURDETTE, F L 127
BURGER, Charles 284
BURGESS, Frances 43
BURKE, Issa 189
BURKETT, James 289
BURKS, Amelia 98 Edith 98 Elizabeth 98 Frank 202 Richard 98
BURNER, Joseph 297
BURNETT, Jemima 10 Martha 200 Patsey 200
BURNS, Ann 232 John 232 Margaret 95 Martha 130 Thomas 95
BURNSIDE, Robert 307
BURNSIDES, Margaret 193
BURROUGHS, John 323
BURRUSS, Bessie 151 Elmer 151 Lucy 34 Rebecca 299 Sally 212
BURT, Elizabeth 314 Hannah 314 John 314 Moses 314
BURTEN, Lavina 89 Samuel 89
BURTON, A 39 David 46 Eugene 262 Jesse 293 M A 85 May 83 Polly 278
BURUM, Catharine 79
BURWAUGH, M C 227
BUSH, Frances 245
BUSHNELL, A D 101
BUSICK, Nancy 283
BUTLER, Delaney 64 Elizabeth 93 165 Jonathan 299 Joseph 299 Mary 93 165 189 Nancy 98 Patrick 93 Phoebe 146 Sarah 299 Thomas 98 William 146 Zachariah 93
BUTTS, Hester 98
BYARGEON, Hilda 167 W 167
BYRNE, Martha 129
CAFFREY, Eleanor 79 John 79
CAGUS, Susan 12 William 12
CAIN, Ann 314 Jeremiah 314 Leonidas 212
CALDWELL, David 323 Eleanor 277 Houston 180 James 323 Robert 194
CALE, John 269 Lisselle 262
CALHOON, A A 283 Alexander 283 Margaret 283 William 283

CALLAWAY, Margaret 95
CALLIS, George 299
CALTHARP, Mary 93
CALVERT, Lydia 266
CAMDEN, Amarella 45 Hyse 45 John 45 Nancy 45 Washington 45
CAMPBELL, Anderson 105 Ann 289 Archibald 40 George 288 John 288 Joseph 126 Lenna 143 Margaret 97 177 Mary 186 Matilda 105 Samuel 217 Susannah 40 Thomas 323
CAMPER, Tilman 53
CANADY, John 65
CANDLER, Hannah 2
CANNADAY, John 53 64
CANNON, Nancy 238 Roger 238
CARGAN, Elizabeth 271
CARGILL, John 254 Margaret 254
CARLILE, Allan 7
CARLTON, Henry 51
CARMACK, Cornelius 134 Jane 134 Jesse 134 Joseph 134 Sarah 134 Susannah 134 William 134
CARMAN, Elizabeth 218 Lucy 100
CARMICHAEL, Ida 327 J C 327
CARNAGEY, John 155
CARNEY, Winford 144
CAROTHERS, William 124
CARPENTER, Ann 161 263 Catherine 129 Cornelius 326 David 129
CARPER, M G 301
CARR, Frank 321 John 177 Lulu 194 Mary 116 271 Mildred 177
CARRELL, James 319
CARRINGTON, Clyde 296 Hennington 34 Poage 34 Powel 34 Sterling 244
CARROLL, Nancy 182
CARSON, Esther 195 Lucy 200
CARTER, Anne 216 Catharine 31 Charles 271 Emma 217 Fanny 284 Frances 284 James 203 Jeduthan 298 Joseph 291 Leah 42 Ponder 272 Richard 327 William 285
CARTHEY, Julier 186
CARTY, Margaret 195
CARUTHERS, Mary 103

CASADAY, James 230
CASE, Charles 47
CASKEY, Matilda 257
CASON, Elizabeth 250
CASSADAY, Daniel 319 Jane 319
CASTLE, Rebecca 22
CASTO, Phebe 232 Sarah 232
CATLING, Mary 267
CATO, Green 274 Martha 274
CATRO, Catharine 231 Charles 231
CAUSEY, Martha 9
CAVE, Belfield 326
CAVENDISH, Alice 207 William 207
CECIL, John 276 Malinda 276 William 276
CESTERSON, Anna 42
CHADWICK, Erna 73
CHAFFIN, Elizabeth 199 Nancy 199
CHALMERS, Alice 256 William 256
CHAMBERLAIN, Mahala 82
CHAMBERS, David 245 Mary 245 Sarah 245 Tabitha 245 Walker 314 William 245
CHAMBLIN, Sarah 299
CHAMPE, George 133 Jane 133
CHANDLER, Lucy 43 Margaret 136 Mary 166 Robert 43 Sarah 43
CHANDLEY, Sarah 145 William 145
CHAPIN, Charles 287
CHAPMAN, E G 64 Reynolds 304 307
CHAPPELEAR, George 49
CHEATHAM, Silas 233
CHENOWETH, John 246 Susan 246
CHICK, James 94
CHIDESTER, Jane 182
CHILDER, Phoebe 146
CHILDERS, Jane 206 Marjory 206 Phoebe 147
CHILES, Ann 304 Susannah 144 William 304
CHILTON, John 56 Joseph 56 Mark 56 Merryman 44 Milly 44 Ralph 44
CHINN, John 314, Sally 314
CHIPMAN, Sally 143
CHISM, John 50 Mary 50

CHIVIS, Ann 270 Elizabeth 270 Henry 270 John 270 Mary 270 Patsey 270 Sarah 270 Thomas 270
CHOICE, Sophia 67
CHRESMAN, Elizabeth 128 John 128
CHRISMAN, Elizabeth 128 John 128
CHRISTIAN, Harriet 110 John 271 313 Thomas 110
CISSNA, Stephen 264
CLAIBORNE, Elizabeth 7
CLAP, Margaret 150
CLAPP, Margaret 150
CLARK, Albert 167 Alfred 270 Benjamin 319 David 330 Francis 267 George 179 Jessie 284 John 281 291 330 Jonathan 323 Laura 167 Lydia 205 Mary 270 Micajah 167 Mourning 71 167 Paulett 313 Robert 307 Samuel 297
CLARKE, Alfred 270 Ann 324 E 300 George 309 Mary 270 Susanna 300, Thomas 20 William 95
CLARKSON, Catharine 48 Elizabeth 47 Mary 47 Polly 47
CLATON, Mary 208
CLAY, Sallie 180
CLAYTON, Henry 99 Mary 208 Winnie 73
CLAYTOR, Margaret 276 Peggy 276
CLEMENT, William 293
CLEMENTS, Anne 312 John 265 Mary 199 Stephen 199
CLEMMER, Mary 123
CLENDENNING, Esther 222
CLETHERLAN, Frances 13
CLEVELAND, Addie 273
CLEVENGER, Reuben 155
CLINE, Philip 84
CLOPTON, Abner 318 James 313
CLOUSE, Catherine 262
CLOYD, Polly 222 Thomas 222
CLUNG, Henry 84
CLUVERIUS, Gibson 143 147 Susan 143 147
CLYNE, Philip 84
COBB, Lamar 51 Thomas 7

COBBS, Mary 132 Polly 132
COCHRAN, John 123 Margaret 123
COCK, Barnabas 213
COCKE, Butler 290 Jane 243
  Pleasant 67 Richard 290 Ro-
  salie 274 Sarah 67 Sally 187
COCKRAN, James 227 Mary 227
COFFEE, Elizabeth 215
COFFEY, Mary 98
COFFMAN, Abigail 128 Elizabeth
  11 George 53 Joseph 128 L N
  144 Paul 11
COFMAN, Paul 11
COGER, Michael 260
COGGIN, Nancy 250
COLE, Ann 33 Daniel 114 Eliza-
  beth 245 Mary 176 299 Robert
  299
COLEMAN, Elizabeth 230 James
  316 Matilda 270 Robert 270
  Thomas 271
COLEY, Albert 299
COLLIER, Ann 174 Charles 174
COLLINGE, N Elena 227 W H 227
COLLINGSWORTH, Covington 42
  Jane 42
COLLINS, Connie 224 Elisha 318
  Elizabeth 93 Elva 106 Gran-
  dison 318 John 329 Richard
  318 Robert 124
COLQUITT, F A 135
COLWELL, John 141 Mary 141
COMBS, Priscilla 313 Sarah 265
  William 237 265
COMPTON, Abbie 309
CONDLY, Sarah 124
CONDREY, John 295
CONGER, Hannah 303 Lewis 303
CONKLIN, John 111 Mary 111
CONNELL, Jesse 16 Nancy 16
CONNELLY, John 144
CONRAD, Margaretta 106
CONTEE, Allice 112, Benjamin
  112 E R 112 Edmund 112 Ed-
  ward 112 Eleanor 112 Philip
  112 R 112 Richard 112 Sally
  112 Sarah 112
CONWAY, C J 247 Verna 122
COOK, Barnabas 317 Clara 180
  James 147 Janet 282 Joseph
  107 Judith 107 193 Mary 181
  295 Pheba 100 Phebe 100 Ra-

COOK (continued)
  chel 107 Rebecca 228
COOKE, Katie 230 William 180
COOKSEY, Lydia 266 Obed 266
COOMBS, John 237
COOPER, Elizabeth 243 James 78
  John 108 Lucy 78 Sarah 67
  253 T M 247 Wine 168 Winne
  168
COPLAN, Benjamin 182 Jane 182
COPLIN, Benjamin 182
COPPAGE, Hannah 315
COPPLE, David 217 Permeley 217
  Permelia 217
COPPUS, Mary 159
CORBIN, Benjamin 63 Dosha 63
  Joanna 63 Nancy 63
CORBLY, Abigail 305 John 305
COREY, Richard 318
CORK, Charles 156
CORYEA, W A 273
COSBY, Barbara 270 David 270
  Elizabeth 271 Mary 270
COTHRAN, M J 16
COTTON, James 26 Nancy 26 Sary
  324
COTTRIL, James 328
COULLER, Susannah 196
COULTER, Susannah 196
COURTNEY, Judith 311
COWAN, John 2 Tabitha 2 3
COWNOVER, Joseph 170
COX, Banister 299 Bartlett 299
  Hannah 299 Herman 299 James
  124 Jane 65 Lucy 24 L K 255
  Martha 251 Priscilla 299 Ra-
  chel 262 Susannah 165
COYLE, Edward 231 Fannie 231
  James 231
CRABB, Miriam 121 Ralph 121
CRADICK, Charles 324 Mary 324
CRAGE, Martha 36
CRAGHEAD, John 70 Margaret 295
  Robert 70 Sucky 70 Susannah
  70
CRAGWELL, Samuel 287
CRAIG, Ann 259 Catherine 78
  Caty 78 Elizabeth 107 Lewis
  78 Margaret 13 Martha 36
  Thomas 14
CRALLE, Ruth 11
CRAWFORD, Elizabeth 215 Frank

CRAWFORD (continued)
  83 John 277 Martin 215 Nancy
  315 Peter 243 Rose 153 Sally
  277 William 315 321 Zacha-
  riah 215
CRAWLEY, William 318
CREAL, John 326
CREATH, William 299
CRESAP, John 290
CRETHEN, Sally 203
CREWS, Margery 170 Mary 249
CREWSON, Elizabeth 203
CRILEY, Bertha 294
CRISMOND, Malinda 62
CRITTENDN, Henry 87 Mary 185
  Polly 185
CROCKETT, Caty 293 Joseph 222
CROCKWELL, John 258
CROOK, Benjamin 223 Nancy 223
CROTHER, Sally 203
CROUCH, Mary 108
CROW, Nathaniel 77
CROWDER, Holly 26 J W 171
CROWELL, John 257 Louisa 257
CRUGER, Lydia 266
CRUM, J Louis 8 W S 35
CRUMB, Anna 192 Christian 192
  Henry 192
CRUMBLE, Mary 44
CRUMP, Abner 310 Beverly 313
  Peggy 138 Thomas 138
CRUMPLER, Mary 44
CRUSE, U G 148
CRUTCHER, James 318
CRUTCHFIELD, Elizabeth 58 Nan-
  cy 160 Stapleton 270
CRYMNS, Thomas 295
CULBERSON, Olin 180
CUMEE, Edward 291
CUMMINS, Elizabeth 8 John 17
  Nancy 63 Robert 63 Sarah 18
CUNDIFF, Elijah 301 Isham 301
  Isom 301 Jemima 301
CUNNINGHAM, Ann 314 Catharine
  85 314 David 314 Elizabeth
  314 James 314 John 85 314
  Katy 85 Lucy 328 Martha 288
  Mary 85 296 314 Nelly 314
  Thomas 314 William 314
CUPPY, Aaron 135 Ruth 135
CURLE, C T 172 Mildred 172
CURRELL, Judith 66

CURTIS, Caleb 86 Elizabeth 86
  James 121
CURTISS, Jeremiah 201
CUSTIS, James 174 W B H 174
DABNEY, Frances 193 Mary 271
  Robert 312 Thomas 308 W O 7
DADE, Lawrence 307
DALTON, Anna 307 Avery 330
  Elizabeth 330 Lewis 307 Pol-
  ly 330 Saluda 330 Samuel 330
DALY, John 299
DALZELL, J M 58
DAME, Catherine 122
DAMSEL, Mary 221
DANCE, Frances 71
DANIEL, Bessie 277 Jane 282
  Mary 281 Peter 281 Thomas
  157 Ursula 132 William 312
DANIELS, A C 91 Louise 91 Nan-
  cy 9
DARLING, T J 71
DAUGHERTY, Sally 126
DAUGHTRY, Ann 32 William 32
DAVEE, H A 76
DAVENPORT, Braxton 231 Mary 54
  Polly 54
DAVIDSON, Andrew 331 Eleanor
  112 John 233 Patsy 183 Ro-
  bert 190
DAVIS, Alta 292 Arthur 321
  Benjamin 243 Caroline 63 Ca-
  therine 251 Charles 272 Da-
  vid 63 Edmund 267 Elizabeth
  187 252 George 266 Grace 266
  Henry 101 John 215 Jonathan
  122 235 L W 292 Martin 188
  Mary 93 186 209 Nancy 71 Ni-
  cholas 93 Peggy 18 Phebe 235
  Rachel 304 Sarah 82 122 224
  243 Thomas 63 229 William
  187 252 252 266 290
DAVISON, Eleanor 112
DAVISSON, David 289
DAVY, Cora 111
DAWES, Fannie 231
DAWSON, Alice 291 Ann 291 Eleanor 112 Frances 112 Frederick 112 George 155 Jane 155
  John 291 Judith 291 Lewis
  291 Martin 321 Mary 112 Philip 112 Rebecca 155 199 Robert 112 William 112 291

DAY, John 323 Samuel 64 William 25 Winifred 64 Winnifred 64
DeJARNETTE, Elizabeth 222
DeMASTERS, Edward 188 John 188
DEAN, Alice 74 Rachel 81
DEANE, Nancy 143 Sarah 143
DEATHERAGE, Abner 307 Betsy 308
DEATON, Lucy 176
DEAS, Martha 49
DEBARD, Mary 204
DEDMAN, Nancy 148
DEES, Charlotte 9
DEJANOTT, James 172 Polly 172
DELANEY, Jane 262
DENNIE, Elizabeth 297 Henry 297
DENNIS, Ainsley 12 Bessie 232 Martha 17
DENTON, Jane 199 Margaret 206 V L 206
DEWEY, E S 178
DEWITT, Nancy 59 Thomas 59
DIAL, Susanna 235
DICK, Archibald 270 Elizabeth 270 J A 194 Lulu 194 Margaret 261 Sarah 270
DICKENSON, Griffith 330
DICKERSON, Agnes 20 Jonathan 254 Nancy 254
DICKEY, Edna 189 Rebecca 237
DICKINSON, Charles 191 Flora John 191 Martin 309 Molley 177 Nancy 191
DICKSON, John 206 Joseph 206
DIGGS, Averilla 259
DILLARD, Joseph 65 Susannah 65
DILLON, Mary 235
DINSMORE, Anna 242 George 242
DISHMAN, Polly 42 Samuel 42 Susanna 42
DISOWAY, Israel 213 Lititia 213
DISOWELL, May 51
DISPONETT, May 51
DIXON, Harry 151 Joel 199 Patsey 223 Sarah 151 228 Telmon 223 Tilmon 223
DODD, Elizabeth 28
DODSON, Hiram 261 Valentin 261
DOLPH, Salina 247

DOLLINS, Sarah 249
DONAHO, Mary 86
DONALDSON, K 295 Thomas 167
DOOLEY, Eva 84
DORSEY, Jessie 118
DOTSON, Mary 261
DOUGLAS, Polly 121 William 265 287
DOUGLASS, Nancy 147
DOVE, William 330
DOWDEN, Nancy 289
DOWDY, Martin 176
DOWNING, Major 258
DOWTY, James 12 Susan 12
DOYAL, Alexander 223
DOYLE, Alexander 223 Juda 223 Judah 223
DOZIER, W S 218
DRAIN, Fanny 317
DRAKE, Joseph 172 Martha 172 Samuel 313
DRAPER, Joshua 127
DREISBACH, Laverda 195
DRENNEN, Catharine 210 Catherine 210
DuPRIEST, Ann 289 Jane 288
DuSHANE, J S 205
DUDLEY, B R 151 Bessie 151 Peter 49
DUKE, Elizabeth 163
DUNAWAY, J R 171 Robert 291
DUNCAN, Elizabeth 80 102 William 80
DUNLAP, Lily 74 Phebe 76 Samuel 316 Walter 227
DUNN, Benjamin 304 E A 140 James 320 Jane 209 John 209 Julia 209 Mary 267 Rebecca 119
DUPUY, Anthony 307
DURBIN, John 231
DURLAND, Theresa 201
DUTTON, H J 249 Rosella 249
DUTTY, George 327 Thomas 327
DUTY, Sarah 94
DUVALL, Mary 256 Polly 256
DYAR, Rachel 12
DYER, Mathew 128 Rebecca 128 Zebulon 309
DYSON, Elizabeth 112 James 320 John 233
EANES, Patsey 46

EANS, Patsey 46
EARLE, Ann 122 Bayles 122 John 122
EARLY, Eleazar 250 251 Jane 250 251
EASLY, Elizabeth 78 John 78
EASTERS, Margaret 306
EASTES, Charles 163
EASTHAM, Ezekiel 259 Martha 259 Miriam 121
EATON, John 122
ECHEBERRY, Catharine 74
ECHOLS, G V 40
EDDY, Catharine 74 Mary 74 Michael 74
EDLE, Elizabeth 240
EDMONDS, Frances 66 Jane 66
EDRINGTON, Thomas 285
EDWARDS, Charles 180 Edwin 290 J C 33 John 323 Julia 300 Mary 321 Nancy 75 R H 50
EGGLESTON, Joseph 243 Richard 243 William 243
EGLE, Susannah 240
ELAM, James 295 Lucy 295 Richard 295
ELDEN, Peggy 275 William 275
ELDER, Ephraim 292 295 Martha 292 295
ELDRIDGE, Mary 311 Rolfe 310 311
ELGIN, Lady 321
ELLINGER, John 259
ELLIOTT, Alcy 74 James 289 Doris 318
ELLIS, Ann 32 107 296 Elizabeth 107 278 Mary 107 William 32
ELLISON, James 134 Peyton 167
ELLSMORE, Jemma 204
EMBERSON, Nancy 78
EMBY, Deborah 11
EMERSON, Jeanette 36
EMMERT, Elizabeth 185 Jacob 185
ENGEL, H E 292
ENGLE, Virginia 94
ENGLISH, Adria 61 Batsey 120 Elizabeth 120 James 120 John 1 William 61
ENNES, Mary 276
ENSMINGER, Mary 264 Philip 264

ERVIN, Maude 171 Mildred 297
ERWIN, Williams 206
ESKRIDGE, Charles 269 320
ESTES, George 230
ESTILL, Wallace 121
EUBANK, John 272 Warner 291
EUSTACE, Alice 49 Ann 49 John 49 113 Nancy 49 Sinah 113
EVANS, Caroline 128 Dudley 297 George 151 Hannah 128 J E 70 Joseph 279 Josephine 128 Obadiah 308 Rebecca 75
EVE, Fanny 18
EVERLY, Eve 176 Michael 330
EVINS, Anna 230 Hannah 239 Nathaniel 230
EWART, Agness 115
EWING, Andrew 222 Eliza 222 James 12 Robert 130 Sydney 130 Victor 13
EZELL, Isabella 172 Urbelo 172
FABER, Jane 177 William 177
FAGAN, Joseph 308 Mary 308
FAIR, Margaret 146
FAISON, Joseph 318
FALK, George 218
FANCHER, Elsie 141 Emmett 141 Martha 141
FARDEN, Aaron 139 Mary 139
FARDIN, Aaron 139 Mary 139
FARGUSON, Nancy 178
FARIS, H P 216 John 216 Sally 216
FARISS, Sarah 153 Sally 153
FARLEY, Sarah 89
FARMER, Henry 295
FARNS, Jacob 43 Polly 43
FARR, Margaret 146
FARTHING, Chester 33
FAULKNER, Elizabeth 41
FAUNTLEROY, Elizabeth 329 Moore 246
FAZEL, John 260
FEAR, Delilah 99 John 99 William 99
FENDALL, L E 112 Sarah 112 Thomas 112
FERGUS, Rachel 171 172
FERGUSON, Elizabeth 9 131 Jacob 184 Robert 298 Samuel 202
FERRIS, Sally 153 Sarah 153

FERRY, Mary 263
FIELD, Henry 126 Nora 161
FIGG, John 309
FIGLEY, Elizabeth 189
FIKE, Henry 92
FINDLAY, Jane 99
FINE, Nancy 111
FINELY, Jane 214 Robert 214
FINK, Catharine 264
FINLEY, Jean 214 Robert 214
FINLY, Jane 214 Robert 214
FINNELL, Elizabeth 105 Mary 138 William 105
FISHBACK, Mary 49
FISHER, Maggie 242 Samuel 192
FITCH, George 289
FITE, John 229
FITZGERALD, Agnes 93 Edmund 298 Francis 321 Matilda 303 Nancy 303 Samuel 298 William 330
FITZPATRICK, James 42 Mary 42
FLANDERS, Martin 286 Mary 120
FLEMING, James 320 Mathew 263
FLEMMING, William 263
FLETCHER, George 269 Pearl 42 Sarah 80
FLIPPO, Mary 179 May 179
FLOOD, Fedners 212 John 212 Judith 253 Lavinia 212
FOARD, D A 20
FOGG, Littleton 77
FOGGERSON, Margaret 178
FOLGER, Frances 78
FONDREN, Juliett 229
FONTAINE, May 75
FOOTE, Mary 173
FORAN, Margaret 322
FORBES, Elizabeth 209 John 209
FORD, Dianna 20 Disey 20 Joel 195 Judith 195 Mary 195 Peter 195 S C 91 William 264
FOREST, Ann 299 Anne 299
FORKNER, Elizabeth 41
FORMAN, Catherine 92 Lelah 91 119
FORREST, Charles 222 Elizabeth 210 280
FORRISTER, Rachel 30
FORSHAY, Obediah 289
FORTNER, Dinah 315 Lewis 315
FOSTER, Elizabeth 37 Frances

FOSTER (continued)
 101 Francis 305 Frankey 37 George 297 James 208 305 Joshua 305 Margaret 216 Nancy 208 Rebecca 235 Robert 305 S W 7 Samuel 267
FOUCHE, Barbara 194
FOUSHEE, William 326
FOWLER, Dora 222 Elizabeth 248 John 222
FOX, Joseph 304 308 Thomas 293
FRAIL, Lucinda 300
FRAM, John 318
FRAME, Mary 279
FRANCIS, Ellen 157 Henry 297 Mary 223
FRANK, Elvisa 34 John 34 Mary 34 Polly 34 Silvaner 8 Thomas 34 Will 34
FRANKLIN, Jesse 306 Mary 306
FRAZER, Susan 165 315
FREEMAN, Ann 48 Benjamin 299 Eleanor 43 Eli 49 Elizabeth 259 James 48 John 259 Rachel 134 Rebekah 259 Sarah 299
FREENEY, June 149
FREMAN, Kit 134 Sally 134
FRENCH, Ann 242 George 242
FRIEND, Elizabeth 104
FRIZELL, Lamme 91
FRU, Olivia 294
FRY, C W 122
FRYATT, Rosanna 209
FRYMIER, Mary 272
FUDGE, Conrad 322
FUGATE, Zachariah 319
FULKS, John 253 Margaret 253
FULTON, Elizabeth 214
FUNDERBURG, Mabel 261
FUNK, Annie 63 Eve 139
FUQUA, Sarah 113
FURGERSON, Elizabeth 157 John 157
GABELL, Polly 228
GADBY, Anna 111 Gabriel 111 Mary 111
GAINES, Edward 290 Elizabeth 189 John 189 LeGrand 189 Polly 290
GAINS, Elizabeth 71 John 71 Nancy 71 Sarah 71
GAMBILL, Clay 30 Nancy 30

GAMBLE, Ann 112 William 112
GAMMEL, John 185
GANAWAY, Tabitha 143
GANNAWAY, Tabitha 143
GANO, Dora 243
GARDNER, Frank 257 Henry 89
  Sarah 89
GARLAND, Mary 243
GARLICK, Gasper 62 Elizabeth 62
GARNET, Henry 264
GARNETT, Granville 157 Susannah 157
GARRARD, J A 42 James 47 John 305 Justice 305
GARRETSON, Catherine 302
GARRETT, Alexander 321 Ira 267 287
GARRISON, Clara 98
GASS, Elizabeth 255
GATES, Bailey 23 Hannah 23 Matilday 23
GATEWOOD, Amey 140 Augustine 254 Barbara 268 Ellen 268 Josephus 254 William 254 268 269
GAYLE, Mathias 271
GEISE, A H 149
GELDER, Tolman 143
GENTRY, Atha 154 Elizabeth 154 John 154 Nancy 318 Rachel 154 Winifred 183
GEORGE, Elizabeth 18 29 Margaret 263 Reuben 29
GERHART, Ora 232
GERKEN, Charles 162
GERMAN, William 14
GEUPEL, Ruby 299
GIBBON, Ola 63 Thomas 63
GIBBONS, M B 107
GIBBS, Charles 329 F L 295 Maria 60 Mary 46
GIBSON, Hannah 290 Jonathan 329 Maria 261 Meredith 290
GILBERT, Alice 87
GILKESON, J H 2
GILL, Elizabeth 186 Erasmus 269 Goode 312
GILLASPIE, Lawrence 124
GILLESPIE, J H 275 Polley 289 Watson 289
GILLET, John 293

GILLIAM, Floyd 29
GILLILAND, Jane 116
GILMORE, Ann 202
GILMOUR, Mary 183
GILTNER, Anderson 70 Susanna 70 Tirsah 70
GIPSON, Martha 314
GISH, Abraham 328 Sany 328
GIVENS, Elizabeth 120 John 219 Rhoda 219 Samuel 120 Sarah 120
GIVINGS, Lucy 24 Susan 24
GLASCOCK, Gregory 314 Jane 313 Jennett 313 Jenny 313
GLASSCOCK, Nancy 96
GLENN, Augusta 242 Dora 243 F H 264 G B 48 Patsy 243
GLOVER, Edmond 311 Ella 231
GOAD, Robert 309
GOBBLE, Abraham 42 Eleanor 42
GODBY, Anna 111 Gabriel 111 Mary 111
GOLDSBY, Elijah 97 Elizabeth 97
GOOCH, Alonzo 287 Stephen 281
GOOD, George 169
GOODE, Catharine 253 David 253 Sarah 187
GOODKNIGHT, Comfort 203 Michael 203
GOODMAN, John 268
GOODNIGHT, Comfort 203 Jacob 266 Michael 203
GOODRIDGE, Jane 306
GOODWIN, Elizabeth 34
GOOLSBY, Celia 285 Selah 285
GORDON, Alexander 227 Effey 227 Elizabeth 107 Isabella 227 John 227 Lucy 37 Margaret 227 Thomas 320 William 227
GOSSETT, John 78 Martha 78
GOTTBERG, Elizabeth 221
GOVERNEUR, Maria 280 Samuel 280
GRADDY, James 239 Susan 239
GRAFTON, Jinnie 285 John 285
GRAGG, Mary 327 Nancy 228
GRAHAM, Ann 303 George 303 Ida 101 Margaret 287 Nancy 288 William 287
GRASSLY, M H 280

GRAVELY, George 307
GRAVES, Benjamin 156 Elizabeth 262 George Anne 156 Richard 293 W W 249
GRAY, Dorothy 101 D S P 313 Isabelle 313 James 240 Margaret 313 William 284
GRAYSON, Jennie 193
GREEN, Barbara 245 Frances 221 Hannah 314 Jennie 125 John 116 206 Margaret 116 Nancy 116 Tabitha 199 William 116
GREENE, Albert 167 Betsy 153
GREENSTREET, Joseph 269
GREER, Elizabeth 314 James 314
GREGORY, Willia 194
GRESHAM, James 291
GRIDER, Rebekah 176
GRIFFIN, Ethel 122 Kathleen 100 Nancy 122 Walter 122 William 122
GRIFFITH, Carrie 302 M Bryant 302
GRIMES, Ruth 141
GRISHAM, John 81 Nancy 81
GROGAN, Alexander 153 Amy 153
GROVES, Elizabeth 126 279 John 279 Lydia 11 Nancy 279
GRUNDY, Felix 222
GUERNSEY, Cadence 300
GUERRANT, John 287 Peter 287
GUEST, Violet 122
GUNALL, Raymond 79
GUNNELL, William 316
GUSTINE, William 104
GUTHREY, Elizabeth 74
GUTHRIE, W A 221
GWIN, Agnes 234 Ann 234 David 234 Nancy 234
GWINN, Agnes 234 Ann 234 David 234 Jesse 298 Nancy 234
HACKMAN, Florence 288 Henry 288
HACKNEY, Priscilla 119
HAFF, Charles 327 Edwin 327
HAGANS, C F 21 Custie 21
HAGLER, Mary 202 272
HAILY, Ann 273 Nancy 273
HAINEY, Jane 156 Jenny 156
HAISLIP, John 248
HALL, Bazil 160 Docia 160 Elisha 131 Elizabeth 156 172

HALL (continued) 175 Horace 287 Isham 89 James 308 John 172 Lucy 287 Margaret 131 172 Matilda 94 Nelly 308 Sally 85 Samuel 131 Sarah 85 89 Thomas 239 William 83 209
HALT, John 307
HALYARD, Sarah 270
HAM, Betsey 85 Elizabeth 85
HAMBLETON, James 328 Susanna 103
HAMER, Mary 14
HAMES, John 313
HAMM, Ann 270 Bruton 270
HAMOCK, Jane 122 Milliman 8
HAMILL, Louis 23
HAMILTON, Frank 303 Mary 223 303 Michael 172 Sarah 284 Thomas 172
HAMLET, Hannah 295 Mary 15 Polly 15
HAMMEL, Margaret 294
HAMMILL, Elizabeth 226 Stephen 226
HAMMON, Ruth 273
HAMMONS, Ambrose 30 Mary 30
HAMPE, Anna 150 Christine 150 Franz 150 Henrietta 150
HAMPTON, Dorothy 49 Emma 5 Patricia 182 Sally 280 Sarah 228 Susannah 144
HANCOCK, Embly 96 John 96 296 Mary 8 Stephen 88
HANDCOCK, William 188
HANDLEY, Alexander 330 Samuel 330
HANEY, Jane 156 Jenny 156
HANGER, B O 291
HANKINS, Rachel 163
HANKS, Richard 3 Susan 239
HANLEY, Alexander 330 J A 330 Samuel 330
HANLIN, L D 134
HANNA, Jane 237
HANNAH, Jane 237
HANNEN, Susan 211
HANNUM, L L 156
HANSBERRY, Nancy 266
HANSBOROUGH, Nancy 266
HANSFORD, Jane 43 John 43
HARADON, Frank 218 Lola 218

HARBERSON, Elizabeth 293
HARBISON, Agnes 284
HARDAWAY, Daniel 243 317 Dicey 120 Grief 120 John 184 Rebecca 184
HARDIN, Mark 87 Susannah 300
HARDISON, Mary 115
HARDY, Eleanor 254 Nancy 13
HARGIS, H C 297
HARLE, Baldwin 259 Isabella 259
HARLOW, Mary 146 Polly 146
HARMAN, John 246
HARMON, Lucy 23
HARNDON, Clarissa 323
HARNESS, David 205 Elizabeth 205 John 323 Mary 205
HARPER, Charles 300 Elizabeth 266 Sarah 100 William 321
HARR, David 116 Mary 116
HARRELL, John 268
HARRES, Nancy 200
HARRINGTON, F B 114 Mary 114
HARRIS, Dosha 312 Elizabeth 66 Escheler 197 Lucinda 58 Mary 240 Mourning 193 Sarah 183 Sidon 52 Silas 66 Thomas 36
HARRISON, Elizabeth 25 J A 123 John 157 Mary 256 Ralph 129 Thomas 157 256 William 316
HART, Anthony 162 Charles 27 John 124 Priscilla 331 Sarah 124 Willie 162
HARTLEY, Joseph 302
HARVEY, Phereba 172
HASKINS, Aaron 295
HASSELL, Mary 37
HATCHER, Charles 287 Edwin 323
HATFIELD, Andrew 208 Catherine 208 Isaac 208 Magdalena 51
HATMAKER, Elizabeth 107 Melichy 107
HAUGHTHAM, Frances 174 Jane 174 Thomas 174 Walker 174
HAUK, Henry 77
HAWES, Cynthia 45
HAWKINS, Ann 158 Caroline 112 Catherine 78 Caty 78 James 197 Jane 251 Josias 112 Marry 197 Moly 197 Philemon 78 Rachel 163 Sally 71 307 Strother 158 Thomas 307

HAY, Catherine 194 Eliza 289 Minnie 79
HAYES, Elizabeth 111 Mary 93 111
HAYMOND, Thomas 302
HAYNER, Sue 93
HAYNES, Anna 105 Mary 140 Thomas 105
HAYNIE, Richard 126
HAYS, Judith 96 Thomas 96
HAYTER, Margaret 13
HAYTOR, Nancy 13
HAZLEWOOD, Daniel 299 Lucy 299
HEARN, Betty 228
HEASTERN, Mary 304
HEASTIN, Mary 304
HEATH, Ann 180 Mary 265 William 181
HEFLEY, Ann 130
HEFLY, Ann 130
HEIGDEN, Charles 42 Mary 42
HEISKELL, Amelia 192 Emily 102
HELSELL, F H 44
HELM, William 301
HELPHENSTINE, Catharine 87 Peter 87
HENDERSON, Anna 86 Catherine 227 Elizabeth 133 Esther 232 Manassah 227 Margaret 135 Rachel 325
HENDLEY, W 44
HENDRICK, James 203 Nancy 203
HENDRIX, Hannah 285 John 285
HENNESSEE, James 222 Jane 222
HENRY, Ann 119 Charles 262 Josiah 219 Moses 300 Patrick 133
HENSLEY, Catherine 135 Ichabod 135
HENTON, Mary 128 Polly 128 William 128
HERNDON, Catherine 29 Fanny 229
HERRING, Jarucia 79 Jerusha 79
HESTER, Jane 299
HEWING, Sarah 114
HEWITT, Martha 267
HEWLETT, Alfred 133 Elizabeth 133
HICKERSON, Mary 62 Ransom 62
HICKEY, Thomas 141
HICKMAN, Lucy 261 Margaret 83

HICKMAN (continued)
  Mary 134 Robert 293
HICKOK, Lelia 281
HICKS, Daniel 299 Mildred 297
HIGGINS, Nancy 135
HIGH, Rachel 255
HILDEBRAND, Susan 159
HILDERBRAND, Mary 175
HILL, Edwin 270 Eliza 270 Fanny 272 Francis 326 Jackson 272 John 311 Nicey 10 Nicy 10 Robert 199 320 Susan 194 T Temple 49 Tabitha 232 Thomas 307
HILLARY, Thomas 308
HILLEBRANDT, Susannah 117
HILLIARD, Peter 25
HILMAN, John 96 Martha 96 William 96
HILS, Sarah 62
HILTON, Lucinda 160
HIND, E O 239 Madeline 239
HINER, Mildred 249
HINES, J Porter 110
HININGER, A J 294
HINMAN, Betsey 121 John 121
HINTON, Lewis 291 Mary 128 Polly 128 William 128
HIPPEN, Betsey 29 Elizabeth 29
HITE, James 231 Rolfe 302 Thomas 231
HITT, James 62 Lewis 326 Malinda 62 Polly 326 William 326
HIX, Susanna 212
HODGE, Elizabeth 214
HODGES, Bess 180 Elizabeth 214 Rachel 327
HODGKINS, Mildred 21
HOFFMAN, Benjamin 326 Fredericka 7
HOFFNAGEL, Millie 14
HOGAN, Polly 39
HOGUE, Leah 126
HOLCOMBE, Sarah 164
HOLDWAY, Jemimah 18
HOLE, John 135
HOLEMAN, Elizabeth 136 Henry 136 Mary 146 Yancey 146
HOLEY, Moses 166
HOLLAND, Biddy 203 Frankey 88 James 301 L P 110

HOLLEY, Winney 296
HOLLIDAY, Elizabeth 101
HOLLIDY, Margaret 216
HOLLINSWORTH, Charity 179 Elizabeth 179 Henry 179 James 179 Mary 179
HOLLISTER, Charles 157 Virginia 157
HOLLYFIELD, Emzay 220
HOLMAN, Alva 73 Richard 232
HOLSOM, A J 216 Emma 216
HOLT, William 327
HONEYCUT, Anne 28
HONNOLD, Ella 245
HOOD, Elizabeth 219 Mary 301
HOOPER, Lettie 37 Meecha 249 Mercha 249 Richard 249 William 37
HOPE, Bethia 255 Bethire 255
HOPKINS, Francis 153 George 322 Hannah 124 Judith 32 Mary 248 317 S D 307
HORD, A H 313 Susan 304
HORE, Ann 16 Edward 16
HORN, Christian 316
HORNER, William 323
HORNOR, Mildred 249
HORNSBY, Albert 179 Elizabeth 179 Julia 179 Maria 179 Ruth 179
HORTON, Ann 82
HOSKINS, James 269 Joseph 269 Mary 269 Nancy 269
HOUGH, Chloe 180 Mamie 128 Moody 180
HOUGHLAND, Betsy 328 Catey 328 Elijah 328 John 328 Mary 328 Nancy 328 Robert 328 Stephen 328 Vina 328
HOUSE, Mary 123
HOUST, Mary 129
HOUSTON, Esther 227 George 83 Ida 92 Margaret 6 Nannie 227 Samuel 227
HOWARD, Betsy 194 Discretion 5 Johnson 233 Mary 8 N F 93 Samuel 233
HOWE, Mary 139
HOWELL, Abner 170 David 168 Elizabeth 320 Jesse 170 Margaret 170 Patsey 170
HOYLE, M N 280

HOWZE, James 97 Lucy 97
HUBBARD, Elizabeth 252 Joel
  138 Joseph 252 Sally 138
  William 252
HUDDLESTON, Daniel 201
HUDGINS, Joice 271 Thomas 302
HUDSON, Jane 299 William 299
HUEY, Nancy 295
HUFFMAN, Joanna 99
HUGHES, Charles 300 Cythea 300
  Gabriel 302 James 212 John
  221 Mary 47 Polly 300 Robert
  310 Sarah 194
HUGHS, Elizabeth 252 Rody 320
  William 320
HULETT, Nancy 55 Reuben 55
HULL, Andrew 115 Calvin 223
  Elizabeth 223
HUMBLE, Keziah 92
HUMPHREY, Benjamin 239 Hannah
  170 Jonah 170 Marcus 170 Mary 170 Nancy 170
HUNDLEY, Frances 100 John 166
  Joseph 301 Mary 166 189 William 166
HUNNIWELL, August 290
HUNT, Hannah 272 James 171 Judith 198 Lulu 170
HUNTER, Archibald 149 Daniel
  105 David 307 Elizabeth 196
  James 140 John 196 304 322
  Jonathan 323 Kate 149 Marianna 149 Martha 83 Mary 105
  Robert 83
HUNTING, Elizabeth 12
HURST, William 231
HUSON, Hobart 38
HUSSMAN, Margaret 319
HUSTAND, John 141 Mary 141
HUSTANT, John 141 Mary 141
HUSTON, George 83
HUTCHENS, Seth 312
HUTCHINSON, John 297
HUTCHISON, Bethea 255
HUTT, J Warren 316
HUTTON, Levina 25
HYATT, Anne 225
HYDE, Jemimah 328
HYDEN, Sarah 96
HYTEN, Sarah 96
HYTON, Sarah 96
IAMS, Mary 1

ICE, Jesse 1
IDEN, James 1, V Gilmore 1
IIAMS, John 1
ILES, William 1
IMHOFF, Frederick 1
INGRAM, Anne 194 Edward 2 Jeremiah 194 John 2 115 Mahala
  109 Mickie 2 Nancy 174 Samuel 2 Saunders 2 William 2
  115
INMAN, Abednego 240 Mary 240
INSCOE, James 2
INYART, Ann 294
IRBY, Anne 3 Betsey 3 David
  298 Elizabeth 2 Hannah 2
  James 3 Joseph 3 Joshua 3
  Mary 2 Nansey 3 Polly 2 Sally 2 Tabitha 2 3 Thomas 3
  William 3
IRION, Robert 3
IRON, Silas 3
IRVIN, Amanda 3 Aylett 3 Caleb
  3 Chrissa 3 Elizabeth 3
  Frances 3 Isaiah 3 4 James 3
  Jane 3 4 John 3 274 Joshua 3
  Letticia 3 Lucinda 3 Margaret 99 Mary 3 Robert 3 Sarah
  100 Stephen 3 Tabitha 3 William 3
IRVINE, Alexander 4 Nancy 312
  Peggy 99 Samuel 4 Will 3
IRWIN, Martha 132
ISAACS, Samuel 4
ISAAKS, Samuel 4
ISABEL, James 4
ISBELL, Benjamin 5 Discretion
  5 Francis 5 Franka 5 James 4
  John 5 Lewis 4 Livingston 5
  Margaret 5 Mary 5 Polly 5
  Prudence 5 Samuel 5 Thomas 5
  William 5
ISGRAGG, Mary 303
ISRAEL, Nancy 5
IVES, Gertrude 210
IVIE, Anselm 6 Benjamin 6 Lucinda 6 Sally 6 Washington 6
JACK, G W 187 Jane 187 John 6
  Margaret 6 Susan 186
JACKMAN, Phebe 6
JACKSON, Abigail 8 Alexander 8
  Ambrose 8 Andrew 6 Ann 9 Benedict 8 Benjamin 7 Bertha 9

JACKSON (continued)
  Betsy 7 Bines 299 Catharine 6 7 29 Caty 8 Charles 9 Charlotte 8 9 Chesley 9 Christiana 9 Cynthia 6 Daniel 8 Edward 8 Elisha 7 Eliza 9 Elizabeth 6 7 8 9 292 Elsafin 9 Elsie 9 Ephraim 8 Eula 9 Frances 9 Francis 8 George 7 8 179 Handcock 8 Hugh 9 Humphrey 7 Isaac 7 J H 9 James 6 8 Jane 7 Jarvis 8 Jemima 10 John 7 8 9 Jonathan 8 Joseph 7 Josiah 9 179 Katharine 7 Kessiah 9 Lee 8 Lorenzo 10 Lottie 263 Loyd 8 Lucy 8 Malinda 6 Martha 9 Mary 8 McKinney 6 Milliman 8 274 Moses 8 Nancy 8 9 215 Nicey 10 Nicy 10 Patsy 7 Peggy 10 Phebe 8 Polly 7 8 9 299 Rachel 6 Rebeccha 8 Reuben 8 Sally 7 9 45 Sarah 6 8 9 45 Spencer 316 Silvaner 8 Stephen 8 Tabitha 7 Temperance 9 Thomas 6 7 Walter 7 William 6 8 Winifred 7 Woody 8 9 Zephaniah 9

JACOB, Ann 12 Susan 10

JACOBS, Alexander 11 Allen 11 Amanda 11 Ann 10 Aquilla 11 Baylor 63 Benjamin 11 Bennett 11 Catherine 11 Deborah 11 Elijah 11 Eliza 11 Elizabeth 10 Ephraim 11 Frances 10 George 11 Jacob 10 11 James 11 John 10 11 Lydia 11 Margret 11 Martin 11 Mary 11 63 Mason 11 Matthew 11 Melinda 11 Milburn 11 Nancy 11 Prudence 10 Pernelleper 11 Polly 11 Priller 11 Robert 10 Roley 11 Sally 11 Sarah 11 173 Sefrona 11 Toliver 11 William 11 Zachariah 11

JAMES, Ainsley 12 Ann 12 23 Bridget 12 Casander 39 Cassandra 11 Elizabeth 12 13 Evelyn 12 Frances 12 Jean 40 Joan 40 John 12 40 56 Margaret 12 Mary 12 Nancy 12 325 Peggy 12 Polly 12 Rosey 12

JAMES (continued)
  Robert 12 123 Sally 12 Susan 12 Thomas 12

JAMESON, Edward 13 George 13 Jane 13 193 John 13 Margaret 13 Martha 13 241 Mary 13 Nancy 13 Patsy 13 Sally 13 Susanna 13 William 13

JAMIESON, Alexander 14 63 Catherine 14 Elizabeth 13 62 Hannah 13 Jane 13 John 13 14 Margaret 13 Mary 14 Robert 14 Thomas 14 William 14

JAMISON, David 239 Frances 13 J E 13 John 13

JARED, Betty 14 Israel 14

JARMAN, Mary 14

JARRELL, Elizabeth 14

JARVIE, Jane 256

JARVIS, Catherine 14 Elenor 14 Field 14 Jane 14 John 14

JASPER, Nancy 311

JAUSSAUD, Louis 238

JAY, John 194

JEAN, Betsy 15 Elizabeth 15 Nancy 15 Sally 14 15 Smith 15 Wyatt 15

JEANNERAL, Betsy 8 Elizabeth 15 Vance 15

JEFFERS, Andrew 15 Dilly 16 Eaton 15 John 15

JEFFRESS, Mary 15 Polly 15 Rebecca 172

JEFFREYS, Andrew 15 Dilly 15 Drury 15 Sarah 178 Thomas 15

JEFFRIES, Ambrose 49 Ann 16 Anne 16 Celia 16 Clarissa 42 Elizabeth 16 George 16 Gowin 16 Henry 16 James 16 Jane 16 John 15 16 Josiah 16 Mariah 16 Martha 16 Moses 16 Nancy 16 Reuben 16 Richard 16 Susan 15 Susanah 16 Washington 16 William 15 16

JEFFRIS, William 16

JEMERSON, Eleaner 16

JENIFER, Walter 16

JENKINS, A J 185 Adam 17 Adison 18 Adolphus 18 Anthony 17 Cynthia 18 David 18 Edward 17 Elijah 18 Elisha 18 Elizabeth 17 18 Eva 185

JENKINS (continued)
  Fanny 18 Frances 18 George
  17 18 Hiram 18 J M 119 J T 2
  Jackson 18 James 17 18 Jaw-
  deck 18 Jemimah 18 Jesse 18
  Job 17 Jonathan 17 John 17
  18 Keseah 18 Kisiah 18 Lewi-
  sa 18 Lucinda 17 Martha 17
  Mary 17 18 29 87 Marwood 18
  Nancy 18 Peggy 18 Polly 18
  Sally 18 Sarah 17 18 Solomon
  18 Stephen 17 Susan 18 Tabby
  18
JENNINGS, Agnes 19 Agness 111
  Ann 19 122 69 Allen 19 Dani-
  el 269 Elizabeth 19 142 Han-
  nah 19 Isabel 91 James 19 20
  Jane 19 John 19 Jonathan 19
  Lucreecy 19 Lydia 19 Martin
  19 Mary 19 Miles 19 Nancy 19
  269 Philadelphia 19 Polly 19
  Robert 19 20 Salley 19 Samu-
  el 19 Sophy 19 Temperance 95
  Thomas 19 Webb 19 William 19
  20 33
JERALD, Nancy 158
JESSE, Anderson 20 Ann 20 Di-
  annah 20 311 Elizabeth 20
  Judith 20 Lazarus 311 Mary
  20 Sarah 20 Thomas 311
JESSEE, William 311
JESTER, C L Rachel 294
JETER, Fielding 20 Hugh 20
  Jane 20 John 20
JETT, Charles 21 Custie 21 Eva
  21 Stephen 21
JEWEL, William 21
JEWELL, Catherine 21 Joseph 21
  Mary 21 Mildred 21 Nancy 21
  Robert 21 Susan 21 Tabitha
  21
JEWETT, Catherine 64
JINKINS, Burrell 21 Mary 21
JOB, Sarah 21
JOBE, Enoch 21
JOHN, Anna 21 Annette 22 Cath-
  erine 21 Edwin 22 Jane 22
  Martha 22 Mary 22 Milley 51
  Milton 212 Morgan 51
JOHNS, Anderson 70 Betsy 22
  Mary 22 Moses 22 Nancy 22
  Sally 70 Susannah 22 Thomas

JOHNS (continued)
  22 William 22
JOHNSON, Abel 27 Abner 26 Ab-
  raham 29 Adin 23 Albert 23
  Alsey 32 Ambrose 30 Amos 25
  Anderson 29 Andrew 23 Ann 25
  32 Anna 23 24 Anne 28 Anner
  25 Arthur 23 Bailey 23 251
  Batsy 32 Benjamin 23 32 134
  Berry 29 Betty 25 Cary 191
  Catharine 24 Catherine 29
  Charles 24 Christina 26
  Christopher 24 Cicero 21
  Clement 29 Cloe 30 Colin 32
  Cornell 24 Cyntha 23 Dalmath
  25 Daniel 23 David 25 28
  Delphia 53 Delphina 22 Dicey
  25 Dillamus 25 Dudley 23 24
  Ebenezer 28 Elijah 23 Eliza
  31 Elizabeth 22 23 24 25 28
  29 31 32 189 Ellet 25 Esther
  27 Fanny 34 Frances 28 30 34
  George 23 30 Gideon 26 Hannah 23 25 28 Harriet 67 Henery 23 Henry 31 Hester 25
  Holly 26 Isaac 22 Isabella
  31 Jacob 28 James 23 25 27
  32 24 226 Jane 22 25 Jemima
  27 Jeptha 12 Jesse 22 23
  John 22 23 25 27 28 30 32 34
  Johney 25 Jordan 30 Joseph
  32 Josiah 27 Judith 32 Julia
  32 Juliet 24 Kinsey 25 Kitty
  29 L W 30 Langston 29 Lantz
  27 Lawson 30 Lemuel 24 Levi
  25 Levina 25 Lewis 30 199
  Louisiana 29 Lucinda 111 Lucy 23 24 27 126 Lydia 30
  Margaret 27 Margaretta 32
  Martha 24 25 29 Marthy 24
  Martin 34 Mary 1 22 24 25 26
  27 28 29 30 31 32 199 235
  Melinda 23 Metilday 23 Milly
  228 Molley 24 Monroe 29 Nancy 23 24 25 26 27 30 31 32
  Nathaniel 23 Noble 25 Nora
  24 27 30 31 33 124 Owen 32
  Patsey 30 126 Patsy 32 Peter
  22 31 34 136 Phebe 23 111
  Pheby 24 Philip 30 Pleasant
  25 Polley 23 Polly 23 29 Rachel 25 30 Rebecca 22 24 28

JOHNSON (continued)
Rebecha 23 Rebecker 25 Reuben 32 Rhoda 25 Richard 24 28 30 Ritter 23 Robert 24 30 31 32 Rosa 12 Sampson 23 Samuel 30 Sarah 22 25 26 27 31 33 191 Seymour 32 Silas 31 Simon 22 Stephen 23 Stewart 26 Susan 29 134 Susannah 22 25 Thompson 25 Thornton 22 Tunis 31 Ursula 26 Wila 25 William 23 24 25 26 27 30 32 320 301 Winny 23 Zadock 23
JOHNSTON, Adin 23 Andrew 209 Ann 33 Bailey 23 Betsey 34 Charlotte 33 Cinthy 34 Elijah 23 Elizabeth 33 Fanny 34 Frances 34 George 34 H H 34 Hannah 23 Henery 23 Henry 34 Hugh 33 313 Jack 34 James 23 27 33 34 249 Jemima 33 Jesse 23 John 23 28 33 34 323 Joice 33 Joseph 29 33 Joyce 23 Julia 209 Larkin 35 Lawrence 34 Louise 32 Lucy 34 Malinda 33 Martilda 34 Mary 33 34 Martin 34 Matilda 34 Melinday 23 Metilday 23 Morgan 35 Moses 29 Murtila 34 Nancy 34 Noble 33 Oney 235 Pamelia 72 Parrinenus 33 Peter 34 35 322 Philip 29 Polly 34 Priscilla 41 Rachel 35 Richard 41 S P 56 Sandford 34 Sarah 33 Uranah 33 W M 98 William 23 33 34 209 313 Willis 2
JOINER, Delilah 35 Elizabeth 36 Henry 36 Jonas 36 Jonathan 36 Mary 36 Matthew 36 Moses 239 Poley 36 Sally 36 Thomas 36
JOLIFF, Margaret 298
JOLLEY, Bourland 36
JOLLY, Edwin 241 Elizabeth 209
JONES, Abraham 43 47 Alford 50 Alse 41 Amanda 311 Amarella 45 Ambrose 36 Ann 48 49 311 Anna 42 43 Anne 40 42 43 Applin 45 Aquilla 37 Barbary 36 Barshaba 41 Benjamin 44 Bertram 37 Betsey 37 40 41

JONES (continued)
48 49 Betsy 37 43 Burnly 46 Caleb 43 Casander 39 Cassandra 39 Catharine 37 41 44 48 Catherine 46 237 Caty 41 Celia 16 39 Charles 36 Chesley 37 Christian 38 Christina 38 Churchwell 41 Clarissa 42 Clarkson 48 Cynthia 45 Daisy 76 Daniel 38 39 48 David 41 321 Dolly 50 Dorcas 37 Dorothy 49 50 Douglas 38 Easter 40 Eda 180 Edee 180 Edmond 39 42 Edmund 43 Edward 39 Eleanor 39 42 Eli 49 Elijah 40 Eliza 48 Elizabeth 6 36 37 39 40 42 43 44 45 46 47 48 49 50 176 Emilia 50 Erasmus 38 Fielding 41 Frances 37 43 46 Francis 39 46 Frankey 44 Freeman 38 G R 37 Gabriel 37 44 George 38 Godfrey 47 H B 286 Harrison 39 Henry 36 47 Hetty 42 Hezekiah 41 42 148 Hizar 41 Hugh 37 44 Hyse 45 Israel 41 J Herbert 39 J Logan 45 James 36 38 40 41 42 46 49 50 299 311 Jane 38 42 44 45 50 Jesse 40 231 Jessie 50 Jienny 36 Joanna 43 John 36 39 40 41 42 43 45 46 47 48 50 281 Joseph 41 43 44 47 50 Joshua 48 Judith 44 Laban 50 Lane 45 Laura 40 Leah 42 Leanah 47 Learnah 45 Leonard 49 Letitia 40 Lettice 39 Lettie 37 Leusendy 39 Levi 37 43 45 Levina 45 Lewis 44 46 Loftis 44 Lucy 36 37 41 44 50 311 Maben 38 Margaret 42 47 49 311 Maria 47 Mariah 44 Malindy 50 Marshall 46 Martha 36 39 50 Mary 36 38 39 40 41 42 43 44 46 48 49 50 Matilda 42 46 Meriah 39 Michael 38 Milberry 41 Milbury 41 Milley 41 Milly 41 44 50 Molly 40 44 Morgan 39 Morton 37 44 Moses 42 Mourning 183 Nancey 49 Nancy 36 42 44 45 46 49 50 90 203 213 Nannie 40 Nel-

JONES (continued)
ly 39 Newton 42 P G 258 Patsey 46 Patsy 50 Peggy 49 Peter 40 Philip 41 Polly 36 43 44 46 47 299 Preston 50 Priscilla 36 39 40 Publius 38 Rachel 39 Rebecca 38 44 303 Rebecky 48 Reuben 42 Rhoda 45 Richard 36 41 44 47 Robert 39 42 Rodham 16 Rolling 48 Ruth 40 Salley 39 Sally 37 39 40 43 44 45 Sampson 46 Samuel 39 40 42 43 311 Sarah 39 40 43 45 46 49 50 215 Shelton 48 Sintha 45 Sinthy 36 Smith 47 Solomon 39 Sophronia 41 Squire 48 Stephen 46 Susan 42 44 45 48 Susanah 49 Susanna 43 48 Susannah 48 49 50 Temperance 50 Tholemiah 39 Thomas 40 41 42 43 44 47 176 Thursee 50 Valentine 37 Viney 50 Virginia 311 W R 37 W S 40 Weldon 39 Wesley 45 Westley 46 Wiley 48 Wilam 36 37 38 39 40 41 42 43 45 46 47 48 49 50 151 311 Willis 299 Winfield 39 Winston 45 Zilla 41

JOUETT, Francis 266

JOYNER, Honor 52 Jonathan 36 Nancy 191 Sarah 52 Thomas 52 William 52

JUNY, J A 120 Margaret 120

JUSTICE, Delphia 53 John 53 Margaret 53 Samuel 53 Susanah 53 Teackle 53

KAHL, Christine 150 John 150

KARNEY, Ruth 53

KARR, James 69

KARREN, Edward 53 John 53 Peter 53

KAUTZMAN, Ann 53

KAY, Ann 184 C W 54 Frederick 54 Gabiel 184 James 54

KAYSER, Jacob 72

KEA, John 54

KEARNEY, Ann 54

KEATH, Mary 54 225 Polly 54 William 56 225

KEATON, John 55

KEBLING, Adam 55

KEEBLE, Charlotte 54 June 54 Mary 54 PM 54 Rebecca 54 Richard 54 Walter 54

KEEBLINGER, Adam 54 61 Elizabeth 54

KEEF, Susan 303 Thomas 303

KEELING, John 154 Mary 154

KEEMLE, Caroline 55 Eliza 55 Maria 55 Rebecca 55

KEETH, John 56

KEETON, Margaret 55 Nancy 55

KEIP, Elizabeth 71 William 71

KEISER, Rosa 59

KEITH, Alexander 56 Elizabeth 56 H H 190 Helen 190 Isham 56 James 56 Jane 56 John 56 Judith 56 Marshall 56 Membrance 56 Nancy 56 Phebe 56 Polly 56 Susannah 56 Thomas 56

KELLA, John 169 Mary 169

KELLAM, Elizabth 57 Houston 246 Margaret 57

KELLAR, Mary 57

KELLER, Abraham 57 Christina 57 Harry 57 Isaac 57 Jacob 57 John 57 Mary 57 Samuel 57 Sophia 57

KELLEY, Abigail 58 Absalom 58 Alexander 60 Ann 58 Barbara 60 Charles 58 Elizabeth 58 59 Jacob 59 James 60 Janice 58 John 58 Joseph 56 Judy 58 Lucinda 58 Mary 58 Mordecai 58 Nancy 57 58 Philadelphia 58 Rose 58 Rutha 58 Sally 58 Samuel 58 Sarah 57 58 Susan 58 William 58 59 60

KELLOGG, Joseph 202

KELLY, Alexander 60 Amy 98 Anderson 322 Barbara 60 Catharine 59 60 Daniel 60 Elizabeth 60 Francis 59 Griffin 57 James 58 59 John 58 59 60 169 Joseph 59 Leah 59 Lydia 60 Maria 60 Mary 59 60 169 322 Maud 58 Nancy 59 60 Nathan 59 Rachel 59 60 Richard 60 Rosa 59 Sally 95 Samuel 59 Sarah 60 Stewart 59 Susan 166 Thomas 59 William 58 60

KELSO, Charles 60 Clarence 61

KELSO (continued)
　James 60 Margaret 60 Wilber 61
KELSOE, Alexander 61 Eleanor 146 Ellen 146
KELSOO, Alexander 61
KELTLINGER, Adam 55
KEMP, Esther 61 Frances 61 James 61 Sarah 61 Thomas 61
KEMPE, Thomas 61
KEMPER, A 83 Alexander 61 Charles 83 Elizabeth 296 Gladys 61 John 61 62 Nancy 176 Peter 62 Sarah 62 Susanna 61 William 61 62
KEMPLEN, Ann 62 Elizabeth 62 George 62 Henry 62 John 62 Mary 62 Nicholas 62 Thomas 62 William 62
KENADY, Jesse 65
KENDALL, Catharine 62 Elizabeth 62 Enoch 62 Harrison 63 Harry 62 Henry 63 Jeremiah 62 Malinda 62 Mary 62 Nancy 62 Paula 62 Peyton 63 Rhoda 62 Robert 62 Warder 62
KENDRICK, Abraham 63 Annie 63 Benjamin 63 64 Benoni 63 Benson 64 Catharine 63 Catherine 63 64 Christopher 63 Clarenda 63 Daniel 64 Dosha 63 Eleanor 63 Elizabeth 63 Fanny 63 64 Francis 64 Frankey 63 Jacob 63 64 James 63 64 Jane 4 64 Jennie 63 Joanna 63 John 63 64 Joseph 63 Juda 63 Judy 63 Mary 63 Mitchell 64 Nancy 63 Robert 63 Sally 64 Samuel 63 Sarah 63 Susanna 64 Temperance 63 Viola 4 Winifred 64 Winnifred 64 William 4 63 64
KENDRICKS, William 64
KENNADAMER, W C 275
KENNAHORN, Delaney 64
KENNAMER, W C 37
KENNEDAY, Elizabeth 76
KENNEDY, Barbara 65 Elizabeth 65 James 65 Jane 65 Jesse 65 John 65 Martha 65 Patsy 65 Pierce 65 Robert 65 Shadrack 65 Sherwood 64 Susannah 65

KENNEDY (continued)
　William 64
KENNELLY, Kathryn 277
KENNER, Elizabeth 65
KENNERLEY, George 65 Samuel 65 273 William 65
KENNERLY, Samuel 65
KENNON, Alice 66 Beverly 66 Elizabeth 66 Emily 66 Erasmus 66 George 66 Lucy 66 Mary 66 Oliver 66 Richard 66 Roberta 66 Sally 66 Sarah 66 William 66
KENSAUL, John 81
KENTON, Mary 328
KENT, Alexander 66 Alice 112 Allice 112 Ann 67 Benjamin 233 Bernice 292 Daniel 66 Elizabeth 67 Harriet 67 James 56 Jane 66 233 Jency 234 John 66 222 234 Joseph 222 Judith 66 274 Julian 234 Sarah 67 Susan 67 Susanna 234
KEPPS, Elizabeth 67
KERBY, David 68 Edmund 67 Elizabeth 67 68 Isaiah 67 Jesse 67 John 67 Leonard 68 Lucy 67 Martin 68 Minor 68 Nancy 67 68 Poley 67 Sarah 67 Sirus 67 Sophia 67 Tully 67 William 67
KERCHEVAL, Charles 68 Elizabeth 68 George 68 Jane 68 John 68 Joseph 68 May 68 Thomas 68 William 68
KERLIN, Elizabeth 157 Hiram 157
KERNES, Sarah 68
KERNEY, Susannah 68 Thomas 68
KERNS, John 69 Rebecca 129
KERR, Anna 69 Benjamin 69 David 77 Eleanor 77 James 53 Jane 78 John 69 Martha 69 Rachel 69 Ruth 69 Sarah 69
KERSEY, Benjamin 69 James 69
KESLER, Catharine 102
KESLING, Elizabeth 83
KESSEE, Betty 100 John 100
KESTER, Conrad 70 Nancy 235
KESTLER, Catherine 70 Emanuel 70 Samuel 70

KETCHAM, Mary 122
KEY, Agnes 71 Alexander 70 Alfred 71 Bingham 71 Elizabeth 52 71 Fathy 70 Harriet 71 Harry 70 Henry 71 James 70 71 Jesse 70 71 John 70 71 Joseph 70 Joshua 71 Lucia 70 Macklin 71 Martin 70 71 McLin 71 Mildred 71 Mourning 71 Nancy 71 Peterson 71 Peyton 70 Sarah 70 Sucky 70 Susan 71 Susannah 70 Tandy 70 71 93 Thomas 70 71 Walter 70 William 70 71
KEYSACKER, Aron 71 Mary 71
KEYSER, Cat 72 Charles 72 Christopher 72 David 72 Elizabeth 72 Fleming 72 George 72 Hester 72 James 72 Jonas 72 Joseph 72 John 72 Kesiah 72 Keziah 72 Pamelia 72 Polly 72 Sally 72 William 72
KIBLER, Elizabeth 72 George 72 Jacob 72 John 72 Margaret 72 Mary 72 Nancy 72
KIBLINGER, Jacob 54
KIDD, Asa 72 George 321 James 73 Jesse 72 John 246 Lucy 72 Thomas 246 William 72
KIDWELL, Erna 73 Hezekiah 73
KILBURN, Henry 73
KILBY, John 268
KILGORE, Avarilla 73 Charles 73 Hiram 73 Reuben 73 Winnie 73
KILLIAM, Thomas 294
KILLION, Becky 73
KIMBLE, Archibald 74 Catharine 74 Fanney 74 Martha 74 Mary 74 Nancy 74
KIMBRILL, Thomas 74
KIMMEY, Margaret 74
KINCADE, Nancy 298 William 298
KINCAID, Alice 74 Alcy 74 Annie 193 Elizabeth 74 Hugh 193 John 74 80 Joseph 74 Nancy 298 Rebecca 74 Thomas William 298
KINCER, Michael 81 Philip 81
KINCHELOE, Allen 75 Caroline 75 Caty 75 Claracey 75 Hannah 75 Jesse 75 John 75 Jo-

KINCHELOE (continued) seph 75 Lewis 75 Mary 75 May 75 Molly 75 Nancy 75 Peggy 75 Phillip 75 Purkins 75 R Perkins 75 Thomas 75 William 75
KINDER, Margaret 75
KINDRED, Bartholomew 75 Edward 75 William 75
KINDRICK, Silas 75
KING, Abigail 78 Amelia 72 Andrew 249 Ann 78 Anne 78 Caleb 76 Catharine 76 79 Catherine 78 Caty 78 Cora 79 David 78 Dicey 79 Dolly 78 Dovey 78 Drury 79 Easter 76 Edmund 78 Edward 76 Eleanor 77 Elizabeth 76 77 Eloner 78 78 79 Frances 143 Garrett 77 George 76 79 Gladden 125 Isham 143 Jacob 77 James 76 78 135 217 Jane 76 78 Jenny 78 Jarucia 79 Jeremiah 85 Jerusha 79 John 76 77 79 275 Joshua 77 Keziah 77 149 Lucinda 78 Lucy 78 79 Lurana 79 Margaret 78 79 Marsha 79 Martha 78 Mary 76 78 79 144 275 Minerva 78 Minnie 79 Nancy 62 78 79 Nathaniel 275 Peggy 78 Permelia 217 Permely 217 Phebe 76 Philip 78 Rebecca 76 Rhoda 78 Sally 75 Samuel 76 Sarah 76 78 Seybert 79 Sibert 79 Susan 16 135 Thomas 77 78 William 76 78 79 Wilson 79
KINGREE, William 327
KINGSTON, Bernard 79 Betsy 79 Edmund 79 Eleanor 79 George 79 John 79 Nancy 79 Nicholas 79 Polly 79 William 79
KINGTON, John 79
KINKADE, Arthur 80 George 80 Isabella 80 James 80 Mary 80 Molly 80 Patsey 80 Sarah 80
KINKAID, Elizabeth 80 Hannah 80
KINNAIRD, David 80
KINNEY, Betsy 81 Charles 285 Claborn 81 Claborne 81 Clayman 80 Emily 81 George 80 81

KINNEY (continued)
  Harrison 81 James 80 81 John
  81 Katharine 81 Lucinder 81
  Margaret 265 Mary 81 Rachel
  81 Rosa 81 Sarah 81 Saul 81
  Solomon 81 Susan 80 81 Su-
  sanna 80 Susannah 81 William
  81
KINNSHAW, Delaney 293
KINSER, Elizabeth 81
KINZER, Michael 81 Philip 81
KIPHART, Jake 81
KIPPS, Catharine 81 Jacob 67
  81 John 81
KIPS, Jacob 67
KIRBY, Betsey 81 Jesse 68 John
  81 Margaret 78 Michael 82
  Nancy 81 Polly 81 Suckey 81
  William 82
KIRCHEVAL, Benjamin 282 Marga-
  ret 282
KIRK, Allen 82 Ann 82 291 Be-
  verly 291 Chester 222 Fran-
  cis 291 George 82 Harvey 82
  Jane 82 James 82 Jemima 204
  John 82 Joseph 82 Mahala 82
  Nancy 82 W M 204 William 291
KIRKLAND, John 82
KIRKNER, Henry 56
KIRKPATRICK, Jane 234 John 83
  Rachel 59
KIRWOOD, Catherine 210 L A 210
KISENCEDERS, Benjamin 83 Jo-
  seph 83 Margaret 83 Sarah 83
KISER, Charles 72 Rose 58
KITCHEN, Andrew 84 Benjamin 83
  Daniel 83 Elisha 83 Eliza-
  beth 84 Jane 84 John 84 La-
  vica 83 Mary 83 84 Molly 83
  Polly 83 William 83 84
KITCHENS, Thomas 84
KITE, George 84
KLAYDER, Paul 322
KLEIN, Philip 84
KLEPINGER, E C 55
KLEIN, Abraham 84 Anthony 84
  Barbara 84 Daniel 84 Eliza-
  beth 84 Eva 84 John 84 Jo-
  seph 84 Mary 84 Michael 84
  Philip 84 Rebecca 84
KLUNCK, Elizabeth 84
KNAPP, Flora 128 Prude 84 Pru-

KNAPP (continued)
  dence 84
KNICK, Adam 85 Betsy 85 Cathe-
  rine 85 Flora 84 John 85 Ka-
  ty 85 Polly 85
KNIGHT, Abigail 85 Amanda 85
  Anna 86 Betsey 85 Betsy 85
  Effey 85 Effie 85 Elizabeth
  85 86 Frances 86 George 85
  Grant 85 Helen 85 James 85
  Jane 85 Jean 85 John 85 86
  321 Joseph 85 Margaret 85
  Mary 85 86 Nancy 85 Orson 85
  Polly 85 Richard 85 Sally 85
  Sarah 85 William 85
KNIGHTEN, Lydia 86 Susannah 86
KNIGHTER, William 86
KNIGHTON, Thomas 86
KNOWLES, Archibald 86 Cathe-
  rine 86 Cathran 86 Elender
  86 Elinder 86 Jane 86 John
  86 Mary 86 Rebecca 164 Ro-
  bert 86 Salley 86 Sally 86
  Samuel 86 Susan 86 Susannah
  86 William 86
KNOX, Paul 322
KOHLMORGAN, Hazel 20
KOOGER, Elizabeth 260
KREMER, Catharine 87 George 87
  Mary 87 Peter 87
KURTZ, Clyde 251
LaRUE, Isaac 117 Jacob 117
  James 117
LACEY, Hannah 25
LACKEY, Agnes 64 Alexander 87
  Andrew 88 Catharine 87 Eli-
  zabeth 88 264 Jane 88 262
  John 898 Joseph 88 Mary 88
  Nancy 88 Peggy 88 Thomas 88
LACY, Betsy 37 Charles 88 Eli-
  za 88 Ellit 88 Frankey 88 J
  Horace 37 Jesse 88 Keziah
  136 Matthew 88 Patsey 88 Pe-
  ter 88 Polley 88 Stephen 88
  Susanna 88 Susannah 88
LADD, John 88 Mary 88 William
  313
LAFFOON, C A 88 Simon 88
LAFON, Anna 89 Anne 89
LAFONG, Mary 89
LAFOY, Mary 89 113
LAHR, Catharine 26

LAIDLEY, Sara 89
LAIN, Drury 89 Elias 89 Henrie 89 Isham 89 94 Joel 89 Joseph 95 Nancy 89 Patesie 89 Patsy 91 Pleasant 89 Robert 89 Sally 89 Sarah 89 Sare 89 Will 89
LAINE, Gisborn 89 Mary 89
LAINHEART, Isaac 89
LAKE, Asa 90 Chloe 89 Esther 90 Ira 90 John 90 Joseph 89 Lidia 90 Lorenzo 89 Martha 90 Milton 89 Rachel 89 Sarah 89 Silas 89
LAMB, Bessie 184 Richard 94
LAMBERT, Abraham 90 Elizabeth 90 Jane 90 John 90 Nancy 90 Rachel 90
LAMKIN, Benedict 232 Joanna 90 John 90 Mary 90 Thomas 90 William 90
LAMME, Agnes 91 Nancy 91 Nathan 91
LAMON, Isabel 91 Mary 91 William 91
LAMPKIN, John 90
LANCASTER, Catherine 91 Mallory 91 Michey 91 Sarah 91
LAND, Elizabeth 91 Franka 5 Ida 91 John 5 91 Joseph 91 Moses 91 Nightingale 91 Obedience 91 Rosanah 91 Philip 91 Thomas 5
LANDALE, Charles 98
LANDER, Catherine 92 Jacob 92
LANDERS, Mourning 92 Nancy 92
LANE, Adelina 94 Agnes 93 Anderson 96 Ann 95 Anna 93 Betsy 96 Carolina 94 Cinda 94 Clear 93 Daniel 96 Esther 93 96 Drury 94 Elizabeth 95 Fountain 96 Garret 93 Hazel 95 Henry 94 95 Hiram 95 Isaac 94 Isham 94 James 95 96 Jane 85 93 Jean 85 Jemima 95 John 93 94 95 Joseph 94 95 96 Louisa 95 Lucinda 94 Margaret 95 96 Mark 95 Mary 93 94 95 Maryanne 95 Micajah 95 Pleasant 93 Polly 96 Rachel 95 Rebecca 95 96 Sally 95 96 Ranson 93 Robert 106

LANE (continued)
Rosa 290 Rutherford 94 Sally 95 96 Samuel 94 Sarah 85 94 95 96 Temperance 95 Theney 93 Thomas 94 95 Tidence 93 94 Truman 95 Vany 94 Waller 96 William 94 95 Z H 304
LANDMAN, William 92
LANDMON, Newman 92
LANDREM, Thomas 93
LANDRES, Keziah 92
LANDRUM, George 93 Joanna 93 Mary 93 Nancy 93 Patsey 140 W R 94 Young 93
LANDS, Polly 93 Unity 93 Zachariah 93
LANEY, John 96 William 96
LANGFIT, Dolly 96 Lucy 96 William 96
LANGFITTE, Embly 96 Margaret 97 Nancy 96 Philip 97 Thomas 96 William 97
LANGHAM, Elizabeth 97 Isham 97 James 97 Jane 97 John 97 Joshua 97 Marshall 97 Martha 97 Mary 97 Samuel 97 Thomas 97
LANGLEY, Lucy 97 Mary 97 Samuel 97 Susan 183 William 97
LANGSDALE, Charles 98
LANDSDEN, Elizabeth 98 Royal 98
LANGSDON, Ann 195 Charles 98 Edith 98 Elizabeth 98 John 98 Mary 98 Nancy 195 William 98
LANGSTON, John 168
LANHAM, A J 98 Betty 98 Catharine 98 John 98 Mathers 98 Pleasant 98 Stephen 98 Susanna 98
LANIER, Amy 98 Elizabeth 98 Esther 98 Hester 98 Isaac 98 James 98 Mary 98 Nancy 98 Noel 98 Sarah 98 Thomas 98
LANTER, Archibald 99 Delilah 99 Hannah 99 James 99 Joanna 99 John 99 Larkin 99 Mary 99 William 99
LANTZ, Andrew 303 Joana 303
LAPSLEY, Margaret 99 153 Peggy 99 Sally 99 Samuel 153

LAREW, Martha 100
LARGE, Adam 100 Debora 100 Deborah 100 Elizabeth 100 Jacob 100 John 100 Lucy 100 Mary 100 Pheba 100 Phebe 100 Sarah 100 Thomas 100 William 100
LARIMER, John 283
LARRANCE, Beheathaland 100 Behesland 100 Eliza 100 George 100 Ida 100 Sarah 100 101
LASHLEY, Delilah 101 Elijah 101 Sarah 101
LASITER, Margaret 156
LASLEY, Frances 101 John 101
LATHAM, Dorothy 101 Frances 101 John 101 Philip 101 Susan 101
LATIMER, Amelia 314 Barbara 314 Elizabeth 101 James 314 Mary 314 Pascow 314 Roe 314
LATTEMER, Margaret 102 Sarah 102
LAUDERDALE, James 102 John 102
LAUGHFLAND, Jane 221
LAUGHLIN, Elizabeth 102
LAUK, Amelia 102 Emily 102 Simon 102
LAURENCE, Catharine 102
LAVENDER, Charles 102 John 102 Lucinda 102 Lucy 102 Sarah 103 Simeon 102 103 William 102 Winston 102
LAW, Anderson 103 Avyrilla 103 Daniel 103 Elizabeth 103 Joel 103 John 103 Mary 103 Polly 103 Sally 103 Susannah 103 Willis 103
LAWHON, Margaret 5
LAWIER, John 106
LAWLESS, Benjamin 103 Edward 103 Henry 103 James 103 Jesse 103 John 103 104 Mary 103 Polley 103 Polly 103 Reuben 103 Sally 103 Susannah 103 William 103
LAWRENCE, Amanda 3 Ann 303 Chester 87 Elizabeth 34 104 Feliska 104 Hanson 3 Isaac 100 Isabella 104 Jacob 104 James 104 John 100 Jonas 104 Margaret 104 Patsey 104

LAWRENCE (continued) Rebecca 104 Richard 104 Sally 104 Thomas 102
LAWS, John 104 Margaret 104 Martha 104 Sally 104
LAWSON, Anna 105 Benjamin 104 Betsy 105 David 191 Delilah 105 Elizabeth 105 Ellen 105 Elva 106 Fabius 104 105 Frances 105 Harmon 105 John 105 106 Joshua 105 106 Lazarus 105 Lewis 105 Lydia 105 Maria 315 Matilda 105 Meliela 105 Mormon 106 Patsey 105 Peter 106 Phoebe 106 Polly 105 Randolph 105 Reynolds 105 Runels 105 Russell 105 Staples 105 William 105
LAWTON, Elvira 309
LAWYER, Eve 106 Elizabeth 106 Margaretta 106
LAYER, Elizabeth 138 John 106
LAYNE, Lewis 106 Rebecca 96
LAYRLE, John 125 Solomon 125 Zachariah 125
LAYTON, Ann 107 Elizabeth 107 John 107 Richard 107 Robert 107
LAZIER, A M 234
LeCHIEN, A T 325
LeSAGE, I 72 I R 297 Josephine 72
LEACH, Amelia 107 Ann 107 Barbara 60 Betsy 107 Elizabeth 107 Fanney 107 George 107 James 107 John 107 Judith 107 Lewis 107 Luis 107 Margaret 159 Mary 40 107 Milly 107 Nancy 107 Polley 107 Rachel 107 Sarah 107 Susan 107 Susanah 107 Susannah 40 Thomas 107 Valentine 107 William 40 107 Willis 107
LEADBETTER, Susan 182
LEAGUE, Cinthia 108 Jane 108 Martha 108 Mary 108 Ryleigh 108
LEAK, Hanna 108 Mask 108 Walter 108
LEAKE, James 108 Judith 108 Mary 108 Mathew 108 William 108

LEANER, Adam 117 Catharina 117
 Daniel 117 David 117 Elizabeth 117 George 117 Jacob
 117 Johnann 117 Margaret 117
 Samuel 117 Susanna 117
LEAR, George 108 Hannah 108
 278 Mary 108 William 278
LEATHERER, Paul 109
LEATHERS, Judith 233 Judy 233
LECKEY, William 109
LECKIE, Elizabeth 109 Griffin
 109 Lucy 109 Polly 109 Sally
 109 Sucky 109
LEDBETTER, E B 109 Elizabeth
 109 Isaac 109 Johnson 109
 Richard 109
LEDBITTER, Richard 109
LEDLIE, James 110
LEDWIDGE, Rebecca 110
LEE, Abner 110 Agness 111 Allen 109 Ailcy 110 Alsy 110
 Andrew 112 Ann 112 Anna 111
 Benjamin 111 Caroline 112
 Charles 111 Davison 112 Docia 160 Drewry 111 Drury 111
 Drusilla 112 Eleanor 112
 Elizabeth 111 112 Enoch 111
 Francis 112 Franky 110 George 111 210 Granville 110
 Greenwood 110 Gresham 113
 Hannah 112 Henry 109 Hiram
 111 James 111 112 John 109
 111 Jonathan 160 Joseph 109
 112 Keziah 111 Lewis 111 Lucinda 111 Mahala 109 Margaret 112 Martha 112 Mary 90
 110 111 112 Maryann 113 Michael 111 Nancy 111 Phebe
 111 Perry 112 Philip 112
 Polly 111 Rebecca 112 Richard 109 112 Sally 110 Samuel
 113 Sarah 110 112 Stephen
 111 Susannah 112 Sytha 111
 Thomas 109 112 William 109
 110 113 121 Willis 111 Zacharias 160
LEECH, Agnes 264 Burdett 107 D
 B 113
LEEYHEW, David 114
LEFTWICH, Augustine 113 Jabez
 113 114 Joel 113 John 114
 Littleberry 114 Mary 113 114

LEFTWICH (continued)
 Peyton 113 Sarah 113 T B 114
 Thomas 113 114 William 113
 114
LEFTWITCH, Augustine 113
LEGG, Hannah 114 Nancy 114
 William 114
LEGGET, John 126
LEGGETT, John 126 Robert 126 W
 Wirt 126
LEGON, Sarah 114
LEGUE, Edmond 108
LEHEU, David 114
LEHMAN, D A 95 H A 135 Hazel
 95
LEIGHTON, Jane 218
LEISTER, Sally 89 Sarah 89
LEITCH, Angelina 107 Burdett
 107 Emelene 107 James 114
 115 John 107 Mary 107 Sarah
 115 William 114
LEMARTY, Elsie 141 Frank 141
 Violet 141
LEMASTER, Benjamin 115 Cathryne 15 Charity 115 Charlott
 115 Dick 103 Elizabeth 103
 115 Isaac 115 James 115 John
 115 Marcus 115 Mary 115 Nancey 115 Richard 115 Saphrona
 115 Thomas 115
LEMASTERS, Sarah 78
LEMAY, Susanna 15
LEMEN, Agness 115 Samuel 115
 William 115
LEMION, Sally 11
LEMMON, Jane 115 John 116
LEMMONS, Mary 116
LEMON, Abraham 11, Lydia 11,
 Robert 91 William 115
LENNARD, Harriet 141
LENOIR, I 116 J P 116
LEONARD, Adam 117 Agnes 117
 Christiana 116 David 117 Edy
 117 Elizabeth 116 117 Frederick 116 Gasper 116 George
 116 Henry 116 Jacob 117 Jenny 116 John 116 117 Margaret
 116 Mary 116 Michael 116
 Nancy 116 Priscilla 117 Samuel 116 117 Susanna 117 Susannah 117 William 116 117
LEPRADE, Joanna 264

LERUE, Abner 117 David 117 Elizabeth 117 Mary 117
LESEUR, Martil 118
LESLEY, John 101
LESTER, Elizabeth 122 Fathy 70 James 118 John 95 118 Nancy 79 William 118
LETCHER, Giles 277 Mary 230
LESUEUR, Betcy 118 Catherine 118 Dorothy 118 Elizabeth 118 Grandason 118 James 118 Ludwell 118 Mosby 118 Moseley 118 Patcy 118 Polly 118
LEVENS, Lucretia 118 Mary 118
LEVI, Elias 119 Mary 118 119 Polly 118 Priscilla 119
LEVISEY, Edmon 119 Elizabeth 119 Enoch 119 George 119 James 119 Jesse 10 Joseph 119 Margaret 119 Mary 119 Nancy 119 Peter 119 Reachel 119 Thomas 119
LEVY, Rice 119
LEWALLEN, Parasida 119 Parazeda 119
LEWIS, Acey 124 Addison 279 Ann 12 122 123 Andrew 120 125 281 Anna 120 Asa 124 125 Barbara 179 Belinda 124 Benjamin 124 Betsey 124 Catharine 123 Catherine 21 122 Charles 119 121 122 124 125 Daniel 122 Deidamia 124 Dicy 120 Edmond 124 Edward 125 Elias 125 Eliza 123 Elizabeth 66 109 120 121 122 123 179 Elnather 120 Francis 124 Gardner 124 George 122 Griffith 124 Hannah 122 124 Helen 121 Henrietta 123 Henry 124 Hugh 123 James 121 122 124 Jane 82 122 123 170 177 Jemima 27 Jennie 125 Jesse 120 John 120 122 123 124 125 Jonathan 122 Joseph 122 Katherine 122 Levi 122 Lewis 123 Lucy 170 Margaret 120 123 125 Margret 124 Mary 120 121 122 123 124 177 198 Martha 109 122 Matthew 12 Merriwether 120 Micajah 121 Mildred 170 Miles 120 Miriam

LEWIS (continued) 121 Nancy 122 124 Nicholas 177 Polly 121 Pollydora 123 Rachel 123 Raul 120 Richard 21 123 Sallie 122 Samuel 120 123 Sarah 122 123 124 270 Stephen 122 Susan 122 123 Susannah 123 Thomas 21 120 123 124 Vincent 122 Violet 122 William 120 121 122 123 124 170 326
LIDDELL, James 226 Nancy 226
LIERLE, Mae 125
LIEUZADDER, Alexander 126 Elizabeth 126 Isaac 126 John 126 Leah 126 Martha 126 Mary 126 Nancy 126 Patty 126 Rachel 126 Sally 126
LIEUZADER, Abraham 126
LIGGETT, John 126
LIGHT, Jane 307 John 307 Jonathon 307 Rachel 307 Rhoda 307 Stacy 307
LIGHTBURN, Alvan 126 John 126 Lucy 126 Martha 126 Patsy 126 Polly 126 Richard 126 Sarah 126 Temperance 126 Thomas 126 William 126
LIGHTBURNE, Richard 126
LIGHTFOOT, Francis 316 Philip 126 Sally 39 Thomas 292 William 175
LIGON, Blackman 126 Edith 127 Elizabeth 126 John 114 126 Joseph 126 Martha 127 Nancy 127 Sally 66 William 66 312
LILJA, Lucinda 241 N A 241
LILLARD, Ben 127 Daniel 127 David 127 Ephraim 127 James 127 John 127 Joseph 127 Lena 127 Polly 127 Thomas 127
LILLISTON, Asa 127 Blanche 127 Elizabeth 127 Lea 127 Sally 127
LINARD, Mary 260
LINCHACUM, Elizabeth 117 Rice 117
LINCOLN, Abigail 128 Abraham 128 Abram 128 Celia 128 David 128 Dorcas 128 Jacob 128 John 128 129 Mary 129 Polly 128 Rebecca 128

LINDER, Ann 170
LINDSAY, Clarissa 128 Hetty
  128 Levi 127 Nancy 151 Walter 129
LINDSEY, Benjamin 128 James
  129 Mary 129 Priscilla 129
LINDSTROM, A J 183
LINE, Abraham 129 Catherine
  129 John 129 Joseph 129 Mary
  129 Rebecca 129 Susanna 129
LINER, Anna 130
LINEWEAVER, Margaret 130
LININGER, Ann 260
LINN, Aaren 130 Adam 130 Andrew 130 Ann 130 George 130
  John 130 Joseph 130 Nancy
  130 Samuel 130 Sydney 130
LINSEY, Ann 100 John 100 Walter 127
LINTON, Ann 131 Elizabeth 131
  John 130 131 Katherine 122
  Mary 130 131
LINVILL, Mary 131
LINVILLE, William 131
LION, Jacob 154 James 154 Meredith 154 Ruth 154 Valentine 154
LIPFORD, Amos 131 C H 131 David 131 Elizabeth 131 Henry 131
LIPPINCOTT, Ephraim 131
LIPSCOMB, A A 132 Ambrose 132
  Catherine 131 Converse 131
  Dorothy 132 Eben 131 Elizabeth 132 168 Fielding 13
  Henry 131 J Roy 131 James
  131 132 John 131 132 Levi
  131 Lucy 131 Mary 132 Polly
  132 Richard 131 Thomas 132
  Vivienne 132 William 132
  Winny 131
LIRELY, S P 125 William 125
LISK, Elizabeth 132 Nicholas 132
LISTON, Elisha 176
LITLE, Martha 132
LITTERAL, Jane 133
LITTLE, Alexander 132 Elizabeth 133
LITTLEPAGE, Amy 133 Elizabeth
  133 Ellis 133 Epps 133 James
  133 John 133 Lucy 168 Polly

LITTLEPAGE (continued)
  133 168 Richard 133 168 Sallie 169 Vivienne 168
LITTLETON, David 133 Elizabeth
  133 John 133 Mary 133 Nancy
  133 Peter 133 Rubin 133 Samuel 133 Sarah 133
LITTRELL, Daniel 211
LITTON, Burton 102
LITZENBERGER, William 133
LIVELY, Co°thel 133 Cotrel 133
  Cottrel 134 Goodwell 133
  Hemphill 133 J H 134 James
  134 Jane 134 Jesse 134 John
  134 Joseph 134 Judith 134
  Lorenzo 134 Madison 133 Mary
  133 Salley 134 Sally 133 134
  Sarah 133 134 William 134
  Wilson 134
LIVESAY, John 119
LIVINGGOOD, Anne 134 Barbary
  134 Catharine 134 David 134
  Jacob 134 Mary 134 Peter 134
  Sarah 134
LIVINGSTON, Anthony 135 Catherine 135 Caty 134 Elizabeth
  134 Frances 134 Henry 135
  James 135 Jesse 135 John 134
  Joseph 135 Nancy 134 Peter
  134 Phebe 134 Polly 134 Rachel 134 Samuel 134 135 Sarah 134 Susan 134 135 Susannah 134 Susannah 134 Thomas
  134 William 134 135
LIVSAY, Jesse 119 Peter 119
LLOYD, Alsey 135 Fanny 135 George 135 James 247 John 135
  Lydia 135 Patience 135 Patty
  135 Sally 111 Sarah 111 247
  Thomas 135
LOCHRIDGE, Ann 135 Anna 135
  John 135 Rebeckah 135 Robert
  135 Thomas 135 William 135
LOCK, Mary 136
LOCKE, Addison 136 Ludwell 136
  Polly 136
LOCKER, Joseph 169
LOCKETT, Edmond 136 Joel 137
  Mary 136 Nancy 136 Polly 136
  Richard 136 Sally 136
LOCKHARD, Margaret 136 Peggy 136

LOCKHART, Adam 137 Martha 25
    Samuel 137
LOCKRIDGE, James 135
LODEN, Susan 137
LOGAN, Agnes 138 Benjamin 87
    138 Bess 180 Drury 138 Elijah 138 Fay 137 George 137
    Hugh 137 138 James 87 Jane
    138 John 138 Joseph 87 138
    Margaret 137 138 Martha 137
    Mary 138 Sarah 137 Sophia
    137 Thomas 138 Timothy 137
    William 137 138
LOGIN, Anney 138 Benjamin 138
    Joseph 138 Levy 138 Moses
    138 Sarah 138 Susaner 138
LOGSDEN, James 138
LOHR, Catherine 143 Michael
    143 Thorressa 143
LONASS, John 139 Mary 139
LONG, Amey 140 Armistead 142
    Betsy 141 142 C Addison 140
    Christopher 111 Catsey 139
    Cookson 139 David 139 140
    Delilah 140 Dicey 141 Elizabeth 139 140 141 142 291
    Esther 139 Eve 139 Frances
    142 Gabriel 140 141 George
    141 Glen 141 Hannah 141 Harriet 141 Helen 140 Isabel
    139 Jacob 142 James 140 141
    142 Jannet 139 Joel 141 John
    139 140 141 Joseph 139 Joshua 286 Kersiah 167 Lavinia
    140 Levi 140 Margaret 141
    280 Margret 139 Martha 139
    141 Mary 139 140 141 Mildred
    140 Nancy 140 Nicholas 141
    Patsey 140 Peggy 141 Polly
    140 Rachel 141 Rebecca 139
    Reuben 140 Richard 142 Ruth
    141 Sally 140 141 Sarah 140
    141 William 139
LONGAM, Ann 156
LONGAN, George 119
LONGEST, Elizabeth 142 James
    142 Richard 142
LONGLEY, Abigail 142 Campbell
    142 James 142 Joel 142 John
    142 Jonathan 142 Joseph 142
    Mary 142 Mercy 142 Priscilla
    142 Sarah 142
LONGLY, William 142
LONGSTREET, Maggie 103 William
    103
LONGWORTH, Ann 122
LOOKADO, Keziah 136 William
    136
LOONY, Nancy 277
LORD, Frances 143 Nancy 143
    Roberson 143
LORE, Catherine 143
LORENS, Mickie 2
LORTON, Elizabeth 143 Francis
    143 Henry 143 Israel 157
    John 143 Joseph 143 Lenna
    143 Martha 143 Mary 143 Mordica 143 Polly 143 Robert
    143 Sally 143 Sary 143 Stewart 143 Susannah 143 Tabitha
    143 Thomas 143 W H 143 William 143
LOUDEN, John 129
LOUDERBACH, Mary 215
LOUDERMILK, G L 27
LOUMPKINS, Dickeson 151
LOUETT, John 52
LOUTS, Elizabeth 143 Isaac 143
LOVE, Agnes 144 Allen 144
    Charles 144 145 Clifford 256
    Daniel 144 Elizabeth 144
    James 144 Margaret 292 Mary
    144 Rebecca 145 Robert 144
    145 Rosanna 144 Samuel 145
    Susanna 299 Susannah 144
    Thomas 144 William 144 299
    Winford 144
LOVELACE, Ann 145
LOVELADY, Nancy 145
LOVELESS, John 145
LOVELL, Johanna 298
LOVERN, Elizabeth 145 Fanny
    145
LOVET, Joseph 146
LOVETT, Aaron 145 Betsy 145
    Comfort 145 Elizabeth 145
    George 145 John 145 Joseph
    145 Mary 145 Moses 145 Sarah
    145
LOVING, Frances 146 Judith 146
    Mary 146 Polly 146
LOW, Eleanor 146 Ellen 146
    John 146
LOWE, Cynthia 146 Elizabeth

LOWE (continued)
 146 Henry 146 John 146 Mary
 146 Richard 146 Ruth 146 Sa-
 rah 146 William 146
LOWREY, Ann 147 Charles 147
 Elender 147 Elizabeth 147
 James 147 John 147 Middleton
 147 Nathan 147 Polly 147
 Shadrach 147
LOWRY, Ann 147 Betsy 227 John
 147 Light 147 Moses 147 Nan-
 cy 147 William 47
LOWTHER, Deidamia 1467 Elias
 147 Jackson 147 Mary 147
 Nancy 147
LOY, Nancy 262
LOYD, Daniel 148 George 148
 Mary 148 Nancy 148 Thomas
 148 William 148
LOYDE, Elizabeth 148
LOZIER, Abraham 148 Christiana
 148 Ezekiel 148 Henry 148
 Israel 148 Jane 148 William
 148
LUCAS, Caty 1150 Charles 149
 Eliza 149 Elizabeth 148 149
 Ferd 126 Francis 148 Henry
 149 James 149 150 Jemima 148
 John 149 150 June 149 Leola
 149 Margaret 149 Martha 149
 Mary 148 149 150 Mildred 290
 Mimy 150 Nancy 149 150 Re-
 becca 149 Robert 148 149
 Sally 149 Samuel 149 Sarah
 149 Susan 149 Tabitha 149
 Theodicia 149 Thomas 149
 William 148 149 Wilson 149
LUCASS, John 149
LUCKETT, William 130
LUDEMANN, Anna 150 Catherine
 150 Christine 150 Rudolph
 150
LUGAR, Adam 150 Margaret 150
LUKER, Susan 151
LUMBLEY, Mary 150 Washington
 150
LUMPKIN, Anthony 151 Catharine
 151 James 151 John 151 Kitty
 151 Nancy 151 Susan 151
LUMPKINS, Dickeson 151
LUMSDEN, Elizabeth 151 Jeremi-
 ah 151 Patty 151

LUNESCH, Ada 92
LURTY, Elizabeth 152 Mary 152
 Moore 152 Robert 152 William
 152
LUSH, Mary 243
LUSK, Charles 152 Joseph 152
 Nancy 152 Samuel 152 William
 152
LUSLEY, G S 141
LUTTERELL, Alfred 152 James
 152 Nancy 152 Thomas 152
 William 152
LUTTRELL, Frances 152 John 152
 Lucy 152 Michael 152 Rodham
 152
LUTZ, Joseph 143 Michael 143
LYLE, Abraham 99 Andrew 99 An-
 na 192 Elizabeth 218 Frances
 99 Frederick 192 Jane 99
 Joel 99 John 99 100 218 Mar-
 garet 99 Martha 99 Mary 218
 Nora 99 Sarah 99 William 99
LYNAM, Andrew 153 Betsey 153
 Betsy 153 David 153 Eliza-
 beth 153 James 153 John 153
 Lee 153 Margaret 153 Rachel
 153 Richard 153 Sally 153
 Sarah 153 William 153
LYNCH, Aaron 153 Amy 153 David
 153 Elijah 153 Isaiah 283
 Jacob 213 James 20 154 Mar-
 tha 153 Patsey 153 Peyton
 154 Peytona 154 Rose 153
 Sally 153 Sarah 153 Thomas
 154
LYNN, Margaret 125 Mary 57
 William 57
LYNOR, Betsey 154 Nancy 154
 Peggy 154 Polly 154
LYON, Austin 154 Elizabeth 154
 Frances 154 Jacob 154 James
 154 155 Jane 154 John 154
 Meredith 154 Nancy 154 Rach-
 el 154 Ruth 154 Solomon 154
 Valentine 154
LYONS, John 154
MacDONALD, William 102
MacKAY, Nancy 220
MacNATT, John 237 Richard 237
MAABE, John 160
MABE, John 160
MABEN, Andrew 155

MABEN, James 155
MABRY, James 155
MACBEE, Israel
MACCLURE, Mary 208 Mary 208
MACCONN, James 155
MACE, Paul 155
MACKALL, Eleanor 155 James 155 Jane 155 John 155 Rebecca 155 Thomas 155
MACKAY, Catherine 155 Matthew 155
MACKY, Ann 156 Anne 156 Elizabeth 156 George 156 Jane 156 Margaret 156 Mary 156 Robert j156
MACON, A Jane 48 Jane 46 Thomas 313 William 313
MACY, J S 83
MADCAP, Gabriel 50 Susanna 50
MADDEN, Jane 156 Jenny 156
MADDOX, Alexander 156 Bernard 157 Betty 310 Cynthia 157 David 157 Delia 157 Delilah 157 Elijah 157 Elizabeth 157 Frances 157 G S 311 Guinn 157 Healthy 157 Henry 157 Jacob 157 James 157 Jenny 157 John 157 Larkin 157 Levi 157 Levina 157 Linna 157 Patsey 157 Polly 157 Preston 157 Prudence 157 Sally 157 Sherwood 157 Thomas 157 William 157 Wilson 157
MADDUX, Hannah 314
MADDY, H B 215 Sally 133 Sarah 133
MADEIRA, Casper 157 Christian 157 Michael 157 Nicholas 157
MADERA, Ann 158 Anna 158 Elizabeth 158
MADISON, Ann 158 Anna 120 Anne 42 Bess 108 Betsey 120 Eliza 120 158 Elizabeth 158 Elnather 130 James 158 Jane 158 Lucy 158 Martha 156 Mira 158 Mirah 158 Myra 158 Nancy 158 Rowland 120 158
MAFFITT, Elijah 158 Elizabeth 158 Henry 158 Peggy 158 William 158
MAGERS, Thomas 162
MAGILL, Augustine 159 Bessie

MAGILL (continued) 159 Buckner 159 Hervey 159 James 159 John 232 Mary 159 Nathaniel 159 Robert 159 Samuel 159 Thomas 159
MAGINNIS, Anna 159 Daniel 159 Elizabeth 159 Margaret 159 Sarah 159 Susan 159
MAGRAW, Mary 119
MAGRUDER, James 229 Louise 229 Margaret 229 William 229
MAGWIER, Aleygone 224
MAHANY, Patsy 265
MAHIN, Mabel 270
MAHOLLAND, Lucy 160 Nancy 160 William 160
MAHONE, Ann 160 Archelaus 160 Cecelia 160 Elizabeth 160 Fanny 160 John 160 Magdalina 160 Mary 160 Micajah 160 Nancy 160 William 160 Zachariah 160
MAHONEY, Benjamin 63 John 255 Joseph 63 Roberta 63
MAHORNEY, Jack 160 Mina 160 Owen 160
MAIB, Alexander 160 Lucinda 160
MAID, Thomas 243
MAIDEN, Docia 160 Sally 160
MAIGHER, Ann 161 Catherine 161 Lydia 161
MAIL, George 161 Priscilla 161
MAIN, Katherine 161
MAINARD, James 164 Simon 161
MAINES, Edgar 161 Isaac 161 Joseph 161 Levi 161 Philip 161
MAINS, George 161
MAJOR, John 161 Nancy 161 Samuel 161 William 161
MAJORS, Samuel 161 William 161
MALING, Elizabeth 323
MALLARY, Philip 162 Robert 162
MALLERY, John 163
MALLETT, William 203, 204
MALLICOAT, Mary 100
MALLICOTE, Augustin 213 Elizabeth 213
MALLIHON, John 162
MALLORY, Catharine 162 Catherine 163 Clairborne 163 Eli-

MALLORY (continued)
zabeth 162 163 Francis 163
Henry 162 James 163 John 163
Myrtle 162 Nancy 152 Pamelia
162 Philip 163 Polly 162 Rebecca 162 Sarah 162 Thomas
163 William 162 Willie 162
MALLOWS, Henry 163
MALONE, Christian 116 Dulaney
116 Elizabeth 116 John 116
MALONEY, Nancy 164 Rachel 163
MANARD, Chaney 164
MANESS, Matthew 21 Tabitha 21
MANEY, Elizabeth 164 James 164
John 164 Keziah 164 Martin
164 Nancy 164 Sarah 164 William 164
MANGUM, Rebecca 164
MANHALL, Francis 299 Jane 299
MANK, William 193
MANKER, Sarah 165
MANLEY, Ancil 165 Ann 165 Caleb 165 Elizabeth 165 Fanney
165 John 165 Polly 165 Susannah 165 Thomas 165 William 165
MANLY, Ancil 165 Ann 165 Caleb
165 Elizabeth 165 Fanney 165
John 165 Polly 165 Thomas
165 William 165
MANN, Agnes 165 Alice 207 Ann
166 James 165 Jane 207 John
166 Martha 166 Mary 166 William 166
MANNAN, James 166 John 166 Letitia 166 Lettice 166 Lucy
166 Mary 166 Nancy 166 Robert 166 Sary 166 Susan 166
Susannah 166 William 166
MANNON, James 166 John 166 Lucy 166 Mary 166 Nancy 166
Robert 166 Sarah 166 Sary
166 Susan 166 Susannah 166
William 166
MANNING, James 167 Susan 167
MANSFIELD, Arletta 258 Betsy
161 Charles 167 David 167 E
A 258 George 167 Henry 167
168 James 59 Kate 167 Kersiah 167 Lucy 167 Mourning 167
Nancy 167 Norman 167 Rebecca
167 Robert 167 Thomas 167

MANSFIELD (continued)
William 167
MANSON, Nathaniel 317
MANY, Elizabeth 164 James 164
John 164 Martin 164 Nancy
164 William 164
MAPP, Cassandra 12 John 12
Littleton 168 Mary 168 Molley 168 Robert 168
MARBERRY, Luke 290
MARBREY, Eleanor 290
MARCH, John 168 Minnie 308
MARCOM, Betsey 168 Edman 168
Elisha 168 Fanney 168 Geley
168 Isaiar 168 Meley 168
Nancy 168 Nathan 168 Patcy
168 Polley 168 Thomas 168
William 168
MARCUM, Betsey 168 Edman 168
Elisha 168 Fanney 168 Fanny
168 Geley 168 Isaiar 168 Meley 168 Nancy 168 Nathan 168
Patcy 168 Polley 168 Stephen
168 Thomas 168 William 168
MARDERS, James 168
MARDIS, Betsy 168 Elizabeth
168 James 168 Lucy 168 Nancy
168 Polly 168 Sallie 168
Stephen 168 William 168 Wine
168 Winne 168 Winny 168
MARHAR, Patrick 160
MARICK, Harriet 169 John 169
MARION, Francis 185 J H 125
MARKHAM, Alfred 169 Archibald
169 Edmund 169 Elizabeth 122
James 65 169 John 169 Josiah
169 Judith 169 Major 169
Margaret 169 Marvel 169 Mary
169 Nelly 169 Peggy 169 Sallie 169 Thomas 169 William
169
MARKLAND, A P 193
MARKRUM, Phalby 197
MARKS, Abel 170 Anne 170 Benjamin 170 Bennet 179 Betsy
170 Catherine 170 Clementine
170 Crissey 170 Deborah 170
Elisha 170 George 170 Hastings 170 Isaiah 170 Jesse
170 John 170 Lucretia 170
Lucy 170 Lydia 170 Margaret
170 Margery 170 Mary 121 170

MARKS (continued)
Peter 170 Polly 121 170 Rachel 170 Samuel 170 Sarah 170 Thomas 170 Ury 170 Watts 170
MARKUM, Anna 170
MARL, James 171
MARLAR, Peterson 170
MARLATT, Ann 170 C L 171 Elizabeth 171 Evaline 171 George 170 Thomas 170 171 Walter 171
MARLOW, Stella 112
MARNEY, Amos 171 Betsey 171 David 171 Phebe 171 Robert 171 Sally 171 Samuel 171 Sarah 171
MARS, Alexander 171 David 171 172 Hannah 171 John 171 Margaret 171 172 Rachel 171 172 Shannon 171
MARSH, Phereba 172
MARSHAL, Jessy 174
MARSHALL, A J 279 308 Alexander 323 Ann 173 174 Beheathland 173 Behethland 173 Bettie 172 Daniel 172 Eleazar 173 Elizabeth 14 172 173 175 Emily 172 Eupham 173 Euphemia 174 G 173 George 172 174 Hanson 172 Henry 132 173 Henson 172 Hersey 173 Isabella 172 J 308 J M 173 James 56 174 Jane 56 173 174 John 173 174 Joseah 172 Joseph 173 Keziah 174 Lillian 126 Lucy 175 Makethea 173 Margaret 173 Marquis 173 Martha 172 Mary 172 173 174 175 Merryman 14 Michael 172 Mildred 172 Milly 175 Nancy 168 172 174 Patience 174 Polly 172 Rachel 173 Rebecca 172 Richard 173 Robert 168 172 Samuel 172 Sarah 173 174 Theophilus 173 Thomas 172 173 175 281 292 Walter 172 Washington 173 175 William 172 173
MARSTON, John 287 Sarah 175 Susanna 175
MARTIN, Abram 180 181 Absalom

MARTIN (continued)
181 182 Alee 180 Alex 180 Amanda 178 Ann 180 182 183 Anna 176 Anne 180 Austin 182 Azariah 175 183 Bailey 176 Barbara 179 Benjamin 176 Betsey 176 C S 178 Catharine 178 Charles 178 Chloe 180 David 175 181 E L 183 Eda 180 Edee 180 Eleanor 226 Ella 183 Elizabeth 11 97 175 176 178 179 180 181 182 Enoch 178 Ephraim 178 181 Eve 176 Fanny 176 Frances 178 George 66 180 181 182 Gincy 178 Grace 183 Henry 177 Hester 182 Hudson 177 Hugh 183 Jacob 178 James 176 178 180 181 182 183 Jane 175 176 181 182 183 Jeffreys 178 Jehoiada 175 Jehoida 175 Joab 182 Joel 177 John 176 177 178 180 181 182 183 265 Jonathan 175 Joseph 178 180 Josiah 182 Leah 126 Leticia 183 Letitia 178 183 Letty 176 183 Lewis 175 178 Liberty 175 Loes 180 Lois 180 Lucy 175 176 180 182 Luther 178 Marey 180 Margaret 177 183 Martha 175 180 183 Marthew 180 Mary 66 92 175 176 177 179 179 180 181 Mildred 177 Moab 176 Moaning 180 Molley 177 Morning 180 Moses 180 Mourning 183 Nancy 175 176 178 179 181 182 183 Nathan 176 Nelson 179 Nicholas 177 Patricia 182 Patsey 180 Patsy 177 183 Peter 11 178 Pleasant 180 Poley 182 Polly 178 Rachel 178 Rebecca 176 Rebeccah 183 Rebekah 176 Rhoda 182 Richard 178 Robert 66 175 181 Sabra 181 182 Sallie 180 Sally 176 Samuel 178 183 Sarah 11 178 182 183 Stephen 180 Susan 42 182 183 Susanna 180 Susannah 176 178 Syrene 182 Talitha 179 Templeton 182 Tinny 182 Tyre 183 Thomas 175 178 179 180

MARTIN (continued)
181 182 Valentine 182 Washington 183 William 1765 177 178 180 182 183 272 310 Wilson 181 Winifred 183
MARTINDALE, James 183 Mary 183 William 183
MARVAULT, Simon 323
MARYE, Jane 21 John 21
MASENGILL, Henry 185
MASON, A G 184 Ann 184 Benjamin 185 Catherine 41 David 184 Elizabeth 185 Eva 185 Frances 184 Jane 202 Jinney 202 John 202 Littleberry 184 Lucy 41 Mary 184 185 228 Milley 41 Nancy 184 Polly 185 Nathaniel 184 Philip 184 Rebecca 184 Robert 184 Smith 254 Thomas 184 William 184
MASSA, O D 185
MASSENGELLS, Henry 185
MASSENGILL, Elizabeth 185 F D 185 G D 185 J T 185 John T 185
MASSEY, Charles 186 188 Edmond 186 Elizabeth 186 Emeline 185 Hannah 187 Henry 186 Jesse 186 John 186 Judith 186 Lovell 186 Margaret 185 Mary 186 Robert 186 Ruth 146 Sarah 185 186 Susan 186 Susannah 186 Thomas 186 William 186
MASSIE, Charles 186 Elizabeth 186 Ellen 187 Eugenia 123 187 Harriet 187 Henry 123 187 John 186 187 Joseph 186 Judith 187 Julier 186 Juliet 187 M D 187 Martha 186 Mary 123 186 Patrick 187 Sally 187 Sarah 123 Shearwood 186 Susannah 123 Thomas 123 186 187 Thornton 187 Waller 187 William 186 187
MASSY, Dolley 188 Elizabeth 187 188 Enoch 188 James 188 Joanna 188 John 188 Kitty 188 Patsey 188 Peter 188 Samuel 188 Sevier 188 Sherrod 188 Thomas 187
MASTERS, Betsey 188 Cornelius

MASTERS (continued)
188 Elizabeth 188 Elvira 188 George 188 John 188 Margaret 188 Nancy 188 Polly 188 Sally 188 Sarah 188 Wiatt 188
MASTERSON, Caleb 188 Edward 188 Elizabeth 188 James 188 John 188 Joseph 188 Lovet 188 Maray 188 Margaret 188 Mary 188 Peggy 188 Richard 188 Robert 188 Sarah 188 William 188
MASTIN, Susan 29
MATHENY, Catharine 86 Cathrane 86 James 86
MATHEW, Benjamin 189
MATHEWS, Adelaide 302 Benjamin 189 Eleanor 189 Elina 189 Elizabeth 189 H 178 Isaac 189 191 James 189 Jane 189 Jeremiah 191 John 189 Joseph 189 Kate 189 Littlebury 191 M A 115 Margaret 189 Martha 125 Mary 189 191 Molly 189 Philip 189 Richard 189 Sampson 189 Sarah 329 Thomas 189 W P/R 189 William 189 318
MATHIOT, Alice 190 Catherine 190 Christian 190 J D 190 Jean 190 Ruth 190
MATHIOTT, George 190
MATHURST, Andrew 229 Frances 229
MATLO, Elizabeth 190 George 190 Hezekiah 190 Sarah 190
MATLOCK, Ann 190 Dolly 190 Elizabeth 190 Jane 190 John 190 Lucy 190 Martha 190 May 190 Susanah 190 Thomas 190 Usly 190
MATTENLY, Nancy 152
MATTHEWS, Albert 191 Betsey 191 Bradley 192 Burrel 191 Burwell 191 Cade 191 Cady 191 Cary 191 Elbert 191 Elijah 191 Esther 190 George 191 H 178 James 191 Jeremiah 191 Louis 191 M A 115 Mahala 190 Mary 191 Nancy 191 Newman 191 Polly 191 Rosey 191 Ruby 191 Sally 191 Sarah 191 Susan 192 Thomas 189 William

MATTHEWS (continued)
191 192 Willis 191
MATTINGLEY, James 192
MATTINGLY, Dykeander 192 Elizabeth 192 Lewis 192 Massie 192 Nancy 192 Thomas 192
MATTOCKS, Jacob 192 Joseph 192 Peter 192
MATTOX, John 3
MAUCK, Matthias 193
MAUK, Andrew 164 Anna 87 192 Anthony 192 Henry 164 165 Mathias 87
MAUPIN, Albert 193 Ann 193 Anna 193 Annie 193 Bernard 193 Clay 193 Clifton 193 Cornelius 193 Cynthia 14 Daniel 91 193 Elizabeth 193 Eva 193 Frances 193 Gabriel 193 George 193 Hannah 114 Henry 193 Jane 193 Jesse 193 John 193 Judith 193 Logan 193 Lurana 79 Margaret 193 Mary 14 318 Mourning 193 Nancy 193 Peggy 193 Polly 193 Samantha 14 Sintha 14 Synthia 193 Thomas 193 Tilman 14 193 Waller 193 Wellington 14 William 14 193
MAURY, Abraham 194 Catherine 194 Elizabeth 194 Fontaine 194 James 195 Willia 194
MAUZY, Fayette 292 300 J H 194 John 194 Sarah 194 Ursula 194
MAWZEY, Susanna 61
MAXCY, Betsey 194 Susan 194
MAXEY, Ann 195 Anna 89 195 Anne 89 195 Beulah 194 Edward 194 195 Elisha 195 Elizabeth 195 Ephraim 89 Esther 61 J H 194 James 195 John 194 195 Josiah 195 Judith 195 Mary 194 195 Nancy 195 R J 195 Radford 195 Rice 195 Robert 195 Shadrach 195 William 194
MAXWELL, Alexander 195 Edward 282 Esther 195 F W 196 Franklin 268 George 195 James 195 Jane 195 282 Jessie 195 John 195 Laverda

MAXWELL (continued)
195 Louisa 195 Margaret 195 Nathaniel 195 Thomas 195 Venie 195 Wallace 195 William 195
MAY, Abram 117 Alexander 196 Ann 311 Asa 197 Booker 195 Charity 197 Charles 196 Daniel 197 David 196 Edmund 196 Elender 197 Elizabeth 196 Escheler 197 George 196 197 James 195 197 Jane 196 John 196 197 255 311 Leroy 197 Mable 197 Marry 197 Martha 196 Martin 196 Mary 117 163 197 Matilda 196 Moses 196 Orpah 197 Peter 197 Phalby 197 Rachel 197 Rhoda 197 Robert 196 Ruth 197 Samuel 197 Sarah 197 Stacy 196 Stephen 196 Susannah 196 Thesolard 197 William 196 197
MAYBERRY, George 198 William 198
MAYER, John 158
MAYES, Andrew 213 Elijah 199 Martha 198 Nancy 198 Susanah 198 Thomas 198
MAYFIELD, Micajah 198
MAYHEW, John 323
MAYNARD, James 164 N L 87
MAYNER, Mary 198
MAYO, John 198 199 Judith 198 Landy 198 Lanty 199 Pearl 199 Rebecca 199 Richardson 198
MAYS, Ann 85 Elizabeth 199 F P 199 Jane 199 Leutitia 199 Lutitia 199 Nancy 199 Prudence 199 Sarah 199 Tabitha 199
McADAM, Charles 199 Charlotte 199 George 199 Tommy 199
McAELHANY, Candace 225 Candis 225
McAFEE, Elia 183
McALEXANDER, Alexander 200 Amelia 200 David 200 Edmund 200 James 200 Jane 200 John 200 Joseph 200 Lucinda 200 Martha 200 Patsey 200 Patsy

McALEXANDER (continued) 200 Samuel 200 William 200
McALLISON, Halbert 45 Susan 45
McALLISTER/McALISTER, Adam 200 George 200 Harvey 200 James 200 John 200 Martha 200 Robert 200
McAMIS, Thomas 202
McANALLY, Charles 200 John 200 Nancy 200 Patty 200
McATTENCE, Mary 227
McBRIDE, Abram 201 Andrew 201 Ann 201 Betsy 201 Evan 201 Hannah 201 James 201 Jeremiah 201 John 201 Martha 201
McCAIN, Frederick 201 Theresa 201
McCALL, Elizabeth 98 283 Mary 98
McCALLISTER/CALISTER, Daniel 200
McCALLY, James 202
McCAMANT, Samuel 298
McCAMPBELL, Andrew 202 Ann 202 202 David 219 Jane 219 John 219 Martha 202 Mary 202
McCAMISH, Jenney 202 Jinney 202 Thomas 202 William 202
McCAN, Mary 202 Patrick 202
McCANDLESS, Alexander 202 Cynthia 202 Jane 202 Jinney 202 Polly 202 William 202
McCANN, Biddy 203 Melville 157
McCANT, Elizabeth 203 James 203 Joseph 203 Susan 203
McCARGO, David 203
McCARMICK, Abraham 203 Andrew 203 Comfort 203 Elizabeth 203 George 203 Hetty 203 Isaac 203 James 203 John 203 Mary 203 Polly 203 Sally 203 William 203
McCARROLL, William 304
McCARTER, Caty 299 Nancy 299 Thomas 299
McCARTNEY, Catherine 204
McCARTY, Ann 204 Anna 204 Anne 204 Daniel 82 316 Ida 315 Jemima 82 204 Margaret 204 Mary 204 Nicholas 204 Sarah 204 William 204
McCARY, Benjamin 204 Kitty 204

McCARY (continued) Louisa 204 Richard 204 William 204
McCASLAND, Dorothea 205 Eleanor 204 Elener 205 J I 205 James 204 205 John 205 Lovina 205 Pheby 205 Sarah 205 Susana 205 William 204 205
McCAULEY, Mary 205
McCHISICK, Daniel 304 Rachel 304
McCHRISTY, Charles 205 Isaac 205 James 205 Jesse 206 John 205 Polly 205 Sally 205 William 205
McCLAIN, Abijah 205 Grace 232 Lydia 205 Margaret 208
McCLANAHAN, Alexander 206 Blair 206 Elijah 206 Elizabeth 206 James 206 Jane 206 John 183 206 Leticia 183 Letitia 183 Letty 193 Margaret 206 Marjory 206 Mary 206 Peggy 206 Robert 206 Sarah 206 Tabitha 206 William 206 281
McCLENAHAN, Alexander 206 Elizabeth 206 Sarah 206
McCLINTIC, Alice 207 Jane 207 Robert 207 William 207
McCLINTOCK, Adam 207
McCLUNG, Elizabeth 207 James 207 Joseph 207
McCLURE, Ann 209 Betty 208 Caty 208 David 208 Elizabeth 45 208 Jane 171 208 209 Janet 208 Jemima 208 Jinny 208 John 208 Leanna 171 Levisa 208 Lulu 170 Margaret 208 Mary 208 Nancy 208 Nathaniel 208 P F 194 Peggy 208 Robert 208 Rosanna 144 Sallie 208 Sarah 208 William 208
McCLURG, James 156
McCOLLOCH, Abram 208 Ebenezer 208 Elizabeth 208 James 208 John 208 327 Margaret 208 Rebecca 208 Samuel 208 Sarah 208 William 208
McCOMAS, Catharine 208 Catherine 209 Isaac 209 Jesse 209
McCOMB, Esther 248

McCONAHEY, John 209
McCONIHEY, John 209 Mary 209
McCONNELL, Abram 209 Ann 209 Elizabeth 209 James 209 Jane 209 Mary 209 276 Rosanna 209 Thomas 209 William 209
McCORD, Charles 210
McCORKEL, Elizabeth 210
McCORKLE, Henry 85
McCORMACK, Alexander 210 Emmett 210 Nancy 210
McCORMICK, Catharine 210 Catherine 210 Isabel 139 Lewis 210 Mamie 203 Myrtle 210
McCOWAN, Agnes 138
McCOY, Agnes 211 General 211 George 211 James 211 Jesse 211 Joseph 88 Lee 23 Susan 211 Thomas 211 William 211
McCRACKEN, Patience 135
McCRAVEY, John 212
McCRAW, Ann 121 Cary 212 Francis 212 George 212 Lockey 212 Martha 212 Mary 121 Miller 212 Sally 212 Susanna 212 Thomas 212 Timothy 212 William 212
McCRAY, Lucretia 303 William 240
McCROSKEY, Margaret 211
McCROSKY, John 211 William 211
McCUBBINS, John 213 Nancy 213 Zachariah 213
McCULLOCH, Catarver 213 Kizia 213 Richard 120 Robert 213 Thomas 213
McCULLOCK, Elizabeth 213 Sarah 213 Thomas 213
McCULLOUGH, Benjamin 213 Catherine 129 Jane 213 Lititia 213 Martha 129 Mary 129 213 W E 275 William 213
McCUNE, Christiana 213 Jack 30
McCURDY, Gretchen 115
McCUTCHAN, Elizabeth 214 Jean 214 Samuel 214
McCUTCHEM, William 214
McCUTCHEN, John 214 Vera 93
McCUTCHEON, Jane 78 Samuel 214
McDANAL, Jeremiah 214 Lucretia 214 Mary 214 Nancy 214 Nathan 214 Phebe 214 William 214

McDANIEL, Alexander 214 Alfred 216 Ann 216 Anne 214 Anny 215 Benjamin 214 Caleb 214 Catharine 215 Catherine 155 Celia 215 Clement 261 Daniel 215 Edward 215 Elizabeth 68 214 215 Emily 214 Ephraim 214 215 Fountain 216 Guy 215 Icher 214 James 45 215 John 214 215 Joseph 216 Livingston 214 M 297 Margaret 215 Martha 215 216 Mary 215 Mumford 187 Nancy 45 215 Samuel 216 Sarah 214 215 Stephen 214 Thomas 215 Walter 215 Winston 216
McDAVITT, Susan 10
McDERMENT, Joseph 216
McDONALD, Catharine 217 Catherine 217 Charles 216 Clara 151 David 217 Elijah 217 Eliza 217 Elizabeth 216 217 Ellen 217 Emma 101 Ezekiel 217 Francis 216 J R 151 James 217 Jane 216 John 215 216 217 Katharine 217 Lucindy 217 Mahala 284 Margaret 216 Mary 51 217 Permeley 217 Permelia 215 Permely 217 Peter 217 Rachel 217 Stacy 269 Susanna 217
McDONOUGH, Jane 217 Margaret 217
McDORMAN, Nancy 218
McDOWELL, Archibald 206 Clyde 215 Hester 218 Isabella 218 J Q 206 James 218 Jane 218 John 218 Juliette 218 Magdalene 218 Mary 218 Nancy 218 Polley 218 Salley 218 Samuel 218 Swepson 218 William 218
McDURMID, Asenath 219 Catherine 219 Jason 219 Margaret 219 Orlesto 219
McELHANEY, Betsy 219 Jane 219 Peggy 219 Polly 219 Sophy 219 Strother 219
McELHANY, E 219 Elizabeth 219 James 219 Rachel 219
McELHENEY, Stephen 219
McELHENNY, Samuel 219 William 219

McELROY, William 82
McELWEE, Abner 219 Ann 219 Dan 219 Elizabeth 219 220 J J 220 James 219 220 L C 220 Mary 219 Rhoda 219 220 Ross 219
McEVER, Catherine 220
McEWING, Polly 220
McFADDEN, James 220
McFALLS, Duram 220 Emzay 220
McFARLAND, Carl 220 Franky 110 Hannah 221 Margaret 221 Mary 221 Robert 220
McFARRAN, Samuel 221
McFARREN, Jane 221
McFAULS, Arthur 220
McFERRIN, John 1 221 William 221
McGANNON, Alexander 221 Alice 221 Aylesey 221 Hugh 221 Jane 221 John 221 Mary 221 Reuben 221 Salley 221 Sally 221 Thomas 221 Zachariah 221
McGAUGHEY, Samuel 221
McGAUGHY, Agnes 221 Jane 221
McGAVOCK, David 222 Eliza 222 Hugh 222 Jacob 222 James 221 Joseph 222 Polly 222 Randal 222 Robert 222 Sally 222
McGEE, Ann 222 Edward 222 Dora 222 Elizabeth 222 223 Estelle 222 Esther 222 Hannah 223 Jackson 222 James 222 Jane 222 John 223 Mary 223 Micajah 222 Polly 222 Olive 222 Olivia 222 Sally 222 223 Samuel 222 Thomas 222 223 Wesley 222 William 222
McGEORGE, Elizabeth 223
McGHEE, Elizabeth 223 Judith 134
McGILL, Helen 251 William 251
McGINNIS, Anna 223 Betsey 306 William 60 223
McGLAMERY, John 290
McGLASSON, Elizabeth 223 James 223 Juda 223 Judah 223 Nancy 223 Patsey 223 William 223
McGLOUGLIN, Ann 223 Anne 223 John 223
McGORHAM, Polly 203
McGOWAN, Daniel 91

McGRAW, Elizabeth 23
McGREGOR, Ezekiel 222 Polly 222
McGUIRE, Aleygone 224 Ann 224 Elijah 224 Everet 224 Fannie 207 James 158 224 John 224 Lidea 224 Merry 224 Moses 224 Nancy 224 Polly 224 Rhoda 224 Robert 125 Williams 224
McHAFFEY, Martha 13 Patsy 13
McHAFFY, Martha 13 Patsy 13
McHANEY, Andrew 235 Fanny 224 Sarah 224 Terence 224
McHENRY, Martin 251 Mildred 251
McILHANY, Cecelia 225 Hannah 225 James 225 324 Louisa 225 Margaret 225 Mary 225 Mortimer 225
McILHENY, Moses 225
McILVAINE, Margaret 82
McILWAIN, W J 122
McINLIN, Thomas 54
McINTIRE, Anne 225 James 225 Nancy 225
McINTOSH, Anderson 225 Anna 86 Candace 225 Candis 225 Charles 226 Daniel 86 Elijah 225 Elizabeth 226 James 226 John 225 Julia 225 Margaret 225 Nancy 225 Nimrod 226 Sena 225 Thomas 226
McINTYRE, Rhoda 62
McIVER, Angus 220
McKALL, H D 155
McKAMEY, Anna 226 Ischela 226 John 226 Malinda 226 Margaret 226 Mary 226 Nancy 226 Pamela 226 Polly 226 Robert 226 Sarah 226 Sinthy 226 William 226
McKAMY, Agnes 226
McKARNY, Agnes 226 James 226
McKAY, A W 227 Adam 227 Alexander 227 Anny 227 Bennett 308 Catherine 227 Daniel 227 George 227 Hugh 226 227 Isabella 226 227 John 227 Lochland 227 Margaret 227 Nancy 226 227 Nell 227 William 227
McKEAN, Dorothea 228

McKEE, Alexander 288 Betsy 227
  Esther 227 James 227 John
  227 Lydia 227 Marthy 288 Ma-
  ry 227 Nancy 227 Nannie 227
  William 227
McKEEVER, Angus 220 Ollie 20
McKELVY, Elizabeth 228 Hugh
  228 John 228 Katharine 228
  Mary 228 William 228 Willis
  228
McKEMY, Alexander 228 Anna
  228 Elender 228 Elizabeth
  228 Hugh 228 Jane 228 Jinny
  228 John 228 Malinda 228
  Nancy 228 Poley 228 Polly
  228 Rebecka 228 Robert 228
  Samuel 228 Sarah 228
McKENNAN, Elizabeth 228 Th M T
  228
McKENNEY, Betsey 228 Elizabeth
  228 Milly 228 Rachel 228 Sa-
  muel 228 Sarah 228 Tully 231
  Wilson 228
McKENNY, Tully 231
McKENT, James 203
McKENZIE, Alexander 229 C F
  214 Catherine 231 Daisy 317
  Dora 214 Jeremiah 229 Jesse
  231 Joshua 231 Martha 229
  Moses 231 Patsy 229 Sarah
  107 231
McKIE, Benjamin 229 Daniel 229
  Elizabeth 229 Fanny 229
  Frances 229 G W 229 Green
  229 Herndon 229 Irene 229
  James 229 Juliett 229 John
  229 Margaret 229 Mariah 229
  Martha 229 Mary 229 Michael
  229 Nancy 229 Polly 229 Sarah 229 Stephen 229 Washing-
  ton 229 William 229
McKINNEY, Anna 230 Catherine
  231 Caty 231 David 230 231
  Elizabeth 230 Francis 231
  Hannah 230 Jane 230 231 Jenny 231 John 230 299 Lucinda
  231 Margaret 230 Mary 230
  231 Nancy 231 Polley 230
  Polly 231 Rebecca 230 Robert
  230 Robinson 230 Sarah 230
  231 William 231
McKINSEY, Sarah 231

McKINZIE, Tabitha 232
McKISSICK, Daniel 304 Rachel
  304
McKITRICK, John 232
McKITTRICK, Thomas 232
McKONKEY, David 209
McKOWN, Elias 232 Gilbert 232
  Isaac 232 Mary 232 Phebe 232
  Polly 232 Sarah 232
McKOY, Thomas 156
McLAIN, James 232
McLARREN, Daniel 233 Harrison
  233 Henry 233 Jane 233 Jency
  233 Susana 233
McLAUGHLIN, Alfred 234 Appy
  234 Archibald 234 Davis 233
  Ephraim 234 Jacob 233 234
  John 233 234 Judy 233 Mary
  233 234 Nancy 234 Neeley 233
  Samuel 234 Stephen 233 234
  Willis 234 Wilson 234
McLAURINE, James 234
McLEAN, Allen 233 Flora 233
  Hugh 227 Laughlan 233 Neal
  233
McLEMORE, John 156 William 156
McLOUGHLIN, Agnes 234 Ann 234
  Jane 234 Nanny 234
McLURE, Andrew 234 Ann 234
  James 234 Jane 234 John 234
  Keziah 234 Mary 234 Robert
  234
McMAHAN, Abner 235 Andrew 235
  C L 235 Elizabeth 235 Gregg
  235 Gregory 235 Henry 235
  James 235 John 235 Joseph
  235 Lucy 235 Mary 235 May
  235 Nancy 235 Oney 235 Phebe
  235 Polly 234 235 Rebecca
  235 Robert 235 Sarah 235
  Thomas 235 William 234 235
McMAHON, Joseph 235 Thomas 235
  William 235
McMannes, Ellen 236 James 236
  Joseph 236
McMANNIS, Felix 236 Fielding
  236 John 236 Margaret 236
  Nancy 236 Polly 236 Sally
  236 Thomas 236 William 236
McMANUS, Charles 236
McMEANS, Mary 159
McMECKIN, Robert 236

McMEEKIN, James 236 Martha 236 Samuel 236 William 236
McMEINS, James 236
McMICKIN, Robert 236
McMILLAN, Mary 236 Mary 236
McMILLEN, Joseph 25 Mary 236 Sabina 236 Salina 236 Sally 25
McMILLIAN, Jane 237 Jeremiah 237 Martha 236
McMILLIN, Mary 175 Thomas 236
McMULLEN, Hannah 237
McMULLIN, John 301
McMURTRY, Lucy 158 Nancy 152
McNABB, Elizabeth 237 Isaac 237 James 237
McNATT, Lucretia 237
McNAUGHT, Jennie 167 Helen 167
McNEAL, Rebecca 223
McNEELEY, David 238
McNEELY, George 237 Martha 237 Nancy 237 Rebecca 237 William 237
McNEIL, Gabriel 238
McNELLY, Mary 238
McNEMAR, George 238
McNICKLE, Neale 238
McNIEL, Robert f238
McNUTT, Margaret 221 222 Samuel 222
McPHEETERS, Margaret 238
McPHEETRS, John 238
McPHERON, Harry 193
McPHERSON, Daniel 238 Elizabeth 238 James 238 Lewin 75 Linda 238 Nancy 238 Sinny 238 Thomas 238
McPROCTOR, Maximillian 238
McQUADDY, John 239
McQUADY, Susan 239
McQUAY, Lucretia 303
McQUEEN, Elizabeth 239 Joshua 239 Sarah 70 Uriah 239
McQUIE, Alexander 231
McQUINN, Polly 240 Timothy 240 William 240
McQUOWN, Mary 240 Solomon 240
McROBERTS, Anna 240 Catherine 240 Charlotte 240 Elizabeth 240 James 240 Josiah 240 Mary 240 Samuel 240 Sarah 240 Thomas 240

McSPADDEN, Elizabeth 240 Polly 240 Susanna 240
McSPEDDEN, Mary 240 Thomas 240
McVANEY, Christopher 241
McVANY, Mary 241
McVERNARS, George 238
McVICKERS, Lucy 231
McWHINNEY, Temperance 63
McWHIRTER, Jane 311 Shelton 311
McWHORTER, Elizabeth 241 H C 241 James 241 John 241 Robert 241 Sally 241 Samuel 241 Thomas 241 William 241
McWILLIAMS, Anna 241 Dorothea 242 Elizabeth 241 Hannah 241 Hugh 241 James 241 Jane 241 John 193 242 Lizzie 242 Maggie 242 Margaret 193 Martha 241 Mary 241 242 Peggy 193 Polly 241 Samuel 241
MEACHAM, Anna 242 Ichabod 242
MEAD, Jane 243 John 243 Minor 243 Patsy 243 Polly 243 Sarah 243 William 243 244
MEADE, Benjamin 243 David 243 327 Elizabeth 243 Hodijah 243 Lincoln 243 Madison 243 Mary 243 Patsey 243 Richard 243 Sallie 243 Samuel 243 Seth 243 William 243
MEADER, Banister 244
MEADOR, Ann 244 Banister 244 Benjamin 244 Bennett 244 Betty 244 Hezekiah 244 Isham 244 Jehu 244 Jesse 244 Job 244 Jobe 244 Joel 244 Jonas 244 Joseph 244 Lydia 244 Martha 244 Merritt 244 Monroe 244 Ruth 244 Sally 244 Susie 244 Virginia 244 William 244
MEADOW, Banister 244 Hilda 244 William 245
MEADOWS, Barbara 245 Benjamin 244 Elizabeth 245 Esthel 245 Frances 245 Francis 215 Henry 245 J R 245 Jacob 244 James 215 Jane 245 Jubal 245 Mary 245 Nancy 245 Rebecca 245 Sarah 245 William 245
MEAGHER, Richard 161

MEAIRS, Alexander 171 David 171 172 Hannah 171 John 171 172 Margaret 171 Rachel 171 Shannon 171 172
MEANLEY, John 246
MEANLY, Emeline 246 George 246 James 246 John 246 Mary 246 Philadelphia 246 Sarah 246
MEANS, John 246 Margaret 241 Nancy 246 Susan 246
MEARS, David 246 Elizabeth 246 George 246 Jesse 246 Joel 246 Nancy 246 William 246
MEDCALF, Absolum 164 John 247 Nancy 154
MEDEARIS, B W H 247 Benjamin 247 Christian 247 Elizabeth 247 George 247 John 245 Margaret 247 Mary 247 Polly 247 Rachel 247 Sarah 247 Washington 247 William 247 Wily 247
MEDEASIS, John 247
MEDKIFF, Mary 247
MEDLEY, Faye 247 Samuel 247
MEDLOCK, Nathaniel 100
MEDOWS, Francis 245
MEEK, Ada 214 Bazel 247 Benjamin 248 Elizabeth 248 Esther 248 Georgia 248 John 247 Mary 248 Pollie 248 Robert 248 Salina 247 Samuel 249
MEEKS, Charles 248 Elizabeth 248
MEFFERD, John 248
MEISNER, M S 81 194
MELLEN, Calvert 78
MELTON, Benjamin 249 Betsey 248 Elizabeth 248 John 248 Nancy 248 Sarah 248 Tebbie 248
MENEFEE, Henry 249 Mary 249 Sarah 249
MENTO, Margaret 329
MERCER, A L 249 George 249 James 322 John 249 Lucy 249 William 249
MERCHANT, Elizabeth 185
MEREDETH, David 249 Davis 249 Elizabeth 249 Jesse 249 Keziah 249
MEREDITH, David 249 James 249

MEREDITH (continued) Jesse 249 Mary 249 Meecha 249 Mercha 249 Rosella 249 Rudolph 314
MEREWETHER, David 250 George 250 Martha 250 Mildred 250 Priscilla 250 Thomas 250 William 250
MERITT, Nancy 250
MERIWETHER, Albert 251 Alexander 250 Catherine 251 David 251 Elizabeth 251 Emily 251 James 250 251 312 Martha 251 Mildred 251 Thomas 250 251 William 251
MERRELL, Elizabeth 251
MERRILL, Andrew 251
MERRIMAN, Dicy 251 Martha 251 Phebe 251
MERRIT, Daniel 251 Levi 251 Samuel 252
MERRITT, Benjamin 251 Daniel 251 David 251 Elizabeth 179 Happey 251 James 252 Laney 251 Lavoiney 251 Lucy 251 Mary 242 Nancy 251 Pallman 251 Poley 251 Saley 251 Samuel 252 Sidney 251 Susanna 251 Washington 251
MERRY, Philip 322 Rose 252
MERRYMAN, Mary 29
MERSHON, Elizabeth 252
MESHAW, Nancy 179
MESSHEU, Jessie 252
METCALF, Anthony 253 Charlton 188 Ellenor 188 James 188 Joseph 188 Letitia 178 Mary 252 Warren 252
METHEANY, Anne 253 Archibald 253 Daniel 253 Elender 253 Ellender 253 Emillia 253 John 253 Joshua 253 Luke 253 Margaret 253 Mary 253 Milley 253 Mily 253 Moly 253 Sarah 253 Sary 253 William 253
MEURE, Olivia 222
MICHAEL, Catherine 253 Elizabeth 253
MICHAUX, Elizabeth 309
MICHEL, David 190 James 190
MICHIE, Betsey 253 Elizabeth 193 Judith 253 Lucy 253 Nan-

MICHIE (continued)
  cey 193
MICHUM, Collin
MICOU, Anna 253 Evelin 253
  James 271 320 Jane 253 Melissa 253
MIDCALF, Absolum 164 Nancy 164
MIDDLEBROOK, Lucy 254 Mary 254
  Sally 254
MIDDLECOFF, J P 92
MIDDLESWART, Elizabeth 254
  Hannah 254 James 254 Jane
  254 Mary 254 Sarah 254
MIDDLESWORT, Jacob 254
MIDDLETON, Aubin 254 Arthur
  254 Benjamin 254 Eleanor 254
  George 254 John 254 Mary 254
  William 308
MIDETON, John 254
MILAM, Edward 255 Henry 255
  Mary 255 Polly 255
MILBURN, Beca 255 Bethea 255
  Bethia 255 Bethire 255 David
  255 Elizabeth 255 Malinda
  255 Mary 255 Nancy 255 Polly
  255 Rachel 255 Sarah 255
  William 255
MILES, Alice 256 Ames 256 Ann
  256 Benjamin 256 Betsey 256
  Byrd 256 Elizabeth 256 Frances
  256 Grace 256 Hannah 256
  Hartwell 256 Heartwell 256
  Louisa 256 Jane 256 Jefferson
  256 John 256 Mary 256
  Patterson 256 Patsey 256
  Patty 256 Phanny 256 Polly
  256 Reuben 256 Sarah 256
  Thomas 256 Wats 256 William
  256
MILLAM, Rush 255
MILLAR, Deborah 257 Martin 257
  Matilda 257 Taliaferro 257
  William 257
MILLBANK, Anny 257 Charles 257
  Elender 257 Elizabeth 257
  Mary 257 Sally 257
MILLENBARGER, Catharine 81
MILLER, Agnes 264 Alexander
  263 Ann 259 260 262 263 Anna
  262 Annis 263 Averilla 259
  Barbara 258 259 Barbary 258
  Barney 72 257 Benjamin 258

MILLER (continued)
  Betsy 254 C 135 Catharine
  258 259 264 Catherine 262
  Cathy 259 Christina 259
  Christopher 258 Daniel 263
  David 259 Delaney 262 E B
  329 Edward 259 Eliza 261
  Elizabeth 258 259 260 262
  264 271 Emanuel 262 Eve 262
  Frances 262 Gabriel 259 Garand 262 George 261 262 Gerard 262 Henry 192 258 259
  260 264 Ichabod 264 Isaac
  258 259 261 262 Isabella 259
  Jacob 258 259 260 262 James
  10 258 259 264 Jane 22 262
  263 Joanna 264 John 258 259
  260 261 262 264 285 Jonathan
  258 Joseph 258 262 Lewis 34
  262 Lois 263 Louis 262 Lucy
  34 261 Luke 258 Margaret 260
  261 263 Martha 264 Mary 72
  289 258 260 261 283 265 268
  Mason 259 Matilda 34 May 47
  Merriman 259 Molly 189 Myrtilla 258 Nancy 262 263 264
  Nathan 264 Nicholas 257 Patsey 259 Philip 258 Polly 259
  262 Presley 258 Rachel 262
  Rebecca 259 264 Robert 262
  263 Sally 110 Samuel 261 Sarah 258 260 Shepard 271 299
  302 Squire 263 Susannah 258
  Teny 261 Thomas 262 264 310
  Tissue 258 Valentine 263
  William 258 259 261 262 263
  264 265 287 296
MILLERWAY, George 265 Isaac
  265 John 265 Nancy 265 Patsey 265 Susan 265 William
  265
MILLIGAN, Mary 265
MILLION, Sarah 265
MILLOWAY, George 265
MILLS, Agness 265 266 Ann 266
  Caty 266 Elizabeth 266 Emily
  299 Frances 266 Francis 266
  Hezekiah 266 J J T 266 Jacob
  267 James 266 Jane 266 Joseph 267 John 266 299 Keren
  267 Letticia 3 Lydia 266 Mary 266 267 Mattie 267 Nancy

MILLS (continued)
228 266 Ruth 266 Sally 267
Samuel 266 Sarah 266 William 266
MILTON, Benjamin 248 Bushrod 268 Caroline 268 Ebin 268 George 268 John 268 Kitty 268 William 268
MILUM, Jordon 255
MILWEE, Thomas 198
MINEAR, Elizabeth 268 Enoch 268 John 268 Jonathan 268 Mary 269
MINER, John 268 Samuel 303
MINGE, John 175 Sarah 175
MINNEY, Barney 22 Susannah 22
MINNIX, Colohill 268
MINOR, Alfred 270 Alice 270 Ann 269 270 271 Annie 270 Archibald 270 Barbara 270 Casandra 268 Coleman 269 Dabney 271 Daniel 269 Edward 269 Eldred 271 Elizabeth 269 270 271 Ephraim 270 Garrit 271 George 268 270 271 Hubbard 270 Jacob 268 James 270 271 Jefferson 270 John 269 271 Joseph 269 270 Larkin 268 Lewis 270 Lucy 270 Malinda 270 Marthy 270 Mary 269 270 271 Matilda 270 Nancy 269 270 Patsey 270 Peggy 269 Rebecca 269 Rebeccah 269 Reuben 268 Robert 242 269 Sarah 270 Spence 269 Stella 270 Thomas 269 270 271 Threesilvolius 271 William 242 268 270
MINSEY, Harriet 169
MINTER, Catherine 271 Johanna 271 Joice 271 Margaret 271 Mary 271
MINTON, Betsey 271 Ebenezer 271 Elizabeth 271 Fanny 271 Isaac 271 Jane 271 Liddie 271 Preston 271 Vardeman 271 Washington 271
MINZEY, Harriet 169
MINZIES, Hannah 272
MITCHAEL, Frances 13
MITCHEL, Amasa 272 Fanny 64 Mark 275

MITCHELL, A 277 Absolute 275 Alfred 275 Andrew 217 Ann 273 275 278 C 276 Chloe 278 Claiborne 277 D E 23 Dagworthy 275 Deborah 275 277 Drewry 274 Drury 274 E L 123 Edward 277 Eleanor 277 Eliza 272 277 Elizabeth 3 273 274 275 Eve 276 Fleming 272 Floodde 273 Frederick 278 George 273 276 Giles 278 Grace 277 Harvey 272 Henry 275 277 Isaac 275 277 J S 273 James 272 273 275 278 Jane 4 John 272 274 277 Jones 275 Kity 217 Labin 275 Letitia 276 Letty 276 Lucy 272 276 Malinda 276 Margaret 276 Martha 194 274 275 Mary 42 272 275 276 277 Nancy 273 277 Nanny 277 Nathaniel 33 Ned 276 Oliva 278 Paul 276 Peggy 275 276 Peyton 277 Philip 278 Polly 275 278 Reuben 276 Rheuben 276 Richard 291 Robert 276 312 328 S D 47 Salley 276 Sally 277 Samuel 273 276 277 Sarah 217 274 276 277 Susannah 275 Theodore 275 Thomas 275 277 William 4 275 277 278 Winny 277
MITCHEN, Isabella 278 Samuel 278
MITCHIAM, Collin 278
MIZE, Wiley 278
MOBELEY, John 111 Keziah 111
MOBELY, Keziah 111
MOBLEY, Isaiah 278 Keziah 111 Sibella 278
MOBLY, Clemmant 278
MODERELL, Robert 278
MOFFETT, Ann 295 Elizabeth 279 Hannah 279 Jesse 323 John 279
MOHN, Elmer 115 Gretchen 115
MOLDING, Amy 250
MOLER, Jacob 279
MOLLIHON, John 279
MOLSBE, William 279
MOLSBEE, William 279
MOLSBEY, David 279 Marget 279

MOLSBEY, Nanny 279 Polley 279
William 279
MONDAY, Elizabeth 28
MONROE, Alexander 280 315 Andrew 280 281 Ann 281 Bernyce 322 Betsey 280 Betsy 281 Elenor 280 Eliza 280 Elizabeth 280 281 Fanny 281 Forest 280 George 280 H E 319 James 290 Jency 281 John 280 281 303 319 Joseph 321 Lillian 280 Lucy 281 Margaret 280 Maria 280 Mary 280 281 Nancy 280 Polly 280 303 Rachel 281 Rebekah 280 Sally 280 281 Sarah 315 Sidney 315 Susannah 281 Waters 280 William 280 282 Winifred 280 Woodson 280
MONTACUE, Peter 281
MONTAGUE, Abraham 281 Ann 281 Augustus 281 Charlotte 281 Clarasa 281 Jacob 281 Jane 281 282 Katharine 281 Katherine 281 Mickebrough 282 Peter 282 Philip 281 282 320 Randolph 282 Rice 281 282 Richard 281 282 Sarah 281 Thomas 281 282 W 281 William 281 282
MONTGOMERY, A B 137 Alexander 283 Ann 87 David 283 Elizabeth 283 Eve 282 F L 4 Fanny 284 Frances 284 George 282 Helen 263 Henry 282 283 Hugh 2 282 Isabella 282 James 87 282 283 Jane 282 Janet 282 Jesse 284 John 282 283 284 Jonah 283 Jordan 284 Joseph 283 Margaret 282 283 Martha 282 Mary 282 Michael 283 Nancy 283 Peggy 282 Richard 283 Robert 282 283 Sarah 282 306 Thomas 284 306 William 87 283
MONTH, Agnes 284 Daphne 284 Mahala 284 Mary 284
MOODY, Alfred 284 Annie 284 Billy 284 Catherine 285 Celia 285 Cely 284 Charlotte 284 David 284 Elsada 284 Fanny 284 Frances 284 Franky

MOODY (continued)
284 Jameson 98 Jefferson 284 Joel 284 285 John 285 Katey 284 Levi 284 Lewis 99 Nancey 284 Phoebe 284 Polly 284 285 Sally 284 285 Sarah 284 Selah 285 W L 98 William 285
MOOK, L C 239
MOOMAH, Christopher 320
MOOMAW, Christopher 320
MOON, Ann 285 Christopher 286 Darcas 304 John 127 Nancy 285
MOONEY, Anderson 286 Bryant 286 Edith 286 Esther 201 John 286 Margaret 286 Mary 286 Mildred 286 Milly 286 Patsey 286 Patsy 286 Richard 286 Thomas 286
MOOR, Michael 292 Robert 293
MOORE, Agnes 290 Alexander 155 Alfred 288 Alice 288 Alicia 252 Alta 292 Amos 287 Andromache 290 Ann 166 287 289 201 294 Anne 288 289 Barbara 292 Betsy 288 295 Blackwell 292 Catharine 293 Catherine 293 Caty 293 Clark 330 Cynthia 18 David 289 290 293 Edward 166 Eleanor 290 Elenor 290 Elisha 206 Elizabeth 287 290 291 292 293 294 Frances 292 Franky 294 George 289 292 295 Hancock 294 Hannah 290 Henry 293 294 Hugh 288 James 288 290 293 294 Jane 288 Jeremiah 294 Jesse 288 John 127 287 288 289 290 291 293 294 Jonathan 291 292 293 294 Josiah 288 Judith 287 291 Levi 289 293 Louise 292 Margaret 292 Marshall 294 Martha 166 288 292 Mary 170 206 286 289 290 292 295 Matilda 288 Mildred 290 Morris 290 Nancy 127 288 289 290 292 293 295 Nell 290 Olivia 294 Phebe 289 Polly 18 170 288 293 294 Rachel 90 288 293 294 Rebecca 289 291 Rhody 289 Robert 288 292 293 S A 81 S McD 287 Sally 287

MOORE (continued)
293 295 305 Sarah 206 229
287 288 293 295 Silas 294
Sukey 293 T A 231 Tabitha
294 Thorressa 143 William
52 123 165 170 288 289 290
292 293 294 306 Winney 290
MOORMAN, Ann 181 Anne 180 Elizabeth 25
MORAN, Margaret 137 Stephen 137
MORBERLY, Patsy 306
MOREHEAD, Ann 295 Anne 300 Armistead 300 Dudley 295 Elizabeth 300 John 300 Julia 300 Mary 300 Robert 300 Susan 300 Susanna 300
MORELAND, Anne 296 Catherine 296 Elizabeth 296 John 296 Malinda 296 Mary 296 Samuel 296 Temperance 296 William 296 Winney 296
MOREN, Hazel 20
MORGAN, Aaron 296 Ann 296 299 302 Anne 299 300 Austin 311 Benjamin 297 Catherine 302 Charles 297 300 301 Cina 302 D 301 Daniel 297 300 301 David 297 302 Drucilla 300 Drusilla 301 302 Edward 208 Eleanor 297 Elizabeth 158 296 297 298 299 300 302 Evan 297 298 302 George 289 Hannah 297 299 Haynes Jacob 300 James 297 299 301 302 Jane 300 Jesse 296 John 295 298 300 302 June 117 Katharine 81 Lucinda 300 Lucy 311 Lydia 301 Margaret 208 298 Mark 298 Martha 127 Mary 88 297 301 302 Morgan 297 300 302 Moses 296 Nancy 297 298 Naomi 298 Nathan 299 Nathaniel 300 Nell 300 Phebe 296 Raleigh 301 Rebecca 297 300 301 Ritta 299 Robert 301 Sally 302 Samuel 302 Sarah 296 299 Simon 300 Sina 302 Stephen 302 Susan 298 Susanna 298 300 Susannah 297 300 William 299 300 Willis 299 Zackwell 302 Zacquil 158 297

MORGAN (continued)
298
MORING, Elizabeth 302
MORLATT, Peter 171
MORRELL, Ann 303 John 303 Polly 303 Susan 303
MORRIS, Aaron 305 Amos 303 Andrew 303 Angelia 304 Ann 303 304 305 Archibald 303 Barton 306 Betsey 305 Betsy 306 Catey 304 Christianna 304 Dabney 304 Darcas 304 Edward 131 Eleanor 306 Elizabeth 304 305 306 Ennis 306 Essie 111 Ethel 144 Frances 43 305 George 303 305 H F 306 Hannah 303 Harry 306 Henry 209 Huston 303 Isaac 303 James 303 305 Jane 306 Janetta 306 Jesse 324 Joana 303 Joanna 303 John 144 205 232 304 Kitturah 306 Leonard 43 Leroy 111 Levi 43 303 Lewis 306 Lot 303 Louisa 306 Lucretia 303 Lucinda 306 Lucy 304 305 Margaret 305 306 Martha 305 Mary 131 304 306 Malinda 303 Micajah 305 Mylls 305 Nancy 303 Patsy 306 Peggy 306 Peria 303 Polley 304 Polly 85 304 305 Rachel 205 232 304 Rebecca 303 Richard 85 304 305 Robert 303 Sally 304 305 Sarah 303 304 Simpson 306 Susan 303 304 305 Tandy 304 Theodore 303 Thomas 85 131 305 306 William 304 305 306
MORRISON, Anna 307 Betsey 307 David 307 Elizabeth 65 306 308 Estelle 210 George 307 James 307 Jane 307 John 307 Martha 307 Mary 310 Maude 307 Nelly 307 Polley 307 Rachel 307 Rhoda 307 Sally 307 W R 16 Wilbur 268 William 307
MORROW, David 308 Jane 308 Margaret 257
MORSE, Alexander 308
MORTIMER, Elvira 309 Emanuel 309 Hazel 308 309 Mary 308

MORTIMER (continued)
 Sarah 309 William 309
MORTIMORE, Famous 309
MORTON, Abbie 309 Anderson 318
 Elizabeth 300 John 300 309
 James 300 Mayme 309 Richard
 309 Susannah 310 William 309
 310 Willis 300
MOSBY, Benjamin 310 Dianna 311
 Elbert 310 Elizabeth 311
 Charles 310 Clarissa 310 Daniel 310 Diana 311 Jacob 320
 James 229 Jesse 311 Joe 228
 John 229 300 Joseph 310
 Littleberry 310 Margaret 229
 Maria 229 Mariah 229 Mary
 310 Michael 229 Nancy 311
 Nathan 229 Samuel 310 Susanna 310 Wade 310 William 229
 Zoradia 229
MOSE, S A 26
MOSELEY, Ann 311 312 Burwell
 312 Daniel 312 Eliza 311
 Elizabeth 312 Francis 312
 Jane 311 Judith 108 311 Lucy 311 Margaret 311 Martha
 311 Mary 311 Matthew 311
 Nancy 311 312 Sally 311 Sarah 100 Thomas 312 Tully 312
 William 311 312
MOSELY, Elizabeth 95 James 311
 Leonard 312 Martha 317 Peter 312
MOSS, Helms 313 Isabelle 313
 Jackson 313 James 313 Jane
 313 Jennett 313 Jenny 313
 Judith 187 Nathaniel 299
 Priscilla 313 Ray 230 Reuben
 187 Samuel 313 Thomas 326
 William 313 314 316 322 326
MOSSOM, Nelly 314
MOSSUM, David 314
MOTHERSHEAD, Alvan 314 Barzilla 314 Elizabeth 314 John
 314 M B 314 Moses 314 Polly
 314 Sally 314 Tabitha 314
 Ruth 314
MOTHERSHED, Nathaniel 314
MOTLEY, Robert 7
MOTT, Polly 305
MOUNT, Catherine 204 Dinah 315
 Mather 314 Mathew 314

MOUNTJOY, Alvin 315 Elizabeth
 315 Mary 315 Richard 315 Sarah 315 Thomas 315 William
 315
MOUNTS, Caleb 315 Jessica 315
 Maria 315 Nancy 315 Providence 315 Polly 315 Rachel
 315
MOURY, Sophia 57
MOUTRY, Lucy 316
MOWRY, Peter 296 Sophia 57
MOXLEY, Hannah 316 Joseph 316
 William 316
MOXTON, Jane 308
MOYER, Adam 331 Henry 331
MOYERS, Peter 316
MOZLEY, Daniel 317 Dixon 317
 Jane 317 Maria 317 Martha
 317 Mary 317 William 317
MUCKLEVAINE, Jacob 317
MUCKLEWAINE, Tunis 317
MUFFETT, Hannah 23
MUIRHEAD, Andrew 317
MULBERRY, Cela 317 Elizabeth
 317 Fanny 317 Mary 317
MULLEN, Joshua 318 Rachel 35
 Sarah 317 William 317
MULLENS, Anthony 318 Betsy 318
 John 318 Joseph 318 319 Joshua 318 Mary 318 Nancy 318
MULLIGAN, Denis 183 Grace 183
MULLINGS, Agnes 318 Amey 318
 Frances 318 Latitia 318
 James 319
MULLINS, Anna 318 Anthony 318
 Coleman 319 Dianna 320 Dorcas 319 Elizabeth 320 Ephraim 319 Gabriel 318 Hosea
 320 James 319 Jane 319 John
 318 Joshua 318 Julia 320
 Mandlin 320 Martha 319 Mary
 318 319 Matthew 318 Nancy
 319 320 Paul 329 Polly 319
 Samuel 320 Sarah 319 Stephen
 319 Susannah 319 William 318
 319
MUMFORD, Mary 72
MUMMA, Christopher 320
MUNDAY, Abraham 321 Ann 320
 Charles 321 Chloe 320 Clark
 321 Elizabeth 320 Evana 321
 Fletcher 320 Isabella 321

MUNDAY (continued)
  Jane 321 Jeremiah 320 Jonathan 320 321 Mary 321 Matilda 321 Monroe 320 Nancy 321 Osbourn 320 Patsey 320 Reuben 321 Rosannah 320 Samuel 321 Spencer 320 Thomas 321 Walker 321
MUNDELL, Charlotte 321 Fanny 321 Joseph 321 Thomas 321 William 321
MUNDLE, John 321
MUNDY, Chloe 320 Fletcher 320 Isaac 321 James 321 John 321 Man 321 Monroe 320 Nancy 321 Reuben 321 Spencer 320 William 321
MUNFORD, Elizabeth 321 Thomas 321 William 321
MUNN, Alice 322 Azuba 322 Eleanor 322 Hannah 322 John 322 Mary 322 Solomon 322 William 322
MUNROE, Spencer 322
MURCER, Daniel 322 Herman 322 Silas 322 Thomas 322
MURDEN, James 323 Mary 323 Polly 323
MURDOCH, John 322
MURDOCHS, James 322 Jane 322 John 322 Joseph 322 Margaret 322 Mary 322 Nathan 322 Robert 322
MURDOCK, John 322
MURELL, Samuel 329
MURPHEY, Alexander 323 Clarissa 323 Elizabeth 323 Eveline 323 Gabriel 324 Hezekiah 324 John 323 Joseph 325 Lucy 323 Mary 323 Murtila 34 Nancy 323 Polly 323 Sally 323 Travis 323 William 326
MURPHY, Albert 325 Ann 324 Anthony 322 Benjamin 324 Cynthia 325 David 325 Delilah 325 Elizabeth 325 Francis 325 Grace 277 Henderson 324 325 Hiram 277 James 323 324 325 John 279 325 Joseph 325 326 Kasiah 325 Ketura 325 Lewis 325 Mabel 325 Magdalin 324 Mariney 325 Martha 325

MURPHY (continued)
  Mary 323 324 Millie 325 Nancy 325 Oratia 324 Rachel 325 Samuel 324 Sarah 324 325 326 Sary 324 Susan 325 Tamfrey 325 William 324 325 326
MURRAH, Abraham 320 All 326 Emanuel 326 Jane 326 Jeremiah 326 John 326 Joseph 326 Joshua 326 Light 326 Lucy 326 Margaret 326 Mary 179 Nancy 326 Robert 326 Sally 326 Williams 326
MURRAY, David 327 Elizabeth 326 F D 326 H H 208 Ida 326 James 326 Lucinda 327 Mary 326 Mildred 326 Simeon 326 Susannah 326
MURRELL, Alis 327 Artemicy 327 Betsey 327 328 Charlotte 327 Elizabeth 328 Geminy 327 George 328 Granville 328 Hezekiah 328 Isaac 327 James 328 Jefferson 327 Jemima 328 Jenney 328 John 327 Lemuel 327 Lucy 327 328 Mary 327 Matilda 327 328 Nancy 327 Polley 328 Rachel 327 Richard 327 Robert 328 Samuel 328 Sarah 327 328 Schuyler 328 Susannah 328 Thomas 327 William 327 328
MURREY, Samuel 316
MURRY, Charles 326 Mark 327 Mary 328 Sany 328
MURSH, Elizabeth 328 James 328 John 328 Rhoda 328 Rhody 328 Sally 328 Sarah 328
MURTLE, John 329
MUSE, Elizabeth 329 Fauntley 329 James 329 John 329 Mary 329 Olive 222 Olivia 222 William 46
MUSGROVE, Abigail 329 Elizabeth 329 Ephraim 329 John 329 Polly 304 Samuel 329 Sidney 329
MUSICK, Abraham 330 Ephraim 330 Lewis 330 Obadiah 330 William 330
MUSTAIN, Drury 330 Joel 330 John 331 Mary 330 Molley 330

MUSTAIN (continued)
  Saluda 330 Seludy 330 Shadrack 330
MYER, John 158
MYERS, Adam 331 Barbara 331 Elizabeth 331 Frederick 331 George 331 Hanah 331 Isaac 331 Jacob 331 John 331 Mary 331 Peter 331 Priscilla 331 Sarah 331 Silas 331 Susannah 331 William 331
NANCE, James 330 Polly 143
NASH, Alpha 239
NATIONS, Mae 125
NEAL, Elizabeth 17 John 330
NEAT, Sally 37
NEELEY, Andrew 206 Elizabeth 105 206 Sarah 206 William 105
NELSON, William 307
NETHERLAND, Jane 282
NETHERTON, Polly 111
NEVILL, James 330 John 205
NEWBERRY, Ann 303
NEWCOM, Eve 106
NEWELL, W H 179
NEWLAND, Magdalin 324
NEWLIN, Magdalin 324
NEWMAN, Alexander 302 Mason 329
NICHOLAS, John 317
NICHOLS, Frank 263 Martha 316 Rachel 6
NICHOLSON, Daniel 83 Lavica 82
NICK, William 83
NIMMO, Ann 189 James 189 John 189
NISBET, Agnes 61 Archibald 61 Nancy 61 Robert 61 William 61
NIX, Elizabeth 20
NOLAND, John 264
NORMENT, W B 30
NORRIS, Sarah 159
NORTHINGTON, Betsy 299
NORTHROP, Henry 199
NUGEN, Elizabeth 111 Mary 111
NUNN, James 246
O'BANNON, Jemima 33
O'DANIEL, Eva 189
O'NEAL, Rosa 247
O'REAR, Daniel 114

OBRIAN, Christiana 213
OBRIEN, Christiana 213
OAKES, Mary 86
OGDEN, James 302
OGLESBY, Z W 108
OLDAKER, Isaac 24 Rebecca 24
OLIVE, Berry 101 Delilah 101 John 101
OLLIVE, Rebecca 110 Thomas 110
OLMAN, Polly 23
OMOHUNDRO, R C 320
ORR, Elender 253 W O 276
ORRICK, Charles 331
OSBORN, Ann 33 Mary 110
OSBORNE, Alexander 41 Beulah 138 C D 138 James 41 Sarah 89
OSTIEN, Olive 232
OTTING, Sena 1258
OTTINGER, Elender 228
OUTTEN, Augustus 291 Elizabeth 291 John 291 Margaret 291 Martha 291 Mary 291 Powell 291 Shadrach 291
OVERFIELD, Sarah 170
OWEN, Abraham 319 James 259 Polly 280 Susannah 319 W O 101
OWENS, Averilla 259 Michey 91 Thomas 259
OWSLEY, Nudegate 87
PACK, Jane 134
PACKARD, Mary 138
PADEN, A D 26
PALMER, Dorothy 132 James 132 Nup 132
PAMPHLIN, William 144
PANCOAST, Carrie 129
PANGLE, Vany 94
PANKY, Susannah 143
PANNELL, Patty 200
PANNILL, William 296 330
PARES, Christian 38 Christina 38
PARK, Catharine 156
PARKER, Ann 48 Elizabeth 258 George 294 Hannah 225 Henry 258 John 48 266 Mary 31 121 Richard 121 322
PARKES, Samuel 74
PARKESON, Mary 196
PARKS, Frances 154

PARMER, Martha 166
PARNELL, James 55
PARRISH, Bessie 298 Christina 38
PARSONS, Abijah 261 Betsey 100 Grant 268 Joseph 247 Mary 247
PASEL, Mary 241
PASSMORE, Charles 181 Susie 181
PATE, Mary 75 Mathew 301
PATERSON, Emilia 50 Milly 50
PATTEN, Lucy 249
PATTERSON, David 285 Edward 221 Jane 250 John 21 Lottie 250 Susanna 250
PATTESON, David 311 J M 311
PATTISON, John 311
PATTON, Elizabeth 25 M B 120 Sarah 40 Will 120
PAUL, Alice 260 Elizabeth 260
PAXTON, Estaline 51
PAYNE, Charlotte 8 Daniel 308 Eleanor 39 Elvira 309 James 308 John 308 Nelly 39 Thomas 275
PAYTON, Richard 291
PEACHY, Alice 49
PEACOCK, Mary 255 Richard 270
PEARCE, Mary 286
PEARSE, James 287 John 287 Lucy 286 Mary 286 Nancy 286 Philadelphia 286
PEARSON, Mary 214
PECK, Christiana 148 Thomas 123 148
PEDEN, Jane 309
PEEPLES, Drury 14 Lewis 263 Sally 14 Wyatt 15
PEGRAM, John 317
PEGUES, Mary 142
PEIRCE, Mary 286
PENCE, Abraham 57 John 126 Reuben 57 Sarah 126
PENDLETON, H L 27 John 254 270 Philip 286 Samuel 232
PENNEY, Martha 27
PENNINGTON, Ann 275 Kichen 277 Kinchen 277 Robert 276
PENNYBACKER, T B 225
PEPPER, Annie 305
PERCY, Sarah 260

PERDUE, John 180 Martha 180 Patsey 180
PERIMAN, W F 308
PERIMMER, Lizzie 26
PERKINS, Archelaus 265 Deborah 277 E K 227 Emma 227 Louisiana 29 Nancy 161 Richard 312 Sally 322 William 161
PERKINSON, Ezekiel 279
PERRIGO, Harry 110
PERRIN, Martha 65 Patsy 65 William 321
PERRY, Betsy 168 John 179 Nancy 179
PERSON, Robert 83 Martha 83
PETTIT, Amos 315 Sally 70
PETTUS, Thomas 318
PETTY, Elizabeth 296
PETUMAN, Susan 149
PEYTON, Ann 123 John 123
PHELPS, Frances 29 Lydia 30
PHILLIPS, J M 94 Margaret 241 Mattie 267 Nancy 245 Sarah 197 Thomas 197 Zachariah 245
PICKENS, John 311 Martha 311 Patty 311
PICKETT, Elizabeth 301 Hannah 108 Lucy 301 Mary 108 175 William 107 301
PICKLE, Margaret 130
PIERCE, Ellen 105 Mary 286
PIERREPONT, A V D 167
PIGG, E L 241 Lewis 241 Sally 241
PILCHER, Elizabeth 107 Mary 107
PILLOW, Mary 26
PINCKARD, May 21
PINKINGTON, John 314 Mary 314
PINKTON, Eleanor 306 Elias 306 Nancy 280
PINNELL, H F 201 Halene 201
PITCHER, Elizabeth 107
PITMAN, Andrew 268 Margaret 268
PITTMAN, Alsey 32 Micager 32 Nancy 32
PLEASANTS, John 123 230 Mary 123 187 Robert 287
POE, Susan 298 Susanna 298
POFF, Adam 316
POINDEXTER, A G 125 John 243

POINDEXTER (continued)
  304 Mary 310 Parke 295 312
  Parker 233
POINTER, Samuel 298
POLLARD, Elijah 295 Fanny 250
  284 Frances 250 284 James
  246 Priscilla 250 Robert 246
  292 308 Robin 269 Sally 250
POPE, Nathaniel 316
PORNELL, James 55
PORTER, Anna 174 Edwin 194
  Elizabeth 228 Ella 231 Eunice 35 James 83 Mary 208
  Phebe 251 Polly 194 Sally
  190 Sarah 83 William 298
PORTERFIELD, Mary 301 William
  301
PORTLOCK, James 325 William
  325
POTTER, Addie 76 207
POTTINGER, Forrest 13 Samuel
  13
POTTS, Francis 190 Margaret
  190 William 190
POULSON, Elizabeth 12 James 12
POWELL, George 263 John 316
  Peyton 315 Peytona 154
POWER, Elizabeth 321 Mary 122
  Thomas 321
POWERS, Jane 182 Sarah 165
PRENTZ, Elizabeth 54 Philip 54
PRESSOR, Henry 60 Rebecca 60
  Sarah 60
PRESTON, Bowker 275 Pleasant
  275
PREWETT, George 42
PRIBBLE, John 322
PRICE, Ann 10 Elizabeth 23
  James 23 Mary 260
PRICKETT, Drusilla 300
PRIGMORE, Kezia 96 Levinia 96
  Lucinda 96 Mahala 96 Malinda
  96 Polly 96 Ruth 96 Sally 96
  Thomas 96
PRINCE, Elizabeth 54 H H 190
  John 190 Philip 54 William
  83
PRIOR, Clarissa 128
PRITCHET, Nancy 283 Zebulon
  282
PRITCHETT, Robert 142
PROCTOR, Abraham 152 Fanny 152

PROCTOR (continued)
  George 152 Hannah 152 Larkin
  152 Lucy 152 Mary 152 238
  Maximilian 238 Newton 152
  Nolley 152 Patsey 152 William 152 Winifred 7
PRUIT, John 233
PRYOR, Elizabeth 90 John 90
  Jane 243 Samuel 25
PUCKETT, Nettie 121
PUCKINGTON, John 314 Mary 314
PUGH, Ann 216 Josiah 259 271
PURDY, Samuel 315
PURKINS, Peggy 75 Richard 75
PURYEAR, Jane 299 Susannah 320
PUSEY, Josiah 320
PUSIE, Mary 241
PUSSE, Mary 241
PUTNAM, Elizabeth 63
PYLE, Jane 171
QUARLES, J C 7
QUARRIER, Alexander 317
QUIMBY, Freeman 295
QUIN, Bertha 9 Elsie 9 Keseah
  18 Kisiah 18
RADFORD, Elizabeth 312 William
  312
RAGSDALE, Amy 250 John 250 Rebecca 250 Richard 250
RAIFORD, Mollie 108
RAIN, Amelia 98
RAINEY, Sanford 320
RAITHEL, Margaret 161
RALSTON, John 214 William 187
RAMBLES, Sarah 317
RAMSEY, Betsy 203 Elizabeth
  203 LeMaire 302 Susan 49 Susannah 49 William 237
RANDOLPH, Charlotte 243 Edwin
  243 Edmund 243 Maria 243
  Peyton 243 Richard 60
RANK, J B 167
RANKIN, James 186 Margaret 186
RANKINS, Ury 170
RANSDELL, Eva 193 Martha 83
RANSEN, Ann 212 William 212
RANSOM, G W 286
RANSOME, Frances 13
RAPELER, Mary 149
RATCLIFFE, Robert 322
RATHBONE, Eliza 277 Lewis 277
RATHER, James 267 Keron 267

RATHER (continued)
    Lucy 267
RAVENSCROFT, Sarah 40
RAWLINGS, Delila 52 John 52
RAY, Sarah 8 Thomas 297 302
RAYLA, Peggy 79
READ, Edmond 114 Edmund 114
    Paulina 114
RECTOR, Sally 79 Sarah 76
    Wharton 97
REDDEN, Margaret 219
REDDING, Sarah 11
REDFORD, Robert 287
REECE, William 301
REED, G R 37
REEDY, Isaac 301
REES, Daniel 315 Malinda 33
REESE, Charlotte 321 George
    321
REHFELDT, F F 247
REICHARD, Henrietta 150
REID, Andrew 287 David 78 Haller 196 Margaret 78 Nora 99 Sally 287 Samuel 331 Sarah 287
REN, Letitia 276 Letty 276 William 76
RENO, Clarecey 75 William 75
RENTFROE, Winiford 96
RESLER, Rebecca 158
RETECKER, Mary 171
REYNOLDS, Cora 79 Elizabeth 247 Louise 240
RHEA, Archibald 184 William 116
RHODES, Mary 39
RHONEMUS, Jessie 17
RICE, Andrew 153 Charles 153 David 274 Helen 263 Polly 153 Rachel 153 William 153
RICHARDS, Elizabeth 300 Jesta 215 John 88 265
RICHARDSON, Catherine 151 F E 313 John 151 318 Kitty 151 Richard 167 Rose 37 Stanard 313 Susan 167
RICHMOND, Catherine 161
RIDDIN, Margaret 219
RIDDLE, Martha 79
RIDER, Mary 275 Polly 275
RIDGEWAY, John 25
RIFFE, Mary 72

RIGGAN, William 79
RIGGS, David 323
RILEY, John 79 Margaret 79 Willshire 239
RINEHART, Mattie 67
RINKER, Edward 316
RITCHIE, Mary 240
RITTERSBACH, David 258
RITZ, P E 246
RIVERS, Amy 149 Elizabeth 149 Martha 149 Nancy 149 Polley 140 Robert 149 Sally 149 Thomas 149
RIVES, Elizabeth 149 Nathaniel 149 Patty 151 William 275
ROACH, Absolom 215 John 17 Mary 17
ROBBERTSON, Catharine 41 Caty 41 Dorcas 128
ROBERDS, W T 91
ROBERSON, Catherine 41 Caty 41 Harriet 71 Sally 45 Sarah 45
ROBERTES, W T 91
ROBERTS, Elizabeth 134 Joshua 134 Mary 249
ROBERTSON, Anna 318 C H 311 James 304 Jane 158 John 50 Lewis 243 N 328 N R 301 Susan 190 Susanna 310 Thursee 50 William 158
ROBINSON, Anna 318 Catharine 41 Caty 41 Gertrude 101 Hannah 75 316 John 41 310 Solomon 316 Winslow 267 318
RODES, Charles 175 Lucy 175
RODGERS, Ann 12 Edward 12 Elizabeth 57 Frances 178 James 12 Jane 12 John 57 274 Margaret 57 Robert 12
ROE, H A 118
ROGERS, Ann 287 Benjamin 151 Charles 287 David 124 Elender 197 Elisbeth 294 Frances 3 G W 91 Jesse 123 John 124 151 Malenna 91 Mager 294 Martha 229 Nancy 151 Paula 62 Thomas 294 William 87 124
ROLFE, Agnes 144
ROMJUE, M A 81 Maud 81
RONEY, Frances 149
ROPER, Elizabeth 188 Grace 232
ROSAMOND, Elizabeth 126 James

ROSAMOND (continued) 126
ROSE, Elizabeth 249 John 316 Robert 249 Susan 192
ROSEMAN, Elizabeth 126 James 126
ROSIER, Hester 72
ROSS, Ellender 275 Polly 314 R N 82 Samuel 314
ROUNDTREE, Hester 182
ROUTH, Betsy 327 Elizabeth 328 Isabel 230 Joseph 327
ROWLETT, Thomas 321
ROYALL, James 331
ROYSTER, David 264 287 Francis 287
RUBAL, Jane 38
RUBLE, Elizabeth 59 Mary 38
RUCKER, Mary 144
RUMSEY, Nancy 277
RUNIONS, James 49 Malindy 49
RUPPLE, Clara 151
RUSSELL, Andrew 322 Caty 266 Joshua 263 Robert 300 Sarah 94 Thomas 94
RUTAN, Clara 151
RUTHERFORD, Mary 18 Rebecca 38 Susannah 88
RYAN, Rebecca 112 William 112
RYDER, Mary 275 Polly 275
SADLER, John 281
SAFFORD, Patience 51
SAMPSON, Francis 312 Joseph 42
SANDELS, Margaret 97
SANDERS, Edward 180 Jesse 307 Lucy 34
SANDRICH, Polly 127
SANFORD, Claud 260 Deborah 275 Mary 27 Whiting 275
SALLEY, Magdala 299
SALMON, John 265
SAP, John 99
SARGENT, Nelson 100
SATER, Louisa 195
SATTERFIELD, Isaac 327
SATTERWHITE, Robert 254
SAUNDERS, Mary 76 Polley 299 Reuben 291 Thomas 299 320
SAVAGE, Elizabeth 12 13 George 316 Michael 12 Peggy 12 Susan 12 Susannah 12
SAWYER, Celia 128 Mary 289

SAYERS, Robert 329
SAYLER, James 83
SCARBOROUGH, Edy 117
SCATES, Louise 229
SCEARCE, Sarah 122
SCHLEICHARDT, Jessie 193
SCHLICHER, George 94
SCHODDE, Anna 150
SCHRIVER, Catherine 243
SCHRYHAUSER, Mary 235
SCHWEIBLE, Faye 247 J F 247
SCHWIMMER, Madeline 239
SCOMP, H A 269
SCOTT, A M 281 Ann 204 270 Anna 204 Anne 204 Francis 270 Maria 12 Mary 221 281 Sukey 283 William 293
SEACHREST, Ella 261
SEAY, Ann 209 Austin 248 Benjamin 209
SEE, Betsy 299 Jesse 299
SEELEY, Jennie 63
SEEMER, Elizabeth 258 William 258
SELBY, Walter 300
SELECMAN, Thomas 266
SELLERS, James 305
SEMLER, Charles 207 Mabel 208
SEMPLE, Charlotte 281 Robert 281
SENATE, Mary 22
SESSIONS, Litsey 71
SEVIER, Joanna 93
SEWARD, Mickie 2 Richard 2
SHACKELFORD, Charles 120 Edward 120 Eliza 120 Elizabeth 120 Jane 120 Joseph 297 302 Lucy 120
SHADD, Susan 80
SHADOWN, Lewis 28
SHAFER, Blanche 326
SHANK, John 135
SHANKLIN, Eizabeth 138 J T 138 Richard 138 William 138
SHANNON, Elizabeth 123
SHARP, Mary 108 Robert 108 William 239
SHEARMAN, Martin 291
SHEARWOOD, Ann 271 Richard 271 Robert 271
SHEILD, Charles 323
SHELBURNE, Charlotte 135 John

SHELBURNE (continued) 135
SHELFATHAM, John 272
SHELTON, Armistead 298 Chloe 320 Elizabeth 298 Emma 28 Henry 298 Josiah 314 Mary 314 Sally 93 Samuel 330 Sarah 101 Thomas 28
SHEPHERD, David 266 Dorothy 50 John 50 Elijah 50 Lydia 266 Mary 154 Moses 266 Ruth 255 Sarah 67 Viney 50 William 67
SHERBURNE, Cora 111 E M 111
SHERER, Keziah 174
SHERLAND, Lillian 36
SHERRY, Martha 282
SHIELDS, Mary 208
SHINAULT, Benjamin 261
SHOEMAKER, June 173
SHORTRIDGE, Elizabeth 144
SHREUES, Tabitha 294
SHREVES, Tabitha 294
SHULL, Magdalena 51 Susannah 51
SHULTZ, Arthur 121 Helen 121
SHUMATE, Celia 215 D L 203 Nancy 181
SHUTTLEWORTH, May 182
SIGMAN, James 267
SILLIVEN, Samuel 201
SIMMONS, Jehu 301 W H 31 W F 61
SIMONS, Mary 149
SIMONTON, Nancy 246
SIMPKINS, James 102 Robert 102
SIMPSON, Louisa 237 Mary 5 Polly 5
SIMS, Mary 327 Nancy 265
SINCLAIR, Ann 320 Arthur 66 Elizabeth 66 George 66 Gilberta 66 James 320 John 321 Sarah 66 Susan 101 William 66
SININGER, Ann 260
SINTER, Margaret 169 Peggy 169
SISK, Andrew 133 Polly 133
SITTON, Elizabeth 109 M W 59
SKINNER, Isaac 329
SLAGLE, Jacob 231
SLAUGHTER, Matilda 328 Nancy 327
SLOAN, J M 108 Joseph 308

SLOME, Easter 76
SMALLEY, A D 141
SMITH, A J 172 Aaron 301 Abner 300 Barbara 65 Beheathland 100 Behesland 100 Carrie 251 Daniel 111 Davidson 241 Deborah 277 Elijah 44 Elizabeth 111 208 Ernest 209 F C 30 Fanny 63 Frances 290 Frank 34 124 Hannah 201 Henry 277 Isaac 271 James 239 John 247 277 Judith 310 Leila 260 Lucretia 44 Margaret 137 Mary 45 126 277 301 Morgan 290 Nancy 56 60 Nicholas 46 Nora 27 30 31 32 33 34 123 Polly 46 Pitman 295 Priscilla 299 Ralph 60 Rhoda 78 Richard 180 Salley 134 Sarah 138 301 328 Thomas 138 W Wayne 34 111 Washington 241 William 56 147 208 299 301
SMITHERMAN, Linda 238
SMOAT, Alice 260 Charles 260
SMOCK, William 176
SMYTH, Tobias 213
SNAW, Elizabeth 154 John 154
SNEAD, Edwin 24 Nancy 90
SNEED, Elizabeth 72 Jean 72 Keturah 72 Richard 72 Salley 72 William 72
SNODDY, Allen 175 233
SNODGRASS, Mary 316
SNORF, Annie 208
SNOW, Elizabeth 154 James 154 Richard 267 320
SOMERFIELD, James 86
SOURBEAR, Catharine 116 Elizabeth 116 Frederick 116 George 116 Mahala 116 Thomas 116
SPARKS, Ann 278 Billey 278 Mary 188 278 Nancy 60 Thomas 278 Wesley 278
SPAULDING, Nancy 238
SPEARS, John 224 Polly 224
SPEER, John 283 Lillie 148
SPENCE, A Kemper 83 Elizabeth 171 Marianna 149
SPENCER, Elizabeth 270 James 270 John 189 270 Joseph 127 Mary 184 Nancy 127 Sarah 127

SPENGLER, Clarenda 63 Eleanor 63
SPILMAN, Henry 302
SPILLAR, Elizabeth 317 Thomas 317
SPILLERS, Elizabeth 317 Thomas 317
SPOTSWOOD, John 61
SPRAGE, Catherine 11
SPRINGER, Drusilla 302 Uriah 330
SPRY, Cornelius 34
SPURR, Virginia 264
STANDAGE, George 289 Mary 289 Nancy 289
STANFIELD, John 8 Sarah 8
STANFORD, Margaret 11
STANLEY, Anny 295 Franck 123 Richard 319 Sarah 107 123 187
STANSBERRY, Lucy 9
STAPLES, Catharine 37 Drusilla Samuel 113
STAPP, Akilles 257 Ann 257
STAR, Mary 18
STARKE, Sally 267
STARLING, Roderick 246
STARR, William 36
STATIN, Polly 103
STATZER, Philip 317
STEARMAN, William 272
STEEL, Agnes 91
STEELE, Agnes 91 David 91 Elizabeth 294 George 234 Nancy 91 Reuben 319 Samuel 174
STEELMAN, Venie 195
STEINER, Betty 14
STEPHENS, James 50 Mary 50 Molly 50 Philip 96 Rebecca 60 Winfield 96
STEPHENSON, Betsey 85 Catherine 63 Effey 85 Elizabeth 85 John 63 Marcia 260 Margaret 260 Mary 85 Polly 85 Richard 85 Sally 85
STEVENS, John 322
STEVENSON, Deborah 257 Fanny 252 L O 111
STEWARD, Catharine 62
STEWART, Catharine 59 Charles 309 David 309 Edward 309 Elizabeth 282 George 287

STEWART (continued)
James 124 Laura 40 Mary 299 Philadelphia 287 Sarah 124 Virginia 178
STILES, William 303
STINNETT, Susan 18
STINSON, Deborah 257 Sarah 329
STITH, Caroline 75 J P 321
STOCKDELL, Nancy 183
STOCKER, Herman 331
STOCKTON, Sophie 273
STODARD, Mary 103 Polley 103
STOFER, Bursy 104 Jacob 104 Maggie 103
STOKELEY, Christopher 279 John 279 Nancy 279
STOKES, Sine 295
STONE, Diana 294 Dinah 294 Donald 7 H W 297 James 120 Joshua 297 Micajah 113 Polly 299 Rachel 288 Sarah 71 113
STONER, Jane 312
STORER, Joicy 293
STORY, Mary 90
STOUGHTON, Elizabeth 239 Nancy 239
STOUT, Susan 182
STOWERS, Anna 130
STRATON, William 323
STRATTON, James 248 John 103 Sarah 103
STRAWHAND, William 323
STRAYER, Dorcas 128 John 129
STREET, Emily 201
STRIBLING, Sigismumd 224
STRICKLAND, Sarah 98
STRICKLIN, Olivetta 151
STRIEBY, Fred 97 Mary 97
STRINGFELLOW, Hannah 316 Nancy 214
STRONG, Mary 27
STROPES, Sarah 8
STROUSE, David 286 Isaac 286
STUART, Archibald 86 Catharine 26 Elizabeth 207
STUBBLEFIELD, Beverly 129 Priscilla 129
STUBBS, Simon 324
STULTZ, Lucretia 175
STURGEON, Aaron 93
STURGES, Jane 250
STUTTS, Elizabeth 174 Marshall

STUTTS (continued) 174
SULLINGER, Martha 105
SULLIVAN, Jane 231 Martha 244 Peter 282 Samuel 201 231
SUMMERS, Elizabeth 121 George 316 Richard 121
SURBER, Adam 208 Mary 208 Thomas 208
SUTHENFIELD, Mary 230
SUTTLES, Hannah 187
SUTTON, Ellen 268 John 317 Sally 57 Sarah 57
SWAIM, Hannah 36 Isaac 36
SWAIN, Quincy 96
SWANN, John 310
SWARINGEN, Lydia 301
SWEZEY, George 208 Martha 208
SWINEBROOD, Ruth 56
SWISHER, D Clay 262
SWISSHELM, C R 223
SWITCHER, Elizabeth 84
SWITZIR, Elizabeth 84
SYBROOK, Henry 153
SYFFERT, George 327
SYMAN, David 312
SYMONS, Charles 117
TABB, John 33
TAGGART, Anna 224 James 86 Margaret 86 Samuel 86
TAIT, Nancy 218 234
TALBERT, P T 24
TALIAFERRO, John 126
TALLEY, Emma 290 William 73
TANDY, Ann 184 Kitty 29
TANEY, John 313
TAPP, Rosanna 300
TAPSCOTE, Samuel 291
TARNES, Lucinda 300
TASSEY, E E 329
TATTERSHALL, George 17 Lucinda 17
TAYLOR, Catharine 215 Charity 197 Christopher 154 Dorcas 37 Elizabeth 270 Frances 37 George 56 Giles 295 James 270 310 314 Jane 56 187 John 313 Martha 200 Mary 158 Polley 23 S N 73 Simon 316 Tazewell 324 Thomas 199 200 William 295 318
TEAGUE, Margaret 330

TELFORD, Mary 296
TEMPLEMAN, Samuel 304
TEMPLETON, Ann 58 John 58
TENLEY, Frances 136
TERRELL, James 287 Mary 271 Thomas 313
TERRY, James 108 Mary 108 Mollie 108 Nathaniel 274 Peyton 113 Rebecca 291 Sarah 113 Stephen 113 Susannah 297 William 113 291 297 298
TETER, Ralph 269
THACKER, Daniel 248
THACKSTON, Mary 136
THOMAS, Betsy 288 Elizabeth 288 John 129 224 Mary 231 Neal 235 Priscilla 129 Rufus 18 Stephen 288
THOMASSON, Polley 307
THOMPSON, Arabella 274 Benjamin 262 Dorothea 228 E St Clair 84 Elizabeth 33 228 Jacob 39 James 173 John 111 228 313 322 Margaret 104 Mary 297 Nathaniel 175 Sytha 111 Thomas 175 Wells 12 William 33 297 298
THOMSON, Archibald 47 Margaret 47
THORN, Esther 98
THORNBURY, John 266
THORNE, Hester 98 J S 326
THORNTON, Anthony 270 George 270 Rosa 290
THOROWGOOD, Sarah 2
THRUSTON, Ann 147 James 77 Kiziah 77 Mary 159 William 147
THURMOND, Philip 272
THWEATT, Sarah 274
TILLER, William 323
TILLETT, James 48 Mary 48
TILLEY, Bennett 5
TILLY, Bennett 5
TIMBERLAKE, John 285 Walker 248
TINCH, Nicholas 179
TINSLEY, Leola 149
TITTLE, Margaretta 32 Peter 32
TODD, Andrew 52 Eliza 52 Elizabeth 52 Jane 52 Johnson 52 Lydia 227 Sarah 52 Simpson 52

TOMPKINS, Christopher 307
TONGATE, Urial 103 Mason 103
TOOLE, Jacob 322
TORRENCE, Hannah 80
TRACY, Wiley 284
TRAMMEL, Martha 317
TRAVIS, J H 41
TRICE, Dolly 199
TRIMBLE, Mary 230 Polly 230
TRIPLETT, Betsey 280
TROWBRIDGE, Elizabeth 122
TROWER, Sarah 140
TROY, James 303
TRUEHEART, Susanna 310
TRUSLOW, Benjamin 270
TUCK, Nancy 266 W H 181
TUCKER, Daniel 299 Eppes 299 Ethel 299 Frances 299 Gabriel 299 Herbert 299 Jesse 78 John 118 119 Luther 180 Mary 118 119 172 Nancy 78 Polly 118 Reuben 299 Robert 299 Susan 299 Thomas 312
TUNSTALL, William 298 330
TURLINGTON, John 246 Nancy 246 Peter 246
TURNER, Benjamin 275 Edith 127 Lucy 254 Martha 275 Mary 113 Miles 275 Robert 300 Sarah 113
TURRENTINE, Alva 73
TYLER, John 303 Rebecca 303 Sally 7
TYREE, David 77 Elizabeth 77
UPDYKE, Rufus 232
VAN, Keziah 164
VAN ANTWERP, Jane 213
VAN METER, Abraham 258 C O 258 Sarah 258
VAN NATTA, T F 279
VAN ZANDT, Ailcy 110 Alsey 110 Isaac 110 John 110
VANCE, David 171 Mary 264 Samuel 171 Sarah 171
VANDIVER, John 10
VANN, Keziah 169
VARNEY, Lena 224
VASS, Elizabeth 194 Henry 281
VAUGHAN, Almond 256 292 Claudia 189 John 327 Mary 52 Patsey 256 Patty 256 Thomas 292 William 52 256

VEECH, John 80 Mary 80
VENABLE, Charles 313 George 120 Mary 66 120
VERDIER, James 316 Susannah 316
VERNON, Catharine 44
VESSELS, Custis 191
VINEY, Rachel 123
VINSON, Ann 9
VINZANT, J L 34
VIOLETT, Edward 231
VOWEL, Parazeda 119 Parisida 110
VOWELL, Banester 119
WADDELL, Alexander 296 Elizabeth 115 George 115 James 115 296 Jane 115 John 115 Mary 115 William 115
WADDLE, Robert 308 Sarah 308
WADDY, George 66
WADE, George 303 Margaret 66 Sarah 230
WAGES, Benjamin 282
WAGGONER, Benjamin 148 Elizabeth 148 Eve 262
WAITE, Harrison 331
WALDEN, E F 244 Susie 244
WALDROP, Lucretia 214
WALKER, Ann 242 Estaline 51 Hannah 256 Jeremiah 100 Laura 91 Lucy 304 Mary 100 Nancy 184 Philadelphia 246
WALL, Hannah 171
WALLACE, James 230 Joseph 230 Margaret 230 Lucy 299
WALLIS, William 49
WALLS, Ray 94
WALMSLEY, Mary 301
WALSH, Katherine 206
WALTON, Eliza 31 John 31 Martin 31 William 330
WARD, Benjamin 243 Conrad 109 Emma 290 F M 319 J H 290 Maria 243 Mary 243 Tabitha 290 Virginia 244
WARDLOW, Cynthia 146
WARE, Anna 224 Elizabeth 214 John 224
WARFORD, Benjamin 157 Delia 157 Delilah 157
WARNE, Elijah 126 Jonathan 126 Martha 126 Patty 126 Thomas

WARNE (continued)
126
WARNECK, Elizabeth 150 Frederick 150
WARREN, Helen 153
WARTHEN, James 118
WASH, Lucy 190
WASHAM, Elizabeth 249
WASHBURN, Gabriel 182 Jane 156 Rhoda 182
WASHER, James 105
WASHINGTON, George 275 291 297
WATERS, N M 222 Philemon 256
WATKINS, Alfred 300 Austin 321 Caroline 268 Charles 300 Francis 309 George 267 John 287 Margaret 215 Martha 45 Mary 45 311 Susannah 151 300 310 Thomas 45 William 45
WATSON, Charles 11 178 David 121 Estella 11 Estelle 178 Frances 121 John 270 321 Mary 121 Nancy 121 Prudence 121 William 121
WATTS, Elizabeth 273 John 312
WAY, Lydia 205 Mary 63
WAYNE, Anthony 293 C E 179
WEAKLEY, William 328
WEAR, Elizabeth 214 Frederick 194
WEAVER, Lewis 149 Mary 209 Theodicia 149 William 209
WEBB, Elizabeth 314 Hannah 99 Isaac 290 James 314 John 99 314 Mary 99 314 Milley 99 Nancy 82 Rachel 228 Simeon 82 Tabitha 290
WEBSTER, Harry 4 Hubert 242 Jessie 242
WEEKLEY, Nannie 40
WEISMAN, Catherine 258
WELCH, Jane 133 S H 230
WELDON, Polly 9
WELLS, Guy 238 Joice 33 Joyce 33 Pallie 248
WELMAN, John 324
WEST, Cina 302 Hezekiah 113 Nancy 56 Obedience 92 Sina 302 Susanna 271 William 323
WESTBROOK, William 181
WESTCOAT, Hezekiah 12 Susanna 12

WESTLAKE, James 217 Jane 216 Thomas 216 217
WESTMORELAND, Mary 133
WHALEY, Mary 296
WHARTON, Rose 252 Samuel 252
WHATELY, Rhoda 224
WHEELER, Altie 210 H H 210
WHELESS, M B 172
WHELON, E Frances 264
WHERLEY, Martha 153 Patsey 153
WHETZELL, Henry 316
WHICKER, Jane 116 Louisa 116 Malvina 116 Martha 116 Newell 116 Samuel 116 Sarah 116 Thomas 116 Willis 116 Zachariah 116
WHIRLEY, Martha 153 Patsey 153
WHITAKER, E M 180
WHITE, Ann 37 Arabella 274 Betsey 166 Catharine 7 Charles 190 257 Goren 15 Hampton 298 Henry 168 172 Hiram 78 Jacob 88 113 John 190 Joseph 274 290 Julina 178 Katharine 7 Mary 88 113 168 236 290 Nancy 168 Nellie 285 Robert 178 Sarah 78 William 287
WHITECOTTON, Elizabeth 306
WHITEHEAD, John 323
WHITELEY, Bettie 173
WHITENER, Eve 262
WHITESIDES, Phebe 8
WHITLEY, A B Elizabeth 173
WHITLOCK, Betsy 142 Elizabeth 142 John 295
WHITLOW, Hannah 4 Thomas 4
WHITMAN, Jesse 58 Lucinda 58
WHITMOND, Jesse 58 Lucinda 58
WHITSETT, Elizabeth 146 Jane 3
WHITTLE, Elizabeth 66 J W 312 William 66
WHORLEY, Martha 153 Patsey 153
WICKERSHAM, Nan 234 235
WIDDICOMB, William 309
WIDOWS, Daniel 32 Julia 32
WIEDMAN, Christian 331 Elizabeth 331 Mary 331
WIGGENTON, Jane 64
WILBORN, Becky 73
WILEY, Agnes 234 Ann 234 Anne 223 Claudia 189 James 234 John 219 Nancy 234

WILKENSON, Temperance 9
WILKERSON, Nelly 169 Ranson 169
WILKINS, Sarah 61 William 61
WILKINSON, R L 25 Sally 81
WILLIAMS, Agnes 264 Andromache 290 Ann 53 Anna 23 195 Anne 195 Belle 33 Casandra 269 Catharine 219 Charles 219 301 Drusilla 301 Elisha 170 Elizabeth 90 216 George 287 Hannah 170 James 170 195 313 319 Johanna 271 John 23 53 216 263 320 323 Joseph 285 Judith 53 Leah 170 Levi 170 Lucretia 327 Margaret 225 229 Milly 170 Nancy 195 Polly 170 Rachel 170 Richard 170 Ritter 23 Robert 216 Samuel 53 127 170 290 327 Sarah 39 Tabitha 206 Thomas 254 Ury 170 W F 33 William 219
WILLIAMSON, Auldin 101 Elizabeth 28 Emmet 309 Mary 301 Nathan 28
WILLIS, Charlotte 135 Henrietta 123 James 176 Mary 103 Polly 103 Salley 176
WILLOUGHBY, Jane 195
WILLS, Charlotte 135 J W 35
WILLSON, William 219
WILSON, Allen 309 Daisy 23 George 23 J W 116 James 254 Jenney 292 Jinney 202 John 183 Joseph 208 Lavica 83 Margaret 183 Rebecca 208 Robert 26 Ruth 260 Sarah 4 Susannah 178 T O'J 136 Thomas 312
WIMBROUGH, Richard 128
WIMSATT, Mary 186
WINDER, Geroge 75
WINDOFFER, Opal 319
WINE, C H 65
WINFIELD, Elizabeth 39 249
WINFREY, Lucy 37
WINGFIELD, Gustavus 325
WINLOCK, Effey 85 Joseph 86
WINN, Mable 197 Margaret 34
WINSLOW, Elizabeth 251
WINSTON, Elizabeth 216 Joseph

WINSTON (continued) 216 Martha 216 Philip 267
WISE, Catherine 217 Catharine 217 Mary 217
WISLER, Betsy 288
WISMAN, Catharine 258 George 258
WITCHER, Ann 100 Vincent 298
WITHERSPOON, Sally 99
WITT, Agnes 71
WOCKENPUSS, Ethel 283
WOLF, Evaline 171 Elizabeth 143 Leanna 171 Margaret 215 Solomon 171
WOLTZ, Ferdinand 286
WOOD, Archibald 266 Baker 152 Edith 297 217 Eldo 207 George 241 Henry 330 Lucy 152 Richard 309 Thomas 287
WOODBY, Elizabeth 296
WOODFIELD, John 289 Mahala 289
WOODFIN, Samuel 234
WOODLY, Elizabeth 296
WOODS, Cadence 300 Charles 37 300 Sarah 191 William 321
WOODSON, Benjamin 212 Charles 312 Dashwood 212 Drury 79 Elizabeth 31 James 212 Lockey 212 Martha 79 Mary 79 Quin 212 Sally 212 Sarah 212 Susannah 212 William 212
WOODVILLE, James 123 Mary 123
WOODWARD, Elizabeth 247 Thomas 247 William 37
WOODY, Benjamin 248
WOODYARD, Ann 266 Calvert 184 Elizabeth 184 Jeremiah 184 John 266
WOOLF, Carvin 190 Elizabeth 190 Emily 190 Lucy 190 Perry 190 Ridden 190 William 190
WOOLFOLK, Sally 250
WOOTON, Silas 318
WORD, Lockey 121 Mary 212 Thomas 212
WORSHAM, Branch 301 312 Frances 46
WORTHINGTON, Betsey 120 Edward 120 Eliza 120 James 120 Jane 120 John 120 Lucy 120 Madison 120 Margaret 120 Mary 120 Patsey 120 Rowland 120

WRIGHT, Archibald 127 Asa 34 George 127 140 John 323 Kelliss 95 Kessiah 9 Mary 140 189 Nancy 34 Patsey 95 Polly 11 Reuben 9 Sarah 11 292 Susannah 186 William 95
WROE, Original 118
WYATT, John 279 Joseph 318 Royal 50 Sarah 50 Susan 270 William 270
WYLLIE, Allan 293
YANCEY, Mary 83
YARBROUGH, Agness 254
YATES, Elizabeth 274 Lydia 161
YERBY, William 291
YOHO, Henry 303
YOKE, Nancy 123 Sam 123
YOST, J W 199 Pearl 199
YOUNG, Elizabeth 253 Frances 174 John 219 236 Judith 178 Letitia 178 Mary 236 Nancy 170 Nathaniel 322 Sarah 247 T C 212 Thomas 174 William 253
YOUNGBLOOD, Benjamin 165 Grace 250 Susan 167
YOWEL, Jane 263
YOWELL, Mary 247 W R 247
ZIRKLE, Elizabeth 67

Other books by the author:

Virginia and West Virginia Genealogical Data from Revolutionary War Pension and Bounty Land Warrant Records: Volume 1
Virginia and West Virginia Genealogical Data from Revolutionary War Pension and Bounty Land Warrant Records, Volume 2 Dabbs-Hyslop
Virginia and West Virginia Genealogical Data from Revolutionary War Pension and Bounty Land Warrant Records, Volume 3 Iams through Myres
Virginia and West Virginia Genealogical Data from Revolutionary War Pension and Bounty Land Warrant Records, Volume 4 Nabors - Rymer
Virginia and West Virginia Genealogical Data from Revolutionary War Pension and Bounty Land Warrant Records, Volume 5 Sacrey-Tyree
Virginia and West Virginia Genealogical Data from Revolutionary War Pension and Bounty Land Warrant Records, Volume 6 Ullum Through Zumwalt
Timesaving Aid to Virginia-West Virginia Ancestors (A Genealogical Index of Surnames from Published Sources)
Virginia/West Virginia Husbands and Wives, Volume 1
Virginians & West Virginians, 1607-1870, Volume 1
Virginians & West Virginians, 1607-1870, Volume 2
War of 1812: Virginia Bounty Land and Pension Applicants
Virginia/West Virginia Husbands and Wives, Volume 2
Genealogical Data from United States Military Academy Application Papers, 1805-1866, Volume 1
Adventures In Genealogy
Genealogical Data From United States Military Academy Application Papers, 1805-1866, Volume 2
Virginians & West Virginians, 1607-1870, Vol. 3
Virginians & West Virginians, 1607-1870, Volume 1
Alexandria City and County, Virginia Wills, Administrations, and Guardian Bonds 1800-1870
Alexandria City and County Virginia Deed Books Extracts1801-1818

CD: *Virginia/West Virginia Revolutionary War Records, Volumes 1-6*

www.ingramcontent.com/pod-product-compliance
Lightning Source LLC
Chambersburg PA
CBHW051624230426
43669CB00013B/2176